STORIES:
CHILDREN'S
LITERATURE IN
EARLY EDUCATION

STORIES:
CHILDREN'S
LITERATURE IN
EARLY EDUCATION

Shirley C. Raines

Rebecca T. Isbell

Delmar Publishers Inc.™

I T P™

Notice to the Reader

Publisher does not warrant or guarantee any of the products described herein or perform any independent analysis in connection with any of the product information contained herein. Publisher does not assume, and expressly disclaims, any obligation to obtain and include information other than that provided to it by the manufacturer.

The reader is expressly warned to consider and adopt all safety precautions that might be indicated by the activities described herein and to avoid all potential hazards. By following the instructions contained herein, the reader willingly assumes all risks in connection with such instructions.

The publisher makes no representations or warranties of any kind, including but not limited to, the warranties of fitness for particular purpose or merchantability, nor are any such representations implied with respect to the material set forth herein, and the publisher takes no responsibility with respect to such material. The publisher shall not be liable for any special, consequential or exemplary damages resulting, in whole or in part, from the readers' use of, or reliance upon, this material.

Cover design by Kristina Almquist Design.
Cover illustration by Robin Brinkman.

Delmar Staff:
Administrative Editor: Jay Whitney
Developmental Editor: Erin J. O'Connor
Senior Project Editor: Andrea Edwards Myers
Production Coordinator: Sandra Woods
Art/Design Coordinator: Karen Kunz Kemp

For information, address Delmar Publishers Inc.
3 Columbia Circle, Box 15-015
Albany, New York 12212-5015

Printed in the United States of America
Published simultaneously in Canada
by Nelson Canada.
a division of the Thomson Corporation

1 2 3 4 5 6 7 8 9 10 XXX   00 99 98 97 96 95 94

Library of Congress Cataloging-in-Publication Data
Raines, Shirley C.
    Stories: Children's Literature in Early Education
    Shirley Raines, Rebecca Isbell.—1st ed.
        p.   cm.
    Includes index.
    ISBN 0-8273-5509-2

    1. Literature—Study and teaching (Early childhood)—United States.
  2. Children's literature—Study and teaching—United States. 3. Children—
  Books and reading. I. Isbell, Rebecca. II. Title.
LB1139.5.L58R35   1994
372.64—dc20   93-28119
                                                                  CIP

Contents

Foreword

What a pleasure it is to have the opportunity to introduce students to *Stories: Children's Literature in Early Education,* because it is so obviously written with them in mind.

Students can't help but be encouraged by the success stories that demonstrate how beginning and more experienced teachers alike have solved a variety of commonplace difficulties associated with presenting literature to all sorts of young children. These brief case histories are culminated by a chapter that describes, in greater depth, how five early childhood teachers conveyed their love of reading fine books to the youngsters.

In addition to this positive emphasis on success, material on multicultural literature is woven consistently throughout the text. Suggestions for literature related to children with special needs are provided as well. The significance of family influence is also recognized in a special chapter that outlines a helpful, overall approach for working with the family.

The book is filled with practical ideas ranging from the room arrangement to suggestions for effective storytelling. This practicality, so badly needed by students, is balanced by presentation of a useful theoretical structure for classifying various types of children's literature.

While the aforementioned virtues make *Stories: Children's Literature in Early Education* a valuable contribution to the field, in my opinion its crowning glory is its focus on truly fine children's literature. In a time when tawdry and often tasteless books for children abound, it is reassuring to come across a text that cites hundreds of beautifully illustrated, well-written books, and to know its use will benefit both teachers and children in their care.

Joanne Hendrick, Ph.D.

reface

Welcome to an exciting era in the history of early childhood education—a new awakening to the value of fine literature shared in dynamic, active learning environments, especially designed for young children. *Stories: Children's Literature in Early Education* is an extensive view of the literature written for children from birth to age eight and a thorough examination of developmentally appropriate ways to interact with children about quality books and stories.

Teachers preparing to teach and those already in programs serving children from birth to age eight are the audience for this textbook. This children's literature book helps the reader make connections between who the child is as a growing and developing learner, quality literature, and the curriculum which engages the child as a thinker. The textbook is also a celebration of the teacher and the child because we tell many teacher and child success stories. These cases of successful teaching are filled with valuable insights for the beginning and the experienced teacher. In the schools, centers, and homes you will visit in this book, the adults and young children are engaged in a celebration of the power of quality literature to teach, to entertain, to connect one generation to the next, to bind up feelings, and to unleash imaginations.

Our goal in writing this book is to provide information, inspiration, and insights the early childhood educator can use to make the classroom and curriculum alive with quality literature.

Organization

Stories: Children's Literature in Early Education is organized in three major sections. Part One, "Inviting Young Children to Good Literature," is comprised of the first three chapters. In Chapter 1,

the reader visits a kindergarten classroom where the teacher uses developmental information about five-year-olds, her own renewed interest in children's literature, and insights about young children's emerging literacy to make changes in her teaching and in the ways she "invites" children to good literature. The teacher success story in Chapter 1 provides a model of how good teachers think. They consider the child, the literature, and the curriculum. In Chapter 2, the reader is reminded of the developmental characteristics of young children and the implications for the classroom and the curriculum. Chapter 3 is an examination of reading and writing in literature-rich early childhood classrooms.

Part Two, "Literature Genres and Forms," is a thorough examination of the various genres and forms of children's literature beginning in Chapter 4 with the picture book. Chapter 5 looks at literature which ranges from folk literature to modern fantasy. Chapter 6 is an exploration of realism in realistic fiction and nonfiction for young children. Chapter 7 is a celebration of poetry and rhythm of expression. In Chapter 8 connections are made between stories in books and the oral language traditions of storytelling, creative dramatics, and puppetry. Chapter 9 is an examination of the rapidly expanding world of stories in film, video, laser disks, computer imaging, and stories presented with an array of technology.

Part Three, "Literature Connections to the Classroom and Curriculum," deals with ways teachers and parents invite their children to quality literature. In Chapter 10, we see an array of ways to design the classroom library which will invite children to interact with books. In Chapter 11, we meet five early childhood educators who face dilemmas in their teaching and curriculum but find ways to solve their problems. The reader meets:

- ☐ a child-care center director who helps parents learn how to read to their infants and toddlers
- ☐ a preschool teacher who engages three- and four-year-olds with books
- ☐ a kindergarten teacher who invites dialogue about skills-based versus literature-based reading
- ☐ a first-grade teacher who moves to a multiage continuous-progress elementary school where reading is taught with children's literature and the curriculum is organized in thematic units
- ☐ a third-grade teacher who challenges the school's pull-out instruction program for children with special needs

Chapter 13 provides examples of how to help parents select quality literature, read to their children more effectively, and support their children as emerging literacy learners.

Inviting Features of this Textbook

The text contains:
- ☐ teacher success stories
- ☐ examples of developmentally appropriate practices for the young child as a literacy learner
- ☐ connections to the curriculum and effective teaching practices

Every chapter features:
- ☐ multicultural literature books
- ☐ an extensive list of quality children's books

- ☐ recommended references for teachers
- ☐ reader-friendly materials which make the text come to life, such as, photographs, illustrations from children's books, highlights of key points, and suggested learning experiences

Appendices include:
- ☐ lists of Caldecott Medal and Honor books
- ☐ bookbinding directions
- ☐ questionnaire about wordless picture books
- ☐ sources of information for parents and teachers
- ☐ children's videos, cassettes, and CDs
- ☐ distributors of computer software for children
- ☐ children's magazine information

The instructor's manual provides:
- ☐ outlines of chapters
- ☐ instructional suggestions for lecture, cooperative learning, active in-class participation
- ☐ materials and books to organize for class presentations
- ☐ follow-up suggestions for out-of-class assignments
- ☐ class projects for individuals and groups
- ☐ overhead transparencies of main points and figures from the textbook
- ☐ possible test questions

The authors and illustrators of the children's books are listed at the end of each chapter by their first and last names to help the reader become acquainted with them. The references for the teacher's resources and professional readings are listed separately in APA style.

Closing Message to the Readers

We believe early childhood educators deserve their own children's literature textbook. As former classroom teachers, child-care center directors, and now as teacher educators, we have listened to teachers and librarians and have written the type of children's literature textbook, they told us they wanted. *Stories: Children's Literature in Early Education* acknowledges the young child's characteristics as a learner and helps teachers plan developmentally appropriate practices which connect the child, the literature, and the curriculum in inviting, engaging, and dynamic interactions.

It is our hope that *Stories: Children's Literature in Early Education* will inform practice, inspire creative teaching, and connect the world of children's literature and the world of the classroom.

Acknowledgments

The acknowledgments section of a children's literature book is the people part of our venture. The first group of people who inspired us to write this textbook are the authors and illustrators of children's books. Thank you for your creative genius, your belief in the child as a worthy audience, and for allowing us to write about and reprint parts of your works.

The second group of people who inspired us are the children who read to us, played with us, and struck up conversations about very simple and extremely complex topics. We are especially grateful to the children at the East Tennessee State University Child Study Center in Johnson City, Tennessee, the Vienna Baptist Children's Center in Vienna, Virginia, and the Centennial Elementary School in Pasco County, Florida.

To the teachers, principals, and center directors of those programs, we thank you for providing access to the children, telling your teaching success stories, and questioning how to make classrooms better literacy learning environments. There are two groups of educators who pressed us far beyond the usual challenges. We are indebted to the teachers and librarians of the Literacy Forum of CARD, the Center for Applied Research and Development at George Mason University in Fairfax, Virginia, and to the Teaching Cases Writing Team from George Mason University and Fairfax County Virginia Public Schools.

The world of children's literature is indeed fortunate to have knowledgeable professionals in children's bookstores and book distributorships around the country. Three bookstore entrepreneurs and their staffs who helped us find the exciting books which "sell themselves" were Lisa Crandall and Catherine Marston of Young Editions in Tampa, Chris Bury of Storybook Palace in Burke, Virginia, and Sheila Egan of A Likely Story in Alexandria, Virginia. One of this country's most knowledgeable professionals in good books for young children is Leah Curry-Rood at Gryphon House, a publisher of teacher resource books and distributor of children's books located in Mt. Rainier, Maryland. Leah and her assistant Lorin Kilby answered our questions and expanded our horizons.

In our lives as teacher educators, we could not function without the support of our colleagues in early childhood education and children's literature at our universities and in the professional organizations, particularly ACEI, the Association for Childhood Education International, and NAEYC, the National Association for the Education of Young Children. We thank our friends at the University of South Florida and at East Tennessee State University who provided the solid critiques, the extra references, and the push to revise one more time. We wish to express particular appreciation to Becky Armstrong, Sarah Clark, Amy Dinsmore, Christy Grant, Helen Lane, Laura Phillips, and Reba Sanders at ETSU, East Tennessee State University, for their research and manuscript preparation efforts. Beth Hogan, assistant professor and librarian at ETSU, provided encouragement, assistance, and diligent pursuit of every piece of information we requested. The majority of the wonderful photographs in the book are by Larry Smith, photographer for the book and for ETSU.

We also appreciate the editorial leadership of Jay Whitney at Delmar who sought us out to write this book, the encouragement of Erin O'Connor whose editorial guidance brought the manuscript through development, Andrea Edwards Myers, the project editor, and Megan

Terry whose tireless quest for permissions to reprint illustrations and quotes made the book come to life for the reader. We are indebted to our reviewers Colin Ducolon, Champlain College, Vermont, William S. Bingman, Frostburg State University, Maryland, Janet Imel, Indiana Vocational Technical College, and Wendy Kasten, University of South Florida at Sarasota for the time, honesty, and clarity they brought to the design of this different type of children's literature textbook.

To our families and friends, thank you for understanding that we have wanted to write a book together since we were doctoral students in the late seventies. Since those days at the University of Tennessee, we have remained good friends, become colleagues in research and writing, and made countless presentations together. Our friendship survived and even flourished in the hurried reality of writing and revising this book. May we always have dreams and the patience, endurance, and strength to do the work to make the dream a reality.

Shirley C. Raines
Rebecca T. Isbell

I

Inviting
Young Children
to Good Literature

*Invitations to Children's Literature
and Teacher Decisions*

*Developmental Characteristics
of Young Children*

*Reading and Writing
in Literature-Rich
Early Childhood Classrooms*

1

Invitations to Children's Literature and Teacher Decisions

Invitation to Children's Literature and Teacher Decisions

Stories: Children's Literature in Early Education is a book about children and teachers, and the ways they interact around good books. Part One of the textbook is a description of the "invitations" teachers issue to young children to become involved in good books, the developmental considerations of the young learner, and how the child grows and develops in the literacy processes. In this chapter you will read about a kindergarten teacher who made changes in her teaching and in the operation of the classroom and the curriculum to become more effective at "inviting" children to good books. She decided to make these changes based on her understanding of developmentally appropriate practices and on an expanded appreciation of children's literature. In Chapter 2 you will review the developmental characteristics of young children, which guided the changes the teacher made. In Chapter 3 you will learn more about the young child's literacy development, what is meant by the reading and writing processes, and the teacher-to-child interactions, as well as activities which support the children's growth as readers and writers.

Stories: Children's Literature in Early Education covers the entire early childhood range from birth to age eight. Each chapter contains a "teacher success story" about classroom problems and their resolutions. The stories are insightful because they present solutions which are sound in theory and in practice. In the process of telling these teacher success stories, it is our hope that the reader will visualize lively and engaging classrooms where children are invited to quality literature and where teachers guide children in their emergent and early literacy experiences.

The chapters on the different genres and forms of children's literature, the developmental characteristics of young learners, literacy processes, and those on curriculum and schooling concerns provide the reader with ways to analyze the teacher stories and apply what is being learned. Throughout the book, a clear discernible model of the teacher as a professional is evident in the decisions teachers make and their well-defined reasons for change.

Stories: Children's Literature in Early Education builds upon three knowledge bases:

1. developmentally appropriate practices found in classrooms for young children (Bredekamp, 1987), derived from child growth and development studies

2. the constructivist view of ways children interact with texts and construct meaning

3. a wide variety of quality books for young children.

To invite children to literature, the teacher must know about practices that are appropriate for children at different ages and stages of development and select books that will interest them because of who they are as learners. To plan selections and interactions that integrate literacy and literary experiences throughout the curriculum and the classroom, the teacher needs a clear concept of how young children construct meaning. To make appropriate book selections, the teacher must also know children's literature.

The chapters on the various literature genres explain how the field of children's literature is organized and also lead the reader to an appreciation of writers and illustrators of children's books. Whether exploring the various genres or perusing the lists of books that have received awards, it is paramount that teachers read a wide variety of children's books and sample numerous authors' and illustrators' works.

To take full advantage of this study of children's literature, we recommend that teachers search for good examples of each genre by browsing through books in the school library and public library. Also, bookstores devoted to children's literature are valuable sources for learning about republished versions of classics and hot-off-the-presses new books and discovering some new author or illustrator who may capture the imagination of the children.

A Kindergarten Teacher's Success Story

In the following pages, you will meet Helene Franklin, an experienced kindergarten teacher who made changes in the ways she presented books to children. You will also learn how she arranged for her class to interact with books and how she helped individual children make connections to quality literature. Helene found avenues to take advantage of the children's interests and to invite them to good books. After Helene's teacher success story, we will analyze her application of the three knowledge bases of developmentally appropriate practices, ways children construct meaning, and good children's literature.

THE TEACHER STORY BEGINS

On Monday morning Helene Franklin began a new procedure. Usually, at the end of group time, she dismissed the kindergartners by having them sing a song together, then they scurried off to the center activities. Today, Ms. Franklin asked each child to state which center he or she would like to visit first. She recorded the children's selections on a chart.

As Helene expected, Jason and his three buddies chose the block area. Monica and Alicia waited for Michelle to say where she wanted to go, then the three hurried to the creative dramatics center. One child chose the writing center. Two wanted to paint at the easel. Three went to the table top activities, which included the small blocks, puzzles, and sorting materials. Five children stayed at the special art table set up for making fall leaf prints. Some went to the sand table to bury treasures, and Damien, while tugging on Ms. Franklin's skirt, asked for a Sesame Street game before rushing over to the computer.

Helene kept a record of the children's center selections at the beginning of choice time and at fifteen minute intervals throughout the hour. The children were not required to change activities, but Helene observed each center for changes at fifteen minute intervals. At the end of the week, she tabulated the results and found there were certain areas of the classroom that were the children's favorites and others they seldom entered. She was surprised to learn that the library was the least used area. While she was convinced that each activity in the room was an important one, and she valued the practice of letting the children chose their activities, Helene decided to make some changes.

As she looked back at her chart, Helene noticed Michelle and Alicia were the two who went to the classroom library most often. They retreated there and seemed to select many of the same books each day. However, two children interested in books were not enough. Helene became determined to find some ways to interest more children in books and stories.

The Importance of Children's Literature

Helene's realization that the children were not choosing to go to the classroom library center meant they were not choosing to interact with books. Since many of Helene's students came from homes where there were few books available, she knew she must find ways to invite them to good books. Recently, through a course she was taking, she had become aware of the research on emergent literacy and how youngsters who are read to and who show interest in stories are more successful in their beginning schooling (Anderson, Hiebert, Scott, & Wilkinson, 1985; Bissex, 1980; Durkin, 1966; Holdaway, 1979; Roser, Hoffman, & Farest, 1990; Stickland & Morrow 1989; Taylor, 1983; Wells, 1986). She knew the research, but she also realized from her years of experience that the same children who enjoyed books in kindergarten were often the ones who did well in later years.

A significant part of an educator's role is to help each child enjoy learning and to open up that child's world to an ever widening set of experiences. And while Ms. Franklin prided herself on keeping as many firsthand experiences as possible in the curriculum, she knew that books and stories helped children go beyond the physical world of their immediate environment, and she found ways to connect the firsthand experiences and good books. When Helene thought about the children who delighted in stories she read to them, she also wanted them to delight in books when she was not around to read to them. It was marvelous to watch five-year-olds engaged in a story, reading the pictures and sometimes the words, relishing the tale which unfolded in their hands from the pages of the book to the pages of the mind.

In addition to understanding the importance of young children developing an interest in books for their future successes as students and adults, Helene also knew that books for young children should be valued because quality literature is inherently interesting and satisfies the deep human needs children have for finding out about the social and physical worlds in which they live. As children relate to stories in books, they understand how they are like others and begin building bridges between themselves and the rest of the world. They grasp new knowledge by being confronted with information and stories which challenge their present levels of understanding.

Louise Rosenblatt wrote so eloquently about this process of constructing meaning through text in her classic book, *The Reader, the Text, the Poem* (1978), when she described aesthetic reading as reading for the joy of the experience. Aesthetic reading is certainly the kindergartners' version of reading. In fact, five-year-olds are so blatantly honest with their appraisals of books and interest in stories that their attention speaks for itself. The story must interest them by connecting with their own lives, or the idea must be so captivating that they are led through the story by some intrigue expressed in words and illustrations.

Ours is a literate culture and the futurists predict that the demands for more advanced reading and writing skills will escalate. Young children who are growing and emerging in their literacy find support in a family and a society that value reading and writing, but even families who have many books in their homes often find themselves pressed for time and energy to engage in reading. Parents report that they know they should read to their children, but when the schedule is tight, reading together is often eliminated (Raines & Isbell, 1989).

Given the many benefits of quality literature in young children's lives, Helene Franklin set about to make changes in her teaching and in her classroom operation which would invite children to books and stories.

A Glimpse Into the Transformed Classroom

Three weeks later, Helene Franklin noted with some pride that she had accomplished her goal. More children were actively engaged in stories and activities which related to them. She knew the transformation of the classroom was successful when she once again compared the children's center selections from the first week when only two children chose to do any book- or story-related activities to their selections of centers and activities now. Michelle and her friends still chose the creative dramatics area first, and Jason and his friends chose the construction materials. The table area with puzzles and math manipulatives was a first choice of many and special art projects always drew a crowd, but there was a marked increase in the number of different children visiting the library and engaging in other book-related activities over the course of the morning.

About twenty minutes into learning center time, the library was buzzing with activity. Michelle and Monica were sitting in a rocking chair giggling about the funny bear covered with blueberries in *Jamberry* (Degen). Damien was looking at *Brown Bear, Brown Bear, What Do You See?* (Martin) and putting pieces on a flannel board to correspond to the sequence in the book. Marissa came to the library, searched for *The Teddy Bears' Picnic* (Kennedy), tucked it under her arm and proceeded

to the housekeeping area to set up a picnic for the stuffed animals she had arranged around the kitchen table. Jason was there with his friends, directing his two followers to put on the headphones, while he fidgeted with the listening station, testing the volume and pointing to where they should look while he turned the pages to *Rooster's Off to See the World* (Carle).

How did it happen? What turned around the interest in the books and stories in this kindergarten class? Helene Franklin:

1. changed her presentation of books;

2. observed children's choices of activities;

3. determined what interested the children; and

4. devised a plan based on kindergartners' and individuals' characteristics.

Teacher Presentation of Books

Helene reserved the first circle time of the day as a major teacher-led time in the schedule. She used the twenty to thirty minutes to introduce concepts associated with the unit she was teaching, announce special activities, help children plan their day, and read a book to the children. Her usual process was to read the book at the end of the circle time. Reading to them seemed to help them listen better and refocus the entire group's attention. Helene decided that if she expected her kindergartners to interact more with books and stories, she must plan more interactions. She began by revamping the way she presented the books during group time and by providing more opportunities for the children to interact with books and stories throughout the day. Helene's changes included:

1. more effective book presentations

2. increasing book exploration time

3. more engaging follow-up interactions with books planned with individuals and small groups in mind

BEFORE, DURING, AND AFTER READING

In her university course, several teachers had modeled how they used enlarged texts, or big books, in their classrooms. The teachers helped their students learn to approach a book the way a proficient reader and a good thinker approaches the reading task. The teachers suggested that the reading session should be thought of in three parts: before, during, and after reading. Before reading, the teachers engaged the children in discussing the main topic of the book. They asked the children to *predict* what the book might be about based on the title, the book cover, or based on their knowledge about the subject. During reading, the teacher paused at a few key points in the story for the children to *confirm* their predictions or *change* them based on new information. After reading, the children *integrated* their new understandings with the old, made associations between this book and others they had read or between the subject of the book and their own lives. The purpose of the three-step interactions with the story in the book was to support the child's construction of meaning from the text.

Many of the big books, as the teachers demonstrated in the course, were of the predictable type or patterned language books. Read more about the literary process and literature interactions in Chapter 3. Chapter 4, The Picture Book, contains more information about big books.

Helene already had several big books in her classroom, but she had not been using them to emphasize the reading process or the distinctive features of the language in books (Galda, Cullinan, & Strickland, 1993). Helene adopted the three-step approach to book presentations, whether she was reading a little book or a big book to the kindergartners. Over the course of the year, Helene made many other changes in her book presentation, but the three-step process of before, during, and after reading provided her a way to plan for better book presentations.

During the university course, Helene also discovered many new books that were excellent sources for the social studies and science units she usually taught. She also began developing some new units of study prompted by the wonderful multicultural books and new ecology-oriented books she read. Helene began reading the stories much more carefully and preparing her three-step presentation by building better connections between the main ideas of the stories and the main concepts in the thematic units.

TRANSITION TIME

In the course Helene Franklin was taking with other teachers from her district, the professor asked a simple question, which prompted her to make a change in her classroom operation. The question was, "When do children explore books on their own?" There were basically two times in the schedule for free exploration of books, a transition time and choice time, when the children were free to choose any area of the classroom. Kindergarten teachers often use the transition times, the few minutes between major activities in the schedule, for book exploration. For instance, in Helene's kindergarten, while some children were finishing cleaning up from center activities and storing materials, the teacher's aide would spread a large number of books out on the carpeted circle-time area. As the children finished cleaning up, they came over and looked at, pretended to read, or read books on their own. Helene had to admit that the few minutes served more as a classroom management function than a book exploration time.

Helene made a simple change in her classroom that helped the children have time to explore the books. Normally, every child was expected to help with cleanup. Instead, Helene printed the children's names on large index cards. On one side their names were printed in green, on the other side in red. When she took roll each morning, she placed their names along the chalk rail under the chalkboard. If their green names were showing, they were to go help with cleanup. If the card showed their names printed in red, they were to stop on the carpet and read books. This simple change in classroom operation provided from ten to fifteen extra minutes for half the children each day to enjoy the books. The aide helped with the cleanup and Helene modeled effective silent reading by selecting a book and reading. After a few minutes, she asked three or four children to show her their favorite illustrations from the books they had read or tell something about the most exciting part. The transition time soon became a few minutes to relax with a good book and explore the story enough to be able to share a brief comment or two with the teacher.

ENGAGING RESPONSES AND INTERACTIONS WITH BOOK AND STORIES

To continue answering the question "When do children explore books on their own?" Helene referred back to her initial observations of the children's choices of center activities. Only two children chose to go to the library area and interact with books during center time. During group time, children were expected to listen to her presentation of the book, and they were expected to read the book or look at books during transition time. Helene knew the true test of whether or not the children were more interested in books would be if they chose to go to the library during choice time. Unfortunately, even Helene's better presentations of books and her rearrangement of transition time for free book exploration did not produce a change in the use of the classroom library. Helene determined that she needed more information to guide any further changes. She decided to:

1. observe the children systematically;

2. determine the characteristics of the activities which interest them; and

3. find ways to connect individuals to reading and literature enjoyment activities.

OBSERVATIONS OF CHILDREN'S CHOICES OF ACTIVITIES

Helene Franklin's observation device was simple and efficient and did not interfere with her usual interaction patterns with the children. Yet, it generated a great deal of information. (See Figure 1.1 for an example of the observation chart.) She made a list of the children's names down one side of a sheet of paper. Across the top of the page, she listed the centers, then drew a column down the paper for each center. She placed a number in the center column to indicate the fifteen-minute time interval for the center when she observed the children. For example, the first fifteen minutes would be *1*, the second fifteen-minute interval *2*, the third *3*, and fourth fifteen minutes would be *4*. The children were free to remain at activities as long as they desired during choice time. If a child stayed in the same center for more than one fifteen-minute period, the teacher wrote *2,3* under the column. At the end of the week, it was evident from the charts which centers were popular and the pattern of activity for each child.

An observation system need not be complicated to be effective. One of Ms. Franklin's colleagues had a parent volunteer come to the classroom and complete a checklist; another teacher asked the children to tell her the centers they liked best then randomly noticed how they were spending their time over the course of the morning. A student teacher, who was making a photo album of her class, took instant print pictures of activities during center time. Some teachers prefer anecdotal notes and simply choose to focus their attention on the library to see who visits the area and what activities take place. They write a collection of notations and often consult with the aide to recall the children's interests. Whatever the system of observation, it is imperative to look at the frequency with which the library area, books, and book-related activities are chosen, by whom, and what the children actually do.

Figure 1.1 Sample Form for Observation of Center Use

Date: (Three weeks into library emphasis)
Comments: (Special activities which may cause traffic in an area)

KEY: A-Art; B-Blocks; C-Computer; HK-Housekeeping including Dress-up; L-Library;
M-Manipulatives, Puzzles, Small motor, Mathematics materials; M/L-Music and Listening;
S-Science Table; TP-Theme Project; W-Writing; WT/ST-Water Table and Sand Table;
Other-Additional special activities, as cooking, carpentry

DIRECTIONS: Scan the room every fifteen minutes and place a numeral under the column indicating the center where the child is at the first fifteen-minute scan (1); at the second fifteen-minute scan (2); at the third fifteen-minute scan (3); and at the fourth fifteen-minute scan (4).

| NAMES | CENTERS | | | | | | | | | | | |
Child	A	B	C	HK	L	M	M/L	S	TP	W	WT/ST	Other
Damien			1,2		3	4						
Jason		1,4				3	2					
Monica				1,3	2				4			

Add totals for the day. How many children went to each center? Which centers were used for longer period of time?

Summary Comments: _____

_____

_____

CHARACTERISTICS OF ACTIVITIES THAT INTEREST YOUNG CHILDREN

Another important piece of information teachers want to know is what centers and types of activities interest the children. After her initial week of observations, Helene Franklin decided to observe more closely the areas the children were choosing and try to find out what characterized their activities. After careful review, Helene made several inferences which guided the changes she decided to make in the classroom.

This year, as with every year's class, the kindergartners were an active group. If the class library was going to become an area the children chose, it would have to become more active. Secondly, many children were very interested in fine-motor manipulatives. The puzzles, small building blocks, cutting and pasting artwork, and the mathematics sorting materials were always chosen. If the library was to become an area they chose, it would have to become more manipulative and include much more fine-motor activity. This group of five-year-olds, like all the classes she had taught before, were social beings. They enjoyed one another's company and, with the exception of a few children who liked solitary activity, made friends easily, and seemed content to form and disband groups. If the library was to become an area the children chose, it must become more of a social area.

Active, fine-motor oriented, social—Ms. Franklin had known these characteristics of five-year-olds for a long time, but she had not thought to use these descriptions as a guide to reinvigorating the interactions with books in her curriculum plans and in the classroom library. When Helene reflected on what she knew about five-year-olds in general and each of the children individually, she began to formulate a plan to increase the children's interest in books.

Helene also soon realized individuals were another key. She began thinking about two types of children in her classroom, the ones who were leaders and the ones who played alone. She decided to begin with them. Among the girls, Michelle certainly qualified as a leader. She enjoyed the role, relished the attention, and even though some of her methods of getting the other children's participation left a lot to be desired, she was the one to whom they turned. Among the boys, Jason, the block builder, was a crew chief. When he declared himself the boss, others followed easily. Then, there were the solitary players. Some were like Damien who engaged in playing with others often, but who enjoyed solitary activity, as well as extraordinarily complex tasks. Whenever Helene thought about her class, she always worried about Katrina, who was young and shy, yet interested enough to at least stay on the periphery of the activity. Ms. Franklin decided to concentrate her first efforts on these four students, Michelle and Jason, the social leaders, and Damien and Patrick, the solitary players.

HELENE'S PLAN: KINDERGARTNERS' CHARACTERISTICS AND INDIVIDUALS' CHARACTERISTICS

On her notepad, Ms. Franklin printed in bold letters ACTIVE, FINE-MOTOR, SOCIAL. Her next chore was to decide which activities to change in the library area to make it more active and fine-motor oriented, as well as a social place. Then, she planned to invite the four children, Michelle, Jason, Damien, and Katrina, and observe what happened. But first some background information on the four children.

The Leaders: Michelle visited the library center often, but primarily with Alicia. Monica was often included in their play group when they went to creative dramatics dress-up area. Ms. Franklin

decided to engage the three friends who were already a social unit by adding something active, a fine motor project that would entice them. Many children's books include stories of characters getting dressed, as Carlstrom's *Jessie Bear, What Will You Wear?* The following morning in group time, Helene brought some props and read the book while Michelle held a small teddy bear and dressed him. When the group time ended, Ms. Franklin asked Michelle to place Jessie Bear in the library and requested that Monica and Alicia each take one of the small suitcases she used for props. They had no idea what was inside, but once over in the library area, they opened it to find the Jesse Bear outfit. Michelle read, actually retold the book, while Alicia and Monica dressed Jessie Bear. Of course, others in the class became interested as well. Behavior among five-year-olds is often contagious, a spark of interest from one child ignites others.

Jason and his buddies from the block area were a bit more of a challenge. Ms. Franklin observed the builders quite closely and reconfirmed that Jason was indeed the leader. While open to other's directions, he retained control. The key to this social unit's participation in the book activities was Jason's leadership. During circle time one morning, Helene brought in the listening station with its four headphones and tape player. She explained how it worked, let Jason experiment with its operation as his buddies tried on the headphones. Helene read Carle's *Rooster's Off to See the World*, and at the end of group time, she asked Jason to help her set up the listening station on the edge of the library area. Of course his usual three followers volunteered to help.

The most difficult task over the first few days was getting Jason to relinquish his teacher role as the page turner for the other listeners. Helene capitalized on his leadership and interested him by letting him select three other books which she and the Jason crew made into listening tape sets, complete with sound effects. The four were eager participants and contributed to the recordings by repeating the recurring phrases from

Gág's *Millions of Cats*, Zemach's *It Could Always Be Worse*, and Rosen's *We're Going on a Bear Hunt*.

Jason was also in charge of recording the page signal for the tape, a clicking sound made by snapping a stapler near the microphone of the tape recorder. It worked. The little group listened to the tapes, reread the books, and Jason solicited other children to come over to hear them. Making recordings for the listening station, operating it, and having the page-turning responsibility became another social experience for the four.

The Solitary Players: The two less social children Ms. Franklin chose to focus on where not keen on being told what to do by a leader. While they were not antisocial, Damien and Katrina seemed content to follow their own interests. Damien enjoyed challenges, tried the most difficult puzzles, played computer games, and was the architect for some elaborate structures of bristle blocks and tinkertoys. Helene knew if she was to attract him to books, there must be a puzzle involved. At first she thought she might simply bring over some puzzles that related to the books on animals, but that was much to simple for Damien. What was puzzlelike with enough of a challenge to keep him involved?

The flannel board or felt board was the answer. Helene had a number of flannel board stories, but only one with the accompanying book, *The Very Hungry Caterpillar* (Carle, 1981). She decided to see if she could peak Damien's interest. She invited him to spread all the flannel board pieces out so he could see them, just like he did when working a puzzle. While she read the book, Damien found the pieces to go on the flannel board. One reading was enough. He immediately took the book from the teacher's hands and said, "Let me do it." This time he turned the pages, reassembled the flannel board pieces and told the story in sequence. On the third session, he was muttering under his breath saying the words, "But he was still hungry," for each turn of the page. Just as Damien had enjoyed working and reworking the puzzles, building and rebuild-

ing the block structures, he became engrossed in building the story from beginning to end. But Helene knew one story puzzle was not enough. If she wanted Damien to continue working the puzzle of the sequence of a story, she needed more flannel board stories to accompany books. She chose another Eric Carle book, *The Very Busy Spider,* and two folktales, *The Mitten* (Tresselt) and *Three Billy-Goats Gruff: A Norwegian Folktale* (Appleby). As Helene made new selections of books for her classroom, she remembered to select some puzzle books, her code word for books that could be turned into good flannel board stories.

The Puzzling Child: Katrina was not like Damien. While she was often alone like Damien, she seemed to be on the periphery of activities. While building or painting, she looked longingly over to groups of children, sat on the edge of the large block area and observed, or stood near the science table watching others experiment. She was quite responsive to Helene's attention and the aide's, but when the two teachers stopped interacting with her, she left the activity and began her sideline routine again.

Helene returned to her original plan: Observe the children, see what interests them, and find a way to connect the activity to the books. Obviously, the only thing that captured Katrina's attention was the other children. She was intrigued by them and their activities. Helene would have to find a way to get Katrina into a social group. She must involve Katrina in something that the other children would want to do.

Helene, the teacher, contemplated several alternatives. Katrina was too shy to be the leader in some fingerplays. She was too quiet to lead a group tape recording of books, and too easily distracted to show others how to operate one of the new computer games. As Helene mulled over the possibilities, she recalled other Katrinas she had taught over the years. While she respected who each child was as an individual, the shy children who wanted to be a part of a group often needed a helping hand. She recalled what worked with other shy children she had taught and decided on puppets. The children's attention would be on the puppet, not on Katrina.

One problem remained — how to keep Katrina an important person with the puppets. Katrina's usual pattern of interaction was to let others take over. The key might be the designation of Katrina as the main character for a week at a time. Going back to folktales again, Helene thought that the main character is the character the children most want to be. In *The Three Billy-Goats Gruff*, it is the big billy goat. In *The Mitten*, it is the mitten, which all the animals squeeze into until it breaks.

For days, Helene involved Katrina and a few others in making stick puppets for *The Three Billy-Goats Gruff* and animals for *The Mitten*. After the puppets were made, Helene designated the characters. She read the book aloud to the small group and they acted out the play. The children interacted with the story and with Katrina. The challenge remained for Helene to find other ways to incorporate Katrina into the children's groups, but for a week, the child's confidence was built as she participated at the center of a group, not on the periphery.

APPLICATIONS FROM HELENE'S CLASS

Ms. Franklin is an experienced teacher who knows children and knows what she wants them to accomplish. What can be extrapolated from this case description of her classroom? Obviously we can apply the same attributes Helene listed to ensure that the activities are appealing. The early childhood classroom library and book invitations should be:

☐ active

☐ fine-motor oriented

☐ social

But there are other suggestions for success that can be derived from Helene's experiences.

☐ Evaluate one's own selection and presentation of books.

☐ Observe the children systematically.

☐ Determine the characteristics of the activities which interest them.

☐ Find ways to connect individuals to reading and literature enjoyment activities.

Helene's plan was brilliant and straightforward. It took advantage of what she knew about the nature of the five-year-old as a learner, but it also was based on what she knew about the individuals in her classroom. There are many more pointers one could take from Helene Franklin's kindergarten. If a videotape camera had been placed in her classroom and recorded the activity when Helene and the aide focused their attention on the library area, it would be readily noticeable that with each addition of materials, Helene and the aide reorganized the space, equipment, and design of the library areas. They brought many new books into the area and kept some of the children's favorites. With the school librarian's help, they located and read books for possible connections they might build between the story and other class activities.

Teacher as Learner

Helene Franklin's own teaching experiences are poignant examples of assimilation and accommodation. In her first year of teaching, Helene set up her classroom, just like the one in which she did her student teaching. The books she read at circle time or group time were the tried and true ones she learned about in her beginning years of teaching. She read them expressively, but until recently, she had not thought of teaching the children to focus on constructing meaning from the text. Similarly, just as in her student teaching, the library center was called the book corner, and it was definitely a quiet place. All the books had to stay in that area of the room, and if a child removed a book, he or she was promptly told that the books must remain in the library corner.

After a few months of teaching kindergarten, Helene found herself rearranging her classroom and making small adaptations by moving centers from one area of the room to another. But, the book corner and her basic understandings of books in young children's lives remained virtually unchanged. In the library area, the books were displayed with their covers facing out. The book shelves were low and easy for the children to reach. There was a table with three chairs and a bulletin board with dust jackets of the books arranged nicely for a visual display. The rules for the children were the same as those of Helene's supervising teacher from her student teaching days. No more than three children in the book corner at one time, and they must remain quiet in that well-defined area.

Gradually, Helene made changes. After visiting another teacher's classroom, she added some comfortable floor pillows for the children to lounge on while looking at books and changed the name from the quaint book corner to the library center. However, there were no basic changes in her concept about children's interactions with books, until she was confronted with a new way of thinking about emerging literacy.

Over the summer break, she read about whole language (Goodman, 1986; Holdaway, 1979; Raines & Canady, 1990) and was confronted with information about young children's emerging literacy and quite different descriptions of interactions with books and stories. Suddenly, Helene began to question her presentations of books to children, the time she planned for children to explore books on their own, and the quiet little book area. It certainly was not the hub of the classroom, with writing centers, art areas, and listening stations radiating out from it, an area alive with activity.

Helene restructured her classroom based on resolving information that conflicted with her present level of understanding. Reconceptualizing is the process of accommodating new information. However, as with all good teachers, Helene began as she always did, with the children. She let her knowledge of their developmental needs and her observations of them as individuals guide the reor-

ganization of her teaching, of the class time, and of materials and activities for more story and book enjoyment. She saw the children's needs differently.

As teachers' concepts of young children's emerging literacy change, so does their use of time, space, and materials in the classroom. Children need many interactions and adult guidance with the text in books to become literate and that realization prompted Helene's investigations of her own classroom operation, which included the center-use observations. However, there was another important factor in the classroom changes, her growing appreciation of children's literature.

In a graduate class, she studied children's literature, laughing as she enrolled and remembering as an undergrad, calling the course "kiddie lit." After a few weeks, as she plowed through the school's library, the public library, and several book stores, reading hundreds of children's books along the way, she developed an appreciation of these books as fine literature. Most importantly, she realized her classroom collection of books needed to be revitalized. There were so many wonderful books that she wanted her students to enjoy.

The Revitalized Classroom Collection

Helene's rediscovery of children's literature began with looking at the various types or genres of children's literature and deciding on some good titles in each category to add to the classroom collection. Helene also located books she would use throughout the year. She wanted the books to connect with the themes of the curriculum units she planned. She kept in mind the young child's developmental needs and possible titles individual children would find of interest.

The revitalized classroom book collection would offer more read-aloud selections, would allow children to explore books on their own, and would include more stories that could accompany activities, which would help the child revisit the story. Revitalizing the classroom book collection required

Helene to become much more knowledgeable about children's literature. She began by:

1. reviewing books;
2. including a wide variety of genres;
3. coordinating books with curriculum units; and
4. finding more multicultural books.

WAYS OF THINKING ABOUT CHILDREN'S LITERATURE

According to Charlotte Huck, "a child's book is a book a child is reading, and an adult book is a book occupying the attention of an adult" (Huck et al., 1993, p. 7). There are many intriguing stories for children that hold adults spellbound. Recently, a father was reading to his two children, one a preschooler and the other a second grader. Not having been read to as a child, the father was determined that his youngsters would hear the famous children's books read aloud. One evening, his wife looked up to see both Nathan and Caroline sound asleep while the father continued reading *The Velveteen Rabbit or How Toys Become Real* (Williams, 1981). When she interrupted him and asked why he was still reading when they were sound asleep, he said, "I just wanted to see how this part turned out."

For the parents and teachers of young children, the early childhood years are a rediscovery of some of the stories they once loved or were deprived of as children and a discovery of how much books for children have changed since they were young. According to *Books in Print Plus* (February, 1993), there are 71,529 juvenile or children's books in print. But how is a teacher to wander through the maze and find the best ones? Three major ways teachers make selections are by reading book reviews in journals and magazines, using lists of award-winning books, and by their own reviews of books in libraries and bookstores.

BOOK REVIEWS IN PROFESSIONAL SOURCES

Listed in Figure 1.2 and Figure 1.3 are some professional journals and periodicals early childhood teachers find helpful for reviewing books and making selections which will coordinate thematic units and children's literature.

Figure 1.2 Journals from Early Childhood Professional Organizations with Columns Devoted to Children's Books

Childhood Education, published by ACEI, infancy through early adolescence books
Association for Childhood Education International
11501 Georgia Ave., Suite 315
Wheaton, MD 20902

Dimensions, published by SECA, infancy through age eight
Southern Early Childhood Association
P. O. Box 5403
Little Rock, AR 72215–5403

Language Arts, published by NCTE, primarily kindergarten through middle grades books
National Council of Teachers of English
111 Kenyon Road
Urbana, IL 61801

School Library Media Quarterly, published by AASL, quarterly, covers all grade levels
American Association of School Librarians
50 E. Huron Street
Chicago, IL 60611

The Reading Teacher, published by the IRA, primarily kindergarten through middle grades books
International Reading Association
800 Barksdale Road
P.O. Box 8139
Newark, Delaware 19714–8139

Young Children, published by NAEYC, infancy through grade three books
National Association for the Education of Young Children
1509–16th Street, NW
Washington, DC 20036

The book reviews in the resources in Figure 1.3 are labeled by age and grade level:

N or Nursery refers to books for children ages birth to four

P or Primary refers to books for grades K–3, ages five to nine

I or Intermediate refers to grades 4–6, ages ten to twelve

A or Advanced refers to grades 7–9, ages thirteen to fifteen.

Figure 1.3 Periodicals Devoted Exclusively to Children's Literature

Book Links: Connecting Books, Libraries, and Classrooms — 6 issues per year
American Library Association
50 E. Huron Street
Chicago, IL 60611

Booklist — Monthly
American Library Association— Monthly
50 E. Huron Street
Chicago, IL 60611

Horn Book Magazine—6 issues per year
Horn Book, Inc.
14 Beacon Street
Boston, MA 02108

The New Advocate—Quarterly
Christopher-Gordon
480 Washington St.
Norwood, MA 02062

School Library Journal — Monthly
R. R. Bowker and Co.
Box 13706
Philadelphia, PA 19101

The WEB: Wonderfully Exciting Books—
Three times a year
The Ohio State University
The Reading Center
200 Ramseyer Hall
Columbus, OH 43210

BOOK AWARDS

In addition to reading reviews in professional journals and teacher magazines, children's book awards can guide teachers to the best books of the year. The Caldecott Medal is of particular interest to early childhood educators because it is given to the illustrator for the most distinguished picture book published in the United States. The award, first given in 1937, is named for Randolph Caldecott, an English illustrator who is credited with adding illustrations to children's stories to make them more appealing. (See Appendix A for a list of Caldecott Medal and Honor Books.) The Newbery Medal, based on literary quality, is named for John Newbery, who was the first publisher of books for children in England. Also administered by American Library Association (ALA), the Newbery tends to go to authors of books for older children. A further discussion of the Caldecott book award and other significant awards and their significance can be found in Chapter 4, where picture books are discussed in more detail. Since the books that win the Caldecott and the Newbery awards are usually automatic purchases for the school and public libraries, many teachers include the award winning books as read-aloud selections and when appropriate incorporate them into thematic units of study.

TEACHERS' PERSONAL REVIEWS OF BOOKS

An organized review of trade books helps teachers keep their reading relevant to both the children's literature and to their students' and the curricular needs. Annotations of the books might include notes on plot, setting, characterization, theme, point of view, and format, including comments on illustrations. It is also helpful to write brief comments about how the book might fit into curriculum units, learning centers, general concept development, or special notes about the simply irresistible stories for story sake. If working with a librarian to order books, it is often helpful to add the ISBN number to the bibliographic information.

Literary Elements

The following section is a brief discussion of the literacy elements used to describe children's books which includes plot, setting, characterization, theme, point of view, and style.

PLOT

Books for young children should have simple plots, with lots of action to move the story along. In picture books with plots, the illustrations extend the action in the text and help the reader and viewer think beyond the immediate text. Stories for young children end with a climax to the story problem, which is satisfying. Young children develop a sense of story forms when the plots follow patterns most associated with the genre. In addition, a good plot develops in ways that are logical to the young child. While children expect characters in a folktale plot to act in a certain way because of their past experiences with the story form, when they encounter stories from realistic fiction, they relate what is happening in story to how their own family or their friends act. Children build expected patterns and understandings of what should come next, yet the story must contain some surprises that peak the child's interest beyond the expected.

Even the simple plots in books for young children should follow a logical sequence of events. The problem to be solved must be one that interests them or through which the author creates a sympathetic character with whom the child can identify. For example, in Charlotte Zolotow's *Something is Going to Happen*, as the family awakens and proceeds to get ready for their day's activities, they have the feeling, "Something is going to happen." With each repetition of the phrase, the listener or reader wonders what it could be. The logical order of events leads to the climax when the family starts to leave the house, each going in his or her own directions, only to open the front door and discover a thick carpet of snow has covered the ground. It continues to fall, gently quieting the outside world.

Right hand! Left hand! Around you go!
Now back-to-back your partner in a do-si-do!
Mules to the center for a curtsey an' a bow!
An' hey there, skinny kid! Show the old cow how!

Courtesy of *Barn Dance*, published by Henry Holt.

In the fantasy book *Barn Dance* (Martin & Archambault), the problem is an imaginary one. A little boy hears music coming from the barn and goes to investigate. At first, he only peeks inside, but eventually the children know he will be dancing with the animals. As the morning light approaches, the suspense builds when he creeps back into his room, hoping not to awaken anyone.

The plot in children's books takes many varied forms. Often conflicts between people are developed as family members and friends struggle to retain or regain their relationship when confronted with a dilemma. Sometimes the problem is one of growing up, as Ira's dilemma about whether or not to take his teddy bear to Reggie's house for his first sleep-over. Children identify with Ira and his personal ambivalence in Waber's *Ira Sleeps Over* as they try to act grown-up and not be thought of as a baby. *Sloppy Kisses* (Winthrop) is the story of a child's dilemma of how to tell her father not to kiss her goodbye in front of her friends. Sibling rivalry is another conflict often found in children's literature. Whatever the dilemma, the climax of the story should be a satisfying resolution of the problem.

Conflicts with nature, such as rescue and survival stories, are ones young children find enticing, as they struggle to understand how the physical world operates. Weller's *Riptide*, a true story of a dog who saves a child's life and Himmelman's *Ibis: A True Whale Story* are good examples. Heroics by children, cheering for the animal to be rescued, or performing some feat to save the family are favorite plot possibilities for books for young children.

Reprinted with permission, *Ira Sleeps Over*, published by Houghton Mifflin.

For one minute,
three minutes,
maybe even a hundred minutes,
we stared at one another.

Courtesy of *Owl Moon*, published by Philomel Books.

A good plot means a good story that will capture the children's interest right from the beginning, hold their attention with actions which move the story along, follow a logical order of events, and end with the problem or dilemma resolved in an interesting, amusing, or satisfactory manner.

SETTING

Time and place of stories affect how children come to know them. The illustrations in picture books help the child immediately identify the setting and era. By looking at the cover of the book, most young children decide whether or not they are interested in the story (Raines & Isbell, 1991). Time and place often define genre. Often in folktales, fairy tales, realistic fiction, and fantasy, the suspense of a mysterious setting adds to the intrigue.

Sometimes the locale of a story is not stated specifically. It may be a farm, playground, city street, haunted house, or castle in a far-off land, but exact locations are omitted. While a book for older readers may state an exact era and geographic location, books for young children allow the listener

and reader license to image the setting.

Fantasy settings are often conveyed with brief references, which immediately place the reader or listener there. For example, "Long, long ago, in a castle by the sea, lived a young maiden." Other fantasy settings are contrived with a mix of reality and fantasy. The little boy's bedroom in *The Bear's Toothache* (McPhail) looks real, but conversations between little boys and bears are fantasy, delightful fantasy.

Setting and mood are related. For example, in *Owl Moon*, (Yolen) the father and child's night walk through a snowy landscape to go "owling" builds suspense, casts a spell of intrigue, and results in a warm, quiet, calm, and satisfying ending. The setting and mood can not be separated.

Similarly, setting, plot, and characters are interdependent combinations. In plots where the problem is a character against the forces of nature, as *Hurricane* (Wiesner), the plot is dependent upon the setting. To understand the story in *Stay Away from the Junkyard* (Tusa), the child must grasp the setting.

CHARACTERIZATION

In books for young children, the main character or characters are quickly identified. Whether animals with human characteristics, children in a modern family, or imaginary creatures in a Seuss fantasy world, the characters must be developed through associations that are easy for the child to make. The young child's identification with the character propels him or her to care about what happens in the story. Whether a memorable Seuss character as the fantasy elephant named Horton, who sits on an egg, or a memorable Sendak character such as Max in *Where the Wild Things Are*, the young child identifies with the main character.

The author of children's books often relies on dialogue to define the character. Youngsters expect Amelia Bedelia to speak in a certain way and always get the meaning mixed-up. Sometimes the voice of the narrator defines the character through description, as *Madeline* (Bemelmans). Another way characters are developed is by some critical incident or problem or the exploits of tall tale characters, as in *The Narrow Escapes of Davy Crockett* (Dewey).

The art of the illustrator is often responsible for bringing the sympathetic main character(s) to life. The Goldilocks and the Cinderella images children visualize are frequently the ones they first encountered in illustrations. The formation of the character in picture books for young children may be left to the devices of the artist with few words conveying the human nature, but the child constructs for himself or herself what the character is like by looking at the pictures. The scowl on the face of a disapproving stepmother in Cinderella or the subtle warm glow in the

To the tiger in the zoo
Madeline just said, "Pooh-pooh,"

Courtesy of *Madeline*, published by Puffin Books.

monsters eyes in *Where the Wild Things Are* tell the true nature of the characters.

Reprinted with permission, *Where the Wild Things Are*, published by Harper & Row.

Some characters become so endearing to young children, that at the very mention of their names, they can predict how the character might act in a different situation. For example, after reading a few of Arnold Lobel's frog-and-toad stories, as *Frog and Toad Are Friends* and *Frog and Toad Together,* when first and second graders wrote their own Frog and Toad tales, the two characters acted in a predictable way (Raines, 1986). After a few *Curious George* (Rey) stories, some preschoolers took the toy Curious George and acted out some new dilemmas, but George always got into trouble and predictably some kind adult helped him out of his problem.

Courtesy of *Jamaica's Find,* published by Houghton Mifflin.

THEME

The theme of children's books is often the literary element that causes teachers to select the book for their classroom collections. The theme is the underlying idea or message the writer is trying to communicate. Teachers implementing a social studies unit on self-concept might choose books where young children solve challenging everyday dilemmas. For example, in *Jamaica's Find* (Howell), the little girl's decision to take a small stuffed animal to the lost and found desk, rather than keeping it for herself, ends with the child feeling good about herself for doing the right thing. Teachers implementing a science unit on the environment could choose books with the theme of how people affect their environment. Such books as *The Great Kapok Tree* (Cherry) and *The Empty Lot* (Fife) are good examples. If respect for the elderly is a key concept in a unit on families, then teachers might select Tomie dePaolo's, *Now One Foot, Now the Other* or Martin Waddell's *My Great Grandpa.*

POINT OF VIEW

Who tells the story conveys the point of view. If some invisible narrator tells the story or the main character remembers an incident, the point of view affects the development of the plot. A parody of the three little pigs is *The True Story of the Three Little Pigs* (Scieszka), which tells the well-known story from the wolf's point of view. Sympathy is built for the main character by the point of view.

Young children have difficulty changing point of view once they have identified with the main character. As preschool and kindergarten teachers can attest, children do not like playing the mean old wolf in Little Red Riding Hood or becoming the troll in *The Three Billy-Goats Gruff*. Bernice Cullinan (1989) explains that young children are so egocentric in this preoperational stage that they can not take another point of view other than the one with which they first identify.

Courtesy of *The True Story of the Three Little Pigs*, published by Viking Kestrel.

STYLE

Style is the illusive quality which defines why some writer's works are so easily identifiable. It is Leo Lionni's poetic turn of phrases in *Frederick* and in *Matthew's Dream*. In E. B. White's *Charlotte's Web*, descriptions of the barnyards are so vivid, the listener or reader is transported right into the barn with Wilbur, the pig. The style of writing is the author's creative voice, and it is the lure for the reader. Whether the use of strong metaphor, a gift for description, genuine humor, or authentic dialogue from another era, the style of writing makes the story memorable.

Similarly, in the picture book, the style of illustration makes the book memorable. The style of illustration must match the mood, drama, setting, and panache of the writer. A magnificently crafted story with style and flare lies dormant with the wrong illustrations. Similarly, no matter how wonderfully artistic the illustrations, if the story is not told in an appealing style, the reader or listener is left bored.

Courtesy of *Matthew's Dream*, published by Alfred A. Knopf.

Wide Variety of Genres and Forms

Children's literature experts recommend selecting from a wide variety of genres and types of books (Cullinan, 1989; Huck et al., 1993; Norton, 1987). However, many children's books defy classification. While adult literature is easily classified as fiction or nonfiction, poetry or prose, when one classifies children's books by genre, the labels become blurred. For example, the form most teachers of young children identify first is picture books. Yet, picture books can be realistic fiction, fantasy, or folk literature. To achieve the balance in variety of types of literature, seek titles in the genres most appropriate for the young learner. Historical fiction and science fiction are seldom written for the preschool and early primary child because the young child lacks historical perspective and is so centered in the present that he or she does not identify with the significance of the past or future orientations necessary to construct the significance of these texts.

PICTURE BOOKS

For teachers of young children, the form which interests them most is the picture book. Picture books tell a simple story through a masterful blend of text and illustrations. As the art of illustration and printing has advanced so significantly, many picture books are remembered most by the illustrations. In fact, numerous authors of picture books are also famous illustrators. Eric Carle, Barbara Cooney, Jan Brett, Tomie dePaola, Leo Lionni, Maurice Sendak, and Pat Hutchins, to name a few. Picture book author/illustrators have contributed greatly to the critical acclaim of the picture book as an enticement to young children to want to read, but illustrators can also be credited with bringing the world of art to the hands of the child. The infinite styles, forms, media, and combinations of media inspire young artists as well as young readers. In Chapter 4, read more about picture books and the awards that help teachers and librarians identify possible additions to their collections.

Alphabet Books: One of the earliest popular forms of picture books is the alphabet book, see Kate Greenaways' *A—Apple Pie*, written in 1886. According to bookstore owners, alphabet books are often the first type of book parents purchase for their youngsters. There are many levels of complexity among alphabet books, from simple illustrations which show the letter and an object or objects that begin with the sound associated with that letter to complex stories, thematic formats, and multicultural interpretations.

Teachers should consider their goal for using the book to decide which ones are most appropriate. For students learning the alphabet, a simple letter to object association is most appropriate. For older students more complex stories can be told with the alphabet format. For a thematic unit on animals, the Jan Thornhill's *The Wildlife A. B. C: A Nature Alphabet Book* provides both beautiful illustrations and in simple text describes an action for which each animal is most noted. For example, "B is for Beaver, felling a tree."

Counting Books: Like alphabet books, counting books can be quite simple or complex and multifaceted. For younger children, recognizing the numeral and counting the objects on the page provide the beginning associations for one-to-one correspondence, as in Hoban's *Count and See*. For older children, story lines, intriguing plots, puzzles, rhymes, and actual problems to be solved provide more of a challenge, as how to divide cookies among friends in Hutchins' *The Doorbell Rang*.

FOLK LITERATURE

Folk literature includes folk tales, fairy tales, tall tales, fables, myths, and legends. Once a part of the oral tradition, folk literature is particularly appealing for young children because the format is predictable. While the storyteller may embellish the tale, or the writer of a retold version enliven the text with more dialogue, the essential framework or the skeleton of the story stays the same. Whether beginning with "Once upon a time," making three wishes, or casting a wicked witch and a generous

Hey diddle, diddle,
The cat and the fiddle,
The cow jumped over the moon;
The little dog laughed
To see such sport,
And the dish ran away with the spoon.

Courtesy of *Mother Goose*, published by Putnam.

fairy godmother, the stories were originally patterned to be easily remembered for oral storytelling. Children soon begin recognizing the skeleton of these tales and find the predictability reassuring. After the second wish, there is always a third wish and the dilemma of the story is solved. The wicked get their just dues and good always triumphs. The characters, settings, and problems encountered follow a predictable pattern, just as the format of the language used becomes predictable.

In addition to folk and fairy tales, Mother Goose nursery rhymes are also a part of this genre. The rhyming pattern of the Mother Goose rhymes makes them retellable, and the fact that they were a part of the oral language tradition places them in this category.

Folk and Fairy Tales: By far the most popular of the folk literature genre is the folktale. Retellings and reillustrations are published each year. For example, "Puss and Boots," is one of the told stories that was first brought to print by Charles Perrualt in the seventeenth century. A recent translation by Malcolm Arthur has been published with award-winning illustrations by Fred Marcellino. "The Gingerbread Boy," "Jack and the Beanstalk,"

Reprinted with permission, *Puss and Boots*, published by Farrar, Straus & Giroux.

Courtesy of *Pecos Bill,* published by Greenwillow.

"Goldilocks and the Three Bears," "Cinderella," "Henny Penny," and "The Little Red Hen," to name a few, have retold, illustrated, and written in parody and republished.

Folktales from many cultures have captured the imagination of publishers and teachers. In addition to the beauty and intrigue of the story, folktales from other cultures help young readers get a flavor of the language patterns, as well as the commonality and the differences between stories. Whether a cumulative tale with characters added at each scene, fairy tales, or magical transformations, various cultures share folk literature formats, but the language and style are unique. Many cultures have variations of the Cinderella fairy tale. Fairy tales are

also a part of folk literature, in that they originated as told versions, however, Charlotte Huck et al. (1993, p. 397) say Hans Christian Andersen's era is the beginning of the modern fairy tale, when the tale was first presented in written form, rather than appearing first in oral form.

Tall Tales: Tall tales are also a part of the genre of folk literature. Pecos Bill, Paul Bunyan, John Henry, Johnny Appleseed, and Davy Crockett are stories about characters with extraordinary strength or feats of endurance. These often told tales were passed around campfires and logging camps of another era. They now live on in children's books with simple versions written for young children. See Ariane Dewey's *Pecos Bill* for a well-written simpler tale with the exciting exaggeration of any tall tale.

Fables: Fables are short tales that were told to illustrate some trait or characteristic, often using animals to exemplify the teaching. Whether the "The Hare and the Tortoise" or "The Fox and the Grapes," Aesop's fables are the most remembered ones. Young children enjoy Paul Galdone's *Three Aesop Fox Fables* and *City Mouse—Country Mouse* illustrated by Wallner. Modern fables, such as Lionni's *Frederick* keep the tradition of fable writing alive. While fables were originally written to impart

Courtesy of *Frederick,* published by Pantheon Books.

some moral truth, such as the pitfalls of vanity or crying wolf too often, young children may not be able to state the significance of the tale, yet still enjoy the tale.

Legends and Myths: Derived from the oral storytelling traditions, legends and myths often focus on creation and nature. The stories use symbolism to explain a significant happening and to teach a lesson. Of the legends printed in books for young children, many

Courtesy of *Rainbow Crow*, published by Alfred A. Knopf.

are retellings or adaptations from a culture. For example, *Rainbow Crow*, retold by Nancy Van Laan, is the Lenape myth of how the crow became black as he brought fire to the earth and saved all the animals from freezing. Tomie dePaola's *The Legend of the Indian Paintbrush* is a retelling of the tale of a young Indian who is given a special gift, the ability to draw and paint, and with it he records what happens to the People.

FANTASY

A revitalized library collection for young children must include wonderful works of fantasy where imaginary worlds come to life, where characters possess supernatural traits, where good triumphs and evil is destroyed. Fantasy for young children evokes strong emotions. According to Bernice Cullinan, "Fantasy is fiction that contains some element not found in the natural world; it hints of things magical" (1989, p. 279). Whether a talking spider or the last friendship of an enchanted time with a Pooh bear, young children savor fantasy. Afterall, their play is fantasy.

REALISTIC FICTION

Characters in realistic fiction are believable members of real-life settings. The language used by the writer is

Courtesy of *Winnie the Pooh*, published by Dutton Shephard..

There weren't any cars. There weren't any streetlights. There weren't any houses. Even the moon had set. And I knew we could never count all the stars.

Courtesy of *How Many Stars in the Sky?* published by Tambourine Books.

POETRY AND VERSE

Poetry seems such a likely match to the young child's fascination with language. Whether giggling at the silly rhymes of Shel Silverstein's in *Where the Sidewalk Ends*, or left with a warm calm after *Listen to the Rain* (Martin & Archambault) or feeling the glow of colors in *Hailstones and Halibut Bones* (O'Neill), children delight in the sounds and the meanings of poems. Any new

natural. The setting, events, and time could be real. Realistic fiction tends to deal with happenings of significant interest or derive some truth with which young children can identify. The point of view of the story narrator or the perspective from which the story is told must make sense to the young listener or reader. The mood and problems in the story are ones youngsters can associate with their own lives.

Many realistic fiction books for young children deal with growing up, families, dilemmas with friends, and dramatic life changes. While the realistic fiction genre is a favorite one for older elementary children, young children also find solace in many books of this genre. A popular growing up book children enjoy is *I Can Do It by Myself* by Leslie Jones Little and Eloise Greenfield. *How Many Stars in the Sky?* by Lenny Hort provides a boy a satisfying feeling of security with the father, while both of them miss the mother who is away from the family. *Something Special for Me* (Williams) shows how a family helps a little girl celebrate her birthday by contributing money to buy her a present. *Ira Sleeps Over* rings true for many young children as they must decide whether or not to accept their first invitation to spend a night away from home.

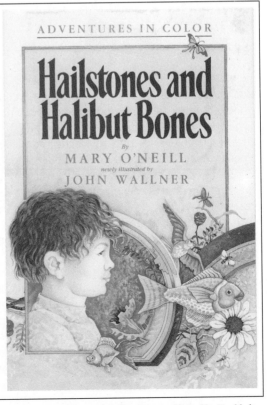

ADVENTURES IN COLOR

Hailstones and Halibut Bones

By
MARY O'NEILL
newly illustrated by
JOHN WALLNER

Courtesy of *Hailstones and Halibut Bones,* published by Doubleday.

library collection must include these poetry books and some favorite poets teachers have come to count on over the years. Some favorites include Jack Prelutsky, Karla Kuskin, Myra Cohn Livingston, John Ciardi, and the ever popular, Eve Merriam.

Addressing Curricular Needs

Teachers often find themselves balancing three major factors in the selection of books that they will read aloud to the children and books that will carry the main concepts of the thematic unit. The books they select as focus for their thematic units of study must be based on these factors:

1. children's developmental needs
2. curricular demands of the school
3. selection of the best literature to accompany units

The breadth of children's development is wide, the curricular demands are extensive, and the selection of books is immense. The next question becomes, "Where to begin?" Often school districts print recommended guides for units at each grade level. Experienced teachers already know the demands of the school system and novice teachers will want to work with mentors to determine what is required and what is recommended. Frequently, beginning teachers forget that the resource guides provided by the schools are just that, resource guides, and not program dictates.

Both experienced and beginning teachers must have extensive knowledge of child growth and development, which becomes the lens through which they examine curricular units, concept development, materials, and activities that are appropriate for the young learner. Three professional organizations have developed position papers that can serve as a refresher for veteran

teachers and as a clear standard for the new teacher for the "developmental lens":

1. *Developmentally Appropriate Practices* (Bredekamp, 1987) from NAEYC, the National Association for the Education of Young Children

2. *The Child-Centered Kindergarten* (Moyer, Egertson & Isenberg, 1987) from ACEI, the Association for Childhood Education International

3. *Literacy Development and Early Childhood (Preschool through Grade 3)* from IRA, the International Reading Association, and endorsed by six other professional organizations

By looking at curriculum guides and resources about books and using their own understanding of children's developmental needs, teachers can approach the task of coordinating the unit topic and appropriate literature rather systematically. For example, armed with the curricular expectations from the school district, which include a list of units, many teachers turn to a variety of sources about children's books to help with the selection process.

AND NOW BACK TO HELENE'S CLASSROOM

Helene Franklin's rediscovery of children's literature and her intensive review provided a wealth of new resources. Clearly, the difficulty arose with balancing, sorting, and selecting from the wide array of good literature. Rather than relying on a rather haphazard approach to selecting books, whatever was on the library shelves at the time, Helene was beginning to feel that finally she had the background knowledge to make wise selections. The next step became how to address curricular needs and connect the literature and the curriculum.

Helene's Approach to Coordinating Unit Themes and Good Books

As Helene Franklin thought about the kindergarten curriculum and reviewed the guides from the school system, she recalled the many good activities she had accumulated over the years that fit the units recommended for kindergarten. As she ran her finger down the list of units, she agreed with the importance of children studying the different seasons and celebrating holidays, but the social themes were the ones she felt she taught especially well, such as self-concept, families, feelings, and friends.

The longer Helene Franklin taught the more she emphasized the connectedness between themes. It was a natural extension for her to begin building better connections between the books she read at circle time and the activities she planned for the classroom. Thematic unit teaching, a long tradition in early education settings, reinforces concepts and helps children build connections to the main ideas in the books and the supporting ideas in the activities (Raines & Canady, 1990).

THEMATIC UNITS WITH A SOCIAL EMPHASIS

Many early childhood teachers in preschool through third grade begin the year with a social studies emphasis in a unit titled, "I am Me, I am Special, Look What I Can Do [Raines & Canady, 1991]." The unit seems to set a positive tone for the beginning of the year. The first book Helene reads to the kindergartners is *Something Special* by David McPhail, in which Sam the Raccoon yearns to be good at something, like all the other members of his family. Finally he finds his own special niche when he discovers painting. After reading the story aloud, teachers can emphasize that all children have special talents and this year they too will discover many new things they can do in their own special way.

After looking for a number of other self-esteem books to add as read-alouds for teaching the unit, Helene was thrilled to find *I Like Me!* by Nancy Carlson. She wanted to add a book that had a female as the main character. And while the girl in the story was a "pretty pink pig," there was no doubt kindergartners would like her.

Families: The community surrounding Helene's school was changing with more ethnic diversity, but also, like the rest of the country, families were changing. There were several children from single parent families, one child living with a grandmother, and

That best friend is me!

Courtesy of *I Like Me!*, published by Viking Kestrel.

Courtesy of *A Baby Sister for Frances,* published by Harper & Row.

a few with stepfathers. As is usual among young families, there also seemed to be a rash of new babies being born for kindergartners to learn to love, with all the accompanying emotional trauma. The families and feelings units seemed to go so well together, since much of the concern about families was the feelings they involve.

All Kinds of Families by Norma Simon is the book Helene uses to launch the unit each year, but she decided to look for some clever books, perhaps with a little humor to lighten the seriousness, which always seemed to surround the unit. Two funny books that are excellent for reading during the families study are Kevin Henkes' *Julius, the Baby of the World* and Marc Brown's *Arthur's Baby*. These two books along with the perennial favorite, *A Baby Sister for Frances* by Russell Hoban, would address the expanding family dilemmas that children seem to face with both tears and delight.

Feelings: From nightmares, teasing, and a fear of the unknown of school or a new neighborhood, understanding one's feelings seems to be a major early education milestone. Teachers emphasize positive feelings of love and affection among families and friends, but for five-year-olds, there are also those dreaded nightmares, fears, and temper tantrums. Mercer Mayer's nightmare books, *There's a Nightmare in My Closet* and *There's Something In My Attic* seem to bring reassurances, and children delight in the humor. Mem Fox, an Australian author, uses animal characters to explain young children's struggles to be good at something. In *Koala Lou* by Mem Fox, a koala thinks she has to win the field

---

Figure 1.4 Thematic Unit Topics Recommended for Young Children

I am Me, I am Special, Look What I can Do!
Families
Friends
Feelings
Animals, Real and Fanciful
Cats, Dogs, and Other Pets
Plants—I Like Growing Things
Science and Nature
Seasons (Each studied separately):
    Fall, Winter, Spring, Summer
Transportation
Whimsical Units
    Teddy Bears and Other Bears
Color All Around Us
1, 2, 3—Everyone Counts Units on Children's
    Literature
    Children's All-time Favorite Books
    Humor for the Young—Tall and Funny Tales
    Poems, Chants, Rhythms and Rhymes
*List adapted from:
Raines, S. C., & Canady, R. J. (1989).
    Story S-t-r-e-t-c-h-e-r-s: Activities to Expand Children's Favorite Books and *More Story S-t-r-e-t-c-h-e-r-s* (1991). Mt. Rainier, MD: Gryphon House.

olympics to have her mother still love her. Given the tremendous pressures on even young children to excel in sports, *Koala Lou* is a good choice to add to the feelings unit.

Friends: The units on families, feelings, and friends seemed to flow together nicely. Finding friends and staying friends concern the children and their parents worry too about whether their youngsters are making friends. The young child's struggles to move beyond their own self-centeredness and consider other's feelings and needs seem to be the source of a great deal of tribulation. Some popular friendship books are: Cohen's *Will I Have a Friend?*, *Best Friends*, and Wilhelm's *Let's Be Friends Again!*

Courtesy of *Koala Lou*, published by Harcourt Brace.

THEMATIC UNITS WITH A SCIENCE EMPHASIS

When Helene first began teaching, science was not her forte, but she worked hard to make the science units as popular as the social studies ones. Now she looked forward to teaching about plants, the environment, and animal life including caring for one's pet. She thought of adding a unit on birds and perhaps one on life in the sea.

Plants: Young children delight in digging in the soil, planting seeds, and watching the first leaves appear. After reading the simple text of the old favorite *The Carrot Seed* by Ruth Krauss, the children often boasted they would need a wagon to take their huge plant home, just like the little boy in the story. Cynthia Rylant's *This Year's Garden* helps the children appreciate how some families rely on gardens for their food through the winter. *Growing Vegetable Soup* by Lois Ehlert seems to appeal to the children who help their families in the kitchen, and a day of cooking soup in the classroom is sure to become a memorable event.

Environment: Helene thought of connecting her units on plant life and the environment. She decided to include a new book she had discovered, *The Great Kapok Tree* by Lynne Cherry as a bridge

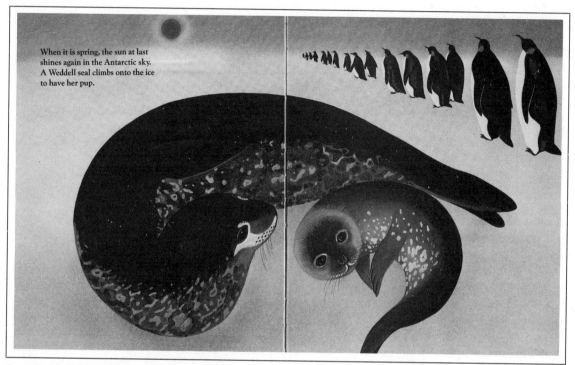

When it is spring, the sun at last shines again in the Antarctic sky. A Weddell seal climbs onto the ice to have her pup.

Courtesy of *Antarctica,* published by Farrar, Straus & Giroux.

into the unit on the environment. According to a children's book store owner, Bill Peet's *Farewell to Shady Glen,* an old environmental favorite, was enjoying a resurgence in sales. Another good environmental book is Dale Fife's *The Empty Lot,* the story of a man who visits the lot he plans to sell and sees so many plants and animals living there that he decides it is not empty after all. Other books on protecting the environment are: Susan Jeffers's rendition of *Brother Eagle, Sister Sky* and Joanne Ryder's *When the Woods Hum.*

Animal Life: When Helene first began teaching, almost all of the books about animals were farm books. Her students still enjoy farm animal books, such as Margaret Wise Brown's *Baby Animals,* republished with new illustrations by Susan Jeffers, and *Big Red Barn,* also republished with new illustrations by Felicia Bond. However, with the interest in protecting animals in the wild, many poignant books, such as Helen Cowcher's *Antarctica* and the true story of *The*

Puffins are Back by Gail Gibbons are becoming popular animal life focus books for a unit. Many of the youngest kindergartners will still enjoy the simple text and beautiful illustrations that match baby animals and their parents in *Whose Baby?* by Yabuuchi. Another book they like is *Big Ones, Little Ones,* a book of photographs with no words.

MULTICULTURAL UNDERSTANDINGS

As the community around Helene's school changed, she realized that she needed more literature representing different ethnic and cultural groups. Over the past few years, the school librarian helped by ordering selections that focused on African-American families, but now that more Asians from many countries and Spanish-speaking families from many cultures were moving into the neighborhood, Helene needed to work on expanding the multicultural books she read to the class.

Even if she had been teaching in a predominately white neighborhood, Helene was convinced that having books with characters from other cultures was an important facet of any good classroom. Over time, Helene had come to realize that children enjoyed a good story, whatever the ethnic backgrounds of the characters, but she was concerned that a stronger identification could be built if children saw illustrations and stories from many cultures.

Helene searched for contemporary fiction, poetry, and beautiful picture books with more cultures represented. She used realistic fiction books with African-American main characters throughout the year, as Ezra Jack Keats' *Hi, Cat!* for her unit on pets. She selected Elizabeth Fitzgerald Howard's *The Train to Lulu's* for the unit on transportation. For the friends unit, Helene always included Lucile Clifton's book, *Everett Anderson's Friend*, which addresses both cultural and gender stereotypes in an interesting story.

The librarian read a lot of Eloise Greenfield's poetry with the children, such as *Nathaniel's Talking* and *Honey, I Love and Other Love Poems*. Both Helene and the librarian realized they seemed to select books with African-American or Caucasian main characters and had few selections with Asian and Latino leads. Unfortunately, it was not easy to find these cultures in realistic fiction books for young children.

After reviewing a number of sources, Helene decided to add some books with other ethnic and cultural groups represented in the illustrations and some with featured main characters. She added two works by Japanese writers and illustrators that are appropriate stories for young children whatever the culture, Soya's *House of Leaves* and Tsutsi´s *Anna's Special Present*, both of which are illustrated by Akiko Hayashi. She also chose *Three Stalks of Corn*, which shows a Mexican-American community in California. The book that seemed to strike a responsive chord with many of the children who were learning English is Ellen Levine's *I Hate English!* in which Mei Mei, who left Hong Kong to move to New York, must now learn a new language.

In addition to these selections, which show young children from different ethnic and cultural backgrounds as the main characters, books are needed that are uniquely representative of a culture. The following books could be incorporated into the class folktales collection: *Toad is the Uncle of Heaven—A Vietnamese Folktale* (Lee); *Bringing the Rain to Kapiti Plain* (Aadema), an African tale; *The Eyes of the Dragon* (Leaf), a Japanese tale.

SUMMARY

Through the story of a successful, experienced kindergarten teacher, we examined the factors she considered when solving a teaching dilemma. She considered the children as learners, what makes a good children's literature collection, and curricular needs. When teachers examine the characteristics of young learners and individual's characteristics, they find appropriate ways to lead children to interact with books. Teachers who know about emergent literacy from the research and from their own experiences find that connecting the child, the curriculum, and the trade book takes advantage of the curiosity, excitement, and individuality of the kindergartner.

Reading books to children, helping them understand the literacy processes, and revitalizing the classroom book collection so that it is relevant to the young learner and to the curriculum requires an industrious review of children's books. To insure a varied collection, teachers must consider the different genres, review books using the literary elements, and select focus books for units that meet their curricular concerns. Concerned teachers who want their students to know and appreciate other cultures also select books that are multicultural, that show children from different ethnic, racial, and cultural backgrounds in the illustrations, as well as selecting books that are uniquely identified with individual cultures.

Helene Franklin's success story is told from the perspective of a knowledgeable teacher who understands young children's developmental needs and who appreciates them as individuals. Most importantly, Helene is a teacher who continues to grow in her own professional development. She makes informed decisions, based on new information and from her own sound judgments supported by years of experience and everyday observations in her classroom. While Helene is a kindergarten teacher, teachers of younger and older children can follow the same decision making steps:

☐ Evaluate one's own selection and presentation of books.

☐ Observe the children systematically.

☐ Determine the characteristics of the activities that interest them.

☐ Find ways to connect individuals to books.

Often, teachers want to take advantage of the new information on early literacy experiences by building the curriculum using children's literature; therefore, the classroom book collection and focus books for curricular units need to be located. Again, using Helene as a model, the four keys to revitalizing the classroom book collection are:

☐ reviewing books;

☐ including a wide variety of genres;

☐ coordinating books with curriculum units; and

☐ selecting more multicultural books.

Helene is just one of many teachers the reader will meet in *Stories: Children's Literature in Early Education*. Teachers can teach us through their success stories. Whether reexamining how the classroom is organized, getting back in touch with the young child as a learner, or struggling to meet new curricular guidelines from a school district, teachers are decision makers. You will read other teacher success stories and the changes made in their instruction and classrooms, as well as the reasons for their decisions. We will follow their observations, their plans for changes, and the ways they manipulated the materials, their schedules, the space, and changed their interactions with children both in group time and in the library to make the classroom a place to link literature and the young child's emerging and early literacy.

SUGGESTED LEARNING EXPERIENCES

1. Observe a teacher presenting a read-aloud selection. Think about the three-step process of before, during, and after reading. How would you help children relate the book to their own experiences?

2. Try Helene Franklin's observation device to determine which learning centers are the most frequently selected ones and the least often chosen ones?

3. Visit an early childhood classroom and sketch the classroom library arrangement.

4. Review a preschool or kindergarten teacher's schedule and see if there is any time for free exploration of books.

5. Talk with a teacher about transition times. How does he or she plan for transitions between major activities in the schedule.

6. Observe a small group of young children playing together. Write a paragraph about each child in the group based on your observations.

7. Interview a kindergarten teacher to determine the thematic units he or she is required to teach and others that might be beneficial.

8. Observe a classroom of children when they are asked to look at or read books. Notice the level of involvement of each child. How can you determine which children are deeply involved in the book and those who are just carrying out the teacher's request.

9. Select five of your favorite childhood books and write annotations of each by writing a sentence about each of the literary elements.

10. Browse through the children's section of a public or school library. Ask the librarian for at least five of the most popular children's books for age three to grade three. Read the books and analyze why you think they are favorites among young children.

ENDNOTE

1. Ms. Franklin's observation idea is adapted from several teachers' classrooms. However, the writers wish to thank Ms. Sharon Winstead, a teacher in Fairfax County, Virginia, who was one of the primary providers of classroom observations and Ms. Jessica Flowers, Director of the Vienna Baptist Children's Center, for insights about individual children.

REFERENCES

Anderson, R., Hiebert, E., Scott, J., & Wilkinson, I. (1985). *Becoming a nation of readers*. Washington, DC: National Institute of Education.

Bissex, G. L. (1980). *Gyns at wrk: A child learns to write and read*. Cambridge, MA: Harvard University Press.

Books in Print Plus. (1993, February). CD Rom Version. New Providence, NJ: R. R. Bowker. Electronic Publishing.

Bredekamp, S. (Ed.). (1987). *NAEYC position paper on developmentally appropriate practices in programs for 4- and 5-year-olds*. Washington, DC: National Association for the Education of Young Children.

Cullinan, B. E. (1989). *Literature and the child*. San Diego: Harcourt Brace Jovanovich.

Durkin, D. (1966). *Children who read early*. New York: Teachers College Press.

Early Childhood and Literacy Development Committee. (1988). *Literacy development and early childhood (Preschool through grade 3)*. Newark, DE: International Reading Association.

Galda, L., Cullinan, B. E., & Strickland, D. S. (1993). *Language, literacy, and the child*. Fort Worth: Harcourt, Brace, Jovanovich College Publishers.

Goodman, Y. M. (1986). Children coming to know literacy. In W. H. Teale & E. Sulzby (Eds.), *Emergent literacy: Writing and reading* (pp. 1–14). Norwood, NJ: Ablex.

Holdaway, D. (1979). *The foundations of literacy*. Sydney: Ashton Scholastic.

Huck, C., Hepler, S., & Hickman, J. (1993). *Children's literature in the elementary school* (pp. 7, 397). Fort Worth: Holt, Rinehart and Winston, Inc.

Moyer, J., Egertson, H., & Isenberg, J. (1987). The child-centered kindergarten. *Childhood Education, 63*(4), 235–242.

Norton, D. E. (1987). *Through the eyes of a child: An introduction to children's literature*. Columbus, OH: Merrill.

Raines, S. C., & Canady, R. J. (1990). *The whole language kindergarten*. New York: Teachers College Press.

Raines, S.C., & Canady, R. J. (1989). *Story s-t-r-e-t-c-h-e-r-s: Activities to expand children's favorite books*. Mt. Rainier, MD: Gryphon House.

Raines, S. C., & Canady, R. J. (1991). *More Story s-t-r-e-t-c-h-e-r-s: Activities to expand children's favorite books*. Mt. Rainier, MD: Gryphon House.

Raines, S. C., & Isbell, R. (1991, April). Book interest and interaction behaviors of young children in the classroom library. Paper presented at Association for Childhood Education International, San Diego.

Rosenblatt, L. (1978). *The reader, the text, the poem*. Carbondale, IL: Southern Illinois University Press.

Roser, N. L., Hoffman, J. V., & Farest, C. L. (1990). Language, literature and "at risk" children. *The Reading Teacher, 43*(8), 554–559.

Strickland, D., S., & Morrow, L. M. (1989). Developing skills: An emergent literacy perspective. *The Teaching Teacher, 43*(1), 82–83.

Taylor, D. (1983). *Family literacy: Young children learn to read and write*. Exeter, NH: Heinemann.

Wells, G. (1986). *The meaning makers*. Portsmouth, NH: Heinemann.

CHILDREN'S LITERATURE REFERENCES

The authors and illustrators of children's books are listed, in all chapters, by their full names to help the reader become acquainted with them. If only one name is listed, the author also illustrated the book.

Aadema, Verna. (1981). *Bringing the Rain to Kapiti Plain*. Illustrated by Beatriz Vidal. New York: Dial Books for Young Readers.

Aesop. (1970). *City Mouse—Country Mouse and Two More Mouse Tales from Aesop*. Illustrated by John Wallner. New York: Scholastic.

Appleby, Ellen. (1984). *Three Billy-Goats Gruff: A Norwegian Folktale*. New York: Scholastic

Bemelmans, Ludwig. (1939). *Madeline*. New York: Puffin Books.

Brown, Marc. (1987). *Arthur's Baby*. Boston: Little, Brown and Company.

Brown, Margaret Wise. (1989). *Baby Animals*. Illustrated by Susan Jeffers. New York: Harper & Row.

Brown, Margaret Wise. (1989). *Big Red Barn*. Illustrated by Felicia Bond. New York: Harper & Row.

Carle, Eric. (1972). *Rooster's Off to See the World*. Saxonville, MA: Picture Book Studio.

Carle, Eric. (1981). *The Very Hungry Caterpillar*. New York: Philomel Books.

Carle, Eric. (1984). *The Very Busy Spider*. New York: Philomel Books.

Carlson, Nancy. (1988). *I Like Me!* New York: Viking Kestrel.

Carlstrom, Nancy White. (1986). *Jesse Bear, What Will You Wear?* Illustrated by Bruce Degen. New York: Macmillan.

Cherry, Lynne. (1990). *The Great Kapok Tree*. San Diego: Harcourt Brace Jovanovich.

Clifton, Lucille. (1976). *Everett Anderson's Friend*. Illustrated by Ann Grifalconi. New York: Henry Holt.

Cohen, Miriam. (1967). *Will I Have A Friend?* Illustrated by Lillian Hoban. New York: Macmillan.

Cohen, Miriam. (1971). *Best Friends*. Illustrated by Lillian Hoban. New York: Macmillan.

Cowcher, Helen. (1990). *Antarctica*. New York: Farrar, Straus & Giroux.

Degen, Bruce. (1983). *Jamberry*. New York: Harper & Row.

dePaola, Tomie. (1981). *Now One Foot, Now the Other*. New York: G. P. Putnam's Sons.

dePaola, Tomie. (1988). *The Legend of the Indian Paintbrush*. New York: G. P. Putnam's Sons.

Dewey, Ariane. (1983). *Pecos Bill*. New York: Greenwillow.

Dewey, Ariane. (1990). *The Narrow Escapes of Davy Crockett*. New York: Greenwillow Books.

Ehlert, Lois. (1987). *Growing Vegetable Soup*. San Diego: Harcourt Brace Jovanovich.

Fife, Dale, H. (1991). *The Empty Pot*. Illustrated by Jim Arnosky. Boston: Little, Brown and Company and Sierra Club Books.

Fox, Mem. (1989). *Koala Lou*. Illustrated by Pamela Lofts. San Diego: Harcourt Brace Jovanovich.

Gág, Wanda. (1928). *Millions of cats*. New York: Coward, McCann.

Galdone, Paul. (1979). *Three Aesop Fox Fables*. Boston: Houghton Mifflin Company.

Gibbons, Gail. (1991). *The Puffins Are Back*. New York: Harper Collins Publishers.

Greenaway, Kate. (1886). *A-Apple Pie*. New York: Warne.

Greenfield, Eloise (1978). *Honey, I Love and Other Love Poems*. Illustrated by Diane and Leo Dillon. New York: Harper & Row.

Greenfield, Eloise. (1988). *Nathaniel's Talking*. Illustrated by Jan Spivey Gilchrist. New York: Black Butterfly Children's Books.

Havill, Juanita. (1986). *Jamaica's Find*. Illustrated by Anne Sibley O'Brien. Boston: Houghton Mifflin Company.

Henkes, Kevin. (1990). *Julius, the Baby of the World*. New York: Greenwillow.

Himmelman, John. (1990). *Ibis: A True Whale Story*. New York: Scholastic.

Hoban, Russell. (1964). *A Baby Sister for Frances*. Illustrated by Lillian Hoban. New York: Harper & Row.

Hoban, Tana. (1976). *Big Ones, Little Ones*. New York: Greenwillow.

Hoban, Tana. (1972). *Count and See*. New York: Macmillan.

Hort, Lenny. (1991). *How Many Stars in the Sky?* New York: Tambourine Books.

Howard, Elizabeth Fitzgerald. (1988). *The Train to Lulu's*. Illustrated by Robert Casilla. New York: Bradbury Press.

Hutchins, Pat. (1986). *The Doorbell Rang*. New York: Greenwillow.

Jeffers, Susan. (1990). *Brother Eagle, Sister Sky*. New York: Dial.

Keats, Ezra Jack. (1970). *Hi, Cat*. New York: Macmillan Publishing Company.

Kennedy, Jimmy. (1983). *The Teddy Bears' Picnic*. San Diego: Green Tiger Press.

Krauss, Ruth. (1945). *The Carrot Seed*. Illustrated by Crockett Johnson. New York: Harper & Row.

Leaf, Margaret. (1987). *Eyes of the Dragon*. Illustrated by Ed Young. New York: Lothrop, Lee & Shepard Books.

Lee, Jeanne M. (1985). *Toad Is the Uncle of Heaven: A Vietnamese Folk Tale*. New York: Holt, Rinehart & Winston.

Levine, Ellen. (1989). *I Hate English!* Illustrated by Steve Bjorkman. New York: Scholastic.

Lionni, Leo. (1967). *Frederick*. New York: Pantheon Books.

Lionni, Leo. (1991). *Matthew's Dream*. New York: Alfred A. Knopf.

Little, Leslie Jones, & Greenfield, Eloise. (1978). *I Can Do It by Myself*. New York: Harper Collins.

Lobel, Arnold. (1970). *Frog and Toad are Friends*. New York: Harper & Row.

Lobel, Arnold. (1972). *Frog and Toad Together*. New York: Harper & Row.

Martin, Bill, Jr. (1983). *Brown Bear, Brown Bear, What Do You See?* New York: Henry Holt and Company.

Martin, Bill, Jr., & Archambalt, John. (1988). *Listen to the Rain*. Illustrated by James Endicott. New York: Henry Holt and Company.

Martin, Bill, Jr., & Archambalt, John. (1986). *Barn Dance*. Illustrated by Ted Rand. New York: Henry Holt and Company.

Mayer, Mercer. (1968). *There's a Nightmare in My Closet*. New York: Dial Books for Young Readers.

Mayer, Mercer. (1987). *There's An Alligator Under My Bed*. New York: Dial Books for Young Readers.

McPhail, David. (1988). *Something Special*. Boston: Little, Brown and Company.

McPhail, David. (1972). *The Bear's Toothache*. Boston: Little, Brown and Company.

O'Neill, Mary. (1961, reissued 1989). *Hailstones and Halibut Bones*. Illustrated by John Wallner. New York: Doubleday.

Peet, Bill. (1966). *Farewell to Shady Glade*. Boston: Houghton Mifflin.

Perrault, Charles. (1990). *Puss and Boots*. Translated by Malcolm Arthur. Illustrated by Fred Marcellino. New York: Farrar, Straus & Giroux.

Politi, Leo. (1976, 1993). *Three Stalks of Corn*. New York: Macmillan.

Rey, H. A. (1941). *Curious George*. Boston: Houghton Mifflin.

Rosen, Michael. (1989). *We're Going on a Bear Hunt*. Illustrated by Helen Oxenbury. New York: Margaret K. McElderry Books.

Ryder, Joanne. (1991). *When the Woods Hum*. Illustrated by Catherine Stock. New York: Morrow Junior Books.

Rylant, Cynthia. (1984). *This Year's Garden*. Illustrated by Mary Szilagyi. New York: Macmillan.

Scieszka, John. (1989). *The True Story of the Three Little Pigs*. Illustrated by Lane Smith. New York: Viking Kestrel.

Sendak, Maurice. (1963). *Where the Wild Things Are*. New York: Harper & Row.

Seuss, Dr. Theodor Co. (1940). *Horton Hatches the Egg*. New York: Random.

Silverstein, Shel. (1974). *Where the Sidewalk Ends*. New York: Harper & Row.

Simon, Norma. (1976). *All Kinds of Families*. Illustrated by Joe Lasker. Niles, IL: Albert Whitman.

Soya, Kiyoshi. (1986). *A House of Leaves*. Illustrated by Akiko Hayashi. New York: Philomel Books.

Thornhill, Jan. (1988). *The Wildlife A. B. C: A Nature Alphabet Book*. New York: Simon & Schuster.

Tresselt, Alvin. (1964). *The Mitten*. New York: Scholastic.

Tsutsi, Yoriko. (1983). *Anna's Special Present*. Illustrated by Akiko Hayashi. New York: Viking Kestrel.

Tusa, Tricia. (1988). *Stay Away From the Junkyard!* New York: Macmillan.

Van Laan, Nancy. (1989). *Rainbow Crow*. Illustrated by Beatriz Vidal. New York: Alfred A. Knopf.

Waber, Bernard. (1972). *Ira Sleeps Over*. Boston: Houghton Mifflin Company.

Waddell, Martin. (1990). *My Great Grandpa*. Illustrated by Dom Mansell. New York: G. P. Putnam's Sons.

Weller, Frances Ward. (1990). *Riptide*. Illustrated by Robert J. Blake. New York: Philomel Books.

Wiesner, David. (1990). *Hurricane*. New York: Clarion Books.

Wilhelm, Hans. (1986). *Let's Be Friends Again!* New York: Crown.

Williams, Margery. (1981). *The Velveteen Rabbit or How Toys Become Real*. Illustrated by Michael Green. Philadelphia: The Running Press.

Williams, Vera B. (1983). *Something Special for Me*. New York: Greenwillow Books.

Winthrop, Elizabeth. (1980). *Sloppy Kisses*. Illustrated by Anne Burgess. New York: Puffin Books.

Yabuuchi, Masayuki. (1985). *Whose Baby?* New York: Philomel Books.

Yolen, Jane. (1987). *Owl Moon*. Illustrated by John Schoenherr. New York: Philomel Books.

Zemach, Margot. (1977). *It Could Always Be Worse*. New York: Farrar, Straus & Giroux.

Zolotow, Charlotte. (1988). *Something Is Going to Happen*. New York: Harper & Row.

2

Developmental Characteristics of Young Children

Developmental Characteristics of Young Children

*H*elping young children develop a love for literature involves more than an adult who has knowledge of books and techniques but one who also understands how young children grow, develop, and learn. A basic knowledge of child development helps the teacher interact with children in developmentally appropriate ways. Understanding children's development can assist teachers as they select books and materials that are meaningful to the children at each unique stage of development. This chapter will examine the patterns of development that serve as a basis for understanding groups of young children, anticipating their needs, and making predications about what is to be expected. But as with any discussion of stages and patterns, it is important to recognize that each child within a given stage progresses at a different pace and has unique interests that make each individual special. Early childhood programs that are working to implement developmentally appropriate practices will consider both the stages of the children in the areas of physical, emotional, social and cognition, and each child's unique pattern, personality, and background (Bredekamp, 1987).

Teachers must use their knowledge of developmental stages and individual differences to plan learning experiences which are appropriate for each child. Joanne Hendrick, in her book, *Total Learning: Developmental Curriculum for the Young Child* (1990, p. 13), emphasizes that teachers must "know what children are like," if they are to plan a curriculum which will provide opportunities for total learning.

Infant/Toddler Development

The roots of literacy begin when a baby is born. In these early days and weeks of development, young infants begin to listen to the voices of important people in their lives. They begin to view the world in special ways and structure their understanding of the world for themselves. During this first year of life, it is important to understand the capabilities of infants so language experiences that are appropriate and effective for this unique period of development can be provided. Although infants develop in a holistic way, it is helpful to look at specific areas of development to clearly understand their beginning capabilities. Developmental characteristics can then be used to guide the design of an environment and determine literature selections that are appropriate for the abilities of infants.

COGNITIVE AND LANGUAGE DEVELOPMENT IN THE INFANT AND TODDLER STAGE

Piaget (1955) and Vygotsky (1962) both describe the inter- relationship of cognition and language development. In the area of cognitive development, Piaget describes infants as being in the sensorimotor stage. During this stage, infants use their physical actions to learn about the world as they explore objects through looking, tasting, and touching and thus form concepts. Tactile books, like *Pat the Bunny*, and *The Touch Me Book* encourage infants to explore in these important ways.

Piaget (1962) described the importance of the development of object permanence, when infants are able to understand that people and objects continue to exist, even if they cannot see them. Object permanence provides a framework for future cognitive advances. A book such as Ahlberg's *Peek-A-Boo* encourages the infant to play with this concept of an object continuing to exist even though it is no longer visible.

Constructivism explains that children acquire language by constructing it for themselves while interacting with the environment. Some of the first words used by toddlers are words they have not heard in their environment but rather are their own creations such as "Ball, gone." These examples clearly indicate that they are constructing language for themselves as they interact with people and objects in their world (Kamii, 1991).

Vygotsky's theory (1962) emphasized the social and cognitive aspects of development. He believed that language makes thought possible, and eventually mediates children's behaviors. In addition, Vygotsky stressed the importance of children's social interactions and their observations of adults as they acquire language. In his first stage, external speech, language-thought development comes through interactions with an adult, usually the parent. The adult's speech attempts to direct the child's thoughts as when an adult asks a child, "What does a dog say?" In the second stage, egocentric speech, the adult's speech is no longer required but the young child speaks out loud as a way of thinking. "Me go bye-bye." This sentence is said by the toddler with no one present and indicates he is thinking about going outside.

Nativistic theorists (Church, 1961; Chomsky, 1969; Slobin, 1971; McNeill, 1970; & Lenneberg, 1966) believe that infants have an innate propensity for language and that the environment has little influence on this development. During the infancy period, there are two universal stages. The first is the preverbal stage, birth to four months, which starts with reflexive crying. Infants begin their first sound productions with cooing, which is an open vowel sound. Around four months, infants start babbling, which includes a consonant and vowel combination. During the cooing and babbling period, infants include many sounds that are not present in their native language. Later, they become more selective in the sounds they produce, eliminating those that are not useful and accelerating the use of others. During this six months, they begin to use the first features of speech, including intonation, juncture, and pause. Observers of infants can hear the similarity of the sound patterns and the sentences they will later use in communication.

In the passive stage, four to six months to one year, older infants begin their quest for linguistic competency. They demonstrate language comprehension when they increase their movements or smile when they hear familiar words or are asked questions. They are receiving language through listening and storing it for future use even though they cannot presently produce the words heard.

Around the first year of life, infants move into the second active verbal stage. During this period, infants produce their first words that are used to identify specific objects or persons in their environment. Their first word may be a word they have created to stand for an important object or person. "Bo Bo" can indicate a loved pet, "Da Da" can identify father, and "Ookie" can request a cookie. Their pronunciation may not be phonologically complete, but it has meaning and is used repeatedly to identify the same item. Some of the first oral productions are holophrastic utterances, and although they contain only one word, it means much more. An example of a holophrase is the infant's use of "up," meaning "I want to be picked up." If this utterance does not effectively communicate the infant's desire, or if the request is not followed, the infant will continue to say, "Up, Up, Up," with increased volume until she is picked up. "Up," a single word, stands for a complete idea.

In the next stage of language development, toddlers begin to use two-word utterances. They use pivot and open class words, which increases the different combinations possible and helps them communicate their ideas more effectively. By using "more" as a pivot word and combining it with changing words, infants can obtain "more milk," "more cookies," and "more juice." During the two-word utterance stage, infants frequently demonstrate that they understand a more complex language structure. If a caregiver asks them, "Would you like applesauce or peas for lunch?," infants can clearly make their preference known through gestures or a single word response. They are able to comprehend this eight word sentence and understand the semantical difference in applesauce and peas, but they cannot produce a sentence of this complexity. Infants receptive language is greater than their expressive language (Harris & Liebert, 1987).

An interesting language pattern that develops during this stage is telegraphic speech. Toddlers send complex messages, using an abbreviated form, leaving out the unimportant words and including the words needed to communicate the idea. These concise messages indicate that toddlers are not only learning vocabulary, but also the structure or syntax of language. In the communication unit "Go ride car-car," the toddler sends the message that "I want to go for a ride in the car." He strips this ten word sentence to the minimum and effectively communicates the same idea with three powerful words in the correct syntactical order.

Another theory that attempts to describe language acquisition is the behavioristic view (Watson, 1924). According to the behavioristic theory, there are three main ways that the environment affects children's behavior. The first is classical conditioning, which involves a simple inborn reflex paired with a stimulus. The second is behavior influenced through rewards and punishments, referred to as operant conditioning.

Figure 2.1 **Summary of Language Acquisition Birth to Two Years**

Summary of Language Acquisition Birth to Two Years		
Form	**Language Sample**	**Approximate Age**
Cooing	"oooo," "aaaa"	two to three months
Babbling	"ba-ba-ba" "do-do-do"	by five to six months
First Words	"Mama," "baba," "baw"	ten to fourteen months
Two-Word Sentence	"More milk." "Big dog."	twenty-one to twenty-four months

Behavioral theorists explain that language acquisition demonstrates how children learn through interactions with their environment. According to behaviorists, infants use the words that are reinforced by their parents; for example, after an infant says "Da Da" the father picks up and praises the baby. Positive reinforcement will ensure that the infant uses this word again. Infants and toddlers also use the words and dialect of their parents, which indicates that they are imitating the adults in their environment. Parents and other important adults serve as models for very young children as they acquire language.

Although these theories of language acquisition differ in their interpretation of the way infants and toddlers develop language, each concludes that the first two years of life are crucial in language development. Each interpretation attempts to describe how the infant grows into the curious two-year-old, full of questioning and trying to find verbal symbols for the world.

SOCIAL-EMOTIONAL DEVELOPMENT IN THE INFANT AND TODDLER STAGE

In the social-emotional domain, infants are totally dependent on their caregiver(s). In these early months, they are unable to separate themselves from this caring adult, but they do influence this reciprocal relationship. Their view of the world is colored by the responsiveness of the adults in their environment and having their basic needs regularly met. A caring adult who attempts to satisfy desires for nourishment and love helps an infant feel secure and establish a trust in the world (Erikson, 1963).

As infants move into toddlerhood, they begin to establish their autonomy and become a separate individual. This transition from dependent infant to independent toddler is filled with progressions, regressions, and frequent changes in their behavior. Books can focus on gaining autonomy. Oxenbury's *I Can* and *Tickle, Tickle* are examples of appropriate content for toddlers. The toddler often asserts individuality through the use of "no" and the refusal to comply with the adult's directions

Skinner (1957) refers to these rewards as reinforcers because he views them as strengthening the behaviors. The third type of behavior is obtained through observation and is usually referred to as social learning. Bandura (1965) has explored the importance of modeling and researched the influence of observations on specific behaviors. The behavioristic view of language emphasizes the environment and experiences that effect learning. Studies of very young infants have focused on environmental influences on their behavior in an attempt to determine how early this influence begins. Meltzoff and Moore (1977) reported that infants as young as twelve to twenty days could imitate an adult model who stuck out his tongue and opened his mouth. They demonstrated that newborns are able to imitate facial expressions and actions of an adult in the first month of their lives.

(Erikson, 1963). Although this behavior is sometimes viewed negatively by adults, it clearly demonstrates the toddler's positive move toward becoming an independent and separate person. Toddlers are learning how the world works, how they can participate, and how they can influence the activities.

PHYSICAL DEVELOPMENT IN THE INFANT AND TODDLER STAGE

Newborn infants can hear and move to the human voice (Alegria & Noirot, 1978). One-month-old infants move their arms and legs in rhythm with chants and music repeated by adults. This synchronized movement demonstrates their very early interest in the patterns of language and the human voice (Condon & Sander, 1974). During the first six months, infants' visual perception progresses from focusing on contrast, lines, and angles to perceiving more complex patterns (Cohen, 1979). As visual perception improves, toddlers begin to focus on details of specific objects in illustrations and begin to label them with words or sounds.

Major changes occur in the first two years of life in the area of physical development. In the first months, very young infants can only control their heads, but by the second year of life, toddlers are capable of walking, climbing, and manipulating small objects. During this period, an infant's physical arena expands from the confines of the crib to the toddler's entire home or rooms in a child-care center. With increased control of their bodies, arms, and legs, toddlers are able to physically examine a new and exciting world.

Infants and toddlers achieve body control following a pattern of directional growth. This principle explains that physical growth proceeds from the head down, cephalocaudal, and from the center of the body to the extremities, proximodistal (Hendrick, 1990; Maxim, 1985). Early in the infants' development, they use shoulder muscles to reach for an object, but by the end of the first year, they can use the pincher grip of fingers to pick up tiny objects, even fuzz, or thread.

The work of Gesell (1928) and Shirley (1933) explains that physical growth evolves through an orderly predictable sequence. Infants will crawl before walking and pick up food with their hands before they use a spoon. Current research indicates that the physical growth process may also be influenced by environmental factors such as nutritional deprivation and will require early intervention.

In the past decade, many changes have occurred in our understanding of the development of infants and toddlers. Theories and research support the view that there is an interrelationship in all areas of development and that this process, which is begun in the infancy period, influences later achievement. We now know that the basis for literacy is also established in the first years of life (Kulleseid & Strickland, 1989; Machado, 1990). As infants listen to books, they store words for future use. As toddlers scribble on paper, they talk about their writing and discuss the message it conveys.

Our new understanding of emerging literacy necessitates that we rethink our environments for infants and toddlers. They learn best when they are actively involved in an experience and have an opportunity to select and control the outcomes. We must immerse the infant and toddler in a language-rich environment where there are many real opportunities to actively use language, to hear stories, and to examine the content of books.

A Planned Environment for Infants and Toddlers

Infants and toddlers in the sensorimotor stage of development are progressing in body control and language abilities. When infants and toddlers interact with people and materials in an environment that is active and responsive, they flourish. Because of the similarity of infant and toddler needs, many environmental factors will be discussed and presented together. It is not suggested, however, that infants and toddlers be cared for in the same space, but rather be provided separate areas that are appropriate for infants and the more mobile toddlers.

The physical environment, at home and in child-care centers, should be both a safe and stimulating place where a child can freely explore and manipulate objects. The environment includes a variety of physical objects, such as squeak toys, rolling musical balls, and push/pull toys. Open space should be available so the infant can roll around on the floor, crawl, cruise by holding onto furniture, and the toddler can walk and run. Some of the toys in the environment should change and others should be continually available so favorite items can be cuddled or transported by the toddlers as they move from place to place.

A space designed for infants should be visually and tactically interesting. Contrasting colors and varieties of textures will provide these sensorimotor learners with opportunities to examine their world first visually, and later through physical manipulation. Simple pictures of familiar people and objects are displayed on the floor and at low

levels of the wall for the baby or toddler to view while lying, crawling, or walking. The toys are safe, washable, and responsive. A musical plastic ball, for example, provides an appropriate toy for infants because it produces movement and a musical sound when touched. A responsive object allows infants to begin to understand a cause and effect relationship and to continue to activate the toy as long as they wish. The area should also include a rocking chair for adults to use while cuddling, soothing, and reading to the infant or toddler.

Adults need to be verbally responsive to the infant early. Caregivers should describe what they are doing to the infants as they prepare their food, dress them, or change their diapers. Caregivers use language to share information, to explain, and to maintain conversations. Talking to the infants while caring for them assists infants in making the connection of sounds and words with the items and activities in their environment.

Adults, caring for infants, should respect and follow the infant's individual schedule. Routine tasks, such as diapering and feeding, are treated as special, individual times to focus on and interact with the child. Honig (1985) emphasized that, "A rich language curriculum must be embedded in everyday caregiving routines [p. 42]." These routine caregiving tasks provide opportunities for language interactions with an adult on a regular basis, including language games ("Peek-a Boo, I see you"), rhymes ("This little piggy went to market"), and songs ("Pat-a-Cake"). The adult can also provide verbal descriptions of the activity as it is occurring such as, "I am fixing your snack," "Today you are having apple juice," "Are you thirsty?", and, "It will be ready soon." The observant caregiver will provide pauses in the narrative to wait for a response from the infant. When the infant indicates she has tired of the exchange, closing her eyes or turning away, the caregiver will conclude the activity.

Adults can also imitate the cooing and babbling sounds the infants produce. As they interact with infants and maintain a cooing conversation, they demonstrate that this is an important and enjoyable activity for both. They provide many opportunities for interactive language by repeating and encouraging the infants' beginning attempts. This turn taking helps infants understand that language is important and that the adults in their world consider them a capable partner (Honig, 1984).

There are many activities that nurture the cognitive and language abilities of the toddlers. During this stage of language explosion, adults should be available to talk with the toddlers, answer their questions, and expand their responses (Stewart, 1982). Language experiences are provided for the individual toddler as well as implemented in very small groups. Books, jingles, and fingerplays are shared throughout the day.

The toddler area has many opportunities for large-motor development. The stimulating environment focuses on action-based sensory experiences for the moving toddler. Toddlers are more cooperative if they have opportunities for making choices and can have some control over the pace of activity (Honig, 1985). Their attempts to care for themselves, become independent, and learn to interact with peers are encouraged. Materials and activities are arranged so toddlers can determine their involvement and leave when they lose interest. A few well-planned toddler centers such as a housekeeping, block area, and art can provide opportunities to participate in small groups and choose the materials to be used.

Simple cooking experiences encourage labeling and discussions between the caregiver and the toddlers in meaningful situations. Toddlers tune into the story content, even though they are not sitting and listening. When a caregiver is sharing a story, and a toddler moves away, the reader continues reading the book. The caregiver knows that eventually, a phrase or picture will rekindle their interest and draw the toddler back to the book. Listening to literature is a "moving" experience for toddlers.

BOOKS THROUGHOUT THE INFANT AND TODDLER SPACES

In both the infant and toddler spaces, books are included in a special library area and are displayed at a low level so they can easily be examined by the sitting or crawling baby or the walking toddler. Very young infants need oilcloth or fabric books that can be tasted and mashed (Honig, 1985). *Baby's Toys 'n Things* is a small book appropriate to use with infants and *Look at Teddy* is a big book that would be effective with toddlers. They need durable and well-constructed, laminated cardboard word books that can be mouthed, bent, and dragged across the floor. Oxenbury's collection, including *Family*, is an example of board books that are appropriate for this stage. The books in the library area should relate to people, objects, and happenings that very young children have experienced. They include simple illustrations that are easy for toddlers to understand and label. Jan Omerod's *Messy Baby* provides label opportunities relating to the toddler's experiences.

Books should be read to infants regularly for they provide an experience with more advanced language while nurturing a love for books. Specific times should be planned for sharing books, but adults should also follow the individual infant's interest in a special book or desire to hear the book again. An adult who reads provides a powerful image for the very young child to emulate. The book *Reading* pictures a father reading to a toddler.

As Dorothy Butler (1980) emphasizes, "Babies need books [p. 1]."

A rocking chair in the area becomes a special place to be cuddled, talked with, and share a wonderful book. For a moving toddler, a rocking chair represents the place where a selected book can be taken and read by an adult as the toddler cruises around the room and then returns to hear more of the story. Toddlers enjoy hearing a story again, and again. They begin to anticipate the content and participate by making sounds, repeating words, or adding movements. A book like Helen Oxenbury's *All Fall Down,* invites the active toddler to join in the literary event. By making reading a pleasurable experience, you can "hook" them on books (Honig, 1985).

Humorous books can help the toddler and caregiver to cope with the stress of the toddlers' desire to do things for "my self" when they don't have the physical dexterity to complete the task. Watanake's *How Do I Put It On?* pictures a character putting a cap on a foot and shoes on the ears. *Tickle, Tickle* also by Helen Oxenbury describes a pleasurable activity while learning control. Funny books provide an emotional outlet for the toddlers working to gain independence and dealing with many frustrations.

Teacher-made books should be available in the toddler area because they are designed to have personal meaning for the infant or toddler. Teacher-made books include pictures of the baby, parents, siblings, home, pets, and other items of importance to the very young child. Additional books could be constructed that include pictures of adults, children, and activities experienced in the center. Personal books help infants and toddlers to begin to understand that books are special and are made to enjoy. Durable books can be constructed by putting photographs inside small plastic bags and taping several containers together with packaging tape. New pages can be added as a child has new experiences. Personal books often become the favorites of many infants and toddlers, and are carried around with them, and even accompany them to their cribs when they sleep.

BOOKS ACROSS THE INFANT AND TODDLER CURRICULA

Curricula specifically designed for infants and toddlers are being developed and expanded as more children are enrolled in child-care (Miller, 1990; Surbeck & Kelley, 1990; Wilson, 1986). Cataldo (1983) stated that an effective program for infants and toddlers must have two purposes. First, the program should help the very young child fully develop competencies needed in growth and learning. The achievement of these skills enables the infant and toddler to become more capable in motor control, experimentation with toys, and communication with others. Touching the pictures in a book to identify the objects in Hoban's *What is It?* allows the very young child to develop book handling skills and labeling of objects for language and cognitive development. A second major purpose of infant and toddler programs is to develop emotionally and socially. As infants and toddlers are developing, they begin to learn to manage their feelings, maintain relationships, and demonstrate their individuality. Books such as Parish's *I Can, Can*

You? and Oxenbury's *Mother's Helper* assist in building self-confidence and understanding of self. Caregivers contribute to the infants and toddlers social development as they provide attention and affection while accepting each individual's behaviors and abilities. An appropriate infant/toddler curriculum includes both planned and unplanned activities and is flexible in design so it can be paced for the individual infant.

Literature experiences for infants and toddlers should take place throughout the day, from arrival time, to individual story sharing, through to the close of the day. Chorao's *The Babies Goodmorning Book*, Oxenbury's *Playing, Dressing,* and Lewison's *Bye, Bye, Baby* are appropriate books for infants and toddlers that can be integrated into their daily activities. During the infancy period, many of these literature experiences will be individual and conducted in the lap of the caregiver. Sharing books should begin in the first months of the infants' life. The books selected to read to infants should be ones the reader enjoys which is demonstrated in the reader's voice and inflections. As the infant is able to focus on a picture, books with appealing and simple illustrations should be added.

In the toddler area, books will be shared individually but time will also be provided for small groups with a shared interest in a book. Some of the appropriate literature-related activities that are planned to provide variety for infants and toddlers include songs, fingerplays, rhymes, puppets, simple stories, and picture books (Jeffery & Mahoney, 1989).

Books can complement the planned activities in both the infant or toddler areas. If some older infants are rolling large balls, a book that shows a ball can be included in the experience. Hoban's book *Of Colors and Things* appeals to toddlers and has individual pictures of many different objects in the infant environment, including a ball. If toddlers are cooking, they can hear and examine a book while they are waiting for the pudding to thicken or the fruit salad to chill. If it is the birthday of an infant or toddler, a book about a celebration could be included, for example Watanabe's *It's My Birthday*. When the toddler class walks around the neighborhood, Shower's *The Listening Walk* could be shared. If a parent brings a rabbit to the classroom, the book *What Bunny Loves* by Szekeres can extend the experience into a literature happening.

Toddlers enjoy stories that have repetition of phrases that they can anticipate and repeat. They also like to label the pictures or make sounds that accompany the book or story. Brown's *The Big Red Barn* has large, simple illustrations with farm

---

Figure 2.2 **Professional References for Infant and Toddler Caregivers**

BOOKS OF FINGER PLAYS:
(SIMPLE FINGERPLAYS WITH EASY-TO-FOLLOW DIRECTIONS)
Finger Rhymes by Marc Brown
Hand Rhymes by Marc Brown
Let's Do Finger Plays by Marion Grayson
Trot, Trot to Boston: Play Rhymes for Baby by Carol Ra

COLLECTION OF SONGS FOR INFANTS/TODDLERS:
Singing Bee!: A Collection of Favorite
Children's Songs by Jane Hart (Ed.)
Lullaby Songbook by Jane Yolen

NURSERY RHYMES:
The Random House Book of Mother Goose selected by Arnold Lobel
Baby's Mother Goose selected by Al Schlesinger

Figure 2.3 Books that Fit the Developmental Characteristics of the Infant Stage

Books about People in Their World:	*Family* by Helen Oxenbury *Reading* by Jan Omerod *Messy Baby* by Jan Omerod
Participation with Tactile Books:	*Pat the Bunny* by Dorothy Kunhardt *I Touch* by Helen Oxenbury *Peek-a-Boo* by Janet and Allan Ahlberg *Misty's Mischief* by Rod Campbell *Bye, Bye, Baby* by Wendy Lewison
Playing with Sounds:	*Baby Says* by John Steptoe *The Baby's Lap Book* by Kay Chorao *Catch Me and Kiss Me and Say It Again* by Clyde Watson *Noisy* by Shirley Hughes
Everyday Happenings:	*The Baby's Good Morning Book* by Kay Chorao *I See* by Rachel Isadora *I Hear* by Rachel Isadora *What Is It?* by Tana Hoban *Playing* by Helen Oxenbury *Dressing* by Helen Oxenbury *Working* by Helen Oxenbury

Figure 2.4 Books for Toddlers

Labeling Books:	*The First Words Picture Book* by Bill Gillham *Max's First Word* by Rosemary Wells *The Wind in the Willows Word Book* by Kenneth Grahamme *The Baby's Catalogue* by Allan and Janet Ahlberg
Learning Autonomy:	*How Do I Put It On?* by Shigeo Watanbe *I Can, Can You?* by Peggy Parish *I Can* by Helen Oxenbury *Jesse Bear, What Will You Wear?* by Nancy Carlstrom *Mother's Helper* by Helen Oxenbury
Books that Include Movement:	*All Fall Down* by Helen Oxenbury *Pat-a-Cake* by Moira Kemp *Here Are My Hands* by Bill Martin, Jr. and John Archambault
Books About Everyday Experiences:	*Goodnight Moon* by Margaret Wise Brown *The Blanket* by John Burningham *William, Where Are You?* by Mordicai Gerstein *Wheels* by Byron Barton *Push, Pull, Empty, Full* by Tana Hoban *Reading* by Jan Omerod
Words and Songs:	*Hush, Little Baby* by Aliki *Over in the Meadow* by Olive A. Wadsworth *Old MacDonald Had a Farm* by Robert Quackenbush *Mary Had a Little Lamb* by Sara Joseph Hale

Storytelling is effective with toddlers also. The story can be compacted or extended, depending on the interest of the individual child. The storyteller can also include the toddlers' names and use vocabulary they understand to maintain their attention.

These first literature experiences are an important component in the curricula because infants and toddlers are building a foundation for literacy. These activities are not just added when there is nothing to do, but are rather an essential part of the program that is carefully planned and joyfully implemented.

animals that prompts the toddler to make the animal sounds at the appropriate time. Participation allows toddlers to be a part of the story and increases their attention to the book. A manipulative book, such as Hill's *Where's Spot*, provides an interesting surprise when the toddler opens the flaps on the pages and finds different animals inside. Becoming involved with the book and the game of finding out the answer, interests the curious and active toddler.

The Preschool Years: Three to Five Years of Age

Preschool age children are at an exciting period of development, for they are growing and learning in many different ways. As they are examining and experimenting with their physical and social world, they are integrating their understandings and relating new ideas with those they already comprehend. A book that clearly illustrates how preschool children take information very literally and apply the idea to what they already know is *The King Who Rained* by Fred Gwynne for which the young child is attempting to understand "a mole on her nose" and "a fork in the road." The pictures indicate that the young child is interpreting these phrases based on his personal experiences with a mole and a fork. The young child is not unintelligent, but rather demonstrating the way he is trying to understand

Daddy says there was a king who rained for forty years.

Courtesy of *The King Who Rained*, published by Young Readers Press.

a very confusing idea: words can have different meanings in different situations.

In the preschool period young children are curious and interested in learning about their world. They meet each new challenge with excitement. Their active learning style and creative nature combines to produce a unique period of development that is very different from the infant and toddler stage. Programs for preschool children should be specifically designed with the developmental characteristics of the young child in mind, while providing an environment where they can acquire knowledge about their physical and social world. Since maturation and experiential background varies for each child, adjustments and adaptations for individual differences are essential in developmentally appropriate programs (Bredekamp, 1987).

COGNITIVE AND LANGUAGE DEVELOPMENT IN THE PRESCHOOL YEARS

In the preoperational stage of development, Piaget (1962) describes young children as thinkers, bound to their experiences. As they process information, they assimilate new information into their existing schemata. He describes this process as being constructed by young children as they interact with the physical world and social world. When encountering new experiences and trying out new information, young children come to the understanding that this knowledge is different and does not fit existing schemata, but requires another category or an additional scheme. As young children actively participate in their learning, they are constantly assimilating, accommodating, and establishing an equilibrium. The young child may see a cow for the first time on a farm and call it a dog. The child has a dog as a pet and has experience with this animal. This field trip to the farm can provide the avenue for the child to concretely see and begin to understand the differences between the two animals. First, the child assimilates the cow into the schema, already established for dogs,

and later he determines that a new category is needed for very large animals that give milk. The assimilation and accommodation process requires young children to be active participants in constructing knowledge through concrete experiences, rather than sitting and listening to information given to them by adults. As they actively participate, they internalize the idea and establish new schema for a concept that is important to them. Books can assist preoperational children as they try to understand their world. For example, *The Big Book of How Things Work* by Butterworth and Green and *My Backyard* by Rockwell can provide another avenue for finding answers and learning about their world.

Young children are egocentric and believe that others see the world in the same way they do. This characteristic can influence their understanding of the world and effect their communication with adults. Piaget (1955) observed young children talking to themselves and called it egocentric speech. Laura, who is building in the blocks center, says, "This is the tallest building in town. I'm going to make it taller." No one is listening to her, but she continues to talk about her block building activities. Piaget believed that much of preschoolers' speech is used without concern for the listener and there is little attempt to make it understood. He concluded that this egocentric language demonstrated their inability to understand another person's point of view.

Vygotsky (1962) interpreted this private speech as the child's way of regulating his or her own behavior. He described how private speech helps children focus their actions on what they are doing and assists them in their activity. During the preschool years, this very prevalent form of speech is an example of their "thinking aloud." Vygotsky said that this private speech is very important during the preschool years as it allows children to focus on their activity and think about what they are doing. As this private speech declines, it becomes internal verbal thought (Harris, & Liebert, 1987).

In the preoperational period, young children demonstrate increased use of symbolic representation. As they develop, they become more involved in pretend play and using symbols in meaningful activity. Piaget (1962) describes preoperational children's ability to imitate other people's behavior, after some time has passed, to indicate they are able to remember behaviors. As young children begin to symbolize their environment and internalize events, they are extending their understanding. Play allows children to use symbols and roles in situations they can control and change. Through play they use language and actions to meet the needs of the situation, adjusting as they communicate with others. Books such as Eve Merriam's *Boys and Girls and Girls and Boys*, *Mommies at Work*, and *Daddies at Work* can expand the roles that young children can reenact in their dramatic play.

In the preoperational period, young children use transductive reasoning which involves drawing a conclusion about the relationship between two objects or experiences using a single attribute. This thinking can lead to interesting conclusions as demonstrated by Mary Ann's question when her father went to the hospital. For example, Mary Ann's neighbor had gone to the hospital and came home with a new baby. When Mary Ann's father went to the hospital, she asked, "Will we have a new baby brother when you come home?"

Young children also frequently demonstrate their animistic thinking, the belief that inanimate objects are alive. The book *Goodnight Moon* captures this view of young children as objects are told good night. Children readily accept that a mouse or frog, in a story, has human characteristics.

In the second span of the preoperational period, the intuitive stage (four to seven years of age), young children's beliefs are based on what they perceive to be true, rather than what adult logic would indicate. The Piagetian task, examining the conservation of liquid using different sizes of containers, demonstrates how young children use this type of thinking. Young children recognize that two containers that are the same size can contain the same amount of liquid. However, when one liquid is poured into a tall, thin container, and the other remains in the low, wide container, they believe that there is more liquid in the taller container. They draw this conclusion because of the visual appearance, which leads them to perceive that the tall container holds more liquid. At this stage of cognitive development, they cannot move beyond the visual focus to reason that although they look different, no more liquid was added to the tall, thin container, therefore it must hold the same amount of liquid as the low, wide container.

Children who are perception bound in their thinking focus on the visual. Several young children became concerned when the last child in their group received a snack of four broken pieces of a single cookie. In this stage of development they believed that Marilyn got a bigger cookie than they did because it looked like more. The ability to conserve or to hold constant an idea even when it is changed in form, is one of the indicators often used to determine when children are moving from the preoperational period to the beginning of the concrete stage of cognitive development.

Young children's visual orientation can be observed as they make book selections. Their book choices are directly influenced by visually interesting covers and captivating illustrations or photographs (Isbell, Floyd, & Fox, 1992). Their visual dependency is also demonstrated by a statement they frequently make during story reading, "I can't see the picture!" Since they are so visually dependent, the illustrations help them understand the story and the events that are occurring.

Vygotsky (1962, 1987) discussed the importance of social interaction on the language development and thinking process of young children. He believed that adults provide more advanced interactions for children when they clarify and extend their ideas. According to Vygotsky's view, there is a collaboration between the adult and child as the adult guides the child to develop understanding beyond the child's level. The adult provides more advanced vocabulary, additional information, and scaffolding, which will encourage a higher level of thinking.

Another important concept of cognitive development that Vygotsky describes is the zone of proximal development. He believed that at each stage, collaboration occurs between the child's cognitive structures and their environment. Because the children will have different experiences and come from cultures that have diverse values, these factors will influence their thinking about the world. Vygotsky emphasizes the spoken interactions between the child and his teacher, parent, or culture as the forces that encourage the child to reach higher levels of thinking than he or she could achieve independently (Dworetzky, 1990).

Language and cognitive development are very closely intertwined. Preschool children talk freely, are interested in new words, and use language as they are involved in meaningful experiences. During this period of language explosion, the young child moves from having a vocabulary of a few hundred words to 2,500 or more words. Literature, containing new words and more complex language, provides additional enrichment for vocabulary development. The preschoolers' sentences are becoming more complex, with longer utterances, and include more diverse vocabulary (Brown, 1973; Cazden, 1972; Dale, 1972).

Preschool children often use conjunctions to string several sentences together. Leslie, age four, said "I went to my grandmother's and we rode in the car and she gave us chocolate chip cookies." At first analysis this communication may be interpreted as a seventeen-word sentence. But under closer scrutiny it can be determined that Leslie used three communications units averaging five words per unit, which could be evaluated as appropriate for a five-year-old child. She used language to communicate happenings that were important to her and that she had personally experienced.

Preschoolers are also developing an understanding of the rules of language, such as using *ed* to indicate past tense. They have not, however, learned the exceptions to the rules and overgeneralize *ed* and *s* ("I goed to the store," "I have two foots.") Overgeneralizing is not an error but rather an indicator that preschool children are internalizing the structure of language. As they refine their language, they will begin to use the exceptions in the appropriate situations (Cazden, 1972). Rather than "correcting" young children's language, it should be accepted and viewed as a demonstration of their level of development. The adult should simply say "Oh, you went to the store. What did you buy?" With this response an adult language model is presented, a question is used to encourage the interaction to continue and the child's communication is accepted.

The preschooler frequently uses words to find out about their world as they ask the questions "Why?"; "What's that?"; and "How does it do that?" This powerful questioning technique allows

---

Figure 2.5 Language Development Pattern Two–Five Years of Age

Language Development Pattern Two-Five Years of Age				
	2 Years Old	3 Years Old	4 Years Old	5 Years Old
Average Vocabulary:	50-200 words	700-900 words	1000-1500 words	2000-2200 words
Sentence Length:	2 word and telegraphic speech	3-4 words	5-6 words	6+ words
Plurals, possessive forms, and verb tenses:	imitation	regular, mastered	over generalization, irregular, not mastered	over generalization, irregular, not mastered
Conjunctions:		uses "and" frequently	adds "but," "because"	adds more conjunctions
Questions:	expressed by intonation only: "Ball go?", "What's that?", "Where go?"	Inversion of yes–no questions. Uses "who," "what"	Adds "when," "why" and indirect questions	Others added
Understandable speech production:	some jargon frequent use of "no"	60% of speech sounds pronounced	80% of speech sounds pronounced	90% of speech sounds pronounced
Language play:	repetitions and rhythmic speech	creating words and phrases	word play, rhymes, simple stories	jokes, word play, stories
Communication:	controls interactions and demand responses, gamelike turn taking	talks to self and and others	talks to self and others	talks with peers, adults, and self
Understanding of syntax:	uses "correct" word order	uses appropriate word order	uses appropriate word order	uses appropriate word order
Diversity of vocabulary:	uses same words over and over in different combinations	expanding diversity	expanding in diversity	diverse vocabulary used

Note: There are many variations from this expected order in individuals. This description can be useful in predicting development in groups of young children.

Adapted from the work of Rubin and Fisher (1982), Dale (1972), and Cazden (1972).

them to influence the communication and continue the interactive process until they wish to conclude the conversation. They also use this technique when they are listening to a story being read or told. Adults who answer these continuous questions and respond by asking questions that require the preschooler to provide more information help young children understand the communication process.

Torrance (1962) has stated that preschoolers are very creative. During this period of high creative ability, preschoolers like to try new activities and to do things their own way. They are persistent in a task that they have chosen and resent interference before it is completed. They like variety in the materials and activities so they have opportunities to use their divergent ideas. Preschooler's creativity can be encouraged by using literature such as *Mouse Paint* by Walsh and *Colors* by Felix.

The beginnings of reading and writing can be observed in the preschool period. Yetta Goodman (1986) has identified five roots of literacy to describe how young children make sense out of print. The root of literacy she describes as most well developed in the preschool years is the awareness of environmental print. Hoban's *I Can Read Signs* matches this interest. They are also developing an understanding of the functions of writing while producing representations that they identify as writing. They are beginning to understand that reading and writing can represent ideas, thoughts, and oral language. Since preschool children are actively constructing their ideas about literacy during this period, it is critical to provide a nurturing literacy environment and observe their participation. Young children's literacy development will be examined thoroughly in Chapter 3.

SOCIAL-EMOTIONAL DEVELOPMENT IN THE PRESCHOOL STAGE

In the preschool stage, Erikson (1963) describes young children as developing initiative. This characteristic involves the young child learning to work toward a goal, to make plans, and to carry them out. Initiative can also be seen as they try to find out how things work and discover new ways of doing routine tasks. In some environments their problem solving is valued and encouraged, and in others it is discouraged and the young child is made to feel guilty about this emerging developmental characteristic. Selecting books such as Cameron's *"I Can't," Said the Ant* and Piper's *The Little Engine that Could* will emphasize the positive aspects of initiative.

Preschool children are often engaged in play where they work with peers and learn social skills. They play beside a peer, parallel play, or participate in associative play as they make attempts to share ideas and take turns. Some young children can be observed involved in cooperative play, working out problems, and adjusting to the interest of the group. They are not, however, ready for games with rules and find it very frustrating to participate in these structured activities. If they are pressured to play rule games, they will change the rules to make winning possible. At this level of development, cooperative activities in small groups are most appropriate and build the young children's confidence. By participating in play activities they develop understanding of roles of others in their world, adjust to group involvement and experience the importance of cooperative efforts. Corey's *Everyone Takes a Turn* and Heine's *Friends* are two books which demonstrate the value of working together.

Nurturing role models are very important to preschool children as they learn by observation the acceptable behaviors in their world. Young children's actions and language demonstrate the models they have observed, including parents, caregivers, and television characters. Children who have observed powerful adults using profanity will use these words without real understanding of their meaning but recognizing that these words have an interesting effect on adults. Young children who have seen caring adults express positive feelings will respond in a similar manner with positive comments and encouragement.

During the preschool years, young children begin to acquire behaviors, standards, and beliefs that help them learn to function in groups and in classrooms. The socialization process is influenced by parents, adults, and peers with whom they interact. Young children learn what is acceptable by observing adult models and peers and noting which behaviors are successful and satisfying. A child who is sharing a toy with a playmate and has an adult comment on the exchanges, will receive encouragement to continue this cooperative play. If the adults are nurturing and liked by the child, they are even more powerful influences guiding the child's behavior.

During this period, the social world of the young child is expanding from family to a broader world filled with new friends, teachers, and other adults. In 1965, only 27.1 percent of young children, three to five years of age, attended preschool programs in the United states. By 1989, the number of three- to five-year-olds attending a program had increased to 54.6 percent (National Center for Education Statistics, 1990). Books such as Cohen's *When Will I Read?* and *Will I Have a Friend?* can be selected to assist young children as they move into new experiences. As their world expands, young children are trying to understand their feelings as well as the feelings of others. They are also examining the roles that are played in their society, related to gender, culture, and work.

Preschoolers demonstrate a range of emotions often changing quickly from pleasure to unhappiness and back to pleasure again. They recover from conflict quickly and can often work out their disagreements. They enjoy slapstick humor and appreciate funny jokes and stories that display humor. The preschooler exhibits certain fears about their world that seem to be universal, including fear of being lost or left, fear of the dark, and fear of certain loud noises or fear of the unknown. As young children are trying to cope with these universal fears, books can provide opportunities to examine their feelings and discuss their concerns. Examples of appropriate books about the fears of preschool children include Preston's *Where Did My Mother Go?* and Mayer's *There's a Nightmare in My Closet* and *There's an Alligator Under My Bed.*

PRESCHOOL CHILDREN'S PHYSICAL DEVELOPMENT

Preschool children are becoming increasingly capable of controlling their bodies in large-motor activities, such as running, climbing, and throwing. They are also beginning to refine their small-motor skills, through activities such as drawing and lacing. Small-motor tasks are very difficult for them and are frustrating if the activity does not match their level of competency and provide them opportunity to be successful. Young children enjoy practicing newly acquired skills in activities that are useful and meaningful to them (Maxim, 1985). Becoming more competent at physical tasks, encourages young children to be more physical and influences their self-image.

During the preschool years there is very little difference in the physical needs and abilities of boys and girls. Both boys and girls are extremely active and need vigorous activities throughout the day. Their high-energy level also necessitates that they have opportunity to participate in quiet activities and have space where they can slow down and relax.

THE PRESCHOOL ENVIRONMENT

Young children learn best in an environment that is specifically designed for them. Classroom and center environments should reflect educational practices that allow for the developmental level and learning approaches of young children. Cowles and Aldridge (1992) summarized the educational principles that should be used to guide the design of physical environment.

1. Children learn by active participation and involvement

2. Children learn from concrete experiences and have opportunities to explore the environment at this level

3. Children need to have both child-initiated and teacher-directed activities

4. A balance is needed between individual and group activities

5. An effective environment provides activities that allow children to work at different paces and in areas that they enjoy.

Since preschoolers are active learners, the environment should be designed to encourage their participation. Materials and activities provide concrete experiences that young children can understand and that relate to their specific level of development. Many real-life experiences are planned where children can actively manipulate both materials and ideas. They need opportunities to observe and question the experiences as they are occurring. Firsthand experiences are provided to increase understanding as well as to provide a base for literacy activities. Centers set up throughout the classroom provide children with choices where they can actively participate in small groups. Some of these centers are available continuously,

such as housekeeping, art, and blocks. Other centers that are available may include: sand/water, carpentry, music, and science. Sociodramatic centers may be set up that focus on the specific theme or unit being studied. For example, a unit focusing on the community leads to a trip to a local grocery store. Later a grocery store is replicated in a classroom enter using real props that were collected, including newspaper advertisements and books about the store such as Rockwell's *The Supermarket*. These dramatic centers allow young children to play out roles, use language to accompany their activity, become involved in cooperative play, and use literacy material in real situations.

In the preschool classroom, literacy is emerging. The schedule is filled with opportunities for talking, listening, reading, and writing to occur throughout the classroom. In the centers, children sign in when they chose the area where they will work. Young children are communicating with peers and adults about activities and projects in context, as they occur. On the bulletin board is an announcement of a puppet show that will be presented next week by a high-school drama group. Every day there is time for the children to read a book of their choice and to "write" down ideas in a journal. At the science table, items are labeled, a science magazine is displayed and books are provided to extend the display. Art work, three-dimensional constructions, and children's writings are artistically displayed with the creator clearly identified. The print-rich environment allows the young children to learn about the functions of literacy in many different ways and in activities that are personally meaningful.

The preschooler should have the opportunity to participate in a child-centered program that encourages choices, activity, and open-ended experiences, where learning is constructed by the child in a developmentally appropriate environment (Bredekamp, 1987). In this classroom there is a focus on the active process of learning rather than the obtainment of isolated skills on ditto sheets. Activities, centers, and experiences are designed to help young children develop confidence in their abilities and view themselves as capable learners.

BOOKS THROUGHOUT THE PRESCHOOL CLASSROOM

The library center should be available throughout the year and designed to encourage involvement with books and other related materials. Collections should include favorite books as well as new and changing books that will capture the attention of active preschoolers. Reference materials, magazines, tapes, and flannel boards add to the variety of literacy choices and draw young children into the area. The inclusion of manipulative books, like Carter's *What's in My Pocket?* encourage active involvement, and sustain their interest.

Books, printed materials, and writing tools are included in all the centers set up in the classroom. For example, the housekeeping center can have books available about families and cooking as well as paper and writing tools for leaving notes or writing "to do" lists. The art center might have a copy of Keat's *Jennie's Hat* to stimulate ideas about decorating hats that could be created by the children. Other books and illustrators can be included during the year. A sociodramatic center set up after a trip to a pet store might include books on pets and pamphlets on the care of pets, along with an appointment book for scheduling pet haircuts or shampoos. The addition of these literacy materials into the regular centers demonstrates that reading and writing are important parts of everyday activities and provide

opportunities for the children to use literacy materials in functional ways. For example, in the veterinarian center, a little girl scribbles a prescription for heartworm medicine and gives it to another child who is pretending to be the owner of a sick dog.

BOOKS ACROSS THE PRESCHOOL CURRICULUM

Story time is an important feature in the preschool classroom. This time occurs each day and is spent focused on a specific book that is carefully selected to match the developmental level and interest of the young children in the classroom. The teacher introduces the book by relating it to what the children know, asking well-designed questions, and reading in a manner that captures young children's attention. After the reading, follow-up questions encourage comprehension and a related activity extends the story to another avenue of expression. Stories can be dramatized, art activities can relate to the story, or puppets can be constructed to retell the story. After the book is shared, it is placed in the library center for the young children to read on their own or share with a friend.

Themes or units are a favorite way to structure an integrated curriculum for young children. Themes or units provide a method for interweaving math, science, social studies, motor activities, language arts, music, and art around a specific topic. Thematic planning helps to organize the week into meaningful experiences for preschoolers rather than filling the day with many isolated and unrelated activities.

A unit with the themes of families would be appropriate for the preschool classroom. The family is important to children of this age, and they have firsthand experiences with roles in the family. A family unit, which could last two weeks, would build on the children's understanding of their family and extend to learning about families that are different from their own. Books used in the unit might include Morris' *Loving,* Hines' *Daddy Makes the Best*

Spaghetti, and Brown's *Arthur's Baby.* Curriculum areas will be covered by selecting activities that focus on the family theme and support the objectives of the unit. A math activity could include the development of a pictorial graph representing the members of each child's family. Science could include taking care of the home of the classroom pet. For social studies, a special day could be planned for grandparents, older neighbors, or guests from a senior citizen's group to visit the classroom and tell stories. In art, a family photographs gallery could be developed and displayed on large cardboard boxes, stacked together to provide a museum display. Other curriculum areas, such as music, movement, health and nutrition, would also relate to the family theme. Some of the centers in the classroom would have new items that encourage the children's play and their talking about the theme.

Figure 2.6 Books that Match the Developmental Characteristics of Three- to Five-Year-Olds

Expanding World:
Come with Me to Nursery School by Edith Hurd
Round & Round & Round by Tana Hoban
My Nursery School by Harlow Rockwell
Will I Have a Friend? by Miriam Cohen
My Backyard by Anne Rockwell
The Big Book of How Things Work
    by Brent Butterworth and Tie Green
I Read Signs by Tana Hoban

Working Together:
Friends by Helme Heine
Everybody Takes Turns by Dorothy Corey

Initiative:
Benny Bakes a Cake by Eve Rice
"I Can't," Said the Ant by Rod Cameron
The Little Engine That Could by Watty Piper

Understanding Feelings:
Go and Hush the Baby by Betsy Byars
The Temper Tantrum Book by Edna Mitchell Preston
On Monday When It Rained by Cheryl Kachenmeister
My Mama Says There Aren't Any Zombies, Ghosts, Vampires,
    Creatures, Demons, Monsters, etc. by Judith Viorst
There's a Nightmare in My Closet by Mercer Mayer
There's an Alligator Under My Bed by Mercer Mayer
Where Did My Mother Go? by Edna Mitchell Preston

Self-Image:
I Like to be Little by Charlotte Zolotow
Spike: The Sparrow Who Couldn't Sing by Tony Maddox
When Will I Read? by Miriam Cohen
Even if I Did Something Awful by Barbara Hazen
The Carrot Seed by Ruth Krauss

Symbolic Play:
Boys & Girls, Girls & Boys by Eve Merriam
Mommies at Work by Eve Merriam
Daddies at Work by Eve Merriam
Martin's Hats by Joan Blos

For example, during these weeks, the housekeeping center could include a baby bathtub with baby dolls for bathing. The block area could contain pictures of their neighborhood, small family dolls, and village pieces. The classroom library would also have new additions related to the family theme.

For preschoolers, four to five years of age, a unit on friends could be used for curriculum design. Books such as Aliki's *We Are Best Friends*, Waber's *Ira Sleeps Over*, and Henke's *Jessica* would serve as the literary base for this unit of study. A letter could be written to a special friend, songs about friendship could be learned, and partner games could be included. Feelings, animals, plants, seasons, pets, and transportation are also effective topics for thematic units for preschoolers. The unit approach to curriculum includes both activities and literature to support the theme and provide concrete experiences to integrate concepts and ideas.

Books can be used very effectively with special projects in the preschool classroom. In the fall, young children may plant bulbs in the outdoor play area. Books and reference materials can assist them as they select and purchase the flower bulbs. Ehlert's *Planting a Rainbow* can assist young children in learning how to visually select bulbs and plant them properly so they will bloom in the spring.

Holiday celebrations are very important to preschoolers. Special days are anticipated with great excitement and books that relate to this celebration become part of this enjoyment. Marc Brown's *Arthur's Thanksgiving* can enrich traditional celebrations and Titherington's

Courtesy of *Fish is Fish*, published by Dragonfly Books.

Pumpkin Pumpkin can accompany the cutting of a jack-o'-lantern.

Developmental Characteristics of Primary-aged Children: Six-, Seven-, and Eight-Year-Olds

Young children in the primary grades (one, two, and three), are continuing to grow in all areas of development: cognitive language, physical, social, and emotional. Although the changes in the primary ages are less dramatic than those in previous stages, they are of great importance for they provide the foundation for later achievement. The development of primary children should be observed and experiences planned that foster their understanding rather than pushing them to perform tasks that focus on rote memory. The drill approach of isolate skills leads to frustration and boredom, resulting in the children learning little about concepts, meaning, and application. In the early grades, young children develop many abilities that are critical for school success but they also develop attitudes that will have an even greater influence on their views of learning and enjoyment of literature. It is not enough that a child can read and write, but there must also be the desire to engage in these activities and to find them pleasurable.

COGNITIVE AND LANGUAGE DEVELOPMENT

At the beginning of this period (six to seven years), most young children are in the preoperational stage. Many of the characteristics discussed in the section about preschoolers continue in these primary years. Young children are actively involved in their learning, constructing their understanding for themselves. Their physical, social, and logico-mathematical knowledge are expanded as they assimilate new information into existing schemata and establishing new schema.

Primary-aged children see the world through their own eyes. An example often used to demonstrate their egocentric view of the world can be found in Lionni's *Fish Is Fish*. When the fish is unable to go out to see the world, the frog comes back to tell his "inseparable friend" about the wide world. As the fish listens to the frog's descriptions of the world, he imagines that a bird is a "flying fish" and that people are "fish wearing clothes." The fish's understanding of birds and people is based on his experiences in his fish world. Primary children also understand their world based on their own experiences.

Primary-aged children continue to learn through concrete experiences that are hands-on, more than abstractions. Their symbolic thinking is developed in play and through real activities as they choose approaches that are meaningful for them. Young children gain understanding while participating in concrete experiences, and only gradually develop the ability to think abstractly independent of real objects. Although pictures are less abstract than letters and numbers, they cannot substitute for primary children's need for real objects and concrete experiences.

Young children's developmental learning pattern can be followed in a thematic unit focusing on the environment. First, the children explore the places they live, take walks, collect items from nature and experience their environment. Next, they move to a semiabstract approach as they look at pictures of their environment and discuss the features they have seen. After many experiences in concrete and pictorial representation will they be able to move to abstract concepts such as waste management. Bowden's *Where Does Our Garbage Go?* can provide visual illustrations to assist understanding of environmental concepts. The study can also be made more concrete by encouraging the children to actively participate in a recycling center that is set up in the classroom. In the center, children can collect and sort items for reuse or to be sold. A concrete base provides opportunities for children to develop their understanding of the concept, as well as time to actively engage in the construction of this knowledge.

In a 1992 study, conducted in the District of Columbia Public Schools, Colker found that structured abstract learning did not promote academic achievement but rather hindered children's later achievement and overall development. The results from the study clearly support active, child-initiated concrete experiences at both the preschool and primary level. The Southern Regional Education Board report (1992), which discussed preparing children for the Challenge of 2000, concluded that developmentally appropriate models should be extended into the primary grades, and academic models should not be forced downward. These and other studies have emphasized the importance of active primary grades where learning is experientially based and appropriate for the developmental level of primary children.

LANGUAGE DEVELOPMENT IN THE PRIMARY YEARS

In the primary grades, young children continue to develop language competencies and expand their vocabularies. They use more complex sentences with increasing length and number of adjectival clauses in their oral language.

Loban's (1976) longitudinal study with children K through twelve provided an in-depth look at the language and literacy abilities of over 300 children. His extensive study analyzed the oral language, reading and writing of children across their years in school and included children from a variety of socioeconomic levels and varying abilities. He found a wide range of language competencies in the children he studied. At the first-grade level, the children identified as the high-language group were very advanced in oral expression, vocabulary, and listening comprehension. The first-grade low-language group did not obtain the same level of language proficiency until the sixth grade. Clearly, a wide range of language abilities are found in the early primary classrooms. In Loban's study, young children who were high in oral language usage at the kindergarten level were the same children who were high in reading and writing at the high-school level. This finding certainly emphasizes the importance of oral language development and the continued need for young children to have opportunities to talk, discuss ideas, and participate in small group activities.

Although primary-aged children have made advancements in their language, it cannot be assumed that this development is complete. Carol Chomsky (1969), in her study of school-aged children, identified that six-, seven-, and eight-year-olds are still in the process of refining their understanding of the structure of language. She found that they confused the meaning of sentences that had similar surface structure, but different deep meanings. She described primary children as unable to distinguish the subtle meanings of the two sentences, "The doll is easy to see" and "The doll is eager to see." These more complex understandings occur as children listen and refine language through use. It is also important to note that each child progresses at a different pace depending on individual experiences and opportunities for responsive interactions in their environment.

First-, second-, and third-grade children are emerging readers and writers. Growth occurs from within the child and as a result of environmental interactions (Teale & Sulzby, 1986). They are moving toward the use of conventional symbols and enjoy demonstrating their ability to write their own stories and read books they have chosen. Further discussion of the reading and writing processes for young children will be included in Chapter 3.

SOCIAL-EMOTIONAL DEVELOPMENT

As primary-aged children observe and interact with more adults and peers, they begin to develop ideas about acceptable behaviors and social roles. These developing views will influence their involvement in group activities and participation with other children.

The development of moral standards progresses from rigid views of right and wrong to the considerations of the situation in determining the outcome of the action. Kohlberg (1981) studied the moral decisions of children, as well as the reasons the decisions were made. His stages are not tied to specific ages, but rather view children as progressing through the sequence at different rates. Most primary children, however, are progressing through the following stages:

> stage 1, where the child chooses to obey the rules to "be good" in order to escape punishment; or
>
> stage 2, where the child conforms to the rules to obtain rewards.

According to Kohlberg, it is not until stages 3 and 4, in the conventional level, that children are concerned with the social expectations of family, groups, or nation. Kohlberg believes all children start at level 1 and most remain at this level until about the age of nine. He has also suggested that boys score higher than girls in moral reasoning. Gilligan (1982) and Gibbs, Arnold, and Buckhost (1984) have presented evidence that girls' moral development progresses as rapidly as boys, but that girls are more concerned about caring for others while boys are focused on justice.

As primary children are constructing their views of right and wrong, they are concerned with rules of behavior and fair treatment. They are also curious about differences in boys and girls and are attempting to understand the roles for each.

Young children are developing friendships that are more sustained. They demonstrate their developing abilities as they work with peers while they participate in sociodramatic play. This advanced level of play is person-oriented and is not focused on materials as in the earlier stages. At this level of play, the children are

1. taking on roles;

2. sustaining involvement on a theme;

3. communicating with language; and

4. adjusting to a predefined theme.

Through play, primary children practice roles and learn problem solving while interacting with their peers. Play situations provide immediate feedback for children to determine the effectiveness of their approach and to refine their social skills. Sociodramatic play is a cooperative group activity where the child can choose and create, but also must work within group-imposed limits (Smilansky & Shefatya, 1990).

Primary children continue to become independent and to develop initiative, as they are allowed to practice decision making: choosing activities and following their sustained interests on a project. Providing choices encourages children to develop independence and encourages them to complete tasks because they have selected what interests them.

PHYSICAL DEVELOPMENT IN THE PRIMARY YEARS

During the primary years, large-motor control is refined and small-motor abilities are continuing to improve. In this period physical growth is less rapid and changes are taking place at a slower pace. Individual variations in the rate of physical maturation, size, weight, interest, and talents become more pronounced. Bodily proportions are becoming more adultlike with primary children having more muscle and less body fat. There are only slight differences in the average weight and height of boys and girls in this period. Physical abilities steadily increase in areas such as grip strength, running speed, hand-eye coordination, balance, and flexibility.

THE PLANNED PRIMARY CLASSROOM ENVIRONMENT

The classroom that is designed to provide for the developmental characteristics of primary children is an active, hands-on learning environment. Individual and group experiences are provided so children can construct their own knowledge and be involved in social interactions. The activity-oriented classroom gives the children many opportunities to explore the environment at the concrete level and to move to more abstract experiences at their own pace.

Active classrooms have learning centers, socio-dramatic play areas, manipulates, science experiments, and many other materials that invite the children to become involved. Opportunities exist for child-initiated activities where materials are easily accessible for the child to create and implement an idea. A variety of activities and materials allows children to work in areas they enjoy while capturing their interest and special abilities (Cowles & Alridge, 1992).

The classroom is a literacy environment filled with talking, reading, writing, and an abundance of children's books. Children are given the opportunity to seek out information and to read and write about their interests. Their work is prominently displayed for others to appreciate. Written language is seen in the chart of the day's activities, the directions for a matching game, a list of books needed from the school library, the classroom phone book with classmates numbers, and a thank-you note to the principal for reading a story to the class. "Print-rich" environments allow children to discover for themselves the importance and usefulness of reading and writing (Fields, Spangler, & Lee, 1991).

Centers are set up in the primary classroom to encourage active participation in small groups. Examples of effective centers found in primary classrooms are writing centers, art and construction centers, as well as science and math centers. Other centers can be added that relate to the unit of study and the exhibited interest of the children. For example, a greenhouse center can be utilized when the focus is on the study of plants. Books such as How a *Seed Grows* (Jordan, 1992) can be used to obtain information about the growing of plants. Centers afford the primary child concrete opportunities to use learning in personally meaningful ways. In centers, primary children use concepts and language as they actively participate. Many of these centers encourage sociodramatic play which assists the children in cognitive tasks such as sustained interest, language expansion, and creative problem solving. Centers are also important in the development of social competencies because

the children learn to adjust roles and work cooperatively with peers.

In the primary classroom, there are both teacher-directed activities and activities that allow the children to shape and influence their learning. The environment that is activity oriented encourages problem solving, making decisions, and working with others while facilitating cognitive, language, and social development.

BOOKS THROUGHOUT THE PRIMARY CLASSROOM

In a classroom that is designed to nurture literacy, books can be found in many places. The classroom library is an essential center for the primary grades where "readers" may chose their books, share a favorite one with a friend, or enjoy a book and tape. A wide range of reading

levels is evident including easy-to-read books, picture dictionaries, reference books, and magazines. Books that relate to the current unit of study are added and changed to support the theme. Posters, brochures, and fliers can extend the variety of presentation of printed material available. The classroom library should include books created and written by children in the classroom made available to check-out, ready with cards and due-date stamps.

In other parts of the classroom, books related to specific activities can enrich the experience. For example, books about the care of a hamster, Fischer-Nagel's *Inside the Burrow: The Life of the Golden Hamster* and Blacker's *Herbie Hamster, Where Are You?*, are available next to the cage of the classroom pet. In the art center, books are displayed that demonstrate collages such as *The Mixed-Up Chameleon* by Eric Carle or Leo Lionni's *Swimmy*. The children can examine these books and choose to try the new technique or explore the artist's medium. In the science area, the children can build an earthworm terrarium following the directions provided in *Earthworms*.

BOOKS ACROSS THE PRIMARY CURRICULUM

Children of all ages, including the primary ages, enjoy hearing a book read aloud. Story reading time should be an anticipated event occurring every day. In a literature-based curriculum, the carefully selected book becomes the stimulus for other activities in the classroom. By linking this quality book with the curriculum areas, children experience the interrelationship of literature and interesting activities. Literature becomes a part of the whole day, instead of a ten to fifteen minute period after lunch.

A literature-based program also provides time each day for reading and writing by the children. Primary children have the freedom to chose much of what they want to read. Writing is done each day in journals, writing centers, and in developing individual books. The teacher also demonstrates the importance of reading and writing during the day as she or he searches reference materials to find information, records an idea, writes plans for the day, or shares a poem. See Chapter 3 for more about the literacy processes.

In a whole language primary classroom, units can be used to integrate curriculum areas around a meaningful theme. An example of an appropriate unit for the primary grades is the study of machines. Primary children are very interested in how things work and they experience many machines every day. *The Big Book of How Things Work* by Butterworth and Green is a guide to inventions and how they work. Gibbons' *Fill It Up* describes how cars and trucks use fuel and require maintenance. Books read to the class could include Tusa's *Stay Away From the Junk Yard* and Cole's *The Magic School Bus at the Waterworks*. A machine shop center could be set up in the classroom and equipped with tools and a collection of broken appliances, including a toaster, mixer, and vacuum cleaner. New books on the theme would be added to the library center and tapes included for the listening area.

Another way to develop a literacy-related unit is to focus on special authors, with activities and centers related to their books. An interesting unit for primary children could be planned around the work of Leo Lionni. On one day, the book *Swimmy* could be highlighted with a study of the author/illustrator, discussion on cooperation, an aquarium setup, and art activities, including painted watercolor paper. Another day, *Alexander and the Wind-Up Mouse* could serve as the literary inspiration. Follow-up activities might include comparisons of real and imaginary, songs about friendship, creating magic pebbles, and writing a wish book. The combination of the study of an author and their works within a unit also demonstrates the importance of literature and authorship in the classroom. Children are immersed in the writing of a featured author and his or her books are everywhere to be read, shared, and to inspire one to write, paint, or draw.

Figure 2.7 Books Appropriate for the Developmental Characteristics of Kindergarten–Grade One

Understanding Based on
Concrete Experiences:

This Year's Garden by Cynthia Rylant
A Tree is Nice by Janice Udry
Big Red Barn by Margaret Wise Brown
Tools by Ann Morris

Interest in Words/Language:

Chicka, Chicka, Boom! Boom! by Bill Martin, Jr.,
& John Archambault
How Many Trucks Can a Tow Truck Tow?
by Charlotte Pomerantz
Best Wordbook Ever by Richard Scarry
Many Luscious Lollipops by Ruth Heller
Chicken Soup with Rice by Maurice Sendak

Friendships:

Will I Have a Friend? by Miriam Cohen
Best Friends by Miriam Cohen
That's What a Friend Is by P. K. Hallinan
Alfie Gives a Hand by Shirley Hughes

Distinguishing Reality and Fantasy:

The Fish Who Could Wish by John Bush
Harold and the Purple Crayon
by Crockett Johnson
Pretend You're a Cat by Jean Marzollo
Alexander and the Wind Up Mouse by Leo Lionni

Socially Acceptable Behavior:

Too Much Noise by Ann McGovern
What Do You Do With a Kangaroo?
by Mercer Mayer
Gregory, the Terrible Eater by Mitchell Sharmat

Independence, Completing Tasks:

Something to Crow About by Megan Halsey Lane
The Little Red Hen by Paul Galdone
I Can Do It Myself by Lessie Jones Little
and Eloise Greenfield

Appreciating Others Who Are Different:

My Friend Leslie by Maxine B. Rosenberg
Arnie and the New Kid by Nancy Carlson
Tacky the Penguin by Helen Lester

Positive Self-Concept:

I Like Me! by Nancy Carlson
Titch by Pat Hutchins
Ira Sleeps Over by Bernard Waber
I'm Terrific by Marjorie Sharmat

Figure 2.8 Books Appropriate for the Developmental Characteristics of Children, Grades Two–Three

Expanding Knowledge of Their World:
World Water Watch by Michelle Koch
A Tree is Nice by Janice May Udry
Bugs by Nancy Winslow Parker
    and Joan Richards Wright
Animals Born Alive and Well by Ruth Heller

More Complex Vocabulary and Language:
The Cat's Purr by Ashley Bryan
Tomfoolery: Trickery and Foolery with Words
    by Alvin Schwartz
A Light in the Attic by Shel Silverstein

Emerging Readers and Writers:
Frog and Toad All Year by Arnold Lobel
The Snake: A Very Long Story by Bernard Waber
Stringbean's Trip to the Shining Sea by
    Vera B. Williams and Jennifer Williams

Concern for Fairness and Rules:
It's Mine! A Greedy Book by Crosby Bonsall
Crow Boy by Taro Yashima
The Reward Worth Having by Jay Williams
Big Brother by Charlotte Zolotow

Forming Lasting Friendships:
Angel Child, Dragon Child by
    Michele Maria Surat
Mrs. Katz and Tush by Patricia Polacco
We Are Best Friends by Aliki

Refining Decision Making:
Chicken Sunday by Patricia Polacco
Sam, Bangs & Moonshine by Evaline Ness
A Color of His Own by Leo Lionni

Expanding Attention Span:
Freckle Juice by Judy Blume
Charlotte's Web by E. B. White
Will We Miss Them? Endangered Species
    by Alexandria Wright

Developing Individual Interests:
Ramona, the Brave by Beverly Cleary
Something Special for Me by Vera B. Williams
Jeremy's Decision by Ardyth Brott

Special events are enriched with the addition of appropriate books. A concert by the high-school band can lead to reading books about musicians, such as Isadora's *Ben's Trumpet* and *The Cat's Midsummer Jamboree* by Kheridian and Hogrogian. Activities might include a classroom touring group, making posters to advertise the performance, and creating a program that will be distributed to the audience before the performance (Lamme, 1990).

Individual Differences

The National Association for Education of Young Children (NAEYC) guidelines for developmentally appropriate practices state that programs serving young children should be both stage appropriate and individually appropriate (Bredecamp, 1987). The characteristics described in this chapter are based on the normal pattern of development that can be identified in specific stages and include predictable changes and growth. It is important to remember that within these stages are many variations that are influenced by the individual child's maturation, background experiences, and intellectual potential. Knowledge of the characteristics of children's development can assist the teacher in designing the space and selecting literature when planning for groups of children. The effective teacher must also make adjustments and vary the pace for individual children within the group. Providing for the needs of both the individual child and the group is a real challenge. To effectively plan for individual differences and specific abilities, careful observation of each child is necessary. Observation of group and individual interests can assist in the selection of literature for reading aloud, additions to the classroom library, and planning challenging activities. A range of available books, as well as times when the child can make personal choices, increases the likelihood that the link between the book and the child will occur. Literature that is appropriate for children in the specific stage of development as well as personally interesting can provide successful experiences that will increase the possibility of book use and enjoyment.

Development and Variations

As programs integrate children with special needs into the classroom, the range of abilities being served will continue to expand. These exceptional children enrich the group and provide many opportunities for students understanding and appreciation of diversity. A brief discussion of special children will focus on characteristics as they specifically relate to literature and the adjustments needed within the regular classroom. These suggestions should only serve as guidelines, for each child within the classroom has abilities and talents that make him or her special.

CHILDREN WITH DISABILITIES

Helping all children reach their potential is an important goal for programs serving young children. In the past twenty-five years, there have been significant advances in understanding young children with disabilities, how they learn, and the best environments to nurture their development. One of the important changes that has recently occurred is the increase of services for young children with disabilities. Public law P.L. 99-457 requires that by age three, services for children with disabilities must begin. Presently all fifty states are providing services for children three years of age and older. There is also an increase of services being provided for infants and toddlers with disabilities as well as "at risk" preschool children. In the fall of 1992, nearly half of the states were providing services for infant and toddlers with disabilities (U.S. Department of Education, 1992).

Research clearly indicates that early identification and appropriate environments are essential in meeting the needs of special young children. Early intervention programs have many positive influences on the development of young children with disabilities.

One basic concept used in planning for young children with disabilities is to provide services in the least restrictive environment for the child, in order for appropriate education to occur. Early childhood programs that are developmentally appropriate are often the places where these guidelines can be effectively met. Through the team efforts of many professionals, including early childhood educators, special educators, and medical personnel, changes and adjustments can be implemented to create an early childhood environment where effective learning can take place. Parents are an essential part of this team because they can contribute information that will help in understanding the unique needs of their individual child.

Inclusion, which combines children with disabilities and "normally developing" children in the same environment, has many values for children. Children with disabilities benefit from having the opportunity to choose friends with whom to play, realize potential skills more fully because of the greater variety of material and activities, and learn from nonhandicapped peers who serve as models expanding the range of behaviors they observe and imitate. Some of the benefits for other young children include learning to accept differences in people, to appreciate how they are alike, to be helpful and caring, and to encourage independence (Morgan, & York, 1981). However, just placing children with disabilities in an early childhood program does not naturally lead to these benefits (Cooke, Ruskus, Apolloni, & Peck, 1981). The most important factor in the successful integration of young children with disabilities into an early childhood program is the ability and attitude of the teacher (Wynne, Ulfelder, & Dakof,

1975). Teacher competencies that lead to positive mainstreaming experiences include the knowledge of normal and atypical stages in children's development, the ability to recognize specific handicapping conditions, the skill in observing and recording behavior of individual children, the ability to prepare goals and objectives which are developmentally appropriate, and the ability to provide activities that are consistent with each child's strengths and weaknesses (Armbruster, & Klein, 1992; Morgan, & York, 1981).

Although it is acknowledged that all children are more alike than different, individual differences must be recognized and considered when planning early childhood programs. Quality early childhood programs can be designed to help all children achieve their potential by building on individual abilities and talents. Labels such as *mentally retarded, visually impaired,* or *physically disabled* are still used but it is important to remember that these terms can limit our understanding of children for each child is different even if they have the same disability label. The severity of the disability can also influence the progress of the child and can range from mildly effecting his abilities to severely limiting development. Young children can be disabled in different ways. Physical disabilities include limited mobility, orthopedic problems, and cerebral palsy. Intellectual disabilities include developmentally delayed, mentally retarded, and learning disabled. In the area of language, difficulties in expressive language and articulation can be present. Other disabilities include auditory, visual, social, and emotional areas. Young children can have special needs in one of these areas or in multiple ways.

LANGUAGE DEVELOPMENT IN YOUNG CHILDREN WITH DISABILITIES

The acquisition of language is a complex process and is influenced by many conditions that must exist to facilitate normal patterns of development. The central nervous systems must be intact and the peripheral sensory systems must function (hearing, vision, and oral tactile). Cognitive development and background experiences directly affect the reception of language as well as the ability to express ideas. Social and affective development also influences language acquisition for young children who need responsive and interactive communication with others in their world.

Other factors can also interfere with language development in children. Auditory disabilities directly influence the learning of speech and language. Although deaf children can be taught to speak and understand language, it is a very difficult task and requires the help of highly trained adults. Even children with mild hearing losses are unable to hear all sounds with equal clarity and therefore receive limited or distorted auditory stimulation (Armbruster & Klein, 1992). Davis (1977), concluded that the longer the hearing loss goes undetected the more likely it will effect development. Auditory-perceptual problems can be the cause of specific language disorders in some children.

Some problems, such as language delay and learning disabilities, may be characterized by an impaired rate of processing acoustical information. Children with this disability often progress at a slower pace in language development and the abilities used in expressing their ideas. They may also have difficulty understanding the thoughts and ideas they hear or read.

Visual disabilities influence the children's understanding of experiences and vocabulary. Because they have a deprived visual environment they need special adaption to encourage language development. For example, they need expanded tactile and auditory experiences, verbal explanations for what is happening, and interactive games. Intellectual disabilities can also cause delay in language development.

Children who are moderately and mildly retarded often learn to talk and understand language in the typical sequence but at a slower pace. For these children it is important to match their language experiences with their level of language development. Interactions should be conducted on a level they can understand and participate actively. Language should accompany their experiences and be useful in understanding the situation.

The lack of stimulation limits language development. Children who have had few experiences and limited opportunities to use language will often be delayed (Armbruster & Klein, 1992). If they have not seen or experienced things in the world, they will be unable to use the vocabulary or have the concepts to understand the happenings.

Muscle control is necessary to produce understandable speech and correct articulation. For example, some children with severe cerebral palsy may have problems producing speech because they lack the muscle control for articulation. The inability to communicate in an understandable way may discourage the child from attempting to talk or ask questions. Every effort should be made to understand the child's attempts at communication and beginning interactions should be nurtured.

A PLANNED ENVIRONMENT FOR INCLUSION OF CHILDREN WITH DISABILITIES

The physical areas that includes young children, both with disabilities and normally developing, should be designed to meet the needs of all children. By expanding the opportunities to meet the needs of children with disabilities, the program is enriched for the entire group (Morgan & York, 1981). Many of the approaches for early childhood programs suggested in previous sections of this chapter are also appropriate for the classroom with children who have special needs. In this inclusion classroom, there should be many opportunities to participate in active, concrete learning. Real experiences are provided, including cooking, sand and water play, blocks, and taking care of class plants and pets. The curriculum is planned to enhance development in all areas: cognitive, language, physical, social, and emotional. Centers are included to allow children to play at their level, chose the materials they like, and interact with other children. Diverse activities, multisensory experiences, and a range of materials are provided that can give all children opportunities to be successful. Children are encouraged to try new experiences and their responses to these new challenges are accepted positively. Conversations are taking place between children and adults as the children expand their language use in meaningful situations. The adult model presents language that is understandable, but includes new vocabulary or another way of relating information to extend the child's understanding. Interactions are focused on activities where the child is participating and language accompanies these actions. Language experiences are functional and their usefulness is understood by the children.

The environment and experiences are designed to encourage the development of independence and the level of assistance is individually determined and decreases over time. The schedule is predictable but also allows flexibility of time periods so children can work on an activity or project that interests them at their own pace and allows them to complete the task. Activities begin at the child's developmental level and assist him in making progress that is appropriate for his abilities. If some children cannot participate in the same way others can, alternative ways are found for them to be involved. Observational records are kept on each child so that progress can be identified and problematic areas can be addressed.

The classroom provides a psychologically safe environment where children feel accepted with their capabilities and limitations. They have opportunities to gain competencies in all areas, to develop confidence in their abilities, and to reach their potential.

BOOKS IN THE CURRICULUM

Books can help young children learn about differences and appreciate diversity. They can provide information about disabilities, develop understanding of some of the difficulties children encounter, and provide an opportunity to discuss their concerns. Stories can also include characters that provide a positive role model for the child with disabilities.

Many excellent books are available to help young children understand more about a specific disability. Some books that develop understanding of visual disabilities are Goodsell's *Katie's Magic Glasses,* Raskin's *Spectacles,* and Keet's *Apt. 3.* Marc Brown's *Arthur's Eyes* is a story about a little boy getting new glasses and how he copes with the teasing from his friends. *See You Tomorrow, Charles* tells about a blind boy and his first days in first grade. He and the other children learn a great deal about each other as they participate in the primary classroom.

Auditory disabilities are examined in several books for young children. Litchfield's *A Button in Her Ear* and Levine's *Lisa and Her Soundless World* explains deafness, using hearing aids, and learning to speak. Sullivan's *A Show of Hands: Say It in Sign Language* and Charlip's & Miller's *Handtalk* encourage children to learn signs and to use them with their classmates. Ancona & Miller's *Handtalk Zoo* focuses on a trip to the zoo and shows signs as they relate to the animals and experience.

Books that deal with intellectual disabilities are Fassler's *One Little Girl* and Lasher's *He's My Brother.* Robert Kraus' *Leo, the Late Bloomer* is a delightful story of a tiger cub who develops at a slower pace than expected.

Physical disabilities are discussed in Fassler's *Howie Helps Himself,* an effective book with children who have physical disabilities, their siblings, and their classmates. Another book which encourages positive attitudes toward the special child is *Nick Joins In* by Lasher. This book shows the many things Nick can do in a wheelchair at school. For primary children, *Kelly's Creek* is about a nine-year-old's struggle to cope with special physical problems.

Acceptance of children with special needs is the focus of *Keith Edwards' Different Day* by Schweir, a picture book and parent/teacher guide. *My Friend Leslie* is a book of photographs about a kindergarten girl with multiple handicaps. *On With the Show: The Kids on the Block Series*, an interesting series of books, features children with disabilities telling stories about their experiences (Aiello, & Shulman, 1989).

Inclusion of books about disabilities and acceptance can lead children to a new understanding of how they are the same and different. Sharing these books also provides a planned time for teacher and children to talk, question, and

Courtesy of *The Big Orange Splot*, published by Hastings House.

empathize about the special problems children encounter. These early experiences with literature may be one avenue to acceptance of those who are different and to the development of new friendships within the early childhood classroom.

GIFTED CHILDREN

Young children can be gifted in many different ways, including intellectual, specific subject area (math, language), the arts, kinesthetically talented, and creativity. Very few children are gifted in all areas, but rather excel in specific domains. Intellectually gifted children often have large vocabularies, high curiosity, and many read two to three years beyond their chronological peers. Intellectually gifted children need opportunities to select books that are appropriate for their reading level and interests. Since intellectually gifted children read three to four times the number of books most children read, they need more opportunities to use the school and community library (Russell, 1961). Young children gifted in specific areas, such as science or history, will read more in-depth and more advanced materials on these top-ics. They need exposure to a wider range of books, requiring higher level thinking, rather than those typically selected for classroom use. Gifted children interested in the arts should have books that build from their strengths, capitalizing on their interests. Within the classroom, all children, including the young gifted child, should be able to read and write on topics that interest them. They should not be required to read and write on the level of their classmates but rather allowed to move at their own pace. Kitano (1982) recommends providing many activities that require decision making, inquiry, and problem solving. Additional drill on concepts they already understand will often turn the gifted child off to the educational system.

CREATIVE THINKERS

Creative children often have difficulty in conforming to the structure of traditional classrooms. Creatively gifted children often come up with many unique ideas making it difficult to focus on a particular idea and bring their work to completion. The creative child demonstrates fluency of ideas, flexibility of thinking, and originality of response

(Torrance, 1962). Creative young children need an environment where different ideas are valued and divergent responses are encouraged.

Books can support the importance of creative problem solving and help the children accept their unusual approaches to life. Pinkwater's *The Big Orange Splot* is an example of a story where the main character was creative and convinced his neighbors to paint their houses in their own ways to represent their uniqueness. In this story the creative person is first viewed as "odd," but, after the neighbors talk with him, they begin to understand him and appreciate his special way of dealing with a problem.

The developmental characteristics of young children can provide a way of understanding groups of children. The similarities of children within a specific period of development can provide the teacher with basic ideas about the group and their needs. These predictable patterns can assist the teacher in designing an appropriate environment that will accept the characteristics of the children and help them reach their potential.

The range of capabilities of young children within any group emphasizes the need for many types of literature and the availability of different levels of printed materials within every early childhood classroom. These variations of abilities also indicate the need for times each day when children can make personal selections and interact with books that are of interest to them. Literature experiences can be appropriate, successful, and personally meaningful.

Figure 2.9 Books that Promote Creative Thinking

The Art Lesson by Tomie dePaola. Describes a creative child in art class.

The Big Orange Splot by Daniel Pinkwater. When one homeowner refuses to be intimidated by "shouldn'ts", he and his neighbors discover new ways to express themselves.

Colors by Monique Felix. A little mouse trapped in a book discovers what colors are.

Color Dance by Ann Jonas. Three girls and a boy create beautiful mosaics of color as they dance.

Elephant Buttons by Norkio Ueno. This wordless book challenges children of all ages to see their environment in new ways.

Imagine by Allison Lester. This book encourages visual imagination through poems and intricate pictures.

Mouse Paint by Ellen Stoll Walsh. Three white mice have a color mixing adventure when they find three jars of paint.

Oh, the Thinks You Can Think by Dr. Seuss. Encourages children to think creatively in numerous ways.

SUGGESTED LEARNING EXPERIENCES

1. Observe a caregiver or parent reading a book to an infant, six to twelve months old. Study the infant's responses and ways he or she demonstrates interest in the reading.

2. Visit a toddler classroom and observe the different behaviors of the toddlers when the teacher is sharing a book with the group.

3. Observe a toddler using telegraphic speech. Write all the language the child uses in a fifteen-minute period. Analyze the child's ability to communicate.

4. Select a book that matches the developmental characteristics of preschool or primary-age children. Write a paragraph explaining your choice.

5. Visit a kindergarten classroom during circle time. Observe the similarities and differences in the children's development in the areas of oral language, social skills, and book interest.

6. Talk with a primary teacher who teaches in a multiage classroom. Discuss with the teacher how the different ages work together on group projects.

7. Tour a child-care facility and visit an infant room, toddler area, preschool classroom, and after-school program. Write a brief summary of the developmental characteristics observed in the four groups.

8. Write a paragraph defending the use of the developmental characteristics in the selection of a book for circle time reading in a kindergarten class.

9. Visit an early childhood classroom which includes children with disabilities that are mainstreamed. Observe the interactions that occur between children during center time.

10. Observe two children who are the same chronological age. Identify their developmental similarities and differences.

REFERENCES

Alegria, J., & Noirot, E. (1978). Neonate orientation behavior towards human voice. *International Journal of Behavioral Development, 1*(4), 292–312.

Armbruster, V. & Klein, D. (1992). Nurturing communication skills. In R. Cook, A. Tessier and V. Armbruster. *Adapting early childhood curricula for children with special needs,* 197-234. New York: Macmillan.

Bandura, A. (1965). Influence of models' reinforcement contingencies on the acquisition of imitative responses. *Journal of Personality and Social Psychology, 1,* 589–595.

Bredekamp, S. (Ed.). (1987). *Developmentally appropriate practices.* Washington, DC: National Association for the Education of Young Children.

Brown, R. (1973). *A first language.* Cambridge, MA: Harvard University Press.

Butler, D. (1980). *Babies need books.* New York: Antheneum.

Cataldo, C. (1983). *Infants and toddler programs.* Reading, MA: Addison-Wesley.

Cazden, C. (1972). *Child language and education.* New York: Holt, Rinehart, and Winston.

Chomsky, C. (1969). *The acquisition of syntax in children 5 to 10.* Cambridge, MA: The MIT. Press.

Church, J. (1961). *Language and the discovery of reality.* New York: Vintage.

Cohen, L. (1979). Our developing knowledge of infant perception and cognition. *American Psychologist, 34*(10), 894–899.

Colker, L. (1992). Getting ready for readiness: A case study. *The ERIC Review, 2*(1), 7–11.

Condon, W., & Sander, L. (1974). Neonate movement is synchronized with adult speech: Interactional participation and language acquisition. *Science, 183*(4120), 99–101.

Cooke, T., Ruskus, J. & Peck, C. (1981). Handicapped preschool children in the mainstream: Background, outcomes, and clinical suggestions. *Topics in Early Childhood Special Education, 1*(1), 73-83.

Cowles, M. & Aldridge, J. (1992). *Activity-oriented classrooms.* Washington, DC: National Education Association.

Dale, P. (1972). *Language development structure and function.* Hinsdale, IL: Dryden Press.

Davis, J. (1977). *Our forgotten children: Hard of hearing pupils in the schools.* Minneapolis, MN: University of Minnesota Press.

Dworetzky, J. (1990). *Introduction to child development* (4th ed.). St. Paul, MN: West Publishing Co.

Erikson, E. (1963). *Childhood and society* (2nd ed.). New York: Norton.

Fields, M., Spangler, K., & Lee, D. (1991). *Let's begin reading right.* New York: Macmillan.

Gesell, A. (1928). *Infancy and human growth.* New York: Macmillan.

Gibbs, J., Arnold, K, & Burkhart, J. (1984). Sex differences in the expression of moral judgement. *Child Development, 55,* 1040–1043.

Gilligan, C. (1982). *In a different voice: Sex differences in the expression of moral judgment.* Cambridge, MA: Howard University Press.

Goodman, Y. (1986). Children's coming to know literacy. In W. Teale & E. Sulzby (Eds.). *Emergent literacy: Writing and reading.* Norwood, NJ: Ablex Publishing.

Harris, J., & Liebert, R. (1987). *The child development from birth through adolescence.* Englewood Cliffs, NJ: Prentice-Hall.

Hendrick, J. (1990). *Total Learning*: Developmental Curriculum for young children. Columbus, OH: Merrill.

Honig, A. (1984). Why talk to babies? *Beginnings.* pp. 3–6.

Honig, A. (1985 Winter). High quality infant/toddler care: Issues and dilemmas. *Young Children, 41*(1), 40-46.

Isbell, R., Floyd, S., & Fox, J. (1992). A study of the effects of environmental factors on the book interest of young children. Unpublished study.

Jeffrey, D. & Mahoney, E. (1989, April). Sitting pretty: Infants, toddlers, and lapsits. *School Library Journal, 38*(8) 37–39.

Kamii, C., Manning, M., & Manning, G. (Eds.). (1991). *Early literacy: A constructivist foundation for whole language.* Washington, DC: National Education Association.

Kitano, M. (1982). Young gifted children: Strategies for preschool teachers. *Young Children, 37*(4), 14–24.

Klein, A. (1992). *Storybook humor and early development.* Childhood Education, 68(4), 213–217.

Kohlberg, L. (1981). *Essays and moral development: The philosophy of moral development.* New York: Harper & Row.

Kulleseid, E. & Strickland, D. (1989). *Literature, literacy and learning*. Chicago: American Library Association.

Lamme, L. (1990). Exploring the world of music through picture books. *The Reading Teacher, 44*(4), 294–300.

Lenneberg, E. (1966). *Biological foundations of language*. New York: Wiley.

Loban, W. (1976). *Language development: Kindergarten through grade twelve*. Urbana, IL: National Council of Teachers of English.

Machado, J. (1990). *Early childhood experiences in language arts*. Albany, NY: Delmar Publishers Inc.

Maxim, G. (1985). *The very young*. Belmont, CA: Wadsworth.

McNeill, D. (1970). *The acquisition of language*. New York: Harper & Row.

Meltzoff, A. & Moore, M. (1977). Imitation of facial and manual gestures by human neonates. *Science, 198*(4312), 75–78.

Miller, K. (1990) *More things to do with toddlers and twos*. Chelsea, MA: Telshare Publishing.

Morgan, D. & York, M. (1981). Ideas for mainstreaming young children. *Young Children, 36*(2), 18–25.

Piaget, J. (1955). *Language and thought of the child* (M. Gabian, Trans.). Cleveland: World Publishing. (Original work published in 1926. Cleveland: Meridian Press)

Piaget, J. (1962). *Play, dreams, and imitation in childhood*. New York: Norton.

Rubin, R. & Fisher, J. (1982). *Your preschooler*. p. 50. New York: MacMillian Publishing.

Russell, D. (1961). *Children learn to read*. Boston: Ginn.

Shirley, M. (1933). *Postural and locomotor development: Vol. 1. The first two years: A study of twenty-five babies*. Minneapolis, MN: University of Minnesota Press.

Skinner, B. (1957). *Verbal behavior*. Englewood Cliffs, NJ: Prentice-Hall.

Slobin, D. (1971). *Psycholinguistics*. Glenview, IL: Foresman and Company.

Smilansky, S. & Shefatya, L. (1990). *The effects of sociodramatic play on disadvantaged preschool children*. Gaithersburg, MD: Psychosocial & Educational Publications.

Southern Regional Education Board. (1992). *Readiness for school: The Early Childhood Challenge*. Atlanta, GA: Author.

Surbeck, E. & Kelley, M. F. (1990) (Eds.). *Personalizing care with infants, toddlers, and families*. Wheaton, MO: Association for Childhood Education International.

Teale, W. & Sulzby, E. (1986). *Emergent literacy: Writing and reading*. Norwood, NJ: Ablex Publishing.

Torrance, E. Paul. (1962). *Guiding creative talent*. Englewood Cliffs, NJ: Prentice-Hall.

U.S. Department of Education (1992) Fourteenth Annual Report to Congress on the Implementation of Public Law 94-142: The Education of all handicapped children act. Washington, DC: Author

Vygotsky, L. (1962). *Thought and language* (Eugenia Hanfmann, E., & Vakar, G., Trans.). Cambridge, MA: MIT Press.

Vygotsky, L, (1987). Problems of general psychology . In R. Rieber & A. Carton (Eds.). *The Collected works of L. S. Vygotsky: Vol. 1*. New York: Plenum Press.

Watson, J. B. (1924). *Behaviorism*. New York: Norton.

Wilson, L. (1986). *Infants and toddlers curriculum and teaching*. Albany, NY: Delmar Publishers Inc.

Wynne, S., Ulfelder, L. & Dakof, T. (1975). *Mainstreaming and early childhood education for handicapped children: Review and implications of research*. Washington, DC: Division of Innovation and Development, Bureau of Education for the Handicapped, U. S. Office of Education.

CHILDREN'S LITERATURE REFERENCES

The authors and illustrators of children's books are listed, in all chapters, by their full names to help the reader become acquainted with them. If only one name is listed, the author also illustrated the book.

Ahlberg, Allan, & Ahlberg, Janet. (1983). *The Baby's Catalogue*. Boston: Little Brown.

Ahlberg, Allan, & Ahlberg, Janet. (1981). *Peek-a-Boo*. New York: Viking.

Aiello, R. & Shulman, J. (1989). *On With the Show: The Kids on the Block Book Series*. Frederick, MD: Twentieth Century Books.

Aliki. (1968). *Hush, Little Baby*. Englewood Cliffs, NJ: Prentice-Hall.

Aliki. (1982). *We Are Best Friends*. New York: Greenwillow.

Ancona, George, & Miller, Mary Beth. (1989). *Handtalk Zoo*. New York: Four Winds Press.

Baby's Toys. New York: Stahlwood Toy Mfg. Co.

Barton, Bryon. (1979). *Wheels*. New York: Thomas Y. Crowell.

Blacker, Terrence (1990). *Herbie Hamster, Where Are You?* New York: Random House.

Blos, Joan. (1984). *Martin's Hats*. Illustrated by Marc Simont. New York: Morrow Junior Books.

Blume, Judy. (1971). *Freckle Juice*. New York: Dell.

Bonsall, Crosby. (1964). *It's Mine!–A Greedy Book*. New York: Harper & Row.

Bowden, Joan. (1992). *Where Does Our Garbage Go?* Designed and illustrated by Pat Paris. New York: Bantam Doubleday Dell Publishing.

Brott, Ardyth. (1990). *Jeremy's Decision*. Illustrated by Michael Marthchenko. Brooklyn, NY: Kane/Miller

Brown, Marc. (1980). *Finger Rhymes*. New York: E. P. Dutton.

Brown, Marc. (1984). *Arthur's Thanksgiving*. Boston: Little Brown.

Brown, Marc. (1985). *Hand Rhymes*. New York: E. P. Dutton.

Brown, Marc. (1987). *Arthur's Baby*. Boston: Joy Street Books.

Brown, Marc. (1979). *Arthur's Eyes*. Boston: Little Brown.

Brown, Margaret Wise. (1947). *Goodnight Moon*. Illustrated by Clement Hurd. New York: Harper & Row.

Brown, Margaret Wise (1989). *Big Red Barn*. Illustrated by Felicia Bond. New York: Harper & Row.

Burningham, John. (1962). *The Blanket*. New York: Crowell Junior Books.

Bush, John & Paul, Korky. (1991). *The Fish Who Could Wish*. Brooklyn, New York: Kane/Miller.

Butterworth, Brent & Green, Tie. (1991). *The Big Book of How Things Work*. Illustrated by Bill Whitney. Lincolnwood, IL: Publications International.

Byran, Ashley. (1985). *The Cat's Purr*. New York: Anteneum.

Byars, Betsy. (1971). *Go and Hush the Baby*. Illustrated by Emily A. McCully. New York: Viking Press.

Cameron, Polly. (1961). *"I Can't," Said the Ant: A Book of Nonsense*. New York: Coward, McCann & Georgheyan.

Campbell, Rod. (1985). *Misty's Mischief*. New York: Viking Press.

Carle, Eric. (1984) *The Mixed Up Chameleon*. New York: Harper & Row

Carlson, Nancy. (1990). *Arnie and the New Kid*. New York: Viking Press.

Carlson, Nancy. (1988). *I Like Me!*. New York: Viking Kestrel.

Carlstrom, Nancy. (1986). *Jesse Bear, What Will You Wear?*. Illustrated by Bruce Degen. New York: Macmillan.

Carter, David A. (1989). *What's in My Pocket?* New York: Putnam.

Chorao, Kay. (1977). *The Baby's Lap Book*. New York: E. P. Dutton.

Chorao, Kay. (1986). *The Baby's Good Morning Book*. New York: E. P. Dutton.

Charlip, Remy. & Miller, Mary B. (1974). *Handtalk*. Illustrated by George Ancona. New York: Parents Magazine Press.

Cleary, Beverly. (1975). *Ramona the Brave*. Illustrated by Alan Tiegreen. New York: Morrow.

Cohen, Miriam. (1967). *Will I Have a Friend?* Illustrated by Lillian Hoban. New York: Macmillan

Cohen, Miriam. (1971) *Best Friends*. Illustrated by Lillian Hoban. New York: Macmillan.

Cohen, Miriam. (1977). *When Will I Read?*. Illustrated by Lillian Hoban. New York: Greenwillow.

Cohen, Miriam. (1983). *See You Tomorrow, Charles*. New York: Greenwillow.

Cole, Joanna. (1986). *The Magic School Bus at the Waterworks*. New York: Scholastic, Inc.

Cole, William. (1974). *What's Good for a Three-Year-Old?* Illustrated by Lillian Hoban. New York: Holt Rinehart & Winston.

Corey, Dorothy. (1980). *Everybody Takes a Turn*. Illustrated by Lois Axemen. Morton Grove, IL: Albert Whitman.

dePaola, Tomie. (1989). *The Art Lesson*. New York: G. P. Putnam's Sons.

Eastman, P. D. (1960). *Are You My Mother?* New York: Random House.

Ehlert, Lois. (1988). *Planting a Rainbow*. San Diego: Harcourt Brace Jovanovich.

Fassler, Joan (1969). *One Little Girl*. Illustrated by M. Jane Smyth. New York: Human Sciences Press.

Fassler, Joan. (1975). *Howie Helps Himself*. Illustrated by Joe Lasker. New York: Human Sciences Press.

Felix, Monique. (1991). *Colors*. New York: Stewart, Tabori, and Chang, Inc.

Fischer, Nagel, Heiderose & Fisher-Nagel, Andrew (1986). *Inside the Burrow: The Life of the Golden Hamster*. Minneapolis, MN: Carolrhoda Books.

Galdone, Paul. (1975). *The Little Red Hen*. New York: Scholastic.

Gerstein, Mordecai. (1985). *William, Where Are You?* New York: Crown.

Gibbons, Gail. (1985). *Fill IT UP!* New York: Harper Collins Child Books.

Gillham, Bill. (1982). *First Words Picture Book*. Photographs by Sam Grainger. New York: Putnam Publishing Group.

Goodsell, J. (1965). *Katie's Magic Glasses*. Boston: Houghton Mifflin.

Grahame, Kenneth. (1989). *The Wind in the Willows Word Book*. New York: Chatham River Press.

Grayson, Marion. (1962). *Let's Do Finger Plays*. Illustrated by Nancy Wehl. Manchester, NH: Robert B. Luce.

Gwynne, Frederick Hubbard. (1970). *The King Who Rained*. New York: Young Readers Press.

Hale, Sarah. (1990). *Mary Had a Little Lamb*. Illustrated by Tomie dePaola. New York: Scholastic.

Hallinan, P. K. (1985). *That's What a Friend Is*, Nashville: Ideals.

Hart, Jane (Ed.). (1989). *Singing Bee!: A Collection of Favorite Children's Songs*. Illustrated by Anita Lobel. New York: Lothrop, Lee, & Shepard.

Hayes, Sarah. (1988). *Clap Your Hands: Finger Rhymes*. Illustrated by Toni Goffe. New York: Lothrop, Lee, & Sheperd.

Hazen, Barbara. (1981). *Even If I Did Something Awful?* Illustrated by Nancy Kincade. New York: Atheneum.

Heine, Helme. (1982). *Friends*. New York: Margaret K. McEdlerry Books.

Heller, Ruth. (1982). *Animals Born Alive and Well*. New York: Grosset & Dunlap.

Heller, Ruth. (1989). *Many Luscious Lollipops*. New York: Grosset & Dunlap.

Henkes, Kevin. (1989). *Jessica*. New York: Puffin Books.

Henwood, Chris. (1988). *Earthworms*. Photographs by Barnie Watts. New York: Watts.

Hill, Eric. (1980). *Where's Spot?* New York: Putnam.

Hines, Anna Grossnickle. (1986). *Daddy Makes the Best Spaghetti*. New York: Clarion Books.

Hoban, Tana. (1972). *Push, Pull, Empty, Full*. New York: Macmillan.

Hoban, Tana. (1983). *I Read Signs*. New York: Greenwillow.

Hoban, Tana. (1983). *Round and Round and Round*. New York: Greenwillow.

Hoban, Tana. (1985). *What Is It?* New York: Greenwillow.

Hoban, Tana. (1989) *Of Colors and Things*. New York: Scholastic.

Hopkins, Lee Bennett. (1980). *By Myself*. Illustrated by Glo Coalson. New York: Thomas Y. Crowell.

Hughes, Shirley. (1983) *Alfie Gives a Hand*. New York: Macmillan.

Hughes, Shirley. (1979). *Up and Up*. Englewood Cliffs, NJ: Prentice-Hall.

Hughes, Shirley. (1985). *Noisy*. New York: Lothrop.

Hurd, Edith Thacher. (1970). *Come With Me to Nursery School*. Photographs by Edward Bigelow. New York: Coward-McCann.

Hutchins, Pat. (1971). *Titch*. New York: Macmillan.

Hutchins, Pat. (1970). *You'll Soon Grow Into Them, Titch*. New York: Macmillian.

Isadora, Rachel. (1979). *Ben's Trumpet*. New York: Greenwillow.

Isadora, Rachel. (1985). *I Touch*. New York: Greenwillow.

Isadora, Rachel. (1985). *I Hear*. New York: Greenwillow.

Isadora, Rachel. (1985). *I See*. New York: Greenwillow.

Johnson, Crockett. (1955). *Harold and the Purple Crayon*. New York: Harper & Row.

Jonas, Ann. (1989). *Color Dance*. New York: Greenwillow.

Jordan, Helene J. (1992). *How a Seed Grows*. Illustrated by Joseph Low. New York: Crowell Junior Books.

Kachenmeister, Cheryl. (1989). *On Monday When It Rains*. Photographs by Tony Berthiaume. Boston: Houghton Mifflin.

Keats, Ezra Jack. (1966). *Jennie's Hat*. New York: Harper Collins Children's Books.

Keats, Ezra Jack. (1971). *Apt. 3*. New York: MacMillan.

Keats, Ezra Jack. (1978). *The Trip*. New York: Greenwillow.

Kemp, Moira. (1987). *Pat-a-Cake*. Los Angeles: Price Stern Sloan.

Kherdian, David, & Hogrogian, Nonny. (1990). *The Cat's Midsummer Jamboree*. New York: Philomel.

Koch, Michele. (1993). *World Water Watch*. New York: Greenwillow.

Kroll, Steven. (1984). *The Biggest Pumpkin Ever*. Illustrated by Jeni Bassett. New York: Holiday.

Kraus, Robert. (1971). *Leo, the Late Bloomer*. Illustrated by Jose Aruego. New York: Windmill.

Krauss, Ruth. (1945). *The Carrot Seed*. Illustrated by Crockett Johnson. New York: Harper & Row.

Kunhardt, Dorothy. (1942). *Pat the Bunny*. New York: Golden Touch and Feel Books.

Lane, Megan Halsey. (1990). *Something to Crow About*. New York: Dial Books for Young Readers.

Lasker, Joe. (1974). *He's My Brother*. Chicago: Whitman.

Lasker, Joe. (1980). *Nick Joins In*. Chicago: Whitman.

Lester, Allison. (1990). *Imagine*. Boston: Houghton Mifflin.

Lester, Helen. (1988). *Tacky the Penguin*. Illustrated by Lynn Munsinger. Boston: Houghton Mifflin.

Lewison, Wendy. (1992). *Bye, Bye, Baby*. Illustrated by True Kelly. New York: Scholastic.

Levine, Edna S. (1974). *Lisa and Her Soundless World*. Illustrated by Gloria Komer. New York: Human Sciences Press.

Lionni, Leo. (1963). *Swimmy*. New York: Pantheon.

Lionni, Leo. (1969). *Alexander and the Wind Up Mouse*. New York: Pantheon.

Lionni, Leo. (1970). *Fish Is Fish*. New York: Dragonfly Books.

Lionni, Leo. (1975). *A Color of His Own*. New York: Random House.

Litchfield, Ada B. (1976). *A Button in Her Ear*. Illustrated by Eleanor Mill. Chicago: Whitman.

Little, Lessie Jones & Greenfield, Eloise. (1978). *I Can Do It Myself*. Illustrated by Carole Byard. New York: Thomas Y. Crowell.

Livingston, Myra Cohn (Ed.). (1985). *Thanksgiving Poems*. Illustrated by Stephen Gammel. New York: Holiday.

Lobel, Arnold. (1976). *Frog and Toad All Year*. New York: Harper & Row.

Lobel, Arnold. (1986). *The Random House Book of Mother Goose*. New York: Random House.

Maddox, Tony. (1989). *Spike: The Sparrow Who Couldn't Sing*. New York: Barron's.

Martin, Jr., Bill. (1967). *Brown Bear, Brown Bear, What Do You See?* Illustrated by Eric Carle. New York: Henry Holt.

Martin, Jr., Bill & Archambault, John. (1989). *Chicka Chicka Boom! Boom!* Illustrated by Lois Ehlert. New York: Simon & Schuster.

Martin, Jr., Bill & Archambault, John. (1987). *Here Are My Hands*. Illustrated by Ted Rand. New York: Henry Holt.

Marzello, Jean. (1990). *Pretend You're A Cat*. Illustrated by Jerry Pinkney. New York: Dial Books for Young Readers.

Mayer, Mercer. (1968). *There's a Nightmare in My Closet*. New York: Dial Books for Young Readers.

Mayer, Mercer. (1974). *Frog Goes to Dinner*. New York: Dial Books for Young Readers.

Mayer, Mercer. (1975). *What Do You Do With a Kangaroo?* Boston: Houghton Mifflin.

Mayer, Mercer. (1987). *There's an Alligator Under My Bed*. New York: Dial Books for Young Readers.

McGovern, Ann. (1967). *Too Much Noise*. Illustrated by Simms Taback. Boston: Houghton Mifflin.

Merriam, Eve. (1972). *Boys & Girls, Girls & Boys*. Illustrated by Harriet Sherman. New York: Henry Holt.

Merriam, Eve. (1989) *Daddies at Work*. Illustrated by Eugenie Fernades. New York: Simon & Schuster.

Merriam, Eve. (1989). *Mommies at Work*. Illustrated by Eugenie Fernades. New York: Simon & Schuster.

Morris, Ann. (1990). *Loving*. Photographs by Ken Heyman. New York: Lothrop, Lee & Shepard.

Morris, Ann. (1992). *Tools*. Photographs by Ken Heyman. New York: Lothrop, Lee & Shepard.

Ness, Evaline, (1966). *Sam, Bangs, and Moonshine*. New York: Henry Holt.

Numeroff, Laura. (1985). *If You Give a Mouse a Cookie*. Illustrated by Felicia Bond. New York: Harper & Row.

Ormerod, Jan. (1985). *Messy Baby*. New York: Lothrop.

Ormerod, Jan. (1985). *Reading*. New York: Lothrop.

Oxenbury, Helen. (1981). *Dressing*. New York: Simon & Schuster Trade.

Oxenbury, Helen. (1981). *Playing*. New York: Simon & Schuster Trade.

Oxenbury, Helen. (1981). *Family*. New York: Wanderer Books.

Oxenbury, Helen. (1982). *Tickle, Tickle*. New York: Macmillan.

Oxenbury, Helen. (1983). *The Birthday Party*. New York: Dial Books for Young Readers.

Oxenbury, Helen. (1985). *I Touch*. London: Walker Books.

Oxenbury, Helen. (1986). *I Can*. London: Walker Books.

Oxenbury, Helen. (1987). *All Fall Down*. New York: Macmillan.

Oxenbury, Helen. (1990). *Working*. New York: Simon & Schuster Trade.

Oxenbury, Helen. (1992). *Mother's Helper*. New York: Dial Books for Young Readers.

Parish, Peggy. (1980). *I Can, Can You?* New York: Greenwillow.

Parker, Nancy Winslow & Wright, Jean Richards. (1987). *Bugs*. Illustrated by Nancy Winslow Parker. New York: Mulberry Books.

Pinkwater, Daniel Manus. (1977). *The Big Orange Splot*. New York: Hastings House.

Piper, Watty. (1954). *The Little Engine That Could*. Illustrated by Richard Walz. New York: Platt & Munk.

Polacco, Patricia. (1992). *Chicken Sunday*. New York: G. P. Putnam's Sons.

Polacco, Patricia. (1992). *Mrs. Katz and Tush*. New York: Bantam Books.

Pomerantz, Charlotte. (1987). *How Many Trucks Can a Tow Truck Tow?* Illustrated by R. W. Alley. New York: Random House.

Prelutsky, Jack. (1986). *Read-Aloud Rhymes for the Very Young*. Illustrated by Marc Brown. New York: Alfred A. Knopf.

Preston, Edna Mitchell. (1976). *The Temper Tantrum Book*. Illustrated by Rainey Bennett. New York: Puffin Books.

Preston, Edna Mitchell. (1978). *Where Did My Mother Go?* Illustrated by Chris Conover. New York: Four Winds.

Quackenbush, Robert. (1972). *Old MacDonald Had a Farm*. New York: Lippincott.

Ra, Carol. (1987). *Trot, Trot to Boston: Play Rhymes for Baby*. Illustrated by Catherine Stock. New York: Lothrop, Lee & Shepard.

Raskin, Ellen. (1969). *Spectacles*. New York: Antheneum.

Rice, Eve. (1981). *Benny Bakes a Cake*. New York: Greenwillow.

Rockwell, Anne. (1984). *My Backyard*. New York: MacMillan.

Rockwell, Anne, & Rockwell, Harlow. (1979). *The Supermarket*. New York: MacMillian Children's Group.

Rockwell, Harlow. (1976). *My Nursery School*. New York: Greenwillow.

Rosenberg, Maxine B. (1983). *My Friend Leslie*. New York: Lothrop.

Rylant, Cynthia. (1984). *This Year's Garden*. Illustrated by Mary Szilagy. New York: Macmillan.

Scarry, Richard. (1963). *Best Word Book Ever*. New York: Random House.

Scarry, Richard. (1987). *Things That Go*. New York: Western.

Scheffler, Ursel. (1986). *A Walk in the Rain*. Illustrated by Ulises Wensell, translated by Andrea Merman. New York: G.P. Putnam's Sons.

Schlesinger, Al. (1957, 1992). *Baby's Mother Goose*. G. P. Putnam & Sons.

Schubert, Ingrid, & Shubert, Dieter. (1985). *The Magic Bubble Trip*. Brooklyn, NY: Kane/Miller.

Schwartz, Alvin. (1973). *Tomfoolery: Trickery and Foolery With Words*. Illustrated by Glen Rounds. New York: Harper & Row.

Schweir, Karin M. (1988). *Keith Edwards Different Day*. Toronto: G. Allen Roemer Inst.

Sendak, Maurice. (1978). *Chicken Soup with Rice*. New York: Harper & Row.

Seuling, Barbara. (1976). *Teeny-Tiny Woman*. New York: Viking.

Seuss, Dr. Theodor Giese. (1975). *Oh, the Thinks You Can Think!* New York: Random House.

Sharmat, Marjorie. (1977). *I'm Terrific*. New York: Holiday House.

Sharmat, Mitchell. (1980). *Gregory, the Terrible Eater*. Illustrated by Jose Aruego and Ariane Dewey. New York: Scholastic.

Showers, Paul. (1961). *The Listening Walk*. Illustrated by Aliki. New York: Thomas Y. Crowell.

Sikorski, Anne. (1988). *Look at Teddy*. New York: Modern Publishing.

Silverstein, Shel. (1981). *A Light in the Attic*. New York: Harper & Row.

Smith, Doris B. (1975). *Kelly's Creek*. Illustrated by Alan Tiegreen. New York: Thomas Y. Crowell.

Stein, Sara B. (1984). *About Handicaps*. New York: Walker.

Steptoe, John. (1988). *Baby Says*. New York: Lothrop, Lee, & Shepard.

Strauss, Barbara, & Friedland, Helen. (1986). *See You Later, Alligator: A First Book of Word Play*. Illustrated by Tershia D' Elgin. Los Angeles: Price Stern Sloan.

Sullivan, M. & Bourke, L. (1980). *A Show of Hands: Say It in Sign Language*. Reading, MA: Addison-Wesley.

Surat, Michelle Maria. (1983). *Angel Child, Dragon Child*. Illustrated by Vo-Dinh Mai. New York: Scholastic.

Szekeres, Cyndy. (1990). *What Bunny Loves*. Racine, WN: Western Publishing Company.

The Real Mother Goose. (1984). Illustrated by Jane Chambless Rigi. Japan: Checkerboard Press.

Titherington, Jeanne. (1986). *Pumpkin, Pumpkin*. New York: Greenwillow.

Tusa, Tricia. (1988). *Stay Away From the Junkyard!* New York: MacMillan.

Udry, Janice M. (1961). *Let's Be Enemies*. Illustrated by Maurice Sendak. New York: Harper & Row.

Udry, Janice M. (1956). *A Tree Is Nice*. Illustrated by Marc Simont. New York: Harper & Row.

Ueno, Noriko. (1973). *Elephant Buttons*. New York: Harper & Row.

Van Allsburg, Chris (1981). *The Polar Express*. Boston: Houghton Mifflin.

Viorst, Judith. (1973). *My Mama Says There Aren't Any Zombies, Ghosts, Vampires, Creatures, Demons, Monsters, Fiends, Goblins, or Things*. Illustrated by Kay Chorao. New York: Atheneum.

Waber, Bernard. (1972). *Ira Sleeps Over*. Boston: Houghton Mifflin.

Waber, Bernard. (1978). *The Snake: A Very Long Story*. Boston: Houghton Mifflin.

Wadsworth, Olive A. (1986). *Over in the Meadow*. Illustrated by Mary Maki Rae. New York: Penguin.

Walsh, Ellen Stoll. (1989). *Mouse Paint*. San Diego: Harcourt Brace Jovanovich.

Watanabe, Shigeo. (1980). *How Do I Put It On?* Illustrated by Yasuo Ohtomo. New York: Putnam.

Watanabe, Shigeo. (1988). *It's My Birthday*. Illustrated by Yasuo Ohtomo. New York: Philomel.

Watson, Clyde. (1983). *Catch Me and Kiss Me and Say It Again*. Illustrated by Wendy Watson. New York: Philomel.

Wells, Rosemary. (1979). *Max's First Word*. New York: Dial Press.

White, E. B. (1953). *Charlotte's Web*. Illustrated by Garth Williams. New York: Harper.

Whitten, Eve & Whitten, Pat. (1961). *The Touch Me Book*. Illustrated by Harlow Rockwell. New York: Golden Books.

Williams, Jay. (1977). *The Reward Worth Having*. New York: Four Winds.

Williams, Vera B. (1983). *Something Special For Me*. New York: Greenwillow.

Williams, Vera B., & Williams Jennifer. (1988). *Stringbean's Trip to the Shining Sea*. New York: Greenwillow.

Wolf, Bernard. (1977) *Anna's Silent World*. New York: J. B. Lippincott.

Wright, Alexandra. (1992). *Will We Miss Them? Endangered Species*. Illustrated by Marshall Peck III. Watertown, MA: Charlesbridge.

Yashimo, Taro. (1955). *Crow Boy*. New York: Viking Press.

Yolen, Jane. (1986). *Lullaby Song Book*. New York: Harcourt Brace Jovanovich.

Zolotow, Charlotte. (1966). *Big Brother*. Illustrated by Mary Chalmers. New York: Harper & Row.

Zolotow, Charlotte. (1987). *I Like to Be Little*. Illustrated by Erik Blegvad. New York: Harper & Row.

3

Reading and Writing
in Literature-Rich
Early Childhood
Classrooms

Reading and Writing in Literature–Rich Early Childhood Classrooms

Young children's development as readers and writers happens best in literature-rich early childhood classrooms where teachers understand the emergent literacy processes. In this chapter we examine the process of children becoming literate by visiting a kindergarten classroom where the teacher, Ms. Warren, is struggling to reconcile her views of young children as developmental learners and the reading instruction she is delivering.[1] Examples are also given from other classrooms at other grade levels where teachers use children's literature in a process approach to literacy instruction.

The classroom examples demonstrate that in a supportive literacy environment children learn to read and write while enjoying the processes. Teachers who are good observers will recognize the many ways children grow in their literacy development as they construct knowledge about print. Responsible teachers provide ways for children to demonstrate their ever-widening knowledge about reading by interacting with the print in books and by constructing print using whatever writing they presently know how to form.

Early childhood teachers have a long and rich heritage of including good books and stories in their classrooms. Because the preschool, nursery school, and kindergarten have often been exempt from textbook adoptions, teachers have been freer to design their instructional programs than in most primary grades. With the emphasis on whole language and literacy processes, early childhood educators in the preschool and kindergarten can influence practice in the primary grades. Similarly, there are some reading and writing strategies which pre-first-grade teachers can borrow from the primary grades which will improve literacy and literature experiences for younger children.

Only a few years ago when kindergarten, nursery school, Head Start, and child-care teachers were asked if they taught reading, their resounding reply was "No." Indeed, child-centered teachers of young children could not advocate the type of primary reading instruction which was composed of extensive lists of sequential skills, decoding rules, and endless phonics exercises of isolated sounds, then linking the sounds together, with the hope that in the end children would read whole words and whole sentences.

Unfortunately, some kindergarten teachers who were part of the primary school began to feel enormous pressures to teach reading in this isolated skills approach. In addition, publishers marketed "reading readiness" materials for the kindergarten. Many kindergarten teachers found themselves a part of the textbook adoption process and the extensive sets of reproducible worksheets and workbooks became the school's view of kindergarten reading instruction.

Today, however, pre-first-grade teachers' views of themselves as reading teachers have changed because of research on emergent literacy and an appreciation of the child as an active learner who constructs knowledge about print. Reading instruction has become more of a developmental process focusing on emerging literacy, and pre-first-grade teachers are beginning to see themselves as reading and writing teachers. Ms. Warren is one such kindergarten teacher.

Ms. Warren's Kindergarten

A quick glance around Ms. Warren's kindergarten classroom reveals her views of the curriculum and the active ways young children learn. The room is organized into learning centers which consist of hands-on materials for multilevel learning. All centers reflect the five-year-olds' needs for concrete, visual, and manipulative materials. In the circle time lesson, Ms. Warren presents a lesson to the whole group, and she helps children make associations between new concepts, their interests, and information they already know.

The reading and writing center is impressive with its attractive display of popular children's books, comfortable chairs, and cushions. "Free exploration" reading is also scheduled so that children can thumb through books quickly or linger over a single book at length. Abundant materials for individual drawing and writing are stored conveniently. In the reading and writing center, as in all centers, the simple procedures to be followed are clearly understood by the children.

The children's drawings and some anecdotal notes on their interests are assembled in portfolios as evidence for parents to view at conferences. However, once one gets beyond the drawings and notes, the folders contain a gross inconsistency in Ms. Warren's apparent philosophy concerning the learning process of young children. Each of the folders contains reading "readiness" and phonics worksheets which are being completed in a predetermined sequence. The reading readiness worksheets consist mostly of "find-the-one-that-matches" pictures and letters. The phonics sheets are designed for children to mark individual letters and their sounds. Another inconsistency in philosophy appears when Ms. Warren calls all of the children to the rug area where they sit in a circle around her rocking chair to "work on their sounds." Ms. Warren produces a series of letters and pictures and expresses her approval or disapproval as the children attempt to determine the sound a particular letter makes by associating it with a picture. Using the prepackaged set of materials does not feel right to Ms. Warren, but she explained that, "These materials go with the reading series our school has adopted. I am expected to use them."

Ms. Warren is concerned about the problems her children are facing in learning to read. She has been struggling to decide what to change in her classroom to emphasize reading more and has been considering adding a workbook. Many kindergarten teachers, like Ms. Warren, have little preparation in the teaching of reading, and therefore feel they lack the knowledge to design a good program and resort to prepackaged sets of materials. They think of teaching reading as "putting their children through the worksheets and workbooks."

However, Ms. Warren, like many other early childhood educators, has studied child development and is a skilled observer. The reading specialist at Ms. Warren's school suggested that she use the same techniques of observation to determine the children's development as readers and writers that she uses to study the children's progress in other areas. This process of observations is one Yetta Goodman (1978) calls "kidwatching."

When asked to describe how young children learn, Ms. Warren is quick to point out that from her observations they are active, social, hands-on learners who are creative problem solvers and enjoy using and playing with the materials in her classroom. They sometimes work alone, with the teacher, and with small groups of other children. Ms. Warren readily explains that young children learn best in a warm, accepting environment where they receive encouragement and are free to try things. Obviously, there is a conflict between Ms. Warren's view of young children's learning and her methods of teaching reading which require exact answers and only one right answer.

Prepackaged Instructional Programs Versus Literacy Process Approach

In Robert Aukerman's book *Approaches to Beginning Reading* (1984), he describes over 500 instructional programs, each claiming to be more effective and each providing empirical research data to support their claims. Given that Aukerman's book is now almost ten years old, many other prepackaged instructional programs have now been added to the list. However, the popularity of whole language education is an indication that teachers are no longer impressed with prepackaged instructional programs which, despite their claims of success, continue to produce a large number of nonreaders and readers who choose not to read. Teachers are using whole language because it is a literacy process approach and because the philosophy supports the natural learning process they have observed (Goodman, 1992).

Through literacy process instruction, teachers are able to capitalize on the effective learning strategies children were using long before they entered school. Teachers are able to keep alive that intense excitement young children feel about learning to read and write by providing learning activities designed around the interests of the students. Teachers are able to personalize instruction because whole language as a literacy process view of development is not based on a preset package of instructional materials. Whole language is based on the teachers' observations of how children learn to read and write naturally.

THE NATURAL LEARNING ENVIRONMENT

Since the 1960's, researchers have observed "natural readers"—those children who acquired literacy on their own, rather than from a sequence of lessons from parents or teachers (Clark, 1976; Clay, 1972; Durkin, 1966; Goodman, 1968; Teale & Sulzby, 1989). Findings from the studies of natural readers indicate that children have already begun the process of learning to read and write long before they enter kindergarten. Children enter kindergarten at various stages in the process of learning to read and write, but most of them come with clear concepts of the reading and writing process (Canady, 1983; Harste, Woodward, & Burke, 1984).

Natural readers and writers were provided with a learning environment which enabled them to learn about reading and writing in the same supportive manner that they learned to speak and listen. In homes and in classrooms where children learn to read and write by being immersed in purposeful reading and writing activities in a non-threatening environment, learning to read and write is a natural, yet expanded part of the communication process (Cambourne, 1988; Morrow, 1983; Teale & Sulzby, 1989).

THE READING PROCESS

Essential to a whole language philosophy of literacy acquisition and development is the acceptance of learning as an active process whereby the learner constructs meaning based on the learner's prior knowledge (Wells, 1986). Although educators do not agree about the best way to teach reading, many teachers support the Goodman Model of Reading which describes the process of reading as 1) predicting, 2) sampling, 3) confirming or correcting, and 4) comprehending or integrating (Goodman, 1968). Psycholinguists who study the relationships between thought (psycho) and language (linguistics) believe that very young children who are in the initial stages of learning to read use a process very similar to the more mature readers.

The following examples are offered in support of the theory that young children, as they explore the print/meaning relationship, use a process which is very similar to what we have accepted as the "reading process." For example, a three-year-old, almost four, who had been read to regularly at home, had "memorized" some of his books. He had begun to notice several words and even point out some letters. When given a children's book which he had not seen before, he looked at the picture of a fire truck and the word "TRUCKS" on the cover of the book. He *predicted* that the book was about fire trucks and firefighters. He then opened the book to the title page, (*sampling* or attending to only part of the text) pointed to the word "TRUCKS" written in large letters and said, "Fire trucks." He turned the next page and saw a picture of a dump truck. On the following page, he found an illustration of a gasoline truck and on the next a fire truck. At this point, he confirmed that the book *was* about fire trucks, but it was also about other kinds of trucks, so he turned back to the title page pointed to the letters and said, "trucks." He *corrected* himself. Then, as he turned each page, he said, "Dump truck, big truck (gas truck), fire truck," which was *comprehending* or *integrating*. The child in the illustration above was already aware of the reading process long before he entered kindergarten. Unfortunately, many teachers, who use prepackaged sets of materials will ignore this previously learned information and will treat him as if he has no understanding of how the reading process operates.

The ultimate purpose of reading instruction is to help students become fluent readers who understand the text. Fluent silent readers skip words, substitute words, and make logical guesses at words they do not know (Goodman, 1968). Whole language teachers strive to provide reading instruction which reflects the reading process.

GUIDANCE FOR EARLY CHILDHOOD LITERACY PROCESS INSTRUCTION

Even though Ms. Warren, the teacher in our case study for this chapter, has a reading and writing center in her classroom, when asked how she teaches reading and writing, the endless stream of reading readiness and phonics worksheets were offered as her method. Before the reading specialist at the school made a presentation on emergent literacy, Ms. Warren saw little relationship between the children's free exploration of the books in her room, their drawing and writing, and ways to support the children's development as readers and writers.

In a joint statement of concerns about present practices in early childhood programs like Ms. Warren's, the International Reading Association provides clear guidance for improvement of literacy process instruction through the position paper, "Literacy Development and Early Childhood (Preschool Through Grade 3)." The position paper has been officially endorsed by five other prominent professional organizations:

Association for Childhood Education International

Association for Supervision and Curriculum Development

International Reading Association

National Association for the Education of Young Children

National Association of Elementary School Principals

National Council of Teachers of English.

Figure 3.1 Literacy Development and Early Childhood (Preschool Through Grade 3)

LITERACY LEARNING BEGINS IN INFANCY. CHILDREN HAVE MANY EXPERIENCES WITH ORAL AND WRITTEN LANGUAGE BEFORE THEY COME TO SCHOOL.

☐ Children have had many experiences from which they can build ideas about the functions and uses of oral and written language.

☐ Children have a command of language and of processes for learning language.

☐ Many children can differentiate between drawing and writing.

☐ Many children are reading environmental print, such as road signs, grocery labels, and fast food signs.

☐ Many children associate books with reading.

☐ Children's knowledge about language and communication is influenced by their social and cultural backgrounds.

☐ Many children expect that reading and writing will be sense-making activities.

BASIC PREMISES OF A SOUND PRE-FIRST-GRADE READING PROGRAM

☐ Reading and writing at school should permit children to build upon their already existing knowledge of oral and written language.

☐ Learning should take place in a supportive environment where children can build a positive attitude toward themselves and toward language and literacy.

☐ For optimal learning, teachers should involve children actively in many thoughtful, functional language experiences, including *speaking, listening, writing,* and *reading*.

☐ Teachers of young children should be prepared in ways that acknowledge differences in language and cultural backgrounds and should emphasize reading as an integral part of the language arts as well as of the total curriculum.

CONCERNS

☐ Many pre-first-grade children are subjected to rigid, formal prereading programs with inappropriate expectations and experiences for their levels of development.

☐ Little attention is given to individual development or individual learning styles.

☐ The pressures of accelerated programs do not allow children to be risk takers as they experiment with written language.

☐ Too much attention is focused upon isolated skill development and abstract parts of the reading process, rather than on the integration of talking, writing, and listening with reading.

☐ Too little attention is placed on reading for pleasure; therefore, children do not associate reading with enjoyment.

☐ Decisions related to reading programs are often based on political and economic considerations rather than on knowledge of how young children learn.

☐ The pressure to achieve high scores on tests inappropriate for the kindergarten child has led to undesirable changes in the content of the programs. Activities that deny curiosity, critical thinking, and creative expression are all too frequent and can foster negative attitudes toward language communication.

☐ As a result of declining enrollment and reduction in staff, individuals with little or no knowledge of early childhood education are sometimes assigned to teach young children. Such teachers often select inappropriate methods.

☐ Teachers who are conducting pre-first-grade programs without depending on commercial readers and workbooks sometimes fail to articulate for parents and other members of the public what they are doing and why.

RECOMMENDATIONS

1. Build instruction on what the child already knows about oral language, reading, and writing. Focus on meaningful experiences and meaningful language rather than on isolated skill development.

2. Respect the language the child brings to school, and use it as a base for language and literacy activities.

3. Ensure feelings of success for all children, helping them to see themselves as people who enjoy exploring both oral and written language.

4. Provide reading experiences as an integrated part of the communication process, which includes speaking, listening, and writing, as well as art, math, and music.

5. Encourage children's first attempts at writing, without concern for the proper formation of letters or correct conventional spelling.

6. Encourage risk taking in first attempts at reading and writing, and accept what appear to be errors as part of children's natural growth and development.

7. Use reading materials that are familiar or predictable, such as well known stories, as they provide children with a sense of control and confidence in their ability to learn.

8. Present a model for children to emulate. In the classroom, teachers should use language appropriately, listen and respond to children's talk, and engage in their own reading and writing.

9. Take time regularly to read to children from a wide variety of poetry, fiction, and nonfiction.

10. Provide time regularly for children's independent reading and writing.

11. Foster children's affective and cognitive development by providing them with opportunities to communicate what they know, think, and feel.

12. Use developmentally and culturally appropriate procedures for evaluation, ones that are based on the objectives of the program and that consider each child's total development.

13. Make parents aware of the reasons for a broader language program at school and provide them with ideas for activities to carry out at home.

14. Alert parents to the limitations of formal assessments and standardized tests of pre-first-graders' reading and writing skills.

15. Encourage children to be active participants in the learning process rather than passive recipients by using activities that allow for experimentation with talking, listening, writing, and reading.

(Reprinted by permission from the International Reading Association.)
Early Childhood and Literacy Development Committee.
Literacy development and pre-first-grade. Newark, DL: International Reading Association.

Fortunately, Ms. Warren, the kindergarten teacher introduced at the beginning of the chapter, described young children's learning in a manner consistent with the recommendations from the emergent literacy research and from the position statement on *Literacy Development and Early Childhood*. Yet, the instruction she delivered in reading and writing was inconsistent with her description of young children's learning.

Changes in Ms. Warren's Kindergarten Literacy Instruction

By making changes in literacy instruction, Ms. Warren can begin planning for children's development as readers and writers in ways which are consistent with her stated views of the conditions under which young children learn best. With assistance from the reading specialist and the librarian at her school, Ms. Warren made the following six changes in her classroom:

1. improved read-aloud presentations;
2. modeled reading strategies, which focused on the reading process;
3. restructured before, during, and after reading presentations of books;
4. read big books through the "shared book experience";
5. planned partner reading; and
6. used story retelling.

READ-ALOUD PRESENTATIONS

Jim Trelease (1989) has become one of the foremost proponents of parents and teachers reading aloud to their children. Read-aloud sessions provide opportunities for adults to introduce children to quality literature, for children to make associations between their experiences and those of others, and to prompt better understanding of the social and physical world we inhabit. Young children bond with the book and story when parents and teachers read to them. They also recognize that reading good literature is something which adults prize.

Another major reason for reading aloud to young children is to provide a good reading role model. The teacher's reading aloud allows the child to hear more complicated texts and imaginative language than the beginning reader could manage. But perhaps more importantly, reading aloud becomes a shared activity where teacher and students meet for a pleasant experience.

A great deal of preparation goes into selecting a book for reading aloud to the children. Deborah Wolter (1992) reminds teachers to keep in mind the developmental level of the children and appropriate expectations of the listeners. No matter how expressive the classroom teacher is as a reader, the effectiveness is lost if the story is too long, the plot too complicated, or not enough preparation has gone into getting the children ready to listen. Establishing a regular reading routine helps children get ready to listen, and introducing the book well helps the students become good listeners.

Ms. Warren reads to the children everyday. In addition to reading to the children during group time, she also reads to them before lunch. With the assistance of the librarian, she began making better selections that were age- and listener-appropriate. She also practiced reading with more expression, worked on eye contact, and made sure the children were seated comfortably and could see the illustrations. However, after studying the reading process, Ms. Warren decided to use one of the two sessions of group reading as a time to model reading strategies. She did not turn each read-aloud session into a specific reading lesson because she recognized that every read-aloud session is an implied reading lesson when children enjoy the story, internalize an appreciation of language and plot structure, and are engaged with the text in a variety of ways, which are uniquely theirs as individuals.

READING STRATEGIES THAT FOCUS ON THE READING PROCESS

In addition to reading aloud to the children, Ms. Warren began modeling reading strategies which focused on the reading process.[2] Before she read the book to the children, Ms. Warren had them *predict* what the book might be about. She then wrote their predictions on a chart tablet or on the board, thus allowing the children to see their spoken words becoming print. She often selected predictable books with recurring word patterns, as in Galdone's *Henny Penny* when the little hen says in each scene, "The sky is falling." The children *predicted* what words would come next by thinking about the order of the words in the text and when they should expect to hear Henny Penny say, "The sky is falling." After the reading, the children drew Henny Penny scenes and the teacher wrote captions for their drawings. Some children wrote their own captions, which Ms. Warren praised, even if their writing had few standard spellings of words. As the children were using parts of the story for their drawings and dictations, they were *sampling* from the book. As the teacher wrote each child's dictated caption, the child who was the artist, writer, reader, and speaker, then became the listener as the teacher read back the dictation. Through the process, the child *confirmed* that indeed he or she remembered Henny Penny correctly. One child was overheard correcting the teacher as she inadvertently substituted the word "acorn" for "nut."

BEFORE, DURING, AND AFTER READING PRESENTATIONS

After the reading specialist modeled some lessons, Ms. Warren began thinking of her own presentations of books in a three-stage process— before, during, and after reading. Before reading, Ms. Warren lead the children in an exercise to predict what the book might be about. She often asked the children to look at the cover of the book and make predictions. She then read the title and the children added to their predictions. Predicting what the story might be about based on the title and the cover illustrations is one of the activities teachers of young children use quite effectively. Predicting helps the children focus on the book, engages their sense of anticipation, and, in some instances, allows the teacher to determine the prior knowledge of the students.

Assessing prior knowledge or activating prior knowledge are reasons for engaging in "before reading" activities. In *Literacy: Helping Children Construct Meaning*, Cooper (1993, p. 122), identifies five different strategies for assessing prior knowledge: free recall, word association, recognition, structured questions, and unstructured discussion. For young children, we prefer free recall, word or concept association, and discussion. For example, when reading a book on a topic that the children could relate to easily, the teacher had them recall all they knew about the topic of the book. A discussion of growing vegetables was preparation for reading *This Year's Garden* by Cynthia Rylant.

Young children readily make associations between the stories in books and their own lives. For example, one first-grade teacher had difficulty getting started reading a book on pets because when she invited the children to talk about their pets, everyone could associate with the topic and had something to contribute. The two processes of recalling information and making associations are highly personal for young egocentric learners.

Many early childhood teachers employ a K-W-L chart, a graphic representation, to help record the children's prior knowledge about a specific topic (Ogle, 1986). The K stands for "what we *know*," the W for "what we *want* to know," and the L for "what we *learned*." (See Figure 3.2, Sample of K-W-L Chart on Growing Vegetables.) Some kindergarten and preschool teachers have modified the K-W-L chart to eliminate the "W." They find their students are very interested in telling what they know and what they learned after hearing the book read, but some young children lack the conceptualization to think ahead about what they might like to know. Other teachers retain the "W" and the teacher generates the questions based on what he or she thinks the children might like to know.

During the reading, teachers often compare the children's predictions and the actual text or may pause to answer questions the children formulated from the K-W-L chart. However, it is important that the "during" reading interruptions are limited so that they do not interfere with the author's story or the way the text is constructed. In a keynote address at a children's literature conference, Charlotte Huck cautioned teachers about "basalizing" quality books by structuring the reading much like the basal readers present texts, which includes interrupting the story often for the teacher to ask questions.[3]

After reading the book or having the book read to them, the children can list what they learned and the answers to their questions. Some teachers also use the K-W-L chart to continue the learning by listing questions not answered in the text and new questions the children may have now that they know more. Second- and third-grade teachers find this practice of expanding the K-W-L chart most helpful.

Certainly, discussion and answering questions are appropriate follow-up for some pieces of literature. However, open-ended questions and higher-level thought questions are preferable to literal recall. One particularly effective second-grade teacher often began the discussion by simply saying, "Tell me something that interested you." Whether the book was fiction or nonfiction, the question prompted immediate replies. There was no right or wrong answer, but the teacher's open-ended question led to the higher-level thought she was seeking.

SHARED READING EXPERIENCE WITH BIG BOOKS

The "shared book experience" is equated with big books, a practice made popular by Donald Holdaway in *The Foundations of Literacy* (1979). In an attempt to approximate lap reading, where an individual child sits on the lap of an adult and experiences the printed text and illustrations close-up, Holdaway suggests enlarging texts so that they can be readily seen by groups of children. Teachers use big books when they are concerned that many of their students have not been read to at home, when helping bilingual children who are experiencing a second language, and as a source for modeling reading strategies.

Figure 3.2 Sample of K-W-L Chart on Growing Vegetables

K (What we *know*) K	W (What we *want* to know)	L (What we *learned*)
We eat vegetables.	Are vegetables hard to grow?	We can grow vegetables.
We buy vegetables at Publix.	Can people grow vegetables, or just farmers?	Vegetables grown on the stalks and bushes.
Vegetables come in cans.	Where do the seeds come from?	Some grow in the ground, like potatoes and carrots.
Some vegetables are frozen.	Do vegetables grow in flower pots?	Gardening's hard work.
Some vegetables are in a special place.		Seeds come from many places.
Vegetables grow in gardens.		You can grow vegetables in big patio flower pots.

Big books may be commercially produced or homemade. While there is no replacement for holding a child on one's lap while reading, the big book does allow for some of the same elements of the lap-reading experience. Children can see the illustrations and print easily and make associations between the rate of reading and the print as it is pointed out by the reader (Raines & Canady, 1990). Big books allow the child to make associations between the spoken and printed word because they can see the print more easily. It is imperative that teachers continue to focus on reading for meaning, rather than just having big book readers repeat words to sound fluent.

Andrea Butler (1988) proposes that choosing the right book for a big book is key to the success of the shared reading experience. Some of her suggestions are true for any read-aloud selection, such as good story line, characters or situations the children identify with, quality illustrations, and humor or warmth (p. 5). Many big books feature language that has rhyme, rhythm, and repetition. Patterned language books allow the child to read the text easily and build the his or her confidence, while the easily remembered phrases promote a closer approximation of the printed text and the spoken words. Predictable texts or patterned language books that use rhyme, rhythm, and repetition are often children's favorite beginning reading materials.

The following sequence is suggested for using big books to model reading strategies. During the first presentation, the big book should be explored like any other story. The teacher might ask the children to predict what the book is about based on the title and the cover illustrations. Next, the teacher should read the story from beginning to end, without stopping to point out words or running a pointer under the print. The story should be enjoyed for the sake of the whole story, so that the child is more likely to construct meaning. After the story is read through the first time, the teacher may use any number of after reading points, such as having the children check their initial predictions against the content, or discussing what interested them, and how the story is like others they know, and so forth. Some teachers have the children retell the story by looking through the illustrations and putting the story in their own words.

The second presentation of the big book could occur on the same day or at a later reading session, depending on the audience's interest and level of development. During the second presentation, a re-reading of the text, the teacher helps the children follow along in the text by running a hand, a pointer, or a ruler under the words of the text. Some teachers mistakenly focus on individual words at this point, rather than helping the children associate fluent reading by moving their pointers under the phrases in a flowing fluent manner. If the story contains repeated phrases, the children might join in and read with the teacher. For example, the teacher may read what the gingerbread man says: "Run, run, as fast as you can. You can't catch me. I'm the gingerbread man," and the children will join in reading the recurring phrases. Again, the emphasis continues on fluent reading.

Teachers can also use this rereading session for other forms of language study, such as high frequency words or noticing the conventions of printed language in spelling, grammar, and punctuation, and sound/symbol relationships. At this juncture, the teacher points out elements of language study, not expecting that all children will master them. The emphasis remains on the reading pleasure while joining in with the combined voices of the teacher and the other students.

The third step in the process of shared book experience with big books is to have the children attempt to read at least parts of the book on their own. Since the students are familiar with the story and the language, they can read it on their own. Reading without the teacher's assistance can be accomplished by children who are reading partners reading from the book directly, listening to a taped version and joining in with the reading, or listening to another child reread the book. The important point for teachers to remember is that children learn to read by reading, and the reading and rereading should be encouraged in many forms and activities (Butler, 1988; Holdaway, 1979; Smith, 1985).

Book publishers have expanded their releases of big books for preschool, kindergarten, and first grades. A word of caution is needed for those teachers adding big books to their classrooms. The best big books were published and successful as good little books before being released in big book format. See the list of predictable and patterned language books found in Chapter 4; many of them are also published as big books.

PARTNER READING

Another confidence builder for young children is to engage in partner reading with peers, older children, or younger ones. Partner reading allows the child to enjoy the story with another while hearing the reading and participating in the actual reading process. Older students can be encouraged

Figure 3.3 Child One's Drawing and Retelling of *The Very Hungry Caterpillar*

Child's Words in Retelling of *The Very Hungry Caterpillar* to accompany drawings
"The moon was out.
The egg was on a leaf.
The sun came out.
There was a tiny caterpillar.
He was hungry.
He ate one pear.
Then he ate two pears.
Then he ate three pears.
Then he ate four strawberries.
Then he ate five oranges.
Then he got fat.
He built him a house.
Then he covered it.
Then he colored it.
He turned into a butterfly."

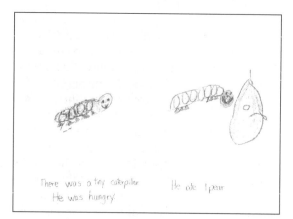

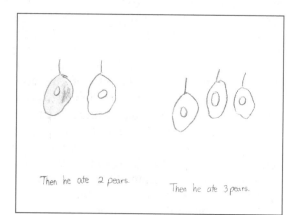

Then he ate 4 strawberries.   Then he ate 5 oranges.

Then he got fat.   He built him a house.

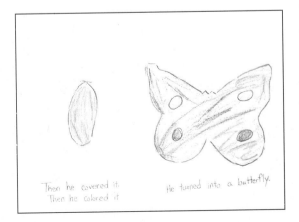

Then he covered it.
Then he colored it   He turned into a butterfly.

to allow younger ones to join them in reading a repeated refrain or reading the pictures, or reading the actual text.

Some teachers encourage older students to select picture books to read to younger students. The older child has practice in considering the audience for the selection, getting to know the reading partner's interests, and anticipating the enjoyment of the story. For example, at Kings Park Elementary in Springfield, Virginia, third-grade children read to kindergartners and first graders. These partnerships are formed at the beginning of the year and are maintained throughout the year. The success of the partnerships vary, but all told, both teachers and students give partner reading high marks. Recently, student teachers extended the partnerships to include writing partners as well. The partners often write notes to each other or write an extended story based on one of their favorite characters; sometimes they compose some sort of jointly authored response or evaluation of an exciting book.

STORY RETELLING

Story retelling is another activity that preschool, kindergarten, and primary teachers find helpful in observing children's knowledge of story structure, language usage, awareness of print forms, and visual literacy or the ability to interpret pictures. For the preschool child, story retelling with a book often takes the form of simply describing or labeling the contents of each picture. Other preschoolers, who have often been read to by their parents, construct elaborate stories based on their recall of the story they may have heard read and the picture clues. Some kindergartners may continue in the labeling stage, rather than the story construction phase. However, most are able to follow the actions of the main characters by looking at the pictures, and many use story language, such as "Once upon a time..." They take visual cues for their story retellings based on their limited reading and the illustrations. Some primary children recall stories almost word for word and often attempt to retell

Figure 3.4 **Child Two's Drawing and Retelling of *The Very Hungry Caterpillar***

Child's Words When Requested to Retell *The Very Hungry Caterpillar*
"A caterpillar went into the forest.
 He met a porcupine, a bear, a monkey, a
  goose, a rabbit, and a deer.
 They all followed him to a little girl's house.
 They saw her and six little dwarfs inside.
 The animals went away."

them as if they were reading the story instead of telling it. The purpose, of course, is for children to place the stories in their own words.

Story retelling is frequently recommended as a step in enjoying literature. Teachers who have not included story retelling in their array of literacy activities may find that children need practice in story retelling. Presented in Figures 3.3 and 3.4 are two children's first attempts at retelling the familiar story, *The Very Hungry Caterpillar* by Eric Carle. The stories were retold by two children in Mary Kay Elwick's class at Liberty School in Sallisaw, Oklahoma.

The child drew the pictures and the teacher wrote the child's retelling of the story. Notice in Figure 3.3 how child one stays very true to the original version. Of particular significance is the way the child described the cocoon as, "He built him a house." Eric Carle describes the cocoon as a house. Since the child is far more aware of houses than cocoons, the house is what appears as a symbol of that part of the story. Similarly,

the child's description of the process is most apropos: "Then he covered it. Then he colored it." Obviously, if a beautiful butterfly is to emerge, then someone has to color it.

They saw her and 6 little dwarfs inside.

The animals went away

In Figure 3.4, notice that the child understands the directions to tell a story about a caterpillar, but decides to take the storyteller's license and diverge a bit from the original version. The illustrated scenes and the child's dictation imply that the child decided to tell several stories at once. (See Figure 3.4.) His first attempt at story retelling may infer that he thought Eric Carle's story a bit too tame, or perhaps, limited exposure to story retelling as a technique was the reason for his elaborated version. Regardless, the teacher ascertained that indeed the child has a well-developed sense of story, just not *The Very Hungry Caterpillar* story.

Children Reading on Their Own

Of course, the goal of any reading program is to have children reading independently. Parents breathe a sigh of relief when their first and second graders begin sounding like fluent readers. Teachers relax when they see a child select a book and read it silently, although often accompanied by an almost audible mumble. We know children are becoming comfortable readers when we observe them laugh out loud at the funny parts, or rush over and read passages to their friends, saying, "Listen, to this."

Yet, there are numerous examples of children becoming readers and enjoying reading long before they reach this level of independence as a reader. One example is of a four-year-old who read the pictures of a Frog and Toad book he had never seen before, but made it sound like real reading by reading/telling the pictures, even including improvised dialogue. Another is of a four-year-old who pretended to read to dolls and imaginary friends by acting out the role of her nursery school teacher. She had the dolls and the imaginary friends sit in front of her, held the books so they each could see, and encouraged everyone to listen whenever she turned the page.

A six-year-old kindergartner who was struggling to learn English was seen organizing pretend school with her younger brothers and sisters. She told/read a book and the little ones listened and clapped at the end. She was overheard to say, "When you go to school, you read books, big books."

Early childhood teachers who are whole language teachers use classroom practices that foster young children's reading on their own such as: 1) library center; 2) transition book times; and 3) "drop everything and read time." The library center will be described in detail in Chapter 10; however, the significant point for teachers to remember is that having a specially designated area of the classroom says to the students, their parents, and other teachers that good children's literature is an important activity and a significant component of the curriculum. In early childhood classrooms where there are large blocks of time for children to choose their own activities, having a well-stocked, well-designed classroom library, promotes children's interests in books.

Traditionally, nursery school, child-care, Head Start, and kindergarten teachers have used children's book explorations as a transition between major activities. For example, in one nursery school, the teacher's aide scattered an array of books out on the circle time carpet. When the children came in from outside play, they gathered on the carpet to look at books, while their friends got drinks of water. In a Head Start classroom, book exploration was used as a transition between clean-up time from play areas to the group circle time. While some children were finishing cleaning up their areas, the others sat on the carpet and looked through books. In some kindergartens, books are used as a transition to the morning's opening activities. As soon as the children arrive in the classroom, they go to the library area, select a book, and return to their tables where they look at or read the books until all the children have arrived from all the buses.

These transition times are certainly appropriate to invite young children to explore books independently. However, it is the teacher's attitude and effective use of this time that is significant. If the teacher sees this brief bit of time as simply a filler in the schedule or a classroom management tool to keep the students under control, then its effectiveness as a period for independent reading is lost. Fortunately, many early childhood teachers have begun to connect the transition times by having children share what they read in the books. It may be as simple as saying, "Jeremy, I see you like the story of *Gregory the Terrible Eater*. Show us one of the funny pages."

We are often concerned about the child who is reticent about books and is simply a page turner. However, if we look at adults and think about how we pass the time in the doctor's office waiting room, page turning exploration of children's books can be compared to page-turning of magazines. There is some entertainment merit and transition time needed in all our lives.

Transition times for book reading are not adequate amounts of time for setting the expectation that all young children will spend part of their day engaged with books. Setting aside time in the daily schedule to look at or read books is appropriate for the early childhood classroom. USSR, Uninterrupted Sustained Silent Reading, or DEAR, "Drop Everything And Read," are specific times when the entire school is reading. When there is not a school-wide observation for focusing on the value of reading, teachers can look at their schedules and select a time in the day when there are few interruptions and schedule a class routine of everyone reading.

One kindergarten teacher we observed used the time right after lunch as a quiet period when she, the teacher's aide, the parent volunteer, any adult in the classroom, and all the children looked at or read books. The teacher often used this time to read through books she planned to read aloud to the children on other days. The teacher's aide, who was also a college student, read her textbook. Parent volunteers often read the same books as the children so they could become familiar with the books and read them to the bilingual children.

Regardless of what the children read, it is important to set up the expectation that the children will read on their own and enjoy the books on their own. Often, it takes a few days to establish the routine. Experienced DEAR teachers recommend starting with ten minutes and building to a longer period, depending on the age of the children. Many proponents of DEAR time suggest that no follow-up or extension activities, or queries about what one is reading, should be planned. They think this is a time for children to savor the book they have selected in their own way, without expectations established by the teacher.

Ms. Warren began to identify herself as a process-approach reading teacher after she learned more about the reading process and refined her read-aloud presentations of books, and developed specific reading strategies that focused on children reading for meaning. By watching the reading specialist and the librarian model lessons that focused on the three phases of book presentations, before, during, and after reading, Ms. Warren found the children more engaged with the content of the books. She used big books and emphasized the reading process. Her presentation of books became a routine part of the morning group time. Partner reading, story retelling, more effective use of transition times, and DEAR became established literacy routines in Ms. Warren's classroom. With the help of the librarian, she added many more books to the kindergarten classroom for the children to explore on their own.

Ms. Warren's Present Approach to Writing Instruction

The writing instruction in Ms. Warren's kindergarten, like the reading instruction, does not reflect young children's development as writers. Ms. Warren, like many other early childhood teachers, thought of writing instruction as handwriting. She felt pressure from first-grade teachers to have all the children recognize and know how to form all the letters of the alphabet. Again, the ditto sheets were her means of writing instruction.

Ms. Warren was convinced to change her view of writing instruction based on an observer's comments. During a thirty-minute visit, the observer asked individual children in Ms. Warren's classroom which letter they were forming. Four of the children identified the letter incorrectly; one said he did not know but said he could show the observer how you do it; and many children asked with questions in their voices, "J?" Writing, like reading, needs to be meaningful to children. Obviously, the "J" ditto exercise had little meaning to the kindergartners.

The Writing Process

Traditionally, teachers have treated writing as a communication skill that follows reading, but close observation of the writing process suggests that children learn to read and write as related processes (Chomsky, 1972; Clay, 1975; Harste, Woodward, & Burke, 1984; Heller, 1991; Morrow, 1993). Writing, like reading, speaking, and listening, is a process that emerges naturally as children explore the various ways people express themselves (Goodman, 1986). In home and school environments were children are engaged in purposeful writing activities and allowed to develop at their own pace, they not only progress through the various stages of writing, but also view writing as a natural and enjoyable vehicle for self-expression and communication.

The various developmental stages of writing and constructing standard spelling usually include the following, as in this example for writing the word "house":

1. scribbling
2. pretend writing using letter-like forms
3. random use of actual letters (usually consonants)
4. single consonants representing beginning sounds of words (h)
5. beginning and ending consonants (hs)
6. addition of interior sound (hws)
7. addition of vowels (hows)
8. correct spelling (house) (Heller, 1991; Temple, Nathan, Burris, & Temple, 1988)

Much has been written concerning the stages and sequence of spelling in children's writing. Writing is a natural learning process of building new knowledge about writing based on what the child has already learned. It is not necessary to place age or time limits on the development of writing (Clay, 1975; Gentry & Henderson, 1978; Graves, 1983). The concern many teachers and parents express is that children will not learn to spell correctly if they are allowed to progress through the writing stages at their own speed (Temple, Nathan, Burris, & Temple, 1989). In a process writing program, children are involved in purposeful writing activities, and in order for them to achieve their purpose, they refine their spelling.

Young children are "constructors" of print. They use the writing they know at present to communicate. If they write by mocking adults' lines of print, but they scribble, that is the print they know how to construct. If they use the letters of their name, a usual first step in letter writing, then they are constructing print using the letters they know. If they borrow letters from print they see around the classroom, then they recognize the need for more information to construct what they want to write. If they write using an array of letters that have no sound/symbol relationships, they are still constructing print using what they know. Gradually, they will use sound/symbol relationships, and their writing will become more readable by adults.

To take advantage of the young child's development as a writer, the seven suggestions listed in Figure 3.5 can guide Ms. Warren's kindergarten process writing.

Figure 3.5 Suggestions for Writing Process Emphasis

1. Write everyday and establish the routine from the first day of kindergarten.

2. Recognize that writing is a composing process.

3. Have the children read their writing.

4. Write for a purpose. Use many functional writing purposes as a part of the classroom routines.

5. Write to communicate with others inside and outside the classroom.

6. Write in response to children's literature.

7. Relate writing and reading.

WRITE EVERYDAY

Writing instruction should begin with the first day of kindergarten when the teacher asks the children to draw and write something about themselves. Some children will say they do not know how to write, but simply suggest they can write any way they choose, to just use the writing they know. One kindergarten teacher placed examples of children's writing from her previous classes all around the room (Raines & Canady, 1990). The writing ranged from scribbling and drawing, to mock letter forms, to letter strings, to invented spelling and standard spelling. In a research study by Elizabeth Sulzby and colleagues (October, 1989, p. 36), in October of the school year, the teacher actually modeled all the different ways children might write. Thus, reassuring children that whatever their level of writing, it was appropriate for kindergarten.

RECOGNIZE THAT WRITING IS A PROCESS

Donald Graves (1983), in his research with primary teachers in New Hampshire, pointed out that writing for young immature writers is as much a composing process as it is for adult writers. The steps he outlined are prewriting, drafting, editing, and publishing. Obviously, the teacher of young children will find that for the very young preschoolers, simply holding a pencil and making a mark is the most of their writing. However, if we examine the writing process as a composing process, then the stages of the writing process make more sense. For example, three-year-olds are not known for their writing abilities; they are scribblers. Yet, the composing process and the physical act of writing are beginnings of the children's demonstrations of what they know about print.

Whole language teachers refer to their writing programs as being a *writing process* or *writing workshop* approach. Just as the process of reading has been identified by observing the strategies used by fluent readers, the writing process has been determined by observation of the strategies used by natural writers. A writing process approach is organized around the steps used by professional authors, from brainstorming ideas for a writing project to the publication of the finished product.

In a literature-based whole language classroom, independent writing plays a key role in each child's daily activities. Every child writes every day. In many primary classrooms, children begin and end the day by writing in their personal journals and a part of each day is reserved for creative compositions. Each student has a writing folder, which contains a self-designed list of possible topics for writing, work in progress, and notes made during the student's conference with the teacher.

Motivation for writing stems from the child's individual interests, daily interaction with good children's literature, and the student desires to become published authors. Early childhood teachers through the primary grades modify the four steps involved in writing for publication to fit their students' needs (Tompkins, 1990):

1. prewriting
2. first draft and reading own writing
3. drafting and revising
4. sharing one's writing

PREWRITING

One preschool teacher made Mothers Day Cards by folding the cards and having the children draw around their hands. Then on the inside of the card, she pasted an instant print picture of the child. On the other side, she asked the child to write a message to his or her mother; all of the children scribbled. She had the child read what the message said, and she wrote under the child's scribbles what the message was so that the parent could read it. The prewriting or planning part of the composing process began when the teacher introduced the writing activity during the morning circle time. Then, when she sat at one of the tables during free-choice time and the children came over to make their cards, many had already decided what they wanted to say. Some composed their messages on the spot by listening to what

others said. Several children told their mothers about the experience of drawing around their hands, while others described themselves in the picture by telling where they were in the classroom when the photo was taken. Children benefit from knowing that their ideas on a particular topic are important enough to be written down by the teacher.

Brainstorming, a concept once used mostly in upper elementary and secondary classrooms, has become an important part of the instructional program in primary writing classrooms as well. The brainstorming process, whether it is done as a group activity or as a part of a teacher-student conference, allows the child to begin the process organizing his or her thoughts. See the example in Figure 3.6 of third- graders brainstorming a tall tale their literature group plans to write after reading about Pecos Bill.

Brainstorming as a preparation for writing is especially important for children who are primarily

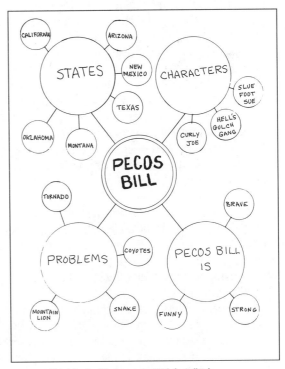

Figure 3.6 Third Graders' Brainstorming Web for Tall Tale

visual learners. Brainstorming sessions, which result in the construction of a web of ideas, help children organize their thoughts and visualize the total story or concept. Brainstorming and cognitive mapping or webbing are used most effectively in the primary grades. Prewriting is a plan to get the writer started with the composing process. It can be as simple as the photo used to stimulate the three-year-olds' compositions for the Mothers Day cards, or it can be an elaborately planned prewriting web reflecting all the characteristics of a certain type of tale.

First Draft and Reading One's Own Writing

To encourage young children to write, teachers must establish from the beginning of the year that writing is meant to be read. Ask each child to read his or her writing and observe how the child reads. It will not be surprising to many teachers that often young children will resort to telling about their picture, rather than reading their writing.

Researchers, such as Elizabeth Sulzby and colleagues (1989), Dobson (1989), and Martinez and Teale (1989), have verified the ways children read their own writing. When children practice reading their own writing, they eventually attempt to match their written text and spoken words. Sometimes, the child will finger-track the letters he or she has written and trace under the letters matching the speed of tracing to the speed of speech. If children are asked to reread their pictures and writing much later in the day or even days later, they often read it differently.

A higher level of writing and rereading, which eventually develops, is the child's attempt to translate speech into print by using letter names. According to Dobson (1989), this higher level of writing using letter names is the child's attempt to keep the writing stable. At this stage, the writer reads the same thing or approximates the reading when read again at a later time. This advanced writing and rereading may occur in kindergarten or may not appear until first grade. When children reach the stage of refining their letter-sound asso-

ciations in their compositions and are using more invented spellings, their rereadings of their writing remain constant.

Given these varying levels of development among the individuals in her classroom, it is crucial that teachers find ways to respond to the child's writing and to their reading of their compositions. Teachers should respond positively and tell the child, "I like seeing what you have written and hearing you read it to me." Most importantly, teachers should expect the kindergartners to make progress if they are given opportunities to write and read what they have written.

There are numerous questions kindergarten teachers ask about writing. However, one of the most often asked is about "overwriting" (Tompkins, 1990). When a child has composed a piece of writing and rereads it, the teacher must decide whether or not to overwrite what the child has written. Some teachers write what the child reads by printing the child's words under the writing. They believe it is important for the child to see the teacher model the child's personal message. Others use post-it notes and write what the child says on the note. Some teachers fold the bottom edge of the drawing paper under. After the children have drawn their pictures and written something, the teacher unfolds the paper edge and writes what the children read of their writing.

Many teachers feel it demeans the child's writing to have the adult writing model below the child's. Others like providing a way to model standard writing. We recommend overwriting pieces that the teacher plans to keep for assessment purposes, to recall the child's progress in "meaning making" as he or she constructed the print.

Drafting and Revising

Children are natural revisers. Kindergarten and first-grade teachers know from experience the number of children who ask, "Can I have a new piece of paper? I want to start over." Their requests are evidence of their initial attempts to self-correct and draft again, whether it is a picture or a piece of writing. The young child will revise in the middle of writing or drawing. The significant point for the preschooler is that they actually make marks on paper. For the kindergartners and first graders who are gaining more control over print, the range will still include from scribbling, to mock letter writing, to using letter names and beginning consonants, to establishing sound/symbol relationships. However, what is important is that the teacher focus on the *meaning* of what the child has written.

In a writing process program, children enjoy using the appropriate terminology for the various steps involved in writing for publication. Visitors to a writing process classroom are often surprised when a young child shares a rather disorganized piece of writing with them and then explains, "This is just my first draft."

First drafts are important for young children, just as they are for professional authors. Professional authors know that before their writing will be ready for publication, it will probably be revised many times. All authors must have the freedom to record their original ideas without concern for correct form or spelling. The success of the writing process approach is due in large part to the fact that children know they can experiment with writing their first draft and then revise it, put it away in their folder for future use, or abandon it completely.

Conferencing to revise. One teacher whose class was composed of first and second graders compared the revisions made by her students (Raines, 1986). To help with the revising process, the teacher modified Donald Graves' recommendations for conferencing about writing. With primary children in New Hampshire, Graves and his colleagues conducted writing conferences where the author of the piece read his or her writing aloud. The students in the editing group told what they liked and disliked about the compositions the group member read to them. As many teachers of first and second graders have experienced, the writing conference in small groups may work well for older children and for group compositions lead by the teacher, but it does not work well with six- and seven-year-olds on their individual pieces of writing.

When the first and second graders attempted to have a writing conference, some praised their friends so much for their writing that the author took the praise to mean that the piece of writing was wonderful. If a piece was wonderful, why bother to revise it? The opposite happened to other writers. The group members criticized the piece of writing so much that the writer was devastated. The children then refused to write, sometimes even crying that their friends did not like their stories. After three attempts at demonstrating the writing conference using a group's composition, the problems persisted when the first and second graders critiqued one another's writing. Finally, the teacher devised the following modifications to the editing conference.

Modifications of Writing Conferences With Young Children. The teacher in the combined first and second grade changed the writing conferences. She continued to have the children conference with others about their individual pieces, but arranged the conferences differently than Graves recommended. When a child finished writing a composition, the teacher looked around the room and found children who were free to be listeners. Some listeners were the students who were illustrating their writing, so she felt they could be interrupted. The teacher did not interfere with those children who were still writing. She called the listeners together and gave them only three rules, "You may not praise. You may not criticize. You may ask questions."

The teacher modeled the "listening conference" by having the author read his or her piece of writing. The audience was then directed to ask questions by thinking, "What else would I like to know?" Some of the questions the listeners often asked the author were, "When did this happen?" and "What happened next?" After several practice sessions, another routine statement became a part of the listening conference. The listeners would say, "I want to know more about the part where . . ."

These listening sessions helped the authors revise their writing. The authors could choose to answer the listeners' questions or not. Since the authors retained control of their own writing, it was up to the author to decide whether or not to make the changes. The teacher found that the second graders chose to make changes more often that the first graders. The first graders frequently answered the children's questions verbally but would still not choose to revise their writing. The first graders who did revise their pieces of writing would simply add a sentence or additional information at the end. Some of the second graders would make minor modifications within the piece of writing, adding a line or two to major scenes.

In an attempt to work on revising, the teacher tried a cut and paste technique to help them take their pieces of writing apart and put them back together in different ways. The teacher had observed this revising technique being used successfully with a third-grade class. After the child had written the piece, the teacher would photocopy it. Then, the child would cut the piece of writing into sentences and rearrange the sentences.

Most of the first and second graders responded to this strategy by seeing it as a puzzle. They simply put the sentences back together to make it look whole again, rather than rearranging the sentences internally. Only one second grader, a child repeating second grade, used the strategy to change his composition.

Teachers who are knowledgeable about Piaget explain this process easily. The young child who is in the preoperational stage is not capable of the reversible thinking needed to reconstruct a piece of writing in a variety of ways. He or she lacks the "conservation" skills to hold constant their original piece of writing while thinking about how to do it differently. Therefore, if they want to make changes, they simply add them on. The teacher labeled these compositions *train pieces*. The children revised by simply adding on sentences or phrases like cars on a train to make their train longer. See Figure 3.7 for a comparison of first and second drafts from one very bright first grader.

However, one child amazed both the teacher and the researcher in the classroom. "K" introduced himself to the researcher by saying, "Hi, I'm "K." I'm a repeater." "K" was repeating second grade and was eight years old. He was clearly in the concrete operations stage, capable of reversible thought, a conserver of information, who could think about his story and edit it internally. He edited one piece seven times and generated a lengthy publication.

Figure 3.7 First Grader's Writing With Revisions

First draft
"I wowc up and want in the livin room. I had a lot uv towis. and I plad and plad and plad." (I woke up and went in the living room. I had a lot of toys. And I played and played and played.)

Second draft
"I wowc up and went in the livin room. I had a lot uv tows. And I plad and plad and plad. I had fun."

Figure 3.8 Eight-Year-Old's Writing With Extensive Revisions

First draft
"Wednesday the oil mill bleuna up. Ploenis come dowe ther. I was sctred that nite." (Wednesday the oil mill blew up. Police came down there. I was scared that night.)

Third draft
"Wednesday the oil mill bleun up. Ploenis come dowe ther. The fierman come dowe ther to. They come dowe by the oil mill. Ploenis tote the plensus to go some weren to spenten the nite. I was sctred that nite and I betna same _____ven plensas. It is sctry to go off to spenten the nite. Wen ploenis tote you."

(Wednesday the oil mill blew up. Police came down there. The fireman come down there too. They come down by the oil mill. Police told the people to go some where to spend the night. I was scared that night and I bet some others were too, even police. It is scarry to go off to spend the night, when police told you.)

SHARING ONE'S WRITING

Children share their writing with the community of writers in the classroom in a variety of ways, such as posting them on bulletin boards, binding and publishing pieces of writing in the classroom, and through "author's chair." The author's chair is a special chair in a place of prominence in the classroom where children sit and read a piece of writing they have selected for their listening audience.

Author's Chair. The author's chair has become identified with Graves' approach to the writing process. After an author finishes her or his piece of writing and has revised it to the point of being ready to share it with an audience, the writer signs up for a time to read. Normally, this is a routinely scheduled time at the end of writing workshop, at the end of the morning, or perhaps at the end of the week. This form of sharing is akin to publishing. In the primary grades, the audience expects a polished piece of writing and the writer expects an appreciative audience.

Young children at the beginning of first grade, kindergarten, and even younger may write, but many will lack the skills of revising that will enable them to create a polished piece of writing. However, this should not preclude the teacher's establishing and using the author's chair. The value of author's chair is that children soon learn that writing is meant to be read.

One kindergarten teacher established the author's chair the first week of class. She had the children draw pictures, then each day students came one at a time to sit in the chair and talk about their pictures. She encouraged each to include some writing. One boy showed the class his name. Another had meticulously copied part of the ABC chart. Some scribbled along the bottom of the page and others gave titles to their pictures, such as "My House," written with invented spelling, "HS."

Some kindergarten teachers begin author's chair by letting the child read a story he or she has dictated for the teacher to write. First and second graders often accomplish elaborate pieces of writing and edit their work with the help of a teacher or a parent volunteer. Whatever the level of writing, the author's chair signifies to the children that writing is meant to be read, is meant to have an audience.

Publishing and Bookbinding. As children become more proficient writers, they may edit a piece until it is ready for publication in book form. Children who choose to continue their writing toward publication discuss their first draft with the teacher and the writing or listening group and use their suggestions for rewriting the story. The suggestions for primary children might include reorganization of the story, adding to or deleting parts of the story, and expanding a part of the story to make it more descriptive.

In a writing process approach, it is important for children to retain ownership of their writing. Teachers should edit children's stories and make suggestions for changes that allow the children to make the final decisions concerning their own writing. Because the children are actively involved every day in children's literature, they are aware that the teacher's suggestions help their stories sound more like the stories they read and hear each day.

Only selected pieces of children's writings are published. When the teacher and child agree that the writing is ready to be published, the final draft is paged and decisions are made concerning the placement of possible illustrations. When the final draft is clearly marked indicating that the text is to appear on the particular pages of the published book, and the spaces to be made available for illustration have been defined, the final draft is given to a parent volunteer for typing. Some parent volunteers assist by spending time in the classroom with the various stages of writing, while others choose to help by typing the book pages at home or in a school publishing center. When the pages of the book are returned to the school, usually on the next day, the child rereads the story and adds the illustrations, which were planned earlier. The book is then ready to be bound.

As part of the writing process program, many classrooms have a publishing center equipped with all of the materials needed for binding children's books. The materials can be precut for ease of construction and the children are able to assist in the construction of their own books. (See the illustrations in Appendix B for bookbinding directions.)

Children's published books become part of the classroom library and may be used for classroom reading or checked out and taken home. Some children's books are chosen for the school library and some neighborhood public libraries even have a section reserved for child-authored books.

Writing to Communicate Within the Classroom

A writing process classroom is one in which writing is also one of the routines of the classroom. For example, in the KEEP program, Kamehameha Early Education Program in Honolulu, Hawaii, the kindergarten teachers devised the morning message as a means of communicating to the children (Kawakami-Arakaki, Oshiro, & Farran, 1989). What began as a simple message, such as "Today is Thursday. We have two new fish in the aquarium," developed into a routine that emphasized the reading and writing processes. Rather than already having the morning message on the board, the teachers began writing it with the children. They used it as a way to begin reading and writing instruction. Later in the year, the children composed four or five lines as a group. After the teacher wrote the morning message, the children analyzed the writing by talking about it. For example, one child may note the root word "day" in today and Thursday. Later in the year, children pointed out commas, question marks, contractions, and notice endings of words.

In Fairfax, Virginia, teachers select one kindergarten child a day to write something on the message board before the group time begins. The child reads what he or she has written, whether scribbles or invented spelling. The teachers simply asks the child to, "Read to me what you have written."

The teacher comments positively about the writing. If the child uses scribbles, the teacher may point out the left to right progression and top to bottom of the page, always finding accurate ways to describe what the child is writing.

In some districts with half-day kindergartens, the morning and afternoon kindergartners become pen pals. Other teachers form reading and writing buddies between their kindergartners and third graders. In literature-rich classrooms, the messages often center around favorite books and recommended authors. The kindergarten children are most eager to receive notes from the older children and by the middle of the year, many of them have progressed from the stage of drawing pictures to composing simple messages.

Functional Writing, Inside and Outside the Classroom

Functional writing provides a way for the children to communicate inside and outside the classroom. Writing preserves the spoken language that needs to be repeated. For example, in September, the children could decide what activities, which areas of the classrooms, and what materials need signs, labels, and directions. Another purposeful writing exercise is listing children who want to participate in certain classroom activities.

In one kindergarten class, the children liked to play Candyland but they seemed to always disagree about the rules. The teacher had the children who were disagreeing try to figure out what should be written so that other children would know the rules of the game. Composing meaningful signs and rules is a powerful tool to communicate to youngsters that the writing in their classroom environment has meaning.

In the routines of the school, there are numerous times when teachers need to communicate information outside the classroom. For example, a kindergarten student teacher received a note from the librarian asking if her children could switch library times with another class. The astute student teacher read the note aloud to the children, and they composed a reply. Lunch counts, permission slips, notes from parents, and notes to volunteers are examples of numerous opportunities to let children in on the writing process as a means of communicating within the world of the school building and outside their classroom walls.

Writing in Response to Children's Literature

The writing program should also include numerous ways for children to write in response to books (Cullinan, 1992). Group, individual, and reading partners' assessments of books can provide a means for children to express their likes and dislikes, as well as respond to specifics about a books.

GROUP RESPONSES

The following examples are of group activities that also allow for individual responses to literature. In a teaching demonstration by the author, Bill Martin, Jr., we observed first graders writing their approval of his book and measuring their responses graphically.[4] After reading *Up and Down on the Merry-Go-Round*, Dr. Martin drew a horizontal line along the middle of a chalkboard and asked each child to place a mark to indicate how much they liked the book. Some children marked an X on the line near the end labeled like, but one child drew a X on the dislike. Bill Martin complimented him on his independent thinking and being honest about whether or not he really liked the book. The next child drew a long vertical line down from the horizontal one. While the child was drawing the line straight down, Dr. Martin said, "Oh, you didn't like this book at all, you don't want to even put your mark on the line." However, before he could finish his statement, the little girl, Heather, drew a heart at the end of the line. Quickly, other children started drawing lines of varying lengths down from

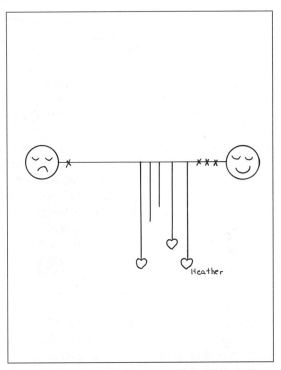

Figure 3.9 Reproduction of a Chalkboard graph Like and Dislike Books

the horizontal one and replying whether or not they liked the book as much as Heather did. The children immediately understood Heather's message and responded in varying degrees with their own. Many did not draw hearts at the end of their lines, indicating that their likeness was not as keen.

Later, when the teacher asked the children to write letters to Dr. Martin thanking him for allowing them to come to his presentation, they began explaining their evaluations of the book. The writing exercise was a genuine communication tool. The children were quite direct. One boy said he did not like the book because he could not read the sounds, meaning the "Oom-pah-pah-pah," in the poetry of the book. Another child said he liked the book because it was about fun things to do, and going to an amusement park was fun. A girl said the merry-go-round horses reminded her of horses, and she loved horses. Some of the children wrote about liking parts of the book more than other parts. One child, concerned that the children's evaluation of the book might disappoint the author, decided to write an encouraging message and implored the author to write more books like *Brown Bear, Brown Bear, What do you See?* because everybody loves that book.

While the first graders who met Bill Martin, Jr., were certainly privileged to meet a great author of children's books, teachers need not have so personal an encounter to routinely include children's assessments of their likes and dislikes about a book as a part of the classroom. A kindergarten teacher composed a "child-graph" of favorite Bill Martin books by having the children tell all the Bill Martin books they liked. They selected the top five—*Brown Bear, Brown Bear, What do you See?*, *Chicka Chicka Boom Boom, Polar Bear, Polar Bear, What do you Hear?*, *The Barn Dance,* and *Listen to the Rain.* Then the children stood in front of a chalkboard and line-up behind the child who held their favorite Bill Martin book. After the entire class was in place, the teacher counted the children, recorded the number in each line of children and taped the numeral onto the chalkboard behind each line of children. Then the book-holders placed their books on the chalkboard rail under the numeral. It is not difficult to predict that their favorite book was *Brown Bear, Brown Bear, What do you See?* Interestingly, because the teacher said her favorite Bill Martin, Jr., book was *Listen to the Rain,* more children lined up behind that book than she expected.

As a follow-up process, she gave the kindergartners sheets of paper and asked them to draw and write something about their favorite book. The responses ranged from a drawing of a little girl and her mother reading the book together to an industrious child who copied word for word most of the text of *Brown Bear, Brown Bear, What do you See?*

Beginning readers find comfort in reading books by the same author. A second-grade teacher commented that invariably her children discover Bill Peet, and a fan club of readers emerges. In the past, before she had her students engaged in a lot of classroom writing, she encouraged oral book sharing of new Bill Peet discoveries. Now, she constructs a bulletin board and the children write messages to the class about their latest Bill Peet finds and what they like about them.

Another second-grade teacher began letting children write post-it notes and stick them on the inside cover of the books. The children quickly moved from writing evaluations of the book to specific messages for their friends who were also Bill Peet fans. On the inside cover of *The Caboose Who Got Loose,* one child wrote, " 'R'., look on page 40—flying caboose." Another wrote a quiz for readers, "How many cars did Katy push?" What ensued was a post-it note argument, because the length of the train varied in different pictures.

INDIVIDUAL AND PARTNER RESPONSES

Reading logs are also productive ways to keep track of individual's preferences in authors, genres, and topics of interests. In their reading logs, the students copy the titles of books they have read and draw or write something about the book. Some teachers also ask the children to write recommendations for other children to read.

In a combined kindergarten and first-grade classroom, Julie's teacher read *Something Special for Me* by Vera Williams as a part of a unit on "Celebrations." Julie, a first grader, wrote the following message to her kindergarten writing buddy about her hopes for a birthday present.

When Julie read her message to her kindergarten reading/writing buddy, the kindergartner replied, "You don't skate on the tennis court. You play ball."

Julie's teacher established writing as a routine response to literature the children read on their own. Each child drew or wrote in response to a book they enjoyed. When the children shared their drawings or writings with the class, it was

Julie

I am going to get a new pair of skates Win I get my skates. I am going to the tennis court and skate. Every Saturday I am going to skate in the tennis court. The End

a form of recommended reading to others. These pieces of writing went into the children's writing folders.

Relating Writing and Reading

Obviously from the previous discussion of the literacy processes of reading and writing and the examples cited, these teachers have helped children relate writing and reading. Their students understand that writing is meant to be read. Similarly, if we look at young children's writing over time, we see evidence of the reading instruction they are receiving and the literary language they are hearing.

It would be difficult to over-emphasize the reciprocal relationship that exists between the reading and writing processes. Children in a process approach classroom feel a kinship with the authors of the stories they hear and read because they know what is involved in writing and publishing a book. They learn the importance of clarity, spelling, punctuation, and expanded vocabulary as they relate to purposeful writing. Teachers who are still reluctant to provide the amount of classroom time required for a successful writing program, need to be aware that the so-called "basic reading skills," such as sound/symbol relationships, word beginnings and endings, high frequency sight words, and so forth can be learned through the writing process. It should also be noted that the steps of the writing process approach involve the child in a tremendous amount of reading, as well as writing.

SUMMARY

This chapter provided a review of Ms. Warren's kindergarten classroom by examining the reading and writing processes. Other process approach classrooms and examples of children's literacy development were presented to help the reader gain an understanding of emergent literacy.

Early childhood educators support literacy process approaches because they are more developmental in nature. Teachers recognize that young children grow and develop over time in their awareness of reading and writing and in their actual use of reading and writing. Whole language teachers advocate the practices that have been deemed appropriate by teachers in good early childhood programs and are endorsed in a number of documents from professional organizations, including the IRA position paper, "Literacy Development and Early Childhood (Preschool through Grade 3)."

A visit to Ms. Warren's kindergarten classroom a year later revealed a very different approach to literacy instruction in a literature-rich classroom, rather than the workbook and dittos from the previous year. Ms. Warren now describes her kindergarten as a whole language classroom that uses a process approach to literacy development. She explains that children are immersed in language in both its spoken and written forms. There is always an emphasis on meaningful communication. Ms. Warren also points out that the kindergartners are figuring out how print works in books and are constructing print and stories through reading and writing. She expects the children to refine their knowledge of print and eventually sound like mature readers and write like mature writers. However, she recognizes this process is a long one developmentally. Yet, she accepts their reading and writing of print as having meaning for them, even thought it does not yet approximate standard reading and writing. Ms. Warren's kindergarten classroom is alive with literacy and literature activities which are appropriate for the young child as a developing reader and writer.

SUGGESTED LEARNING EXPERIENCES

1. Observe a librarian read aloud a book to a group of children. Describe what makes the librarian's presentation of the book effective.

2. Visit a kindergarten or first grade class and note the big books in the classroom. List the titles.

3. Ask a reading specialist in a school how he or she works with classroom teachers to model different reading strategies.

4. Survey a group of children to discover the titles of their favorite books.

5. Read at least five of the books recommended by the children and determine what makes them appealing.

6. Try the teacher's exercise of making a human graph of favorite books from a single author.

7. Examine samples of children's writing. What can you determine they know about print and how it functions by looking at their writing?

8. Observe a big book lesson. Interview the teacher about the steps he or she uses in presenting the big book, as well as follow-up activities.

9. Volunteer to read to a group of children on a regular basis.

10. Start a pen pal arrangement between your college or university class and a classroom of children.

ENDNOTES

1. Ms. Warren is a fictitious name; however, the case is of an actual kindergarten teacher.

2. Portions of this article appeared in *Oklahoma Children*, Vol. XII, No. 2., a newsletter of the Oklahoma Association on Children Under Six.

3. Dr. Charlotte Huck. (1991). Keynote Address: A Celebration of Children's Literature. Fairfax, VA: George Mason University.

4. Dr. Bill Martin, Jr. (1988). Presentation to the Children's Literature Conference. Fairfax, VA: George Mason University.

REFERENCES

Auckerman, R. C. (1984). *Approaches to beginning reading.* New York: John Wiley.

Butler, A. (1988). *Shared book experience.* Crystal Lake, IL: Rigby.

Cambourne, B. (1988). *The whole story: Natural learning and the acquisition of literacy in the classroom.* New York: Ashton-Scholastic.

Canady, R. J. (1983). Beginning reading programs: How can we begin what has already begun? In S. Raines (Ed.), *The Wesleyan papers: Keeping the child in childhood* (pp. 19–28). Rocky Mount, NC: North Carolina Wesleyan College Press.

Chomsky, C. (1972). Stages in language development and reading exposure. *Harvard Educational Review, 42*(1), 1–33.

Clark, M. (1976). *Young fluent readers.* London: Heinemann.

Clay, M. M. (1972). *Reading: The patterning of complex behavior.* London: Heinemann.

Clay, M. M. (1975). *What did I write?* Auckland: Heinemann.

Cooper, J. D. (1993). *Literacy: Helping children construct meaning.* Boston: Houghton Mifflin.

Cullinan, B. E. (1992). Whole language and children's literature. *Language Arts, 69*(6), 426–430.

Dobson, L. (1989). Connections in learning to write and read: A study of children's development through kindergarten and first grade. In J. Mason (Ed.). *Reading and writing connections* (pp. 83–101). Boston: Allyn and Bacon.

Durkin, D. (1966). *Children who read early.* New York: Teachers College Press.

Early Childhood and Literacy Development Committee. Literacy development and early childhood (Preschool through Grade 3). Newark, DL: International Reading Association.

Gentry, J. C., Henderson, E. H. (1978). Three steps to teaching beginning readers to spell. *The Reading Teacher, 31*(6), 632–637.

Goodman, K. S. (1968). The psycholinguistic nature of the reading process. In K. S. Goodman (Ed.). *The psycholinguistic nature of the reading process* (pp. 13–26). Detroit: Wayne State University.

Goodman, K. S. (1992). I didn't found whole language. *The Reading Teacher, 46*(3), 188–199.

Goodman, Y. M. (1978). Kidwatching: An alternative to testing. *National Elementary School Principal, 57*(4), 41–45.

Goodman, Y. M. (1986). Children coming to know literacy. In W. H. Teale & E. Sulzby (Eds.). *Emergent literacy: Writing and reading* (pp. 1–14). Norwood, NJ: Ablex.

Graves, D. H. (1983). *Writing: Teachers & children at work.* Exeter, NH: Heinemann.

Harste, J., Woodward, V., & Burke, C. (1984). *Language stories and literacy lessons.* Portsmouth, NH: Heinemann.

Heller, M. F. (1991). *Reading-writing connections: From theory to practice.* New York: Longman.

Holdaway, D. (1979). *The foundations of literacy.* Sydney: Ashton Scholastic.

Kawakami-Arakaki, A., Oshiro, M. E., & Farran, D. C. (1989). Research to practice: Integrating reading and writing in a kindergarten curriculum. In J. Mason (Ed.). *Reading and writing connections* (pp. 199–218). Boston: Allyn and Bacon.

Martinez, M., & Teale, W. H. (1987). The ins and outs of a kindergarten writing program. *The Reading Teacher, 40*(4), 444, 451.

Morrow, L. M. (1993). *Literacy development in the early years: Helping children read and write.* Boston: Allyn and Bacon.

Ogle, D. (1986). The K-W-L: A teaching model that develops active reading of expository text. *The Reading Teacher, 39*(6), 564–570.

Raines, S. C. (1986). Teacher educator learns from first and second grade readers and writers. *Childhood Education, 62*(4), 260–264.

Raines, S. C., & Canady, R. J. (1990). *The whole language kindergarten.* New York: Teachers College Press.

Smith, F. (1985). *Reading without nonsense.* New York: Teachers College Press.

Sulzby, E., Barnhart, J., & Hieshima, J. A. (1989). Forms of writing and rereading from writing: A preliminary report. In J. Mason (Ed.), *Reading and writing connections* (pp. 31–63). Boston: Allyn and Bacon.

Teale, W., & Sulzby, E. (1989). Emergent literacy: New perspectives on young children's reading and writing. In D. S. Strickland & L. M. Morrow (Eds.), *Emergent literacy: Young children learn to read and write* (pp. 1–15). Newark, DE: International Reading Association.

Temple, C., Nathan, R., Burris, N., & Temple, F. (1988). *The beginnings of writing.* Boston: Allyn and Bacon.

Tompkins, G. E. (1990). *Teaching writing: Balancing process and product.* Columbus, OH: Merrill.

Trelease, J. (1989). *The new read-aloud handbook.* New York: Penguin.

Wells, G. (1986). *The meaning makers.* Portsmouth, NH: Heinemann.

Wolter, D. L. (1992). Whole group story reading? *Young Children 48*(1), 72–75.

CHILDREN'S LITERATURE REFERENCES

The authors and illustrators of children's books are listed, in all chapters, by their full names to help the reader become acquainted with them. If only one name is listed, the author also illustrated the book.

Carle, Eric. (1981). *The Very Hungry Caterpillar.* New York: Philomel.

Galdone, Paul. (1968). *Henny Penny.* New York: Seabury.

Martin, Bill, Jr. (1983). *Brown Bear, Brown Bear, What Did You See?* Illustrated by Eric Carle. New York: Henry Holt.

Martin, Bill, Jr. (1991) *Polar Bear, Polar Bear What Do You Hear?* Illustrated by Eric Carle. New York: Henry Holt.

Martin, Bill, Jr., & Archambault, John. (1986). *Barn Dance!* New York: Henry Holt.

Martin, Bill, Jr., & Archambault, John. (1989). *Chicka Chicka Boom! Boom!* Illustrated by Lois Ehlert. New York: Simon and Schuster.

Martin, Bill, Jr. & Archambault, John. (1988). *Listen to the Rain.* New York: Henry Holt.

Martin, Bill, Jr. & Archaumbalt, John (1986). *Up and Down on the Merry-Go-Round.* New York: Henry Holt.

Peet, Bill. (1971). *The Caboose Who Got Loose.* Boston: Houghton Mifflin.

Rylant, Cynthia (1984). *This Year's Garden.* Illustrated by Mary Szilagyi. New York: Macmillan.

Sharmat, Mitchell. (1980). *Gregory, the Terrible Eater.* Illustrated by Jose Aruego and Ariane Dewey. New York: Scholastic.

Williams, Vera. (1983). *Something Special for Me.* New York: Greenwillow.

II

Literature Genres

and Forms

The Picture Book

*From Folk Literature
to Modern Fantasy*

*Realism in Realistic Fiction
and Nonfiction for
Young Children*

4

The Picture Book

The Picture Book

*P*art Two of *Stories: Children's Literature in Early Education* is "Literature Genres and Forms." From this section, the reader will gain knowledge of children's literature, teachers' successful uses of each genre or form, and a listing of recommended authors and illustrators. Chapter 4 looks at the picture book, the form most often associated with early education. Chapter 5 provides information about literature which ranges from folk and fairy tales to modern fantasy. In Chapter 6 the theme is "realism," and books which are classified as realistic fiction and real-life nonfiction are featured. Chapter 7 presents poetry and rhythm of expression. In Chapter 8 the oral language traditions of storytelling, creative dramatics, and puppetry are discussed. Chapter 9 examines the rapidly expanding world of technology and discusses stories that are available on film, video, laser disk, and computer imaging.

Each chapter in "Literature Genres and Forms" contains teacher success stories, briefings on appropriated teaching practices, issues to be considered, suggested learning experiences, as well as teacher references, and recommended children's books.

Teacher Success Story: Sarah, a Student Teacher

Sarah was nervous about her student teaching in first grade. Ms. O'Connor, who had a reputation as an excellent reading teacher, had been emphatic at their get-acquainted meeting. She wanted Sarah to read aloud to the children every day and plan lessons in which the first graders read, wrote in response to literature, and composed their own stories.

Sarah wondered if she would ever feel so confident and relaxed as Ms. O'Connor appeared. On Sarah's very first day in the classroom, Ms. O'Connor pointed to the bookshelf and said, "Look through the picture books and find three or four you know well enough to read aloud to the children. I'll look at your selections and help you choose one the children will really like."

Sarah found the four books quickly and beamed with pride when the teacher complimented her good taste. With guidance from Ms. O'Connor, Sarah selected *Something Special for Me* by Vera B. Williams. The first graders liked the story and leaned closer to Sarah to get a glimpse of the bright watercolor illustrations which brought them into the world of the little girl, Rosa. As they listened, they felt sympathy for Rosa's mother who worked so hard and saved the tip money she earned at the Blue Tile Diner to buy Rosa a special birthday present. When Rosa's birthday finally arrived, she went shopping with Mama to select her special presents. The story continued with all the things she considered buying and ended with a surprise when she selected an old accordion.

Relieved that the children actually listened to her, Sarah couldn't help noticing when Ms. O'Connor went over and sat by a child who was beginning to whisper and pull on his friend's shirt. She wondered what she would have done if Ms. O'Connor hadn't been there to redirect his attention.

Immediately after reading the book, Sarah expected Ms. O'Connor to step in and take over the class, but she didn't. She sat looking up at Sarah just as intently as the children sitting in the semicircle on the carpet, waiting for her to continue. Sarah almost panicked and thought, "What do I do now?" At the end of this chapter, read the rest of "Sarah's Story."[1]

Introduction

Even on her first day of student teaching, Sarah demonstrated her knowledge of children's books, young children's interests, and effective techniques for reading aloud. She accomplished the first task done by any teacher who uses children's literature effectively. She selected a good picture book, one which would engage the children's attention.

Picture books, a story told in words and pictures, have often been called the "twice-told tale."

However, for the young child, there is no separation of the text and pictures. The picture storybook is an imaginative interaction of text and illustrations used to tell a story. The combination of text and illustrations to create a story are as intermingled as the lyrics and melody that create a song. The picture storybook is an enticement to begin reading, a way for the young child to visualize a story, to approach a book, to revisit a story; it is a primary source of engagement.

Librarians and teachers tend to call these books that create stories with few words and many pictures, *picture books*, while parents and children often call them storybooks. When asked to recall their beginning literacy experiences, many adults describe their favorite picture book. In fact, they also remember when their reading instruction turned to chapter books and how much they missed the pictures.

The picture book is the form most associated with the early childhood years. It is the only type of book named for its format rather than content. Picture books can be of many varieties: folklore, fantasy, poetry, or realistic fiction.

In this chapter we examine picture books more closely. We present criteria teachers and student teachers, like Sarah, can use to make good selections, examine ways to classify picture books, and consider the associations between the content and the format of the book. Our intent is that teachers and student teachers extend their appreciation of the story and the artistry of the illustration in picture books.

Selecting Picture Books

When early childhood teachers find their first teaching positions, they begin selecting books for their classroom from many sources. They often choose books they knew and loved as children, those they discovered in their college children's literature courses, and books that were part of classrooms in which they completed their field experiences. The familiar books that have stood the test of time are almost always included in the experienced teachers' classroom collections and are a good beginning point for the student teacher or beginning teacher to consider.

Who can imagine a preschool or kindergarten classroom without these favorites: Eric Carle's *The Very Hungry Caterpillar*, Margaret Wise Brown's *Goodnight Moon*, Bill Martin, Jr.'s *Brown Bear, Brown Bear, What Do You See?*, Ezra Jack Keats' *The Snowy Day*, or Ruth Krauss' *The Carrot Seed*? They are so commonly associated with classrooms for young children that a classroom is somehow empty without them.

Who can imagine a first- or second-grade classroom without H.A. Rey's *Curious George*, Arnold Lobel's Frog and Toad stories, Maurice Sendak's *Where the Wild Things Are*, Robert McCloskey's *Make Way for Ducklings*, and Dr. Seuss's *Green Eggs and Ham*? While the preschool and kindergarten teacher may have read these stories aloud, the first- and second-grade teachers claim them as stories they can count on the children wanting to read for themselves.

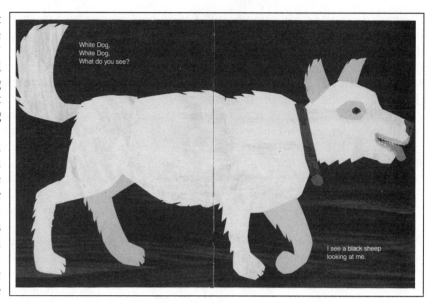

Courtesy of *Brown Bear, Brown Bear*, published by Holt.

Frog & Toad, reprinted with permission by Harper & Row.

These picture storybooks are both teacher tested and child tested. Each of these books is very different in manner of presentation of the content and quite different from one another in illustration. Nonetheless, they hold some of the common characteristics of all good picture books.

Criteria for Picture Book Selections

APPROPRIATENESS AND APPEAL

Of course the first criterion for selecting picture books for young children is the appropriateness of the book for the age and interest of the children. Each of the titles previously mentioned has become a part of the culture of the early childhood classroom because it appeals to the young child's interest. Whether engaging children in answering questions, as in *Brown Bear, Brown Bear, What Do You See?*, appealing to the young child's sense of rhythm and rhyme as the story of Sam-I-Am in *Green Eggs and Ham*, or identifying with all young children's attempts to stay awake as in *Goodnight Moon*, the successful picture book connects with the young child through its interactive organization, or its play with language, or its content is aligned with who they are developmentally. While the question, "Is the story appropriate for the young child?" is rather simple, the answers are many and complex and should be followed up with the related question, "What makes the story appealing to young children?" Remember these two questions:

☐ Is the picture book appropriate for the young child?

☐ What makes the book appealing to young children?

MATCH OF TEXT AND ILLUSTRATION

When asked why they like a particular picture book, teachers and children often say, "The pictures are just beautiful," or "I like the story." When teachers and students vacillate and can't decide whether they like the illustrations or the text better, then a good match of text and pictures has been achieved. The best of the picture books, like those previously mentioned, contain illustrations and text which compliment each other and are dependent upon each other to the point that one would be ineffective without the other.

Jane Yolen's *Owl Moon* is an example of a superior text/illustration combination. John Schoenherr was awarded the Caldecott Medal in 1988 for his illustrations of Yolen's poetic story. *Owl Moon* is the story of a father and his daughter going

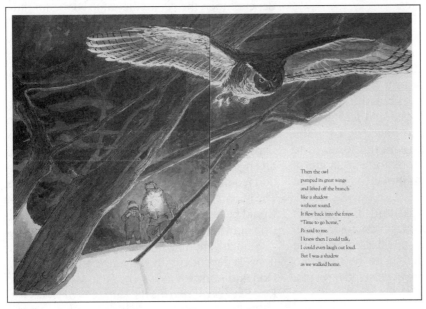

Courtesy of *Owl Moon*, published by Philomel.

"owling" on a moonlit winter night. The author and illustrator captured the pleasure the child feels just being with her father in a quiet, peaceful, and natural world. The emotionally warm, yet suspenseful story, is told from the child's point of view. The magnificent winter scenes in watercolor and ink draw the reader back again and again to enjoy the mood. The elusive owl's appearance at the end of the book is a magnificent illustration (Raines & Canady, 1991, p. 128).

And we'll both eat it all up. YUM!

Courtesy of *The Little Mouse, the Red Ripe Strawberry, and the Big Hungry Bear,* published by Child's Play.

The first step in selecting a good picture book is to read it. We suggest enjoying the story and the illustrations as a whole first, then going back to the book to examine the illustrations and see if there is a good match between the text and pictures.

One kindergartner we know did not like the paperback version of Slobodkina's *Caps for Sale,* usually a favorite story among five-year-olds. When asked why he didn't like the story, he said, "The caps are not brown." In the illustrations, the caps look ocher, but the text says they're brown. To the five-year-old learning his colors, it was disturbing to have the caps the wrong color. After looking more closely, the teacher tried to say the caps were a shade of brown, but the little boy continued to insist that the caps were not brown.

The match between text and illustrations includes many more subtleties than color correspondence. The illustrations should also convey the mood, match the setting, and invite the child into the text visually, adding to the understanding of plot and theme of the story.

APPROPRIATENESS OF ILLUSTRATION TO STORY TYPE

As we discussed in Chapter 1, the criteria for evaluating the content of a good children's book depend upon the genre; the same is true for illustrations. The pictures should enhance the tale because they are appropriate for the type of story. Tomie dePaola's stylized drawings in *The Legend of the Indian Paintbrush* are an example of a good match with the type of story. Ariane Dewey's illustrations in *Pecos Bill* fit the tall tale characteristic of exaggeration. Similarly, the mood of fancifulness is created with delicate lines and muted colors in David McPhail's tale of a little boy dreaming he is an engineer in *The Train.* By its nature, realistic fiction requires, realistic visual representations of life. The impact of the story of *William's Doll* by Zolotow would be less without William Péne du Bois' realistic drawings of family and play life.

Similarly, humor, from slapstick to subtle renditions, is dependent upon the text and illustration. Don and Audrey Wood's *The Little Mouse, the Red Ripe Strawberry, and the Big Hungry Bear* works well as a story because of the bold, comedic, and expressive visual humor. Imagine a tiny mouse wanting the same strawberry that a big hungry bear wants; at least that's what the narrator leads Little Mouse to believe. The type of story is determined by the way the story is told and the type of illustration is determined by the type of story. Again, the form-and-function mixture of illustration and text becomes inseparable.

When selecting picture books, ask yourself, "Are the illustrations appropriate for the type of story?"

ILLUSTRATIONS OF ACTIONS

The way the action in a story is conveyed partly determines the type of story it is, whether it's the magical "poof" of a fairy godmother's wand producing Cinderella's elegant carriage or the outlandish campfire saga of Paul Bunyan's giant blue ox drinking an entire lake dry, the action of the story is made visible in the illustration and moves the story along. The illustrators of children's books are responsible for making those printed action-words come to life for the young child, even before he or she can read. Good stories for young children are dependent upon lively action. Remember to note if the illustrations focus on the action.

ILLUSTRATIONS TO CREATE MOOD

Right from the beginning, the mood of a story is set by the illustrator's use of color, light, and line. Don and Audrey Woods' *The Napping House* is an excellent example of the use of color to create mood. Because of the use of a grayish blue with white accents in the illustrations, the reader knows immediately that the grandmother in the story is taking an afternoon nap, not tucked away in her feather bed for the night. The time and place are easily conveyed by the color and light, and the unusual color accents, varied perspectives, and comical expressions make the reader turn the pages to see what comes next.

There are illustrations that create the mood of the story by enhancing what the author has written,

and then there are books where the primary purpose is to create a mood. For example, James Endicott's illustrations of Bill Martin, Jr. and John Archambault's *Listen to the Rain* create the mood of this enchanting poem which tells the story of a rainstorm.

The sound effects build from the beginning "whisper of the rain" to the steady "singing of the rain" on to the driving force of the "roaring pouring" rain. As the poem proceeds, the rainstorm recedes and the listener is left at the end with the "wet, silent, after-time of rain." The beautifully simple and elegant illustrations, and even the dark blue endpaper pages of the book, are a perfect setting for the drama of the rainstorm (Raines & Canady, 1991, p. 98). Intrigue, suspense, homey reassurance, magical dreams, or the mysteries of nature can be communicated in the picture book by the illustrator's artistry with color, light, and line to convey or create the mood. Note if the illustrations of your selection create or enhance the mood of the story.

ILLUSTRATIONS TO UNDERSTAND SETTING

Understanding another time and place is not easy for young children. They interpret the world from their knowledge of the immediate present.

Listen to the quietude,
the silence and the solitude
of after-rain,

Courtesy of *Listen to the Rain*, published by Henry Holt.

Their understanding of place is limited to the places they have experienced. Therefore, the young child is dependent upon illustrations to enter a story from another era or set in a place that he or she has not experienced.

Cynthia Rylant's *When I Was Young in the Mountains* cannot be understood by young children without Diane Goode's illustrations. This Caldecott Honor Book is a collection of scenes from a little girl's childhood in the mountains where she lived with her grandfather and grandmother. Rylant evokes a special warmth as she recalls how Grandfather looked when he came from working in the mines, Grandmother's wonderful cooking, the swimming hole, and the Crawfords' general store. The reader can see mountain life, pumping water from a well, going to church and baptisms, posing for a traveling photographer, shelling beans on the front porch, and listening to the sounds of the birds. Diane Goode's delicate misty colors help children think of the story occurring in another time and place (Raines & Canady, 1992, p. 166).

Another time is conveyed by more than dressing the characters in a different style of clothing. Place is conveyed by more than the city or country scenes. Consider for example, Barbara Cooney's *Miss Rumphius* and the way she transports the reader back through the places and times of the life of Alice and how she became known as the Lupine Lady.

As a child she made three promises to her grandfather, to live by the sea, to travel to faraway places, and to make the world more beautiful. When she grew up, she became Miss Rumphius, the librarian. In her old age, she made the world more beautiful by sowing blue, purple, and rose-colored lupines (Raines & Canady, 1992, p.162).

Barbara Cooney's distinctive style of fragile lines yet strong message is painted in acrylics with pencil. She captures the stages and places of Alice's life—childhood, adult Miss Rumphius, and the aging Lupine Lady—with an exquisite, delicate touch. Remember to ask yourself, "Do the illustrations help the young child understand time and place?" when reviewing illustrations.

AVOID STEREOTYPES

The picture book for young children should avoid all the stereotypes, including race, gender,

Courtesy of *Miss Rumphius*, published by Viking Press.

and age. Controversy swirls around stereotyping. Certainly books published today should avoid stereotypes; however, some of the folktales that have been passed down for generations have fallen into disapproval, even censorship, for some of the images portrayed. For example, *The Five Chinese Brothers* was thought to perpetuate the myth that all Chinese look alike. However, according to Kay Vandergrift,

> *It is true that if there is only a single book, or a very few available about a culture or group of people, that work may exert undue influence on children's perception of those people. Nonetheless, the remedy is not to remove a book such as The Five Chinese Brothers but to increase the availability of other types of stories dealing with the Chinese people (Vandergrift, 1980, pp. 75-76).*

The tales from the past are particularly poignant examples of stereotyping. Some African-American families object to stories which use black dialect. Yet, Patricia C. McKissack's *Flossie & the Fox* has won critical acclaim and become a favorite among many modern families:

> *Set in another era, this folk tale-like story is about a little girl who outsmarts a sly fox by refusing to believe he is the fox. Told using some black dialect, Flossie's cunning, quick-thinking retorts have children cheering for the heroine. In the author's note, Patricia McKissack attributes this tale to her grand-father (Raines & Canady, 1992, p. 164).*

The fact that the dialect represents the grand-father's voice makes it acceptable to most families because many recall dialect speakers from their childhoods. As educators gain more of a linguistic appreciation of dialects, we become less concerned about the form of language and more concerned about the quality of the story and the lasting impression of the characters.

Similarly, as we become more aware sociologically of the influence of stereotypes on chil-

dren's understanding of sex roles and gender issues, the illustrations and stories in children's picture books have come under more scrutiny. Having Daddy cook spaghetti and Mother coming home from the office is appropriate sex-role identity; however, to have all fathers cooking and all mothers returning home from the office would also do a disservice to the young reader. What the early childhood teacher looks for is a balance of books that portray boys and girls and men and women engaged in the wide variety of activities that are a part of living, rather than limiting them to the types of tasks once associated with gender.

Achieving this balance requires diligent efforts on the part of the teacher. Finding female characters as the leads in picture book is imperative. More books have male rather than female leads. Many of the picture books have animal leads, but even then, maleness is inferred by the name of the character, dress, or actions (Rudman, 1984).

Older citizens also express concern about the way grandparents and other older and elderly people are portrayed in children's picture books. The stereotypical plump little grandmother with white hair, glasses, and a long apron, somehow does not capture the energetic grandmother of today. Grandparents approve of Betty Jo Stanovich's *Big Boy, Little Boy,* an inviting story of an afternoon shared by a little boy and his grandmother. Virginia Wright-Frierson illustrates the grandmother dressed in slacks and a sweater, has her gray hair cut in an easy style, not the stereotypical old woman with a long dress, bun on her head, and wire-rimmed glasses (Raines & Canady, 1989, p. 60). It is important to determine whether the picture books avoid stereotyping. See Chapter 6 for an in-depth discussion on avoiding stereotypes.

Purpose for the Classroom

There are many reasons teachers choose books for their classrooms—to read aloud, to place in the library, to associate with a concept, to extend or elaborate upon on a theme, or for children's independent reading. Therefore, the selection of a picture book for the classroom is highly dependent upon the purpose for which the book is intended. Some books are meant purely to entertain, others to inform, some to inspire. Many are stories for stories' own sake, because they connect us culturally, address our human frailties and strengths, or help us see beyond ourselves.

Making the right selection of picture books for the classroom depends on the ways teachers anticipate using them. For example, selections for group time are needed to connect to the social studies or science thematic unit, which organizes the early childhood curriculum. Picture books that match the theme, support the main ideas or build associated concepts are appropriate choices. Whether it's called group time, circle time, or story time, the label the teacher gives to the time he or she reads aloud places certain demands on the illustrations. Obviously, when reading to a large group of young children, the pictures need to be large and clear enough for them to be seen at a distance. Some smaller books can still be read aloud to young children when the illustrations are bold and have a great deal of contrast.

At times, the reason for selecting a particular book is related to the reading process. If predictable books are needed as confidence builders for beginning readers, there are many helpful lists available from reading specialists and librarians. If a picture book is needed because of a child's keen interest in a topic or some new influence in the family, such as a new baby's arrival, then just the right picture book can be found to fit the occasion.

Book Awards

The early childhood teacher who seeks guidance for selecting good picture books can turn to the various book awards. Many teachers and librarians routinely purchase each year's Caldecott Medal winner. The Caldecott Medal winner and Honor Books are selected annually by the Association for Library Services to Children, a part of the American Library Association. The Caldecott Medal is named for Randolph Caldecott, a nineteenth-century British illustrator. The Caldecott Medal, given since 1938, recognizes "the artist of the most distinguished American picture book for children." (See Appendix A for a List of the Caldecott Medal and Honor winners.)

Figure 4.1 Questions to Guide Picture Book Selections

Is the picture book appropriate for the young child?

What makes the book appealing to young children?

Is there a good match between text and illustration?

Do the illustrations focus on the action?

Are the illustrations appropriate for the type of story?

Do the illustrations create or enhance the mood of the story?

Do the illustrations help the young child understand time and place?

Do the picture books avoid stereotyping, such as by race, gender, or age?

Will the picture book fit the purpose for which it will be used in the classroom?

In addition to the American Library Association's Caldecott Medal and Honor Books, many other awards recognize the picture book. Some are given to new authors, as the International Reading Association Children's Book Award. Other authors and illustrators are honored for special content, as the Coretta Scott King Awards, given to an African-American author and illustrator for "outstanding inspirational and educational contributions to literature for children." There are also the National Jewish Book Awards and the Catholic Book Awards. According to the Children's Book Council, over 100 awards are recognized in the field of children's literature. (Huck, Hepler, & Hickman, 1993, p. 30).

There are numerous state and regional awards, many selected by children. The competitions are sponsored by library associations, reading councils, and colleges of education. Several awards are given from newspapers and magazines. Chief among these are the New York Times Best Illustrated Children's Book of the Year, the Washington Post/Children's Book Guild Nonfiction Award, and the Boston Globe-Horn Book Awards. Parents often notice the stickers on the covers of children's books showing the award from Redbook and from Parents Magazine, publications they read routinely. In the last few years, a new seal has appeared on numerous picture books; the Reading Rainbow oval, which signifies that the book was read on the popular Public Television Series.

Perhaps the award that has gained the most attention among teachers is not an award at all, but rather a list. The International Reading Association's Children's Choices list, published in the October issue of *The Reading Teacher,* represents voting by thousands of children on favorite books from a preselected assortment. Patricia Cianciolo analyzed the Children's Choices and found that children prefer books set in the present, fantasy of any type, humorous and exaggerated tales, and realistic or cartoonlike illustrations that are bright, colorful, and full of detail. (Cianciolo, 1983)

Types of Picture Books

Picture books may be classified in many ways: by content, type of illustrations, story form, or organizing format. In addition to the storybook, alphabet books, counting books, and wordless books are a part of this broad category of books, which we classify as picture books. There are numerous other types, which will be addressed in more detail in other chapters. Mother Goose and nursery rhyme books, as well as other types of folk literature are presented in Chapter 5.

ALPHABET BOOKS

Traditionally, some of the first books parents purchase for their children are the simple alphabet books. ABC books have a long literary history, dating back to the 1500's when the "horn books" contained the ABCs and a few illustrations. The horn book was a paddle-shaped wooden board to which papers were tacked and a sheet of thin transparent cow's horn was placed on top to protect the papers. Later, chapbooks—folded pieces of cardboard—had the alphabet and funny illustrations printed on them. During colonial times, the Puritans used the alphabet to organize religious teachings. (Cullinan, 1989) The ABC book remains popular today for young children.

There are basically five types of alphabet books:

1. letter and one-object picture associations
2. letter and multiple object associations
3. simple stories or narratives
4. question or riddle ABCs
5. theme alphabets

The complexity of the ABC book is usually the factor used to determine the age for which the book is best suited. Infant and toddler ABC books tend to be simple with only one picture associated with the letter, such as Charles Reasoner and Vicky Hardt's *Alphabite! A Funny Feast from A to Z.* In this ABC board book for young children, the book begins with someone taking bites from various foods. The book begins, "A this someone ate apples, tart and red," and on the next page, "Then took a big bite of banana bread." The ABC board book is appealing because of the rhyme, the mystery, and the fact that the foods are ones which toddlers are beginning to recognize.

The purpose of these simple ABC books is not to teach the alphabet, but for children to begin recognizing pictures of common objects. Labeling and naming things also appeals to three and four year olds who tend to enjoy the letter and multiple object associations in the pictures, as in Tana Hoban's *A, B, See!* and Helen Oxenbury's *A, B, C of Things.*

Courtesy of *David McPhail's Animals A to Z*, published by Scholastic.

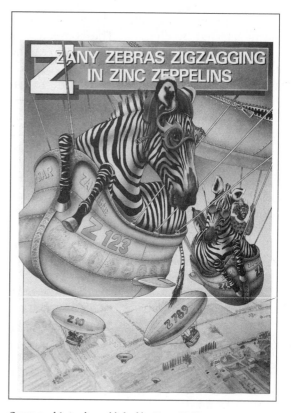

Courtesy of *Animalia*, published by Harry N. Abrams.

Kindergartners and early primary children seem to enjoy the simple stories, rhymes, question or riddle ABCs, and the theme alphabets. An example of a rhyming ABC book is Martin and Archambault's delightful story of *Chicka Chicka Boom Boom* about the letters of the alphabet attempting to climb the trunk of the coconut tree and chanting as they are joined by other letters until the trunk begins to bend and they all tumble off. One of the riddle ABC books is Jan Garten's *The Alphabet Tale*. The reader is asked to guess the identity of the animal based on information found in the rhyme and the picture of the tail of the animal. The animal's identity is shown on the following page.

Theme alphabet books tend to be of people and places, animals, or plant types. Anita Lobel and Arnold Lobel's *On Market Street* is a simple story of a child shopping and meeting tradespeople who are shaped in the letter of the alphabet. However, each of the letters is created by the shape of the objects. For example, the "B" for bookperson is drawn with stacks of books.

Another of the people-and-places ABC books is Margaret Musgrove's *Ashanti to Zulu: African Traditions*, illustrated by Leo and Diane Dillon. The book is the only ABC book to have ever won the Caldecott Medal. In a description of 26 different African tribes, from A to Z, the people are illustrated in tribal dress, showing their homes, animals, and treasured possessions. Another book with an African theme is Tom and Muriel Feelings' book, *Jambo Means Hello*, which is based on the Swahili language.

Animals are popular subjects for alphabet books. In *David McPhail's Animals A to Z*, there is no print, except the letters. The book begins with an aardvark staring at an ant. The B has a picture of a bear in a boat, reading a book. The animal theme is also the subject of Ann Jonas' *Aardvarks, Disembark* in which Noah calls many endangered species and lesser-known animals from the ark.

Emily earned an Easter lily for Florence.

Allison's Zinnia, reprinted with permission of Greenwillow.

In a book suitable for older second and third graders, Jerry Pollotta wrote *The Furry Alphabet Book* with little known animals. The A is for the "Aye-Aye," which looks like a monkey and lives in Madagascar. Each unusual animal is described in three or four sentences.

Another primary grades ABC book picturing animals is Jane Yolen's *All in the Woodland Early,* and illustrated by Jane Breskin Zalben. Yolen's verses and Zalben's illustrations represents each letter with an animal, a bird, and an insect in the natural woodlands setting. While Yolan's book is based on reality, the well-known Graeme Base's *Animalia* is packed with fantasy and fanciful illustrations. In the foreword, he challenges the reader to find a thousand things. In addition to illustrating the phrase for each letter, he ladens each inch of each picture with additional objects, living and fanciful things that represent the letter. In *Animalia,*

B is for "Beautiful blue butterflies basking by a babbling brook."

Plants are presented in ABC format in a beautifully illustrated book by Anita Lobel, titled *Allison's Zinnia.* The charming, appealing narrative combines the word play of ABCs, girls' names, herbs and flower names to create an absolutely delightful and beautiful book to look at and read. The alphabet book begins "Allison acquired an Amaryllis for Beryl." Rich in detail, each illustration is a flower painting (Raines & Canady, 1992, p. 214).

COUNTING BOOKS

Like alphabet books, counting books add to children's language as they begin to hear, see, and read the vocabulary of counting. While counting alone does not represent mathematical understanding of numbers and numeration, the counting book can help reinforce those associations.

Counting books range from the simple to the complex:

1. simple numeral and picture associations showing one-to- one correspondence

2. numeral, objects, and number word associations

3. addition and subtraction

4. story problems

Most counting books for young children begin with one and end with ten. Eric Carle's *My Very First Book of Numbers* is a simple counting book. The simplicity is appealing also in Tana Hoban's photographic format in *Count and See,* but rather than stopping with the number ten, she continues to one hundred and develops the concept of sets of ten. One hundred peas is pictured as ten peas in ten pods. Helen Oxenbury's *Numbers of Things* also goes beyond ten and follows the usual process of counting by tens, but with a surprise ending showing an astronaut asking, "How many stars?"

Anno's Counting Book is one of the books children can enjoy for its simplicity and complexity.

Courtesy of *Ten, Nine, Eight,* published by Greenwillow.

The young children can count the stack of cubes in the margins and associate them with the numeral. Older children make the connection of the twelve months of the year and the seasonal activities, as well as the puzzle of finding different sets of objects that represent the number. As in the eleventh month, there are the obvious eleven houses; but, there are also eleven people, eleven birds in the sky, eleven evergreens on the hilltop, eleven sheep on the path, and so forth.

Counting in another language is the format for *Moja Means One* by Muriel and Tom Feelings. A parallel book to their alphabet book, *Jambo Means Hello,* the numbers are represented by groups of Swahili people.

One of the favorite children's literature books of all times is often thought of for the story, *The Very Hungry Caterpillar,* and not necessarily for number concepts. Helping young children understand quantity, the Very Hungry Caterpillar ate through "one apple, but he was still hungry." As the story continues, the caterpillar eats through two pears, three plums, and so forth (Carle, 1969).

Another story/counting book we highly recommend all teachers read to their children is Molly Bang's *Ten, Nine, Eight.*

This Caldecott Honor Book is the poem a father says to his little girl to get her ready for bed. It starts with "ten small toes all washed and warm" and continues counting down to finally "one big girl all ready for bed." (Raines & Canady, 1989, p. 172).

A number book illustrating subtraction is the text to a popular children's song, *Roll Over, A Counting Song* by Merle Peek. Peek illustrates this favorite counting song by showing a little boy who keeps rolling over in bed. Each time he rolls over, he imagines an animal falling out of the bed. By the time he counts backwards from ten to one, all the animals have fallen out of the bed and he has fallen asleep (Raines & Canady, 1989, p. 168).

Figure 4.2 Appealing Counting Books by Age Group

Counting Books to be Read With Children

Infants and Toddlers	*1, 2, 3,* Tana Hoban *Who's Counting,* Nancy Tafuri
Threes and Fours	*Ten, Nine, Eight,* Molly Bang *The Very Hungry Caterpillar,* Eric Carle
Fives and Sixes	*Anno's Counting Book,* Mitsumasa Anno *How Many Snails?,* Paul Giganti, Jr. and Donald Crews
Sevens and Eights	*The Doorbell Rang,* Pat Hutchins *Moja Means One,* Muriel and Tom Feelings

It was Peter and his little brother.
"Come in," said Ma.
"You can share the cookies."

Courtesy of *The Doorbell Rang,* published by Greenwillow.

While seldom classified as a counting book, Pat Hutchin's *The Doorbell Rang* is an example of a mathematical story problem embedded in the plot.

One afternoon Ma made cookies for Victoria and Sam, and they complimented her on her baking. To which she replied, "No one makes cookies like Grandma." As Victoria and Sam are counting out the cookies to share, the doorbell rings and their friends Hannah and Tom arrive. They continue to share their cookies with other friends whose arrival is signaled by the doorbell ringing. Finally, when there is only one cookie per child, the doorbell rings one last time. It's Grandma with more cookies (Raines & Canady, 1989, p. 174).

When evaluating counting books, the first criterion is the same one as for any picture book: "Does it appeal to the age and interest level of the readers?" A good match between the text and illustrations is particularly important for the counting book. The child, as reader, listener, or viewer of the page, should be able to make easy associations between the number of objects, the numeral, and the number world.

CONCEPT BOOKS

Alphabet books and counting books are concept books. The child's concept book is in some ways like the adult information book in its simplest form. A concept book helps the child understand by making associations. As the young child's vocabulary expands, she or he begins to use descriptive words that classify by color, shape, function, and other attributes.

Using photographs as the medium, Tana Hoban's has written and illustrated numerous books of the concept variety that appeal to preschool and kindergarten children. Her books illustrate a wide array of concepts that are a part of the early childhood curriculum. (See Figure 4.3 for a partial list.) The reader can easily determine from the titles the main concept of the book.

Several other authors are known for concept books. Donald Crews, for example, has published a series of books about transportation; *Truck, Freight Train, Flying , Harbor, School Bus,* and *Bicycle Race.* Another author who writes enjoyable concepts books, but who isn't always as fully appreciated by teachers, is Richard Scarry, who uses cartoonlike drawings and humor in his illustrations. For example in his book *Cars, and Trucks*

Courtesy of *Dig, Dump, Drill, Fill*, published by William Morrow.

and *Things that Go,* there is a drawing of a pickle car. The children enjoy the entertainment of Scarry's books, and since the books are so engaging, children make the concept associations.

Anne and Harlow Rockwell's books on community helpers are also well known among teachers. *My Doctor, My Dentist, The Emergency Room,* and *Fire Engines* are frequent selections for teacher's social studies units. Other Rockwell

---

Figure 4.3 Partial List of Concept Books by Tana Hoban

Big Ones, Little Ones
Circles, Triangles, Squares
Dig, Drill, Dump, Fill
Dots, Spots, Speckles, & Stripes
I Walk and Read
Is it Larger? Is it Smaller?
Is It Red? Is It Yellow? Is It Blue?
Is It Rough? Is It Smooth? Is It Shiny?
Look Again
Over, Under, Through
Push Pull, Empty Full
Round, & Round, & Round
Shapes, Shapes, Shapes
Take Another Look

books fit nicely into teaching units, particularly at the preschool and kindergarten levels. For a unit on simple machines, teachers might select *Machines* and *The Toolbox.* For a unit on community, *The Supermarket* and *Our Garage Sale* are appropriate.

Preschool and primary teachers often organize units around the seasons. Anne Rockwell's *Apples and Pumpkins,* illustrated by Lizzy Rockwell, has become a staple for a unit on fall. In simple text and bright simple illustrations, the story is told of a trip to a farm where there is an apple orchard and a pumpkin patch (Raines & Canady, 1991, p. 112).

The demarcation line between what a concept book is and what is classified as an information book becomes cloudier when the concept book is written for older children. Concept books for first and second graders tend to fall more into the child version of adult information books. Byron Barton's *Building a House* shows an intriguing process from digging the foundation through each step of construction until the time the family moves in.

Wordless Picture Books: A Valued but Neglected Resource—"Do you want to hear me read it again? I can do it another way, too." Six-year-old Lauren's question to her teacher captures the essence of the value of the wordless picture book—it is the variations in interpretations of the story that make the wordless picture book a creative medium.

In the next section of this chapter, we present a more expansive view of one type of picture book, the wordless book. The wordless books deserve expanded treatment as a vehicle for children's developing language abilities, visual appeal, sense of story, and pleasure of interacting with books. Why then, do preschool and elementary teachers neglect to use this valued resource in their classrooms?

We asked 128 teachers from five states questions about the availability, selection (see the questionnaire in Appendix C), and use of wordless picture books. (Raines & Isbell, 1988; Riley 1992) When asked, "Do you use wordless picture books in your classroom?," approximately one-third of the teachers responded, "No." Of the remaining two-thirds who answered, "Yes," the majority of them stated they use wordless picture books by placing them in the library corner of the classroom for browsing, indicating a low-level of instructional usage. When asked, "How often do you use word-less picture books in your classroom?," most answered three to five times a year. As was expected, the greatest percentage using wordless picture books were preschool and kindergarten teachers. However, regardless of grade level, teach-ers consistently identified three problems:

1. There are few wordless picture books available in library collections.

2. They do not know how to select quality wordless books,

3. Few know the variety of instructional uses for wordless picture books.

FEW WORDLESS BOOKS IN COLLECTIONS

To address the concern about the availability of wordless books in collections, we suggest that librarians and reading specialists, as well as cur-riculum coordinators in early childhood settings, plan some sessions on the uses of wordless picture books. When teachers understand the extensive possibilities for wordless picture books, they will be eager to request more for their school's collec-tions, will seek them out in public libraries, and will include them in book orders for their classrooms.

SELECTING QUALITY WORDLESS BOOKS

To address the issues concerning teachers not knowing how to select quality wordless picture books, we suggest they examine wordless picture books in much the same manner as they review

other books. Examine the quality of the story and the quality of the illustrations by reviewing books using the following steps.

THE INSTRUCTIONAL VARIETY CONCERN

The third finding of the study was that teachers do not realize the variety of instructional uses for wordless picture books. The following suggestions are some of the many possibilities for readers and writers at different stages of their literacy and lan-guage development. We separated the wide array of uses into three categories:

1. teaching ideas for young children

2. teaching ideas for the primary grades

3. teaching ideas for proficient readers

The ideas listed for each category are followed by a few descriptions of teachers who value and use wordless picture books.

Teaching Ideas: Wordless Books and Young Children—Ask the children to:

1. Label pictures in concept books.

2. Tell actions on each page.

3. Dictate the story to teacher or parent volunteer.

4. Write captions for action pages.

5. Arrange sequence pictures of wordless books.

6. Pretend dialogue with a partner.

7. Role-play favorite scenes.

8. Tape-record different versions of the story.

By using these teaching ideas, the teacher can easily analyze the language development of the child and evaluate the child's use of story struc-ture. For example, during free-choice time, one preschool teacher assisted individual children who were at the labeling stage of language devel-opment to examine concept books in the library corner. One of the children's favorites was Lustig's *The Pop-Up Books of Trucks.* For more mature language users, she encouraged verbal composition of stories and first helped the children practice following the action of the main character throughout the story, then she requested their storytelling. One of their favorites was Emily McCully's *First Snow.*

A kindergarten teacher selected wordless picture books with clear emotional overtones with which her children could identify. For example, youngsters eager to prove their physical prowess identified with the little boy in Martha Alexander's *Bobo's Dream,* and the children who are frightened by new experiences related to Emily McCully's *First Snow.* Eric Carle's *Do You Want To Be My Friend?* appealed to those younger children seeking friends at school. The kindergarten teacher found she could better evaluate their language development and sense of story structure when she matched the developmental needs of her students and the underlying emotional appeal of the books.

Teaching Ideas: Wordless Books and Primary Children—Ask the children to:

1. Select one character and describe actions
2. Write captions for key action pages.
3. Create new endings in written form.
4. Retell the story to a small group.
5. Tell a group story.
6. Write character descriptions, emphasize adjectives.
7. Identify similarities and differences between characters.
8. Select a character and write a new adventure.
9. Focus on improvisation and create dialogue.
10. Draw a cognitive or semantic map of the story.

After using wordless picture books throughout the school year, one group of first graders enjoyed telling group stories by imagining the conversations between characters. In one class for instance, for Mercer Mayer's *A Boy, A Dog, and A Frog* three children played the characters and invented dialogue for each page of the story. In a second-grade class where several different languages and cultures were represented, the children used both of their languages to tell stories. One Mexican-American girl tape-recorded her two versions of Jan Omerod's *Moonlight.* The perceptive teacher then selected key Spanish words from the

Courtesy of *First Snow,* published by Harper & Row.

child's story and taught them to the entire class with the aid of the pictures from the wordless book.

Teaching Ideas: Wordless Books and Proficient Readers—Ask the students to:

1. Write imagined characterization by placing the character in another setting.
2. Role-play new scenes to add to a wordless book.
3. Add a character and retell the story.
4. Discuss how cause and effect are shown visually.
5. Draw a talking mural with add-on scenes that continue.
6. Tape-record a variety of versions of wordless books to give to younger children.
7. Create a wordless book and read it to younger children.
8. Find wordless books to accompany social studies themes.
9. Display a series of wordless books by the same author.

Table 4-1 Story quality

1. Examine the book and determine if it is a concept book or a story book. Concept books, such as Brian Wildsmith's *Circus,* present a collection of illustrations organized around a concept, and are appropriate at the labeling stage and for vocabulary development. The reader simply labels what is seen in the pictures. The storytelling wordless picture book, such as Emily McCully's *Picnic,* follows a main character or characters through actions to a satisfying ending.
2. Choose concept books designed to intrigue by the nature of the idea.

Likewise, choose storybooks that intrigue by the nature of the problem to be solved by the main character(s).

3. Determine which facets of the book capture the imagination, the plot, the setting, an unusual character, or unusual series of events that happen to a character with whom the children can identify.
4. Review the wordless book for the ease of following the actions in the story.
5. Speculate about one of your brightest children's responses to the storyline, then look at the book and consider a less advanced student's reactions.

Illustration quality

1. Remember three key words: *simplicity, complexity,* and *predictability.*
2. Turn the pages and follow the main character(s). Can the reader follow the storyline without losing the visual image of the main character(s) in a barrage of visual details?
3. Examine the illustrations for complexity. Are the illustrations complex enough to: support the actions of the main character(s); convey their relationships to one another and to the problem they most solved; forward the plot?
4. Review for predictable actions and characterizations. Stop after viewing a few pages and predict what will happen next. Is your prediction confirmed and if it is not, is the surprise turn of events easy to identify and follow throughout the story?

A third-grade teacher captured the imaginations of her students when she displayed a collection of John S. Goodall's wordless books. The Edwardian-style drawings did not interest them at first until they hypothesized what Porky Pig, the cartoon character, would do if he met Paddy Pork, the wordless picture book hero. This simple connection persuaded them to add accents and humor to their verbal rendition of the stories inferred in the illustrations.

When preschool and primary teachers and teachers of proficient readers expand their vision of the possibilities of uses for the wordless picture book, then this resource will become valued and used, not neglected.

Common Themes, Characters, and Situations in Picture Books

The diversity of story in picture books is immense, whether of the wordless book type or those with narrative. And while the diversity of stories and plot structures are great in picture books, there remain some common themes, characters, and situations which appeal to the young child. Stories are told by humanlike animals, talking toys, personification of objects, fantasy, humor, and realism.

HUMAN-LIKE ANIMALS

Dearly loved animal friends, such as the animals Frog and Toad in the series of books by Arnold Lobel, are entertaining and identify with the young child's concerns. Frog and Toad love, accept, and help each other out with the simplest of problems, like being embarrassed about a new swimsuit in the story, "The Swim" from *Frog and Toad Are Friends.* Another favorite story is about the dilemma of mustering enough willpower when faced with a

cookie jar filled with freshly baked cookies in *Frog and Toad Together.*

Another couple of animal friends who have become popular among the primary-aged children are George and Martha. The two hippopotamuses share a day together. Children like the humor and relate to the outrageousness of two hippos with friendship problems. Each of the five stories in James Marshall's *George and Martha: One Fine Day,* has a clear moral, which is cleverly and kindly exposed. For example, in "The Tight Rope" story, George's comments make Martha lose her confidence when she is walking the tightrope, but as soon as he realizes his words are making her shaky, he compliments her and she does some fancy footwork for George to see (Raines & Canady, 1989, p. 36).

While humanlike animals display human characteristics and emotions, children delight in the humor and recognize their frailties as well. For example, children identify easily with Frances the badger in *A Baby Sister for Frances:* Russell

Courtesy of *George and Martha: One Fine Day,* published by Houghton Mifflin.

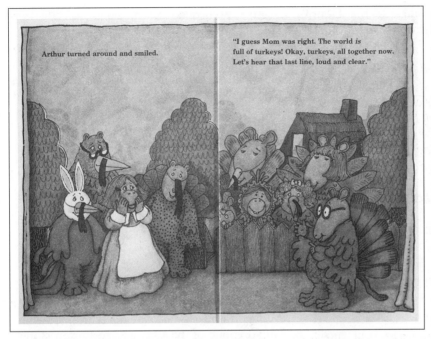

Courtesy of *Arthur's Thanksgiving*, published by Joy Street Books.

Hoban captures "the ambivalent feelings of a child confronted with her jealousy of the new baby in the family and her pride at becoming a big sister" (Raines & Canady, 1989, p. 24). Russell and Lillian Hoban have written and illustrated numerous Frances books, a testimonial to the personality they developed through Frances and to the appeal of talking animals with human characteristics.

Some animal stories are so humanlike that they have almost lost their animal identity. For example, Marc Brown's character Arthur has become a favorite among first- and second-grade readers and as a read-aloud selection for the whole class. Arthur the aardvark has five buddies, Francine, Muffy, Brain, Buster, and Binky Barnes, who always appear in the stories with him. Over the years since the first Arthur story, *Arthur's Nose*, Marc Brown has sketched Arthur to look less and less like an aardvark. At the author's guest appearances at children's bookstores, the question is often asked, "What kind of animal is Arthur?" Marc Brown replies that Arthur is an aardvark with a nose job.

Regardless of how Arthur has changed over the series of books, his character has become very well developed, more human than animal. The stories are set in Arthur's home or at school. We particularly like *Arthur's Thanksgiving* because it "provides a few insights into the problems of "being in charge" when Arthur was chosen as the director of the school Thanksgiving play" (Raines & Canady, 1991, p. 114).

Other picture story books with animals as main characters have their own series of books. They include H. A. Rey's unforgettable *Curious George*, the monkey who is always into mischief and must be rescued by his friend and keeper. Bernard Waber's *Lyle, Lyle the Crocodile* series shows Lyle with a family in the city and how his help is always needed to solve all kinds of problems. And of course, the venerable Beatrix Potter's *Peter Rabbit* series of books and Peter's misadventures continue to entertain young children today.

Other animal characters have not developed into full-blown series, but the characters are forever etched into our memories based on a single story. Leo Lionni has created numerous memorable one-story characters. Who can forget *Swimmy*'s heroism when one lone fish teaches a whole school of little fish how to avoid being eaten by the bigger fish? Also memorable is *Frederick*, who taught the other little mice the value of words and poetry during the long dreary winter days. The latest of Leo Lionni's unforgettable animal characters is in *Matthew's Dream:*

> *Matthew the mouse and his family live in a dusty attic surrounded by old newspapers, discarded toys and broken furniture. Matthew's parents want him to grow up to be a doctor, but Matthew doesn't know what he wants to be until the day he goes with his classmates to an art museum. There he becomes enchanted with the paintings and with a mouse named Nicoletta who loves art. In classic Lionni style, the story and the art complement each other, simply, boldly, and beautifully (Raines & Canady, 1991, p. 30).*

TALKING TOYS COME TO LIFE

Toy animals who talk like humans are often main characters in children's books. For example, A. A. Milne's Winnie the Pooh is a toy bear who likes honey like real bears but who talks as if he is human. His friends Tigger and Eeyore the donkey have similar human and animal-like qualities, while clearly in the illustrations they are toy stuffed animals. The personification of toys has a long tradition in children's literature and continues today.

A most popular toy for picture books is the teddy bear. There are teddy bear alphabet books, counting books, talking teddies, lost and found teddies, teddy bears having fun, teddy bears at school, teddy bears and other toys, and teddy bears and children.

An early childhood teacher's unit on Teddy Bears would not be complete without Don Freeman's *Corduroy* books. While the story does not have Corduroy speak, his thoughts, feelings, and reactions are explained in humanlike terms as the toy comes to life. In the first Corduroy story, we meet an adventuresome toy bear who wanders around in a department store at night (Raines & Canady, 1989, p. 144). Another Corduroy adventure occurs after he is home with his new owner. In *A Pocket for Corduroy,* the little bear wants a pocket for himself and searches for one in a laundromat. He gets lost and has to spend the night alone there.

TALKING MACHINES, TRAINS, AND TRUCKS

In addition to personified toys, machines and trains come to life in children's literature. *Mike Mulligan and His Steam Shovel* (named Mary Anne) is one of the Virginia Lee Burton stories, which preschool and kindergarten teachers read

Corduroy is a bear who once lived in the toy department of a big store. Day after day he waited with all the other animals and dolls for somebody to come along and take him home.

Courtesy of *Corduroy,* published by Viking Press.

With my red lights turning
and my blue lights winking
and my headlights burning
and my green lights blinking,
I'm doing my job,
I'm proud as can be,
with three tows swinging
in back of me!

Three tows in a row are dangling back there—
rear wheels on the ground, front wheels in the air.
The other tows doze, but I'm wide awake.
I talk to my tires, my engine, and my brake:

Courtesy of *How Many Trucks Can a Tow Truck Tow?* published by Random House.

aloud to their children, and first and second graders enjoy reading on their own.

Put out of work by more modern machines in the big city, Mike Mulligan and Mary Anne the steam shovel take on the challenge of digging a new city hall for the little town of Popperville. In a comical style, Virginia Lee Burton has the reader cheering for Mike and Mary Anne, while giving credit to the little boy who saved the day with his good ideas (Raines & Canady, 1992, p. 166).

Virginia Lee Burton has another machine that comes to the rescue in *Katie and the Big Snow*, where Katie the snowplow saves the town with characteristic "pushing on" against great odds, persevering, then receiving the praise of the village.

Of course, one of the most famous personified objects is the talking train in Piper's *The Little Engine That Could*. The book is so popular that it continues to be used as a metaphor for never giving up: "I think I can, I think I can, I think I can."

The tradition of having machines come to life is still evident in stories of today. While often reserved for the preschool and kindergarten child, beginning readers also flock to these tales. Preschoolers and kindergartners enjoy *How Many Trucks Can a Tow Truck Tow?* by Charlotte Pomerantz. The story told in rhyme is a tongue twister to read but a delight to hear. The children will cheer the little tow truck when each new turn adds another tow truck to be towed, and the littlest truck is the hero of the day. One can almost hear the little tow truck saying the same words as the little engine, "I think I can, I think I can, I think I can" (Raines & Canady, 1991, p. 210).

Bill Peet's *The Caboose Who Got Loose* is a favorite among first and second graders. Katy is a caboose, a machine confined to the tracks, but she wants to be free. One day, the coupling breaks between the train cars. When Katy goes around a mountain curve, she is flung free. She lands between two evergreen trees and becomes a happy home for squirrels and birds (Raines & Canady, 1991, p. 118).

FANTASY

The category of fantasy is most often associated with picture books. Talking hippos, steam shovels, cabooses, and persevering trains are certainly fanciful characters. Dream stories and fantasy creatures are clearly associated with the fantasy label. Fantasy also includes the use of magic in fairy and folk tales which are discussed in Chapter 5.

"Go away, Nightmare, or I'll shoot you," I said.

Courtesy of *There's a Nightmare in My Closet,* published by Dial.

Dream Fantasy—*Harold and the Purple Crayon* by Crockett Johnson is an excellent example of a dream fantasy. In this imaginative tale, first published in 1955, Harold takes his crayon with him on a walk where he proceeds to draw adventures, supplying everything he needs. When he needs more light, he draws a moon to shine on his path. When he wants a walk in a forest, he draws a tree. But occasionally, Harold's drawing has some unexpected results, as the dragon he drew so frightens him that he shakes his crayon and accidentally draws a sea. In the end, Harold's purple crayon come to the rescue, and we find him safely tucked in bed (Raines & Canady, 1991, p. 188).

Purple shades are used quite effectively to create a dreamy mood by another artist/storyteller, David McPhail, in his story *The Bear's Toothache,* in which a tiny boy assists a huge bear by pulling his aching tooth. As a reward, the bear gives the boy the giant tooth to put under his pillow.

McPhail's tale is illustrated in layered colors with line drawings on violet and charcoal backgrounds to create the dreamy night mood (Raines & Canady, 1989, p. 236).

The fantasy of mythical creatures, like dragons and ghosts and nightmares that come out at night, are also common occurrences in the picture book genre. Conquering one's fears is a childhood developmental task. As the young child attempts to separate reality from fantasy, the fantasy characters in a real-life setting help the child make the distinction. For example, many parents appreciate Mercer Mayer's books for helping them put the young child's fanciful nightmare creations to rest. In *There's a Nightmare in My Closet,* a suspenseful, yet humorous tale, Mayer expresses a child's nightmares and lets the child heroically invite the nightmare to share his bed. This 1968 book with a simple text has become a best seller and a childhood favorite. Characteristic of many Mayer tales, the scary monster turns into a friendly, slightly adorable companion (Raines & Canady, 1991, p. 70). In *There's an Alligator Under My Bed,* Mayer uses the same theme. His drawings of the facial expressions of the little boy translate the humor and imagined fears most effectively.

HUMOR AND EXAGGERATION

Clearly, Mercer Mayer's nightmare tales are humorous and imaginative and fit the category of fantasy with their invented nightmare creatures. However, there is another type of picture book which also has a great deal of appeal to young children, the story told with humor and exaggeration. *Imogene's Antlers* and *The Giant Jam Sandwich* are humorous and exaggerated to the point of silliness, but both are funny stories that children request teachers to read aloud often.

Imogene's Antlers, by David Small, is the outrageously funny tale of a little girl who wakes up one day to find she has grown antlers. An embarrassment to her family and terribly inconvenient, Imogene's dilemma perplexes the doctor, the school principal, and even her brother, Norman, who declares she is turning into an elk. After trying many

On Thursday, when Imogene
woke up, she found she
had grown antlers.

Courtesy of *Imogene's Antlers,* published by Crown Publishers.

invaded by four million wasps. The nasty wasps harass the picnickers, drive the farmers from their fields, sting Lord Swell's bald head, buzz and dive and eat everything in sight. The story ends with all the wasps eating the jam while the villagers lower a mammoth slice of bread down on top of the wasps, trapping them inside. The illustrations are witty, inventive, and invite several perusals for a few extra giggles per reading (Raines & Canady, 1989, p. 230).

REALISTIC FICTION

The picture book genre is not all imagination, exaggeration, and giggles; perhaps the greatest increase in publication over the last ten years has been in the category of the realistic fiction book. Common plots include children successfully resolving everyday childhood problems of family and friends. Another type of realistic fiction attempts to deal with very serious problems of abusive situations, divorce, even concern about drugs, violence, and diseases.

Children find realistic fiction books quite reassuring in that the main characters are real children with real problems and plausible solutions. *How Many Stars in the Sky?* by Lenny Hort is a realistic

silly disguises, Imogene wakes up the next day to find her antlers gone. However, she is surprised to find when she goes downstairs to breakfast that she has a beautiful fan of peacock feathers on her behind. The book is a winner of the Parent's Choice Award (Raines & Canady, 1992, p. 240).

Imogene's Antlers is supposedly set in a real family household, but *The Giant Jam Sandwich* by John Vernon Lord with verses by Janet Burroway requires a more expansive imagination to visit a village named "Itching Down," which has a serious problem. They are

Courtesy of *How Many Stars in the Sky?* published by Tambourine Books.

fiction book primary-grade children particularly enjoy. Father and son drive out into the country and look up at a sky so clear that they can see the Milky Way. Finally, exhausted, they lie down in the bed of the pickup and sleep under the stars. The story of family feeling, of missing Mama yet sharing a special time with Father, is much more than a story about counting stars. James E. Ransome's realistic oil paints are rich and deep with interesting visual perspectives (Raines & Canady, 1992, p. 44).

While there are literally thousands of friendship books for young children, Miriam Cohen's book *Will I Have A Friend?* seems to always strike a responsive chord among young children. The problem is a universal childhood worry about starting school and finding, making, and keeping a friend.

Art and Illustration in Children's Picture Books

In the picture storybook, there is an interdependent relationship between the two elements of story and pictures. Some picture storybooks contain illustrations that are of such extraordinary quality that they could stand alone as works of art. Others are illustrations of the story and have little meaning without the accompanying text.

One of the books that is a work of art rather than just illustration, is *Riptide* by Frances Wade Weller with pictures by Robert J. Blake. *Riptide* is the true adventure of a dog who became the nineteenth lifeguard at a beach because of his heroism in saving a little girl from drowning. Robert J. Blake's oil paintings are indeed works of art with deep blue, turquoise and azure seas, white-capped waves, sandy beaches with lapping surf and beautifully sunny days with billowing clouds, as well as scenes of stormy skies (Raines & Canady, 1992, p. 156). Blakes' realistic paintings illustrate the story and bring the child into the aesthetic world of the seashore, filled with the beauty and peril, which is the essence of the story.

Regardless of the medium, the artist/author combination can make the picture book both a

Courtesy of *Riptide,* published by Philomel.

literary and an aesthetic experience. Unlike Blake's oil paintings, each page a work of art, many artists subdue their art to illustration for most of the book and show their art separately on the cover or in a pause in the story for dramatic effect. For example, *Minou* by Mindy Bingham is illustrated by Itoko Maeno. Set in Paris, *Minou* is the story of a cat whose painter/owner dies. Itoko Maeno's exquisite watercolors of the street scenes of Paris and familiar landmarks are wonderful impressionistic art.

The match between the artist's choice of medium and the story are critical. Blake's oil paintings and Maeno's watercolors fit the two stories perfectly. The use of color and style of painting to suit the story are also critical. One superb example is Margaret Leaf's story *Eyes of the Dragon*, which is illustrated by Ed Young. "Bold reds and greens on the cover and beautiful full-page pastel chalk drawings lure the reader and listener into this folk tale set in China" (Raines & Canady, 1992, p. 180).

The illustrator of children's books is often an artist, but illustrations do not have to be great works of art to convey the meaning of the story. For example, primary-age children enjoy the funny Amelia Bedelia stories by Peggy Parish. Lynn Sweat's drawings of Amelia Bedelia are not great works of art in the same sense as Robert Blake's oil paintings for *Riptide*, Itoko Maeno's impressionism watercolors in *Minou*, or Ed Young's chalk drawings in *Eyes of the Dragon*, but her illustrations have so captured the character of Amelia Bedelia that they are associated with the mixed-up maid.

The amount and quality of illustration

Courtesy of *Make Way for Ducklings*, published by Viking Press.

also change depending on the function of the book. Many poetry collections do not have pictures for each poem, while others are illustrated versions of one poem. While many of the easy-to-read books are still in the picture book category, they may not have illustrations on each page. Even Arnold Lobel's beloved *Frog and Toad: All Year* series does not have each page illustrated, but there is at least one illustration for facing pages. The *Little Bear* series by Else Minarik and pictures by Maurice Sendak is another example of the variance in the amount of illustration. The child reader gets the impression from the drawings provided, but the illustrator highlights only key scenes, rather than supplying a visual interpretation for each.

AWARD WINNING ARTISTS AND THEIR MEDIA

The artist's or illustrator's choice of medium affects the story and the aesthetic appreciation of the picture storybook. While personal style of expression is key to an artist's success, some experiment with medium to make just the right connection with the text. Clearly, many of the Caldecott Medal winners and Honor Books are good examples.

Awarded the Caldecott Medal in 1942, Robert McCloskey's *Make Way for Ducklings* is less colorful than most of the present day winners, but the expressiveness of the policeman who stops traffic for the Mother Duck and her little brood to cross the street, and the artist's effective use of expression, perspective, and landscape continue to make the selection appropriate fifty years later. The much heralded book claimed international attention a few years ago when USA First Lady Barbara Bush presented then USSR First Lady Raisa Gorbachev with bronze statues by Nancy Schon of the mother duck and eight ducklings, just like the ones that stand in the Boston Public Gardens (Shepard, 1991, July).

Artist Ezra Jack Keats created numerous books that children have taken to heart because the stories were so in tune with the young child, such as *Peter's Chair*, *Hi, Cat!*, and *Whistle for Willie*. The book for which Keats won the Caldecott in 1963, *The Snowy Day*, remains just as popular today, thirty years later. "Keat's marvelously simple illustrations are graphic collages of big shapes textured with fabric prints and chalk shadings to

Courtesy of *Tuesday*, published by Clarion.

add depth" (Raines & Canady, 1989, p. 122). Collage and mixed media artwork were rare in illustrations of children's books at the time.

In 1976, Leo and Diane Dillon won the Caldecott for their unusual applications of paint in their illustrations of *Why Mosquitoes Buzz in People's Ears*, an African tale retold by Verna Aardema. The artists created elaborately decorative pictures using airbrushes, a type of stenciling, painting, and glazing, with layers of color on color (Dillon & Dillon, 1976).

In the 1980's Chris Van Allsburg won the Caldecott Medal twice, for *Jumanji* in 1982 and for *The Polar Express* in 1986. In contrast with the shades of black, white, and gray in *Jumanji*, the deep color of *The Polar Express* is created by layered shades of color. Perhaps Van Allsburg is best known for his unusual perspectives. Whether it is the unique visual point of view in *Jumanji*, as the reader looks down onto the table top of two children playing a game in which imagination becomes reality or the magical story perspective of continuing to believe in Santa Claus in *The Polar Express*, Van Allsburg creates a perfect meld of story and picture.

The two Caldecott Medal winners named during the writing of this book are David Wiesner's *Tuesday*, awarded in 1992, and Emily McCully's *Mirette on the High Wire*, awarded in 1993. *Tuesday* is a wordless picture book, which Wiesner illustrates as a surrealistic tale of flying frogs on lily pads making their way into a surprised town. In *Clarionews*, Wiesner credits today's children with much visual literacy and likes the child's interpretation of story to be heard instead of the writer's voice (*Clarionews*, 1992).

Courtesy of *Mirette on the High Wire*, published by Putnam.

Courtesy of *Honey, I Love*, published by Harper & Row.

Emily McCully is the 1993 Caldecott Medal winner for *Mirette on the High Wire*, illustrated in watercolors. Mirette is the daughter of the owner of a boarding house. There she meets a highwire artist who has lost his nerve for performing. Mirette's curiosity and her desire to learn to walk the wire, charm the performer into an attempted comeback. McCully's illustrations are as charming as the story, which set around the turn of the century in Paris.

VARIETY OF MEDIA

The illustrator's choice of a medium has a great deal to do with the effectiveness of the story in the picture book, whether painting with oils, watercolors, and acrylics, or printing from wood or linoleum block cuts. The tools and instruments of drawing with plain pencils, charcoals, pastels, pen and ink, markers, and crayons can be as varied as the paints. Some artists illustrate by constructing unusual visuals with paper cuts, photography, or elaborate mixed media collages. Artists often vary their choice of media to suit the story. For example, Leo and Diane Dillon, used airbrushing, stenciling, and glazing layers of paint in *Why Mosquitoes Buzz in People's Ears,* but illustrated *Honey, I Love by Eloise Greenfield,* with charcoals. The Dillons' illustrations for Greenfield's book are a creative combination of charcoal drawings of the little girl, whose feelings are featured, and childlike etchings in a smaller size overlaid at either the top or the bottom of each page.

PAINTING IN OIL, WATERCOLORS, ACRYLICS, AND TEMPERA

Oil paintings give picture book illustrations a depth and substance that other media do not achieve. In addition to Robert Blake's oil paintings of *Riptide,* be sure and examine Mike Wimmer's illustrations for Diane Siebert's *Train Song*. The poem takes the reader to stations in different geographic areas and includes the freight trains with boxcars, auto hauler, and hopper cars, as well as passenger trains with sleepers, diners, and observation cars (Raines & Canady, 1991, p. 213).

Watercolors can be subdued and dreamy, as those used by artist Uri Shulevitz in his book *Dawn*. Particularly associated with the medium, the watercolors fluidity lends itself to the artist's theme. *The Empty Pot* by author and illustrator

Courtesy of *The Empty Pot*, published by Henry Holt.

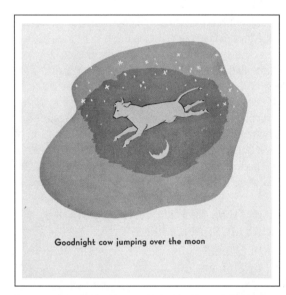

Goodnight cow jumping over the moon

Courtesy of *Goodnight, Moon*, published by Harper & Row.

Demi has lovely fine-line watercolor illustrations to accompany this moral and memorable story told in folktale form. A Chinese emperor devises an ingenious plan to choose his successor by having the children of the land plant seeds. Ping, the main character, planted his seeds carefully and took good care of them, but nothing grew. On the last day of the year, he had to go to the emperor with an "empty pot," while all the other children came with beautiful plants. The emperor choose Ping because he did his best and was honest. The seeds had been cooked and none of them would grow. Demi's watercolor illustrations are the most appropriate medium for the beautiful flowers, Chinese vases, and palaces. (Raines & Canady, 1991, p. 92)

Watercolors do not have to be subdued, muted, and delicate; they can also be bold, bright, and patterned, such as those used by Vera B. Williams in *A Chair for My Mother*. A loving and exciting rendering of the pictures gives vitally to this story of a little girl's desire for and experience of saving for a chair for her mother, who works all day in a diner.

Acrylics are particularly appealing to illustrators of picture books because of their clarity, intensity, and ability to show bright colors. Jose Aruego's illustrations of Robert Kraus' *Whose Mouse Are You?* is an excellent example. The bright yellows and oranges stand out graphically and make it a particularly appealing book to read at circle time, since the illustrations can be seen easily by groups of children.

Tempera paints or powdered color paints, including gouache, are a favorite medium among picture book artists. Perhaps the most famous of the tempera paint books is Maurice Sendak's *Where the Wild Things Are*. Sendak's artistry and gift for color, contrast, shading, and texturing give depth to the usually flat medium.

DRAWING WITH PEN AND INK, PENCILS, MARKERS, CRAYONS, CHARCOALS, AND PASTELS

Pen and ink, plain pencils, colorful makers, and layers of waxed crayons are also appropriate media choices. Often pen and ink drawings are washed with watercolors or combined with other coloring tools. Beatrix Potter's *Peter Rabbit* books are exquisite examples of pen and ink with watercoloring. Another famous book, *Goodnight Moon* by Margaret Wise Brown includes pen and ink drawings and colors in a different arrangement. The illustrator, Clement Hurd, arranged bright colors on facing pages followed by black and white pages to lull the viewer into the mood of the story (Raines & Canady, 1989, p. 72).

Doubtless many artists begin with pencil sketches and choose other media for their final product, but the deft sketches of an illustrator fit many children's stories. Marcia Brown's rendition of Perrault's *Cinderella* is delicately drawn with a hand so light that the magic and mystical mood of the story is apparent. In contrasting style, Bill Peet's sketches are cartoonlike and he is a favorite author/illustrator among primary-age

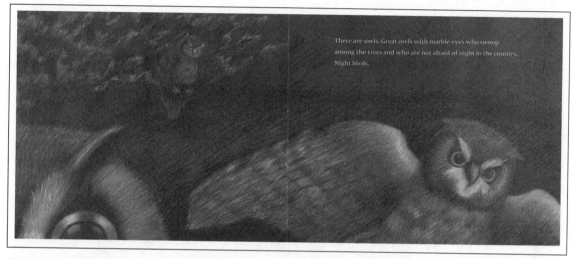

There are owls. Great owls with marble eyes who swoop among the trees and who are not afraid of night in the country. Night birds.

Courtesy of *Night in the Country*, published by Bradbury Press.

children. James Stevenson's cartoonlike drawings work well in *Will You Please Feed Our Cat?*, "a zany, preposterous tale which entertains and fits young children's sense of responsibility for pets" (Raines & Canady, 1992, p. 154).

Artists often use markers and crayons to color their drawings. Children recognize the use of markers in Susie Shenk's illustration for Elaine W. Good's *That's What Happens When It's Spring!* Layering colored markers is another technique artists use to create mood. In Cynthia Rylant's *Night in the Country*, Mary Szilagyi's illustrations make the reader want to linger in the scene and enjoy the almost silence and the almost stillness of a country night. The drawings look like layered crayons with just enough of the darkness scrapped away to expose an animal or a scene from the night (Raines & Canady, 1989, p. 80).

Drawing and shading with charcoals and pastels takes a tremendous amount of physical control of the medium. David McPhail's illustrations in *Lost!* are soft chalk drawings, yet rich with color and shadows to compliment the story of a bear who crawls into a delivery truck, falls asleep, and awakens to find himself deep in the city, instead of deep in the woods.

PRINTING WITH WOODBLOCK AND LINOLEUM CUTS

Perhaps the woodcut print that most early educators recognize is Ed Emberley's illustrations of *Drummer Hoof*, created by using three colors. Marcia Brown, a three time Caldecott winner, used woodcuts in her *All Butterflies*, the ABC book. Linoleum cuts, like wood block prints, create a clean, simplicity of design. In *A Year of Birds*, Ashley Wolff used linoleum blocks to illustrate the seasons. Tejima's *Fox's Dream* is a striking woodcut book with the textures and contrasts of the outline of the fox set against the sights of the forest on a winter night. *Fox's Dream* was the winner of the New Times Best Illustrated Children's Book Award.

PHOTOGRAPHY

Tana Hoban's photography in both color and black and white is the medium for the concept books for which she is well known. (Refer to Figure 4.3.) The popularity of photography books has grown as a medium for nonfiction for young children.

A photography book that always gathers an audience is Joanna Cole's *My Puppy Is Born*, which was photographed in color by Margaret Miller. The photographs record the birth process and the young narrator's joy at welcoming the new puppy and watching her grow. Teachers can review this book to use in a unit on pets.

For a unit on families, we highly recommend the photographic essay book *Loving* by Ann Morris with color photographs by Ken Heyman. Families from many cultures from around the world in both city and country life are shown eating together, dressing, walking, talking, reading, playing, and expressing their affections (Raines & Canady, 1991, p. 46).

18   They teach you how to ride a pony

Courtesy of *Loving*, published by Lothrop, Lee & Shepard.

For a unit on friendship, *My Friend Leslie: The Story of a Handicapped Child* is a pleasingly honest book by Maxine B. Rosenberg that tells of Leslie's capabilities and limitations. Karin and Leslie's friendship is apparent through George Ancona's black and white photographs and can be interpreted by children without reading the text.

TEXTURING WITH COLLAGE, PAPER, PLASTICINE, OR CLAY

Cutting and pasting, good early childhood art techniques, are also employed by some great illustrators of children's books. Collage materials add texture and depth to the composition. Some artists are famous for their collage works. Ezra Jack Keat's used fabric swatches to illustrate the patterned wallpaper and Peter's pajamas in *The Snowy Day*. Eric Carle's technique of painting,

then cutting out the characters and pasting them onto a background, adds depth and creates his characteristic clean lines. Also, every child who has read *The Very Busy Spider* recalls the texture Carle created by adding clear plastic lines, which the child can rub to feel the spider's web. Leo Lionni is famous for use of collage and torn paper. In his most recent book, *Matthew's Dream*, collage materials illustrate the dusty attic where Matthew's family is surrounded by old newspapers, discarded toys, and broken furniture. Paper cutting is also a way of texturing and adding depth. Molly Bang's *The Paper Crane* is an excellent example.

Plasticine, molded like clay, is used effectively in Edith Newline Chase and Barbara Reid's book *The New Baby Calf*. A recent multi-material collage book is Jeannie Baker's *Where the Forest Meets the Sea*. With clay to model

Courtesy of *Berlioz, the Bear,* published by Putnam.

the figures of the man and boy who explore a shoreline and bits of shell, fabric, and wood, Baker's illustrations are highly texturized and give great depth perception to the landscapes and seascapes.

Artistic Style and the Elements of Design

Many artists have so distinguished themselves that they have created a signature style that is instantly recognizable. Whomever the artist and whatever the medium chosen for artistic expression, the design of the work is created through line, space, color, and perspective. The signature styles that are highly recognizable use these elements effectively; but to create their highly personalized style, the artists emphasize different elements. Eric Carle's simple use of bold, graphic colors, sparse lines, and white space for contrast are signature elements. For examples, look at *Brown Bear, Brown Bear, What Do You See?* and *The Mixed-up Chameleon.*

In contrast, while using bright colors, Jan Brett covers all of the canvas of the page and lavishly decorates each inch. She layers decorative borders over the illustrations, adds intricate details on clothing with many lines, and tells subplots of the story through creating pictures that go beyond the text. See *Berlioz, the Bear, Annie and the Wild Animals,* and *Goldilocks and the Three Bears* for beautiful examples.

Courtesy of *Where the Forest Meets the Sea,* published by Greenwillow.

Some artists are known for their interesting perspectives, or point of view. Chris Van Allsburg's *Two Bad Ants* is an example of an imaginative perspective. Telling the story visually from an ant's eye view is ingenious. The gray, taupe, and brown colors, the lines, and textures heighten the sense of adventure—of something unusual happening. An interesting perspective is clearly a Van Allsburg signature.

The Physical Structure and Form of the Picture Book

From the front cover to the back cover, the format of the picture book is a visual experience. Whether a toy pop-up book, a miniature, a big book, one with die-cut pages, one with a mostly vertical or mostly horizontal layout, with or without dust jackets, the way a book is constructed and assembled is vital to the young child's acceptance and interest in the book.

All books have covers, endpapers, and title pages. For classrooms, if books have book jackets, we recommend those that repeat the cover of the book because young children manipulating the book soon separate the jacket from the book. Since young children usually select a book by its cover, the plain cloth cover is not as appealing as the fully illustrated jacket.

Book size and shape are key to the book's acceptance by the young child as well. Some of the palm-sized editions are too hard for little children to hold and turn the small pages, while some of the large formats cannot be easily held by the child and must be placed on the floor. The recent popularity of big books in the classroom is discussed in more detail in Chapter 3. Board books and shape books cut in the shape of the main idea of the story are popular choices for infants and toddlers. Young children also enjoy

Courtesy of *Two Bad Ants*, published by Houghton Mifflin.

toy or pop-up books, but most are not durable enough to stand up to classroom use.

In recent years, illustrators have begun carrying the theme of the story throughout the physical presentation of the book. The cover and dust jackets are colorfully illustrated and even the endpapers are decorated. For example, in Lynn Cherry's *The Great Kapok Tree*, the endpapers are a map of the tropical rain forests of the world, bordered with small drawings of the insects and animals that inhabit them.

The layout of the book, the spacing of the text and illustrations on the pages, the style and size of print, the texture of the paper, the way the pages are sewn, and even the density or opaqueness of the paper (so that print does not show through from one page to the other), help to create the physical appearance of the picture book and make it a pleasing aesthetic or distracting experience. The quality of the design,

The man awoke with a start. Before him stood the rain forest child, and all around him, staring, were the creatures who depended upon the great Kapok tree. What wondrous and rare animals they were!

Courtesy of *The Great Kapok Tree*, published by Harcourt Brace Jovanovich.

special, a toy, computer games, even presents for their parents' birthdays and Mother's and Father's Day. They talked about what they did to earn money, where they kept the change, and how slowly it added up.

By the time Ms. O'Connor interrupted to say it was time for the children to get ready to go to music, almost every child had participated in the discussion. When the children left the room, Ms. O'Connor put her arm around Sarah's shoulder and said, "You handled that really well. I'm looking forward to seeing how you can extend the idea for a writing project. Give it some thought and we'll discuss it tomorrow."

Success, and on the first day, Sarah almost danced down the hallway of the school.

layout, and physical construction are hardly noticed by the young child, but they are the physical skeleton upon which the story and illustration depend to engage the young child's attention and sustain interest.

Sarah's Story Continues

Remember Sarah, the student teacher you met in the opening paragraphs of this chapter? The picture book and its connections to real life helped Sarah succeed on her first day of student teaching.

SARAH'S DILEMMA

When Sarah realized Ms. O'Connor expected her to continue after she finished reading *Something Special for Me,* she swallowed hard, took a deep breath, and began telling the children about something she saved for when she was a little girl. She wanted a skateboard like her older brother's, so she saved her money to buy one.

Instantly, the children's hands went up and they began to tell about saving for something

EPILOGUE

Sarah went on to have many successful teaching experiences. The following day she ask the children to draw pictures of their experiences saving for something special. Some children drew themselves doing extra chores to get money. One child drew a picture of the piggy bank where she kept the money she was saving. Others drew themselves shopping for presents and some illustrated the scenes where they gave presents to their parents. All the first graders wrote captions for their pictures, but some of the children decided to write longer stories.

Sarah described her semester of student teaching as mountain tops and valleys. Her elation when a lesson went well was often followed by despair when the next one fell apart. Ms. O'Connor had high expectations for the children in her class-room and Sarah often thought unrealistic expectations for her as a student teacher. Ms. O'Connor did not hesitate to criticize Sarah's teaching, but she also was quick to praise when the lessons went well.

Over the semester, Sarah's confidence grew. Reading to the children seemed to work well for her. The children would focus on the book or story. Sarah's dramatic reading voice seemed just right for the first graders. At times, she really "hammed it up," then dramatically let her voice fall almost to a whisper. Just as she had done in reading *Something Special for Me*, Sarah continued to select books that connected to something in the children's lives, so that they could discuss the book after she read it aloud to them.

Ms. O'Connor convinced Sarah to put that same dramatic voice to work in her regular classroom instruction, to "ham it up a bit," get excited about the lesson, use her voice inflection for emphasis, and make connections between the lesson and the children's lives. In many ways, the story picture book lesson became the model for Sarah's teaching.

5. Read/tell a wordless book to a class. Ask the teacher to let you work with two children. Have one child retell the wordless book you read and ask the other child to change the story in some way.

6. Compare two humorous illustrators' styles, such as Don and Audrey Wood to James Marshall.

7. Examine David Wiesner's Tuesday. Look at the book with a child and assess the child's reaction.

8. Among the illustrators whose works appear in this chapter, select five that appeal to you. Find the complete works and read the books.

9. Compare Emily McCully's artwork in the wordless picture books First Snow and her Caldecott Medal book Mirette on the High Wire.

10. Compare the Caldecott Medal books and the Honor Books. Do you agree with the judges decisions or would you have awarded the medal to one of the books that was an Honor Book?

SUGGESTED LEARNING EXPERIENCES

1. If you were Sarah and were given a choice of books to read to first graders, what three books would you select?

2. Examine the Caldecott Medal winners for the last five years. Determine which medium each illustrator used. Which books are particularly appealing to you and why?

3. Read at least one of the Caldecott Medal winners to a child. Let the child tell you which illustrations she or he likes.

4. Review the section on wordless picture books. Visit a library and compare wordless books which are the story variety and those which are concept books.

REFERENCES

Cianciolo, P. J. (1983). A look at the illustrations in children's favorite picture books. In N. Rose & M. Firth (Eds.), *Children's choices: Teaching with books children like.* Newark, DE: International Reading Association.

An interview with David Wiesner. (1992, Spring). *Clarionews*, 5.

Cullinan, B. E. (1989). *Literature and the Child*. San Diego, CA: Harcourt Brace Jovanovich.

Dillon, L., & Dillon, D. (1976). Caldecott Medal Acceptance. *Horn Book*, 52(4), 376.

Huck, C. S., Hepler, S., & Hickman, J. (1993). *Children's literature in the elementary school*. Fort Worth, TX: Harcourt Brace Jovanovich.

Raines, S. C., & Canady, R. J. (1989). *Story s-t-r-e-t-c-h-e-r-s: activities to expand children's favorite books*. Mt. Rainier, MD: Gryphon.

Raines, S. C., & Canady, R. J. (1991). *More Story s-t-r-e-t-c-h-e-r-s: activities to expand children's favorite books*. Mt. Rainier, MD: Gryphon.

Raines, S. C., & Canady, R. J. (1992). *Story s-t-r-e-t-c-h-e-r-s for the primary grades: Activities to expand children's favorite books*. Mt. Rainier, MD: Gryphon.

Raines, S. & Isbell, R. (1988). *An array of teaching ideas using wordless picture books.* ACEI Annual Study Conference. Salt Lake City, UT.

Riley, B. (1992). *Bibliography of wordless picture books.* (Available from Oklahoma State Department of Education, 2500 Lincoln Boulevard, Oklahoma City, OK 73105).

Rudman, M. K. (1984). *Children's literature: An issues approach.* New York: Longman.

Shepard, L. (1991, July 30). Summit — first ladies. Moscow: Associated Press.

Vandergrift, K. (1980). *Child and story.* New York, Neal-Schuman.

CHILDREN'S LITERATURE REFERENCES

The authors and illustrators of children's books are listed, in all chapters, by their full names to help the reader become acquainted with them. If only one name is listed, the author also illustrated the book.

Aardema, Verna. (1975). *Why Mosquitoes Buzz in People's Ears.* Illustrated by Leo and Diane Dillon. New York: Dial.

Alexander, Martha G. (1970). *Bobo's Dream.* New York: Dial.

Anno, Mitsumasa. (1975). *Anno's Counting Book.* New York: Thomas Y. Crowell.

Baker, Jeannie. (1988). *Where the Forest Meets the Sea.* New York: Greenwillow.

Bang, Molly. (1985). *The Paper Crane.* New York: Greenwillow.

Bang, Molly. (1986). *Ten, Nine, Eight.* New York: Greenwillow.

Barton, Byron. (1981). *Building a House.* New York: Greenwillow.

Base, Graeme. (1986). *Animalia.* New York: Harry N. Abrams.

Bingham, Mindy. (1987). *Minou.* Illustrated by Itoko Maeno. Santa Barbara, CA: Advocacy Press.

Bishop, Claire Huchet. (1938). *The Five Chinese Brothers.* Illustrated by Kurt Wiese. New York: Coward-McCann.

Brett, Jan. (1985). *Annie and the Wild Animals.* Boston: Houghton Mifflin.

Brett, Jan. (1991). *Berlioz the Bear.* New York: G. P. Putnam.

Brett, Jan. (1987). *Goldilocks and The Three Bears.* New York: G. P. Putnam.

Brown, Marc. (1986). *Arthur's Nose.* Boston: Little, Brown & Company.

Brown, Marc. (1983). *Arthur's Thanksgiving.* Boston: Joy Street Books.

Brown, Marcia. (1974). *All Butterflies.* New York: Scribner.

Brown, Margaret Wise. (1947). *Goodnight Moon.* Illustrated by Clement Hurd. New York: Harper & Row.

Burton, Virginia Lee. (1942). *Katie and The Big Snow.* Boston: Houghton Mifflin.

Burton, Virginia Lee. (1939). *Mike Mulligan and His Steam Shovel.* Boston: Houghton Mifflin.

Carle, Eric. (1971). *Do You Want to Be My Friend?* New York: Crowell.

Carle, Eric. (1985). *My Very First Book of Numbers.* New York: Harper Collins.

Carle, Eric. (1984). *The Mixed-Up Chameleon.* New York: Harper & Row.

Carle, Eric. (1984). *The Very Busy Spider.* New York: Philomel.

Carle, Eric. (1969). *The Very Hungry Caterpillar.* New York: Philomel.

Chase, Edith N., & Reid, Barbara. (1984). *The New Baby Calf.* New York: Scholastic.

Cherry, Lynne. (1990). *The Great Kapok Tree.* San Diego, CA: Harcourt Brace Jovanovich.

Cohen, Miriam. (1967). *Will I Have A Friend?* Illustrated by Lillian Hoban. New York: Macmillan.

Cole, Joanna. (1991). *My Puppy Is Born.* Photography by Margaret Miller. New York: Morrow.

Cooney, Barbara. (1982). *Miss Rumphius.* New York: Viking Press.

Crews, Donald. (1985). *Bicycle Race.* New York: Greenwillow.

Crews, Donald. (1987). *Flying.* New York: Greenwillow.

Crews, Donald. (1978). *Freight Train.* New York: Greenwillow.

Crews, Donald. (1982). *Harbor.* New York: Greenwillow.

Crews, Donald. (1984). *School Bus.* New York: Greenwillow.

Crews, Donald. (1980). *Truck.* New York: Greenwillow.

Demi. (1990). *The Empty Pot.* New York: Henry Holt.

dePaola, Tomie. (1988). *The Legend of the Indian Paintbrush.* New York: G. P. Putnam.

Dewey, Ariane. (1983). *Pecos Bill.* New York: Greenwillow.

Emberley, Barbara. (1967). *Drummer Hoff.* Illustrated by Ed Emberley. Englewood Cliffs, NJ: Prentice-Hall.

Feelings, Muriel. (1974). *Jambo Means Hello: Swahili Alphabet Book.* Illustrated by Tom Feelings. New York: Dial.

Feelings, Muriel. (1971). *Moja Means One.* Illustrated by Tom Feelings. New York: Dial.

Freeman, Don. (1968). *Corduroy.* New York: Viking Press.

Freeman, Don. (1978). *A Pocket for Corduroy.* New York: Viking Press.

Garten, Jan. (1964). *The Alphabet Tale.* Illustrated by Muriel Batherman. New York: Random House.

Giganti, Paul, Jr. (1988). *How Many Snails?* Illustrated by Donald Crews. New York: Greenwillow.

Goodall, John. (1983). *Paddy Pork's Odd Jobs.* New York: Atheneum.

Good, Elaine W. (1987). *That' What Happens When It's Spring!* Illustrated by Susie Shenk. Intercourse, PA: Good Books.

Greenfield, Eloise. (1978). *Honey, I Love.* Illustrated by Diane and Leo Dillon. New York: Harper & Row.

Hoban, Russell. (1964). *A Baby Sister for Frances*. Illustrated by Lillian Hoban. New York: Harper & Row.

Hoban, Tana. (1982). *A, B, See!* New York: Greenwillow.

Hoban, Tana. (1976). *Big Ones, Little Ones*. New York: Greenwillow.

Hoban, Tana. (1974). *Circle, Triangles & Squares*. New York: Macmillan.

Hoban, Tana. (1972). *Count and See*. New York: Macmillan.

Hoban, Tana. (1992). *Dig, Drill, Dump, Fill*. New York: William Morrow.

Hoban, Tana. (1987). *Dots, Spots, Speckles, & Stripes*. New York: Greenwillow.

Hoban, Tana. (1984). *I Walk and Read*. New York: Greenwillow.

Hoban, Tana. (1985). *Is It Larger? Is It Smaller?* New York: Greenwillow.

Hoban, Tana. (1978). *Is It Red? Is It Yellow? Is It Blue?* New York: Greenwillow.

Hoban, Tana. (1984). *Is It Rough? Is It Smooth? Is It Shiny?* New York: Greenwillow.

Hoban, Tana. (1971). *Look Again*. New York: Macmillan.

Hoban, Tana. (1987). *Over, Under & Through*. New York: Macmillan.

Hoban, Tana. (1972). *Push, Pull, Empty, Full: A Book of Opposites*. New York: Macmillan.

Hoban, Tana. (1983). *Round & Round & Round*. New York: Greenwillow.

Hoban, Tana. (1986). *Shapes, Shapes, Shapes*. New York: Greenwillow.

Hoban, Tana. (1981). *Take Another Look*. New York: Greenwillow.

Hort, Lenny. (1991). *How Many Stars in the Sky?* Illustrated by James E. Ransome. New York: Tambourine Books.

Hutchins, Pat. (1986). *The Doorbell Rang*. New York: Greenwillow.

Johnson, Crockett. (1955). *Harold and the Purple Crayon*. New York: Harper & Row.

Jonas, Ann. (1990). *Aardvarks, Disembark!* New York: Greenwillow.

Keats, Ezra Jack. (1970). *Hi Cat!* New York: Macmillan.

Keats, Ezra Jack. (1967). *Peter's Chair*. New York: Harper & Row.

Keats, Ezra Jack. (1962). *The Snowy Day*. New York: Viking Press.

Keats, Ezra Jack. (1964). *Whistle for Willie*. New York: Viking Press.

Kraus, Robert. (1970). *Whose Mouse Are You?* Illustrated by Jose Aruego. New York: Macmillan.

Krauss, Ruth. (1945). *The Carrot Seed*. Illustrated by Crockett Johnson. New York: Harper & Row.

Leaf, Margaret. (1987). *Eyes of the Dragon*. Illustrated by Ed Young. New York: Lothrop, Lee & Shepard.

Lionni, Leo. (1967). *Frederick*. New York: Pantheon.

Lionni, Leo. (1991). *Matthew's Dream*. New York: Alfred A. Knopf.

Lionni, Leo. (1963). *Swimmy*. New York: Pantheon.

Lobel, Anita. (1990). *Allison's Zinnia*. New York: Greenwillow.

Lobel, Arnold. (1976). *Frog and Toad: All Year*. New York: Harper & Row.

Lobel, Arnold. (1970). *Frog and Toad Are Friends*. New York: Harper & Row.

Lobel, Arnold. (1971). *Frog and Toad Together*. New York: HarperCollins.

Lobel, Arnold. (1989). *On Market Street*. Illustrated by Anita Lobel. New York: William Morrow.

Lord, Jane Vernon. (1972). *The Giant Jam Sandwich*. Verses by Janet Burroway. Boston: Houghton Mifflin.

Lustig, Loretta (1974). *The Pop-up Books of Trucks*. New York: Random House.

McCloskey, Robert. (1941). *Make Way for Ducklings*. New York: Viking Press.

McCloskey, Robert. (1957). *Time of Wonder*. New York: Viking Press.

McCully, Emily. (1985). *First Snow*. New York: Harper & Row.

McCully, Emily. (1984). *Picnic*. New York: Harper & Row.

McCully, Emily. (1992). *Mirette on the High Wire*. New York: Putnam.

McKissack, Patricia C. (1986). *Flossie and the Fox*. Illustrated by Rachael Isadora. New York: Dial.

McPhail, David. (1989). *David McPhail's Animals A to Z*. New York: Scholastic.

McPhail, David. (1990). *Lost!* Boston: Little, Brown.

McPhail, David. (1972). *The Bear's Toothache*. Boston: Little, Brown.

McPhail, David. (1977). *The Train*. Boston: Little, Brown.

Marshall, James. (1978). *George and Martha: One Fine Day*. Boston: Houghton Mifflin.

Martin, Bill, Jr. (1983). *Brown Bear, Brown Bear, What Do You See?* Illustrated by Eric Carle. New York: Holt.

Martin, Bill, Jr. & Archambault, John. (1989). *Chicka Chicka Boom Boom*. Illustrated by Lois Ehlert. New York: Simon & Schuster.

Martin, Bill, Jr., & Archambault, John. (1988). *Listen to the Rain*. Illustrated by James Endicott. New York: Henry Holt.

Mayer, Mercer. (1967). *A Boy, A Dog, and A Frog*. New York: Dial.

Mayer, Mercer. (1987). *There's An Alligator Under My Bed*. New York: Dial.

Mayer, Mercer. (1968). *There's A Nightmare in my Closet*. New York: Dial.

Milne, A. A. (1926, 1988). *Winnie-The-Pooh*. Illustrated by Ernest H. Shepard. New York: Dutton.

Minarik, Else, H. (1957). *Little Bear*. Illustrated by Maurice Sendak. New York: Harper & Row.

Morris, Ann. (1990). *Loving*. Photographs by Ken Heyman. New York: Lothrop, Lee & Shepard.

Musgrove, Margaret. (1976). *Ashanti to Zulu: African Traditions*. Illustrated by Leo and Diane Dillon. New York: Dial.

Omerod, Jan. (1986). *Moonlight*. New York: Lothrop, Lee & Shepard.

Oxenbury, Helen. (1972). *A, B, C of Things*. New York: Watts.

Oxenbury, Helen. (1983). *Helen Oxenbury's Numbers of Things*. New York: Delacorte Press.

Parish, Peggy. (1977). *Teach Us, Amelia Bedelia*. Illustrated by Lynn Sweat. New York: Greenwillow.

Peek, Merle. (1981). *Roll Over! A Counting Book*. New York: Clarion Books.

Perrault, Charles. (1954). *Cinderella*. Illustrated by Marcia Brown. New York: Scribner.

Peet, Bill. (1971). *The Caboose Who Got Loose*. Boston: Houghton Mifflin.

Piper, Watty (1929, 1954). *The Little Engine That Could*. Illustrated by George Hauman and Doris Hauman. New York: Platt and Munk.

Pollotta, Jerry. (1991). *The Furry Alphabet Book*. Illustrated by Edgar Stewart. Watertown, MA: Charlesbridge Publishing.

Pomerantz, Charlotte. (1987). *How Many Trucks Can A Tow Truck Tow?* Illustrated by R. W. Alley. New York: Random House.

Potter, Beatrix. (1902). *The Tale of Peter Rabbit*. New York: Frederich Warne.

Reasoner, Charles, & Hardt, Vicky. (1989). *Alphabite! A Funny Feast From A to Z*. Los Angeles, CA: Price, Stern, Sloan.

Rey, H. A. (1941). *Curious George*. Boston: Houghton Mifflin.

Rockwell, Anne. (1989). *Apples and Pumpkins*. Illustrated by Lizzy Rockwell. New York: Macmillan.

Rockwell, Anne, & Rockwell, Harlow. (1986). *Fire Engines*. New York: Dutton.

Rockwell, Anne. (1972). *Machines*. Illustrated by Harlow Rockwell. New York: Macmillan.

Rockwell, Anne. (1984). *Our Garage Sale*. Illustrated by Harlow Rockwell. New York: Macmillan.

Rockwell, Anne. (1985). *The Emergency Room*. Illustrated by Harlow Rockwell. New York: Macmillan.

Rockwell, Anne, & Rockwell, Harlow. (1979). *The Supermarket*. New York: Macmillan.

Rockwell, Anne. (1971). *The Toolbox*. New York: Macmillan.

Rockwell, Harlow. (1992). *My Doctor*. New York: Macmillan.

Rockwell, Harlow. (1975). *My Dentist*. New York: Greenwillow.

Rosenberg, Maxine B. (1983). *My Friend Leslie: The Story of a Handicapped Child*. Photographs by George Ancona. New York: Lothrop, Lee & Shepard.

Rylant, Cynthia. (1986). *Night in the Country*. Illustrated by Mary Szilagyi. New York: Bradbury Press.

Rylant, Cynthia. (1982). *When I Was Young in the Mountains*. Illustrated by Diane Goode. New York: Dutton.

Scarry, Richard. (1974). *Richard Scarry's Cars & Trucks & Things That Go*. Racine, WI: Western Publishing.

Schulevitz, Uri. (1974). *Dawn*. New York: Farrar, Straus.

Sendak, Maurice. (1963). *Where the Wild Things Are*. New York: Harper & Row.

Seuss, Dr. (Geisel, Theodor Seuss). (1960). *Green Eggs and Ham*. New York: Random House.

Siebert, Diane. (1990). *Train Song*. Illustrated by Mike Wimmer. New York: Thomas Y. Crowell.

Slobodkina, Ephyr. (1940). *Caps for Sale*. New York: Harper & Row.

Small, David. (1985). *Imogene's Antlers*. New York: Crown Publishers.

5

From Folk Literature
To Modern Fantasy

From Folk Literature To Modern Fantasy

The Teacher's Lost Keys Tale

Barbara was returning home late one night from a committee meeting, where she had been helping to plan the next state Early Childhood Conference. As she started to park her car, Barbara saw her neighbor obviously searching for something. She was down on her hands and knees patting the ground and muttering to herself, "Where are they?"

Barbara went over to her neighbor and asked, "What's the problem?"

The neighbor, interrupted in her search, looked up, and in exasperation said, "Oh! I've lost my keys."

Barbara quickly volunteered, "I'll help you look for them. Where do you remember having them last?"

And they proceeded to reenact the whole scene.

The neighbor recalled, "I got out of my car. I had my keys then. I went around to the trunk to get out the children's books I picked up at the library. That's the stack of books over on the steps. I had the keys then to open my trunk."

Barbara interrupted, "And what did you do next?"

They proceeded to follow her every move. Finally, the teacher went over to the mailboxes, several feet away, and there lying in the dark were her keys.

The neighbor said, "I just knew they had to be over here."

"Pardon me," said, Barbara. "If you knew your keys were over here in the dark, why were you crawling around on the ground over there under the street light?"

The neighbor replied, "Oh, I was just looking over there, because the light was better."

Introduction

Numerous versions of the "search for the lost keys under the street light story" have been told by speakers in a variety of settings to illustrate their points. We don't know whether or not an incident like this ever happened. The two authors of this book have heard variations of this story told from conference podiums, in pulpits, at Girl Scout leadership trainings, and even at a political convention. Like folktales from the past, "the lost keys search" is a tale with an oral tradition that the teller modifies to fit his or her situation.

The lost keys story fits our purposes as well because in these days of "reinventing classrooms," teachers are "trying to find their keys." Many are looking in the wrong places. Early childhood teachers who are searching for guidance in becoming language and literature process teachers need to remember that the keys to successful whole language instruction lie with understanding children as learners, and linking the learners to good children's literature.

Traditional Literature Keys

To take the key analogy a bit further, imagine three types of keys teachers hold in their hands. These keys represent the field of children's literature.

First, visualize a beautiful old brass key, ornately cast and decorated. The beautiful old key is heavy in our hands. Imagine the immense old wooden doors, tall, carved, massive doors from another era, which this key opens. Behind these doors lie some powerful old stories from the past.

These stories from the past are our legacy, the tales that people from other centuries told to entertain, to enlighten, and to emphasize morals. The tales, like our key story, have been passed down to us. They are the folk tales, fairy tales, fables, legends, and myths from many cultures that have survived because of

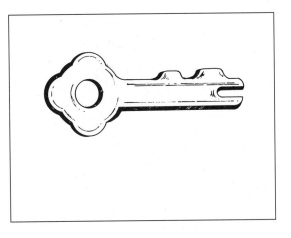

their roots in the oral tradition. The tellers of these tales organized a story that could be easily remembered.

APPEAL OF FOLK LITERATURE

All societies possess stories that have been passed down for centuries. Their survival is evidence that these story forms satisfy some universal human needs. Whether folktales, legends, myths, or the simple Mother Goose nursery rhymes, the traditional folk literature appeals to young children and to adults' cultural concerns for a variety of reasons.

First, the themes in the folk literature connect with all cultures universally because the morals are apparent. Good eventually wins over evil. Resorting to trickery and deception leads to no good ends. One should be thankful for the life he or she is given, rather than coveting another's riches or position. Hard work, perseverance, and kindness will be rewarded.

Secondly, the most obvious reason that the stories have survived is that they come from an oral tradition, thus they are easily remembered by adults and children. Over the years, the stories have been honed, exaggerated, and structured in ways that make them easy to recall, and also easy for the young child to gain a sense of story. According to Arthur Applebee (1978), a well-developed sense of story serves the child well for success as a beginning reader.

Thirdly, the language of the tales is very appealing to the young child who enjoys the rhythm and rhyme of the repeated phrases. Hearing the tales told or read aloud evokes an immediate response. For example, children say the rhymes and repeat the phrases that mark the action. They repeat the giant's verse in *Jack and the Beanstalk* and the alliteration in "Fee, fi, fo, fum" rolls off the tongue, letting the child know something is about to happen.

A fourth appeal of the folk literature is humor. The trickster tales, the exaggerated tall tales, the sillies and noodlehead stories are examples of stories that are easily remembered because they are so outrageously funny and create such strong visual pictures. While the child and the adult's senses of humor differ greatly, nonetheless, what is laughable, "giggleable," to the young child is the same type of rather primitive humor found in many folktales. (Jalongo, 1985)

Lastly, folk literature appeals to the young child's sense of fantasy. Separation of reality from fantasy is something that happens in the early primary grades. According to André Favat (1977), because children's play life is filled with fantasy, they relate well to the fantasy literature of the fairy and folktale variety. Favat's review of literature indicates that children's interest in folktales correlates well with their developmental stages. In preschool and early primary years, children show a preference for folktales. As they grow older and separate reality and fantasy more, they begin to think more rationally and prefer realistic stories. Favat's findings support Piaget's and Inhelder's (1969) writings about children's play and their belief in animism and use of fantasy as a tool for expression.

Bruno Bettelheim, writing in the *Uses of Enchantment: The Meaning and Importance of Fairy tales* (1976), emphasizes that children clearly identify with the good fantasy characters and they cheer as evil is conquered in the resolution of the problem. They identify with the basic drives of the tales—survival, love, gaining control. The moral behaviors and steps in problem solving have clear consequences. The fantasy allows the children to identify with the characters who are conquerors against horrendous odds, not dissimilar to what it is like to be the youngest and smallest in our society. (Butler, 1989). (For additional essays on fantasies, see Chesterton, 1989; Cullinan, 1989; Fadiman, 1989; Stewig, 1988, and Tolkien, 1989).

Mother Goose Rhymes

Mother Goose books have a long literary heritage. They are a part of the folk tradition of literature derived from oral storytelling and singing, which was later collected and printed. Mother Goose has stood the test of time, although not unscathed by criticism for the violence and sexism used in many verses (Minard, 1975).

The first printed version of the rhymes and stories is reported to be Charles Perrault's 1697 publication of *Histoires ou contes du temps passé, avec des moralities* (Stories or tales of time past, with morals) (Opie & Opie, 1974). The name Mother Goose is supposedly derived from the illustration in the book of an old woman spinning and telling tales. Iona and Peter Opie provide more insights into the history and origin of Mother Goose in *The Oxford Dictionary of Nursery Rhymes* (1951). Regardless of her origin and the criticism, Mother Goose continues as a favorite book, one often purchased by parents and grandparents who remember their own childhood reading of the nursery rhymes.

What is the appeal of Mother Goose nursery rhymes? For infants and toddlers, the participation suggested by the rhymes is the beginning of their literary experiences. The parent who reads "Pat-a-cake, pat-a-cake," usually adds the clapping of the hands, often holding the infants hands and clapping them together. One toddler we knew associated reading with "Pat-a-cake," and would start clapping his hands together at his mother or father's suggestion of reading a book. The ritual of beginning their reading together with the rhyme was his first association with the pleasure of reading. Of course, "This Little Piggy Went to Market," is also one of the first participation rhymes, which many parents do with their children.

Even though some of the nursery rhymes are not understood by children, they experience the rhyme and the sound of the language while visualizing the funny pictures. Who can forget the fun of trying to repeat "Peter Piper picked a peck of pickled peppers"? Even though young children do not often know what pickled peppers are, they enjoy the sound of the verse. The ticking rhythm of "Hickory, dickory, dock, the mouse ran up the clock" keeps running through the mind, long after one has forgotten the picture of a mouse on a clock. Children who have had some of the traditional Mother Goose verses read to them will enjoy a Jim Aylesworth's *The Completed Hickory Dickory Dock*, which begins with the old verse and adds humorous versions.

"Simple Simon Met a Pieman" and "Old Mother Hubbard" survive as rhymes and short narrative stories with simple problems and simple solutions. Other Mother Goose rhymes narrate a very simple scene.

Courtesy of *Nick Butterworth's Book of Nursery Rhymes*, published by Viking Press.

> Jack and Jill went up the hill
> To fetch a pail of water.
> Jack fell down and
> Broke his crown
> And Jill came
> Tumbling after.

The verse is rhymed, is funny, and if you like slapstick falls, also tells a little story. In a new twist on making collections of Mother Goose rhymes, Leonard Marcus chose eighteen rhymes for *Mother Goose's Little Misfortunes*, a book first through third graders will enjoy.

Humorous characters are also part of the appeal of Mother Goose. Humpty-Dumpty sitting on the wall, The Little Old Woman Who Lived in a Shoe, and The Crooked Man are funny to visualize. The cat and the fiddle and a cow jumping over the moon, as well as a dish running away with a spoon are preposterous but funny to the young listener. The humorous illustrations in *Nick Butterworth's Book of Nursery Rhymes* casts the old rhymes in a new light. Kindergartners like the mouse pole-vaulting over the candlestick and other whimsical variations.

Little Bo-Peep, Little Boy Blue, and The Three Little Kittens who lost their mittens evoke sympathy from young children. While no muffets and tuffets are apparent in today's life, the common experience of being scared by a spider is a part of the child's world, just as it was for Miss Muffet.

Mother Goose books tend to be of two types, the collection editions and the single version illustrations. *Brian Wildsmith's Mother Goose* is beautifully illustrated with bright watercolors in purples, pinks, and blues. However beautifully illustrated, it is not the sweet version of the rhymes. He shows the farmer's wife about to cut off the tails of the three blind mice with the carving knife. Tasha Tudor's *Mother Goose* is

Courtesy of *Tomie de Paola's Mother Goose*, published by G. P. Putnam.

exquisite in costume and reminiscent of the old-fashioned drawings often associated with earlier Mother Goose books. Tomie dePaola's *Mother Goose* contains over 200 nursery rhymes and is illustrated in bright colors with a bold, almost graphic, style. Lucy Cousins' *The Little Dog Laughed and Other Nursery Rhymes* contains fifty rhymes, but the unusual childlike illustrations and large print, with pictures for each rhyme, make it particularly appropriate for preschoolers. Another unusual illustration approach is Tedd Arnold's photographs of cross-stitched verses from *Mother Goose's Words of Wit and Wisdom: A Book of Months.*

Among many preschool and primary teachers, two favorite Mother Goose collections are the illustrated versions by Alice and Martin Provenson and James Marshall. The variety and number of illustrated versions highlight the contrasting styles

artists choose for the old verses and stories.

Other illustrators of children's books have published versions of Mother Goose in the single verse or story version. Paul Galdone's *The Three Little Pigs* and *Old Mother Hubbard* are two that preschool and kindergarten children like. A more recent publication, Janet and Allen Ahlberg's, *Each Peach Pear Plum* includes an "I Spy" game as a part of the visual enjoyment and keeps kindergartners and first graders returning to the book to read it for its rhyme and the game. Peter Spier's *London Bridge Is Falling Down* is enjoyed by older children with the landmarks and the history of the bridge included.

The appeal of Mother Goose is likely to draw other illustrators to publish other collections or single story versions in the future. Parents, grandparents, and teachers can rest assured that their children will have fresh, new versions, parodies, and comical interpretations to delight so that Mother Goose will never quite lose her charm.

Folktales

Folktales have been told and retold in the oral tradition and finally appeared in print after they became a part of the cultural heritage of diverse societies. Since the stories have been shared across

Courtesy of *Each Peach Pear Plum*, published by Puffin Books.

time, they also have crossed cultural boundaries. Like Charles Perrault, who was believed to have been the first to place French tales of the common folks in print, Jakob and Wilhelm Grimm collected folktales and published *Kinder-und Hausmarchen* in 1812 and 1815 to preserve the German tales. The stories were translated into English and illustrated by George Cruikshank under the title of *German Popular Stories* in 1823. What distinguished the stories of the folktale variety were that they were first told by the common *folk*. (See a more detailed discussion in Huck, Hepler, & Hickman's *Children's Literature in the Elementary School*, 1993.)

The story elements of folktales make them particularly appropriate for the young child. The setting, plot, characters, style, and theme of folk literature tend to be simple in nature. The time and place of the tales are construed to be vague. "Once upon a time in a land far, far away," "Long, long ago in a kingdom by the sea," "Once, so the story goes, a poor. . ." and the time and place are left to the imagination.

The plot of the stories are usually single-focused, with only one problem to be resolved. By the very nature of folktales and fairy tales, the characters are stereotypical. The wicked witch and the stepmother are always evil. The fox is always cunning and the donkey is always stubborn. The style

of writing in folk literature is based on the oral tradition and is usually told with story markers, such as repeated phrases, new characters joining the adventure, or more perils around the turn of the bend on the long journey.

The themes of folktales hold universal attraction. The poor become rich. The ugly become beautiful. The good conquer and the evil get their just dues. The small and humble endure great peril on behalf of family or friends and in the end are rewarded for their unselfish nature. Through the folktales, the common people's dreams, aspirations, and values are expressed.

Numerous patterns or motifs have been identified by folklorists. The characters and plot of the story are described by these commonalities. Whether it is the fragile and beautiful damsel in distress or the sly, deceptive wolf lurking in the forest, the characters are stereotypical. The action or plot of the story may be laced with magic, spells, and enchantment. The problem has no resolution without the magic ingredient, the magic beans, the curse, or the enchanted forest where trees can speak.

The three structures of folktales that appeal most to preschool and kindergarten children are the chained and cumulative tales, such as "The House That Jack Built," the talking animal tales, such as "The Three Billy-Goats Gruff," and the wonder tales, such as "Jack and the Beanstalk." The primary-aged child likes the pourquoi, or "why" tales, such as Aardema's *Why Mosquitoes Buzz in People's Ears* and the noodlehead stories, such as Zemach's *The Three Sillies*.

Figure 5.1 Examples of Motifs in Familiar Folktales for Young Children

Stereotypical Characters
(wicked witches, stepmothers,
fairy godmothers, etc.)

The Long Sleep or Enchantment	*Hansel and Gretel, Sleeping Beauty*
Magic Objects	*Jack and the Beanstalk*
Magic Transformations	*The Frog Prince*
Wishes	*The Three Wishes*
Trickery	*Stone Soup*
Noodlehead	*The Three Sillies*

CHAINED AND CUMULATIVE TALES

One chained tale, which won the Caldecott Medal in 1972, is Nonny Hogrogian's *One Fine Day*, an adaptation of an Armenian folk story. When an old woman put down her pail of milk to gather firewood, a fox came along and drank the milk. The angry old woman chopped off his tail. When the fox begged for his tail back, the old woman told him it would be returned when he

Courtesy of *The Mitten*, published by Putnam.

replaced the milk. And the chain of events that follow are linked back to the fox's quest to regain his tail. He searches for a cow who will give milk to replace the pail he drank, but the cow will not cooperate unless he goes to the field and asks it for some grass, and so the story goes on, chaining one event to the next.

In the cumulative tale, characters are added to the story in each scene and are linked together because of some problem or event. For example, *The Mitten* by Jan Brett is an adaptation of an old Ukranian folktale with numerous animals. In Brett's version, Nicki convinces his grandmother to make him some snowwhite mittens. She reluctantly agrees but warns him that they will be difficult to find if they are lost in the snowy woods. The tale is the story of what became of the mitten when animals from the forest crawled inside to keep warm.

In an earlier version of *The Mitten* by Alvin Tresselt, illustrated by Yaroslava, the mittens are yellow, edged with fur, and lined with red wool. The mitten is lost while the grandson is out gathering firewood, and the animals are different also.

Animals are often involved in cumulative tales and sometimes come to the rescue of their human friends. For example in *The Mouse and the Potato*, a farmer grows an enormous potato, but he can't pull it out of the ground. Finally a little mouse adds himself onto the long line of "pullers" and the huge potato explodes from the ground, leave all topsy-turvy. The farmer's wife cooks a huge plate of potato scones for the hungry family and their helpers (Raines & Canady, 1991, p. 94).

Quite often the cumulative tale is one of some enormous vegetable or fruit. From the Russian, Tolstoy collected the peasant tale of *The Great Big Enormous Turnip*. According to Catherine Storr (1986), it is thought that many of the enormous food folktales originated because the peasants and common folk were preoccupied with hunger, with finding enough to eat, and someday having their hunger satisfied beyond belief.

TALKING ANIMAL TALES

The Three Little Pigs, *The Three Bears*, *The Three Billy-Goats Gruff* not only have the commonality of "three-ness" prevalent in many folktales, but they are also examples of talking animals that have human voices. "Three-ness" helps the young child remember the tale, as there are three main events in each story: three bowls of porridge, three chairs, and three beds—one for each of the three bears.

Talking animal stories continue to be popular throughout the early childhood years. Kindergartners and first graders like *The Little Red Hen*. The familiar version by Paul Galdone is one of the most used folktales in the early childhood curriculum. When the Little Red Hen solicits help from the cat, the dog, and the mouse to plant a few grains of wheat, the animals reply, "Not I." She continues to ask their help to tend the wheat, cut the grain, mill the flour, and bake the cake. The children chime in at the refrain from each of the animals who reply, "Not I," to the Little Red Hen's requests. Finally, when Little Red Hen bakes the cake, all the animals want to help her eat it, but she eats it all by herself. Of course, as with any good folktale, there is a lesson to be learned. From that day forward, whenever "there was work to be done, the Little Red Hen had three very eager helpers."

Courtesy of *The Little Red Hen*, published by Houghton Mifflin.

WONDER OR TRANSFORMATION TALES

Magical objects, curses, spells, and wishes are the vehicles for transformations to occur in folktales, classified as wonder tales. Whether with Jack's beans, the spell cast on Sleeping Beauty, or the Fisherman and his Wife's three wishes, magical transformations take place. Transformation tales are a part of the folk literature of many cultures.

From the sea islands off the coast of South Carolina, the African-American tale of *Sukey and the Mermaid* is retold by Robert San Souci, with scratchboard and oil pastel illustrations by Brian Pinkney. Sukey, a young woman, seems doomed to a life of drudgery by a mean "step-pa" until she meets a beautiful black mermaid, named Mama Jo. While Mama Jo offers riches and escape, it is Sukey's kindness that rewards her with the love of a husband and her mother.

Wonder and transformation tales are the stories of ordinary humans or humanlike animals who are transformed because of their extraordinary kindness, or for rising to an unexpected challenge, or are rescued from their plight by true love. Other wonder tales are the stories of seemingly foolish people, like Jack and his magic beans, who redeem themselves by accomplishing some daring feat and ending with a pot of gold. The illusive pot of gold and unexpected riches befalling the poor are also a part of the folktale tradition.

POURQUOI TALES

Pourquoi tales frequently include the word *why* in their titles to explain why animals look and act as they do, why the world of nature exists as it does, or why particular customs have been adopted (Huck, Hepler, & Hickman, 1993, p. 240). Many African cultures include tales of why animals look and behave as they do. For example, Sandra Robbins' *How the Turtle Got Its Shell*, told with African animals, will appeal to children because of the story and the unusual Swahili phrases. The well-known *Why Mosquitoes Buzz in People's Ears* by Verna Aardema won the Caldecott Medal in 1976 for Leo and Diane Dillon, the illustrators.

TRICKSTERS IN FOLK LITERATURE

The trickster is common in folktales from numerous cultures. In African tales, Anansi, the spider, plans to outwit others, but in the end is often outwitted. For example, in a recent Anansi tale, *Anansi Goes Fishing*, retold by Eric A. Kimmel, "Anansi the spider plans to trick Turtle into catching a fish for his dinner, but Turtle proves to be smarter and ends up with a free meal. The tale explains the origin of the spider webs through the creation of a fishing net." (Kimmel, 1992)

Another popular Anansi tale is Gerald McDermott's *Anansi the Spider: A Tale From the Ashanti*, which tells why the moon is in the sky. The Anansi tales were brought to America and other countries by African people when they were slaves.

Brer Rabbit is an African-American version of the trickster character. While there are many versions of the Brer Rabbit stories, such as Julius Lester's *The Tales of Uncle Remus: The Adventures of Brer Rabbit,* they are best reserved for older students. There are some tales that have been rewritten and can be appreciated by the older second and third graders. Priscilla Jacquith's *Bo Rabbit Smart for True: Folktales from the Gullah* have the storyteller language of repeated phrases and humor that amuse young children.

In Native-American folktales, the trickster may be the coyote or the raven. *Quail Song,* told by Valeria Scho Carey, is a Pueblo tale about the innocent-looking quail who outwits the coyote. In a collection of stories from Emerson and David Coatsworth, *The Adventures of Nanabush: Ojibway Indian Stories,* Nanabush is the trickster. Most of the stories are appropriate for kindergarten through third grade; however, a few require more abstract thought and are best reserved for older elementary students.

TALL TALES AND LEGENDARY FIGURES

When Americans think of tall tales, immediately Paul Bunyan and Pecos Bill come to mind. These tales were conceived around the campfire or the logging camp and were meant to entertain: The heroes never lived. As legend has it, *Pecos Bill,* (Dewey) was a Texan who was raised by coyotes. When he grew up, he met a cowboy named Curly Joe, and that is when his adventures began. He tamed a rattlesnake and made a lasso out of it, rode a mountain lion, captured outlaws, lassoed eagles in flight, and roped entire herds of cattle, to name only a few of Pecos Bill's adventures.

Some of the legendary figures in tall tales are based on real people who once lived but whose exploits have become so exaggerated that they have become tall tales. Some historical figures who have become legends are Daniel Boone, Johnny Appleseed, and Davy Crockett. Until recently, few of the stories of these legendary figures were written with young children in mind, although the tall tale by its nature contains the exaggeration, humor, and fantasy, which appeal to the young listener and reader. One of the recent tall tale books is another one by Ariane Dewey, *The Narrow Escapes of Davy Crockett.*

Other tall tale and legendary figures include John Henry, "a steel driving man," and Mike Fink, a river man who knew every twist and turn

---

Figure 5.2 Folktale Types for the Early Childhood Classroom

Cumulative tales	*The House That Jack Built*
	Henny Penny
Talking animal tales	*The Three Little Pigs*
	The Three Billy-Goats Gruff
Wonder tales	*Jack and the Beanstalk* (magic objects)
	Sleeping Beauty (magic spells)
	The Frog Prince (magical transformation)
Pourquoi tales	*Why Mosquitoes Buzz in People's Ears*
	Why the Sun and the Moon Live in the Sky
Noodlehead stories	*The Three Sillies*
	The Twelve Clever Brothers and Other Fools

on the "mighty Mississippi." Recently, we read Sandra Robbin's tall tale about an African-American woman, *Big Anne*, a flatboat captain who sang to children along the riverbanks and who, on one fateful day, delivered presents to the children when one of the big ships could not get through because of a storm. The tall tale is based on a Creole women who lived in New Orleans (Robbins, 1990).

Noodlehead Tales

Noodlehead tales, because of their different humor, do not appeal to preschoolers and kindergartners, but are enjoyed by some primary-aged children. As children begin to develop more logical thought, they delight in pointing out the foolish decisions, silly consequences, and irrational thoughts of these characters. Many cultures have noodlehead tales, fool stories, or blundering simpleton characters. *The Three Sillies*, illustrated by Margot Zemach, is a tale of a man who searches for three people sillier than his future in-laws.

Fables

Like many stories in folk literature, fables have morals, except that in the fable the moral is explicitly stated. Aesop's fables, attributed to a Greek slave, are short didactic tales specifically told to illustrate the moral. Most of Aesop's fables are about animals. The plot is simple, the characters few, and the resolution of the problem and the moral are clear.

Preschool and kindergarten children enjoy Aesop's story of "The Hare and The Tortoise" and understand the moral that the sure and steady win the race. While young children may lack the language and abstract thought process possible to state the implications of the moral, they can still enjoy the story. However, it is important to point out that preschoolers, kindergartners, and many young primary-grade children should not be expected to understand the satire and generalize a moral.

After hearing their teacher read John Wallner's *City Mouse—Country Mouse and Two More Mouse Tales from Aesop*, the children were asked which fable they liked best. The other two tales were "The Lion and the Mouse," in which a tiny mouse befriends a huge lion by gnawing through the hunter's ropes, and "Belling the Cat," in which clever mice device a plan to put a bell on the cat so they can hear her coming. All the children preferred the story of the City Mouse—Country Mouse. Few could explain why, but instead related the story to times when they had visited the country.

Many of the common fables require more sophisticated levels of thought in order to interpret them. Therefore, preschoolers, kindergartners, and first-grade children tend to like the story for the animals or for the action. The story quality is more important than the moral it is supposed to teach. Older second and third graders are able to interpret some of the meanings of the fables by writing their own versions. One teacher read "The Boy Who Cried Wolf" and the children were asked to write modern versions that applied to their lives. Interestingly, the children were able to write from various accounts of tattling on their siblings, acting seriously hurt when they were not, and asking for help just to get attention, clear inferences derived from the results of crying wolf too often.

Early childhood teachers associate some of the best fable collections by the illustrators who are popular for other picture books, such as Paul Galdone, Eric Carle, Alice and Martin Provensen, Ed Young, and James Marshall. Their books have illustrations of the ancient tales, and are sometimes rewritten in a simpler form or dressed-up with dialogue and interesting prose.

Myths and Legends

Myths are stories meant to explain the creation of the world and nature. Greek and Norse myths are not appropriate literature for the early years, but fit better with upper elementary students. However, some of the Native-American and African myths and legends about creation, natural phenomena, and tales of why animals look

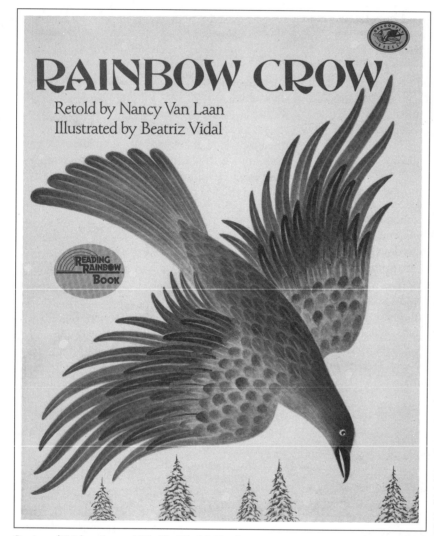

RAINBOW CROW

Retold by Nancy Van Laan
Illustrated by Beatriz Vidal

Courtesy of *Rainbow Crow,* published by Alfred A. Knopf.

the story is told of how birds and animals came to earth. Jerrie Oughton tells the Navajo legend that explains the stars in *How the Stars Fell Into the Sky.* (See Elleman, 1992 for additional Native American references.)

Rainbow Crow is an example of a Native-American tale that explains how fire came to earth and how the crow came to be black. The story, retold my Nancy Van Laan, is an adaptation of the "Lenape tribe's legend of the fire bearer, as told by Elder Bill 'Whippoorwill' Thompson. Crow was once a beautiful bird with rainbow-colored feathers who rescued the forest animals from a snowstorm by bringing fire to earth to melt the snow. In the process of bringing the fire from the Great Spirit, Rainbow Crow's feathers were burned and blackened" (Van Laan, p. 172). Beatriz Vidal's bright, colorful, full-page illustrations of *Rainbow Crow* are magnificent.

The Story of Light, a retelling of a Cherokee myth by Susan Roth, explains how Spider brought the sun to the animals on earth. Tomie dePaola's *The Legend of the Indian Paintbrush* is an example of a tale meant to explain how this flower, which grows so profusely in Texas and Wyoming, came to be. Little Gopher is a young Plains Indian who paints pictures of the hills and meadows. While Little Gopher has a great talent as a

and behave as they do are appropriate choices to read to young children.

Cultures close to nature include tales of how animals look and about how the world and its natural phenomena came to be. A recent book by Kristina Rodanas, *Dragonfly's Tale,* is a Zuni legend about respecting nature and all creatures. Many Native-American tales explain how the earth and the life inhabiting it came to be. In Bierhorst's *Ring in the Prairie: A Shawnee Legend,*

Courtesy of *Bringing the Rain to Kapiti Plain,* published by Dial.

More than seventy years ago, Sir Claud Hollis, a famous anthropologist camped near a Nadi village in Kenya. He published a version of the story in 1909. It is reported that he learned many folktales from the Chief Medicine Man and from the Nandi children. (Aardema, 1981).

SONGS AS FOLK LITERATURE

Part of the legacy of literature originating in the oral form is the folk song. Songs were invented and passed down from one generation to the next to make the work go faster, to entertain after the work was done, or to teach simple concepts. Because of the rhythm and rhyme, the songs are easy to remember and are also quite appropriate for the young child.

painter, he is small and wishes he could be like the other children and learn to hunt and be brave. As a reward for staying true to his talent, Little Gopher's paintbrushes become the Indian Paintbrush flowers, which emblazon the countryside every spring, and his people rename him He-Who-Brought-the-Sunset-to-the-Earth.

African tales also speak often of natural phenomena and explain how some young innocents come to the rescue. For example, Verna Aardema's *Bringing the Rain to Kapiti Plain* is a Nandi tale from Kenya. The bright full-color illustrations by Beatriz Vidal and the rhyming pattern with repeated phrases make it irresistible to young listeners and readers. Ki-pat is a herdsman who watches his cows go hungry and thirsty because there is no rain to make the grass grow. When a huge cloud shadows the ground and it still does not rain, Ki-pat makes an arrow from an eagle feather and shoots it into the cloud. It rains.

On an information page about the book, there is a description of how the tale was discovered.

Lullabies, songs with actions, rhymes for the seasons, and songs for chores are a part of our cultural tradition from the past. Jane Hart collected and Anita Lobel illustrated *Singing Bee!: A Collection of Favorite Children's Songs,* which includes 125 songs, many of which originate in folk literature.

Songs with lively actions, played as group participation, are also a part of the musical literature. Many songs from the English include "Pop! Goes the Weasel," "The Farmer in the Dell," "Ring Around A Rosy," "The Mulberry Bush," and "Go Round and Round the Village." Many of these popular old musical songs continue to be childhood favorites for their actions, and teach young children to listen and take turns.

Other folk songs for children are of the American tradition, such as the animal songs, "Go Tell Aunt Rhody" about the choice goose, and "Old

MacDonald Had a Farm" in which children learn animal names and the sounds they make. Then there are the railroad songs, such as "She'll Be Coming Around the Mountain" and "Working on the Railroad."

Some of the songs were meant to instruct the young and make the task of remembering easier. For example, the counting songs, "Roll Over" and "Five Little Chickadees" are very popular in preschool and kindergarten classes. Another favorite is "Over in the Meadow," which uses numbers, associates animals' actions, their homes, and colors in a playful rhyme:

"Over in the meadow, in the sand, in the sun, Lived an old mother frog and her little froggie one" (Hart, 1982, p. 44).

Many of the folk songs tell stories, such as the American version of "The Bear Went Over the Mountain." Song versions of the popular nursery rhymes are a natural accompaniment to reading the Mother Goose verses. There are musical versions of many of Mother Goose's popular rhymes, such as "Sing a Song of Sixpence," "Mistress Mary," "Jack and Jill," and "Hickory Dickory Dock."

Fairy Tales as Folk Literature

Folktales include fairy tales; however, as teachers and parents we think of fairy tales as a separate category. We recall our childhood dreams of Cinderella's evening at the beautiful ball. We look with sympathy on the princess who has been cheated of her rightful throne. We are amazed that one ugly frog could be magically transformed to one so handsome. As Catherine Storr stated, "Folk stories are fables of the effort to remain alive. Fairy tales are fables, myths, if you like, of the struggle to become human, to attain a unique identity, to attain the stature of an individual." (1986, p. 66). There is romance and adventure in the saga of the humble person becoming a prince

or a princess, of a great journey to slay the dragon, or some daring proof to show that the peasant is the rightful heir to the throne.

Interestingly, as Storr points out, the fairy tale is about the younger generation. (1986, p. 66). It is the story of the new princess, the chance to win the daughter's hand in marriage, and the hero's claim to a better land. It is about the young going out into the world to prove themselves.

Fairy tales are also of the wonder-tale type and are populated with royalty and magical objects, spells and curses that transform people and animals, and enchanted places where all these happenings become possible. The fairy tale is set in a distant land and a distant time, unidentifiable. In some ways, the fairy tale is like the modern soap opera. It is about the people of power falling on hard times and the common people finding great riches and power.

A child of today may enjoy fairy tales from many cultures. The French "Cinderella" and the German "Snow White" are perhaps the best known of the fairy tales. Many variations of the classic fairy tales have been identified in other cultures. There are numerous versions of "Sleeping Beauty" and "Beauty and the Beast," including the recent Disney movie, which retold the story in yet another medium. The fairy tale with the most variations appears to be the rags-to-riches story of Cinderella. *Yeh-shen* by Ai-Ling Louie, illustrations by Ed Young, is the Chinese version of "Cinderella." The Cinderella story also appears in Native-American tales. Rafe's *The Rough-Face Girl* is a Cinderella tale from the Algonquins.

Cinderella-type tales of the poor mistreated little sister who is made to work while another sister or sisters enjoy their leisure, can be found in the American South. One such tale, *The Talking Eggs*, is retold by Robert D. San Souci, with illustrations by Jerry Pinkney. The story varies in that there is only one sister and the riches are provided by talking eggs and a haggard old woman. In the end, Blanche, the good sister goes off to live with her riches in the city and her mother and sister Rose are doomed to wander the woods always searching, but never finding, the talking eggs. The impressive tale is thought to have been brought to Louisiana by French émigrés, but Cajun and Gullah variations have also been heard in the rural South. *The Talking Eggs* was a Caldecott Honor Book for Jerry Pinkney's illustrations and also won the Coretta Scott King Award for nonviolent social change.

For a most intriguing look at Cinderella stories, see *Cinderella: A Case Casebook,* edited by Alan Dundes for essays on the story from many cultures and time periods (1983). Also, it is intriguing to read some of Marian Roalfe Cox reviews of the 345 variations of the Cinderella theme (1983). For a critical look at stereotyping in fairy tales, read *Womenfolk and Fairy Tales* (Minard, 1975).

Modern illustrations and retold versions of *Cinderella* have met with much acclaim. Marcia Brown's rendition won the Caldecott Award in 1955. For the early childhood years, we recommend Susan Jeffers' illustrations in the *Cinderella* story edited by Amy Ehrlich. Since the original fairy tales collected by Perrault in France and the Grimm Brothers in Germany contained a great deal of violence, later versions have been rewritten to fit different audiences. Because folk literature is based on the oral tradition of the storyteller who takes the structure and jest of the story and tells his or her own version, it is thought by many that the author's liberties are appropriate for the genre.

PASSING ON OUR LITERARY HERITAGE

We, as teachers, hold in our hands, this beautiful, ornately cast and decorated key of stories from past. They are beautiful, but they are weighty in our hands. If we are to link our learners to literature, we must use this ancient key from the past and unlock the power of old tales to connect the learner and literature.

MODERN LITERARY TALES OF FANTASY AND FOLKLIKE LITERATURE

To return to our key analogy, the folk literature is represented by the heavy old brass key, but the modern fantasy is represented by rather ordinary looking keys. Just as the printing press changed the

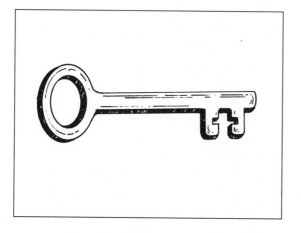

mold of the story form from the oral tradition to that of the written word, the key changed as well. A modern stamping machine began pressing out modern versions of keys, just as the printing press began pressing out modern versions of stories, which resembled the old, but had a form of their own. Whether the heavy ornately cast keys of the past or the modern stamped metal keys of today, one's shape influenced the other. They are still key-shaped.

Like the folktales and fantasy of the past, today's works derive their story shape in much the same form as the tales of old. There are modern folktales of persons with extraordinary abilities, talking animals, trickster tales, magical experiences, and stories of kindness, goodness, and persevering against great odds. The folktale-type, the cumulative tale, the magical object or event story, the animals who tell stories, and the literature based on song are written by authors who understand what interests young children—but mostly they tell a good story.

FAIRY TALES ORIGINATING IN PRINT

Fairy tales that first appeared in literary form, such as Hans Christian Andersen's stories, have the flavor of the old folk literature, but they do not fit the definition of folktales because they originated in the written form first (Huck, Hepler, & Hickman, 1993, p. 48). The literary tale, versus the folk fairy tale, has become so much a part of the culture that it is difficult for many people to separate them. Hans Christian Andersen adopted a style of writing that made the tale sound like the folk stories from the oral tradition. This same pattern and illustrative language continues today in the modern fantasy of many writers.

Many of the Hans Christian Andersen tales are part of the literary heritage of fantasy that young children savor. Much like the folktale, the fantasy story often reinforces values we hold dear, such as the appreciation of a thing of beauty in *The Nightingale,* the truth as seen by a child in *The Emperor's New Clothes,* or the triumph of even a small boy who has courage in *Tom Thumb.*

Hans Christian Andersen's literary tales mark the beginning of modern fantasy. Yet, modern fantasy contains more than the fairy-tale-type story. Stewig separates fantasy into simple fantasy, literary folktales, stories about animals with special abilities, unearthly creatures, people with special abilities, toys and dolls, magical objects, trips through time and space, changes in size, transformations, and conflicts with evil powers (1988, p. 523-562). As one can easily read from the categories, many of the features of a good fantasy story are comparable to the ones in good folk literature.

The early childhood educator who has read widely from the vast array of children's literature recognizes that some of the classics and favorite stories are of the fantasy genre. Some of the best writers indulge their imaginations and we are the recipients of their creativity. Beatrix Potter's *Peter Rabbit* and E. B. White's *Charlotte's Web* have main characters who are talking animals. Margery Williams' *The Velveteen Rabbit* is the story of a magical transformation from a toy stuffed rabbit to a real one. Other fantasy stories of later publication have become a part of the popular literature of this genre. They include talking elephants, *The Story of Babar* (DeBrunhoff), talking teddy bears, *Paddington the Bear* (Bond), and even a talking donkey in *Sylvester and the Magic Pebble* (Steig). Perhaps it is because these stories contain some of the magical quality of the old tales that we remember them so fondly.

The world of make-believe so often associated with young children and their play fits appropriately with the world of fantasy in literature. According to Stewig, "in writing fantasy, authors must create characters, setting, and action that are so interesting that the reader (or listener in the case of the young child) is willing to suspend disbelief and enter the world presented" [1988, p. 507]. The fantasy story is charmed with language, style, setting, and characters that, despite their imaginary worlds, meet some undeniable needs. We long for the happy ending, for courage to tackle the seemingly insurmountable task, and for the peace of the well-

The years passed and other koalas were born — brothers and sisters for Koala Lou. Soon her mother was so busy she didn't have time to tell Koala Lou that she loved her.

Although of course she did.

Courtesy of *Koala Lou*, published by Harcourt Brace Jovanovich.

ordered kingdom. The child's fantasy world is also a world of the sensory imagination. Whether smelling the distinctive odor of Wilbur the pig's barnyard in *Charlotte's Web*, hearing the trains whistle in Paddington's stories, or seeing the gilded mechanical bird in *The Nightingale*, they are vivid sensory experiences.

The types of fantasy stories that are particularly appealing to young children are those with talking animals, magic and transformations, and small worlds. Talking animals who have humanlike traits are popular and capture the hearts and imaginations of the young. The classic ones, such as Wilbur and Charlotte in *Charlotte's Web* and Peter Rabbit and his brothers and sisters in *The Tales of Peter Rabbit*, live in a world of animals and people. Wilbur the Pig's barnyard is a part of the Arable family farm and Peter Rabbit's burrow is near Mr. MacGregor's garden.

In many talking animal fantasies, the stories are set in jungles, fields, and farms. One of the most famous fantasies is Rudyard Kipling's *The Jungle Book*, influenced by tales from India. The alliterative language and the unusual animals in Kipling's *Just*

So Stories are very entertaining. Many of the tales are pourquoi tales, such as "How the Leopard Got His Spots." The popularity of the funny animal story, which Rudyard Kipling made famous, continues today. A recent one is *"Stand Back," Said the Elephant, "I'm Going to Sneeze!"* by Patricia Thomas.

In some modern stories, the animals' world is fraught with common human problems. *Koala Lou* by Mem Fox is a fantasy story of a child koala living in a family with younger brothers and sisters. Koala Lou is her mother's delight and tells her often by saying, "Koala Lou, I do love you." But when Koala Lou's mother has other babies, she is too busy to notice every little thing that Koala Lou does. Koala Lou decides the one best way to get her mother's attention is to win one of the games in the Bush Olympics.

Attempting some great feat to win approval is an old theme in folk stories from both past and modern children's literature. Animals who want their mothers to tell them they love them, sibling rivalry, wondering if one will have a friend—the problems are human, but the stories are from the mouths of the talking animals.

Courtesy of *Anatole*, published by Bantam.

Another of the talking animal type of story is "the animal with special abilities." A popular example is Beverly Cleary's *The Mouse and the Motorcycle,* in which the mouse talks only to the child in the story:

While on a vacation trip, Keith's toy motorcycle becomes a real motorcycle for Ralph, the mouse. Their attempt to keep the secret from the people and the mice in the story leads to intrigue. Ralph, usually a timid mouse, feels very brave riding the motorcycle. He has his bravery tested when he risks his life to deliver an aspirin to Keith's room and saves the boy from the ravages of a high fever (Raines & Canady, 1992, p. 114).

The first story of *The Mouse and the Motorcycle* was so successful, Beverly Cleary continued the adventure and Ralph starred in other books.

The plot of a small animal with special abilities coming to the rescue of the humans is part of the fascination of the *Anatole* tales by Eve Titus. *Anatole* is the story of a little mouse who secretly earns his keep by becoming the taster in a cheese factory.

TRICKSTERS

In modern literature, the trickster continues to play a role. Talking animals who trick one another or who attempt to trick innocent people are motifs that the modern writer has borrowed from the past. Kindergarten and primary children will enjoy Patricia McKissack's *A Million Fish . . . More or Less,* which is a fishing story from the Bayou Clapateaux in Louisiana. The main character is a little boy who enjoys listening to the exaggerated fishermen's tales. When something extraordinary happens to him, catching a million fish, more or less, Hugh meets several animal tricksters who trick him out of his fish.

Primary-grade children like the humor in *Little Tricker the Squirrel Meets Big Double the Bear* by Ken Kesey, with equally amusing illustrations by Barry Moser. Little Tricker the Squirrel meets a big hungry bear roaming the Ozark Mountains. Complete with a chant, "I'm honnngry. I ate the high hills raw and the foothills bare and now I'm going to Eat! You! Up!," Big Double terrorizes all the little animals until he meets Little Tricker the Squirrel.

MAGIC AND TRANSFORMATIONS

Another type of modern fantasy that children think delightful contains magic. Magical objects, curses, spells, or magical transformations add to the suspense and intrigue of the story. For example, both the appearance of a magical object and a transformation take place in William Steig's *Sylvester and the Magic Pebble.* In a moment of fright, Sylvester, a donkey, asks his magic pebble to turn him into a rock, which it does. Now the question is, How can he wish himself back into his own shape again? This well-loved Caldecott Medal winner has a happy and affectionate ending.

A modern fantasy book that involves the listener or reader suspending belief is that of a magic hat, *Rembrandt's Beret or the Painter's Crown* by Johnny Alcorn. While a little girl's grandfather is painting her portrait, she stares at a Rembrandt painting of a child in a beret with a feather. She thinks the boy has the same eyes as her grandfather. While she poses, Grandfather tells her a story about when he was a little boy and the famous paintings in the museum came to

Courtesy of *Rembrandt's Beret,* published by Tambourine Books.

life. Cleverly written and masterfully painted, the story's mystery, secrets and adventure let children imaginatively enter the world of art (Raines & Canady, 1992, p. 190).

Not all the magic in stories happens with magical objects such as Sylvester's pebble or Rembrandt's beret. Magic also happens by some strange event occurring in seemingly ordinary households. Take for example *Flat Stanley* by Jeff Brown, illustrated by Tomi Ungerer, a terrifically silly adventure that lures the young listener and reader into imaginary possibilities: One night while Stanley is sleeping, a huge bulletin board falls on him. When he awakes, he is flat.

Transformations in fantasy stories can also take place by wishing, but one has to be careful what is wished for, it just might come true: *The Fish Who Could Wish* by John Bush and Korky Paul is an excellent example. Told in rhyme, this is the story of a magic fish who gets anything he wishes for—a castle, a car, snow under the sea, and a number of other funny and unexpected wishes for a fish.

PARODIES AND FRACTURED FAIRY TALES

As a part of the movement to help little girls recognize that they do not have to wait for some handsome prince to rescue them, several parodies of fairy tales, often call fractured fairy tales, have been written, such as *Prince Cinders* by Babette Cole and *Sleeping Ugly* by Jane Yolen. Parodies and the levels of comparative thought required are best reserved for the older elementary child. The only exceptions we recommend for the preschool and primary child are those very simple ones based on stories the children know well, such as the recent book by Jon Scieszka, *The True Story of the Three Little Pigs,* told from the wolf's perspective. Also, the children understand the wordless picture book of the reverse

Courtesy of *Jim and the Beanstalk*, published by Coward-McCann.

Courtesy of *Tom Thumb*, published by Harcourt Brace Jovanovich.

story of the Three Bears, *Deep in the Forest* by Brinton Turkle. Primary children also enjoy Raymond Brigg's tale of *Jim and the Beanstalk* in which Jim befriends an aging giant by cooking for him and even making him some false teeth. Steve Johnson's illustrations in the recent parody *The Frog Prince Continued* is a comedic delight for the story written by Jon Scieszka. For example, even after the frog becomes a prince, he still can not control his appetite for flies.

SMALL WORLDS

The small world is a place of fantasy in which the magic of elves, brownies, fairies, and tiny children have great adventures. Two of the most famous tales of small worlds are by Hans Christian Andersen: "Thumbelina," about a girl who is only one inch tall, and "Tom Thumb," a boy who is no bigger than his father's thumb. A recent publication of *Tom Thumb*

was retold and illustrated by Richard Jesse Watson. The magnificent tempera and watercolor illustrations have exciting perspectives and display the fantasy world of elves, knights, and frightening ravens, and show Tom's bravery, wit, and heroic deeds. In modern fantasy, E. B. White's *Stuart Little* is also captivating. "Stuart, born with the size and shape of a mouse but with a boy's sense of mischief and ingenuity, delights young readers with his frequently dangerous adventures [Shelton, 1989, p. 48]."

The small world is also where the forces of nature live. A 1906 German tale retold by Sibylle von Offers, *The Story of the Root Children,* is about the coming and going of spring. In the spring, the root children awaken, sew their new capes, paint the beetles and bugs in pastel colors, and dance in a procession as Mother Earth opens the door into the sunshine.

Many of Joanne Ryder's books published in the last two decades also take children into a small world and help them imagine what it would be like to be a tiny animal. In *The Snail's Spell,* the little child imagines being a tiny snail, exploring the plants in the garden. In *Chipmunk Song*, the beautiful pictures are scenes from nature with a little child imagining the life of a chipmunk.

TOYS AND DOLLS

Fantasy stories with talking toys and dolls excite young listeners and readers. In the classic Milne's *Winnie-the-Pooh*, while Winnie is drawn as a toy bear, he has desires like real bears. For example, he will do most anything for a pot of honey, which often lands him in some undesirable circumstances. Once, he spent several days stuck in Rabbit's front door because he ate so much honey.

Jane Hissey's teddy-bears-come-to-life stories have a great deal of appeal for read-aloud selections and for recording on tapes for a listening station. The story of *Little Bear's Trousers* is inventive and hilarious. Throughout the day different toys use Little Bear's trousers for a variety of purposes. Another Jane Hissey teddy bear story is *Old Bear*, in which a group of toy animals try various inventive ways of rescuing Old Bear from the attic.

Famous Writers Continue Popular Features From the Past

Let's look at some of the famous modern writers popular in today's classrooms and associate them with the characteristics of some of the best folk and fantasy literature from the past. Authors of today write cumulative tales, which rely on prediction, talking animal tales, modern fables, magical transformations, and modern fantasy worlds, and use rhymes and chants to tell the story or teach a concept.

From folk literature we have cumulative tales, which allow the child to predict what will happen next. The author chains the characters together to solve some problem; continues adding characters for the main character to invite to join a journey; or connects the characters by a repeated set of actions with each new encounter. Today's writers have developed a number of prediction devices that allow the young listener or reader to predict what will happen next in the story and to grasp the structure of the story.

So you run—
dashing quickly
   stopping here
      stopping there
looking for food
watching for danger.
You are fast—
leaping over a rock
scooting under a bush
where the last
bright berries hang.
You stretch up high
to eat the sweet berries,
grasping each one
in your furry paws.

Courtesy of *The Chipmunk Song*, published by E.P. Dutton.

And on that dog
there is a cat,
a snoozing cat
on a dozing dog
on a dreaming child
on a snoring granny
on a cozy bed
in a napping house,
where everyone is sleeping.

Courtesy of *The Napping House*, published by Harcourt Brace Jovanovich.

AUTHORS' USE OF PREDICTION

The predictable tale, which help the child feel the structure of the story and allow the child to participate because of the repetition, is a device folk literature used and today's authors manipulate so skillfully. Prediction can be based on repeating characters, as in Audrey Wood's *The Napping House*, having characters join one another on a journey, as in Eric Carle's *Rooster's Off to See the World*, or having the main character interact with each new encounter in the same way as in Marjorie Flack's *Ask Mr. Bear*.

Audrey Wood's *The Napping House*, illustrated by Don Wood, is an excellent example of a chaining tale, where one character and action is linked to the next. The winner of the New York Times Best Illustrated Children's Book Award, the story is of a "snoring granny on a cozy bed in a napping house, where everyone is sleeping." She is soon joined in the bed by a "dreaming child" followed by a "dozing dog" and a "snoozing cat," and so the story continues repeating itself until the end when a "wakeful flee" ends the nap.

Eric Carle is a masterful writer who creates stories young children enjoy for the action, their animal characters, the marvelously bright illustrations, and because his tales, like folktales of the past, are constructed in ways that make them easy for the young child to remember. In *Rooster's Off to See the World*, Carle spins another delightful journey tale which is as enticing visually as it is dramatically. One rooster in his vibrantly colored plumage decides to take a trip around the world and invites two cats, three frogs, four turtles, and five fish to join him. Carle uses two prediction devices most effectively, in that Rooster interacts with each character in the same way, thus allowing the children to predict what Rooster will say and do. In addition, the use of counting helps the children to make predictions.

Ask Mr. Bear by Marjorie Flack has been popular for a number of decades. "Danny is trying to

Courtesy of *Rooster's Off to See the World,* published by Picture Book Studio.

Courtesy of *Ask Mr. Bear,* published by Macmillan.

find the perfect birthday present for his mother. He consults with several of his animal friends for their suggestions. The hen offers him some eggs; the goose some feathers; and the sheep some wool. But Danny's mother already has those things. Then the cow sends Danny to ask Mr. Bear for a suggestion. The wonderful gift Mr. Bear suggests is one that only Danny can give [Raines & Canady, 1989, p. 48]."

Teachers can count on patterned language books working with the children because, through prediction, the child becomes engaged with the text. From research on children's book interests, we know that, when given a choice of books, young children will select books to read and look at that the teacher has read aloud to the class. Among these, the most popular ones are the patterned language books, the predictable books, which allow the listeners to join in with the teacher reading

because there is some recurring phrase, or cumulative pattern of characters who are repeated; therefore, the children can predict what will come next (Martinez & Teale, 1988). Patterned language books, or predictable books, are confidence builders for young readers, because they enable the children to approach the text with confidence, knowing that she or he can read it.

TODAY'S AUTHORS OF ANIMAL TALES

Talking animals who conveyed many of life's lessons were used most effectively in the oral tradition of folk literature. Robert Kraus is a modern writer whose stories are excellent examples of animal tales with humanlike traits and humanlike problems. In most of Robert Kraus's stories, the narrator tells the tale. In the three described as follows, Jose and Ariane Aruego illustrate the stories in their inimitable style—colorful, almost cartoonlike. Preschool and kindergarten children enjoy hearing the Robert Kraus stories read aloud and beginning readers select the stories as some of their first reading books.

Every early childhood teacher who deals with parents' concerns knows and appreciates *Leo, the Late Bloomer*. The tiger family members act like humans, and father is worried about Leo who seems to be late in everything he does, including talking and drawing. Mother encourages Leo's father to be patient because Leo is simply a late bloomer. Finally, Leo's father quits watching Leo so closely and Leo blooms.

Tigers seem unlikely candidates for human stories, but Herman, the Octopus, is an even more unlikely subject in *Herman, the Helper*. Herman lives in the sea and the characters are sea animals, but their traits are human. Herman likes being a helper to everyone and glows in the independence of being able to also help himself.

Other authors are famous for writing stories with animals who actually talk and convey their own stories. Many of them are so humanlike that children often forget that the characters are animals. Kevin Henkes' characters are mice, but they live, act, and play like humans. For example, in his story *Chester's Way*, Chester is a mouse with a good friend Wilson:

> *The two are always together and always doing things just alike. They cut their sandwiches in diagonals just alike, double-knot their shoes just alike, even play croquet and baseball just alike. Then when Lilly arrives in the neighborhood, they notice she has her own way of doing things. Chester and Wilson avoid her. They would not even talk with her on the telephone until that fateful day when Lilly came to their rescue and scared away some bigger guys with her scary disguise. After that, Lilly taught Chester and Wilson how to live a more adventuresome life by cutting their sandwiches with cookie cutters, dressing up in disguises and popping wheelies. The three are inseparable—until Victor moves into the neighborhood (Raines & Canady, 1992, p. 52).*

TODAY'S FABLES MEANT TO TEACH

While the fable is an old type of folk literature, it is also a story structure for new tales. Arnold Lobel won the Caldecott Medal in 1982 for Arnold Lobel's *Fables*. The modern fables are entertaining and the morals have a ring of truth. Younger children delight in the funny illustrations and older primary students enjoy the fable and can make the association with the moral. One that children readily grasp is "The Pelican and the Crane," in which Pelican's table manners are atrocious, yet he wonders why no one asks him to come to tea. "King Lion and the Beetle," the story of how a small beetle can bring a mighty king down to his level, has the sound of some of the ancient fables. Children and adults seem to sense there is truth in the last fable of the book, "The Mouse at the Seashore," in which a small mouse leaves his mother and father and sets out to see the sea, only to wish in the end that they were there with him to see the beautiful colors of the sunset.

While not fitting the story form of the ancient Aesop's fables and the modern *Fables* from Lobel, Leo Lionni's *Frederick* is often called a fable. The story quality and the illustrations make it a child and teacher's favorite, but it is the truth at the end of the story that makes the reader think of it as a fable:

> *Frederick, a field mouse, lives with his family in an old stone wall near a deserted barn and granary. While the other field mice are busy in the fall, Frederick sits quietly. When the four mice ask him why he does not work, Frederick tells them he gathers "sun rays for the cold dark winter days." When winter does arrive, Frederick rescues them from the cold, helps them remember the beautiful colors in the meadow, and cures their boredom with his poetry (Raines & Canady, 1989, p. 108).*

MODERN MAGICAL TRANSFORMATIONS

In fantasy of the past, the magical transformation that changed a person or an animal into someone they wanted to become is firmly ingrained

1. A cat-nap in progress. Illustration from *Puss and Boots*.
   Reproduced by permission of Farrar, Straus & Giroux.

2. *Miss Rumphius* admires her
beautiful flower garden.
Reproduced by permission
of Viking Press.

3. Autumn is at its peak in this
illustration from *Where Butterflies
Grow.* Reprinted by permission
of Lodestar.

Tina tended a Tulip for Ursula.

4. These tulips are alive with vibrant color in this excerpt from *Alison's Zinnia*. Reproduced by permission of Greenwillow.

5. The nighttime setting here adds a dream-like mindset. From *Where the Wild Things Are* by Maurice Sendak. Reprinted by permission of Harper & Row.

6. A panoramic view of the garden from the book *The Empty Pot*, courtesy of Little, Brown and Company and Sierra Club Books.

7. The dramatic underlighting creates an intense feeling in this illustration from *Mirette on the Highwire*. Reprinted by permission of Putman.

He'll draw a picture.

8. This illustration shows just what a mouse can do *If You Give a Mouse a Cookie*, courtesy of Harper & Row.

9. Dynamic imagery and painterly style create excellent movement in this illustration from *Rembrandt's Beret,* courtesy of Tambourine.

10. The artist's choice of color gives depth to the already threatening night sky. Illustration from *Roosters Off to See the World* by Eric Carle. Reprinted by permission of Picture Book Studio.

11. Tom Thumb and his forest friends stalk the noble knights. The detail lends
realism to this illustration from *Tom Thumb* by Richard Jesse Watson. Reproduced
with permission of Harcourt Brace Javonovich.

Trainberry
Trackberry
Clickety-clackberry

12. Work is fun on the *Jamberry* train, a book by Degen. Reproduced with permission of Harper & Row.

13. Try to tame these Flying Frogs from *Tuesday*. Illustration courtesy of Clarion.

14. A playful plethora of unicorns break out of
bounds in *Animalia*. Reproduced by permission
of Harry N. Abrams.

At first, his grandmother, Baba, did not want to knit white
mittens.
"If you drop one in the snow," she warned, "you'll never
find it."

But Nicki wanted snow-white mittens, and finally Baba
made them.

15. A handsome young lad from *The Mitten*.
Reprinted with permission of G. P. Putman.

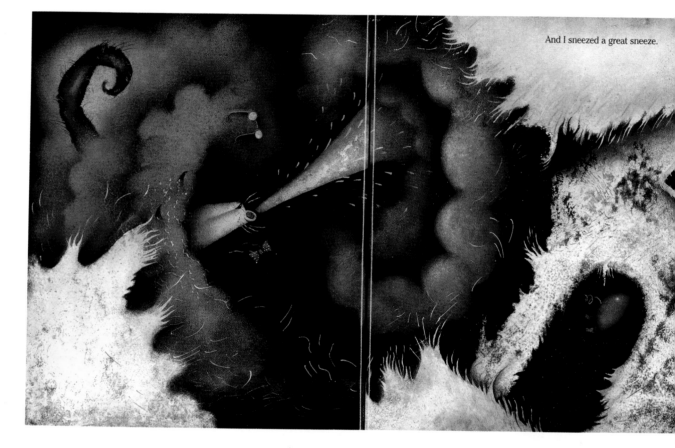

And I sneezed a great sneeze.

16. A hardy gust of wind from the wolf scares the occupants. Illustration from *The True Story of the Three Little Pigs*, courtesy of Viking Kestrel.

17. Christopher Robin and friends. Illustration from *Winnie the Pooh Story Book*.
Reproduced with permission of Dutton Shepherd.

as a plot structure. One of today's writers who uses this same technique most effectively is Eric Carle:

In recognizable Eric Carle style, *The Mixed-up Chameleon* is both a literary and artistically appealing story. When Chameleon envies all the beautiful colors of other animals, he wishes he could be like the animals in other ways, as well. Each time he wishes, Chameleon magically receives a part of the animal, as the deer's antlers, the fish's gills, the flamingo's wings. Growing more absurd looking with each wish, finally Chameleon sees a fly, becomes hungry, and wishes he could be himself again. Magically, he becomes Chameleon and is mixed-up no more (Raines & Canady, 1991, p. 190). Like any good fable, the moral is clear: to appreciate one's own strengths, rather than envying those of others.

FANTASY WORLDS

Few fantasy writers have received as much acclaim as Maurice Sendak, who was awarded

Courtesy of *Frederick*, published by Pantheon.

the Hans Christian Andersen Medal in 1970. Chief in popularity is *Where the Wild Things Are*:

This exciting, yet reassuring tale, has won the author critical acclaim for both text and illustrations, but for the children, it is Max's story. It is the story of a child sent to bed without his supper for making a "smart" remark to his mother. Max dreams a most adventuresome tale of a faraway land where there were wild things. Max was able to tame them by staring into their yellow eyes and then even to enjoy them as playmates in a "wild rumpus." But Max grew hungry and homesick and sailed back through his dreams to awaken to supper on a tray in his room. Maurice Sendak's illustrations in Where the Wild Things Are won the Caldecott Medal in 1964 (Raines & Canady, 1989, p. 164).

Another master at creating the fantasy world is a writer who has not always received critical acclaim (Kaufer, 1991, October). To millions of children and now a generation of adults, Dr. Seuss, Theodor Geisel created entire fantasy worlds, where cats dance with fish bowls on their heads, creatures have funny names like Zooks and Yooks, and a compassionate elephant named Horton sits on an egg high atop a tree. Theodor Geisel captured the imagination and the conscious of children and adults in the much embattled *Butter Battle Book*, in the television production of *How the Grinch Stole Christmas*, and in his promise to all who are young and any who seek their fortunes in *Oh, the Places You'll Go*. From the innocent phrases of *The Cat in the Hat*, which many adults and children cite as the first book read without an adult's assistance, to the provocative *Butter Battle Book*, a "metaphorical depiction of the nuclear arms race" (Carlsson-Paige & Levin, 1986, p. 37), Dr. Seuss's stories have entertained, taught, and provoked moral discussions. Seuss has accumulated a number of detractors and supporters (Dow & Slaughter, 1989; Van Cleaf & Martin, 1986); however, children are not in the detractors' ranks (Bernstein, 1991). Many preschool and kindergarten children know

Courtesy of *Green Eggs and Ham,* published by Random House.

A favorite chant most early childhood teachers, camp leaders, and girl and boy scout leaders know is "Going on a Bear Hunt." The tale of the bear hunt is told with the teacher leading the chant and the children repeating phrases. It is popular because it involves large muscle movements, action words, and sound effects, with the suspense building at the end as the family enters a cave and finds a bear. Then, they have to reverse all the actions to arrive safely home. Now there is a book, *We're Going on a Bear Hunt*, and the chant

about Dr. Seuss from their teachers' reading of *Green Eggs and Ham* and ultimately discussing if they want to at least try the strange menu.

Today's Literature Based on Song and Rhyme

It is an immense pleasure to visit in early childhood classrooms where teachers have created a literature-rich environment. Even in kindergarten and preschool classrooms, we see young children reading on their own, not in the stilted manner of a basal reader series but in the natural manner of a young child enjoying the rhythm and the rhyme of the language. One of the popular ways young children read is through song and rhyming patterns. They have learned the words to songs, chants, fingerplays, jump-rope jingles, commercials, and then they read them from books, in stories, on chart tablets, and class "big books" that they make themselves. (See Chapter 3 on Reading and Writing in Literature-Rich Early Childhood Classrooms.)

is retold in story form by Michael Rosen and illustrated by Helen Oxenbury with delightful drawings of a father, baby, older brother, and two sisters.

Marc Brown's *Hand Rhymes* is a collection of fourteen familiar hand games or fingerplays with detailed drawings for each rhyme. Joanna Cole's *Anna Banana: One Hundred and One Jump-Rope Rhymes* includes the famous "Teddy Bear, Teddy Bear, Touch the Ground," "Red-Hot Peppers!," "I Love Coffee, I Love Tea," and "Cinderella Dressed in Yellow." Some of the jump-rope rhymes of today's playgrounds and sidewalks include commercials. Recently, on a neighborhood playground, a group of third and fourth graders were seen jumping rope to a McDonald's commercial, "Two all beef patties, special sauce, lettuce, cheese, pickles, onions, on a sesame seed bun."

Like chants and fingerplays, there are numerous childhood songs that are a part of the early childhood culture. One of the favorites is "The Wheels on the Bus." Several author/illustrators have published versions of the song; however, we like the book by Maryann Kovalski because it tells a story:

> "*Grandma, Jenny, and Joanna went shopping for new winter coats and tried on everything on the racks. After making their purchases, they went to the bus stop to wait for the bus. To entertain the two girls, Grandma had them sing, "The Wheels on the Bus." They became so excited and preoccupied with their singing and doing the motions that they missed the bus and end the day by taking a taxi home (Raines & Canady, 1991, p. 206).*

Another nursery school and kindergarten favorite song used to teach young children their colors is "Mary Wore A Red Dress." Merle Peek has taken the familiar song and turned it into a story, *Mary Wore Her Red Dress and Henry Wore His Green Sneakers.* Peek draws animal characters and dresses them in different colors, as they get ready for Mary's birthday party.

Like the chants and rhymes children know and then find included in a story, the songs that are adapted to story form allow the young listener or reader to predict what will come next. Similarly, through the songs and rhymes in the folk literature of Mother Goose, the lullabies, and old-fashioned games, the child can predict the rhythms and rhymes easily. These chants, rhymes, and songs become sources of confidence-building reading materials. Predictable materials allow the reader to approach the text and know that she or he can read it.

These functional keys on our "key rings" symbolize the features of literature that emerged in the folk literature but which continue to be used effectively by today's writer of books for young children. Like the folk literature of the past, we have come to depend on these writers for their stories and the way they structure them with cumulative tales, talking animals, new legends, magical transformations, fantasy worlds, and the use of song and rhyme. We could not function without our keys and the

classroom could not function without these books. They are keys to concepts we want to teach, keys to intriguing stories, keys to confidence builders, and keys to the books that interest our children most. These books are the familiar key books, the tried- and-true literature of today that we can always count on appealing to the young child.

These authors of today are keys to early childhood educators creating literature-rich classrooms. Just like keys, we can count on them to unlock doors to beginning literacy. These writer's books always work to entice children into reading, to build their confidence as readers because writers of today recognize the power of story forms—many of which evolved from our rich traditional literature heritage. We, as teachers, must know these authors, their stories, and keep them with us, handy on our "key ring" because we know they open doors everyday.

The Third Key: New Books

The third key in the early childhood teacher's hand is a new type of key. This new key is the kind of key the hotel guest receives when checking into a modern hotel. Sometimes it is a small rectangle of plastic with holes punched in it. Other times, it is a plastic card with a magnetic strip on the back, like a credit card. The guest simply slips this little piece of plastic into the slot of a lock and click the door opens. A new kind of key for a new kind of lock.

This plastic key represents what is "new," the new books that come on the market each day. According to Connie Wright Eidenier, the editor of *Children's Writer's and Illustrator's Market*, the number of children's books published doubled during the 1980's and shows no signs of regressing. (1990). The trend of publishing more than 5,000 children's books per year continues in the 1990's. This new key represents the hundreds of new books, which may someday become the familiar ones and which may eventually become a regular part of our early childhood classrooms. Some of these new books are just the right ones to connect to those certain children in the classroom who show little interest in books or who have quite different tastes than most of the class.

A problem that new books on the market face is finding their audience. Before the book can reach the hands of the child for whom it was written, the

new books must appeal to the adult who will purchase them. Teachers, librarians, parents, and grandparents purchase books that satisfy their own tastes and, of course, they also consider what the young child will like.

Interestingly, in the selection of the books for the *Story S-t-r-e-t-c-h-e-r* series (Raines & Canady, 1989, 1991, 1992) of teacher resource books, many of the children's books that teachers recommended did not pass the test when we asked groups of children to give us a "thumbs-up" or a "thumbs-down" on the book. However, another problem also arose: Each of the three *Story S-t-r-e-t-c-h-e-r* books contains ninety children's books, and in selecting these books, we realized that we also had biases. The following story illustrates how children confront our biases with their tastes.

A PROFESSOR'S DELAYED SUCCESS STORY

We encouraged the teachers in our graduate classes to bring in children's books that their students enjoyed and to let us decide if we wanted to include them in our teacher resource books. On one occasion, Suzanne, who teaches fours and fives in a low-income area, brought Degen's *Jamberry* to a graduate class meeting and heartily recommended it.

However, when the professor read *Jamberry* she disagreed with the teacher's recommendation and said, "I'm sorry Suzanne. I just don't think this book is a good choice. There's no story and the silly illustrations don't mean a thing."

Suzanne had taken several courses from the professor and usually called her by her first name but today, she put her hands on her hips and said, "Well, I dare you to come out to my center and read this book to the children and then tell me it is not a good choice."

Needless to say, university professors are not accustomed to being dared to do something. What else could the professor do? She went out to

Suzanne's classroom and read *Jamberry* to the children.

With the boys and girls seated around her on the carpet, she said, "Today, I'd like to read *Jamberry* to you." She introduced the book by showing the cover, and immediately, a little boy said, "Jamberry, all right." Other children chimed in and said, "Yeah, Jamberry."

When the professor began reading, "One berry, two berry, pick me a blue berry," one child said, "You ain't doing it right."

The surprised professor said, "Pardon me." University professors are also not accustomed to people telling them, "You ain't doing it right." The professor invited him to show her how to do it and the little boy said, "You got to move your shoulders." So she asked him to stand up with her and the professor tried it again, but this time she moved her shoulders up and down when she read,

One berry,
Two berry,
Pick me a
    Blueberry.

Courtesy of *Jamberry*, published by Harper & Row.

At this point, a little girl sitting on the other side of the circle said, "You're still not doing it right." So the professor invited the little girl to show her what she should do. The little girl directed the professor, "You got to move your knees." With the little girl on one side and the little boy on the other, the professor started over again. And as she read this time, the children clapped their hands together in rhythm with the words, to the beat of *Jamberry*.

Before the professor finished reading the book, she was moving her shoulders up and down, bending and straightening her knees, and dancing to the rhythm of the language. Every child in Suzanne's class could read *Jamberry*—read it, sing it, and dance it. Needless to say, *Jamberry* became one of the books included in *Story S-t-r-e-t-c-h-e-r-s: Activities to Expand Children's Favorite Books*.

Remember the new plastic key. This key represents the "different books," the books that may not

be particularly appealing to teachers, just as *Jamberry* was not appealing to the professor. This key represents the different book, the one with an unusual turn, a surprise ending, rib-tickling illustrations, or some enchanting feature, like *Jamberry*, which endears the book to the children.

Getting beyond our own biases about what "good" literature for children should be is an important factor in connecting the child, the literature, and the curriculum. The authors of this textbook also learned this important point when conducting research on low book-interest children.

LOW BOOK-INTEREST CHILDREN

When asked to rank children with the highest book interest to those with the lowest book interest, teachers can usually identify three or four students who seem to show little interest in books. Low book-interest children are the ones who never choose the library corner during center time or choose books to read when they have a few free minutes. They are the ones who are the last to come to the carpet area of the classroom and pick up a book to read or look at during drop-every-thing-and-read time. They are the ones who never scoot up close while the teacher is reading aloud.

We researched twelve low book-interest children's behavior in our study, "Identification and Description of Four Year Olds' With Low Book-Interest Behaviors in Three Classroom Contexts," which appeared in the *School Library Journal Annual* (*30*, p.119-127). We found some intriguing information from our study. The books we were finally able to use with the low book-interest children could be symbolized by the new plastic key and the new lock. The children liked the "different book," the toy or manipulative book, the books with a lot of humorous illustrations, and those with more interactive texts.

During transition time, when the preschoolers were expected to come from their cleaning-up chores to a circle-time carpeted area and select a book or books and look at them on their own for five to ten minutes, the low book-interest children were often the last to come to the circle area. Most of their interactions with the books were thumbing through or flipping through the pages, sometimes one at a time and at other times turning several pages at once. Most of the low book-interest children went through several books at a session, usually from two to four in this page-turning fashion, pausing only briefly to examine a picture more closely. One child was observed flipping through eight books before pausing to look with any interest at a picture. The book that caused the child to pause was *Baby Animals: A Change A Picture Book* by Larry Shapiro. The action book has circles that the reader can turn to show different stages of an animal's life.

On another occasion, one of the low book-interest children selected Eric Hill's *Opposites*, a peek-behind-the-flap type of action book. The child did not make many verbal comments about the content of the book, but instead took the book to the teacher and opened and closed the flaps, later calling it the book with "doors."

Over the twelve weeks of the study, all of the subjects did occasionally pause to look at specific pictures. When comments were made to other children about the books, they tended to focus on funny pictures. The subjects would giggle, as the child who commented about the illustrations in Richard Scarry's *Cars & Trucks & Things That Go*. He pointed to the picture of the "pickle-shaped car" and got the attention of another child who also laughed about the illustrations.

While all young children enjoy humorous books, we found humorous books were one type that could interest the low book-interest children. Since the study ended, we have located a number of books that appeal to the child's humor. Like the visual humor of a "pickle-shaped" car, Don and Audrey Wood crafted a feast of blatant visual and subtle verbal humor in *The Little Mouse, The Red Ripe Strawberry, and the Big Hungry Bear*. In this story, a little mouse is tricked into sharing his strawberry before the big hungry bear can find it. Little mouse tries numerous ways to hide the strawberry and himself, including using a Groucho Marx disguise with a big nose, bushy eyebrows, and dark-framed glasses.

In addition to the manipulative toy books and the humorous books, one interview with a child in the study, Scott, led us to recommend more interactive texts. When we asked Scott which books he liked, he said, "I like puzzles." After trying to redirect the question, thinking he had misunderstood, and letting him know the question was about books, not puzzles, he modified his answer and said, "I like puzzle books." When we asked him to go to the library corner and find a puzzle book, he returned with Deborah Guarino's *Is Your Mama A Llama?*

The book contains the recurring question, "Is your mama a llama?," starting a series of rhyming riddles, which the child tries to answer based on the clues given in the verse. What Scott meant by "puzzle books" was riddle books. While there are few riddle books written for young children, many stories for young children do include the suspense

or how it is disguised.

Courtesy of *The Little Mouse, the Red Ripe Strawberry, and the Big Hungry Bear,* published by Child's Play.

of adding up what is happening in the plot to guess what might happen next. When we analyzed what else Scott and the other preschoolers liked about *Is Your Mama A Llama?,* it was the fact that they had to "think" about what they were hearing to predict what would come next. Like a puzzle, the child assembles the pieces and creates a picture. We are presently trying the idea of seeing a story as a puzzle as one possible means to engage children more with texts.

After our experience with Scott, we've started searching for more story puzzle books and actually turning books into story puzzles. We followed up with Scott by making flannel boards and calling them story puzzles for him to work. His first one was *The Very Hungry Caterpillar.* He liked putting the stories together like a puzzle and retelling the story as he went. We found him taking the book from the shelf and checking to see if he had it right.

We are still finding out which books appeal to low book-interest children. We know that they

like "very different books," silly books, outrageous books, hilarious books, books with pickle-cars, elements of surprise, toy or pop-up books, and we know they like books that are thinking puzzles. To conduct the study and to find books and activities that will engage the low book-interest children, we had to lay aside our own biases about books. Many teachers and librarians, like us, are "snobs" unknowingly and think less of the toy pop-up books, the silly books, and find little story in some of the puzzle books; however, if we are to engage the low book-interest child, we must use what interests them as a beginning point.

Summary

This chapter, "From Folk Literature to Modern Fantasy" uses three keys as symbols. The beautiful ornate brass key represents stories from the past—powerful old stories from the oral tradition, which have stood the test of time. The functional keys, everyday keys we keep on our key rings, symbolize the rich good literature of today, which children want to hear read again and again and represents those superior authors who understand the power of a good story. The new plastic key represents the new books, which come on the market everyday.

As early childhood educators and whole language teachers, our challenge is to find the good stories and types of books that will connect to the young child who has shown little interest in books. To accomplish this, we must observe these children closely and find ways to connect them to the literature; but first we need to get beyond our own biases and be open to the unusually formatted book, like the toy books, the outrageously silly books, which do not appeal to our adult sense of humor, and find more books that cause the children to "think" along with the story and put the story "puzzle" together.

Through literature we tell the stories of our culture, the tales, poems, jokes, riddles, and story traditions that connect one generation to the next. Through the literature we choose to read to our students, we teach values, bring reassurances, and help children understand themselves. Through the literature we charm and delight, but much more than simply being a motivating moment in the day, a good book captivates the imagination.

Children explore books, listen to us read and enjoy retelling stories because they want to "own" what it means to be literate. We must celebrate the children's enjoyment of story and accept the challenge of creating a literature-rich environment, and in the process we will transform our classrooms to whole language environments.

SUGGESTED LEARNING EXPERIENCES

1. Compare different versions of Mother Goose collections. Read articles that criticize Mother Goose stories and decide if you agree or disagree with the author's points.

2. Find songbooks with traditional songs. Survey your friends for their top five favorites.

3. Recall tall tales you read as a child. Read one of the tall tale books mentioned in this chapter.

4. Compare Native-American stories of the "fire bringer," the animal who brought fire to earth.

5. Read several Cinderella stories from different cultures and compare them. Read Robert D. Sans Souci's *The Talking Eggs*. What elements are similar to the Cinderella story that you recall?

6. Read a modern fantasy selection. How is it like and different from traditional fantasy?

7. Ask a school librarian for some titles of humorous books that young children enjoy.

8. Observe a classroom of children for a morning and try to decide who the low book-interest students are. How were you able to identify them?

9. Select a fairy tale and rewrite it as a fractured tale.

10. Visit a children's bookstore and look at the new folk tales on the market. Write down the titles and the parts of the world represented. Don't forget the American folktales.

REFERENCES

Aardema, V. (1981). About the tale. *Bringing the rain to Kapiti Plain* (pp. not numbered) New York: Dial.

Applebee, A. (1978). *The child's concept of story: Ages two to seventeen*. Chicago: University of Chicago Press.

Bernstein, P. W. (1991, October 7). Epitaph: Green eggs and me. *U.S. News and World Report*, 111(15), p. 18.

Bettleheim, B. (1976). *The uses of enchantment: The meaning and importance of fairy tales*. New York: Alfred A. Knopf.

Butler, F. (1977, 1989). Afterword on fantasy and the child. In F. Butler (Ed.), *Sharing literature with children: A thematic anthology* (pp. 437-463). Prospect Heights, IL: Waveland Press.

Carlsson-Paige, N., & Levin, D. E. (1986). The butter battle book: Uses and abuses with young children. *Young Children*, 41(3), 37-42.

Chesterton, G. K. (1989). The ethics of elfland. In Butler, F. (Ed.) *Sharing literature with children: A thematic anthology* (pp. 472-477). Prospect Heights, IL: Waveland Press.

Cox, M. R. (1983). *Cinderella: Three hundred and forty-five variants*. New York: Folklore Society, David Nutt.

Cullinan, B. E. (1989). *Literature and the child*. San Diego, CA: Harcourt Brace Jovanovich.

Dow, A. J., & Slaughter, J. P. (1989). The butter battle book and a celebration of peace. *Childhood Education*, 66(1), 25-27.

Dundes, A., (Ed.), (1983). *Cinderella: a casebook*. New York: Wildman.

Eidenier, C. W. (Ed.), (1990). *Children's writer's and illustrator's market*. Cincinnati: Writer's Digest Books.

Elleman, Barbara. (1992). The inside story: Shonto Begay's *The Mud Pony*. *Book Links*, 1 (6). Chicago, IL: American Library Association.

Fadiman, C. (1989). A meditation on children and their literature. In Butler, F. (Ed.) *Sharing literature with children: A thematic anthology* (pp. 477-483). Prospect Heights, IL: Waveland Press.

Favat, F. A. (1977). *Child and tale: The origins of interest*. Urbana, IL: National Council of Teachers of English.

Huck, C. S., Hepler, S., & Hickman, J. (1993). *Children's literature in the elementary school*. Fort Worth, TX: Harcourt Brace Jovanovich.

Jalongo, M. R. (1985). Children's literature: There's some sense to its humor. *Childhood Education*, 62(2), 109-114.

Kanfer, S. (1991, October 7). The doctor beloved by all. *Time*, 138(4), p. 71.

Kimmel, E. (1992). *Anansi goes fishing* (Quote from inside cover). New York: Holiday House.

Martinez, M., & Teale, W. H. (1988). Reading in a kindergarten classroom library. *The Reading Teacher*, 41(6), 568-572.

Minard, R. (Ed.), (1975). *Womenfolk and fairy tales*. Boston: Houghton Mifflin.

Opie, I., & Opie, P. (1951). *The Oxford dictionary of nursery rhymes*. London: Oxford University Press.

Opie, I., & Opie, P. (1974). *The classic fairy tales*. London: Oxford University Press.

Piaget, J., & Inhelder, B. (1969). *The psychology of the child*. New York: Basic.

Raines, S. C., & Canady, R. J. (1989) *Story s-t-r-e-t-c-h-e-r-s: Activities to expand children's favorite books*. Mt. Rainier, MD: Gryphon House.

Raines, S. C., & Canady, R. J. (1991). *More story s-t-r-e-t-c-h-e-r-s: Activities to expand children's favorite books*. Mt. Rainier, MD: Gryphon House.

Raines, S. C., & Canady, R. J. (1992). *Story s-t-r-e-t-c-h-e-r-s for the primary grades: Activities to expand children's favorite books*. Mt. Rainier, MD: Gryphon House.

Raines, S. C., & Isbell, R. T. (1992). Identification and description of four year olds with low book interest behaviors in three classroom contexts. In J. Bandy Smith, & J. G. Coleman, Jr. (Eds.), *School library media annual: Vol. 10*. (pp. 119-127). Englewood, CO: Libraries Unlimited.

Robbins, S. (1990). *Big Annie: An American tall tale*. Roslyn, NY: Berrent.

Shelton, Helen H. (Ed.) (1989). *Bibliography of books for children*. Wheaton, MD: Association for Childhood Education International.

Stewig, J. W. (1988). *Children and literature*. Boston: Houghton Mifflin.

Storr, C. (1986). Folk and fairy tales. *Children's Literature in Education*. 17(1), 63-70.

Tolkien, J. R. R. (1989). Tree and leaf. In F. Butler, *Sharing literature with children: A thematic anthology*. Prospect Heights, IL: Waveland Press.

Van Cleaf, D. W., & Martin, R. J. (1986). Seuss' butter battle book: Is there a hidden harm? *Childhood Education*, 62(3), 191-194.

CHILDREN'S LITERATURE REFERENCES

The authors and illustrators of children's books are listed, in all chapters, by their full names to help the reader become acquainted with them. If only one name is listed, the author also illustrated the book.

Ahlberg, Janet, & Ahlberg, Allan. (1978). *Each Peach Pear Plum*. New York: Puffin Books.

Aardema, Verna. (1981). *Bringing the Rain to Kapiti Plain*. Illustrated by Beatriz Vidal. New York: Dial.

Aardema, Verna. (1975). *Why Mosquitoes Buzz in People's Ears*. Illustrated by Leo and Diane Dillon. New York: Dial.

Aesop. (1984). *The Hare and the Tortoise*. Adapted by Janet Stevens. New York: Holiday House.

Alcorn, Johnny. (1991). *Rembrandt's Beret or the Painter's Crown*. New York: Tambourine Books.

Andersen, Hans Christian. (1949). *The Emperor's New Clothes*. Illustrated by Virginia Burton. Boston: Houghton Mifflin.

Andersen, Hans Christian. (1985). *The Nightingale*. Translated by Anthea Bell. Illustrated by Lisbeth Zwerger. Saxonville, MA: Picture Book Studio.

Andersen, Hans Christian. (1979). *Thumbelina*. Retold by Amy Ehrlich. Illustrated by Susan Jeffers. New York: Dial.

Arnold, Tedd. (1990). *Mother Goose's Words of Wit and Wisdom: A Book of Months*. New York: Dial.

Aylesworth, Jim. (1990). *The Completed Hickory Dickory Dock*. Illustrated by Eileen Christelow. New York: Atheneum.

Berger, Thomas. (1990). *The Mouse and the Potato*. Illustrated by Carla Grillis. Edinburgh, Scotland: Floris Books.

Bierhorst, John. (Ed.) (1970). *The Ring in the Prairie: A Shawnee Legend*. Illustrated by Leo and Diane Dillon. New York: Dial.

Bond, Michael. (1960). *A Bear Called Paddington*. Illustrated by Peggy Fortnum. Boston: Houghton Mifflin.

Brett, Jan. (1989). *The Mitten*. New York: G. P. Putnam.

Briggs, Raymond. (1980). *Jim and the Beanstalk*. New York: Coward-McCann.

Brown, Jeff. (1964). *Flat Stanley*. Illustrated by Tomi Ungerer. New York: Harper & Row.

Brown, Marc. (1985). *Hand Rhymes*. New York: E. P. Dutton.

Bush, John, & Korky, Paul. (1991). *The Fish Who Could Wish*. Brooklyn: Kane/Miller.

Butterworth, Nick. (1990). *Nick Butterworth's Book of Nursery Rhymes*. New York: Viking Press.

Carle, Eric. (1972). *Rooster's Off to See the World*. Saxonville, MA: Picture Book Studio.

Carle, Eric. (1975). *The Mixed-up Chameleon*. New York: Harper & Row.

Carle, Eric. *(1981)*. The Very Hungry Caterpillar. New York: Philomel Books.

Carey, Valerie Scho. (1990). *Quail Song*. Illustrated by Ivan Barnett. New York: Putnam.

Cleary, Beverly. (1965). *The Mouse and the Motorcycle*. Illustrated by Louis Darling. New York: Avon Camelot.

Coatsworth, Emerson, & Coatsworth, David. (1980). *The Adventures of Nanabush*. Illustrated by Francis Kagige. New York: Macmillan.

Cole, Babette. (1987). *Prince Cinders*. New York: Putnam.

Coles, Joanna. (1989). *Anna Banana: One Hundred and One Jump-Rope Rhymes*. Illustrated by Alan Tiegreen. New York: Morrow.

Cousins, Lucy. (1989). *The Little Dog Laughed and Other Nursery Rhymes*. New York: E. P. Dutton.

DeBrunhoff, Jean. (1960). *The Story of Babar*. New York: Random House.

Degen, Bruce. (1983). *Jamberry*. New York: Harper & Row.

dePaola, Tomie. (1988). *The Legend of the Indian Paintbrush*. New York: G. P. Putnam.

dePaola, Tomie. (1985). *Tomie dePaola's Mother Goose*. New York: G. P. Putnam.

Dewey, Ariane. (1983). *Pecos Bill*. New York: Greenwillow.

Dewey, Ariane. (1990). *The Narrow Escapes of Davy Crockett*. New York: Greenwillow.

Ehrlich, Amy. (1985). *Cinderella*. Illustrated by Susan Jeffers. New York: Dial.

Flack, Marjorie. (1932). *Ask Mr. Bear*. New York: Macmillan.

Fox, Mem. (1989). *Koala Lou*. Illustrated by Pamela Lofts. San Diego: Harcourt Brace Jovanovich.

Galdone, Paul. (1982). *Jack and the Beanstalk*. New York: Clarion.

Galdone, Paul. (1960). *Old Mother Hubbard and Her Dog*. New York: McGraw Hill.

Galdone, Paul. (1973). *The Little Red Hen*. Boston: Houghton Mifflin.

Galdone, Paul. (1984). *The Three Little Pigs*. New York: Clarion.

Galdone, Paul. (1973). *The Three Billy-Goats Gruff*. New York: Seabury.

Guarino, Deborah. (1989). *Is Your Mama A Llama?* Illustrated by Steven Kellogg. New York: Scholastic.

Hart, Jane. (1982). *Singing Bee!: A Collection of Favorite Children's Songs*. New York: Lothrop, Lee & Shepard.

Henkes, Kevin. (1988). *Chester's Way*. New York: Greenwillow.

Hill, Eric. (1982). *Opposites*. Los Angeles, CA: Price/Stern/Sloan.

Hissey, Jane. (1987). *Little Bear's Trousers*. New York: Philomel.

Hissey, Jane. (1986). *Old Bear*. New York: Philomel.

Hogrogian, Nonny. (1971). *One Fine Day*. New York: Macmillan.

Jaquith, Priscilla. (1981). *Bo Rabbit Smart for True: Folktales from the Gullah*. Illustrated by Ed Young. New York: Putnam.

Kesey, Ken. (1990). *Little Tricker the Squirrel Meets Big Double the Bear*. Illustrated by Barry Moser. New York: Viking.

Kimmel, Eric. (1992). *Anansi Goes Fishing*. Illustrated by Janet Stevens. New York: Holiday House.

Kipling, Rudyard. (1972). *Just So Stories*. Illustrated by Etienne Delessert. New York: Doubleday.

Kipling, Rudyard. (1964, originally 1894). *The Jungle Book*. New York: Doubleday.

Kovalski, Maryann. (1987). *The Wheels on the Bus: An Adaptation of the Traditional Song*. Boston: Little, Brown and Company.

Kraus, Robert. (1974). *Herman the Helper*. Illustrated by Jose Aruego and Ariane Dewey. New York: Simon & Schuster.

Kraus, Robert. (1971). *Leo the Late Bloomer*. Illustrated by Jose Aruego. New York: Crowell.

Lester, Julius. (1987). *The Tales of Uncle Remus: The Adventures of Brer Rabbit*. Illustrated by Jerry Pinkney. New York: Dial.

Lionni, Leo. (1967). *Frederick*. New York: Pantheon.

Lobel, Arnold. (1980). *Fables*. New York: Harper & Row.

Louie, Ai-Ling. (1982). *Yeh-shen: A Cinderella Story From China*. Illustrated by Ed Young. New York: Philomel.

McDermott, Gerald. (1972). *Anansi the Spider: A Tale From the Ashanti*. New York: Holt, Rinehart & Winston.

McKissack, Patricia C. (1992). *A Million Fish . . . More or Less*. Illustrated by Dena Schutzer. New York: Alfred A. Knopf.

Marcus, Leonard S., & Schwartz, Amy. (1990). *Mother Goose's Little Misfortunes*. Illustrated by Amy Schwartz. New York: Bradbury.

Marshall, James. (1979). *James Marshall's Mother Goose*. New York: Farrar, Straus & Giroux.

Milne, A. A. (1926). *Winnie-the-Pooh*. Illustrated by Earnest H. Shepard. New York: E. P. Dutton.

Oughton, Jerrie. (1992). *How the Stars Fell Into the Sky*. Illustrated by Lisa Desimini. Boston: Houghton Mifflin.

Peek, Merle. (1985). *Mary Wore Her Red Dress, and Henry Wore His Green Sneakers*. New York: Clarion.

Perrault, Charles. (1954). *Cinderella*. Illustrated by Marcia Brown. New York: Scribner.

Potter, Beatrix. (1902). *The Tale of Peter Rabbit*. New York: Frederich Warne.

Rafe, Martin. (1992). *The Rough-Face Girl*. Illustrated by David Shannon. New York: Putnam.

Robbins, Sandra. (1990). *Big Annie*. Illustrated by Iku Oseki. New York: Berrent Publications.

Robbins, Sandra. (1990). *How the Turtle Got Its Shell: An African Tale*. Illustrated by Iku Oseki. New York: Berrent Publications.

Rodanas, Kristina. (1992). *Dragonfly's Tale*. New York: Clarion.

Rosen, Michael. (1989). *We're Going on a Bear Hunt*. Illustrated by Helen Oxenbury. New York: Margaret K. McElderry Books.

Roth, Susan L. (1990). *The Story of Light*. New York: Morrow Junior Books.

Ryder, Joanne. (1987). *Chipmunk Song*. Illustrated by Lynne Cherry. New York: E. P. Dutton.

Ryder, Joanne. (1988). *The Snail's Spell*. Illustrated by Lynne Cherry. New York: Puffin Books.

San Souci, Robert D. (1992). *Sukey and the Mermaid*. Illustrated by Brian Pinkney. New York: Four Winds Press.

San Souci, Robert D. (1989). *The Talking Eggs*. Illustrated by Jerry Pinkney. New York: Penguin.

Scarry, R. (1974). *Richard Scarry's Cars & Trucks & Things That Go*. Racine, WI: Western Publishing.

Scieszka, Jon. (1991). *The Frog Prince Continued*. Illustrated by Steve Johnson. New York: Viking.

Scieszka, Jon. (1989). *The True Story of the Three Little Pigs*. Illustrated by Lane Smith. New York: Viking Kestrel.

Sendak, Maurice. (1963). *Where the Wild Things Are*. New York: Harper & Row.

Seuss, Dr. (Geisel, Theodor Seuss). (1984). *Butter Battle Book*. New York: Random House.

Seuss, Dr. (Geisel, Theodor Seuss). (1957) *The Cat in the Hat*. New York: Random House.

Seuss, Dr. (Geisel, Theodor Seuss). (1960). *Green Eggs and Ham*. New York: Random House.

Seuss, Dr. (Geisel, Theodor Seuss). (1957). *How the Grinch Stole Christmas*. New York: Random House.

Seuss, Dr. (Geisel, Theodor Seuss). (1990). *Oh the Places You'll Go*. New York: Random House.

Shapiro, Larry. (1979). *Baby Animals: A Change A Picture Book*. Los Angeles: Franklin Watt.

Spier, Peter. (1967). *London Bridge Is Falling Down!* New York: Doubleday.

Steig, William. (1969). *Sylvester and the Magic Pebble*. New York: Simon & Schuster Inc.

Stobbs, William. (1983). *The House That Jack Built*. London: Oxford Press.

Thomas, Patricia. (1971). *"Stand Back," Said the Elephant, "I Think I'm Going to Sneeze!"* Illustrated by Wallace Tripp. New York: Lothrop, Lee & Shepard.

Titus, Eve. (1955). *Anatole*. Illustrated by Paul Galdone. New York: Bantam.

Tolstoy, Alexei. (1969). *The Great Big Enormous Turnip*. Illustrated by Helen Oxenbury. New York: Franklin Watts.

Tresselt, Alvin. (1964). *The Mitten*. Illustrated by Yaroslava. New York: Scholastic.

Tudor, Tasha. (1972). *Mother Goose*. New York: Henry Z. Walck.

Turkle, Brinton. (1976). *Deep in the Forest*. New York: E. P. Dutton.

Van Laan, Nancy. (1989). *Rainbow Crow*. Illustrated by Beatriz Vidal. New York: Alfred A. Knopf.

von Olfers, Sibylle. (1990). *The Story of the Root-Children*. Edinburgh, Scotland: Floris Books.

Wallner, John. (1970, 1987). *City Mouse—Country Mouse and Two More Mouse Tales From Aesop*. New York: Scholastic.

Watson, Richard Jesse. (1989). *Tom Thumb*. (Retold). San Diego, CA: Harcourt Brace Jovanovich.

White, E. B. (1952). *Charlotte's Web*. Illustrated by Garth Williams. New York: Harper & Row.

White, E. B. (1945). *Stuart Little*. Illustrated by Garth Williams. New York: Harper & Row.

Wildsmith, Brian. (1965). *Brian Wildsmith's Mother Goose*. New York: Watts.

Williams, Margery. (1981). *The Velveteen Rabbit or How Toys Become Real*. Illustrated by Michael Green. Philadelphia: The Running Press.

Wood, Audrey. (1984). *The Napping House*. Illustrated by Don Wood. San Diego, CA: Harcourt Brace Jovanovich.

Wood, Don, & Woody, Audrey. (1989). *The Little Mouse, The Red Ripe Strawberry, and the Big Hungry Bear*. Illustrated by Don Wood. London: Child's Play.

Yolen, Jane. (1981). *Sleeping Ugly*. New York: Coward, McCann.

Zemach, Margot. (1963). *The Three Sillies*. New York: Holt.

6

Realism in
Realistic Fiction
and Nonfiction
For Young Children

Realism In Realistic Fiction and Nonfiction for Young Children

The characteristic that binds realistic fiction and nonfiction together is "reality." While the word fiction is used in the label realistic fiction, the significance is the emphasis on reality. In realistic fiction stories, the plot must be plausible, something that might actually happen to real people. The second section of this chapter deals with nonfiction—real stories, lives, places, and events that actually happen or have happened. Nonfiction books introduce children to the excitement of gaining knowledge about the real world. The litmus test of the literature that appears throughout this chapter is reality.

Contemporary Realistic Fiction

Given young children's attraction to the world of magical powers, mythical creatures, majestic castles, and monumental deeds, can realistic fiction hold a candle to fantasy? Emphatically, the answer is yes. The contemporary realistic fiction book appeals to children as they identify with the human characters and the main problem of the story. Identifying with the characters or the problem is a mark of growing sensitivity, of inferential, evaluative, and judgmental thought processes. The young child's curiosity, sensitivity, and remarkable openness to knowing about the world bring the possible, the plausible, and the created reality into sharper focus. The mind's amazing capabilities to transform, transport, and captivate the attention and the imagination, as well as young children's expanding ability to think beyond the printed word, enable them to become the actors in the drama of the story. By making inferences, reading between the lines, or listening between the phrases, the child interprets the plot, may fantasize herself or himself as the main character, or associate the actions of the people to persons she or he knows.

Realistic fiction is also enjoyed simply because it is a good story. Yet, what makes realistic fiction good is quite complex. In order to select quality realistic fiction that stimulates children's interests, teachers must consider the connections between the young child as a learner, as a member of a culture, and as an individual. In addition, good teachers use realistic fiction in curricular units to help children make associations between their lives and their ever-expanding social and real-world environments.

Some librarians, editors, and children's literature specialists only associate realistic fiction with the upper elementary, middle grades, or junior high students. Yet, many stories for young children meet all the criteria for the realistic fiction genre. By the nature of young children as learners and their experiences and capabilities with print, many of the realistic fiction books written for the young child are of the picture book type. However, we define realistic fiction for the young as stories based on true-to-life occurrences with human characters, with incidents that could possibly happen, and that help young children understand their physical and social world.

APPROPRIATE REALISTIC FICTION BOOKS FOR THE YOUNG CHILD

Bernice Cullinan, a former President of the International Reading Association and author of numerous publications about children's literature, describes realistic fiction eloquently as "a window through which we see the world" (1989, p. 390). "Literature mirrors our perceptions of life; we see in stories reflections of our own values, disappointments, and dreams [Cullinan, 1989, p. 394]."

A child is a member of a family, a culture, and a community. While literature helps the child understand life by viewing a world outside his or her own, the mirror that exposes the reality of life also begs the questions of "How much reality?" Whose reality?" and "Which real problems?" are appropriate content for the young reader and listener. Certainly, early childhood educators are concerned about the developmental appropriateness, as well as the individual appropriateness of the story. As educators, we also consider community

appropriateness. We must think of the individual child and her or his interests, while considering the child as a part of a family group with a cultural heritage. Therefore, it is imperative that we understand the communities where the children we teach live.

As the realistic fiction book has gained in popularity, several appropriateness issues swirl around it. Some teachers and librarians equate realistic fiction with the "serious problem book," which deals with themes heretofore reserved for older children, such as divorce, aging, death and dying, even anger and aggression. Many of the so-called problem books are written for the purpose of expounding the problem and a particular point of view, rather than an individual who encounters the problem and resolves it as a part of the plot. Thus, some of the problem books are poorly written and lack the quality of good stories that allow the child to identify with the characters and the situational problem.

THE INNOCENCE ISSUE

The issue of what is appropriate at different ages and for individual children must be considered in selecting realistic fiction. Of paramount importance is the issue of innocence. When should children be exposed to certain problems of society and when should they be protected? The answer lies in knowing child growth and development, as well as the standards and expectations of families and communities.

While the serious problem book, once reserved for the intermediate ages, is now entering the market for the younger child, it is meeting with mixed reviews from librarians, teachers, and parents. The issue is whether or not the problem books will alarm young children unnecessarily. Some argue that the problems of today's society are so pervasive that books for the early childhood years must address them. Others are of the opinion that the books are best reserved as a bibliotherapy type, ones to be used when teachers know children are experiencing these problems.

REALITY IS NOT ALL PROBLEMS

In many ways it is unfortunate that the realistic fiction book has become equated with the problem book. Not all of life is a major societal problem. Much of what children attempt, accomplish, and learn about themselves and their relationships in the physical and social world is not major in terms of the whole of society, but it is major in the lives of the individual or the family. There are the everyday occurrences in family living, joyful realistic experiences, and comfortable reassurances, which are also a part of the child's world and which can be effectively presented in realistic fiction.

The Young Child's Developmental Needs

Teachers and librarians who make wise decisions about realistic books for young children must take into consideration who the young child is as a learner. Many of the problem books and the everyday realistic fiction stories dwell on emotional and social concerns, therefore, the child's cognitive and psychosocial development and abilities to understand these problems must be taken into account. Teachers can make age-appropriate selections that honor the young child's cognitive development, if they use the Piagetian characteristics of the preoperational child and the young concrete-operational child as a guide (Donaldson, 1979). Erikson's descriptions of psychosocial development helps teachers consider appropriate emotional and social development concerns (1963). Some of the characteristics of the preoperational child include rapidly expanding language and concept development, egocentrism, and the time perspective of the present. (See Chapter 2 for a more in-depth discussion.)

Since the preoperational stage covers roughly from ages two to seven, the stage holds several milestones that influence the topics of interest to young children and the format in which they are presented. For example, through seriation, classification, and interpretation based on what is seen, books for the youngest of the preoperational children tend to be those with simple plots, categorization by seriation, and events that are exposed in the pictures and text that are descriptive or show clear cause and effect relationships.

Seriation is the basic story format of *Titch* by Pat Hutchins. Children who are the youngest in the family will identify with the plight of Titch who has the smallest of everything. Titch is smaller than Mary, who is smaller than Peter. Titch's tricycle is smaller than Mary's big bike, and Mary's big bike is smaller than Peter's great big bike. Titch's pinwheel is compared to Mary's kite that flew above the houses and Peter's kite that flew above the trees. Then, one day, Titch plants a seed, which grows and grows into a huge plant that is the envy of the family. Pat Hutchins tells a humorous story, encouraging the youngest and the smallest to take heart, regardless of size (Raines & Canady, 1989, p. 32).

and grew.

Courtesy of *Titch*, published by Macmillan.

In the intuitive stage of preoperational development, the child's imaginative play, interest in fantasy, and awareness of herself or himself in relationship to others takes on new meaning. While still egocentric, the young children from about four years to seven are in the comparison stage. Their awareness of who they are, their places within families, and finding ways to make associations with friends and family are made by comparisons. While still viewing the world from their own perspective, they begin struggling with understanding other's feelings when the problem to be solved is one that has meaning for the child (Donaldson, 1979). (See Margaret Donaldson's *Children's Minds*, Chapter 2, for descriptions of changing egocentrism at the intuitive level.)

An example of a book that focuses on the young child's ability to make comparisons is Marya Dantzer-Rosenthal's *Some Things Are Different, Some Things are the Same*.

> *Josh and Stephan are friends. When Josh visits Stephan's house, he compares their houses, including the playrooms, kitchens, bedrooms, bathrooms, and the family junk room. He compares their favorite toys, their pets, and even how their families handle arguments about sharing toys (Raines & Canady, 1989, p. 54).*

As described in Chapter 2, Erikson's stages of psychosocial development are significant for the early childhood educator. Erikson labels development in terms of conflicts that must be resolved before the child can move on to the next level. The second stage, "autonomy versus doubt" is the theme of many books for young children. The major character begins to make decisions, no matter how small, and establishes her or his autonomy. She or he can decide what to eat, what to wear, and what to play. Often books for the toddler and three-year-olds focus on the youngsters' struggle for autonomy and learning to do things for themselves.

An excellent example is the popular *Red Is Best* by Kathy Stinson:

But my red pyjamas keep the monsters away when I'm sleeping. I like my red pyjamas the best.

Courtesy of *Red is Best*, published by Annick Press.

> *A little girl says her mother does not understand about red. The child likes her red barrettes, mittens, boots and her red cup. She even likes red paints the best because they "put singing in her head." Children sympathize with the little girl's desire to make her own color selections and they understand her logic and love of the color red (Raines & Canady, 1989, p. 180).*

The third stage, "initiative versus guilt," is particularly significant for the preschool through kindergarten or first grade. In this stage, children further develop their autonomy by taking initiative without parents' or teachers' directives. The underlying social dilemma's of considering one's wants versus what is expected is the problem. As the child is confronted with the problems of a new baby in the family, remembering to take care of the family pet, or establishing friendships in the ever-expanding physical world of preschool, child-care, or early grades, the place of self in comparison to others is the source of interpersonal conflicts.

An example of a type of reality-based book that highlights the stage of initiative versus guilt is that of the older brother or sister who prefers not to have a tag-along younger sibling when they play with friends of their own age. In *Jamaica Tag-a-Long*, Jamaica wants to join her big brother's basketball game, but she is turned away. When she meets little Berto, she thinks about how it feels to be the youngest and decides to play with him (Gryphon House Early Childhood Book Catalog, 1992, p. 34).

The fourth stage, "industry versus inferiority," raises a question that stretches from the late second and early third grade and continues through to about age eleven. In this stage, the individual's concern is accomplishing something, whether it is improving one's physical prowess to be on a sports team, learning something difficult, solving a mystery, rescuing an animal, or taking on the cause of figuring out one's unique personal style. The dilemmas are to face what one has the power to do or risk feeling inferior. This stage is marked with numerous books that help the second and third graders establish who they are.

The popular series of Encyclopedia Brown books by Donald J. Sobol now number over twenty-five and many of them contain a mystery per chapter. Third graders in Ms. Peggy Sander's class at Cub Run Elementary in Fairfax, Virginia, enjoyed *Encyclopedia Brown and the Case of the Disgusting Sneakers*.[1] From the front dust cover, the book is described as follows: "Who knows how a handleless teacup can point to a thief? What a pair of soggy sneakers has to do with three stolen fishing rods? How the word 'crabcake' reveals the identity of a kidnapper? [Sobol, 1990]"

The Cub Run Elementary third graders read enough of the mysteries to understand how to decipher the clues. They began to appreciate Encyclopedia's thinking ability, but they also learned to notice how the author slipped the clues into the story. They found most of their detective work was rereading the stories to find out what had been said or done that could be interpreted more than one way. They also enjoyed thinking like Encyclopedia Brown, who was ten, while most of them were eight-year-olds and a few of them were

Courtesy of *Encyclopedia Brown and the Case of the Disgusting Sneakers*, published by Morrow.

nine-year-olds. They liked being as smart, alert, and perceptive as a ten-year-old.

Meeting a challenge is an appropriate cognitive task, as well as a social and emotional one for youngsters in the concrete-operational stage as Piaget described them and in Erikson's industry versus inferiority stage. During this stage, children are establishing their identities, as we see in the Beverly Cleary series of books about Ramona.

In *Ramona and Her Mother*, a second grader tries a number of different ploys to get her mother's attention. Ramona is torn between just being seven and one-half years old and trying to be responsible by doing household chores, taking care of a younger child who comes to visit, and acting more grown-up like her big sister. She decides she can not earn her mother's affection and packs to run away. In the end, mother and daughter gain a new sense of each other's needs, but Ramona's deliberations about who she is and what she can do are significant reminders of the growth ambivalence children feel in the primary grades.

Interpreting School and Community Standards

Knowing and interpreting the school and community standards is crucial for the classroom teacher when selecting realistic fiction. The place of the problem book, which exposes difficult family and societal problems, is a highly sensitive issue. With the addition of books on homosexual families, AIDS, alcoholism, and inappropriate touching, the teacher must act responsibly by carefully selecting those books that further the curriculum, those that meet the standards of quality literature, and those that are appropriate to meet children's needs. (See the list of books in the references by Girard, Jordan, Stanek, and Vigna.)

"Censorship in Children's Literature: What Every Educator Should Know" by Mary Renck Jalongo and Anne Drolett Creany provides some helpful distinctions between selection and censorship (Jalongo & Creany, 1991). The early childhood educator is helped to come to grips with school, community, and cultural standards. Jalongo and Creany propose six guidelines to handle the inevitable complaints that will arise.

Of equal significance is the tendency of some teachers and librarians to eliminate books from the shelves that they think might be a problem, and in effect they become censors. According to Burress, when parents complain about books, they are removed about 40 percent of the time and complaints from school personnel resulted in removal of books about 75 percent of the time (1989). Similarly, there is the censorship that occurs without a complaint, when the librarian anticipates a problem with a book and never orders it. Being responsible without being an overly sensitive censor is a major predicament for librarians and for teachers. Occasionally, with very bright children who read beyond their years, teachers and parents must also cooperate to decide which topics are best reserved for the later grades. It is imperative that the teacher or librarian know the children well, interpret curriculum guidelines, and gain an appreciation of the children as individuals and members of the community and culture.

Figure 6.1 Ways Teachers Can Handle Censorship Issues (Jalongo & Creany, 1991)

1. Keep current in the field by knowing the sides of the issues, elements which are offensive, and know the children's books.

2. Obtain selection criteria from national professional organizations.

3. Communicate with parents.

4. Evaluate books with children.

5. Prepare a school policy statement about book selections and attempts at censorship.

6. Adopt a formal complaint procedure, such as the NCTE's "A Citizen's Request for Reconsideration of a Work."

A CASUAL COMPLAINT ABOUT A BOOK—ONE TEACHER'S STORY

A regular among the few parent volunteers in Ms. deAngeles' first grade said, "I didn't really like the book you asked me to read with Marti. The two little girls in the book pushed each other and had a fight. I don't want my daughter or the new girl, Marti, or anyone at this school thinking that is how to settle arguments. Really, I think you need to emphasize peaceful solutions."

Ms. deAngeles thanked the volunteer for her concern, but reminded the parent that the reason she had asked her to read the book with Marti was that the little girl was new in class. The story is about a little girl who moves to a new house in the city and has to leave her house in the country.

Linda deAngeles took the book from the shelf and leafing through the pages, she remembered how excited she was when she found the book. She liked it immediately because there are so few books with female main characters where the little girls act like real children. She also chose the book because it was about moving and since so many of her children's families moved, she seldom ended the year with the same children with which she started the year. Linda was pleased to add the book to the classroom collection.

Nonetheless, after the volunteer's complaint, she carefully read over the content of Nola Langer Malone's book, *A Home*.

The book opens with scenes of Molly saying good-bye to her old house and her favorite places to play. At the new house, nothing seems right until she meets one of her neighbors, Miranda Marie, a girl who is Molly's age. They play throughout the day, "pigs in the mud," "fish in the water," "caterpillars dancing," until it is dark outside, and they end the day with a silly fight over who sees the first star. The argument includes some pushing and poking. Lonely and upset, Molly returns to the new house, feeling dejected, until she looks out the window and sees Miranda Marie looking out the window directly across from her. They wave to each other and declare they will play again tomorrow (Raines & Canady, 1991, p. 54).

Yes, there was a scene where the two little girls pushed each other, but they regretted the incident and found a way to stay friends.

What would you do if you were Ms. deAngeles, considering the fact that the parent volunteer is giving her time to the school? What should Ms. deAngeles say to the parent the next day she comes to volunteer? Should the teacher remove the book from the classroom? Consider these questions, then turn to the end of the chapter and read the Epilogue of what Linda deAngeles did and decide if you agree with her actions.

Selecting Quality Realistic Fiction for Young Children

Using the literary elements as a means of describing the genre of realistic fiction helps the classroom teacher select quality realistic fiction books that are appropriate for the young child. Considering the plot, setting, theme, characterization, point of view, and style of writing enables the reviewer of realistic fiction to evaluate the quality and appropriateness of the story, in light of what we know about child growth and development. In the following sections, we will cite some of the realistic fiction books that use the literary elements in a particularly effective manner for the young reader or listener.

PLOT

Realistic fiction plots include events that could happen in real life to real people. The story rings true as an authentic event or series of events based on a real-life situation. For active young children, there must be enough momentum and action in the story with clear steps leading to the resolution of the problem.

Ira Sleeps Over by Bernard Waber has clear sequential steps with logical actions that make

Courtesy of *Ira Sleeps Over*, published by Houghton Mifflin.

sense to young children. The book is the story of a little boy's dilemma about whether or not to take his teddy bear to his friend's house for his first time sleeping away from home. The added dimension of reality is the way Ira's sister taunts him, saying he won't be able to sleep without his teddy bear Tah Tah and that Reggie, his friend, will laugh at him (Raines & Canady, 1991, p. 58).

SETTING

Place and time, the setting elements, are crucial to the definition of a realistic fiction book. The place in most realistic fiction for young children is one they know, such as home, school, or community. If it is a different type of setting than most children understand, there must be enough associations built between what they expect in the setting and what they know from experience. The era or time is also crucial. Because the young child is oriented to the present and has little historical perspective, the realistic fiction book is best set in the present.

Young children from ages three through six seldom understand retrospectives and have difficulty with a time perspective other than the present. Some seven- and eight-year-olds can appreciate the immediate past and a past that they have experienced. However, most of the more popular realistic fiction books take place over a brief period of time.

By far, the home setting is the one most often used in realistic fiction books for the preschooler. As children enter kindergarten and first grade, the stories include more school settings. Late second and third graders' books expand to the community.

Daddy Makes the Best Spaghetti by Anna Grossnickle Hines is particularly enjoyable to preschoolers. The place is a child's home and the story transpires in one afternoon and evening when Corey and Dad cook spaghetti dinner for Mom. They shop for ingredients, cook, enjoy the meal, and clean up the kitchen. Dad's antics after dinner and the clever transition to bath, bedtime reading, and good-night kisses displays the warmth, imagination, and sheer delight the family members feel for one another (Raines & Canady, 1991, p. 40).

Kindergartners, first graders, and primary-aged children find Miriam Cohen's books about school settings of great interest. The plots of most of her books usually occur in a short time frame of a day; however, Cohen manages a longer time period and does accomplish the retrospective view in a book more appropriate for the end of first grade or the beginning of second. In *See You in Second Grade*, the children take a nostalgic look back at their first grade from the vantage point of the end-of-the-year picnic and wonder if second grade will be as much fun. The time span of the book works because children can make easy associations with the events.

The ever-widening physical environment of the community is appealing to second and third graders as they venture beyond the security of home and school. In *I Can Do It Myself* by Lessie Little Jones, Donny is determined to buy his mother's birthday present all by himself, even though it means walking past a ferocious dog, finding his way to the right shop, talking with adults, and paying with real money.

The journey story is another realistic fiction in which physical setting and a controlled span of time help young children keep the story in their

"Spaghetti," I say. Daddy makes the best spaghetti.

Courtesy of *Daddy Makes the Best Spaghetti*, published by Clarion Books.

minds. A book that focuses on conquering one's fears and anxieties about travel is *The Train to Lulu's* by Elizabeth Fitzgerald Howard:

Beppy is responsible for her little sister, Babs, for a nine-hour train trip from Boston to Baltimore. Their parents send the two little sisters, with suitcases, paper dolls, crayons, a teddy bear, and lunch boxes off on the train ride. In Baltimore, there are aunts and uncles waiting to greet them, and finally they see Great-aunt Lulu's white hair above the crowd. Hugs and kisses start their summer with Great-aunt Lulu (Raines & Canady, 1989, p. 208).

THEME

The theme is the reason the author chooses to write the story. In a well-developed home or school reading environment, children take away from the book the main idea of the story, even though they may not be able to state it in their own words. Their understanding of theme is evident in their play, in their drawings, and in their associations between books that are alike. They recognize the likenesses and differences with their own lives, think about what happened to the characters, and often derive the reason for the story's existence.

Themes for young children appear to be simple on the surface, but the good story has several levels of meaning. Popular themes in realistic fiction for the young child are appreciating one's self, relating to family members, overcoming fear, and acting responsibly. For example in *Jamaica's Find* by Juanita Havill, "a little girl finds a stuffed toy dog at the park and takes it home with her. After, some soul-searching, she decides to take it to the lost and found office at the park. The next day she meets the child who lost the toy and in the end, the two become friends [Raines & Canady, 1991, p. 60]."

CHARACTERIZATION

The characters in realistic fiction must be believable human beings who look, act, feel, and think like children and adults in a real world. Authenticity is key to believability. The characters in the stories may have some idiosyncracies, but underneath it all, they are like the children who read or listen to the stories.

One character who has won the hearts of young readers is Beverly Cleary's Ramona. In a series of books, Ramona grows from being a "pesty" kindergartner, to a seven and one-half year old who copes with her mother returning to work and her staying

Courtesy of *Train to Lulu's*, published by Bradbury.

with a sitter (Ramona the Pest and Ramona Quimby, Age 8). Then as an eight-year-old, she learns to help her father study when he goes to college. Ramona grows up and acts and thinks more responsibly, but her inventive, unexpected, "pesty" quality, her idiosyncracies make her come to life.

POINT OF VIEW

Young children's appreciation of story is often dependent upon point of view. Since they are egocentric, a story that is told from the point of view of the character who is most like them will interest the young child. Another point of view approach more frequently used by authors is a narrator who tells the story about the main character. This omnipresent narrator sees and hears all and lets the young reader or listener in on the story.

In Eloise Greenfield's, *She Come Bringing Me That Little Baby Girl,* the story is told through the child's voice. The young son's disappointment and jealousy over a new baby sister are dispelled as he becomes aware of his new role as a big brother.

The narrator often is the teller of the tale as the main character's story is presented from an observer's perspective. In *A Walk in the Rain* by Ursel Scheffla, the narrator tells the story of an afternoon walk in the rain that Josh and his grandmother enjoy. Dressed in his new yellow rain slicker, Josh makes many discoveries during their walk through the city streets and out into the forest. The adventure heightens when Barney the dog temporarily disappears.

STYLE OF WRITING

Illusive as it may seem, the quality of the book is dependent upon the style of writing. A writer's style is what makes the story identifiable as belonging to that writer. Whether it is Charlotte Zolotow's sensitive descriptions of families, Eloise Greenfield's stories told through the eyes of children, or Judith Viorst's humorous twists to everyday events, the writing style stamps the story with the personality, pizzazz, and flavor of that particular writer.

Fantasy books have an easily discernable style. It is easy to recognize Leo Lionni, Beatrix Potter, Eric Carle, Bill Martin Jr., Maurice Sendak, and Margaret Wise Brown's eminent styles in fantasy. Yet, the realistic fiction writers, while not as exaggerated as the fantasy writers, possess finely honed qualities that clearly identify them as well.

Whether the story is crafted with a touch of humor, surprise endings, tense dialogue, or mood-setting descriptions, the style of the writing determines whether or not the reader or listener becomes invested in the story. Judith Viorst's stories are realistic fiction, but are almost always marked with a touch of endearing humor. Children and adults recognize themselves and members of their family. In the ever-popular *Alexander and the Terrible, Horrible, No Good, Very Bad Day,* the terrible day begins with Alexander waking up with chewing gum in his hair and continues with so many irritating events that he thinks the only way to survive is to move to Australia.

Courtesy of *Alexander and the Terrible, Horrible, No Good, Very Bad Day,* published by Macmillan.

Using the Realistic Fiction Book in Social Studies Themes

Early childhood teachers in preschool, kindergarten, and the primary grades are accustomed to organizing instruction around curriculum units or themes. Teachers often plan thematic units, such as "I am Me, I am Special, Look What I can Do!" and "Feelings." Some units are based on social adjustments children will make as they become a part of a classroom, such as "Making Friends" and "How Our School Works." Many units focus on social and emotional growth and children's relationships with others, such as "My Family" and "Grandmothers and Grandfathers." The themes of these units are social.

Frequently, teachers worry about repetition of these units, since children have studied them in preschool and they are repeated in kindergarten or in the primary grades. However, as children grow and develop, the literature the teacher uses to bring the unit to life and the activities planned for the students vary. These themes are not *outgrowable*. A quick perusal of magazines for adults and television listings for talk shows verify that these are the same themes that endure because we are human beings engaged in understanding our own development, enjoying others, and finding avenues to fuller lives through our relationships with families and friends.

Teachers also organize curriculum units around the time of the year, such as studies of each season and the holidays. This mix of science and social studies, the changing of the seasons and the celebrations, are founded on basic, yet significant scientific and cultural understandings. When a child studies the present season, takes into account the weather, observes changes in plant and animal life, and recognizes how the seasons influence her or his activities, the study is meaningful and relevant.

SELF-CONCEPT

Teachers enhance young children's self-concepts by providing a wide variety of experiences and activities that lead to a sense of accomplishment (Raines & Canady, 1990, p. 119). The self-concept unit of study is accomplished by selecting the books to be read aloud and those to be displayed in the classroom library, as well as a variety of activities through which each child can appreciate her or his uniqueness and likenesses with others. In addition to concern that a positive self-concept means better emotional development and mental health, how a child perceives herself or himself will determine the eagerness the child feels to learn by experimenting, questioning, and enjoying the challenges of being a student.

For the preschool child, self-concept books often focus on ways children describe themselves and how others perceive them. Growing and recognizing how one changes is another theme of self-concept books. Teachers frequently choose to read aloud the carefully selected self-concept books that focus on children's uniqueness. The title of one self-concept unit, "I Am Me, I Am Special, Look What I Can Do," can be interpreted in three parts. "I Am Me" implies being true to one's own self, rather than trying to be like others. Similarly, "I Am Special," focuses on the uniqueness and appreciation we feel as a special individual, meaning, there is no one else exactly like me. The phrase "Look What I Can Do" emphasizes another element in the self-appreciation theme. As young children become aware of themselves, their changing bodies, and their changing abilities, they naturally want others to notice their accomplishments. Being true to one's own self, individuality, and accomplishments are the elements to use as guides for selecting good self-concept books for young children.

For example, in Hoffman's *Nancy No-Size*, a middle child in the family describes herself and thinks she doesn't look like nor fit any of the ways the family describes her older sister or the baby. Eventually, at her birthday party, Nancy sees herself as she is, five years old, big, tall, "Nancy-shaped,"

She is just the right age and size
to go to school.
And so are all her friends.

Courtesy of *Nancy No Size*, published by Oxford University Press.

and her place is right in the middle of the family.

Accomplishment builds self-esteem. Numerous books for young children help them feel a sense of accomplishment through emphasizing tasks such as dressing themselves. As children get older, they become interested in physical accomplishments,

some as simple as whistling. Remember Ezra Jack Keats' *Whistle for Willie*, the story of Peter's desire to learn to whistle so he can call his dog, Willie.

Milestones in one's life are also celebrated in children's literature. In *The Day of Ahmed's Secret* by Florence Parry Heide and Judith Heide Gilliland, one

My donkey pulls the cart I ride on. I have many stops to make today. The streets are crowded. Everyone is going somewhere. Like me, everyone has something important to do. And they are making such a noise of it!

Courtesy of *The Day of Ahmed's Secret*, published by Lothrop, Lee, and Shepard.

of those milestones was reached and disclosed at the end of the book:

> *Ahmed is a young boy who works in the city of Cairo selling bottled gas and making deliveries with his donkey drawn cart. As he travels through the day, selling, meeting and greeting people, eating, resting and thinking of his family, he has his secret with him to give him a special feeling. At the end of the day, Ahmed gathers his entire family to tell his secret—he can write his name. The story ends with Ahmed's beautiful thought that perhaps his name will live like the old buildings in the city, live for a thousand years. Ted Lewin's watercolors are more than illustrations, they are exquisitely rich paintings filled with the colors, sights, bustle, and character of the ancient city (Raines & Canady, 1989, p. 32).*

FAMILIES

The early childhood classroom is a microcosm of society's changing family structures and roles. Teachers have students in their classrooms whose parents are divorced and the children split their time between two households. Many include single parent families, children dealing with remarriages and placing two families together, adopted children, foster children, and youngsters living with extended family members. A study of the family as a part of social studies is crucial to the child's understanding of herself or himself, as well as appreciating the ways others live. Additionally, families of young children are changing because there are new brothers and sisters being born.

Children's literature is replete with books dealing with families; however, there is not enough good literature that shows families with different structures. There are the "problem" family books, but the incidental setting of different families where the focus is not the family structure is less common.

A good classroom collection of books that support the family theme must have both the books that deal directly with changes in family structure and those that are incidental.

Norma Simon's book *All Kinds of Families* is a must for any early childhood unit on families. Simon's book is an excellent beginning for a families unit because it warmly and affectionately portrays many different types of families and family life. The text and illustrations help children think of themselves as family members and to see what changes in families and what remains the same. The book celebrates family special events, holidays, stories, and feelings at both sad and happy times (Raines & Canady, 1989, p. 40).

Other books that contribute significantly to literature and help the teacher make selections that will answer children's questions about themselves and their families include Linda W. Girard's *Adoption Is for Always* and Shirley Gordon's *The Boy Who Wanted a Family*.

Adoption Is for Always has received critical acclaim from *School Library Journal* as one of the

Courtesy of *All Kinds of Families*, published by Albert Whitman.

He curled up next to their fireplace to get warm.

He watched the six o'clock news on TV.

He tasted their dinner.

He tried out their beds.

Courtesy of *Charlie Anderson*, published by Margaret K. McElderry.

range of emotions a boy feels when he finds out that his parents are getting a divorce.

Divorce as a topic is the central theme in the books just mentioned, but few children's books incidentally inform the reader that a child lives with Mother and spends the weekends with Dad, or vice-versa. Barbara Abercrombie's book *Charlie Anderson* is supposedly a story about a cat. However, the theme of this realistic fiction book is that a cat can have two homes and be happy:

best books about adoption for young children. Celia's parents answer her questions about adoption, but it is still confusing and the child faces some anger and fear, until her parents reassure her that "adoption is for always." In Gordon's *The Boy Who Wanted a Family*, a seven-year-old moves from foster home to foster home as he waits a year to finally be adopted. Foster homes are seldom presented as settings in children's books; however, Patricia Maclachlan writes of a happy foster home experience in *Mama One, Mama Two*, which is appropriate for late second and third graders.

Divorce is so common in today's world, and many authors are approaching the topic in sensitive, yet realistic fashion. Linda W. Girard has also written the family oriented book *At Daddy's on Saturdays*. Reviewers have called it a bibliotherapeutic approach, one that would be helpful for parent/child use or for a class discussion. In the book, the little girl is reassured that divorce is not the child's fault. A boy is the main character in Jane Madsen and Diane Bockoras's book *Please Don't Tease Me*, which takes the reader through the

Two girls, Elizabeth and Sarah, take in a stray cat which they name Charlie. One stormy night, Charlie does not come home and the two girls go searching for him. They continue their search the next day and find him at the house of another family which calls him by the name of "Anderson." Charlie Anderson, the cat, has two homes, a daytime home and a nighttime home with Elizabeth and Sarah, who also have two homes, one with their mother during the week and one with their father on the weekends. (Raines & Canady, 1991, p. 194).

Albert Whitman and Company publishes an extensive list of books, such as the two by Linda W. Girard, which approach difficult societal problems and face many of the issues that some critics find questionable because they are concerned about protecting children's innocence. A review of some of the Albert Whitman and Company titles listed for preschool through grade two indicates that the "problem" book is no longer reserved for the middle grades:

- ☐ *I Wish Daddy Didn't Drink So Much*
- ☐ *The Saddest Time*, a book about death
- ☐ *Don't Hurt Me, Mama*
- ☐ *All Alone After School*
- ☐ *My Mom Can't Read*
- ☐ *My Big Sister Takes Drugs*
- ☐ *Nobody Wants a Nuclear War*
- ☐ *She's Not My Real Mother*
- ☐ *Losing Uncle Tim*, a book about AIDS

GRANDPARENTS IN REALISTIC FICTION

Families in children's books often contain a mention of extended families, and there are a number of books about aging, death, and dying that center around grandparents. Thankfully, there are a few good books that show vibrant, energetic grandpar-

Courtesy of *The Wednesday Surprise*, published by Clarion Books.

ents who have special relationships with their grandchildren. Karen Ackermans' *Song and Dance Man*, which won the Caldecott Medal for Stephan Gammell, is an excellent example. Three children learn to appreciate the past by seeing it through their grandfather's eyes. They look at posters and pictures, and dig through the attic trunk and pretend to be on stage. But Grandpa is the one who makes the past come to life when he puts on his tap shoes, his striped vest and bowler hat and becomes the vaudeville *Song and Dance Man*. (Raines & Canady, 1992, p. 160).

Special relationships between grandchildren and grandparents have taken on new significance. For example, in Eve Bunting's *The Wednesday Surprise*, the family thinks Grandmother is just babysitting every Wednesday. Much to their surprise Anna has been spending her Wednesday afternoons teaching her grandmother to read.

Fortunately, there are a number of good books for young children that show both grandparents living and that illustrate the always popular "going for a visit" to the grandparents' house. In Edith Thacher Hurd's *I Dance in My Red Pajamas*, a little girl recalls all the busy and noisy reasons she likes visiting her grandparents. The highlight of the evening is when Grandmother plays the piano and the little girl dances in her red pajamas (Raines & Canady, 1989, p. 64).

The reality of grandchildren and grandparents is that they do not always get along. In Anna Grossnickle Hines' book *Grandma Gets Grumpy*,

Slowly, he starts to tap. His shoes move faster and faster, and the sounds coming from them are too many to make with only two feet.

Courtesy of *Song and Dance Man*, published by Alfred A. Knopf.

when five cousins spend the night at Grandma's, they see that while her house is a special place for family, Grandma has her limits. She sets limits quite firmly when her patience wears thin as the children romp out of control.

GRANDPARENTS GETTING OLDER

Numerous good books deal with children's relationships with grandparents, such as those just mentioned. In the last few years, books for young children have begun to address the process of aging. In *My Great Grandpa*, Martin Waddell tells the story of a little girl and what she and her Great Grandpa do when she takes him for a ride in his wheelchair. They go down familiar streets, and he watches her play in the park. When they stop to look at the house where he used to live, he tells her stories about her great grandmother. One day Great Grandpa gets overheated and has to spend several days in bed resting. Granny and the little girl take good care of him until he can return again to their

Courtesy of *We Are Best Friends*, published by Greenwillow.

wheelchair rides around town (Raines & Canady, 1991, p. 44).

Another of the grandchild-grandparent relationship books, is one that involves illness, Tomie dePaola's *Now One Foot, Now the Other*. When his grandfather suffers a stroke, Bobby lovingly teaches him to walk again, just as Grandfather once taught him.

FRIENDS

Friendship is a major concern for the young child who is learning to live and work in the social environments of the classroom, the playground, and the community. For a number of years, friendships among children were sweet, no anger or aggression was ever shown, and everyone took turns, shared toys, and played the games by the rules. Handling disagreements and resolving problems was seldom seen from the child's perspective. In reality and in later realistic fiction, friendship among children is fraught with a number of emotions and problems.

The realistic fiction story stays true to young children's actual feelings. The friendship theme about the dilemma's of friends is becoming more prevalent in books for young children. For example, in Winthrop's *The Best Friends Club*, Lizzie learns that she can share her best friend with another child, yet remain best friends without being jealous.

Other popular books with a friendship theme focus on children losing friends when they move away. Several that are popular for kindergartners and primary-aged children include Bernard Waber's *Ira Says Goodbye*, Aliki's *We Are Best Friends*, and Nola Langer Malone's *A Home*. In *Ira Says Goodbye*, Ira's sister breaks the news that his best friend Reggie is moving to Greendale. The following days are filled with sadness and excitement. Ira is sad and feels betrayed that Reggie is excited about the move. Reggie brags about his new house, new people he will meet, and new fun things he can do when he moves to Greendale. How the children express their feelings as well as how they plan to keep in touch are meaningful to primary-aged children whose friends move often (Raines & Canady, 1992, p. 58).

In Aliki's *We Are Best Friends*, Robert is devastated by the news that Peter is moving away. Robert

Courtesy of *Wilfrid Gordon McDonald Partridge,* published by Kane Miller.

thinks he will never find another friend like Peter, and he hopes that Peter will miss him too. Eventually after many days of longing, both boys find new friends, but remain best friends and keep their friendship alive by drawing pictures and writing letters (Raines & Canady, 1991, p. 52).

Friendships among children of different ages are rare in children's books and rarer still are friendships between children and older adults. One of a number of excellent books by Mem Fox tells of the extraordinary friendship of a little boy, *Wilfrid Gordon McDonald Partridge*, who lived next door to an old people's home.

FEELINGS

The thematic units of self-concept, families, and friends all revolve around children's feelings about themselves, their parents, brothers, and sisters, and finding and keeping friends. As young children learn to express themselves and deal with their emotions in a positive manner, the "feelings" book provides a vehicle for classroom discussion and expression of vicarious feelings, which may not be possible for the child to show at other times.

Growth ambivalence, anger, frustration, love, hate, joy, grief, compassion, empathy, sadness—the range of human emotions—can be found in the realistic fiction book for young children. However, in the past most of the books were written with animal characters rather than playing out the stories with humans. Today, many more feelings books with humans as main characters are in the market place.

There are a number of good books that explain a variety of feelings; however, the texts include a minimal storyline and are written instead for the purpose of labeling what each emotion looks like. Three that fit this format are *One Monday When It Rained* (Kachenmeister), which uses photographs of a child's expressions, *Sometimes I Like to Cry* (Stanton), and *I Was So Mad* (Simon), which explain anger and what children can do about it. Other books have stories devised to teach children what to say about their feelings, such as Conlin's *Nathan's Day* and *Ellie's Day*, which associate feelings at school with words children can use to talk about their emotions.

COMMON FEARS

Books containing authentic stories are usually more pleasing to children and less didactic. Many of the common fears books are about situations that young children find fearful, such as starting school, sleeping in a room alone, and loss of affection when a family has a new baby. There are good books about starting school and childcare, such as Ann Tompert's *Will You Come Back for Me?* and Janet and Allen Ahlberg's *Starting School.* Children's nightmares and fears are imaginatively written about in fantasy books, but little realistic fiction addresses the issue.

The loss-of-affection fear is often told through a story about the arrival of a new baby in the family. In Scott's *On Mother's Lap* reassures Michael that he can still sit on mother's lap even after the baby is born. The question is asked differently in Hazen's *Even If I Did Something Awful,* when the child asks,

Even if I did something awful?

Courtesy of *Even If I Did Something Awful,* published by Macmillan.

"Would you love me no matter what I did?" The parents' reassuring answers and expected responses, such as, "Yes, but I'd make you clean it up," or "But I also might be mad and yell some things," provide honest responses to the questions.

DEATH AND DYING

The subject of death and dying is rare in stories for young children. One of the books that second and third graders seem particularly touched by is Judith Viorst's *The Tenth Good Thing About Barney,* the story of the death of the family pet. *I'll Always Love You* (Wilhelm) is the story of a little boy growing up and his dog, Elfie, who is growing older. One night Elfie dies. Grief stricken, the boy remembers that every night he told Elfie, "I'll always love you."

Many of the realistic fiction books about death and dying center around the loss of a pet. Seldom do books for young children deal with the death of a parent, a sibling, or grandparents. Lucile Clifton's *Everett Anderson's Goodbye* is an exception. It is the story of a little boy who is coming to grips with his father's death.

In *Nana Upstairs, Nana Downstairs,* dePaola reminisces about his grandmother and great-grandmother. In the story, both grandmothers die. Yet, the love and tenderness of the story do not focus on the death of the grandmothers, but on the special times they shared and how he will remember each of them every time he looks up at the stars.

Avoiding Stereotypes

Stereotypes cast all the members of a certain age, race, sex, ethnic faction, religion, or other background in the same light. Stereotypes do a disservice to individuals and a disservice to the groups and cultures they supposedly represent. Whether issues of gender, race, age or other demographics, avoiding stereotypes must be of prime concern when selecting literature for the classroom.

Grace went into battle as Joan of Arc . . .

Courtesy of *Amazing Grace*, published by Penguin.

In Chapter 5 on folktales and folk literature, we discussed the ways females are often portrayed in a derogatory manner. Similarly, stereotyping based on age, racial, ethnic, religious, or national background can be equally detrimental.

One of the relatively new books dealing openly about racial stereotyping is *Amazing Grace* by Mary Hoffman. Grace loves stories and loves to act out the most exciting parts. When her skeptical classmates tell her she can not play the part of Peter Pan, Grace tries out anyway and wins the part. Believing in one's individual talents, perseverance, and facing racial prejudice are powerful themes for this beautiful, well-written story which is receiving much critical acclaim.

ELDERLY STEREOTYPES

An honest portrayal of the aging process and the elderly comes through in good books for young children; however, just as there are grandparents who are in poor health, there are also many who are energetic and actively engaged in their own lives. The classroom collection needs to include an array of good books. The stereotype no longer fits of the little old grandmother with glasses, her hair in a bun on the back of the head, standing on the front porch of the farmhouse. Some preschoolers and early elementary children have grandparents who are in their fifties, usually an active decade. So, since grandparents age and children must deal with changes in their grandparents' lives and even loss of life, good books can and must be found.

SEX-ROLE STEREOTYPING AND GENDER ISSUES

Another of the social issues is that of sex-role stereotyping of main characters and family members. Reviewing for sex-role stereotyping is done by examining both the text and the illustrations for the ways the boys, girls, men, and women are portrayed. Gender bias and gender issues are particularly important in the realistic fiction book, which is supposed to portray real life. Since family roles have changed, teachers must look for books that help girls see possibilities for themselves as working outside the home, while still having families and good relationships with their children. In a recent release by Barbara Shook Hazen, *Mommie's Office*, a little girl sees that what her mommy does at work all day is in some ways very like what she does at school. Similarly, books that show fathers doing work at home are also important.

Some books tackle the subject of stereotyping and address them in story form. Martin's *Three Brave Women* is an example of how females sometimes feel bound by how others perceive them:

> *While sitting on the front porch swing with Mama and Grammy, Caitlin screeches that she hates Billy Huxley because she thinks he will tell everyone she is afraid of spiders. The three of them hatch a plan to show Billy that Caitlin isn't afraid. In the process, all three women decide they can be brave, and Caitlin finds Billy isn't always brave either (Raines & Canady, 1992, p. 66).*

Boys and men are often portrayed in stereotypical ways, as well. Yet, some of the most sensitive books about family life also include a look at the stereotypes. Charlotte Zolotow's *William's Doll,*

published over twenty years ago, is a contemporary question that many little boys face:

> *William would like a doll so that he could play with it like his friend Nancy does with her doll. At the very thought of a little boy with a doll, his brother and his friend call him creep and sissy. William's father buys him a basketball and a train, instead of a doll. William becomes a very good basketball player and he enjoys the train set, but he still longs for a doll. Finally, when William's grandmother comes for a visit, she buys him a doll and explains to his father that having a doll will be good practice for him when he grows up and has a real baby to love (Raines & Canady, 1989, p. 50).*

Courtesy of *William's Doll,* published by Harper & Row.

The gender issue of sex-role stereotyping is a significant one for books about family life and for books from other realistic settings. Some of the themes and obvious illustrations of roles ascribed by gender are easy to read and see; others are much more subtle. The number of female leads in books for young children is easy to count; however, the way the supporting characters are portrayed, as well as the problems the females are asked to solve, may paint a quite different picture. Girls are often shown in more passive roles or sitting on the sidelines while the boys are engaged in the action that moves the story along. Teachers who are eager to build a good classroom collection for their units on families will need to look for books that show family members engaged in a variety of activities, without regard to gender.

Acknowledging and Appreciating Likenesses and Differences

Young children are engrossed in the process of self-discovery, learning their capabilities, and appreciating themselves. In the preschool, kindergarten, and early primary grades, children often compare themselves, their families, and their friends to others. By their egocentric natures, they often think of their families' ways as best. However, as they experience other families and friends, they begin to accept and appreciate likenesses and differences.

Young children often focus on how they are alike and different physically. Whether it is comparing the shades of each other's skin, how their hair feels, or how tall or short they are, they focus on physical differences and make comparisons. The mainstreamed exceptional child who is physically limited provokes immediate inquiries from young classmates. There are a number of good books that allow children to think about the ways they are different and the ways they are the same, including the needs of exceptional students. Joan Fassler's *Howie Helps Himself* is about a young boy with cerebral palsy and his struggles to learn to control his wheelchair by himself.

Multicultural Literature in Our Diverse Society

An appropriate developmental task for young children is to grow in appreciation of themselves as individuals, as family members, and as members of a culture in their communities. Individual, family, and cultural identities are exposed and celebrated in multicultural literature. As social studies teachers, early childhood educators are concerned that children also develop an appreciation of others, as well as of themselves and the groups to which they belong.

While much of the attention to multicultural literature is attributed to the civil rights and great society movements of the 1950's and 1960's, increased attention is now being paid to multicultural literature because of the increasing diversity of our society (Donahue, 1992, March). According to the 1990 US Census, during the 1980s the Hispanic population of the United States increased by 56 percent (Barringer, 1991, March). The Asian population more than doubled in the same period. Therefore, in addition to our concerns about racial minorities and ethnic representation, educators realize there is a need for appreciation of cultural diversity, whether the minority is rising in population or not. Concern about how Native-American people and African Americans are represented in literature are crucial.

According to Harris (1992) and Bishop (1992), the publication of multicultural literature appears to wax and wane with the social and political climate. Currently, there is a call for more multicultural literature. In a review of a number of popular press articles, such as *Time, Newsweek, U.S. News and World Report, The Atlantic Monthly,* and *The New Republic,* Joel Traxel noted the debate about multicultural heritage that exalts racial and ethnic pride versus an American cohesion. Traxel ends his essay with a call for writers, editors and publishers, and the academic and critical establishment to take up the challenge of social responsibility and seize the opportunity our present day affords (1992).

Violet J. Harris' *Teaching Multicultural Literature in Grades K–8* provides guidance to teachers in selecting multicultural literature (1992). She defines multicultural literature as those selections about people of color both in the United States and outside. Other writers also include multicultural literature to refer to Appalachians and other regional and religious cultures. In a chapter titled, "Multicultural Literature for Children: Making Informed Choices," Rudine Sims Bishop calls for the "need for cultural authenticity," selecting various types of multicultural literature, and "reading extensively in literature written by 'insiders.' (1992)" By insiders, Bishop means 'literature' written by members of that culture. In addition, it is suggested that teachers select books that show the diversity within and across cultures.

The test of good children's literature is whether it accurately portrays the humans, their communities, and cultures so that they are not stereotypes, but are realistic. If the story is realistic fiction, then the characters must be measured against their qualities as individuals and not against some stereotypes of the members of a group.

In Chapter 5 we presented folk and fairy tales, and many subgenres of the traditional literature, which is the literary heritage of many cultures. Traditional literature comprises much of the multicultural literature available to teachers. While we are indeed fortunate to have preserved the old tales from many cultures and the revival of much interest in preserving the stories as a tribute to one's culture, there is a scarcity of literature representing present-day minority peoples' concerns, values, and lifestyles. We need literature that:

1. portrays the uniqueness of present day cultures;
2. celebrates understanding cultural differences and likenesses; and
3. shows many cultures as a part of a shared community;

MULTICULTURAL LITERATURE THAT PORTRAYS THE UNIQUENESS OF THE PRESENT CULTURE

Authors can use young children's interests advantageously by presenting the story of another culture through the eyes of a child, whether using realistic fiction or nonfiction books. An excellent realistic fiction books that helps children understand the uniqueness of a present culture is *A Birthday Basket for Tia* by Pat Mora, the story of an affectionate relationship between Cecilia, a young child, and her ninety-year-old great-aunt. Cecily Lang's colored cut-paper illustrations fit the details of the daily lives of the Mexican-American family and the traditions of food, music, dance, and games, which are a part of the birthday celebration story.

MULTICULTURAL LITERATURE THAT CELEBRATES UNDERSTANDING CULTURAL DIFFERENCES AND LIKENESSES

Understanding and appreciating cultures different from one's own is not an easy task for a young child who has had limited exposure. When confronted with someone who is different from them, young children express their curiosity in a variety of ways. Unfortunately, children from minority cultures experience teasing and embarrassment because they are different. Books confronting these unfortunate incidents can be helpful in fostering more understanding of differences and likenesses. One realistic fiction book that confronts these problems is *Angel Child, Dragon Child* by Michele Maria Surat, with pictures by Vo-Dinh Mai. Ut is a Vietnamese child who has started school in America. Raymond picks on Ut and teases her about her speech and her dress, but when he learns that Ut's mother is still in Vietnam, it is Raymond who suggests a Vietnamese fair to raise money to bring Ut's mother to live in America.

MULTICULTURAL LITERATURE THAT SHOWS CULTURES SHARING COMMUNITY

In Bernard Ashley's *Cleversticks*, the classroom is the shared community. The children and teachers in this classroom represent several different cultures, including Asian, Indian, African-American, and Mexican-Americans although the cultures are only identified by the children in the background illustrations. Ling Sung feels embarrassed that he does not know how to do what the other children know. When the children and teachers try to eat with chopsticks, Ling Sung has to teach them. The teachers and children learn from Ling Sung about how to eat with chopsticks and he learns about all the school activities from the other children.

There is a need for much more multicultural literature that meets the high standards of all good literature. Lyn Miller-Lachmann's *Our Family, Our Friends, Our World* is a valuable resource for making quality selections for cultures around the world. The guide is not limited to realistic fiction books. The annotated guide reviews approximately 1,000 significant multicultural books for children and teachers. The eighteen chapters of the resources are devoted to various cultural groups: African Americans, Asians, Hispanics, and Native Americans, and cultures from Canada, Mexico, the Caribbean, Central and South America, Great Britain, Ireland, Western Europe, Southern Europe, Eastern Europe and Russia, the Middle East, North Africa, Sub-Saharan Africa, South Africa, Southern and Central Asia, East Asia, Southeast Asia, Australia, New Zealand, and the Pacific. In the foreword to the book, James Comer praised the guide: "The best of these works provide children with a sense of their past, a compelling treatment of current dilemmas, and positive models for solving problems, developing identity, and building self-esteem [1992]."

SUMMARY: CONTEMPORARY REALISTIC FICTION AND THE YOUNG CHILD

The young child from preschool through the primary grades identifies with contemporary realistic fiction because the settings, characters, and problems of the stories are like the child's real world. In the preoperational and concrete-operational stages of development, young children are immensely interested in themselves, their families, friends, schools, and communities. Teachers who use contemporary realistic fiction as a part of their classroom curriculum, collection, and read-aloud selections can:

1. Foster young children's understandings of themselves through self-concepts units.

2. Provide avenues for children to face their social and emotional dilemmas.

3. Encourage appreciation for how children as individuals and members of families and communities are alike in many ways.

4. Develop an appreciation of individual, family, community, and cultural differences.

Nonfiction for Young Children

An area of growing popularity in children's literature is nonfiction for the young child. Beverly Kobrin, notably one of the best reviewers of nonfiction for children, has written a most helpful teacher resource book, *Eyeopeners!: How to Choose and Use Children's Books About Real People, Places, and Things* (1988). In the title of Kobrin's book lies the definition of nonfiction—real books about real people, places, and things. These nonfiction books are not textbooks, but rather are trade books.

Only a few years ago, many teachers shunned the nonfiction trade books because many looked, read, and felt like miniversions of textbooks. If you are one of those teachers, it is time to revisit the bookstores and discover the excitement and vitality of the writing, the illustrations, the pictures, and the format of today's nonfiction books.

In the world of early childhood and whole language classrooms, the word *authentic* is used as a measure of whether or not the curriculum, the assessment, and the interactions meet our exacting standards. Given our concerns about authenticity, the nonfiction book is a welcomed addition to the classroom. The facts, ways and means of how the physical and social worlds work, and our lives and times of the present are fascinating. Yet, nonfiction books need the same careful scrutiny as contemporary realistic fiction.

Reviewing and Selecting Good Nonfiction Books

Nonfiction books must: be accurate; portray as complete a picture as possible for the audience for which it was intended; be written by an authority or one who has developed expertise in order to convey the material; contain information presented in an interesting manner in both words and illustration; and possess the vitality and substance of any good book. In addition, the nonfiction book must have a format that appeals

from cover to cover. Often, because the material is real, the authors and illustrators rely on the inherent interest of the topic and do not invest as much energy in the layout and production values of the nonfiction book as is done for fiction. As Kobrin so aptly points out, the book must be attractive enough that the child wants to take it off the library or bookstore shelf.

With these selection points in mind, teachers, librarians, and parents can look more closely at some of the finer points of review. For example, real books about real people, places, and events can be written with a vitality that appeals to the young reader or listener, or they can be written in a deadly boring manner. A book with vitality is one that consider's what the reader or listener probably wants to know. Like a good opening sentence, an attention-getter, or a hook drawing the reader into the text of an exciting adventure novel, the nonfiction writer must find some means to capture the attention, right from the start.

Secondly, after the attention is gotten, the materials should be organized in a way that lets the reader associate with the topic or build a bridge between the known and the unknown.

Thirdly, the nonfiction writer must present this interesting information in a way that will sustain the reader's interest. Good nonfiction writing can be compared to the difference between reading an article on baseball in *Sports Illustrated* to reading the back of a baseball card. The information about the player may be the same, but the raw data does not capture the energy, the personality, the ups and downs, and the struggles of playing the game.

Fourthly, the writer of nonfiction material must appreciate the audience. Young children need not be talked down to, but should be appreciated for their curiosity and their rapidly expanding vocabulary and concepts. For example, in a

and DINOSAURS
who are extinct, but they were reptiles, too.

Courtesy of *Chickens Aren't the Only Ones,* published by Grossett and Dunlap.

kindergarten classroom where baby chicks were being hatched, the teacher had collected a number of good books. None of the kindergartners shied away from content, the illustrations, or the vocabulary of Ruth Heller's *Chickens Aren't the Only Ones:*

> This wonderfully illustrated science and nature book is told in rhyme and has many surprises. Heller begins with a concept children usually know, "that chickens lay eggs," and expands the idea to every wild or tame bird, to snakes, lizards, crocodiles, turtles and dinosaurs. She continues with amphibians, frogs, toads, and salamanders. The fish, including seahorses, sharks, rays, and the octopus, are set on watery deep blue and green pages. She adds the spiders, snails, and insects in glowing, beautiful detail. The ending of the book refers back to the beginning and gives the children a new word to say, "Everyone who lays an egg is O VIP A ROUS." (Raines & Canady, 1989, p. 102)

Ruth Heller has written other wonderful nonfiction books that appreciate the interest and intelligence of the young child, such as *Animals Born Alive and Well* and *Plants That Never Ever Bloom.*

All of Heller's books have a "revisitable" quality. At each reading and each perusal of the illustrations, there is more the child can learn. Good nonfiction has a lasting quality because it is well researched, well written, and well illustrated, with enough density of material to invite the reader to revisit the information found there.

In the selection process, there are a few cautionary notes. First, children with little experience of the world often have misconceptions that can be exaggerated or at the very least not clarified when the nonfiction book fails to illustrate sizes, and uses anthropomorphism or teleology. For example, one preschooler was overheard calling a photograph of a salamander, "a dinosaur." Indeed, up close the salamander does look like the animated Saturday morning cartoon dinosaur. *Anthropomorphism* attributes human characteristics to animals. The dog may be said to be smiling when he is actually panting. *Teleology* refers to a way of describing a naturally occurring event that makes it sound planned. For example, "The rose opened just for little Sarah." The rose opened because of many reasons, but in nonfiction books it should be made clear that it could not will itself to open.

Figure 6.2 Guidelines for Selecting Quality Nonfiction

Accuracy
Authority
Interesting style of writing
Appealing format
Speaks to age of audience
    without talking down
Attractive, "revisitable" quality

FORMAT AND ILLUSTRATION

The format of nonfiction books ranges from the ABC types, rhymes, and lavish narrative descriptions to wordless books. The illustrations range from black and white stark photographs of the barest essence to richly drawn and detailed pictures. As with all good children's picture books, the illustrations are key to the credibility of the text.

Often when teachers and librarians think of nonfiction, they recall the concept books illustrated with photographs. Frequently, the writers and photographic essayists become known for a certain type of book. Tana Hoban's array of colorful photography books is well known to early childhood educators. (See the extensive list in Chapter 4, on picture books.) Two of her recent photography concept books are *Exactly Opposites* and *Spirals, Curves, Fanshapes, & Lines.* Ann Morris, the author, and Ken Heyman, the photographer, have a collection of the more elaborate essay type of concept book, which treats the subjects in a variety of ways and provide views from many different cultures around the world. They have teamed up for books on *Hats, Hats, Hats, Tools, Bread, Bread, Bread, On the Go,* and *Houses and Homes.*

The black and white photograph can be used effectively for illustration of the nonfiction story or concept book. However, teachers may need to help children appreciate black and white photog-

Courtesy of *Houses and Homes,* published by Lothrop, Lee, and Shepard.

raphy because students will usually select books illustrated with color. Two particularly effective writers and photography teams who use black and white photos are Maxine Rosenberg and George Ancona, whose stories deal with exceptional children, and Cheryl Kachenmeister and Tom Berthiaume, who created the feelings book *One Monday When It Rained.*

Listed below are a number of additional authors/illustrators/photographers whose books are particularly appealing to the young child and support good classroom teaching of curricular units.

Figure 6.3 Authors/Illustrators and Photography Book Titles for Curriculum Units

Author/illustrator	Color/B & W	Titles	Units
Tricia Brown/Fran Ortiz	B & W	*Someone Special Just Like Me*	Exceptional Children
Ron Hirschi/ Thomas D. Mangelson	Color	*Winter*	Seasons
Cheryl Kachenmeister/ Tom Bethiaume	B & W	*On Monday When It Rained*	Feelings
Bruce Macmillan	Color	*Growing Colors*	Plants
Meyer Seltzer	Color/B & W	*Here Comes the Recycling Truck*	Environment
Seymour Simon	Color	*Big Cats*	Animals

PEOPLE, PLACES, AND EVENTS

The biography of someone who has historical, social, or political significance within our culture is not particularly appealing to young children below third grade because they do not yet have an historical perspective, nor societal and patriotic concerns. Some third graders may be interested in present day leaders and sports or entertainment figures. Few biographies of an entire life can be written to hold the attention of the young child. Instead, an incident from a famous person's life may be fleshed out, elaborated upon, and the details recalled to make an interesting story. For example, primary children often read about famous Americans as they relate to children. See *Martin Luther King, Jr: A Biography for Young Children* and *Elizabeth Cady Stanton: A Biography for Young Children* by Carol Hilgartner Schlank and Barabara Metzger. Some biography-type stories include incidents from the famous person's

Courtesy of *My Friend Leslie*, published by Lothrop, Lee, and Shepard.

childhood. See for example, Carl Sandburg's *Abe Lincoln Grows Up.*

Often the "people" books in the nonfiction category for the young child are about the lives and work of people in exceptional circumstances. Two that children can relate to easily are *Our Teacher's in a Wheelchair* by Mary Ellen Powers and Role's *Where's Chimpy?* the story of a Downs Syndrome child.

Mental and learning difficulties are often hard for young children to understand. The extraordinary book *My Friend Leslie: The Story of a Handicapped Child* by Maxine B. Rosenberg is a nonfiction book with the theme of friendship between two girls, one an exceptional child. It is a must for the early childhood classroom library. Leslie and Karin are best friends in kindergarten. The text that accompanies the black and white photographs is Karin's story about her friend Leslie who has multiple handicaps. Seen through a child's eyes, Leslie is accepted as a real friend to enjoy, a capable friend whose ways of acting and means of getting things done are different. Karin tells about Leslie's behaviors, her special hearing aids, and ways the teachers and other children help her. It is a pleasingly honest book, which tells of Leslie's capabilities and limitations (Raines & Canady, 1991, p.56).

NONFICTION BOOKS AS MULTICULTURAL LITERATURE

Nonfiction books about people, places, and events are particularly significant in multicultural literature. The nonfiction books that present a culture accurately and interestingly can foster young children's understandings of other cultures.

A nonfiction book portraying the uniqueness of a present culture is Diane Hoyt-Goldsmith's *Pueblo Storyteller* with photographs by Lawrence Migdale. Ten-year-old April tells about her daily life in the Cochiti Pueblo and the pueblo traditions that her grandparents and she keep:

I am a pueblo child and I love to listen to my grandparents tell stories. From their example, I learn to take what I need from the earth to live, but also how to leave something behind for future generations. Everyday I am learning to live in harmony with the world. And every day, I am collecting memories of my life to share one day with my own children and grandchildren [quote from book jacket, 1991].

Another nonfiction book celebrating how cultures keep their traditions alive in modern day family life is Susan Kuklin's *How My Family Lives in America*. In a photographic essay, we meet three children,

Sanu, who is learning how to braid her hair and to cook the same African meal her father makes; Eric, (from a Puerto Rican family), who loves to play baseball with his dad and dance the merengue with his family; and April, who works hard on her Chinese writing and tries to keep up with her family's challenging games [book jacket description, 1992].

Place and the alphabet are also used as ways of organizing the nonfiction book. For example, Stephanie Feeney's *A is for Aloha* is an alphabet book showing Hawaiian preschoolers engaged in a variety of activities at many different places. Other place-organized books include *Big City ABC* by Alan Moak and *City Seen from A to Z* by Rachel Isadora.

In addition to the array of places introduced through the alphabet book, there are a number of nonfiction books about places, such as *Airport* by Byron Barton, *The Erie Canal* by Peter Spier, and *In My Garden* by Helen Oeschli.

Stories for young children about people may fit categories of people, such as farmers, health-care workers, community helpers, teachers, friends, and families. The nonfiction book about people may focus on how people work, their unusual work, how they get from one place to the other, or how they feel emotionally and relate socially. The people and places books can be read together in a unit of study so that youngsters can more fully develop the inherent concepts. For example, Ray Brockel's *Fire Fighters* could be read on the same day as Gail Gibbons *Fire! Fire!*

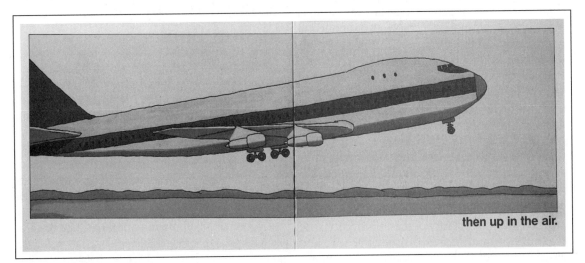

then up in the air.

Courtesy of *Airport*, published by Crowell.

Informational Books

"How-to" books and "all-about-it" books are popular staples for adult readers. Books that contain information are only beginning to become available for young children. Among the new best sellers are a book by David Macaulay, *The Way Things Work,* and the Earth Works Group's *50 Simple Things Kids Can Do to Save the Earth.* These books and others can spark new interests and assist children as they learn about their world.

The dividing line between the nonfiction book for the young and the informational book is not clear. Because the text for the young reader or listener is often sparse, the concept book, the nonfiction book on a particular topic, and the informational book are closely related. For example, when a group of teachers and librarians were asked to classify Byron Barton's book *Building a House,* they listed the book in three different categories. This book is informative, helps develop children's understanding of the process of building a house, and also fits into the category of nonfiction.

Information books can be concept books, how-to books of crafts, cooking, experiments, and other topics, or they can be photographic essays of the life of people, plants, and animals or usual and unusual happenings in ordinary and extraordinary places. In addition, the photographs and limited text in identification books, such as nature guides, can provide young children with an important introduction to the use of reference materials.

SELECTION CRITERIA FOR INFORMATIONAL BOOKS

The criteria for the selection of informational books for young children is similar to that of the nonfiction book. The key evaluation points are: accuracy and clarity of the information; the organization and format of both the text and illustrated material; the quality of the illustrations; and the quality and style of the writing. Often, accuracy and visual appearance are the factors considered first by many teachers. It is, however, very important to select well-written informational books. Well-chosen adjectives, descriptive pictures created with words, and vivid language can make any book memorable. Similarly, because the text of informational books for children can be sparse, the photographs or illustrative materials need to clearly extend the child's understanding and facilitate conceptualization of the information.

The informational book is often meant to be reference material providing a tool for young children to find answers. In many kindergarten and primary classrooms, young children can be observed intently reading the informational book from cover to cover. It is important to include this category of books in the early childhood classroom, for some young children are enthralled by the expansive information that may help them understand some natural phenomena or mechanical information, or answer questions of personal interest.

Curriculum Units With Nonfiction and Realistic Fiction Books

Preschool, kindergarten, and primary teachers can plan intriguing topics of study in the areas of social studies and science that include fiction and nonfiction books. Science teachers often look with disdain on early childhood teachers who read *The Very Hungry Caterpillar* by Eric Carle as part of a unit on metamorphosis. Certainly, caterpillars do not eat salami, pickles, and lollipops as does the Very Hungry Caterpillar; however, they do have a ferocious appetite.

A good unit on butterflies might include the nonfiction book *From Egg to Butterfly* by Marlene Reidel, in which the author describes the metamorphosis of a butterfly through its stages of egg, caterpillar, pupa,

Courtesy of *Where Butterflies Grow*, published by Lodestar.

Courtesy of *Bugs*, published by Mulberry.

and finally of butterfly. The addition of the realistic fiction book *Where Butterflies Grow* by Joanne Ryder will help children learn more about the ecological environment of a butterfly meadow:

In this magnificently illustrated book, the facts of science and the wonder of nature merge with the reader's own imagination. The story of the metamorphosis of the black swallowtail butterfly begins with the invitation to imagine being small and hidden in a tiny leaf. In a poetic voice, we are invited to imagine the growth from egg to creeper to cocoon to swallowtail. We see a lovely meadow of plants, a few small animals, and bird in the full-page illustrations, which are beautiful in nature's colors. On a few pages, enlargements show the details of the caterpillar's changes. At the end of the book, the teacher is given directions for growing a butterfly garden and keeping a caterpillar in a terrarium (Raines & Canady, 1991, p. 100).

An effective comparison could be made based on nonfiction and realistic fiction books. The teacher presents information children need on

caterpillars turning into butterflies and provides accurate pictures and text but uses the fiction book for a point of comparison and helps children see what is real and what is imagined.

In the following list, there are social studies and science units for young children that are taught often and some good nonfiction books that accurately support that unit teaching. The quality realistic fiction books, which can add facts and provide the context for the concept and main ideas of the theme, are also presented.

The classroom teacher who wants to add more reality in the unit will entertain the idea of using both selections of fine nonfiction and contemporary realistic fiction, which reflect what is plausible and possible. For example, for a unit on insects, one of the best nonfiction books is *Bugs* by Nancy Winslow Parker and Joan Richards Wright.

In an usual combination of rhymes, scientific facts, and illustrations, the authors invite young readers to enjoy the book from many different levels. On the left side of the open pages, a rhyme about a person and a bug is printed with clear, simple, colorful illustrations. On the right side of the open pages, Parker and Wright provide a scientific drawing of the bug and the authors discuss facts about the insects. The book ends with a picture glossary of growth stages of bugs, a phylum chart, and a bibliography of the sources. Cleverly conceived and well-executed, the book interests children on an everyday occurrence level, yet introduces them to the fascinating world of fifteen common insects and one slug (Raines & Canady, 1991, p. 104).

To add to a unit on insects, a good contemporary realistic book is *When the Woods Hum* by Joanne Ryder. In this intergenerational story, Papa shows Jenny a cicada he has kept for seventeen years. The story parallels the seventeen years between the cicadas' appearances and Jenny's growing up. At the end of the story, seventeen years later, Jenny tells her son, Ray, about the cicadas as Papa, now a grandfather, walks with them through the woods. The warm, affectionate life cycle story is told through lovely watercolor and ink drawings showing the lush greens of the beautiful woods (Raines & Canady, 1992, p. 90).

The curriculum unit is strengthened by the combination of excellent nonfiction books with accurate information presented in interesting, straightforward ways and the realistic fiction book, which places that information in a story context of the contemporary world.

SUMMARY

Young children's curiosity, fascination with the real physical and social world, and their need to know provide the rationale for the expanding category of reality-based books. Good teachers take into account who the young child

---

Figure 6.4 **Examples of Units — Nonfiction (NF) and Realistic Fiction (RF) Books**

UNITS	BOOKS
Families	(NF) *Loving* by Ann Morris
	(NF) *All Kinds of Families* by Norma Simon
	(RF) *How Many Stars in the Sky?* by Lenny Hort
	(RF) *Daddy Makes the Best Spaghetti* by Anna Grossnickle Hines
Friends	(NF) *My Friend Leslie: The Story of a Handicapped Child* by Maxine B. Rosenberg
	(RF) *Ira Sleeps Over* by Bernard Waber
Animal Life	(NF) *Animals Born Alive and Well* by Ruth Heller
	(NF) *The Puffins Are Back* by Gail Gibbons
	(NF) *Whose Baby Are You?* by Masayuki Yabuuchi
	(RF) *Baby Animals* by Margaret Wise Brown
	(RF) *Nate's Treasure* by David Spohn
Plant Life	(NF) *Plants That Never Ever Bloom* by Ruth Heller
	(NF) *From Seed to Pear* by Ali Mitgutsch
	(RF) *The Seasons of Arnold's Apple Tree* by Gail Gibbons
	(RF) *This Year's Garden* by Cynthia Rylant

See the following sources for additional selections. Raines, S. C., & Canady, R. J. (1989, 1991, 1992). *Story S-t-r-e-t-c-h-e-r-s: Activities to Expand Children's Favorite Books. More Story S-t-r-e-t-c-h-e-r-s. Story S-t-r-e-t-c-h-e-r-s for the Primary Grades.* Mt. Rainier, MD: Gryphon House.

is developmentally and individually and make selections that support both individual and age-stage appropriate development.

In the category of reality, whether contemporary realistic fiction and nonfiction, authenticity and accuracy are the hallmarks. Yet, to make the book appealing to the young child, the illustrative materials must be informative and match the text, often pushing the information beyond the limits of the words. The young child's appetite for knowledge is a compelling charge for the teacher to select quality literature in the reality-based categories.

A Teacher's Success Story: "A Casual Complaint About a Book—One Teacher's Success Story"

Linda deAngeles telephoned the parent volunteer and asked if she would help with a group-time lesson. The volunteer agreed and they planned to meet after school the following day to make their plans.

The young teacher was a bit nervous about the meeting and had to think just how to approach the parent volunteer who had expressed displeasure at the use of the tradebook, *A Home*. Ms. deAngeles was concerned that she might become too defensive.

At the afternoon planning session, Ms. deAngeles thanked the mother for volunteering so much of her time and expressed that she was pleased the parent felt comfortable enough in the classroom to express her opinion about the book, *A Home*. Linda went on to say she wanted to read the book to the whole class and after reading it pause to discuss the pushing incident between the two girls.

The teacher wisely invited the parent to predict what the children might say and then asked if she would tell the first graders what she said to her child about fighting and pushing. Ms. deAngeles wanted to find a way to incorporate the parent's concerns into the next day's lesson.

During the morning of the group time, the teacher and the parent greeted each other warmly, but a bit nervously, then taking a cue from the teacher, the parent sat in a chair at the front of the carpeted circle area. The lesson went very well, although initially when asked what they would do if a friend pushed them, the animated first graders started a few mock fist swings and the teacher feared the lesson would deteriorate. However, she quickly intervened and told a story about how hurt she was as a child when her best friend and she argued. Then she turned to the parent volunteer and asked her to say what she tells her daughter about fighting and pushing.

The children quickly interjected what their parents say to them. Ms. deAngeles ended the lesson by reading the pushing scene from *A Home* again and asked the children to tell what they would say to the two girls. She concluded the whole group session by finishing the reading of the book.

Afterward, the parent volunteer said, "Now, that wasn't so bad. I think the children could have that book in the classroom now, but I still wouldn't want my daughter to read if you hadn't done this lesson."

Suggested Learning Experiences

1. Inquire of a librarian or a school principal how parents' complaints about books are handled.

2. Read the full Jalongo and Creany article on "Censorship in Children's Literature: What Every Educator Should Know" from the Association for Childhood Education International Journal, *Childhood Education* (1991).

3. Select some multicultural books you think are positive ones in representing cultures different than your own. What makes them particularly effective?

4. Look through at least ten popular children's picture books and list the numbers and ways minority children are included.

5. Read a realistic fiction book about a minority culture and a nonfiction book. Evaluate each for their appeal to young children. If possible, read them to a classroom of children and follow up the reading by discussing what they learned from each book.

6. Read at least five realistic fiction books by different authors and evaluate each using the literary elements.

7. Select an early childhood program near your college or university and find out the cultural make-up of the program.

8. Select at least five non fiction books on topics you think will interest young children. Evaluate the books using Guidelines for Selecting Quality Nonfiction found in Figure 6.2.

9. Compare a realistic fiction book and a nonfiction book on the same subject. Plan a lesson using both books.

10. Review Beverly Kobrin's *Eyeopeners! How to Choose and Use Children's Books About Real People, Places, and Things* (1988). Using the reference as a tool, select at least five titles that would interest primary grades children.

ENDNOTES

1. Based on classroom observations in Peggy Sander's third grade, Robyn Ake, student intern, at Cub Run Elementary, Fairfax, Virginia. Cub Run is a Professional Development School for George Mason University and Fairfax County Public Schools.

2. Ms. deAngeles' story is based on an actual experience; however, the teacher's name has been changed for the sake of anonymity, and the parent volunteer's name has not been used.

REFERENCES

Barringer, F. (1991, March 11). Census shows profound change in racial makeup of nation. *New York Times*.

Burress, L. (1989). *Battle of the books: Literary censorship in the public schools (1850 - 1985)*. Metuchen, NJ: Scarecrow.

Comer, J. (1992). Foreword. In L. Miller-Lachmann (Ed.), *Our family, our friends, our world* (pp. xi-xii). New Providence, NJ: R. R. Bowker.

Cullinan, B. C. (1989). *Literature and the child*. San Diego, CA: Harcourt Brace Jovanovich.

Donahue, D. (1992, March 19). Satisfying a hunger for ethnic variety. *USA TODAY*, pp. 1D, 2D.

Donaldson, M. (1979). *Children's minds*. New York: Norton.

Erickson, E. H. (1963). *Childhood and society*. New York: Norton.

Harris, V. J. (1992). Contemporary griots: African-American writers of Children's Literature. In V. J. Harris (Ed.) *Teaching multicultural literature in grades K-8* (pp. 55-109). Norwood, MA: Christopher-Gordon Publishers.

Jalongo, M. R., & Creany, A. D. (1991). Censorship in children's literature: What every educator should know. *Childhood Education, 67*(3), 143-148.

Kobrin, B. (1988). *Eyeopeners! how to choose and use children's books about real people, places, and things*. New York: Penguin.

Raines, S. C., & Canady, R. J. (1992). *Gryphon House early childhood book catalog*. Mt. Rainier, MD: Gryphon House.

Raines, S. C., & Canady, R. J. (1989) *Story s-t-r-e-t-c-h-e-r-s: Activities to expand children's favorite books*. Mt. Rainier, MD: Gryphon House.

Raines, S. C., & Canady, R. J. (1991). *More story s-t-r-e-t-c-h-e-r-s: Activities to expand children's favorite books*. Mt. Rainier, MD: Gryphon House.

Raines, S. C., & Canady, R. J. (1992). *Story s-t-r-e-t-c-h-e-r-s for the primary grades: Activities to expand children's favorite books*. Mt. Rainier, MD: Gryphon House.

Raines, S. C., & Canady, R. J. (1990). *The whole language kindergarten*. New York: Teachers College Press.

Sims, Bishop, R., (1992). Multicultural literature for children: Making informed choices. In V. J. Harris (Ed.), *Teaching multicultural literature in grades K-8* (pp. 55-109). Norwood, MA: Christopher-Gordon.

Traxe, J. (1992). The politics of children's literature: Reflections on multiculturalism, political correctness, and Christopher Columbus. In V. J. Harris (Ed.), *Teaching multicultural literature in grades K-8* (pp. 1-33). Norwood, MA: Christopher-Gordon.

Sobol, D. (1990). *Encyclopedia Brown and the case of the disgusting sneakers* (Book cover). New York: Morrow.

CHILDREN'S LITERATURE REFERENCES

The authors and illustrators of children's books are listed, in all chapters, by their full names to help the reader become acquainted with them. If only one name is listed, the author also illustrated the book.

Abercrombie, Barbara. (1990). *Charlie Anderson*. Illustrated by Mark Graham. New York: Margaret K. McElderry.

Ackerman, Karen. (1988). *Song and Dance Man*. Illustrated by Stephen Gammell. New York: Alfred A. Knopf.

Ahlberg, Janet, & Ahlberg, Allan. (1988). *Starting School*. Illustrated by Janet Ahlberg. New York: Penguin.

Aliki. (1982). *We Are Best Friends*. New York: Greenwillow.

Ashley, Bernard. (1991). *Cleversticks*. Illustrated by Derek Brazell. New York: Crown.

Barton, Byron. (1982). *Airport*. New York: Crowell.

Barton, Byron. (1981). *Building a House*. New York: Greenwillow.

Broekel, Ray. (1981). *Fire Fighters*. Chicago: Children's Press.

Brown, Margaret Wise. (1989). *Baby Animals*. Illustrated by Susan Jeffers. New York: Harper & Row.

Brown, Tricia. (1984). *Someone Special, Just Like You*. Photographs by Fran Ortiz. New York: Henry Holt.

Bunting, Eve. (1989). *The Wednesday Surprise*. Illustrated by Donald Carrick. New York: Clarion Books.

Carle, Eric. (1981). *The Very Hungry Caterpillar*. New York: Philomel Books.

Cleary, Beverly. (1979). *Ramona and Her Mother*. Illustrated by Alan Tiegreen. New York: Morrow.

Cleary, Beverly. (1968). *Ramona the Pest*. Illustrated by Louis Darling. New York: Morrow.

Cleary, Beverly. (1981). *Ramona Quimby, Age 8*. Illustrated by Alan Tiegreen. New York: Morrow.

Clifton, Lucile. (1983). *Everett Anderson's Good-bye*. Illustrated by Ann Grifalconi. New York: Holt, Rinehart and Winston.

Cohen, Miriam. (1989). *See You In Second Grade*. Illustrated by Lillian Hoban. New York: Greenwillow.

Cole, Sheila. (1985). *When the Tide Is Low*. Illustrated by Virginia Wright-Frierson. New York: Lothrop, Lee & Shepard.

Conlin, Susan, & Friedman, Susan Levine. (1989). *Ellie's Day*. Illustrated by Kathryn Smith. Seattle, WA: Parenting Press.

Conlin, Susan, & Friedman, Susan Levine. (1991). *Nathan's Day at Preschool*. Illustrated by Kathryn Smith. Seattle, WA: Parenting Press.

Dantzer-Rosenthal, Marya. (1986). *Some Things Are Different, Some Things Are the Same*. Niles, IL: Albert Whitman.

dePaola, Tomie. (1978). *Nana Upstairs, Nana Downstairs*. New York: Penguin.

dePaola, Tomie. (1981). *Now One Foot, Now the Other*. New York: Putnam.

Earth Works Group. (1990). *50 Simple Things Kids Can Do To Save The Earth*. New York: Andrews & McMell.

Fassler, Joan. (1974). *Howie Helps Himself*. Illustrated by Joe Lasker. Niles, IL: Whitman.

Feeney, Stephanie. (1980). *A Is for Aloha*. Photographs by Hella Hammid. Honolulu: University of Hawaii Press.

Fox, Mem. (1985). *Wilfrid Gordon McDonald Partridge*. Illustrated by Julie Vivas. Brooklyn, NY: Kane/Miller.

Gibbons, Gail. (1984). *Fire! Fire!*. New York: Crowell.

Gibbons, Gail. (1991). *The Puffins Are Back*. New York: Harper Collins.

Gibbons, Gail.(1984). *The Seasons of Arnold's Appletree*. San Diego, CA: Harcourt Brace Jovanovich.

Girard, Linda W. (1986). *Adoption Is for Always*. Illustrated by Judith Friedman. Niles, IL: Albert Whitman.

Girard, Linda W. (1987). *At Daddy's on Saturday*. Illustrated by Judith Friedman. Niles, IL: Albert Whitman.

Gordon, Shirley. (1980). *The Boy Who Wanted a Family*. Illustrated by Charles Robinson. New York: Harper & Row.

Greenfield, Eloise. (1974). *She Come Bringing Me That Little Baby Girl*. Illustrated by John Steptoe. New York: J. B. Lippincott.

Havill, Juanita. (1986). *Jamaica's Find*. Illustrated by Anne Sibley O'Brien. Boston: Houghton Mifflin.

Havill, Juanita. (1989). *Jamaica Tag-a-Long*. Illustrated by Anne Sibley O'Brien. Boston: Houghton Mifflin.

Hazen, Barbara Shook. (1992). *Even If I Did Something Awful*. Illustrated by Nancy Kincade. New York: Macmillan.

Hazen, Barbara Shook. (1992). *Mommie's Office*. Illustrated by David Soman. New York: Macmillan.

Heide, Florence Parry, & Gilliland, Judith Heide. (1990). *The Day of Ahmed's Secret*. Illustrated by Ted Lewin. New York: Lothrop, Lee & Shepard.

Heller, Ruth. (1982). *Animals Born Alive and Well*. New York: Grossett and Dunlap.

Heller, Ruth. (1981). *Chickens Aren't the Only Ones*. New York: Grossett and Dunlap.

Heller, Ruth. (1984). *Plants That Never Ever Bloom*. New York: Grossett and Dunlap.

Hines, Anna Grossnickle. (1986). *Daddy Makes the Best Spaghetti*. New York: Clarion Books.

Hines, Anna Grossnickle. (1988). *Grandma Gets Grumpy*. New York: Clarion Books.

Hirschi, Ron. (1990). *Winter*. Photographs by Thomas D. Mangelson. New York: Cobblehill.

Hoban, Tana. (1990). *Exactly the Opposite*. New York: William Morrow.

Hoban, Tana. (1992). *Spirals, Curves, Fanshapes, & Lines*. New York: William Morrow.

Hoffman, Mary. (1991). *Amazing Grace*. Illustrated by Caroline Binch. New York: Penguin.

Hoffman, Mary. (1987). *Nancy No-Size*. Illustrated by Jennifer Northway. New York: Oxford University Press.

Hort, Lenny. (1991). *How Many Stars in the Sky?* Illustrated by James E. Ransome. New York: Tambourine.

Howard, Elizabeth Fitzgerald. (1988). *The Train to Lulu's*. Illustrated by Robert Casilla. New York: Bradbury.

Hoyt-Goldsmith, Diane. (1991). *Pueblo Storyteller*. Photographs by Lawrence Migdale. New York: Holiday House.

Hurd, Edith Thacher. (1982). *I Dance in My Red Pajamas*. Illustrated by Emily Arnold McCully. New York: Harper & Row.

Hutchins, Pat. (1971). *Titch*. New York: Macmillan.

Isadora, Rachel. (1983). *City Seen From A to Z*. New York: Greenwillow.

Jordan, Marykate. (1989). *Losing Uncle Tim*. Illustrated by Judith Friedman. Morton Grove, IL: Albert Whitman.

Kachenmeister, Cheryl. (1989). *On Monday When It Rained*. Photographs by Tom Berthiaume. Boston: Houghton Mifflin.

Keats, Ezra Jack. (1964). *Whistle for Willie*. New York: Viking Press.

Kuklin, Susan. (1992). *How My Family Lives in America*. New York: Bradbury Press.

Little, Lessie Jones, & Greenfield, Eloise (1978). *I Can Do It Myself*. Illustrated by Carole Byard. New York: Thomas Y. Crowell.

Macauley, David. (1988). *The Way Things Work*. Boston: Houghton Mifflin.

Maclachlan, Patricia. (1982). *Mama One, Mama Two*. Illustrated by Ruth Lercher Bornstein. New York: Harper & Row.

Malone, Nola Langer. (1988). *A Home*. New York: Bradbury.

Madsen, Jane M., & Bockoras, Diane. (1983). *Please Don't Tease Me*. Illustrated by Richard Cuffari. New York: Doubleday.

Martin, C. L. G. (1991). *Three Brave Women*. Illustrated by Peter Elwell. New York: Macmillan.

Mitgutsch, Ali. (1971). *From Seed to Pear*. Minneapolis, MN: Carolrhoda.

Moak, Alan. (1989). *Big City ABC*. Plattsburgh, NY: Tundra.

Mora, Pat. (1992). *A Birthday Basket for Tia*. Illustrated by Cecily Lang. New York: Macmillan.

Morris, Ann. (1989). *Bread, Bread, Bread*. Photographs by Ken Heyman. New York: Lothrop, Lee & Shepard.

Morris, Ann. (1989). *Hats, Hats, Hats*. Photographs by Ken Heyman. New York: Lothrop, Lee & Shepard.

Morris, Ann. (1992). *Houses and Homes*. Photographs by Ken Heyman. New York: Lothrop, Lee & Shepard.

Morris, Ann. (1990). *Loving*. Photographs by Ken Heyman. New York: Lothrop, Lee & Shepard.

Morris, Ann. (1992). *On the Go*. Photographs by Ken Heyman. New York: Lothrop, Lee & Shepard.

Morris, Ann. (1992). *Tools*. Photographs by Ken Heyman. New York: Lothrop, Lee & Shepard.

Oeschli, Helen. (1985). *In My Garden*. Illustrated by Kelly Oeschli. New York: Macmillan.

Parker, Nancy Winslow, & Wright, Joan Richards.(1987). *Bugs*. Illustrated by Nancy Winslow Parker. New York: Mulberry Books.

Powers, Mary Ellen. (1986). *Our Teacher's in a Wheelchair*. Niles, IL: Albert Whitman.

Rabe, Berniece. (1987). *Where's Chimpy?* Illustrated by Linda Shute. Photographs by Diane Schmidt. Niles, IL: Albert Whitman.

Reidel, Marlene. (1974). *From Egg to Butterfly*. Minneapolis, MN: Carolrhoda Books.

Rosenberg, Maxine, B. (1983). *My Friend Leslie: The Story of a Handicapped Child*. Photographs by George Ancona. New York: Lothrop, Lee & Shepard.

Ryder, Joanne. (1991). *When the Woods Hum*. Illustrated by Catherine Stock. New York: Morrow.

Ryder, Joanne. (1989). *Where Butterflies Grow*. Illustrated by Lynne Cherry. New York: Lodestar.

Rylant, Cynthia. (1984). *This Year's Garden*. Illustrated by Mary Szilagyi. New York: Bradbury.

Sandburg, Carl. (1926, 1928, 1954). *Abe Lincoln Grows Up*. Illustrated by James Daughtery. San Francisco, CA: Harcourt Brace Jovanovich.

Schlank, Carol Hilgartner, & Metzger, Barbara. (1991). *Elizabeth Cady Stanton: A Biography for Young Children*. Illustrated by Janice Bond. Mt. Rainier, MD: Gryphon House.

Schlank, Carol Hilgartner, & Metzger, Barbara. (1990). *Martin Luther King, Jr: A Biography for Young Children*. Illustrated by John Kastner. Mt. Rainier, MD: Gryphon House.

Scheffler, Ursel. (1986). *A Walk in the Rain*. Illustrated by Ulises Wensell. Translated by Andrea Mernan. New York: G. P. Putnam's Sons.

Scott, Ann Herbert. (1972). *On Mother's Lap*. Illustrated by Glo Coalson. Boston: Houghton Mifflin.

Simon, Norma. (1976). *All Kinds of Families*. Illustrated by Joe Lasker. Niles, IL: Albert Whitman.

Simon, Norma. (1974). *I Was So Mad*. Illustrated by Dora Leder. Niles, IL: Albert Whitman.

Simon, Norma. (1986). *The Saddest Time*. Illustrated by Jacqueline Rogers. Niles, IL: Albert Whitman.

Simon, Seymour. (1991). *Big Cats*. New York: Harper Collins.

Sobol, Donald J. (1990). *Encyclopedia Brown and the Case of the Disgusting Sneakers*. Illustrated by Gail Owens. New York: Morrow.

Spier, Peter. (1970). *The Erie Canal*. New York: Doubleday.

Spohn, David. (1991). *Nate's Treasure*. New York: Lothrop, Lee & Shepard.

Stanek, Muriel. (1985). *All Alone After School*. Illustrated by Ruth Rosner. Niles, IL: Albert Whitman.

Stanek, Muriel. (1983). *Don't Hurt Me, Mama*. Illustrated by Helen Cogancherry. Niles, IL: Albert Whitman.

Stanek, Muriel. (1986). *My Mom Can't Read*. Illustrated by Jacqueline Rogers. Niles, IL: Albert Whitman.

Stanton, Elizabeth, & Stanton, Henry. (1978). *Sometimes I Like to Cry*. Illustrated by Richard Leyden. Niles, IL: Albert Whitman.

Stinson, Kathy. (1982). *Red Is Best*. Illustrated by Robin Baird Lewis. Toronto: Annick Press.

Surat, Michele Maria. (1983). *Angel Child, Dragon Child*. Illustrated by Vo-Dinh Mai. New York: Scholastic.

Tompert, Ann. (1988). *Will You Come Back for Me?* Illustrated by Robin Kramer. Niles, IL: Albert Whitman.

Vigna, Judith. (1988). *I Wish Daddy Didn't Drink So Much*. Niles, IL: Albert Whitman.

Vigna, Judith. (1990). *My Big Sister Takes Drugs*. Morton Grove, IL: Albert Whitman.

Vigna, Judith. (1986). *Nobody Wants a Nuclear War*. Niles, IL: Albert Whitman.

Vigna, Judith. (1980). *She's Not My Real Mother*. Niles, IL: Albert Whitman.

Viorst, Judith. (1972). *Alexander and the Terrible, Horrible, No Good, Very Bad Day*. New York: Macmillan.

Viorst, Judith. (1971). *The Tenth Good Thing About Barney*. Illustrated by Eric Blegvad. New York: Atheneum.

Waber, Bernard. (1972). *Ira Sleeps Over*. Boston: Houghton Mifflin.

Waddell, Martin. (1990). *My Great Grandpa*. Illustrated by Dom Mansell. New York: G. P. Putnam.

Waber, Bernard. (1988). *Ira Says Goodbye*. Boston: Houghton Mifflin.

Wilhelm, Hans. (1985). *I'll Always Love You*. New York: Crown.

Winthop, Elizabeth. (1989). *The Best Friends Club*. Illustrated by Martha Weston. New York: Lothrop, Lee & Shepard.

Yabuuchi, Masayuki. (1985). *Whose Baby?* New York: Philomel.

Zolotow, Charlotte. (1972). *William's Doll*. Illustrated by William Pene duBois. New York: Harper & Row.

7

Poetry and
the Rhythm of
Expression

Poetry and the Rhythm of Expression

When Maya Angelou read her poem, "On the Pulse of Morning," at the inauguration of President William Jefferson Clinton on January 20, 1993, much of the world paused. Listeners experienced the power of poetry to express deep spiritual truths and to convey meaning through the simplest of symbols—a rock, a river, and a tree. Angelou's poem inspired the humble and the proud, bound us in common histories, and urged us to heal our wounds, and to find some light for our tomorrows. Influential leaders were seen with tears in their eyes as the poet read in a voice that was strong, true, and filled with a sense of a higher calling. The listeners were swept along on the currents of language, the rise and fall of rhythms, and the drama of pauses, which burst with anticipation of the next lines.

The fact that this auspicious moment in history was celebrated with a poem is fitting. In our heights of jubilation, in our sense of celebration, and in the depths of despair, we write poetry. It is the literature form that touches the soul, has deep biological and psychological reasons for its existence, and renders all who embrace it as captives to the passion, the pleasure, and the pain we share because we are human.

In this chapter, we invite you to the celebrations of poetry, its forms, its effects, and its uses in the early childhood classroom. It is our hope that among the children we teach, a Maya Angelou of the future will embrace this literary form and help the next generation appreciate the ways poetry satisfies our deep human needs for expression. If we are to inspire poets of the future, then our classrooms must be filled with poetry. Unfortunately in many schools, poetry is treated as an optional activity, something to be done if time allows. Poetry is not only an integral part of literature-based curriculum that effective early childhood educators embrace, but it is essential to the child as another of the invitations to the world of good literature.

The chapter is organized around the following topics:

1. Goals of poetry instruction
2. Children's sense of poetry
3. Descriptions of poetry
4. Elements of poetry
5. Poetry throughout the curriculum
6. Guidance for a literature unit on poetry

Goals of Poetry as a Part of the Classroom

Teachers have the opportunity to enhance the fascination young children have for rhythmic language and to make poetry a natural part of their development of language and appreciation of literature. But first, teachers must develop within themselves a love and understanding of poetry and project that attitude to their students. Many teachers who feel uncomfortable presenting poetry to their students are themselves victims of poor poetry instruction. The attitude persists in many classrooms that poetry reading, like art and music, is an activity for a few talented individuals. Early childhood educators who have a process language orientation have long since abandoned that notion, and the results have been that all children in their classrooms enjoy listening to and reading poetry, and therefore, poetry is an important part of the literature program.

Similarly, some teachers only think of poetry as rhyming verses and limit their selections to childhood nursery rhymes, rhyming chants, and simple fingerplays, rather than exposing children to the full range of poetry. The fingerplays, chants, and motion rhymes that are a part of preschools, kindergarten, and child-care classrooms are often referred to in the literature as *rhymes*. These selections are appropriate for the early childhood classroom, but our goal is to have children experience and appreciate a wide range of poetry. Children should be exposed to numerous poetry forms, have poems incorporated into daily activities, and include poets, as well as authors of stories, in literature studies (Denman, 1988).

Every parent and early childhood teacher knows that children respond to repetitive patterns, and they should be given many opportunities to listen to and participate in rhythmic language activities. However, one of the earliest understandings we need to communicate is that poems do not have to rhyme. Children need to experience poetry in its broadest sense. The responsibility teachers of young children have is not so much to teach children about poetry and the rhythm of language, rather it is to keep alive the love of poetry and rhythm the children bring to the classroom.

SELECTION AND QUALITY

Children's preferences for certain poetry forms, topics that the students enjoy, and a wide variety of poetry and poets' works should be considered when making selections. Children's preferences should be taken into account; however, with exposure, children's preferences can broaden. Research by Fisher and Natarella (1982) rank young children's poetry preferences. While preschoolers and kindergartners were not included, the study revealed that first, second, and third graders liked narrative poetry, limericks, rhymes, free verse, lyric poetry, and haiku, in that order.

Huck, Hepler, and Hickman warn that children's poetry should reflect real emotions: "Poetry that is cute, coy, nostalgic, or sarcastic may be about children, but it is not for them [1993, p.453]." Teachers who tend to like a certain poetry form, poet, or particular poetic mood must be careful to go beyond their own personal preferences. Children should have a steady diet of poems that reflect a broad range and variety of forms, poets, subjects, and moods that they enjoy, so that the poetry is for them.

The quality of the poetry for the young child is always an issue. To be assured of selecting good quality poetry, teachers can select poems from outstanding poets and anthologists who know and understand young children. Figure 7.1 is a list of poets children from preschool through third grade enjoy. While we can count on these poets and noted anthologists' selections, it is also imperative that teachers choose poetry with their own classroom of children in mind.

Children's Sense of Poetry

Observers of young children's language have discovered the important role rhythm and rhyme play in the early acquisition and continuing development of oral and written language. Most parents and teachers of young children are aware of the fascination young children have with the rhythm of language and their sensitivity to rhyming and repeated language patterns. Even young babies will respond to the sounds of their mothers' voices and then smile or giggle when the mother speaks in rhythmic and repeated phrases. Some think our appreciation of rhyme can be traced to the biological impulses to repeat sounds, such as those in our first rhymes: "ma-ma," "da-da," "ba-ba," "wa-wa" (Chukovsky, 1963).

Even before young children are able to speak, they make sing-song sounds, which they repeat over and over. They delight in hearing rhythmic phrases, such as "gitchie-gitchie-goo." Rhythmic language not only appeals to the child's senses but enhances her or his natural learning process. Early childhood teachers have known for a long time of the effectiveness of rhythm and rhyme in learning.

Descriptions of Poetry

Ironically, many attempts to define poetry also describe the language of young children. Adjectives such as creative, unusual, rhythmic, imaginative, visual, artistic, condensed, and intuitive, which are used to describe poetry, are also used to describe the language of the young child.

Figure 7.1 Poets for the Early Childhood Years*

Arnold Adoff
Jill Bennett
Margaret Wise Brown
John Ciardi
Lucille Clifton
Beatrice Schenk de Regniers
Eleanor Farjeon
Aileen Fisher
Eloise Greenfield
May Ann Hoberman
Felice Holman
Lee Bennett Hopkins
Leland Jacobs
Karla Kuskin
Nancy Larrick
Edward Lear
Patrick Lewis
Myra Cohn Livingston
Arnold Lobel
Bill Martin, Jr.
    and John Archaumbault
Eve Merriam
David McCord
Lilian Moore
Mary O'Neill
Jack Prelutsky
Christina Rossetti
Cynthia Rylant
Diane Siebert
Shel Silverstein
Robert Lewis Stevenson
Judith Viorst
Valorie Worth
Jane Yolen
Charlotte Zolotow

*One is always hesitant to make a list, lest someone be left off; however, we recommend that teachers start their own lists and add the new poets whose works are entering the children's literature market.

Speaking in rhythmic, repetitive patterns is as natural to young children as breathing. Their creative, rhythmic language is familiar to teachers and parents. Authors and book publishers recognize the appeal of rhythmic language and include much of story and poetry in rhyming and lyrical forms to please their young audience.

Few educators have contributed more to the literature of the young child and emphasized the need for rhythmic language in literature for the classroom than Bill Martin, Jr. At a young authors conference in Tulsa, Dr. Martin said, "In our zeal to cover the basic skills, we have all but destroyed the 'music of the language [1984].'" At a similar conference, Dr. Martin gave new meaning to the term *poetry* when he read a column from the sports page with such eloquence that it sounded like a verse from Longfellow.

Perhaps the reason the term poetry has been so difficult to define is because poetry is its own definition. It has to be experienced to be understood. Children understand and appreciate many things that are undefinable to them. Poetry can be defined as using words in unusual ways to stimulate the senses and create pictures in the heads of the listeners or readers. Children can learn to appreciate the language and images of poetry. A writer of poems is a painter of pictures with words; whether the poem is read by Maya Angelou from the inaugural program or Bill Martin, Jr., from the sports page.

Poetry for young children expresses sensory images in imaginative ways. It describes feelings, evokes emotions, and introduces children to the language of symbolism. The poet, Felice Holman (1985) said, "The things I see and feel and think about come to be songs in my head and some of them turn up as poems [p. 9]." Through the images and sounds of the language, the poet crafts a compressed meaningful whole that evokes more response from the reader and listener than simply the sounds of the words. The poet's use of sound means that poetry must be read aloud to appreciate the sounds and the rhythm of the language.

Figure 7.2 **Young Children's Descriptive Rhythmic Language**

"Sliding tickles my stomach."	(going down the slide)
"He's giganticer."	(describing his monster toy)
"Cars can't fly."	(first child)
"Mine can. Watch."	(second child, with sound effects)
"Mine can, mine can, Mine can. Mine can, mine can!"	(repeating, then zooming off)
"Scotty potty, potty Scotty."	(toddler talking in bathroom)

Poetry Elements and Forms

Poetry is described in terms of its elements and forms. The poet uses imagery, figurative language, rhythm, sound, and patterns to craft poems. The ways poems are constructed, look, and sound determine their form. Some poetry forms presented in this chapter include narrative poems, limericks, lyric poems, concrete poems, cinquain, haiku, and free verse. The poetic elements and forms are used to describe the poem, but these are for the teacher's understanding and need not be required of the young child. We do not expect children to use the terms, but to enjoy the richness of the world of poetry because of the elements and variety of forms.

Young children are particularly drawn to poems that are descriptive. Since they are explorers of their ever-widening physical and social world, the descriptive poem appeals to their senses. They like the descriptions that help them imagine sights, sounds, and physical movements. They enjoy the comparisons the poet makes when creating an image. The poet uses imagery and the figurative language of simile and metaphor to create pictures in the mind. Eve Merriam's "Cat's Tongue" in the book of poetry *Blackberry Ink* is an excellent example of a descriptive poem:

Courtesy of *Birdwatch,* published by Philomel.

> Cat's tongue,
> Cat's tongue,
> Pink as clover.
>
> Cat's tongue,
> Cat's tongue,
> Wash all over.
>
> Lick your paws,
> Lick your face,
> The back of your neck
> And every place.
>
> Lick your whiskers,
> Smooth your fur,
> Prick up your ears
> And purr, purr, purr.
>
> Cat's tongue,
> Cat's tongue,
> Pink as clover.
>
> Cat's tongue,
> Cat's tongue,
> Clean all over.

Merriam's description makes it easy for the child to visualize how the cat looks and moves while licking with its "pink as clover" tongue.

FIGURATIVE LANGUAGE

Another literary element the poet uses is figurative language, which compares the subject of the poem to another subject. Figurative language, such as "high as a kite," is a part of our everyday speech, but the poet also uses figurative language to strike new images. In Jane Yolen's *Birdwatch*, a collection of seventeen poems about birds, the illustrator, Ted Lewin, positioned a single red cardinal at the top left of a two page spread of snow. In the lower right Yolen's poem emphasizes winter's page.

> *The Cardinal*
> A showy gesture
> on autumn's stage.
> A brilliant blot
> on winter's page.
> A witty comment
> on early spring.
> And summer's own
> bright darling.

Lewin's illustrations show the brilliant red blot of the cardinal's colors on a white page of snow. The figurative language and the illustrator's art combine for an exquisitely simple poem, which is a delight to read, to visualize, and to see in illustration and in print on the page.

Poets help readers and listeners make memorable associations when they describe objects. Mary O'Neill's color poems in *Hailstones and Halibut Bones* are filled with memorable associations. John Wallner's rich illustrations of O'Neill's poems also comprise collages of visual associations for the reader.

> WHAT IS YELLOW?
> What is Yellow?
> Yellow is the color of the sun
> The feeling of fun
> The yolk of an egg
> A duck's bill
> A canary bird
> And a daffodil.
> Yellow's sweet corn
> Ripe oats
> Hummingbird's
> Little throats
> Summer squash and
> Chinese silk
> The cream on top
> Of Jersey milk
> Dandelions and
> Daisy hearts
> Custard pies and
> Lemon tarts.
> Yellow blinks
> On summer nights
> In the off-and-on of
> Firefly lights.
> Yellow's a topaz
> A candle flame.
> Felicity's a
> Yellow name.
> Yellow's mimosa
> And I guess,
> Yellow's the color of
> Happiness.

Poets use simile, metaphor, and personification as figurative language to compare and contrast their subject to other memorable images. A line from Jane Yolen's "Woodpecker" vividly describes the sound of the woodpecker's "ratatatatat" as a "jackhammer on a city street." We recognize simile when we read "like" or "as." The use of simile is effective because it is the comparison of two unlike things that share some commonality, such as the jackhammer and the woodpecker.

METAPHOR

Metaphor is a device the poet uses that goes beyond simple comparisons and describes one thing as if it is something else. In *Explore Poetry* by Donald Graves (1992), a child is reported telling Ruth Hubbard how he thinks, "Well, I hit rewind, then I hit forward, and when I come to what I want to say or write, I hit stop [p. 61]." The child used the metaphor of a tape recorder to describe his mind. In Nancy White Carlstrom's poem, the little girl's name is a metaphor for how she feels about nature, *Wild Wild Sunflower Child Anna*.

PERSONIFICATION

Personification means giving human qualities to things. In *Mojave*, Diane Siebert uses personification when she begins the poem with the desert speaking,

> I am the desert.
> I am free.
> Come walk the sweeping face of me.

Poetry and Rhythm— Poetry and Rhyme

RHYTHM

Rhythm is the beat, the pace, and the pattern of the language that moves the reader and the listener along. All of language has a rhythm. The chunks of words, the pauses for breath, and the semantic groupings cause the reader, the writer, and the listener to construct the language with a flow that feels natural; some would say even biological, since the pause is associated with breathing. The cadence, the tempo, the meter, and the overt and covert rhythms of language pace the poetry reader, listener, and writer. Whether the listener or reader are swept along in breathless anticipation of a climax, steadily drummed into an expected beat, or lulled into a restful mood, the rhythm of the poem communicates beyond the words.

RHYME

The sound of the rhyme in poetry delights young children. They play with language and recall it by the sounds that seem almost natural to the ear. From jump-rope rhymes, counting songs, religious chants, refrains in commercials, and repeated verses in songs, the rhyme infiltrates the mind and plays there in almost instant recall. Rhyme, with words that sound alike at the end, is the most readily identifiable sound structure in poetry.

ALLITERATION

Children enjoy alliteration, a repetition of beginning consonant sounds, with its range of subtle to almost tongue-twister repetitions. Old time favorites are:

> Peter Piper picked
> a peck of pickled peppers...
> How many pecks of pickled
> peppers did Peter Piper pick?

In "What is Yellow?," O'Neill used the repetition of consonant sounds in

> Dandelions and
> Daisy hearts

Alliteration is used effectively by Eve Merriam, Jack Prelutsky, Shel Silverstein, and many other poets who are listed as children's favorites. Alliteration is often used in humorous lines and plays upon the name-rhyming children experiment with when they are young. Children often request rereadings of humorous poems, such as Eve Merriam's

> Bertie, Bertie
> Dirty Bertie,
> Why don't you take a bath?

Courtesy of *Train Song*, published by Crowell.

ONOMATOPOEIA

Onomatopoeia refers to words that sound like their sounds, for example, *splash, clickety-clack, crack, screech,* and others. Diane Siebert's poetry often contains a rich variety of onomatopoeia, especially "Train Song" with the opening lines,

> out in back
> railroad track
> clickety-clack
> clickety-clack . . . .

Later in the poem she describes the train song as "singing-clickety-song."

REPETITION

Repetition is another way the poet uses the sounds of language. Repetition can also shape the form of the poem. Whether the repeated phrase rhymes with another or punctuates the mood of the poem by creating emphasis, repetition is a tool to carve out the potent parts of the poem. Poets may repeat a phrase as an opening line for each verse as in Jack Prelutsky's "Today Is Very Boring" in *The New Kid on the Block:*

> Today is very boring,
> it's a very boring day,
> there is nothing much to look at,
> there is nothing much to say,
> there's a peacock on my sneakers,
> there's a penguin on my head,
> there's a dormouse on my doorstep,
> I'm going back to bed.
> Today is very boring,
> it is boring through and through, . . .

Repetition is also used to emphasize the main concern of the poem. For example, in *Flap Your Wings and Try* Charlotte Pomerantz repeats the question, capturing the mood and main idea of the poem in the first stanza.

> I'm a little baby bird
> Wondering how to fly.
> See my Grandma in the sky,
> Why can't I, can't I.

POETRY FORMS

The form upon the printed page, the way the refrain is repeated, the rhyming pattern, and the free verse without constraints of rhyme are examples of how poetry looks, is read, and sounds. The forms we discuss in this chapter are:

- ☐ narrative poems that tell stories
- ☐ limericks with five line rhyming schemes
- ☐ lyrical poems akin to songs
- ☐ rhyming motion songs and chants
- ☐ concrete poems that outline a subject or feeling
- ☐ cinquain, diamonte, and haiku, constructed by syllable patterns
- ☐ free verse, without constraint of rhyme and syllable patterns

STORY IN POEMS

Stories can be told in long narrative forms or short poems. Narrative poems tell the story of a particular event. A famous one that instantly comes to mind is Clement Moore's "A Visit From St. Nicholas." On the popular PBS television series, "Reading Rainbow," the producers often include narrative poems to tell stories to children. One book selected for the program was *Barn Dance!* by Bill Martin, Jr. and John Archambault, a narrative poem about a little boy who hears the faint sound of music coming from the barn. He sneaks down to the barn to find the scarecrow playing his fiddle and all the farm animals dancing. Finally, he can resist the music no longer and joins in the fun. Just when the owl calls that it is almost morning, he finds his way back through the barnyard and the house, and crawls into bed. *Barn Dance!* is truly a celebration of the sights and sounds of a young boy's vivid imagination. Ted Rand's illustrations are line drawings with watercolors. The night scenes with the full moon lend just the right magic to the mood.

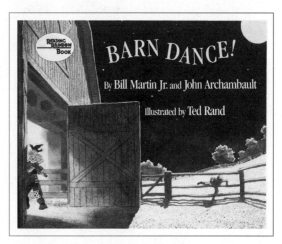

Courtesy of *Barn Dance!* published by Henry Holt.

Many long narrative poems use repeated language patterns to mark the change of scenes. For example, in *Bringing the Rain to Kapiti Plain*, the story is told of Ki-pat the young herdsman who watches his cattle on Kapiti Plain.

> This is the cloud,
>   all heavy with rain,
> That shadowed the ground
>   on Kapiti Plain.
> This is the grass,
>   all brown and dead,
> That needed the rain
>   from the cloud overhead—
> The big, black cloud,
>   all heavy with rain,
> That shadowed the ground
>   on Kapiti Plain.

In a series of short narrative poems, Eloise Greenfield tells Nathaniel' stories. In the book, *Nathaniel Talking*, we meet Nathaniel B. Free, a nine-year-old who tells us what he thinks in raps, chants, and poems with questions. Eloise Greenfield succeeds again in reflecting the spirit of one African-American child. In letting the reader know Nathaniel, she teaches us the depth of a nine-year-old's feelings and thoughts. Nathaniel's questions, ambivalence about growing up, his city neighborhood, his family, his pain, and his joys are explored brilliantly. Jan Spivey Gilchrist's black and white pencil illustrations

include stark silhouettes and muted shadings to accompany gentle poems, and throughout the book, there are beautifully sketched faces.

LIMERICKS

Limericks are humorous poems with a five line scheme of rhymes. Many adults remember their first attempts at writing poetry to fit within this mold. Children in the primary grades will enjoy the humor of the limerick, but preschoolers and kindergartners do not understand this type of humor. Perhaps limericks appeal because they are usually humorous and use the fifth line as a punch line. The rhyming follows a pattern of *a a b b a*. Generally, the first and last line are of the same length, and the third and

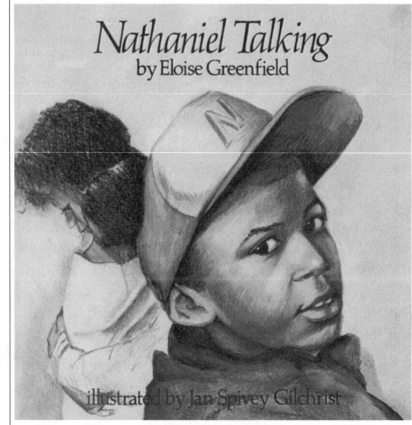

Courtesy of *Nathaniel Talking*, published by Black Butterfly Children's Books.

The Church

This is the church,

This is the steeple.

Open the doors

And see all the people!

fourth lines are shorter. Perhaps the best-known limerick writer was Edward Lear, whose *A Book of Nonsense* contained the humorous and satirical tongue twisters and poems that poked fun at human foibles.

> There was an Old Man with a beard,
> Who said, "It is just as I feared!
>   Two Owls and a Hen
>   Four Larks and a Wren
> Have all built their nests in my beard.

Limerick writers and their works appealing more to children in the younger years are Arnold Lobel's *The Book of Pigericks,* David McCord's *One at a Time: Collected Poems for the Young,* and William Jay Smith's *Laughing Time.*

LYRICAL POEMS AKIN TO SONGS

While the lyric poem is like the ballad in that it is often sung, it is different than the ballad because it does not tell a story. The lyric poem creates a mood, such as those found in lullabies and mood verses. Children's lullabies and some of the traditional songs of childhood can be read or sung.

As we discussed in other chapters, nursery rhymes are examples of the cultural literature that links one generation to another. Popular nursery rhymes continue to be published as collections and in single books of one rhyme. For example, in 1992 Michael Hague published new illustrations for the classic lyrical verse, *Twinkle, Twinkle, Little Star,* written by Jane Taylor in 1806. The rhymes survive because they are easy to remember, were often sung, and also because they evoke such strong visual images.

> Twinkle, twinkle,
> little star
> How I wonder
> what you are!

RHYMING MOTION SONGS AND CHANTS

Many teachers introduce young children to rhymes and rhythms through the fingerplays and motion chants that have become a part of the culture of the early childhood classroom. Whether sung or chanted, these hand rhymes are part of a well-prepared preschool and kindergarten teacher's repertoire. Marc Brown has collected and illustrated fourteen familiar fingerplays in *Hand Rhymes.*

Kittens

> Five little kittens, sleeping on a chair,
> One rolled, off, leaving four there.

> Four little kittens, one climbed a tree
> To look in a bird's nest. Then there were three.

> Three little kittens, wondered what to do.
> One saw a mouse. Then there were two.

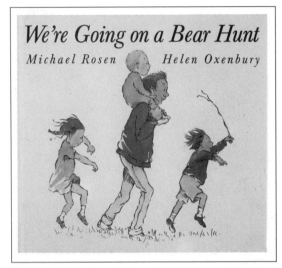

Courtesy of *We're Going on a Bear Hunt*, published by Margaret K. McElderry.

Two little kittens, playing on a wall.
One little kitten, chased a red ball.

One little kitten, with fur soft as silk,
Left all alone, To drink a dish of milk.

Brown illustrated the motions for the hand rhymes on a vertical strip in the left margin. The directions are easy to follow.

In *Read-Aloud Rhymes for the Very Young*, Marc Brown illustrated a collection assembled by Jack Prelutsky of counting rhymes, silly verses, weather poems, jump-rope chants, celebrations of holidays, and expressions of young children's emotions. There are rhymes for almost every conceivable unit in a preschool and kindergarten classroom as well as skills such as counting.

In recent years, the culture of the early childhood classroom has been enriched by the addition of illustrated versions of famous action chants, such as Michael Rosen's retold version of *We're Going on a Bear Hunt*, illustrated by Helen Oxenbury. The action chant has long been a favorite among early childhood teachers. The tale of the bear hunt is told with the teacher leading the chant and the children repeating phrases. It is popular because it involves large muscle movements, action words and sound effects, with the suspense building at the end as the family enters a cave and finds a bear! Then, they have to reverse all the actions to arrive safely home. Now, the tale is told in book form with father, baby, older brother, and two sisters. Their trek through the tall grasses, the cold river, the oozy mud, the dark forest, and even a snowstorm, before entering the gloomy cave, which is presented in charcoal drawings. On alternating pages where the sound effect words are printed, the illustrations are marvelous watercolors.

Few preschool, kindergarten, and first-grade teachers can refuse the cheerleader-type chant and prance of *Chicka*

Courtesy of *Chicka Chicka Boom Boom!* published by Simon & Schuster.

Chicka Boom! Boom! by Bill Martin, Jr. and John Archambault. This ABC book tells an unusual rhyme in Lois Ehlert's usual, bright, bold graphics. With the opening line of the chant, the reader and listeners are caught up in cheering the letters up the trunk of a coconut tree.

> Chicka Chicka Boom Boom
> A told B,
> and B told C,
> "I'll meet you at the top
> of the coconut tree."
>
> "Whee!" said D
> to E F G,
> "I'll beat you to the top
> of the coconut tree."

Motion songs and chants, echoing phrases, and rhythmic poems that naturally call for movement are appealing to the young active child. In some books for the young, the writers and illustrators invite interactions with the illustrations.

For example, in *Each Peach Pear Plum* Janet and Allan Ahlberg write a pictorial "I-spy" book with nursery rhyme and storybook characters. The rhyme tells the reader what to look for hidden things. For example, on the page facing the rhyming couplet,

> "Cinderella on the stairs
> I spy the Three Bears,"

the child searches the picture to see the Three Bears peaking in through a small window.

CONCRETE POEMS

Concrete poems literally form a physical outline of the subject of the verse: The words of the poem are shaped like the object. Concrete poems entertain, delight visually, and help the child writer find a vehicle for structuring what might be said.

Children enjoy writing and drawing concrete poems that do not have a rhyme. Some teachers

include concrete poems to accompany holidays, such as a shamrock for St. Patricks, a valentine for Valentine's Day, or a Jack-o-lantern for Halloween.

Cinquain, Diamonte, and Haiku

Patterns of lines and syllables are used to describe cinquain, diamonte, and haiku poetry. Both cinquain and diamonte are patterns that primary teachers can write with their children by emulating the form. One teacher wrote cinquains for each of her students.[1]

Beverly
Bold beautiful
Bubbling, bothering, boldering
Eagerly soaking up each bright idea
Beverly.

Instead of using a synonym for the title, she repeated each student's name as the last line. The usual pattern is to associate line one with a noun that is also the title; line two describes the noun; line three shows action; line four is a feeling or mood; and line five is a synonym. Like the teacher who wrote "Beverly," and the children who wrote "Rain," students' attempts to write poetry should not be constrained by form but should be encouraged to restructure the form to fit their needs:

Rain
Drippy, Droppy
Misting, Drizzling, Pouring
Soothing, Refreshing, Cleansing, Peaceful
Showers

Diamonte is another poetry form that teachers often use to model writing poetry. In some literature books, it is referred to as "diamond poetry," because when written it is shaped like a diamond.

Writing
Thoughts, Ideas
Wondering, Scribbling, Wandering
Pencil, Paper, Computer, Screen
Composing, Drafting, Editing
Dreams, Schemes
Print-Out

Haiku is composed of three lines of seventeen syllables. The first line has five syllables; the second, seven syllables; and the third has five syllables. The haiku refers to nature, focuses on a single topic, and does not rhyme:

Summer to Autumn
Leaf colors announce the change
Wondrous exhibit.

While haiku is usually reserved for intermediate-aged children, some poets and illustrators have teamed up to create haiku collections that speak to primary-aged children. For example, Richard Lewis' *In a Spring Garden* is appreciated by young children when they see Ezra Jack Keats' illustrations. Perhaps the secret of sharing haiku with young children is to recognize their need for more concrete descriptions and provide illustrations. Young children should not be expected to explain or write; however, they can find it enjoyable by making associations between the descriptions and a well-illustrated collection.

Free Verse

When young children think of poetry, they think of rhymes. When the teacher shares free verse with the children, it "frees" them from their constrained view of poetry. Free verse does not rhyme, but it does have strong descriptive qualities and highly compressed speech, dense with meaning and mood. Poets who write in free verse use all the qualities of good poetry, except structured rhyme. Free verse may have a line or two that rhyme or have some repetitive phrasing. A good example is "My Cat" from Judith Viorst's *If I Were in Charge of the World and Other Worries.*

> My Cat
> My cat isn't stuck up
> Even though
> He's the handsomest cat in
>   the world,
> And smart,
> And brave,
> And climbs the highest trees.
> My cat will sit on my lap and
>   let you pet him.
> He won't mind.
> He thinks human beings are
> Almost as good
> As he is.

ANTHOLOGIES, SPECIAL COLLECTIONS, SINGLE POEM BOOKS

To have good poetry at one's fingertips, the teacher needs several anthologies. Anthologies are collections of poems by many different poets on numerous subjects, in many forms, and expressing the range of emotions. While there are numerous anthologies available, three that are particularly appealing to early childhood teachers and that contain poems on a variety of topics, moods, and poetry forms are:

> *The Read-Aloud Treasury: Favorite Nursery Rhymes, Poems, Stories, & More for the Very Young* (Cole).
>
> *Sing a Song of Popcorn: Every Child's Book of Poems* (deRegniers).
>
> *The Random House Book of Poetry* (Prelutsky).

Joanne Cola, a well-known writer of children's books, and Stephanie Calmenson have collected over 200 poems for *The Read-Aloud Treasury....* As the title implies, the anthology has a balance of the old and new. The volume is particularly suited for the preschool and early primary grades because the poetry is arranged from simple verses for the young child and includes old and new favorites.

Sing a Song of Popcorn: Every Child's Book of Poems is edited by Beatrice Schenk de Regniers and illustrated by nine Caldecott Medal artists. The collection of 128 poems represents a full range of contemporary poets and ones from the past. The volume contains hilarious poems and sentimental ones, spooky ones and pretty ones. The nine Caldecott Medal artists are: Marcia Brown, Leo and Diane Dillon, Richard Egielski, Trina Schart Hyman, Arnold Lobel, Maurice Sendak, Marc Simont, and Margot Zemach. The Mostly Nonsense section is filled with entertaining selections sure to delight young children.

Jack Prelutsky selected the poems for *The Random House Book of Poetry,* which Arnold Lobel illustrated. This extensive collection of 572 poems contains a wide array of the classics, but many more of contemporary poets. Teachers find the extensiveness of the volume helpful when trying to select just the right poem. This volume is most appropriate for the primary grades.

SPECIAL COLLECTIONS

Special collections are organized around some theme, such as nature, seasons, holidays, animals, city or country life, and feelings. Special poetry collections span the age range and the topic range. The special collection edition allows the teacher to have at her or his fingertips poems that fit into curriculum units or themes, as well as to celebrate those everyday occurrences and feelings that are a part of childhood. Several anthologists are known for their special poetry collections. Lee Bennett Hopkins, Nancy Larrick, Myra Cohn Livingston, and Bobbye Goldstein are four whose selections the early childhood educator can count on for being appropriate for the preschool through primary grades. Lee Bennett Hopkins is the author and anthologist of more than fifty books.

While there is an extensive list of special collection volumes, four we heartily recommend are:

Secret Place (age three through elementary)

Birthday Rhymes, Special Times (age three through grade three)

Flit, Flutter, Fly: Poems about Bugs and Other Crawly Creatures (age three through grade three)

The Trees Stand Shining (primary grades)

Charlotte Huck's *Secret Places* is a collection of thirty-one poems by well-known poets who celebrate the secret places where we allow our imaginations to soar and those where we seek refuge. Some of the favorites from the collection will ring true to children: "The Maple" by Elizabeth Coatsworth; "This Is My Rock" by David McCord; "Sleeping Outdoors" by Marchette Chute; and "From Your Own Best Secret Place" by Byrd Baylor.

Birthday Rhymes, Special Times, collected by Bobbye S. Goldstein, contains thirty-two poems. The teacher might select a different poem for each child's birthday, print the poem on child-artist birthday cards and send them home for the celebration. Rose Fyleman's "The Birthday Child" is particularly appealing.

> *The Birthday Child*
> Everything's been different
> All the day long,
> Lovely things have happened,
> Nothing has gone wrong.
>
> Nobody has scolded me,
> Everyone has smiled.
> Isn't it delicious
> To be a birthday child?

Teachers must also remember the children whose birthdays may come when school is out for the summer or holiday break. Jack Prelutsky's "My Birthday's in August" takes the tone of a child's complaint.

Flit, Flutter, Fly: Poems About Bugs and Other Crawly Creatures, one of Lee Bennett Hopkins' many special collections, is a wonderful compliment to nature studies. The collection includes such well known poets as Karla Kuskin, Langston Hughes, Lilian Moore, Myra Cohn Livingston, and Margaret Wise Brown. Most are rhyming poems, which children will enjoy hearing read, reading on their own, and matching to their studies of insects and other fascinating crawly creatures.

The Trees Stand Shining is a collection of thirty-two poems of the North American Indians, selected by Hettie Jones with paintings by Robert Andrew Parker. Parker, a Caldecott Honor artist, portrays the essence of many of the poems in full-page impressionistic paintings. Sixteen different Native-American peoples contributed poems that focus on nature and the significance of time, the physical world, and beauty. Reverence for and delight in nature are expressed simply and eloquently in these lean verses, without titles. According to Jones, the poems were originally songs, prayers, lullabies, short stories, or war chants. The collection takes its title from a line in a Papago poem.

> At the edge of the world
> It is growing light.
> The trees stand shining.
> I like it.
> It is growing light.

COLLECTIONS OF POEMS BY A SINGLE AUTHOR

There are two primary types of poetry books by single authors; the theme book by a single author and a collection of poems on varied subjects and in different forms by one poet. An example of the theme book of poems is Shirley Hughes' *Out and About*, which has a little girl and her baby brother playing their way through each season of the year. Emotions and incidences that prompt special feelings are favorite themes among poets. *Honey, I Love and Other Love Poems* by Eloise Greenfield is an excellent example of "feelings" poetry. The collection of fifteen poems begins with the poem contained in the title. "I Look Pretty," the third poem in the book, expresses the delight a little girl feels when she dresses up in Mama's clothes. "Way Down in the Music" celebrates individuals' responses to their own musical soul-stirring. Although advertised for seven- to eleven-year-olds, the sentiments and clarity of expression make the

HARRIET TUBMAN

Harriet Tubman didn't take no stuff
Wasn't scared of nothing neither
Didn't come in this world to be no slave
And wasn't going to stay one either

"Farewell!" she sang to her friends one night
She was mighty sad to leave 'em
But she ran away that dark, hot night
Ran looking for her freedom

Courtesy of *Honey, I Love,* published by Harper & Row.

poems lovely choices for younger ones as well. As with many poetry selections, the feelings Greenfield expresses transcend the age lines.

Perhaps the best-selling poet of our time is Shel Silverstein whose *Where the Sidewalk Ends* is a collection of his poems. The book made publishing history by topping the New York Times Best Seller List for a number of months and has now sold over a million copies. Another famous Silverstein collection is *A Light in the Attic.* Children, parents, teachers, and librarians enjoy Silverstein's humor, savvy recollections of childhood, and indelible caricatures.

A quick survey of *Where the Sidewalk Ends* reveals many poems early childhood teachers have adopted, such as "Hug O' War"; "Jimmy Jet and His TV Set," the narrative poem about the perils of watching too much television; "For Sale," a sibling rivalry wish about selling a sister; and "Boa Constrictor," a poem that tells about being eaten from toe to neck by a boa. Many teachers have turned "Boa Constrictor" into a chant with motions.

Jack Prelutsky's poetry collections have gained widespread popularity for many of the same reasons that Shel Silverstein's poetry is critically and popularly acclaimed. Both Silverstein and Prelutsky write humorous and narrative poetry, in styles children find appealing. Prelutsky's *The New Kid on the Block* is filled with surprises, jokes, riddles, and giggles. Appealing to primary-aged children, the 107 poems range from rhymed couplets to long narratives. The fun animal poems are only surpassed by the hilarious people poems. Prelutsky's collection is a good one for read-aloud sessions and for primary children to read on their own. Other volumes by Prelutsky that primary teachers will enjoy collecting are *Beneath a Blue Umbrella, Ride a Purple Pelican,* and the two very funny collections, *Something BIG Has been Here!* and *For Laughing Out Loud: Poems to Tickle Your Funny Bone.*

John Ciardi's *You Read to Me, I'll Read to You,* first published in 1961 and released again in 1987 has stood the test of time. Ciardi alternates a poem simple enough for primary children to read easily followed by a poem for the adult to read aloud to the child. An often quoted and anthologized poem from the collection is "Mummy Slept Late and Daddy Fixed Breakfast."

SINGLE POEM BOOKS

The single poem book is a staple in the early childhood literature collection. Several popular ones teachers connect to the curriculum are Mary Ann Hoberman's *A House Is a House for Me*, Ted Rand's illustrated version of Robert Louis Stevenson's *My Shadow*, and Bill Martin, Jr. and John Archaumbault's *Listen to the Rain*.

Hoberman's *A House Is a House for Me* is a favorite among children and their teachers. With the theme of houses, this long rhyme gallops across scenes of insects, animals, people, and things. The recurring phrase "a house is a house for me," ends each verse. Also available in big book format, the patterned language and associations make the book an excellent choice for beginning readers, and its cleverness calls older readers back to the verse just to enjoy the sights and sounds.

Teachers often have children compose lines patterned after those Hoberman has written. The poem can be connected with art activities and a study of science and nature habitats, as well as using the pattern of the poem to add some original lines from the class poets.[2] After reading the poem through once, the teacher can read the poem through again and have the listeners join in saying the recurring refrain, "a house is a house for me."

Betty Fraser, the illustrator, decorated each letter of the poem title as if it was a house. For example, the "A" is a tepee. The teacher might ask the children to draw the letters of their first names in decorative styles and then decorate the letters as houses. For a science and nature study of houses and habitats, the children could look through the poem for all the animals pictured, then illustrate the animals' homes on large index cards. The children could then match the animal names and the habitats. For a writing exercise, one teacher requested that the chil-

dren add their own lines to the poem. Since the teacher read the poem in February, one child added, "A heart-shaped box is a house for valentine candy."

My Shadow is the classic Robert Louis Stevenson poem, with cheerful illustrations by Ted Rand of children from around the world playing with their shadows. Each phrase of the poem is illustrated with a child or children and the ever-present shadows. This single poem book is a delightful celebration of individuals, of friends, and of their discoveries of shadows. The possibilities for connecting *My Shadow* to the curriculum are almost endless. Both the content of the poem and the illustrations prompt a number of inventive responses, such as shadow silhouettes for art, shadow puppets, bouncing balls—all based on the line of the children who are playing with "an India-rubber ball." The whole idea of what balls are made of, ball games one can play alone, those with a friend, and how the ball and the shadows interact make for fascinating illustrations in the book. Identifying children and their homelands from around the world could provide quite a geography investigation for older primary children.

Bill Martin, Jr. and John Archaumbault wrote *Listen to the Rain*, which was illustrated by James Endicott. This single poem book is the enchanting story of a rainstorm. The sound effects build from the beginning "whisper of the rain" to the steady "singing of the rain" on to the driving force of the "roaring pouring" rain. As the poem proceeds, the rainstorm recedes and the listener is left at the end with the "wet, silent, after-time of rain." The beautifully simple, yet elegant illustrations, and even the dark blue endpaper pages, provide a perfect setting for the drama of the rainstorm poem.

Listen to the Rain can inspire numerous related activities for a variety of curricular areas, such as water drop splash prints and rainstorm pastels for art, listening to tapes of rainstorms, music and movement activities with rain themes, and science and nature studies. Children could use the animals and objects pictured in the book and investigate what happens to birds, insects, plants, shells, and fish when it rains.[3]

Poetry Throughout the Classroom and Curriculum

From the discussion of the single poem books and related activities, it is clear that poetry has its place as literature study and in other related curricular areas. In this section, there are recommendations for the teacher's presentation of poetry, children's reading, writing poetry, using poetry for special events and projects, and linking poetry to units of study and themes. Listed in Figure 7.3 are some overall suggestions for teachers to keep in mind when reading, selecting, and studying poetry.

TEACHER READING POETRY ALOUD

Since poetry is meant to be read aloud, the teacher needs to be comfortable with reading. The best way to be at ease is to rehearse the poem by reading it aloud. Select ahead of time the poems to be read and practice reading them to get just the right tempo, rhythm, stress, and pauses. If the teacher is inexperienced or hesitant about poetry reading, we suggest she or he select humorous poems and narrative poems since these two types of poems are ones children prefer.

One of the mistakes teachers of young children often make is to read too much poetry at one sitting. However, unless it is a long narrative poem, sometimes one short poem is insufficient. There are numerous ways to group poems in poetry presentations. The teacher might read two or three different poems on the same topic. For example, a preschool teacher might read Bruce Degan's *Teddy Bear Towers* and select a poem or two from Kathleen Hague's *Bear Hugs*. A kindergarten teacher might pair two poetry books, reading one at the opening of the morning group time and another during the afternoon reading, or a few selections from *Birdwatch* could provide the morning reading and the afternoon reading could be from *Flap Your Wings and Try*.

Eloise Greenfield's *Nathaniel Talking* provides an excellent example of how to read to primary children from a collection of poems. Teachers should rehearse the poetry and try the rhythmic pattern Greenfield suggests for "My Daddy." In just one read-aloud session, the teacher might begin with "Nathaniel's Rap" and read it at least twice. Then, she or he could teach the children the repeated phrases and let them join in. The reading can be continued by having the children listen to "Nine" and "Knowledge." At another session, teachers can create a different mood by asking the children what the pictures tell them about Nathaniel's feelings before reading "Mama" and "Missing Mama." At a third read-aloud session, a teacher could share the poems about Nathaniel's family and neighbors.

After a poetry read-aloud session, the children can discuss the poem, but not for its technical merits or for a sophisticated analysis of the elements. It is important that the children tell what they liked about the poem, how it made them

---

Figure 7.3 Suggestions for Teachers— Poetry in the Classroom

1. Read and enjoy poetry for its own sake.

2. Share poetry that you like reading aloud to the children.

3. Read a wide variety of poetry and poets.

4. Teach children to read poetry by the way it is printed and punctuated; avoid sing-song renditions.

5. Write poetry with children.

6. Encourage poetry writing or writing responses to poetry.

7. Keep the emphasis on enjoyment, not on analysis.

8. Accept and appreciate children's poetry preferences.

feel, any expressions they thought were unique, and which phrases brought pictures to them as they were hearing the poem. The teacher should follow the lead of the children in the discussion.

Preschoolers and kindergartners often make associations and tell something of which the poem reminded them. For example, in response to Eve Merriam's "Cats Tongue," almost all the preschoolers wanted to let the teacher know that their cats licked themselves clean, too. The teacher, following the children's lead, went on to ask about how and where their cats slept, and how kittens were different than cats. They also looked at a cat calendar and the children who had cats like the different breeds talked about their pets. She ended the session by reading "Cats Tongue" again.

When primary children respond to poetry, they can talk more about the images and descriptive qualities of the poem. Primary teachers may find their children making many of the same associations as the preschoolers and kindergartners. Indeed, if children connect poetry to their own lives and their own worlds, they are more likely to think of poetry as a means of self-expression. How much analysis of poetry elements young children can assimilate is debatable. There is concern that if children are required to analyze poems, they will become disenchanted with the genre.

In "Poetry as Direction for the Imagination," (*The Reading Teacher*, 1992) two first-grade teachers Duthie and Zimet incorporate a poetry unit in their whole language classroom. When they conducted minilessons on poetry elements, they found the children did recognize and respond to the strongest element in each poem, such as repetition, rhyme, and alliteration, and noted how the poem was lined. These teachers would have been remiss if they had emphasized the poetry elements to the exclusion of the meaning associated with the poem or the simple enjoyment of poetic language. Similarly, the immersion of their students in poetry throughout the year prepared the children for the poetry unit.

CHILDREN READING POETRY

To help children become good readers of poetry, you should read the selection first. After the children have heard the poem read aloud, teach them how to read it. It is important to avoid the sing-song renditions that children often fall into when reading with a group. Model how to pause at the punctuation and which phrases to stress.

One kindergarten we visited had a chart stand of poems hanging from metal rings. Each poem chart was made of heavy posterboard or oak tag. The words were printed in the form in which they originally appeared on a page. One of the mistakes some teachers make when they copy poems onto charts is not lining them properly and spacing them on the page in the way the poet wrote them. The positioning of the words will help the children to read them with the right inflection.

Tape-recording the children reading poetry also seems to prompt better inflection. Be certain to allow the children to select the poem they want to record and let them practice it. Tape the reading more than once, until the child is happy with the reading.

Choral reading of poetry is another activity that allows the children to experience the pleasure of many voices. However, reading in unison often deadens the inflection. Younger poetry readers can join in poems that have refrains, lyric poems, chants, and nursery rhymes. A number of poems have lyrics that are echoed, such as those found in Joanna Cole's *Anna Banana: 101 Jump-Rope Rhymes* and Cole and Calmenson's *Miss Mary Mack and Other Children's Street Rhymes*. Paul Fleischman's *Joyful Noise: Poems for Two Voices* provides a chance for best friends to perform together.

Primary-grade children who have developed well as oral readers will enjoy poetry that is read in parts. Half the class might read the first verse and the other half the second. Other poems can be divided by parts. Both Shel Silverstein and Jack Prelutsky's poetry books have numerous narrative poems that can be sectioned for children to read in a choral manner. If there are a number of different scenes or voices as a part of the poem, the teacher can let children volunteer for the different parts. For example, Audrey Wood's "Silly Sally" begins with

> Silly Sally went to town
> walking backwards, upside
> down.

Along the way Silly Sally meets a number of animals, including a pig who dances a jig, a dog who played leapfrog, a loon who sang a silly tune. Each character could be read by one child or a small group of children could read the part together.

Many teachers find that reading poetry, particularly rhyming poetry, helps the young reader who needs confidence to approach a text. Rhyming poetry, recurring phrases, and repeated stanzas provide excellent material for practice for the beginning reader, without requiring complete independence. These selections can be confidence builders because the rhythm and often the rhyme of the poem help the reader predict next lines or words.

Writing Poetry

Writing poetry with young children takes many forms, depending on the age and stage of development of the writers. Preschoolers and kindergartners can help their teachers add verses to existing poems, as in the previous discussion of adding to Hoberman's *A House Is a House for Me.* Teachers can focus on expanding the children's descriptive language through improving observations. Teachers can call attention to published poets descriptions and encourage their students to make inventive associations. These ideas are appropriate for language development, regardless of whether they are used for writing poetry or are seen as language expansion.

In *Explore Poetry,* Donald Graves provides many insights into how to teach children to write poetry. Teachers who are aware of the writing process recognize that all good teachers of writing, write. (See Chapter 3.) They model the writing process. They do not simply show the children something they have

written, but they inform and include the students in the composing process. Teachers share all the drafts of their work, involve children in helping them revise, and finally reach a point of publication or public reading of the poem.

Teaching primary-aged children to write poetry is the same as for all writing: it is the process approach. Before children should be expected to write poetry, they must be immersed in it. A heightened awareness of their physical and social environment will provide children with the content for their poetry. Poetry describes things, people, animals, and events in unusual and memorable ways. Poetry writing can be enhanced by helping children become more intense observers, brainstorming ways to describe their sensory experiences and making unusual associations.

Most children can find at least one poetry form that fits their interests. However, for the budding writers we prefer to let children decide whether they want to write a poem or write what they like about a particular poem. When writing in their journals, we often read language that has poetic quality. For example, when writing about the Shel Silverstein poem, "Jimmy Jet and

---

Figure 7.4 Suggestions for Writing Poetry in Early Childhood Classrooms

Adjust poetry writing expectations depending on the age and grade level.
Encourage use of descriptive language.
Write poetry for special class events.
Use a known poetry structure and have children write poetry with their teacher.
Model the writing process from prewriting through publication.
Seek inspiration for writing from the world the children know.
Find role models in published poets' works.
Allow children to take liberties with poetry forms.
Have children read their poetry aloud.
Publish the students' poetry in a variety of ways.

His TV Set," a second grader said, "My mom would like this poem. She is always bugging me, bugging me, bugging me. Mom she just bugs me about the tv, tv, tv." The most important point about writing and poetry is to have the children interacting with poems and finding their own voices for responding.

POETRY FOR SPECIAL EVENTS AND PROJECTS

Special events in the life of a school or a classroom call for reading and writing poetry. At an elementary school we visited, there was a tree planting ceremony as a part of the entire school's emphasis on saving the environment. Several third graders read a poem from each classroom in the school, pre-k through third grade. A parent printed the poems in calligraphy and they were framed for the reception area of the school.

TEACHER SUCCESS STORY

The teacher success story of Carol's experience is an example of using poetry for a special event. Carol, a pre-k teacher, found herself in one of those awkward positions of wanting to say "no" to the Parent Teacher Association President's request but recognizing that she was expected to say "yes." The program committee had requested that all of the pre-k and kindergarten teachers have their classes perform something for the parents.

In an attempt to avoid putting performance pressures on young children, the pre-k teachers decided not to prepare a program but simply to have their children do some of their usual classroom activities. One teacher had the children do the chant and hand motions for "We're Going on a Bear Hunt." Another teacher had the children sing three or four of their favorite songs. Carol decided to have the children recite a poem. She browsed through several anthologies, trying to decide which poem the children might enjoy doing; however, during the science lesson, Carol and the children "invented" their own.

A new aquarium had been added to the pre-k classroom a few days earlier. The children were fascinated with the names of the fish. A discussion ensued about the names of fish they liked, such as goldfish, zebra fish, angel fish, and guppies.

Figure 7.5 Language Expansion Poem From an Observation

Column one was written by children answering, "What do fish do?" Column two was written by children answering, "What are fish doing?" The poem was read as a choral reading with the teacher reading the first column and the children saying the second column.

LIVE IN AN AQUARIUM	LIVING IN AN AQUARIUM
swim	swimming
float	floating
flap	flapping
eat	eating
move fish kiss lips	kiss lipping
go around	circling
go up and down	upping, downing
hide	hiding
touch	touching
swish tails	swishing
look sideways	sidewaying
slip under	slipping
swim, swim, swim	swimming, swimming, swimming

Small groups of children observed the fish closely for a few days and then helped their teacher compose the following chart of words and phrases. Carol began the lesson by asking the children what they saw the fish do. They composed the first list. Then she asked the children to add *ing* to what they were saying, and they came up with the second list.

Carol suggested a title for each of the columns after the list was completed. When she read the list in a poetic voice, with inflection and pauses, several of the children looked at one another. At the end, she asked the children which word they think of most often when they think of fish. Their ending word was swim, and she added a poetic twist by repeating the word three times. While the poem is not ready for publication, it does have descriptive language that captures the life of fish in an aquarium, as well as containing some unusual ways of describing the children's observations.

Perhaps the most remarkable part of Carol's lesson was her openness and acceptance of the children's language. The two children who were joking were surprised that the teacher accepted their remarks. The "fish kiss lips" was a child's attempt to put into words the way humans pucker their lips, suck in their cheeks, and try to mimic a fish. The children were also surprised when the teacher accepted a child's suggestion of "lipping." Another child contributed the observation that fish "look sideways." The whole group added the "ing" and said, "looking sideways." A child teasingly said, "sidewaying" and the teacher accepted the unusual description. This child too was surprised to see "sidewaying" on the list. Several children said that wasn't a word and one boy said it was a word because the teacher wrote it. Finally, Carol added to the discussion by saying that poets sometimes invent words to express what they see.

The children's invented poem became their presentation for the PTA program. The children each drew and painted a fish on a large sheet of manilla paper, then cut out the fish shapes. On the night of the PTA program, they trooped on stage holding their painted fish. Carol explained the origins of the poem and the science concept of observation, which had prompted the writing.

Parent volunteers distributed copies of the poem for the audience to follow along with the reading. The children performed the poem as a choral reading. The teacher read the first column and the children said the extension column. Carol, the teacher, announced, "Live in an aquarium," and the children responded, "Living in an aquarium." To add to the drama of the poem, the children ended by placing their painted fish shapes down on the stage floor, puckering up their lips, putting their arms out in front of them, and swimming off stage. The applause was resounding and the laughter appreciative.

LINKING POETRY TO UNITS OF STUDY

Special events and projects are built into the early childhood classroom because we organize the curriculum in thematic units. Each unit usually contains some initiating activity that launches the unit and a culminating activity that celebrates what the children have learned. During initiating and culminating activities are excellent times to have poetry accompany the special event.

As an initiating activity for a unit on animals, the teacher read *Animals Born Alive and Well* by Ruth Heller. The book, written in rhyme, begins with

MAMMALS
are
animals with fur or hair
who nurse their young
and breath fresh air.

Heller's book is beautifully illustrated, contains key scientific concepts, and includes so much inherently interesting information that children enjoy reading it over and over again. The entire text is a long narrative poem with rhyming words, interesting lists of descriptions, and inventive placement of the print on the page to emphasize facts. During the unit, the teacher also read *My Grandma Lived in Gooligulch* by Graeme Base, a rollicking verse that tells the story of an eccentric grandmother who shared her house with an array of animals from Australia. She knew bandicoots, goannas, emus, kangaroos, pelicans, and wombats, to name a few. Another book the teacher included in the animal unit was *The Wildlife ABC: A Nature Alphabet Book* by Jan Thornhill, which uses rhyming couplets to move the reader through the animal alphabet.

Throughout a unit on friendship, one first-grade teacher collected friendship poems and added one a day to the poem rail. The poem rail was the rail underneath the chalkboard. She printed each poem on construction paper, laminated them, and lined them along the rail. Adding a poem to the rail became an expected event everyday during group time.

As a culminating activity, for a science unit on birds, the children found pictures of birds who had visited their winter feeder. With the help of the school librarian, they found poems about their birds. Then, they careful copied the poems into a book, which they illustrated. Diane, their teacher, noticed two writers who just could not seem to find a poem about a gold finch, so they composed their own.

> Finch, it's a cinch
> to clinch some
> seed.
> If you eat at
> the feeder
> outside Jenny
> and Marianna's door.

The teacher overhead Jenny saying to Marianna, "What rhymes with seed?" On cue, Marianna said, "All poems don't have to rhyme." Consequently, we have an obvious rhyme at the beginning and an abandoned effort for the second verse.

Figure 7.6 Poetry Books for Science Units for Preschoolers

Unit Topic	Recommended Poetry Books*
Animals	*Guess Who?* (Ayres)
	Cats Are Cats (Larrick)
	Whose Mother Are You? (Fisher)
Birds	*Flap Your Wings and Try* (Pomerantz)
Environment	*Over in the Meadow* (Wadsworth)
	The Wildlife ABC (Thornhill)
Insects	*Flit, Flutter, Fly!* (Hopkins)
Seasons	*Caps, Hats, Socks, and Mittens* (Borden)
	Out and About (Hughes)
Weather	*What Will the Weather Be Like Today?* (Rogers)

*While we have divided the selections into two categories, preschool and K through three, many older children will enjoy reading the simpler poems for preschoolers, and similarly many younger children will enjoy hearing poems for older students.

Figure 7.7 Poetry Books for Science Units for K Through Three

Unit Topic	Recommended Poetry Books*
Animals	*Animals Born Alive and Well* (Heller)
	My Grandma Lived in Gooligulch (Base)
	Whose Mother Are You? (Fisher)
Birds	*Birdwatch* (Yolen)
Environment	*Heartland* (Siebert)
	Mojave (Siebert)
	The Wildlife ABC (Thornhill)
	Wild Wild Sunflower Child Anna (Carlstrom)
Insects	*Flit, Flutter, Fly!* (Hopkins)
Weather	*Listen to the Rain* (Martin and Archaumbault)
	Winter (Hirsch)

*While we have divided the selections into two categories, preschool and K through three, many older children will enjoy reading the simpler poems for preschoolers, and similarly many younger children will enjoy hearing poems for older students.

The poetry book of birds became the culminating activity for the second graders. It celebrated their experiences of making the bird feeder, observing the visitors, worrying about whether or not there was enough seed and water during a hard freeze, and appreciating each bird by describing it in poetry form.

In the following section, we list some common curriculum units found in the early childhood classroom and suggest some books to use with each. Some books are particularly good for starting a unit of study. From the earlier discussion, an entire unit on birds could be stimulated by Jane Yolen's book, *Birdwatch,* or a unit on insects could be inspired from reading Lee Bennett Hopkins' *Flit, Flutter, Fly: Poems About Bugs and Other Crawly Creatures.* Other books are significant in summarizing and stretching the imagination even further. (See Figures 7.6 and 7.7.)

Thematic units of study are also the major ways that social studies concepts are presented in the early childhood curriculum. There are numerous poems that fit the social studies themes of self-concept, families, friends, feelings, neighborhoods, transportation, holidays and celebrations, and traditions in different cultures. Concern for the environment is both a science and social studies endeavor, since protecting our planet is a social responsibility, as well as a scientific one.

In the self-concept area, there are numerous poems, but a type of poem children find particularly appealing is the humorous poetry. After reading "I'm Thankful" by Jack Prelutsky, some children in *The New Kid on the Block* wrote their own "thankful poems":

I'm Thankful
I'm thankful for my baseball bat,
I cracked it yesterday,
I'm thankful for my checker set,
I haven't learned to play,
I'm thankful for my mitten,
One is missing in the snow,
I'm thankful for my hamsters,
They escaped a month ago. (first verse, p.28)

Teachers can also use poems to help children appreciate how we are all alike and different in many ways, and should be enjoyed for our differences. Jack Prelutsky's "I'm the Single Most Wonderful Person I know" in *The New Kid on the Block* is a celebration of a child's enjoyment of himself and his imagination. The poem begins,

I'm the Single Most Wonderful Person I Know
I'm the single most wonderful person I know,
I'm witty, I'm charming, I'm smart,
I'm often so brilliant I actually glow,
I'm genius in music and art.

For a self-concept unit, teachers might help children write cinquains about themselves, like "Beverly" mentioned earlier.

There are friendship poems in every poetry form and most are by poets who write with the young child in mind. For the preschoolers there is *Are You My Friend Today?* by Gyo Fujikawa. Kindergartners like *Best Friends,* a collection by Lee Bennett Hopkins, because the poems tell about things that friends do together. First and second graders like narrative poems that tell stories about events that happen to friends. In the lead poem of Jack Prelutsky's *The New Kid on the Block,* the child decides he doesn't like the new kid on the block and ends the poem with, "I don't care for her at all."

While we have mentioned poems and poetry books by age level, poetry does transcend the all ages and grades. Teachers should read the poetry and decide if it will be effective with their students. For example, one third-grade teacher read Judith Viorst's poems from *If I Were In Charge of the World and Other Worries.* She was surprised when Kendra, a third grader, asked to borrow the book to take it to read to her kindergarten reading buddy. The teacher was hesitant thinking most of the poems seemed too advance, but she allowed the child to borrow the book. The girl read, "Since Hanna Moved Away," which is about a child's feelings about being left behind. After hearing the poem, the five-year-old sighed and said, "It's sad." Then the two girls proceeded to talk about friends who had moved away.

POETRY UNIT FOR LITERATURE STUDY

Poetry units for young children can be legitimate literature studies; however, they should not: focus on analyzing poetry for the teacher's or general interpretation; be memorized for performance sake; show preference to a certain form; nor be studied for achievement testing. Follow these guidelines:

1. Poetry should be enjoyed. Therefore, children must be given great freedom in selecting the poetry they want to read.

2. A variety of poetry forms should be shared with the children to broaden their experiences with poetry, and also to help them develop their personal preferences and tastes.

3. Poetry as a literature unit of study might include more information about some of the children's favorite poets.

4. The poetry unit should focus on expanding the child's interests.

In "Poetry Is Like Directions for Your Imagination!" classroom teachers Christine Duthie and Ellie Kubie Zimet (1992) describe the ways they immerse their first graders in the reading and writing of poetry. The teachers teach poetry using the same strategies that they do for teaching prose. They read poetry to the children throughout the year, not just during the poetry unit. Each day the children read a poem, which the teacher copies and sends home. By the time they begin the poetry unit, the first graders have read and responded to over 100 poems. The teachers include a daily time for writing in journals and responding to poetry, and teach poetry using instructional strategies they have developed for all literacy instruction. They have specific lessons with the whole group, small groups, and minilessons. The poetry unit ends with the children creating two anthologies. Each child selects her or his favorite poems for an individual anthology, and the class as a whole creates an anthology of poems they have written.

From our survey of teachers, most preschool and kindergarten teachers say that they do not have separate literature unit studies on poetry. The way a few early childhood teachers conduct a literature unit of study is to focus on a poet whose writing the children particularly enjoy, and instead of having a poetry unit, they have a poet unit. There are so many prolific poets who would be excellent subjects for a poetry unit for kindergartners, such as Karla Kuskin, Myra Cohn Livingston, Bill Martin, Jr., Eve Merriam, Jack Prelutsky, Shel Silverstein, and Jane Yolen to name a few.

Poetry and Cultural Diversity

Throughout this book we have incorporated literature that represents many cultures and points of view. Poetry is one of the most personal of genres, therefore, the voice of the culture that the poet represents is significant. Eloise Greenfield's *Nathaniel's Talking* and *Honey, I Love* are excellent examples of poetry written about African-American children, but the literary quality of the poetry makes it appealing to all children. "Night on Neighborhood Street" and "Under the Sunday Tree" are compelling peeks into the culture of the extended African-American family and neighborhood.

African-American poets have particularly poignant voices for minority children. Nikki Giovanni's *Spin a Soft Black Song: Poems for Children* appeals to children and touches adults. One should be careful designating the appeal of poets by their racial or cultural backgrounds, or even intended audience. These are poets for all children. Poets of all backgrounds express images that are intensely personal, as well as universally human. Eloise Greenfield, for example, writes about her experiences as an African American, as well as a person sharing this world with other people and all the wonder, excitement, trouble, and celebration that sharing evokes.

Arnold Adoff has written *My Black Me*, which third graders and older children will find compelling and perhaps is best known for *All the Colors of the Race* and *Black Is Brown Is Tan*. These books are particularly important for children to learn to appreciate their heritage, and as family members of different races, to learn to live together.

Recently, a number of Native-American publications have been issued. Most Native-American poetry is written for third graders and beyond. Ann Nolan Clark's *In My Mother's House* is the story of a family living in a pueblo in an earlier farming era. *The Trees Stand Shining*, discussed earlier, is a collection of poetry from Native-American Indians. Much of the poetry published by Native-Americans is based on their historical past rather than today's child.

So little poetry is published for children by minority poets. In a review of *Our Family, Our World, Our Literature* (Miller-Lachmann, 1992), the preschool to grade three category had few poetry selections from minority cultures. Among the eighteen different minority cultures, there were few poetry citations for this age group. The few listed were African American, Latino American, and Native American.

SUMMARY

Poetry is a genre that we often associate with the simplicity of childhood rhymes and chants to the sophistication of carefully crafted inaugural poems meant to inspire the nation. We know young children grow in appreciation of poetry when they have a teacher who enjoys reading good poetry to them. To entice the young child into the world of poetry and the possibilities for the genre, we need to expose them to a wide variety of poetry forms, poets, moods, and content.

The poetry forms and elements that describe poetry are simply guides for making certain that we include a wide array.

In this chapter we presented some suggestions for selecting poetry, guidelines for the teacher to read poetry aloud, how to help children become better poetry readers, writing poetry with and for children, creative responses to poetry, and finding ways to include poetry throughout the day and throughout the curriculum. We presented a number of suggestions for units early childhood teachers often use to organize the science and social studies curriculum. In addition, we outlined poetry unit studies and shared recommendations for how to use poetry as a form of language expansion.

Throughout the chapter, an overarching concern was expressed that for the children to enjoy poetry, their teacher must enjoy it. Cautionary notes were scattered throughout the chapter advising teachers to avoid over-analyzing poetry and to find ways for children to make associations, respond to the content, and appreciate the language, rather than dissecting it for literary merit.

ENDNOTES

1. The original concrete, cinquain, diamonte, and haiku poems presented in this chapter were written by a group of teachers in a graduate language-arts course, taught by the author, at Northeastern State University in Tahlequah, Oklahoma.

2. The poetry selections and associated teaching ideas for *A House Is a House for Me* and *My Shadow* are suggested in Raines, S. C., & Canady, R. J. (1992). *Story S-t-r-e-t-c-h-e-r-s for the Primary Grades*. Mt. Rainier, MD: Gryphon House.

3. The teaching ideas for *Listen to the Rain* are from Raines, S. C., & Canady, R. J. (1991). *More Story S-t-r-e-t-c-h-e-r-s: Activities to Expand Children's Favorite Books*. Mt. Rainier, MD: Gryphon House.

REFERENCES

Angelou. M. (1993, January 21). On the pulse of morning. *New York Times*. Vol. 142, p. 1.

Chukovksy, K. (1963). *From Two to Five*. (Morton, M., Trans.). Berkeley, CA: University of California Press.

Denman G. (1988). *When you've made it your own . . . teaching poetry to young people*. Portsmouth, NH: Heinemann.

Duthie, C., & Zimet, E. K. (1992). Poetry is like direction for your imagination. *The Reading Teacher, 46*(1), 14–24.

Fisher, C. J., & Natarella, M. A. (1982). Young children's preferences in poetry: A national survey of first, second and third graders. *Research in the Teaching of English, 16*(4), 339–354.

Graves, D. H. (1992). *Explore Poetry*. Portsmouth, NH: Heinemann. p. 61.

Holman, Felice. (1985). *The Song in My Head*. Illustrated by Jim Spanfeller. New York: Scribner.

Huck, C. S., Helper, S., & Hickman, J. (1993). *Children's literature in the elementary school*. Ft. Worth, TX: Holt, Rinehart and Winston.

Martin, B., Jr., (1984, March). Keynote address to teachers. *Young Author's Conference*. Tulsa, OK.

Miller-Lachmann, L. (1992). *Our Family, our Friends, our World*. New Providence, NJ: Bowker.

CHILDREN'S LITERATURE REFERENCES

The authors and illustrators of children's books are listed, in all chapters, by their full names to help the reader become acquainted with them. If only one name is listed, the author also illustrated the book.

Aardema, Verna. (1981). *Bringing the Rain to Kapiti Plain*. Illustrated by Beatriz Vidal.

Adoff, Arnold. (Ed.) (1984). *My Black Me*. New York: Dutton.

Adoff, Arnold. (1982). *All the Colors of the Race*. Illustrated by John Steptoe. New York: Lothrop, Lee & Shepard.

Adoff, Arnold. (1973). *Black Is Brown Is Tan*. Illustrated by Emily McCully. New York: Harper & Row.

Ahlberg, Janet, & Ahlberg, Allan. (1978). *Each Peach Pear Plum*. New York: Viking Press.

Ayres, Pam. (1987). *Guess Who?* Illustrated by Julie Lacome. New York: Alfred A. Knopf.

Base, Graeme. (1990). *My Grandma Lived in Gooligulch*. New York: Harry N. Abrams.

Borden, Louise. (1989). *Caps, Hats, Socks, and Mittens*. Illustrated by Lillian Hoban. New York: Scholastic.

Brown, Marc. (1985). *Hand Rhymes*. New York: E. P. Dutton.

Carlstrom, Nancy White. (1987). *Wild Wild Sunflower Child Anna*. Illustrated by Jerry Pinkney. New York: Macmillan.

Ciardi, John. (1961, 1987). *You Read to Me, I'll Read to You*. Illustrated by Edward Gorey. New York: Lippincott.

Clark, Ann Holan. (1941, 1991). *In My Mother's House*. Illustrated by Velino Herrara. New York: Viking Press.

Cole, Joanna. (1989). *Anna Banana: 101 Jump Rope Rhymes*. Illustrated by Alan Tiegreen. New York: Morrow.

Cole, Joanna, & Calmenson, Stephanie. (1990). *Miss Mary Mack and Other Children's Street Rhymes*. Illustrated by Alan Tiegreen. New York: Morrow.

Cole, Joanna, & Calmenson, Stephanie. (Eds.). (1988). *The Read-Aloud Treasury: Favorite Nursery Rhymes, Poems, Stories & More for the Very Young*. Illustrated by Ann Schweninger. New York: Doubleday.

Degen, Bruce. (1991). *Teddy Bear Towers*. New York: Harper Collins.

de Regniers, Beatrice Schenk. (Ed.). (1988). *Sing a Song of Popcorn: Every Child's Book of Poems*. Illustrated by nine Caldecott artists. New York: Scholastic.

Fleischman, Paul. (1988). *Joyful Noise: Poems for Two Voices*. Illustrated by Eric Beddows. New York: Harper & Row.

Fujikawa, Gyo. (1988). *Are You My Friend Today?* New York: Random House.

Fyleman, Rose. (1993). "The Birthday Child." In Goldstein, Bobbye S. (Ed.). *Birthday Rhymes, Special Times*. p. 17. Illustrated by Jose Aruego and Ariane Dewey. New York: Doubleday.

Giovanni, Nikki. (1985). *Spin a Soft Black Song: Poems for Children*. Illustrated by George Martins. New York: Hill and Wang.

Goldstein, Bobbye, S. (Ed.). (1993). *Birthday Rhymes, Special Times*. Illustrated by Jose Aruego and Ariane Dewey. New York: Doubleday.

Greenfield, Eloise. (1978). *Honey, I Love*. Illustrated by Diane and Leo Dillon. New York: Harper & Row.

Greenfield, Eloise. (1988). *Nathaniel Talking*. Illustrated by Jan Spivey Gilchrist. New York: Black Butterfly Children's Books.

Hague, Kathleen. (1989). *Bear Hugs*. Illustrated by Michael Hague. New York: Henry Holt.

Heller, Ruth. (1982). *Animals Born Alive and Well*. New York: Grosset & Dunlap.

Hirsche, Ron. (1990). *Winter*. Photographs by Thomas D. Mangelsen. New York: Dutton.

Hoberman, Mary Ann. (1982). *A House Is a House for Me*. Illustrated by Betty Fraser. New York: Penguin.

Hopkins, Lee Bennett. (Ed.). (1986). *Best Friends*. Illustrated by James Watts. New York: Harper & Row.

Hopkins, Lee Bennett. (Ed.). (1992). *Flit, Flutter, Fly: Poems About Bugs and Other Crawly Creatures*. Illustrated by Peter Palagonia. New York: Doubleday.

Huck, Charlotte.(Ed.). (1993). *Secret Places*. Illustrated by Lindsay Barrett George. New York: Greenwillow.

Hughes, Shirley. (1988). *Out and About*. New York: Lothrop, Lee & Shepard Books.

Jones, Hettie. (1971). *The Trees Stand Shining: Poetry of the North American Indians*. Illustrated by Robert Andrew Parker. New York: Dial.

Larrick, Nancy. (Ed.). (1988). *Cars Are Cats*. Illustrated by Ed Young. New York: Philomel.

Lear, Edward. (1946). *The Complete Nonsense Book*. New York: Dodd Mead.

Lewis, Richard. (1964, 1989). *In a Spring Garden*. Illustrated by Ezra Jack Keats. New York: Dial.

Lobel, Arnold. (1983). *The Book of Pigericks*. New York: Harper & Row.

Martin, Bill, Jr., & Archambault, John. (1986). *Barn Dance!* Illustrated by Ted Rand. New York: Henry Holt.

Martin, Bill, Jr., & Archambault, John. (1989). *Chicka Chicka Boom Boom*. Illustrated by Lois Ehlert. New York: Simon & Schuster.

Martin, Bill, Jr., & Archambault, John. (1988). *Listen to the Rain*. Illustrated by James Endicott. New York: Henry Holt.

McCord, David. (1977). *One at a Time*. Illustrated by Henry B. Kane. Boston: Little, Brown.

Merriam, Eve. (1985). "Cat's tongue." In *Blackberry Ink*. Illustrated by Hans Wilhelm. New York: William Morrow.

Merriam, Eve. (1985). "Dirty Bertie." In *Blackberry Ink*. Illustrated by Hans Wilhelm. New York: William Morrow.

O'Neill, Mary. (1961, illustrations 1989). "What Is Yellow?" In *Hailstones and Halibut Bones*. Illustrated by John Wallner. New York: Doubleday.

Pomerantz, Charlotte. (1989). *Flap Your Wings and Try*. Illustrated by Nancy Tafuri. New York: Greenwillow.

Prelutsky, Jack. (1990). *Beneath the Blue Umbrella*. Illustrated by Garth Williams. New York: Greenwillow.

Prelutsky, Jack. (Ed.). (1991). *For Laughing Out Loud: Poems to Tickle Your Funnybone*. Illustrated by Marjorie Priceman. New York: Knopf.

Prelutsky, Jack. (1986). *Ride a Purple Pelican*. Illustrated by Garth Williams. New York: Greenwillow.

Prelutsky, Jack. (1990). *Something BIG Has Been Here*. Illustrated by James Stevenson. New York: Greenwillow.

Prelutsky, Jack. (1984). "The New Kid on the Block." In *The New Kid on the Block*. Illustrated by James Stevenson. New York: Greenwillow.

Prelutsky, Jack. (1984). "Today Is Very Boring." In *The New Kid on the Block*. Illustrated by James Stevenson. New York: Greenwillow.

Prelutsky, Jack. (Ed.). (1986). *Read-Aloud Rhymes for the Very Young*. Illustrated by Marc Brown. New York: Alfred A. Knopf.

Prelutsky, Jack. (Ed.). (1983). *The Random House Book of Poetry for Children*. Illustrated by Arnold Lobel. New York: Random House.

Rogers, Paul. (1989). *What Will the Weather Be Like Today?* Illustrated by Kazuko. New York: Greenwillow.

Rosen, Michael. (1989). *We're Going on a Bear Hunt*. Illustrated by Helen Oxenbury. New York: Margaret K. McElderry.

Siebert, Diane. (1989). *Heartland*. Illustrated by Wendell Minor. New York: Thomas Y. Crowell.

Siebert, Diane. (1988). *Mojave*. Illustrated by Wendell Minor. New York: HarperCollins.

Siebert, Diane. (1981, Illustrations 1990). *Train Song*. Illustrated by Mike Wimmer. New York: Thomas Y. Crowell.

Silverstein, Shel. (1981). *A Light in the Attic*. New York: HarperCollins.

Silverstein, Shel. (1974). *Where the Sidewalk Ends*. New York: HarperCollins.

Smith, William J. (1990). *Laughing Time*. Illustrated by Fernando Krahn. New York: Delacorte.

Stevenson, Robert Louis. (1990). *My Shadow*. Illustrated by Ted Rand. New York: Putnam.

Taylor, Jane. (1992). *Twinkle, Twinkle, Little Star*. Illustrated by Michael Hague. New York: Morrow.

Thornhill, Jan. (1988). *The Wildlife ABC: A Nature Alphabet Book*. New York: Simon & Schuster.

Viorst, Judith. (1981). "My Cat." In *If I Were in Charge of the World and Other Worries*. Illustrated by Lynne Cherry. New York: Macmillan.

Viorst, Judith. (1981). *If I Were in Charge of the World and Other Worries*. Illustrated by Lynne Cherry. New York: Macmillan.

Wood, Audrey. (1992). *Silly Sally*. San Diego, CA: Harcourt Brace Jovanovich.

Yolen, Jane. (1990). *Cardinal*. Birdwatch. New York: Philomel.

8

Stories, Storytelling, Creative Dramatics, and Puppetry

Stories, Storytelling, Creative Dramatics, and Puppetry

*M*elissa, a third-grade teacher in New Mexico, wanted to develop a thematic unit on the Pueblo culture. She had been interested in this culture for many years but a new book that she found, Hoyt-Goldsmith's *Pueblo Storyteller*, sparked her enthusiasm to develop a unit for her class. This book included information about the creation of storyteller figurines. From the book she learned that the figurine depicted a Native-American storyteller who was surrounded by children listening intently to his story. As she prepared the materials for the unit she gained additional information from references, museums, and interviews with Native Americans in her area. During the process of collecting information, Melissa wondered what is so compelling about storytelling that a culture will symbolize this tradition by fashioning a figure to represent the experience? Can this oral tradition be used today to enrich the literature experiences of primary children? Can the children in my classroom benefit from the addition of storytelling, creative dramatics, and puppetry?

The Story of the Storyteller Doll[1]

Many years ago, in the Cochiti Pueblo in New Mexico, a little girl listened to her beloved grandfather, Santiago Quintana, tell stories. He was known as a gifted storyteller who told true stories about his life and traditions that he wanted preserved. To signal the beginning of a story he would say, "Come children, it's time [Babcock & Monthan, 1990, p. 96]." These storytelling events were cherished by his granddaughter, Helen Cordero. In 1964, at the age of forty-five, Helen created her first storyteller figure and revived a Cochiti tradition of figurative art. These first storyteller dolls have become collectors' items and have inspired many other potters in the New Mexico pueblos to expand their figurative creations. Helen's symbolic representation of her grandfather depicts him telling a story with many children sitting on his shoulders, knees, arms, and legs while listening attentively. Cordero's ideas spawned other Pueblo artists who began making storyteller figures. The proliferation of storyteller dolls by other Pueblo potters indicates, that they, too, remember experiences with a grandmother, grandfather, or another important adult who told them cherished stories of their culture.

The storyteller figures represent the power of the story. There are people blessed with the gift of story, but the power of story is not unique to the Native American culture or to the gifted one; it is universal and exists in many cultures. It is the power to remember, to entertain, to teach, to inspire, to create, and to know.

THE POWER TO REMEMBER

The power of story as "the power to remember" was well known to our ancestors who passed information by word of mouth. The folktales, legends, and myths of the past have been passed down for centuries, preserved because they were organized in story form, easy to remember, and could be told again and again.

Children who had the opportunity to hear these stories internalized the structure of each story form and knew that: after the second wish, there will always be a third; after the wicked witch there will be a rescuer; after the fateful event, the animals were changed forever; and after the wrath of the vengeful one, good would prevail.

Children can remember these powerful tales of the past when adults share the rich literature derived from "oft-told" stories that have survived the centuries. Similarly, we can link children to their elders by capturing the adults' "power to remember." Amy, a teacher who grew up in Tennessee, was anxious to preserve the oral tradition of her heritage. On the first weekend in October, she and thousands of other teachers went to historic Jonesborough, Tennessee for the annual storytelling festival of the National Association for the Preservation and Perpetuation of Storytelling

(NAPPS). According to Jimmy Neal Smith (1992), a former teacher and the executive director and founder of the storytelling festival, teachers come to the oldest town in Tennessee for an autumn weekend in celebration of the story. Inside one multicolored tent, teachers, families with children, librarians, and scholars gather to hear storytellers. The storytellers include: South Carolina Islanders telling Gullah tales, an Appalachian man spinning Jack tales, an African-American historian reminiscing about her childhood in the South, a Western cowboy telling stories in poetry form, and an Irishman using a Celtic harp to accompany his story. Beginning storytellers gather at the "swapping place" in the center of town and volunteer to tell stories to all who will stop. Here, many teachers timidly, then confidently, practice their storytelling techniques.

All over this little picturesque town, circus tents are set up on the hills and in the valleys. In one tent there are many resource books on using stories to teach, collections of stories to be told, and tapes of famous storytellers. One father in the tent purchased several tapes of storytellers for his eight-year-old daughter to listen to on their journey back home to the White Mountains of New Hampshire. At this festival it is evident that parents and teachers have recognized the value of the story to remember and to teach.

THE POWER TO ENTERTAIN

Whether laughing out loud or chuckling to himself, Pop can start a story at the drop of a hat. The phrase "that reminds me of the time . . ." identifies for the adults and the children at the family reunion that one of Pop's stories is about to begin. As the story progresses, the children participate in the ritual by asking, "And then what happened, Pop?" Whether it is a tale of two young boys trying to find an escape from the hot summer farm work by dashing for the cool of the pond, or an escapade in search of some sure-fire way to make enough money for the county fair, the humor, the good natured teasing, the gestures, and the pauses invite the listeners into the story. The simple story becomes an entertainment event. The tales capture an era, another time and place that our children would not and could not understand without the storyteller intending to entertain.

The entertaining story in print is the enticement used to capture young readers. The adventure of Lobel's *Frog and Toad*, the mischief of Rey's *Curious George*, the mayhem of Parish's *Teach Us, Amelia Bedelia*, will invariably inspire the young child to read. When the teacher pauses at an expectant moment, she mimics Pop's invitation to participate, and the young listeners ask aloud with the turn of the page, "And then what happened?" Young children's first story readings often imitate that of their parent or teachers. They use the inflections and rituals of reading, pretending to read as they tell about the picture, or retell a memorized version, often pausing with each turn of the page and saying, "And then what happened?"

Drawn into the story form, young children predict how the story will unfold and as surely as they were entertained by the tale, they begin reading, assured that Frog and Toad will always be friends, Curious George will always get into trouble, and Amelia Bedelia will always get things mixed up. The stories consistently entertain and entice, build a predictable structure, a recognizable content, and characters that the child depend upon. Like the listeners to Pop's tales, the child who reads to be entertained owns the power of the story and the power to be entertained by the printed text.

THE POWER TO TEACH

Kieran Egan of Simon Frazer University has written *Teaching as Story Telling: An Alternative Approach to Teaching and Curriculum in Elementary School* (1986), the premise of which is that the "mind organizes best in story form." Egan proposes reorganizing the curriculum by connecting what is to be learned into a story.

While storytelling is widely recommended as an effective teaching practice, it is not often used on a regular basis (Cooter, 1991; Medina, 1986; Morrow,

1979; Nelson, 1989; Nessel, 1985; Peck, 1989; Roney, 1989). There is, however, a resurgence of interest in storytelling as an art and teaching form. This rebirth has led to thinking of storytelling as a means to teach descriptive language, visual imagery, cultural appreciation, effective communication, and the understanding of feelings and emotions. The story is valued for its affective, aesthetic, and creative influences on the learner. Teachers and children gain confidence from telling stories and having an appreciative audience. They learn story form and story structure, value the told story as literature, and make connections to the historical past through the collective remembrances of another era. The "truths" in embellished, flavored, and imaginatively exaggerated tales still prevail as the truth. Morals need not be preached but can be taught, told, and illustrated in entertaining and memorable stories.

THE POWER TO INSPIRE

From the pulpit, the political podium, and the conference speaker's platform, people assemble to tell and to hear the inspiring story. Newspaper editors and television journalists add human interest stories to their print and broadcast media to inspire the human race and remind us that violence, crime, and disaster are not all there is in our world. The human interest story is told for inspiration.

In the corporate world, American businesses have been influenced by telling stories of the company's shaky beginnings, fledgling stabs at entering the marketplace, and uncompromising service to their customers. The culture of the company is conveyed by the stories its leaders choose to tell at meetings and put into print and by those individuals they choose as heroes. Stories of risk takers who finally succeed can build a psychologically safe environment where a new approach can be tried. Stories of leaders and stories of inventive workers ignite a vision of possibilities that go far beyond the usual management style or the union contract.

School principals have adopted a similar strategy to inspire children and teachers to tackle some seemingly impossible task, such as reading a "thousand books in a week." After the children meet the challenge, the principal performs some daring feat, such as spending the day on the school roof, bungee jumping from a crane, or running a hundred laps around the playground. The story of the event lives on to inspire students to tackle difficult problems and becomes a retold story as part of the school's culture.

Teachers often select inspiring stories to instill qualities they value in their students. Stories of persistence in the face of difficulty, working with others, and bravery when attempting something new can also inspire young children to accomplish the difficult and follow the example of a real or imagined character in good children's literature, whether found in print or in the told story form.

THE POWER TO CREATE

Stories in and of themselves are a creative venture. Many young children's first adventures in storytelling are sketches of what happened to them, embellished and told with breathless excitement. In dramatic play, children compose stories and participate as both the authors and the actors. At first they are the characters and the dramatic play helps them put life experiences into perspective. Later, they use more fantasy in their play as they create imaginary characters and select elements to include in the story for the effect. Very early in these play sequences there are recurring patterns and the need for resolution in the story is demonstrated (Raines, 1990; Smilansky & Shefatya, 1990).

As children learn to be writers, they write the story as it actually happened and then enrich it for the sake of the story. These colorful "embellished" versions of their stories allow children to use realism or fantasy while maintaining the central theme and characters. In these creations, the unique and original is valued and variations are accepted as appropriate for the sake of the story. Like adult "fish stories" which are often more exciting than catching the fish, children's creative stories are excitingly "fishy."

Northrop Frye (1964) concluded that stories are a primary means for developing an educated imagination. Through stories, observations can be refined, perceptions of the world changed and sensitivity developed. These expanded capabilities make the child aware of the many possibilities available and gain the personal confidence needed to accept new challenges. A good story engages children in a created world providing a unique aesthetic experience that only literature can provide (Vandergrift, 1980).

THE POWER TO KNOW

Stories provide a way of knowing. A personal experience with a story helps children gain a sense of identity, a sense of control, and a sense of connection with others in the world. The story provides an avenue to explore the world, to extend experiences, and to have power over them. Through story, children learn how to organize the many experiences that bombard them every day. Bettelheim (1976) explains that story is the material children use in forming their concepts of the world and provides the ideas they can use to function in society.

As children construct knowledge, they use their previous experiences as the base and add new experiences to build expanding systematic representations. Each new experience modifies the representation and the process is continuously growing and changing. As certain aspects of the experiences are repeated or a consistent pattern is identified, children are able to use this constancy to understand concepts of the story or build meaning based on a particular story. The understanding of story is constructed through past and present experiences with literature. The accumulation of story experiences provides structure for understanding the world and the literature that represents the world. As this story system is being constructed, children are constantly questioning, developing hypotheses, and trying to gain meaning (Applebee, 1978).

In many Native-American cultures, young children and adults sit together in the presence of the storyteller and listen to the same story. The young Cherokee child who hears how an opossum got his skinny tail thinks of this as a funny story about a real opossum. But the older listener understands that the moral of the story is the peril of false pride. The interpretation is in the mind and life experiences of the listener who constructs the meaning. The story symbolizes a great truth which the listener will grow to understand after hearing it many times and will use the lesson as a way of understanding the world.

THE POWER TO REVISIT

Leland Jacobs wrote, "... through story, biography, poem, a child can, with aesthetic feelings, enter into questing, copings, circumstances, longings, happenings that are possible for the individual in no other way [1980, Forward, p. xii]." Kay Vandergrift (1980) explains that both the understanding and appreciation of story is developmental and cumulative. Each experience with a story builds on previous interactions and provides a structure for those that will follow. "The connection between child and story is threefold: it is personal, it is communal, and it is critical [Preface, p. xiv]."

Stories loved by children are never really left behind but experienced again and again. The preschooler hears the story of Curious George during story time. When he is a kindergartner, he enjoys it again, and in second grade he reads it for himself enjoying it in a new way. In high school he sees a Curious George book in the public library and he privately reads the loved story again. Later in life, when he becomes a father, he selects a Curious George story to read to his own toddler, enjoying the story again and introducing that joy to his child. Stories provide a pleasurable experience that can be repeated again and again.

In the early childhood classroom, when a wonderful story was shared at circle time, children applauded and shouted, "Read it again!" After the story was read again, the teacher placed it in the classroom library area. Moments later a little girl revisited the story in the twice-read book, and she

was heard to say, "I want to read it for myself." After a teacher told a group of five-year-olds the story of the "Gingerbread Boy," the children pleaded in unison, "Tell it again." As children hear the story again and again, they build their understanding and have the opportunity to repeat the enjoyment as they revisit the story. When they are encouraged to retell the stories, they revisit them, often rehearsing and savoring the language as they play "Run, run as fast as you can. You can't catch me. I'm the Gingerbread Man." These numerous opportunities to return to the story are beneficial to young children as they learn how stories work.

The Development of the Concept of Story

Arthur Applebee describes the development of children's understanding of story in his book *The Child's Concept of Story* (1978). Since young children cannot describe their internal cognitive processes, Applebee used the stories children tell as a way of investigating their understandings of stories and how they work. He concluded that although each child experiences stories personally and constructs understanding individually, this process is influenced by the literature they experience. Children in the spectator role look on, trying to find structure and meaning but are not concerned about breaking the story apart or interpreting the story. In this role, children learn that others see the world as they do, have some of the same problems, and experience similar joys. Later, in the participation role, children are more directly involved in the experience by questioning, judging, and discussing ideas presented in the story.

CHARACTERISTICS OF CHILDREN'S STORIES

Young children's compositions can demonstrate the features they have learned to expect. After collecting and analyzing 350 original stories from children ages two through ten, Brian Sutton-Smith (1981) described children's beginning storytelling as an "embryonic stage." If they have the opportunity to tell stories to others, this stage will mature into true folktale forms. He concluded that the character of the narrative is a universal mental activity. All cultures and ages use narratives as a way of communicating ideas and stories.

Pitcher and Prelinger (1963) collected stories told by children two to five years of age which were later reanalyzed by Applebee. The children's use of conventions such as *Once upon a time* and *the end* were seen as indicators of their understanding of the organization of stories and the structure needed to communicate. Applebee found that 70 percent of the two-year-olds studied had begun to distinguish stories from other forms of communication by using at least one of the three conventions: formal opening, formal closing, and consistent past tense. From the ages of two to five, there was a significant increase in the use of all three conventions and by five years of age, 47 percent of the children in the study used all three in their story tellings.

As young children gradually begin to use formal conventions of story, they are also developing understanding of reality and fantasy. The ability to distinguish fact and fiction is a difficult process for children and requires a high level of cognitive development as well as exposure to a variety of literature. Although some young children are beginning to question the reality of the story content, even children six to nine years of age are still convinced that the stories they hear are real. At age six, only half of the children studied understood that Cinderella was a fictional story. It was not until the age of nine that 90 percent of the children recognized that Cinderella was not a real person. These changes indicate that learning to distinguish fact from fantasy in stories is a complex process and requires children many years to acquire (Applebee, 1978).

Another aspect of children's understanding of story is their expectations for the behaviors of characters. Their first views of the characters in the

stories are based on real and everyday experiences with people: mommy and daddy, teacher and grandparents. As children hear more stories told or read, they begin to use conventional story characters, and by age five many include characters such as lion, wolf, fox, fairy, and witch (Applebee, 1978). It is not until children are eight and nine years of age that the roles characters play are clearly understood and include both fantasy and real characters in their stories.

The works of Sutton-Smith, Pitcher, Prelinger, and Applebee clearly indicate that very young children use some conventions of story but these inclusions gradually increase as they have more experiences with literature. The stories, people, places, and the vocabulary used can assist young children in developing understanding of both the world and the way literature works. These rich experiences aid them as they begin to retell and compose stories for themselves.

Storytelling

Reading and telling are effective ways to communicate stories to children and both methods should be used in the early childhood classroom. There are however, differences between the two approaches and the way they influence both the adult and children involved in the literature event. When the story is being read, the reader is conscious of the written text and the words in the book. Attention to the text ties the reader to the book and allows occasional eye contact with the children in the audience. In contrast, the storyteller is able to maintain eye contact with the audience throughout the story and provide immediate response to their reactions. The storyteller can match the story and vocabulary with the audience, making adjustments and clarifications when these are needed to increase understanding. Storytelling is a personal experience for both the teller and the listener for they are constantly interacting with each other and building rapport (Morrow, 1979). The storyteller and children actively participate as they interact in the creation of the story. Storytelling is a powerful medium which captures children's attention because the process is personal, entertaining, and responsive.

Stories presented in oral form are enriched by the tellers personality, voice, and style. The talented storyteller can pull children into a story that is descriptively told, making them feel a part of the story experience. The unique style of the individual storyteller, the facial expressions, intonation, gestures, and word selection create a new world for young children. The storyteller shares an adventure with the children: his life as a cowboy, being a child in Africa, or tracking bears in Alaska. This magical power helps children connect with the teller and the story as they experience the literature in a new way. This enjoyment of the teller and story can motivate young children to move into the literature arena as a storyteller, story reader, and story writer.

In storytelling, the pace and length of the story being told can be expanded or compacted to fit the developmental level of the children who are listening. The magic of Slobodkina's *Caps for Sale* can be enjoyed by either toddlers or seven-year-olds and the story line, characters, and repetitive phrases are maintained when presented to either audience. In the telling of the story, however, the number of caps and the actions imitated by the monkeys can be adjusted to the interest of the children listening. The match of story and audience encourages attention to the content and helps maintain involvement throughout the telling (Nessel, 1985). When storytellers capture children's attention, they encourage their listeners to creatively imagine the happenings in their mind's eye.

In a research study (Isbell, 1979) investigating the effects of storytelling and story reading on young children's understanding of story, significant differences were found between the two approaches. In the study, young children three to six years of age were randomly assigned to literature groups for an eight-week period. During the sessions, literature was presented that could be effectively used in both story reading and storytelling. One group of children had the stories read to them three times a week while the other group of young children had the same stories presented to them three times a week by the teacher as the storyteller. At the end of the study, both groups of children were asked to retell stories they had heard and their oral language was taped and analyzed using several measures of oral language development including fluency of telling, diversity of vocabulary, and length of communication unit (T-Unit). Retellings were also analyzed using Applebee's story conventions: beginning, ending, characters included, sequence of events, and narrative used. An interesting pattern emerged in the two groups' retelling of the stories. Children who had participated in the storytelling group included significantly more story conventions in their retellings. Their stories were longer, included more diverse vocabulary, and were more sequential in composition. One little girl in the story reading group said, "I can't tell the story. I don't have the book." Young children, who are often visual learners, are attentive to the illustrations and many lose the story line when a picture book is read. This study demonstrated the need to include storytelling as a regular part of the early childhood classroom in addition to daily story reading. Storytelling can provide another avenue to expand young children's oral language and increase comprehension of the story (Isbell, 1979).

Storytelling, in the oral tradition and in books, provides children an opportunity to imagine visually. Today's young children have a world filled with ready made visual images: television, movies, computers, and video games. These media do not allow the children to imagine or create a visual picture for themselves. When a picture book is read aloud, young children often concentrate on what they see in the illustrations. In storytelling, young children can imagine what the "rickety house" or "tattered old clothes" look like by the verbal descriptions they hear. Creating mental pictures allows children to work with the structure presented and extend their visual images from this language base (Maguire, 1985).

Storytelling involves three essential elements: the story, the listener, and the teller. If these three elements work in harmony, there will be mutual enjoyment for all involved and the storytelling experience will be repeated again and again.

THE STORY

Throughout human history storytelling has been one of the major ways people have been educated. Through oral stories children come to understand the mysteries of life that surround them, the culture of their community, and the simple truths that link people together (Baker & Green, 1977). When the story told is simple, the language repetitive, the sequence predictable, and the telling enthusiastic, young children catch the spirit and join in the telling while actively constructing their understanding of the story.

The narrative story is told to young children in one session and the variety of content available to tell is limitless. Stories can describe everyday experiences, magical happenings, the struggle between good and evil, or the depths of a human experience (Colwell, 1980). The storyteller, as the narrator, uses the story literature to paint a verbal picture of the setting, characters, and events.

SELECTING STORIES FOR TELLING

In selecting a story for telling, storytellers must find stories that appeal to them personally. It is necessary to read and try many different stories until the storyteller finds the special story that captures his or her interest and inspires the telling. A storyteller's love of the story goes a long way in helping the story come across with sincere positive appreciation. The story should also contain some quality that makes it worth sharing with children. Are there truths, images, discoveries, or understandings that the children in the audience will find valuable? Will it stimulate their imagination and help them

discover that words can be used to visualize time, place, and events? Will the story assist them as they gain understanding of themselves and others? Will the story help them find meaning in the world around them (Barton, 1986)? Some storytellers believe that a good story is a good story for any audience and can be adjusted in length, complexity, and vocabulary to match the developmental level of those who are listening. In this active process, the storyteller becomes the intermediary for the story, embellishing or refining it in harmony with the audience. Close observation of the children and their responses can make the storytelling experience more exciting for both the storyteller and the children.

Barton (1986), identified three literature levels that can serve as a guide in story selection. He suggests that the teller study the composition of the group and determine the experiences the children have had with storytelling before making the final selection. His approach to story selection indicates that regular planned experiences with storytelling leads children to more complex understanding and increased interest in listening to diverse story forms.

Folktales, like *The Little Red Hen* or *The Gingerbread Boy*, work extremely well with young children who are less experienced with storytelling. These stories have been passed down for generations, their morals are clear and their characters are easily understood by the most inexperienced listener. Folktales, which have been told orally, include wonderful descriptive words and a clear story line. The cumulative progression of these stories makes it easy for young children to follow and make predictions about what will happen next. Other qualities that make these tales so wonderful for storytelling include action packed sequences, memorable characters, and interesting language patterns. These characteristics offer children the opportunity to build their story comprehension while actively participating in the presentation (Barton, 1986; Maguire, 1985).

Figure 8.1 Guidelines for Story Selection

Guidelines for Story Selection
Adapted from Barton (1986) and Maguire (1985).

Characteristics of Children	Features of Story	Suggestions
LEVEL I: Wide range of ages (toddlers to school age). Inexperienced with storytelling. Difficult to hold attention, lose interest easily	Clear opening and closing. Characters are distinctive. Content is presented slowly and clearly. Story line is easy to follow. Audience participation is encouraged. Content of story within their experiential background.	Simple folk tales. Participation stories. Simple, authored stories about everyday experiences. Retelling of favorite stories. Predictable story with short repetitive line.
LEVEL II: Homogeneous group in similar developmental level. (Example: classroom of kindergarten children) More experienced with storytelling and have been involved previously.	Dramatic beginning to story. Humor involved. Story sequence easy to follow. Material matches level of development. (Not too difficult or too babyish.) Realistic story. Beginning use of fantasy.	Longer folk tales, authored stories, stories from other cultures, legends, fables.
LEVEL III: Participates in storytelling experiences regularly. Listeners are excited about storytelling. Building repertoire of stories they enjoy.	More refined listening permits use of more complex text and story structure. Longer story can be used. Time is taken and each moment is captured in the story. More descriptions of characters, scenes, and underlaying meaning can be communicated.	Include all types of literature: fables, folktales, fairy tales, myths, legends, and adventure stories. More complex stories with more characters can be used. Meanings and truths can be more subtle.

Contemporary children's books can be effectively used in storytelling if their content reflects situations that directly relate to young children's experiences. Krauss's *Carrot Seed* is an excellent book for storytelling since most young children have had experience with "big people" who tell them that something will not work. If children are captivated by the simple story, the content can be expanded by adding more people who look at the seed and repeat the refrain, "It won't come up." This involvement in the storytelling builds understanding of the predicable story pattern and increases the child's personal identification with the feelings of the character in the story. At the conclusion of the story, the child's seed has grown into an enormous carrot, demonstrating to all listening the reward for not giving up.

Figure 8.2 Suggested Folktales to Tell to Young Children*

It Could Be Worse by Margot Zemach
Millions of Cats by Wanda Gag
Stone Soup by Marica Brown
The Gingerbread Boy by Paul Galdone
The Little Red Hen by Paul Galdone
The Turnip by Katherine Milhous
    and Alice Dalgiesh
Three Wishes by Paul Galdone

Contemporary Authored Stories That Are Effective for Telling

Alexander and the Wind-Up Mouse by Leo Lionni
Caps for Sale by Esphyr Slobodkina
Corduroy by Don Freeman
Dandelion by Don Freeman
Fat Cat by Jack Kent
The Man Who Didn't Wash His Dishes
    by Phyllis Krasilovsky

*All of the suggested folktales and authored stories are also available in book form and can be used to extend the storytelling to an interest in print.

There are also many wonderful stories in books that have out-of-date illustrations or were printed when a limited number of colors were used. These treasures can be released from the book and activated by the storyteller. A great story, *The Man Who Didn't Wash His Dishes*, written by Krasilovsky, is hidden in a book printed in 1950. In this story, a man cooks his supper each evening, and when he finishes he is too tired to wash the dishes. After being too tired to wash the dishes for many nights, he resorts to piling the dirty dishes all over the house and eating out of all kinds of unusual objects. In the end, he realizes that he must wash his dishes each evening no matter how tired he is. This cumulative story has a modern theme, the possibility of many extensions, and a clear message. The storyteller can use the picture book content in an oral presentation that will excite young listeners and provide a new story for their collection.

Fast moving stories that have humorous happenings seem to appeal to large groups and audiences composed of children of different ages. Elements of surprise in the story work well regardless of the size and composition of the audience and lead to their request, "Tell it again!" *The Judge, The Fat Cat,* and *The Snake That Sneezed* are examples of stories that appeal to large or small audiences.

Stories that have proven to be effective for storytelling sessions often include a small number of interesting characters, lots of action, a plot that involves a conflict, building suspense, and a satisfying solution (Wilson, 1991). A lengthy description of a setting or incident can lose young listeners who are more interested in what the characters are doing and the action in the story. Stories that are liked by young children can be shared again and again. "Each time a story is told, it is born again for both the listeners and the storyteller [Barton, 1986 p. 24]."

For older children the inclusions of myths, legends, and fairy tales can provide new types of literature for storytelling. Myths and legends lead to understanding about different people and their culture. *The Legend of the Bluebonnet: An Old Tale of Texas* tells of a young Comanche girl who sacrifices her most valuable possession to save her people from famine. This story helps children appreciate cultural diversity while leading them to understand the deep feelings that all people experience. Fairy tales encourage children to enter the world of fantasy and to vicariously experience the conflict of good and evil. Primary children will enjoy the telling of favorites from the Brothers Grimm and Hans Christian Andersen.

Collections of stories that can be used in storytelling sessions are a valuable classroom resource for the teacher storyteller. The combination of many different stories in one volume allows the teacher to quickly read and select a story that will match the interest of the children in her group. It will also encourage sharing many stories that are on the same topic, use the same story form, or originate from the same culture.

THE LISTENER

Storytelling offers children opportunities to develop listening comprehension, including literal, inferential, and appreciative thinking. Children who listen to stories are developing understanding as they use their imaginations and background experiences to activate the story in their minds.

Figure 8.3 Storytelling Selections for Primary Age Children

Little Beaver and the Echo by Amy MacDonald
The Legend of the Indian Paintbrush by
    Tomie dePaola
The Little Match Girl by
    Hans Christian Andersen
The Mud Pony: A Traditional Skidi Pawnee Tale
    by Caren Cohen
The Night of the Stars by Douglas Gutierrez
The Snow Child by Freya Littledale
Strega Nona: An Old Tale by Tomie dePaola
Such A Noise by Aliana Brodmann
The True Story of the Three Little Pigs
    by Jon Scieszka

Meaning develops when the story is understood and the content affects the listener personally. This process depends on how closely the children identify with the story and the background of experience they bring to the interpretation (Nelson, 1989). Children listen carefully to stories told and discriminate the verbal clues used by the storyteller. By listening to a variety of stories and storytellers, children learn to distinguish and evaluate styles, enjoy dialects and story content, and establish personal meaning. Listeners participate in the storytelling process as they provide feedback for the

---

Figure 8.4 Collections of Stories Appropriate for Telling

Animal Stories Retold by David Kherdian,
    David Kherdian
Best Loved Folktales of the World,
    Joanna Cole
The Blue Fairy Book, Andrew Lang
Easy to Tell Stories for the Very Young,
    Annette Harrison
Favorite Folktales from Around the World,
    Jane Yolen
Giant Treasury of Brer Rabbit, Joel C. Harris
The Girls Who Cried Flowers; and Other Tales,
    Jane Yolen
Grandfather Tales, Richard Chase
Great Children's Stories, Frederick Richardson
Juba This and Juba That, Virginia Tashjian
Keepers of the Animals: Native American Stories
    & Wildlife Activities for Children,
    Michael Caduto and Joseph Bruchac
The Little Old Woman Who Used Her Head and
    Other Stories, Hope Newell
The Magic Orange Tree and Other Haitian
    Folktales, Diane Wolkstein
Native American Stories, Joseph Bruchac
Tales for Telling From Around the World,
    Mary Medlicott
Talk That Talk: An Anthology of African-
    American Storytelling, Linda Goss and
    Marian Baines
Twice Upon A Time, Avery Hall and John Korty

teller, interject sounds, or repeat phrases. Children who have listened to a story on several occasions demonstrate their understanding of the content as they cover their ears when the "big bad troll" comes from under the bridge. They are predicting that he will shout "Who is that trip trap tripping on my bridge?" This anticipation demonstrates their understanding of the sequence of the story and what will happen next (Peck, 1989).

Hearing a story told several different times gives young listeners opportunities to clarify, to fill in gaps, and make important connections. Children increase their control over stories when they hear them again and again. Although sharing a variety of stories is important, young children also need the opportunity to appreciate and revisit familiar stories whether in spoken or written form (Martinez & Roser, 1985). Through repeated tellings children can build a collection of stories they enjoy hearing. They remember the joy they felt when they first heard the story and repeat those feelings as they experience it again and later tell it to others. During these retellings children quickly recognize any changes in the content or the words used by the storyteller. A storyteller shared *Millions of Cats* with a group of young children in the fall of the year. In the spring, the storyteller created a story about rabbits that followed the same story structure and sequence as *Millions of Cats*. At the conclusion of the second session, almost six months after the first telling, a four-year-old listener told the storyteller, "I have heard that story before but the last time there were millions of cats instead of millions of rabbits." This comment demonstrated that the young child was not only listening to the words in the telling but also learning the underlying structure of the story and how the content was communicated.

THE STORYTELLER

The term storyteller often conjures up an image of a famous performer who has a unique style and distinctive voice that mesmerizes audiences: Richard Chase, telling a Jack tale with dialect, Jackie Torrance's melodic voice leading into a chilling story, or the folktellers, Connie Regan-Blake and Barbara Freeman, taking turns and using distinctive voices to tell a humorous story. These models, however, should not discourage a teacher from becoming a storyteller, but rather provide an example of what the art can accomplish when effectively used with children. Every teacher can become a storyteller by just preparing and sharing one story orally. A teacher who has told the first story and experienced the enthusiastic response of young children in the audience takes a step toward becoming a storyteller forever. The personal contact with the audience allows the storyteller to capture the children's interest and carry it with them as the story unfolds and reaches a satisfying conclusion.

The power of story coupled with an inspiring storyteller can awaken the attention of even the most disinterested child who has been impossible to reach. In the kindergarten, Jeremy was always the last child to come to the circle for story time. During the reading of books he wiggled, punched his neighbor, and rolled his head in a circular direction. Today, the kindergarten teacher tells the story of "The Tailor" (in Schimmel's *Just Enough to Make a Story*) to Jeremy and his classmates. Jeremy is mesmerized by the story and intently listens to the entire telling. For the first time, Jeremy is drawn into a story and his interest is demonstrated by his focused attention and fascination with each fabric transformation. The teacher storyteller made the important connection of story and child possible. Finding a way to involve even the difficult child can certainly inspire the early childhood teacher to collect stories and include more storytelling sessions in the classroom.

Beginning storytellers need time to refine stories and become familiar with the content. Although each storyteller must find the technique that assists him or her in learning a new story, some procedures recommended to use in the learning period include reading the story several times, tape recording the reading of the story, or writing an outline of the story. The story is not memorized but rather the content and characters are remembered. Making a story one's own involves using imagination to explore all aspects of the story and finding personal ways of relating the content to the audience. As the story is learned, the teller studies the structure of the story, the sequence of events, a recurring pattern, and the moral of the story. The storyteller also examines the characters in the story to understand their unique qualities and those they share with others. It is also helpful to understand the motivation of the characters in the story and how this contributes to the events. In the learning process, the style and pattern of the language should be examined so the sound of the story is maintained and the meaning communicated in the telling.

After reading or hearing the story several times, the storyteller may want to develop a story card that will aid when first telling the story or to review

Figure 8.5 "How To" Storytelling Resources

Creative Storytelling: Choosing, Inventing, and Sharing Tales for Children by Maguire
Family Storytelling Handbook by Pellowski
Just Enough to Make a Story: A Source Book for Storytelling by Shimmel
Stories in the Classroom by Barton
Students as Storytellers by Griffin

Figure 8.6 Story Card

DANDELION Freeman, Don (1964) *Dandelion.* New York: Viking Press.   **FRONT**

Characters: Dandelion
         Jennifer Giraffe
         Lou Kangaroo
         Theodore the Tailor
         Happy

Dandelion is invited to a tea party and is so excited that he gets his hair trimmed, a shampoo, a manicure, and a perm. Then he buys a new jacket, a hat, and cane. He goes to the party and rings the bell, but Jennifer Giraffe doesn't recognize him and won't let him in. Dandelion is very sad. He walks around and the wind blows. His hat flies away. It rains so his hair straightens out and he takes off his wet jacket. Dandelion decides to go back to the party and try one more time to join his friends. Jennifer Giraffe opens the door and says, "If it isn't our friend, Dandelion, at LAST!"
DANDELION   **BACK**

QUESTIONS:
  1. If you were invited to a party, what would you do to get ready?
  2. What did Dandelion do to get ready to go to the tea party?
  3. Describe how Dandelion looked when he went to Jennifer Giraffe's party.
  4. How did Dandelion feel when Jennifer would not let him in the door to her party?
  5. What did the wind and rain do to Dapper Dan?
 	
  PROPS: A Party Invitation
 	
  FOLLOW-UP ACTIVITY: Creative drama using the story. Dressing up for a party with before and after pictures.

the story. This 5 x 8 card should include the bibliographical information about the story or the reference collection where the story was found. This will help locate the book later when it is added to the library area for children to examine. The card may also include a brief outline of the story, the plot and the characters in the order they appear. If there are phrases that are repeated or exact words that need to be maintained in the telling, they are included in the

write-up. It is also helpful to list questions that could be used at the beginning and ending of the story to develop the listener's comprehension. It is important to include questions that ask more than factual information so that the child is drawn to make conclusions or judgments about the story. Other information could be added, including props to be used, follow-up activities, or other books on a similar topic. Story cards help the busy teacher build a repertoire of stories that can be used throughout the year and assist in a quick review for retelling the story the following year.

Once the story is outlined on the card, the teacher will need to tell the story in her own words, first alone and later with a small group of children. These first experiences are often difficult, for the storyteller is overly concerned that every word be included and nothing be left out. As teachers become more familiar with the story and their confidence increases, they will begin to be more adventurous in moving away from the exact words in the book toward language that is comfortable for them and their audience. After the story has been practiced in the storyteller's own words, it is a good idea to return to the original source and reread the story. In this final review, the storyteller may look for words, phrases, or insights that will improve the story. At this time it would also be helpful to examine the beginning and ending of the story for these two conventions are very important in the successful presentation of the story. An intriguing beginning captures the children's interest and a powerful conclusion provides the listeners personal satisfaction and resolves the story (Barton, 1986).

Oral practices of the story with the story card can help the storyteller feel more comfortable in the first sessions with a new story. Storytellers who love the story they are telling have taken the time to adequately prepare the story, and have made the necessary changes to enrich the telling become powerful literature models for children.

PERFORMANCE

Before beginning a storytelling session, the teacher should draw the children around him or her by using a familiar signal that indicates this is a very special happening. Lighting a candle, singing a special song, or repeating a chant can capture the attention of the young audience and signify that a story is about to begin. In traditional storytelling, the tellers used only their voices to communicate to the listener. This method of presentation is very effective for nothing comes between the teller and listener. The rhyme of the words, the tone of the voice, and the focus of the eyes maintain interest in the story, which gradually unfolds to a spellbound audience.

Today, early childhood storytellers use many different ways to vary the presentation of stories. One variation in the storytelling experience can be achieved through the use of props. Props are real or representative objects the storyteller can use to capture interest, build suspense, or surprise the listeners. A prism can be used to spark interest in Freeman's *A Rainbow of My Own,* a drum can inspire "The Boy with the Drum" from Harrison's *Easy to Tell Stories for Young Children,* and a quilt can introduce the Johnston's book, *The Quilt Story.* The addition of these simple props works best with children four years of age or older. The younger toddler or three-year-old will find the object distracting and will want to continually manipulate the prop, interfering with comprehension of the story. Older children will use the prop to move them into the story and assist in their focus on the content (Jalongo, 1992).

It is extremely important to involve young children in the story presentation as it increases their listening. In a participation story, the storyteller has the major role, but the audience is joining in segments of the telling. To clarify the participation of the audience, a set of cues and responses in the form of actions, words, or sounds is established prior to the telling. "When you hear the word horse, slap your legs." Sometimes the storyteller does not tell the children how they should respond, but rather invites them to create the action to accompany the story presentation. For some stories this active participation involves pulling on *The Turnip* (Milhous and Dalgiesh) or calling for help for in Kaplan's *Tikki Tikki Tembo.* Teale's story of *The Little Woman Who Wanted Noise* can be effectively adapted into a participation story for young children. During the telling, several children can make the sounds representing the animals as they accumulate in the story. At the clue "they all made

good noise," all the sounds are made by the children. This story builds to a climax when all the sounds of the animals, cars, and children are made together and the woman goes to sleep. Actively listening for the cues and participating in the telling encourages children to enjoy and comprehend the story. Other cumulative stories about noise that can be used as participation stories include Zemach's *It Could Always Be Worse* and *Such a Noise!* by Brodmann. This involvement in the story presentation maintains the audience's attention to the story and assists their understanding of the events that are occurring. As children increase their involvement in the story, they will develop their confidence and move to creating stories of their own. With older children, more actions can be used in the story and complex involvement can be rehearsed before the telling. The field trip to the farm in Nobel's *The Day Jimmy's Boa Ate the Wash* can become more interesting if the students make the sounds of the school children, tractor, and animals as well as screaming along with the farmer's wife (Wendelin, 1991). Young children who are active listeners enjoy stories that include sound effects, patterns that can be repeated, or gestures that invite them to participate.

Music is often used in telling stories and can involve the entire group. Stories may have musical phrases that are repeated throughout, as in *The Magic Fish.* The old man calls the fish, "Little fish, little fish, I have a wish," and this musical line is repeated throughout the story. After hearing the pattern several times, the children will join in the singing of the phrase each time it is used by the storyteller. Some cumulative songs lead to storytelling activities. *I Know an Old Woman Who Swallowed a Fly* by Rowds could be an introduction to an expanded version, of Wadsworth's *Over in the Meadow.* This combination of story and music demonstrates another way to capture the interest of young children.

Follow-up activities can help to develop and refine children's comprehension of the story. The choice of the follow up activities will depend on the ages, abilities, and interest of the children in the classroom. They should be directly related to the story and enjoyable for the children involved (Nessel, 1985).

CHILDREN AS STORYTELLERS

Children who have regularly listened to stories told by teachers, parents, or guest storytellers will be interested in telling stories of their own. These retellings and original tellings should be encouraged in the early childhood classroom for they provide many positive benefits to developing young children. After guided retelling, children improve in their literal, interpretive, and critical comprehensions of stories they have heard (Morrow, 1985).

The Storytime Exchange

Children listen

Teacher or children tell stories

Children tell own stories

Children read own stories

Children write own stories

Figure 8.7 Cliatt, M., & Shaw, J. (1988). The Storytime Exchange: Ways to enhance it. *Childhood Education, 64*(5), p. 294.

As children tell stories, they begin to develop a better understanding of themselves and the world around them and to internalize a sense of story. Storytelling also builds confidence and skills needed when speaking before a group. If young children are systematically given this experience, it is speculated that they will be less afraid of sharing information with peers when they become older (Hamilton & Weiss, 1991).

Morrow (1985), in a study of nursery schools and kindergarten classes, found that children seldom have the opportunity to retell stories to the teacher. In a follow-up study, she provided young children with frequent opportunities to retell stories guided by an adult who focused on the structural framework of the story. The adult offered suggestions such as "What happened next?" or "And then?" She found that frequent retellings, as well as involvement with an adult during the process, increased the children's use of theme and sequencing and lengthened the story retelling.

Hough, Nurss, and Wood (1987) investigated children's telling of story with pictures, wordless books, and their original stories. Some of these original stories were about their own experiences and others were adaptations of stories they had heard. The children's original stories were more complex and included more oral language than those told using pictures or books. When they used the pictures or books in their telling, they simply labeled and described the actions of each individual picture and did not create a story. The language used in telling their own story was, however, cohesive and contained a central theme. The researchers concluded that an effective way to stimulate oral fluency is to encourage children to tell their own original stories.

Making up an original story demands creativity on the part of young children. It requires logical thinking, sequencing, and cause-and-effect reasoning, modeled after the stories they have heard. These original stories told by children can also lead to written compositions. The process moves from children hearing stories told, to telling stories of their own, to writing down the stories they want to read in order to share with others.

The beginnings of storytelling can be heard in a toddler's tale of the rabbit she saw at the pet store. The simple story relates a personal experience. "We went to see the rabbit. The rabbit was fat and fluffy. Me feed him lettuce. That's all." In the preschool years, children can be heard telling friends a story their teacher told in circle time. "Sit down and listen. Once there was an old man . . ."

The narrative is continued until the entire story is retold and the child storyteller concludes with "and that's all there is." Throughout the early childhood years, children continue to tell stories about things they have experienced and about people in their lives. As they gain experience with literature, they move into telling stories in the new forms they have heard. These retellings provide a safe framework that increases the possibilities for success since they know and understand the story. Children, like adults, continue to develop their use of storytelling as they move further away from the original stimulus and create stories that are uniquely their own.

When children become interested in a new story for telling, they learn throughout the preparation process. As they choose a story to tell, they develop awareness of the types of literature available and make judgments about the effect of the content. They learn techniques of gaining and holding their audience's attention, such as eye contact, volume of voice, and the use of gestures. They learn to appreciate a good story and the effort it requires to be an effective storyteller. A story that inspires tellers is *The Talking Bird and the Story Pouch* by Lawson. In this playful story, a magic pouch that contains a wonderful collection of stories is passed down from the grandfather and father. At the conclusion of the story, the bird finds that he too is a storyteller. Children will enjoy the magic pouch story while building their belief that they too can be storytellers.

Cooperative storytelling is an approach that seems promising for young children. As children are beginning to understand how stories work, they will enjoy creating stories with adults or other children. These interactive story events are enjoyable and extemporaneous. In the first stage, there is simply a turn taking between the teller and the listener with each adding an important element to the story. As young children build confidence in their abilities, they will begin to assume more responsibility in the story content and development of the solutions. This technique is similar to a verbal scaffolding which is used with young children to encourage their early language development. In this story scaffolding, the cotellers influence the direction of the story and work together to develop cohesiveness in the content. The teacher may begin the story, "Once upon a time there was a beautiful butterfly. Each morning the butterfly would spread her enormous wings and fly out to see _____?" The child would continue the story, "To see her friend, the cat." The teacher repeats after the children, "The butterfly went to see her friend, the cat, but nobody was home. The butterfly wondered where her friend could be, so she flew to a neighbor's house and asked _____?" The child fills in the missing information with, "Have you seen my friend the butterfly?" This process continues until the story reaches a shared conclusion. When young children participate in this safe and responsive way, their ability to create stories will be enhanced (Trousdale, 1990).

In the kindergarten and primary grades, children will continue to enjoy sharing stories with their classmates. Experiences in the primary classroom should also be non-threatening and build the children's confidence in their capabilities so they will want to continue participating in storytelling. Real experiences continue to provide rich content for some of the children's storytelling as they recall their first day of school, the best present they ever received, or the funniest thing they ever saw. Many primary children enjoy telling a joke, riddle, or tongue twister to their classmates as a beginning experience. The addition of Leonard Kessler's *Old Turtle's 90 Knock-Knocks, Jokes, and Riddles,* Alvin Schwartz's Witcracks, or similar books to the classroom library encourages the children to experiment and explore this literature with their classmates.

Retelling of stories also offers children the opportunity to share content they know and want to interpret. Retelling can aid comprehension since it enables children to reconstruct the story. This active internal construction of the story assists the children's understanding of the story and ability to arrange the content in sequential order. After guided retelling, children improve in the literal, interpretive, and critical comprehension of the stories they have heard. Although sequencing is difficult for kindergarten children, retelling can improve their performance on this skill (Morrow, 1985). Sequence cards of important events in a story can be placed in order by the child before the retelling. The teacher and children can discuss the sequence of the happenings in the story, using the flannel board and story pieces.

In the primary grades, a storytelling unit may be included in the curriculum providing opportunities for children to work together while learning about the effective presentation of stories. During this unit of study, children learn to choose, prepare, and tell stories to their classmates. The children will also hear many stories told by teachers, librarians, special guest story tellers, and their classmates during their study. Videotapes of professional storytellers may add another dimension to the storytelling unit by providing variety and diverse approaches in story presentation. The American Storytelling Series (1986) visually presents twenty-one stories including myths, legends, folktales, literary classics, and personal reminiscences told by well-known storytellers. Cassette tapes of storytellers may be added to the

library area of the classroom for additional listening opportunities. Other tapes can be made that include parents and grandparents as storytellers, relating stories they have enjoyed. Through these experiences, primary children will stimulate their imaginations, develop communication skills, expand their understanding of other cultures,

Figure 8.8 Storytelling Videos

American Storytelling Series, available from
H. W. Wilson
Twenty-one stories told by professional storytellers. Myths, legends, folktales, literary classics, and personal reminiscence.

Tell Me A Story, Chuck Larkin, available from
Kartes Video
Stories told by leading storytellers. To see the storyteller is a very special experience. Designed to spark the creative imagination of children.

Tell Me A Story, Lynn Rubright, available from
Kartes Video
Enchanting stories by leading storytellers

Tell Me A Story, Nancy Shimmel, available from
Kartes Video
Enjoyable collection of children's stories

Figure 8.9 Storytellers on Tape

De Spain, Pleasant. *Pleasant Journeys*
Stories told by the speaker include "The Turnip," "The Silly Farmer," and "The Extraordinary Cat."

Freeman, Barbara and Regan-Blake, Connie. *Tales to Grow On*
ALA notable recording. Wonderful telling of stories including "Apples and Bananas," "Soddy Sallyraytus," and "Mama, Mama, Have You Heard?"

Jeffe, Nina. *The Three Riddles: A Jewish Folktale*.
Inspired by folk traditions of Eastern Europe. Includes riddles, Yiddish proverbs, and songs.

Leiberman, Syd. *A Winner and Other Stories*.

Leiberman, Syd. *Joseph the Tailor and Other Jewish Tales*. ALA Notable Children's Recording, 1989.

Leiberman, Syd. *The Tell-tale Heart and Other Terrifying Tales*.
ALA Notable Children's Recording, 1992.

Parent, Michael. *Sundays at Grandma's*.
Grandma's memories provide entertaining stories.

Seeger, Pete. *Stories and Songs for Little Children*.
A collection of songs and stories, sung and told by the famous lyricist, designed to delight little children.

Simms, Laura. *There's a Horse in My Pocket*.
Stories from African, Indian, and American Native cultures.

Torrence, Jackie. *Classic Children's Tales*.
Includes "The Little Red Hen," "The Three Little Pigs," "Gingerbread Man," and eight others told in Torrence's wonderful dialect.

appreciate diversity, preserve history, and become tellers of stories (Hamilton & Weiss, 1991).

Through telling stories, children learn to actively manipulate language and shape story content. Children, as storytellers, have the power to direct the story, to create the characters, and to resolve the conflict in ways not possible in the adult-oriented world.

CHILDREN'S STORIES LEAD TO UNDERSTANDING

Teachers can learn a great deal from listening to young children tell stories. These stories can give the teacher an indication of children's cognitive development, literature background, language competencies, social skills, and special interest. Vivian Paley, in *The Boy Who Would Be a Helicopter* (1990), tells the story of Jason, who was an isolated outsider in her preschool classroom. Paley's sensitive account of her journey to understanding Jason and his move into storytelling will inspire any teacher to become a collector of children's stories. In her classroom Paley values stories told by children and uses them as a vehicle leading to understanding. She believes that play and storytelling are the primary ways young children approach language and thought. In storytelling the young child says, "This is how I interpret what is on my mind." Paley clearly states that young children do not pretend to be storytellers; they are storytellers. (Paley, 1990, p. 17).

Drama With Young Children

Dramatization encourages young children to become actively involved in literature happenings when they use pantomime, role-playing, and puppets to interpret the story. Drama provides an arena where all ideas are heard, considered, compared, interpreted, and acted upon. Each child's individuality and creativity is respected. In addition, when participating in group drama activities, individuals learn to work cooperatively in problem solving. In drama, young children have the opportunity to be both performer and audience, allowing them to appreciate the work of others while identifying ways to change their presentation (Isenberg & Janlongo, 1993). In this play with words and story, young children are able to activate their ideas and influence action. The simplest form of creative dramatics involves the pantomime of an event or happening. In this type of drama young children are not limited by their language or concerns for correctness. During the enactment, children use their body movements and facial expressions to communicate their message. These pantomime activities may focus on a story character such as Galdone's *The Teeny Tiny Woman*, an event in a story such as the wolf blowing on the three little pigs houses, or recreate the entire story line from *Peter and the Wolf* by Prokofiev or Tolstoy's *The Great Big Enormous Turnip*. Pantomime provides young children a safe way to participate individually or in groups without concern for speaking parts.

ROLE-PLAYING

Throughout the early childhood period, young children are actively involved in play activities. Much of this play is spontaneous, changing and adjusting to the children involved and influenced by the materials available. In sociodramatic play children assume roles, adjust their actions, and cooperate in an activity while focusing on a theme for a sustained period of time (Smilansky, 1962). This advanced level of play provides the active involvement necessary for cognitive and language development in children. Yawkey (1986) concluded that involvement in this sociodramatic play also facilitates the growth of creativity, imagination, and expressive language abilities. In sociodramatic play young children take roles they understand and have experienced.

In classrooms for young children, role-playing is often encouraged through centers such as housekeeping and blocks, and dramatic centers such as the grocery store, bakery, and doctor's office.

Centers that relate to a book or a specific type of literature can also be designed for the early childhood classroom. Preschoolers and kindergartners may enjoy packing up the housekeeping center after hearing a story about moving, such as Malone's *A Home*. Primary children may be inspired to role-play in a colonial center, equipped with old objects and dress-up clothes after listening to *Pioneer Children of Appalachia* by Anderson. A recycling center might be developed by primary children after they have read *What a Load of Trash* by Skidmore. In this center children may dramatize stories or create their own while playing the roles of early americans. A castle center, built from cardboard boxes, can coincide with a literature unit on fairy tales. These centers provide young children with a play environment where they can try out roles, use language, and interact with classmates as they make another connection with literature.

STORY ENACTMENT

Children who have participated in pretend play, interacted in sociodramatic centers, and pantomimed actions can easily move into creative dramatics. This form of drama matches the developmental level of young children for there are no fancy props or costumes, the actors have no lines to memorize, and the length of the play is adjusted to the children involved. In creative dramatics there is no pressure for a perfect performance but rather emphasis is on the process and the successful involvement of the children. A story with a few characters, simple story line, and lots of action is read or told to the group. After the reading and discussion of the story, the children are allowed to choose the roles each would like to have in the play. Children clearly know what amount of involvement they want and this should be respected. Next, the group works together to decide how they will reenact the story and what the characters may say. Then the group will present their play to the other children in their own creative way, changing and adjusting as the interactions demand. This free and creative expression allows children to enjoy the process without the fear or stress of a script production while remaining in the context of the story. This type of creative drama, often used as a follow-up of story reading, has lead to increased comprehension in kindergarten, first-grade and second-grade children (Galda, 1982).

Vivian Gussin Paley (1990) originated a unique vehicle for inviting children to become both writers and actors in drama. In her early childhood classroom, children came to her story table and dictated stories. These stories provided a window for observing the children and these writings became the plays they acted out. During the dictation of the story, Paley questioned the child about any content that was unclear or that she may have interpreted incorrectly. The focus was on clarifying the meaning so all would understand the content: the actors, audience, and narrator. In this process children tell stories, the teacher writes them down, she reads the story aloud, and finally the story is dramatized by the children. She related that once the children have seen their story in action they will never again be satisfied until their story is dramatized. "A child storyteller is a story player [Paley, 1990, p. 7]."

SCRIPT PLAY

Simple plays, such as those derived from folktales, are an excellent way to introduce primary children to scripts. These stories, with their predictable patterns and repetitive lines, allow children to experience reading the script, following others' parts, and joining in the drama. Stories, such as *Three Billy-Goats Gruff* or *The House that Jack Built*, are appropriate for the beginning efforts of primary children. After experiences with a script play, primary children may move into creating original plays and performing them for others. At this age level, plays should be created and produced for the enjoyment of the actors as well as the audience. Often, script plays emphasize the actors' performances and characterizations, which is inappropriate for young children. Teachers should avoid having children memorize complicated lines, listen for subtle clues or participate in many rehearsals. These stressful demands negate the positive aspects of using drama as an invitation to literature.

The Puppet Connection

Storytelling and puppetry are ancient forms of oral expression that developed historically in similar ways. The story told was passed from generation to generation and became a binding link for families and cultures. The puppeteer often augmented the storytelling by providing visualization and surprise elements to the story presentation. The design and use of puppets has been greatly influenced by the culture and society of the puppeteer. The diverse cultural influence can be seen in the ornate Chinese shadow puppets and the pure geometric forms of the African rod puppets. From these roots of oral language and cultural transmission, a new view of puppets has emerged. Current use of puppets allows for more personal expression and the variety of designs appeal to wider audiences. These changes have moved puppetry from being exclusively entertainment into an acceptable tool to use in education, therapy, and communication. Jim Henson's Sesame Street Muppets had a powerful influence on this transformation. His popular use of large expressive muppets has lead to the increased value of puppets as an important tool for educating and communicating with children (Champlin & Renfro, 1985; Rountree, Shuptrine, Gordan, & Taylor, 1981).

Young children are drawn to puppets and this magnetic quality can provide a powerful connector to literature. Puppets can be used by both teachers and children in the early childhood classroom. The teacher can use the puppet to introduce a new book, to play a character in the story, to encourage conversation about the text, or discuss the moral in the story. When the teacher becomes the puppeteer, she or he is transformed into a different person whom children quickly identify as

someone who brings pleasure and excitement too (Hunt & Renfro, 1982).

MATCHING CHILDREN'S DEVELOPMENT

Puppets are wonderful facilitators in literature activities for young children who begin to identify with the character. Children in the animism stage (Piaget, 1928) view inanimate objects as real. They often believe that the puppets are "real" and that they can trust the puppet. A teddy bear puppet is real, has feelings, and copes with problems such as being lost. Young children understand this fear and are willing to talk to the puppet about a concern they share. In a classroom, a four-year-old child, Darrell, is talking to a bear puppet that was used by his teacher when sharing Don Freeman's *Corduroy*. The puppet has been placed on an aluminum drink can on a low shelf in the library area. Darrell, with an intense look on his face, tells the bear puppet his own personal experience of being lost at the fair grounds. It is clear to the teacher that Darrell is sharing this painful experience with a puppet as if he is a trusted confidant. This freedom to express ideas and personal views provides an avenue for young children to develop in both the affective and cognitive domain.

Primary-aged children enjoy puppets. At this age, however, they are aware that the actions of puppets are controlled by someone else. Now they choose to "pretend" that the puppet is alive and want to share information with this special friend. They enjoy listening to a wonderful story presented by the puppet or telling the story using the puppet. They also like more diverse stories shared with content expanded into fantasy and adventure (Champlin & Renfro, 1985).

PUPPETS TO USE WITH YOUNG CHILDREN

A small collection of puppets, either purchased or made by the teacher, can be used with many different children's stories. A bear puppet can be used with *Ask Mr. Bear, Corduroy, A Pocket for Corduroy, Jesse Bear, What Will You Wear?, Little Bear* series, *Lazy Bear, The Bears' Picnic,* and *The Bear and the Fly.* A chicken can be used in stories such as *Rosie's Walk, Chicken's Child,* and *The Little Red Hen.* A lion puppet can be used with *Dandelion, Leo Lion Looks for Books,* and *The Happy Lion.* Many wonderful children's stories include mice characters. A mouse puppet can introduce, act out, or lead a follow-up discussion about *Alexander and the Wind-up Mouse, Mouse Tales, Tillie and the Wall, Do You Want to be my Friend?,* and *If You Give a Mouse a Cookie.* Rabbit puppets can relate to *The Rabbit Who Wanted Red Wings, Mr. Rabbit and the Lovely Present,* and *The Runaway Bunny.* These few puppets could begin a collection that the teacher might use throughout the year to add excitement to the classroom and the literature program.

The teacher, using the puppet to tell the story, should select stories that have a few characters, an easy-to-follow sequence of events, and a clear plot. The teacher, as puppeteer, does not need a stage or box in which to hide the puppet nor does the teacher need to be a ventriloquist for young children tend to ignore the teacher and focus their attention on the "real character" they see before them (Hunt & Renfro, 1982).

Story gloves can be used to tell a story, *Five Little Monkeys Jumping on the Bed,* introduce a finger play from *Finger Rhymes,* or accompany the singing of a song such as *The Barnyard Song.* These can be made from gardening gloves with Velcro pieces on each finger. The characters in the story are constructed from pompons and felt and mounted on Velcro. The glove can be used with many stories by changing the characters attached to the fingers of the glove.

Stories in boxes combine storage with the puppet and may include additional props that can be used to expand the telling. These story boxes can be made from cardboard shoe boxes and contain items that can stimulate ideas about the story and expand the telling. *A Fat Cat* story box could include a cat puppet and items representing what he ate.

The large polyfoam puppets, patterned after the Muppets, are difficult to construct but they are definitely worth the effort. The life-size characters are operated by one of the puppeteer's arm and hand.

The puppeteer's other arm becomes the arm and hand of the puppet. With a little practice, the teacher can produce natural movements by the puppet and create a character with a distinctive voice and personality that will make this puppet very special. Most children have grown to love the Muppets on "Sesame Street" so there is an immediate fascination with this new addition to the classroom. A puppet of this type can make the most difficult activity interesting and capture the most inattentive listener. A muppet could be used to introduce a new story to the class each week or call on the children to participate in the repetitive phrases in the presentation. Children never seem to tire of an interesting puppet character sitting in their teacher's lap, allowing the same character to be used again and again.

PUPPETS YOUNG CHILDREN CAN CONSTRUCT AND USE

Puppets can also be made and used by children. They can use commercial or child-made puppets to dramatize a story they have heard or to supplement a story they are composing. In an informal puppet dramatization, it is not necessary to have an audience or a stage. The story is presented informally for the enjoyment of the child or for sharing with a few friends. The focus is not on the perfection of the performance but rather the process in which they are participating. In a supportive environment, children are encouraged to create, to make changes, and to expand the story as they desire. Each child has the opportunity to personalize the story with no pressure to present "in the correct way." This allows children to reconstruct the story and use the puppet at their level of understanding while building self-confidence in their expanding abilities. Often children let the puppet be the narrator and tell the story. This "puppet telling" is an informal method for sharing literature and does not imply putting on a show for an audience. This storytelling puppet can assist the child in identifying with the story, provide a high-interest motivator, and allow personal exchanges with the story character.

During the year, the teacher can provide planned sessions where children construct simple puppets for themselves. These puppet making sessions should include designs that are easy to construct, provide varied materials that encourage unique creations, and include opportunities to use the final products in meaningful ways. Puppet making requires the teacher to allow the children

freedom to create while providing sufficient directions to ensure that the puppet will work effectively. Some of the puppets that young children can successfully construct include: paper cup puppets, stick puppets, paper bag puppets, handkerchief puppets, and box puppets.

Mitt puppets can be used by young children and are easily adapted to their developmental level. Toddlers can move the mitt puppet to accompany a story and kindergarten children can construct the puppet by gluing the fabric together and adding felt pieces for the features. Unique puppets can be constructed out of household items such as wooden spoons, pot holders, sponges, paper rolls, milk cartons, and rag mops. This use of every day items helps the children experience creative flexibility and encourages them to think of other materials that can be transformed into puppets.

One of the most popular puppets with young children is a sock puppet. This simple puppet has a mouth that can be opened and closed by a child's small hand while synchronizing the speech and movements. The addition of felt eyes and yarn hair make the generic character easy to use in many different stories and become a person or animal.

There are several books that children can use to assist them in the construction of puppets. Chernoff's *Puppet Party* (1971) and Roundtree et al. *Creative Teaching With Puppets* (1981) include directions for easy puppets that young children can make. The illustrations provide clear step-by-step instructions for children and teachers. The addition of these books to the puppet-making activity demonstrates to young children that useful information can be obtained from illustrations and print.

Shadow puppets can be another addition to the early childhood classroom. The shadow puppets can be made out of poster board and may have movable parts (arms, legs, and head) that can be attached with wire. Children can move these puppets behind a large screen with a lamp or overhead projector producing the dark shadows. These unique puppets can inspire focused attention on the characters and actions of the story. The puppets can be used to retell a story or to dramatize extemporaneously (Davies, 1985).

String puppets or marionettes are not appropriate for young children but can be successfully manipulated by older children who have more refined small-motor skills. Primary-aged children can construct two string marionettes and understand the mechanical workings while practicing their use. Primary children, however, continue to enjoy the same puppets as young children but use them in different ways. The primary child increases the complexity of the stories she or he tells and adds more detail to the puppets she or he constructs.

Sometimes older children become interested in producing a more elaborate puppet show. They may practice the play, design backdrop props, and invite other classes to view their production. When this interest is demonstrated, the teacher may extend the process by encouraging their design of posters to advertise the event and the distribution of tickets. This performance comes from group interest, is directed by the children, and meets their requirements for the refinement of production.

Although improvisation is most frequently used with puppets, a prepared script can also be preformed by primary children. They can write their own original script or adapt a story they know. When a script is used, it is important to limit the rehearsal schedule to three or four sessions. If too many rehearsals are required the children will lose interest and the production will lack spontaneity. These puppet shows bring together children of varied interest, abilities, and talents. Since there are so many elements in a puppet performance, there is something for everybody to do, no matter how varied their interest or abilities may be. Primary children will enjoy presenting their puppet play to preschool and kindergarten classrooms because this audience is very responsive and they applaud enthusiastically throughout the production.

A Puppet Area

For children to use puppets in the classroom, there must be proper storage and easy accessibility. A puppet center can provide a place where children select the puppet they want, interact with the puppet spontaneously, and return the puppet when their play is completed. A clothes line, skirt hanger, hanging baskets, clear plastic boxes, or low open shelf can provide storage that allows children to readily see the puppets that are available for their use (Hunt & Renfro, 1982).

A simple stage can be constructed and added to the area to encourage dramatizations and children working together in group productions. It is not necessary to build a complex theater for young children enjoy using their imagination while designing the stage. A table turned on its side can provide an immediate stage in an early childhood classroom. Other stages can be constructed by the children from refrigerator boxes, chairs, or fabric strung across a door way. These stages are available for the children's use when they chose to present stories.

PUPPETS AND BIBLIOTHERAPY

Books can be used to help children develop skills they need to function in life. The selection of appropriate books can assist young children in sharing, working with others, understanding feelings, and recognizing acceptable behavior. By combining these books with puppets, young children can hear the message and act out the behaviors with a puppet. Koberstein and Shepherd (1989) used puppets and literature to help preschool children learn about sharing. They found that this combination increased the sharing they observed in the young children included in their study.

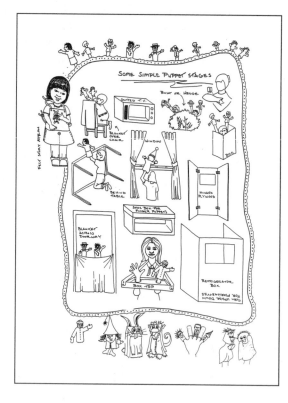

After reading and talking about Viorst's *Alexander and the Terrible, Horrible, No Good, Very Bad Day*, a classroom teacher used a puppet to talk about the misfortunes of Alexander in the story. One girl in the group seemed especially concerned about the problems of the character in the story. After listening carefully to the puppet, she began to relate things that had happened that made it "a bad day for Jackie." Used effectively, puppets can allow children to talk about and deal with their emotions.

Melissa's Success Story

Melissa's unit on the Pueblo cultures was successful in her third-grade classroom. She introduced her children to another culture, helping them understand and appreciate diversity. She invited Native-American storytellers to the classroom. The children heard stories told in the traditional ways. During the unit of study, they searched for other books about Native Americans in New Mexico. The children also collected family stories and began their own storytelling festival. The signal to begin the storytelling festival was the beating of the class drum, like the one the Native-American storyteller used in his story.

As Melissa evaluated the effectiveness of her unit, she concluded that her primary children had grown in their understanding of others and their interest in literature. These stories exposed the children to diverse vocabulary, more complex sentences, story structure, and the use of creative oral expression. Cognitive frameworks were developed as they learned how stories worked while acquiring the conventions used in these forms. As the children were exposed to a variety of stories, presented in different ways, they extended their understanding of how language can be used and were motivated to actively participate in the process. The stories read, told, and performed had served as a powerful catalyst for the children as they built their understanding and appreciation of literature.

SUGGESTED LEARNING EXPERIENCES

1. Recall a story you heard as a child. Retell the story to a friend and ask her to relate a story from her childhood.

2. Compare and contrast story reading and storytelling. Write a paragraph supporting the importance of including both in an early childhood classroom.

3. Visit a library or media center and critique a video of a storyteller.

4. Practice using the cooperative storytelling approach with a child. Record the interaction and listen to the tape to improve the technique.

5. Ask two preschool children to tell a story. Write down the stories as they are told and later identify the story conventions they used.

6. Create a story box that is designed to use with a specific book that is appropriate for primary children.

7. Construct a sock animal puppet. List all the stories that this puppet can be used with in a kindergarten class.

8. Write three story cards and practice telling the stories using the outline. Tell the story to a small group of preschoolers and observe their responses.

9. Visit an early childhood classroom during center time and observe a sociodramatic center such as housekeeping, grocery store, or beauty salon. Identify a book or other printed material that could be added to the center observed.

10. Plan a puppet show with a group of primary children. Include books that can be used to obtain directions for the construction of the puppets and stage.

ENDNOTE

1. Excerpts from this chapter appear in Shirley C. Raines and Rebecca T. Isbell, *Childhood Education* (1994), "The Child's Connections to the Universal Power of Story," Albany, NY: Delmar Publishers 70(3), 164–167.

REFERENCES

Applebee, A. (1978). *The child's concept of story*. Chicago: The University of Chicago Press.

Babcock, B., Monthan, G. & Monthan D. (1990). *The pueblo storyteller*. Tucson, AZ: The University of Arizona Press.

Baker, A. & Green, E. (1977). *Storytelling: Art and techniques*. New York: Bowker.

Barton, B. (1986). *Tell me another*. Markham, Ontario: Pembroke Publisher Limited.

Barton, B. (1990). *Stories in the classroom*. Portsmouth, NH: Heinemann.

Bettelheim, B. (1976). *The uses of enchantment: The meaning and importance of fairy tales*. New York: Alfred A. Knopf.

Champlin, C., & Renfro, N. (1985). *Storytelling with puppets*. Chicago, IL: American Library Association.

Cliatt, M., & Shaw, J. (1988). The storytime exchange: Ways to enhance it. *Childhood Education, 64*(5), 293–298.

Colwell, E. (1980). *Storytelling*. London: The Bodley Head.

Cooter, R., (1991). Storytelling in the language arts classroom. *Reading Research and Instruction, 30*(2), 71–76.

Davies, D. G. (1985). Hand, finger & shadow puppets. *Perspectives, 3*(5), 14–16.

Egan, K. (1986). *Teaching as story telling: An alternative approach in teaching and curriculum in the elementary school*. Chicago, IL: University of Chicago Press.

Frye, N. (1964). *The educated imagination*. Bloomington, IN: Indiana University Press.

Griffin, B., (1989). *Students as storytellers*. Medford, OR: Author.

Hamilton, M., & Weiss, M. (1991). Teacher's guide to storytelling. *Instructor, 100*(9), 27–31.

Hough, R., Nurss, J., & Wood, D. (1987). Making opportunities for elaborated language in early childhood classrooms. *Young Children, 43*(1), 6–12.

Hunt, T., & Renfro, N. (1982). *Puppetry in early childhood education*. Austin, TX: Nancy Renfro Studios.

Isbell, R. (1979). A study of the effects of two modes of literature presentation on the oral language development of four and five-year-old children. Unpublished Doctoral Dissertation, University of Tennessee, Dept. of Curriculum and Instruction, College of Education. Knoxville, TN.

Isenberg, J., & Jalongo, M. (1993). *Creative expression and play in the early childhood curriculum*. New York: Macmillan.

Jacobs, L. (1980). Foreword, p. xii. In Vandergrift, K. *Child and Story*. New York: Neal Schuman.

Jalongo, M. (1992). *Early childhood language arts*. Needham Heights, MA: Allyn & Bacon.

Koberstein, J., & Shepherd, T. (1989). Books, puppets and sharing: Teaching preschool children to share. *Psychology in the Schools, 26*(3), 311–316.

Maguire, J. (1985). *Creative storytelling: Choosing, inventing and sharing tales for children*. Cambridge, MA: Yellow Moon Press.

Martinez, M., & Roser, N. (1985). Read it again: The value of repeated readings during storytime. *The Reading Teacher, 38*,(8) 782–786.

Medina, E. (1986). Enhancing your curriculum through story-telling. *Learning, 15*(3), 58–61. Morrow, L. (1979). Exciting children about literature through creative storytelling techniques. *Language Art, 56*(3), 236–243.

Morrow, L. (1985). Retelling stories: A strategy for improving young children's comprehension concept of story structure and oral language complexity. *The Elementary School Journal, 85*(5), 647–661.

Nelson, O. (1989). Storytelling: Language experience for meaning making. *The Reading Teacher, 42*, (6) 386–390.

Nessel, D. (1985). Storytelling in the reading program. *The Reading Teacher, 38*, (4) 378–381.

Paley, V. (1990). *The boy who would be a helicopter*. Cambridge, MA: Harvard University Press.

Paludan, L. (1974). *Playing with puppets*. London: Mills & Boon.

Peck, J. (1989). Using storytelling to promote language and literacy development. *The Reading Teacher, 43*(2), 138–141.

Pellowski, A. (1987). *The family storytelling handbook*. New York: Macmillan.

Piaget, J. (1928). *Judgement & Reasoning in the child*. (A. Tomlinson, & J. Tomlinson, Trans.). NY: Harcourt, Brace & World.

Pitcher, E. & Prelinger, E. (1963). *Children tell stories: Analysis of fantasy*. New York: International Universities Press.

Raines, S. (1990). Representational Competence: (Re)presenting experiences through words, action, and images. *Childhood Education, 62*(4), 260–264.

Roney, R. (1989). Back to the basics with storytelling. *Reading Teacher, 42*, 520–523.

Rountree, B., Shuptrine, M., Gordan, J., & Taylor, N. (1981). *Creative teaching with puppets*. Tuscaloosa, AL: The Learning Line.

Schimmel, N. (1982). *Just enough to make a story: A source book for storytelling*. Berkley, CA: Sister's Choice Press.

Smilansky, S. (1962). *The effects of socio-dramatic play on disadvantaged preschool children*. New York: Wiley.

Smilansky, S., & Shefatya, L. (1990). *The effects of sociodramatic play on disadvantaged preschool children*. Gaithersburg, MD: Psychosocial and Educational Publications.

Smith, J. (1992). Telephone interview with Rebecca Isbell. National Association for the Preservation and Perpetuation of Storytelling (NAPPS), Jonesborough, TN.

Sutton-Smith, B. (1981). *The folkstories of children*. Philadelphia, PA: University of Pennsylvania Press.

Trousdale, A. (1990). Interactive storytelling: Scaffolding children's early narratives. *Language Arts, 67*(2), 164–173.

Vandergrift, K. (1980). *Child and story: The literary connection*. (p. xiv) New York: Neal-Schuman Publishers.

Wendelin, K. (1991). Students as storytellers in the classroom. *Reading Horizons, 31*(3), 181–188.

Wilson, L. (1991). Stories from the heart. *Momentum, 22*(1), 64–66.

Yawkey, T. D. (1986). Creative dialogue through socio-dramatic play and its use. *Journal of Creative Behavior, 28*(1), 52–60.

CHILDREN'S LITERATURE REFERENCES

The authors and illustrators of children's books are listed, in all chapters, by their full names to help the reader become acquainted with them. If only one name is listed, the author also illustrated the book.

American Storytelling Series. (1986). (Wilson video resource collection). Bronx, NY: Wilson Company.

Andersen, Hans Christian. (1968). *The Little Match Girl*. Boston: Houghton Mifflin.

Anderson, Joan (1986). *Pioneer Children of Appalachia*. Photographs by George Ancona. New York: Clarion.

Asbjornsen, Peter, & Moe, Jorgen. (1957). *Three Billy-Goats Gruff*. New York: Harcourt Brace Jovanovich.

Bailey, Carolyn S. (1978). *The Little Rabbit Who Wanted Red Wings*. Illustrated by Chris Santoro. New York: Platt.

Berenstain, Stan & Berenstain, Jan. (1966). *The Bear's Picnic*. New York: Beginner Books, Random House.

Brodmann, Aliana. (1989). *Such a Noise!* Translated by David Fillingham. Brooklyn, NY: Kane-Miller.

Brown, Marcia. (1947). *Stone Soup*. New York: Scribner.

Brown, Marcia. (1980). *Finger Rhymes*. New York: Dutton Children's Books.

Brown, Margaret Wise. (1972). *The Runaway Bunny*. Illustrated by Crockett Johnson. New York: Harper & Row.

Bruchac, Joseph. (1991). *Native American Stories*. Golden, CO: Fulcrum Press.

Caduto, Michael, & Bruchac, Joseph. (1991). *Keepers of the Animals: Native American Stories & Wildlife Activities for Children*. Golden, CO: Fulcrum Publishing.

Carle, Eric. (1971). *Do You Want to Be My Friend?* New York: Harper & Row.

Carlstrom, Nancy. (1986). *Jessie Bear, What Will You Wear?* Illustrated by Bruce Degen. New York: Macmillan Publishing.

Chase, Richard. (1948) Grandfather Tales. Illustrated by Berkeley Williams, Jr. Boston: Houghton Mifflin.

Cohen, C. (1988). *The Mud Pony: A Traditional Skidi Pawnee Tale.* New York: Scholastic.

Cole, Joanna. (1983). *Best Loved Folktales of the World.* Illustrated by Jill K. Schwartz. New York: Doubleday.

Chernoff, Goldie Taub. (1971). *Puppetry Party.* Illustrated by Margaret Hartelius. New York: Walber & Co.

Christelow, Eileen. (1989). *Five Little Monkeys Jumping on the Bed.* New York: Clarion Books.

dePaola, Tomie. (1975). *Strega Nona: An Old Tale.* Englewood Cliffs, NJ: Prentice-Hall.

dePaola, Tomie. (1983). *The Legend of the Bluebonnet: An Old Tale of Texas.* New York: Putnam.

dePaola, Tomie. (1988). *The Legend of the Indian Paintbrush.* New York: Putnam.

DeSpain, Pleasant. (Speaker). (1986). *Pleasant Journeys.* (Cassette Recording). Seattle: Merrill Court Press.

Domanska, Janina. (1973). *Little Red Hen.* New York: Macmillan.

Fatio, Louise. (1954). *The Happy Lion.* Illustrated by Roger Duvoisen. New York: Scholastic.

Flack, Marjorie. (1932). Ask Mr. Bear. New York: Macmillan.

Frasconi, Antonio. (1958). *The House That Jack Built.* San Diego, CA: Harcourt Brace Jovanovich.

Freeman, Barbara, & Regan-Blake, Connie. (Speakers). (1982). *Tales to Grow On.* (Cassette Recording). Weston, CT: Weston Woods.

Freeman, Don. (1968). *Corduroy.* New York: Viking Press.

Freeman, Don. (1978). *A Pocket For Corduroy.* New York: Viking Press.

Freeman, Don. (1964). *Dandelion.* New York: Viking Press.

Freeman, Don. (1966). *A Rainbow of My Own.* New York: Viking Press.

Galdone, Paul. (1961). *Three Wishes.* New York: McGraw-Hill.

Galdone, Paul. (1973). *The Little Red Hen.* New York: Seabury Press.

Galdone, Paul. (1976). *The Gingerbread Boy.* New York: Houghton Mifflin.

Galdone, Paul. (1986). *The Teeny-Tiny Woman.* New York: Ticknor & Fields.

Gág, Wanda. (1928). *Millions of Cats.* New York: Coward-McCann.

Glazer, Tom. (Arranger). (1973). "The Barnyard Song." In T. Glazer's *Eye Winker, Tom Tinker, Chin Chopper: Fifty Musical Finger Plays With Piano Arrangements and Guitar Chords.* Garden City, NY: Doubleday and Company, Inc.

Goss, Linda, & Baines, Marian F. (Eds.). (1989). *Talk That Talk: An Anthology of African American Storytelling.* New York: Simon & Schuster.

Gutierrez, Douglas. (1988). *The Night of the Stars.* Translated by Carmen D. Dearden. New York: Kane-Miller Books.

Hall, Avery, & Korty, John. (1983). *Twice Upon a Time.* NY: Simon & Schuster Trade.

Harris, Joel C. (1991). *Giant Treasury of Brer Rabbit.* Avenal, NJ: Outlet Book Co.

Harrison, Annette. (1992). *Easy to Tell Stories for Young Children.* Jonesborough, TN: National Storytelling Press.

Hartelius, Margaret. (1977). *Chicken's Child.* New York: Scholastic.

Hoyt-Goldsmith, Diana. (1991). *Pueblo Storyteller.* NY: Holiday House.

Hutchins, Pat. (1971). *Rosie's Walk.* New York: Macmillan Children's Books.

Jaffe, Nina. (Speaker). (1989). *The Three Riddles: A Jewish Folktale.* (Cassette Recording and Book). New York: Bantam Books.

Johnston, Tony. (1985). *Quilt Story.* Illustrated by Tomie dePaola. New York: Putnam.

Kaplan, Carol B. (1989). *Tikki Tikki Tembo.* Studio City, CA: Players Press.

Kent, Jack. (1971). *Fat Cat.* New York: Parents.

Kessler, Leonard. (1991). *Old Turtle's 90 Knock-Knock Jokes, and Riddles.* NY: Greenwillow.

Kherdian, David. (Ed.). (1992). *Animal Fables Retold by David Kherdian.* Illustrated by Nonny Hogrogian. Chicago, IL: Hogrogian.

Krasilovsky, Phyllis. (1950). *The Man Who Didn't Wash His Dishes.* Illustrated by Barbara Cooney. New York: Doubleday.

Krauss, Ruth. (1945). *Carrot Seed.* Illustrated by Crockett Johnson. New York: Harper & Brothers.

Lang, Andrew. (1965). *The Blue Fairy Book.* Illustrated by Henry Justice Ford and George Percy Jacomb-Hood. New York: Dover.

Lawson, Amy. (1987). *The Talking Bird and the Story Pouch.* New York: HarperCollins.

Larkin, Chuck. (Speaker). (1986). *Tell Me a Story.* (Video Series). Irwindale, CA: Kartes Video Communications.

Leiberman, Syd. (Speaker). (1986). *A Winner and Other Stories.* (Cassette Recording). Evanston, IL: Metro Mobile.

Leiberman, Syd. (Speaker). (1988). *Joseph the Tailor, and Other Jewish Tales.* Evanston, IL: Metro Mobile.

Leiberman, Syd. (Speaker). (1992). *The Tell-Tale Heart and Other Terrifying Tales.* (Cassette Recording). Evanston, IL: Studiomedia.

Leydenfrost, Robert. (1970). *The Snake That Sneezed.* New York: G. P. Putnam's Sons.

Lionni, Leo. (1969). *Alexander and the Wind-Up Mouse.* New York: Pantheon.

Lionni, Leo. (1989). *Tillie and the Wall.* New York: Knopf.

Littledale, Freya. (1967). *The Magic Fish*. New York: Scholastic Books.

Littledale, Freya. (1989). *Snow Child*. New York: Scholastic.

Lobel, Arnold. (1992). *Frog and Toad Together*. New York: Harper & Row.

Lobel, Arnold. (1972). *Mouse Tales*. New York: Harper & Row.

MacDonald, Amy. (1990). *Little Beaver and the Echo*. New York: G. P. Putnam's Sons.

Malone, Nolaih. (1988). *A Home*. New York: Bradbury Press.

McLeod, Emilie W. (1975). *The Bear's Bicycle*. Boston: Little, Brown.

Medlicott, Mary (Ed.). (1991). *Tales for Telling From Around the World*. New York: Kingfisher Books.

Milhous, Katherine, & Dalgiesh, Alice. (1990). *Turnip: An Old Russian Folktale*. New York: G. P. Putnam's Sons.

Minarik, Else H. (1967). *Little Bear*. Illustrated by Maurice Sendak. New York: Harper & Row.

Newell, Hope. (1962). *The Little Old Woman Who Used Her Head and Other Tales*. Illustrated by Margaret Rose. New York: Thomas Nelson.

Noble, Trinka. (1984). *The Day Jimmy's Boa Ate the Wash*. Illustrated by Steven Kellogg. New York: Dial Books Young Readers.

Norfolk, Bobby. (Speaker). (1992). *Why Mosquitoes Buzz in People's Ears*. (Cassette Recording). Chicago, IL: Earmig Music.

Numeroff, Laura Jaffe. (1985). *If You Give a Mouse a Cookie*. Illustrated by Felicia Bond. New York: Harper & Row.

O'Callahan, Jay. (Speaker). (1985). *Little Heroes*. (Cassette Recording). Fairview, NC: Arthana Records, High Windy Audio.

Pape, Donna. (1972). *Leo Lion Looks for Books*. Illustrated by Tom Eaton. New Cannon, CT: Garrard.

Parish, Peggy. (1977). *Teach Us, Amelia Bedelia*. Illustrated by Lynn Sweat. New York: Greenwillow.

Rey, H. A. (1941). *Curious George*. Boston: Houghton Mifflin.

Parent, Michael. (Speaker). (1988). *Sundays at Grama's*. (Cassette Recording). Charlottesville, VA: Author.

Rounds, Glen, Illustrator. (1990). *I Know an Old Woman Who Swallowed a Fly*. New York: Holiday House.

Richardson, Frederick, Illustrator. (1938). *Great Children's Stories: Classic Volland Edition*. Northbrook, IL: Hubbard Press.

Rubright, Lynn. (Speaker). (1986). *Tell Me a Story*. (Video Series). Indianapolis, IN: Kartes Video Communications.

Schimmel, Nancy. (Speaker). (1986). *Tell Me a Story*. (Video Series). Indianapolis, IN: Kartes Videorecording.

Schimmel, Nancy. (1987). *Just Enough to Make a Story: A Sourcebook for Storytelling*. Berkley, CA: Sisters Choice.

Schwartz, Alvin. (1973). *Witcracks*. Illustrated by Glen Rounds. NY: Lippincott.

Scieszka, Jon. (1989). *The True Story of the Three Little Pigs*. Illustrated by Lane Smith. New York: Viking Kestrel.

Seeger, Pete. (Speaker). (1989). *Stories and Songs for Little Children*. (Cassette Recording). Fairview, NC: High Windy Audio.

Simms, Laura. (Speaker). (1991). *There's a Horse in My Pocket*. (Cassette Recording). Racine, WI: Western Publishing.

Skidmore, Steve. (1991). *What a Load of Trash*. Brookfield, CA: The Millbrook Press.

Slobodkina, Esphyr. (1947). *Caps for Sale*. New York: W. R. Scott.

Tashjian, Virginia A. (1969). *Juba This and Juba That*. Boston: Little, Brown & Company.

Teal, Valentino. (1967). *The Little Woman Who Wanted Noise*. Illustrated by Robert Lawson. New York: McGraw.

Tolstoy, Alexei. (1969). *The Great Big Enormous Turnip*. Illustrated by Helen Oxenbury. New York: Frankin Watts.

Torrence, Janice. (Speaker). (1989). *Classic Children's Tales* (Cassette Recording). Cambridge, MA: Rounder Records.

Viorst, Judith. (1972). *Alexander and the Terrible, Horrible, No Good, Very Bad Day*. Illustrated by Ray Cruz. New York: Macmillan Children's Books.

Wadsworth, Olive A. (1985). *Over in the Meadow*. Illustrated by Mary Mati Rae. New York: Penguin

Wildsmith, Brian. (1973). *The Lazy Bear*. England: The H.W. Wilson Company.

Winter, Paula. (1976). *The Bear and the Fly*. New York: Crown Publishers.

Wolkstein, Diane. (1987). *The Magic Orange Tree and Other Haitian Folktales*. Illustrated by Else Henriquez. New York: Schocken.

Yolen, Jane. (1974). *The Girls Who Cried Flowers and Other Tales*. Illustrated by David Palladini. New York: Crowell.

Yolen, Jane. (1988). *Favorite Folktales From Around the World*. New York: Pantheon.

Zemach, Harve. (1969). *The Judge*. Illustrated by Margot Zemach. New York: Farrar, Strauss & Giroux.

Zemach, Margot. (1976). *It Could Always Be Worse: A Yiddish Folktale*. New York: Farrar, Straus & Giroux.

Zolotow, Charlotte (1962). *Mr. Rabbit and the Lovely Present*. Illustrated by Maurice Sendak. New York: Harper & Row.

9

Books and Stories in Other Forms

Books and Stories in Other Forms

Before the beginning of school, a team of primary teachers met to plan the thematic units they would use during the year. They decided to rotate the units of study through their multi-aged classrooms so they could collect and share materials. As they brainstormed the units that could be used, they discussed the background and interest of some of the children in their groups. As they shared ideas about the units, they concluded that many of their young children were interested in movies, television, videos, and computers. On the third day of inservice, the primary teachers asked Vanassa, the library media specialist, to meet with them. They knew that she could assist them as they planned their units of study and suggest materials from the media center on a variety of topics. During the meeting the teachers described some of the materials they had used in the past and Vanassa identified new materials she had available. As they planned the units, they discussed the use of media in the classroom. They disagreed. Some urged that videos and tapes should not be used in early childhood classrooms when children are viewing so many at home. They felt films and tapes in the classroom interfere with classroom book reading. They wondered if media could be used to stimulate primary-aged children's interest in books and literature.

Media Options for Children

Throughout history, stories have been told to young children and since the invention of the printing press, stories have been read to them from books. Today, stories are presented to children in many different ways, transmitted through diverse media, which have significantly changed the form and content of the literature they experience. Electronic technology has moved stories into forms that stimulate the visual and auditory senses, bombarding children with fast-paced stimulation that does not wait for their responses. In this new age filled with media, "television has emerged as the dominant media in which stories are presented to children [Meringoff, 1980, p. 240]." Now, stories from books cross media lines and are presented on television, film, cassette tapes, videos, and CD-ROM. Young children can hear a story read by their teacher, watch a film of the same content in the library, view the story on television at home, and listen to an audiotape, seek additional information stored on a CD-ROM, and write about the content on a microcomputer.

Teachers of young children cannot ignore the powerful influence of media, and must therefore review and study the constantly changing array of materials. With knowledge of the characteristics of media and the options available, educators can use these new tools effectively with young children. Although the magic of a classic book shared by an enthusiastic teacher can not be replaced, outstanding audio and visual productions can enhance the appeal of some children's stories. For literature to be effectively adapted to media it should:

1. preserve the quality of the original work
2. effectively use the special capabilities of the medium
3. interest children in exploring the book (Rickelman & Henk, 1990)

Thirty years ago, Marshall McLuhan (1964) made the revolutionary statement, "The medium is the message." He believed that each medium of communication produces social and psychological effects on its audience, and a particular way of thinking that is independent of the content being transmitted.

Print was the first mass medium to be developed, and since its inception, it has been closely tied to formal education. Print continues to be viewed by many educators as the most important medium. Today, however, children live in an environment where they are exposed to print, radio, television, films, audio and video tapes, compact disks, computers, and video games. Greenfield (1984) concluded that each medium can be used to enhance the impact of the other and each has its own message. The cognitive message of print provides the opportunity for reflection. The message of television and film is presented in audiovisual form and provides opportunities for interpreting two-dimensional representations. Listening to audio tapes encourages visual images and, combined with a read-along text, can demonstrate the story and print relationship. Some video games and computers provide their message through interactive learning. Each medium produces a unique pattern for dealing with and thinking about the world (Olson & Bruner, 1974). Each form provides another way to experience and interpret literature.

VISUAL PRESENTATIONS

There are many similarities between films, television, and videos since they communicate in both the auditory and visual form. The first films adapted from children's books were produced in America in 1950. The Disney studios adapted three outstanding picture books to short motion pictures: Burton's *Little House*, Gnamatky's *Little Toot*, and Lawson's *Ferdinand the Bull*. These film versions altered stories—the focus was changed and they were developed for an audience of adults and children. In 1952 *Madeline* by Bemelmans was produced on film using both the original text and the original illustrations.

Later Schindel developed the "iconographic" technique, which simulated motion by moving a camera over still illustrations. Some of the films, which were carefully reproduced from children's books using this technique, were McClosky's *Make Way for Ducklings* and Gág's *Millions of Cats*. A more recent iconographic presentation is Brown's *Arthur's Pet Business*, which describes Arthur's adventures with pet sitting. The development of filmstrips provided another way for the teacher or librarian to read a story to young children with the added benefit of large visual illustrations (Schindel, 1981). The filmstrips of Ezra Jack Keats' *The Snowy*

Day and Joe Lasker's *Lentil* are quality productions that use the original illustrations in the presentation of the story.

It is obvious that technology has influenced the means used in communicating stories. Films, which are shown on large screens, can captivate an audience of twenty-five to thirty children of similar age in a classroom or library setting. When stories are presented on television, a disinterested child can switch instantly to another program and the content is constantly interrupted by commercials. These factors require that television programs be produced with different concerns specifically related to immediately attracting the audience and increasing the number of viewers. For example, Maurice Sendak's *Nutshell Library* was completely redrawn and set to music to make it appealing for the television viewers. Only a few writers of classic children's books have ventured into the arena of television. Theodore Geisel (Dr. Seuss) and Maurice Sendak have worked directly to bring their works to millions of children through this medium (Schindel, 1981).

Some productions on film or videocassette maintain the original content with few variations. Weston Woods has produced a number of films on videocassette that demonstrate a strong link between the visual presentation and the original story. Two films based on McCloskey's *Homer Price* and more recently *Books by Ezra Jack Keats*, which includes *Goggles, A Letter to Amy* and *Peter's Chair*, are wonderful enlarged replicas of the original books. Some video productions use the book as a base but actually improve on the presentation. Irene Wood uses the example of *The Snowman* to demonstrate that a video can sometimes increase the effectiveness of the story (Donavin, 1992).

Animated films require the development of thousands of new illustrations. To create the illusion of movement, animators must produce many drawings that are very close to the original illustration. For example a ten minute animated version of a children's book might require over 7,000 drawings to create the perception of movement (Rickelman & Henk, 1990). Gene Deitch (1978), a leading animator of children's books, believes that media produced in this era of telecommunication should not keep children from books but rather draw them to books.

Today fewer films are being produced for classroom use, but the market is filled with children's videos. Children can see folktales, legends from around the world, replays of young people's specials, and programs dealing with personal crisis. They can also see and hear their favorite author describing the development of a new book or talking about the characters they have created.

Television

The influence of television on young children's development has been a topic of great debate for over forty years. Much has been written about the effects of television including *The Plug-In Drug* (Winn, 1977) and *Children in Front of the Small Screen* (Noble, 1975) and *Literacy in the Television Age: The Myth of the TV Effect* (Newman, 1991). Several major themes have surfaced in attempts to explain the relationship between children and television. The displacement view refers to the vast amount of time young children spend watching television and the subsequent reorganization of their other activities. In this theory the concern focuses on the amount of time children spend watching television, thus limiting their involvement in other activities that may be more worthwhile. With young children watching four to five hours of television per day, it is reasonable to conclude that their extensive viewing is displacing other activities that are critical to their development, such as play, reading, and physical activity (Neuman, 1991). By the time the average child reaches the age of eighteen, she or he will have spent more time with television than any other activity except sleep (Signorielli, 1991).

The information-processing theory examines the influence of television on children's thinking and concludes that this form of communication requires children to gain meaning from auditory and visual symbols while quickly attempting to organize incoming information. Children must draw conclusions about the content at a preestablished pace presented on the medium. This view concludes that television is training children to process information differently from their school environment. Winn (1977) and Singer and Singer (1980) have expressed concern about the frequent use of short and unrelated sequences in some television programs, such as "Sesame Street." They believe this technique does not allow children to process information effectively because of the quick pace of the content. Children presented information at this speed begin to rely on passive memory rather than actively processing the information. When children have the option of self-pacing, they are able to review the text for improved comprehension. This individual control of the content increases the possibility of stopping, elaborating visual images, and sorting information in the brain (Singer & Singer, 1981). Television does not allow this cognitive process to be controlled by the child.

Neil Postman (1985) maintains that television has produced children who expect immediate gratification. Television has demonstrated to children that life should be entertaining and should not require any effort. There are others (Comstock, 1980; Potter, 1976; Collins, 1983) who maintain that television can enhance children's learning. Even though young children watch television primarily for entertainment, they believe that children are learning in unplanned and informal ways. They conclude that television opens a new world to young children and moves them beyond their direct experiences. These expanded experiences enrich their learning and stimulate new interest. They further suggest that children who have seen a program on television may become interested in reading a book or exploring that topic in greater depth.

Studies (Hollenbeck & Slaby, 1979; Lemish & Rice, 1986) have found that visual attention to television starts as early as six months of age and increases from the ages of one to five, reaching its maximum in the year before a child begins attending elementary school. Young children's comprehension and understanding of television content varies depending upon a number of factors including cognitive abilities, general knowledge of the world, the viewing experience and the formal features of television (Audersm & Collins, 1988; Collins, 1982; Pingree & Hawkins, 1982).

What distinguishes television from other media? Many researchers believe that television's form is the distinguishing factor. The visual images presented are constantly changing and are generated by techniques that cannot be replicated in real life: zooms, fast motion, shots from several cameras, flash backs, and other special visual effects. Television is readily available to quickly turn on for instant entertainment. Although illustrated children's books and television both deliver content using visual images, only television is able to depict movement and action that can be simulated in book illustrations. In the auditory realm, programs contain dialogue, music, sound effects, and canned laughter (Wright & Huston, 1983). Television has its own system of codes and formal attributes; some of which are learned easily at an early age, others that are developed when children have the necessary cognitive skills, and others that are not learned until children have sufficient experience with the medium (Signorielli, 1991).

Although there is disagreement over the effects of television, there is clear evidence that television is a powerful influence in young children's lives (Neuman, 1991). Nancy Signorielli (1991) has concluded that in the past forty years, television has become children's primary storyteller.

Whether we view television as a positive or negative force, it is important to realize that we do not have the option of eliminating television from young children's lives. Today's children watch great amounts of television and are very interested in the medium. Busch (1978) found that when second graders were offered the same story on television or in book form 69 percent chose television and by the third grade 86 percent preferred this form of presentation. It is critical that this interest be captured and used to influence children's involvement with literature and print. Early childhood educators cannot ignore television but should become familiar with the medium and the programs that children are watching, so they can discuss the content and use this interest in positive ways.

USING TELEVISION TO EXPAND LITERACY ACTIVITIES

"Sesame Street" is a television program designed to prepare preschoolers for school. Some researchers (Huston, et al., 1990) found that three- to five-year-olds spent two-thirds of their informative viewing time devoted to "Sesame Street," which has highly repetitive settings, characters, and content. The creators of this program identified the techniques that attracted young children and used these elements: animation, puppets, and sound effects to capture their audiences' attention. There are many printed materials available that build on young children's interest in this program including books, collections of favorite stories, puppets, audio cassettes, and video tapes. *The Muppet Magazine* is an entertainment publication featuring the program characters, and *The Sesame Street Magazine* features activities that support learning presented on the television program. Selective inclusion of these materials in an early childhood classroom can make an important print and interest connection for children who enjoy watching "Sesame Street" and the characters that regularly appear.

Mr. Rogers in "Mr. Rogers' Neighborhood" invites young children to participate as he asks questions about feelings and personal experiences allowing a pause for the young listeners' response. Books and activities that relate to the content presented in Mr. Roger's program are also available commercially. Examples of books written by Fred Rogers relating to his television segments include: *When A Pet Dies,* which uses photographs and information about the death of a pet, and *Going to the Doctor* and *Going to Daycare,* which discuss first experiences of young children. Both "Sesame Street" and "Mister Roger's Neighborhood" have large audiences of young children (Neuman, 1991). Children's interest can be channeled toward printed material and books related to the program.

Other popular shows on Public Broadcasting Service (PBS) include "The Electric Company" and "3-2-1 Contact." "The Reading Rainbow" is devoted to presenting children's books on television. On each show LeVar Burton hosts a field trip that includes a visual adaptation of a great children's book. The program also contains reviews by children on books with related titles. The range of books and topics coupled with the high quality of the production makes this an excellent tool to lead to story enjoyment and extension to books. This series is also available on video to use in the classroom or to introduce a specific book in a different way.

Magazines that focus on many of these television programs can provide a connection of print to the auditory-visual presentation viewed by many young children. Many books and magazines based on television characters and events, referred to as *TV tie-ins,* are widely available in supermarkets, bookstores, and through book clubs. These popular materials have proven to be extremely successful in the market place (Neuman, 1989). They can form a reading connection to children's viewing experiences while capitalizing on their interest in the television program and characters. Children with low book-interest may be drawn to materials that relate to television and will be provided with a pleasurable experience with printed materials. Although these materials may not be of the literary quality one would like children to read, they may be the high interest material that captures the child's attention.

CLASSROOM USE OF TELEVISION

One of television's major weaknesses is the passivity of the viewer. If television is used in the classroom to transmit information, news, or special events, it is important to include class discussion lead by the teacher (Greenfield, 1984). Young children's learning from television can be significantly enhanced by interaction and discussion with adults during and following the event (Corder-Bolz, 1980; Lull, 1980). Cooper (1984) found that after young children watched a televised version of a children's story they wanted to discuss its meaning, explore the story, and go to the book. Television is not a substitute for interaction with an adult, but the combination can enhance the influence for some children. The extension of television to discussion and print will provide children with multiple presentations of the story and clarify understanding of content while building an important connection with the media.

Television has the potential to extend learning and literacy in the classroom, and can be used to enhance the comprehension and enjoyment of literature. A number of popular children's books, such as Dr. Seuss's *How the Grinch Stole Christmas* and Margery Williams' *The Velveteen Rabbit,* or *How Toys Become Real* have been adapted to television. These books increased in popularity after their presentation on television. Interest in a television program can also lead children to read similar stories or make certain books popular in the classroom or library. In 1984, Margaret Cooper reported that television viewing can have an influence on children's choices of reading material. Enjoyable television programs can draw a child to read a story she or he may not have considered previously. A major factor that determines whether a book is read after the television program is viewed is the availability of the book. Several children in Cooper's study indicated that after watching the television version of a book, they found the book in the school library, while others located it in a bookstore. It is interesting to note that none of the children indicated that they found the book in their classroom. The teacher who understands the powerful influence of television will attempt to keep current with the television shows children are watching as well as specials that are appearing. This knowledge of the medium and available programming can lead to the inclusion of books and stories in the classroom that are related to the television children are watching. A book, readily accessible in the classroom, will increase the likelihood that the child will follow up the viewing by exploring the story content in a book. Experiencing stories through different media and discussion encourages children to become aware of the unique characteristics of each medium, while distinguishing the adaptations and events presented from their favorite stories.

Kindergarten and primary-aged children can benefit from a unit of study focused on television. Some units include topics related to television production, such as plots, characters as actors, reality/fantasy, construction of settings, and information about advertisements. Other television units deal with the content; entertainment programs, viewers choices, and evaluation of personal viewing. These units can assist children as they learn about the medium. Children can also apply the information they gain by preparing their own television productions, writing a script, dramatizing the story, and creating commercials.

Studying television in the classroom is one way to help children evaluate programs and become more critical viewers. Children in a second-grade classroom participated in a unit focusing on television. They used newspaper listings and television guides as they determined the television programs they would watch. They constructed a graph of the programs most frequently watched by their class. They dramatized and videotaped their adaptations of favorite shows. As a part of the unit, the children were asked to limit their television viewing to one hour a night. They made their selection at school, recorded their choices in a television journal, and evaluated the program after viewing. In a primary classroom, two children were recording their choices in their journals. As they were writing their evaluations, they were heard discussing their television choices for the previous night. One concluded, "I sure wouldn't have wasted my hour watching that program if I had known how stupid it was going to be. Next week I'm going to watch a different show." Studying television can enable children to become more selective and can encourage critical evaluation of the television they watch.

Audio and Video Presentations

Young children enjoy listening to literature on cassettes. A simple and durable tape player can be used by an individual child or shared by four children using headphones at a listening station. Several companies offer packages including a cassette and a book, which can be used together in the listening activity. Benefits acquired from the inclusion of story tapes include:

1. recorded audio media, which can be played repeatedly
2. professional narration, which provides an expressive presentation of the story
3. realistic sound effects and appropriate music to enrich the literature experience (Rickelman & Henk, 1990)

It can also be advantageous to have teachers, parents, and older children make story reading tapes, since these are nearer to the child's dialect and include familiar voices. Many children's books are available from Opportunities for Learning on audio tapes and include such favorites as *Come Back, Amelia Bedelia, Stone Soup* and *Little Bear*. Weston Woods offers many high quality book/cassette read-along packages. Scholastic also produces many classic stories for young children on cassettes with books. Some sets include a big book, standard size books and cassettes for such selections as: *The Doorbell Rang, A House Is a House for Me,* and *The Snowy Day*.

Compact disks, which provide another way of listening to a story, are not as readily available as cassettes, but their distribution is expanding. The increased availability and durability of the compact disk have lead many to suggest that in the future their use may surpass the cassette in early childhood classrooms. Windham Hill Records has produced a series of award winning compact discs in their *Rabbit Ears Story Book Classics* (1990) series. This collection of thirteen popular stories is told by well-known narrators including Meryl Streep, Robin Williams, and Jack Nicholson. Among the stories included in this series are *The Ugly Duckling, Thumbelina* and *The Legend of Sleepy Hollow*. Two of the stories, *The Elephant's Child* and *Pecos Bill*, received Grammy awards for Best Children's recordings. All of the stories in the series are accompanied by beautifully illustrated companion books created by Picture Book Studio (Rickelman & Henk, 1990).

An important development in the 1980's was the proliferation of the VCR (videocassette recorder) in children's homes. In 1978 only 1 percent of homes with TVs had a VCR, but by 1990 that number had risen to almost 75 percent (Dominick, Sherman, & Copeland, 1990). Children's programs and recorded tapes of television programs are a large portion of both videotape sales and rentals. Many parents of young children use rental tapes and their own taped episodes to influence the kinds of programs their children watch (Signorielli, 1991). These tapes become like favorite stories that children enjoy seeing again and again (Barcus, 1988).

Videotapes are compact and easy to manipulate, which explains their increased use in early childhood classrooms. These audio-visual presentations of stories provide another avenue for seeing, hearing, and enjoying stories. Teachers have observed that visually oriented young children are often captured by this medium and inspired to read about the story or draw illustrations that accompany the content. Weston Woods has adapted over 300 classic children's books on filmstrips, film, and now VHS videocassettes. These include such children's favorites as Sendak's *Where the Wild Things Are*, McClosky's *Make Way for Ducklings*, and Hans Christian Andersen's *The Emperor's New Clothes*. Excellent collections are available including: *Five Lionni Classics: The Animal Fables of Leo Lionni, The Maurice Sendak Library, The Dr. Seuss Video Festival: Horton Hears A Who and How the Grinch Stole Christmas,* and Don

Freeman's *Corduroy and Other Bear Stories*. There are also several series that include high quality videos while consistently providing varied approaches to children's literature. These series include: *Stories to Remember*, which is book based with beautiful art work; *Storybook Classics*, which includes fairy tales, folk and literary classics with original art work, clear narratives and appropriate musical accompaniment; and *We All Have Tales*, which presents international folktales with celebrities as narrators, fitting music and art work in such productions as *Anansi* and *Peachboy*.

The presentation of these videos should follow the same plan recommended for reading a book or telling a story to a classroom of young children. An interesting question can be asked or an important event described to capture the attention of the audience before the viewing occurs. The teacher should also build background knowledge, make predictions from the title and relate information to what the children already know. After the completion of the showing, a discussion should focus on content presented to clarify discrepancies or unclear segments of the video. The video should be extended by the use of an appropriate follow-up activity that is inspired by the visual presentation. These planned procedures can make the video an important and integrated component of the curriculum rather than an unrelated quiet time.

Live-action literature-based films use actors and actresses to bring the story to life. These live action films are rare because of the difficulty presented in incorporating live action while preserving the charm of the original book. The *Faerie Tale Theatre* has distributed live-action performances of classic fairy tales that are humorous adaptations of old favorites created by Shelley Duvall. Performers in the series include Robin Williams, Jean Stapleton, and Billy Crystal. These creative productions are especially effective with primary-aged children who are already familiar with the classic fairy tales. Some of these include *Alladin and His Wonderful Lamp*, *The Dancing Princesses*, and *The Nightingale*. These videos could also stimulate writing and dramatization of the children's

adaptations of other familiar stories. Beverly Cleary's Romona Stories appear in a series of ten hilarious dramatizations that relate to family misunderstandings. These funny adaptations can interest children in discussing and writing about their own experiences, as well as prompting them to read the books for themselves. Some video versions combine elements of iconographic and animated presentations, for example, Seuss's *If Ran the Zoo*, and Grimm's *Rumpelstiltskin*.

In *Meet Marc Brown*, the author is seen visiting a school where he demonstrates how to draw Arthur and gets suggestions from the children about new books in his series. In the *Meet the Author Series*, young children can see the writers of their favorite books and listen to them describe the writing process, ideas, and production. For older children, *Meet the Newberry Author: Cynthia Rylant* shows the author relating the effect that her early childhood had on her writing. She recalls the loving environment she enjoyed while she lived with her grandparents in West Virginia while her newly divorced mother went to college. *The Relatives Came* and *When I was Young in the Mountains* reflect that period of her life. This interview with Rylant, including pictures from the family album, can give children a personal insight about a young author. Through the use of these videos, young children can see and hear an author reading his own work or telling about her experiences. This personal encounter with the writer of a book can provide a new dimension to a child's understanding and appreciation of the literature.

The Storytellers Collection includes stories told by talented storytellers, such as Joe Bruchao with Native-American tales, Alice Mcgill telling African-American tales, Jon Spelman with southern mountain stories, and Olga Loya sharing Hispanic tales. These videos bring famous guests into the classroom and, through their presentation, inspire a love for the literature they share.

Some videos based on books for early readers are available. *Bank Street Read-Along Story Videos* series includes *Not Now Said the Cow*, which is a mixture of live action photography, original cartoons from the book, and the narration. The story is read twice; first by the narrator alone and then with the narrator accompanied by subtitles so children can read along. This video encourages children to be actively involved in a successful reading experience complete with accompanying visuals.

Videos can also supplement units of study and provide visual extensions for a group to view. A unit on machines can be enriched by the viewing of *Moving Machines,* which shows children playing with small vehicles and then the real versions of the same machines. The study of insects can be enhanced by the video *Bugs Don't Bug Us.* These videos provide children with visual representations for their units of study and enrich their literature experiences. Careful selection and planning can insure that videos are integrated into the classroom curriculum, that they support the learning process, and that additional activities are provided that relate to the content presented.

Computers With Young Children

The microcomputer is a machine in which symbols are used to represent language, mathematics, music, and to create products such as stories, poems, and songs (Davidson, 1989; Sheingold, 1986). Young children are in a developmental stage characterized by their beginning use of symbols. When they are playing, they use a doll to represent a baby. When they are pretending to cook, they use ingredients that are imagined represen-

tations of the real thing. During these early years, young children are expanding their symbolic capacities as they use language, pictures, three-dimensional objects (clay, blocks, manipulates), movement, music, sociodramatic play, numbers, and logical knowledge (Gardner, 1983). Young children are also beginning to understand written language that represents oral language. The symbolic stage of development in young children seems to match the symbolic nature of the computer. It is, however, critical to examine how children use the computer and determine if the programs support their way of learning.

Much of the early software developed for use with young children consisted of the drill-and-practice approach to learning. In some cases, this approach was designed to look like a game, but the basic format focused on teaching letter and number recognition through repetition. This rote memory approach to learning was viewed by many early childhood educators as inappropriate for young children and lead to the recommendation that computers not be used in early childhood classrooms. Haugland and Shade (1988) effectively communicated this view in their statement, "Whether workbook or software, inappropriate educational materials are inappropriate [p. 41]." Although some of these same programs are still in use today, there are many other types of software available designed to give children the power to interact and control the action of the computer. Children can now paint with a brush, create pictures, arrange shapes in an original design, or compose their own story. Children can give instructions to the computer by using a mouse, paddle, or joy-stick, as well as the keyboard. Children can even directly control what happens on the screen by touching it with a light pen. Special pads have been developed for young and special children using fewer or different symbols from the regular keyboard making the computer more accessible for all children. The new flexibility of the computer and software make it a medium that can now be used for children to use in writing, drawing, and illustrating in many different ways.

Critics of the use of computers with young children suggested that their use decreased social interaction. Recent studies, however, have concluded that computers can encourage social interaction when children are allowed to work cooperatively to discover how to make programs work (Clements, Nastasi, & Swaminathan, 1993). It is beneficial for two or more children to gather around the computer, exploring software and encouraging peer teaching. If young children have appropriate software, they can work together or independently at the computer, providing a choice for their involvement.

Computers may also provide opportunities to use thinking skills as children determine the steps and methods needed to implement their ideas (Papert, 1980). "Logo," for instance, has been found to increase skills with children six years and older in areas of fluency, originality, and divergent thinking. "Logo" is a programming language needed to create graphic designs and programs, simplified for easier use by children. Computers can help children as they construct and revise their ideas (Clements & Gullo, 1984). Young children can experience concepts related to computer use as they explore the use of the backspace key or move

the paint brush. The computer can stimulate children's play as they explore this medium, when they use open-ended software. Although this computer play should not and cannot replace dramatic play, it does provide another medium for exploratory activity, when using appropriate programs. The immediate response to the action of the children also provides instant feedback for their actions and encourages their continued involvement.

Observers of young children using microcomputers report a high level of motivation, longer attention span, and enjoyment while interacting (Campbell & Schwartz, 1986). These observable behaviors indicate that the inclusion of computers into the early childhood classroom can provide an additional experience that will capture the interest and attention of some children.

Using appropriate software can develop a positive view of computers and can influence children's attitudes toward the use of the machine in the future. Inappropriate use can have a negative affect on young children, but a successful and enjoyable computer experience can lead to positive feelings toward the computer (Hyson & Morris, 1985; Wright & Samaras, 1986).

Some research (Clements, 1987; Scott, Cole, & Engle, 1992) indicates that boys may use computers more than girls. Watson, Nida, and Shade (1986) have suggested that the use of computers by both boys and girls in the early years may ensure that both have the interest and competencies to use this tool. The observation and assistance of both sexes to insure their involvement with computers in early childhood classrooms is important and may have positive consequences for children who are living in the computer age. One first-grade teacher observed that when two of her students, Brad and Jennifer, were at the computer table together, Jennifer would let Brad control the computer while she observed the action on the screen. By pairing Jennifer with another girl in a computer activity, the teacher was able to move the observing girl into the leadership role.

Questions do remain, however, related to computer use with young children. Are the skills required too abstract for preoperational children? Does using a computer decrease opportunities for language use and interaction with adult models? Are the activities on computers too structured and set up as a workbook? Would this time be better spent in concrete and real experiences? More research is needed before these difficult questions can be answered.

Davidson (1989), in her book *Children & Computers Together in the Early Childhood Classroom,* concludes that the computer is a medium with many potential benefits. If it is used wisely it can be an important addition to a developmentally appropriate early childhood classroom. She further states that the most appropriate use for the computer with young children is as a tool and thought provoker. Haugland and Shade (1988) describe the computer as an educational tool similar to a pencil or crayon that provides children with a way of dealing with information. Experiences with the computer can be designed to reflect a developmentally sound approach to learning. Papert (1980) has applied Piaget's theory to children's experiences with computers by explaining that the children must be in control of the action and make events happen. He believes that these discovery-oriented interactions with computers enhance children's learning while providing new ways to use ideas and intellectual skills.

SOFTWARE

The value of the computer with young children depends on the selection of appropriate software. Software is the computer program, which makes the computer complete its functions. The software can make the computer function as a word processor, an easel, a workbook, a story board or a musical instrument. If the software is carefully selected to match the developmental level and interest of the children using the computer, it can be an interactive experience that is controlled by the children in a meaningful exchange (Davidson, 1989).

The massive quantity of software available often makes selection a difficult process for the teacher or librarian. When choosing the software, use many of the same questions that are helpful in determining the appropriateness of any material to be used with young children (Davidson, 1989, pp. 48; Dodge & Colker, 1992, pp. 303–306):

1. Does the content of the program support the goals and objectives of the curriculum of the early childhood program?

2. Does the software match the developmental level and interest of the children in the classroom?

3. Is the software open ended to provide opportunities for exploration and flexible use?

4. Will the child be able to independently use the program without constant assistance?

5. Does the program allow the child to control the actions?

6. Does the program involve the child in a sufficiently challenging activity?

When evaluating the operations of specific software, the teacher will review the clarity of the instructions, the number of different keys needed to activate the program, the level of control provided to the children, and the pace of the presentation. It is also important that the software maintain children's interest after they have initially explored the program, so it will continue to be used by the children (Dodge & Colker, 1992). Teachers should determine the software that is appropriate for their classroom by a hands-on evaluation. It is only with actual use of the software that the teacher can decide the effectiveness of a specific design and the match with classroom curriculum. The teacher should examine the software in computer stores, in libraries, at workshops, and at conferences. Some software companies will allow programs to be previewed for thirty days and returned if they are not appropriate. This procedure is especially helpful for the classroom teacher or librarian.

There are several reference books that provide descriptions of programs, price, suggested age levels, and a brief description of the content of software programs. These books can help identify specific software that the teacher would like to evaluate. The High/Scope Educational Research Foundation provides yearly guides to early childhood software in *Survey of Early Childhood Software.* They use three major factors in their evaluation of software for young children: user friendliness, content, and instructional design. Each year they identify excellent software for young children, and recognize programs that are of a high quality, have appropriate early childhood content, provide room for creativity, and allow children to print their computer-created product. Some of the software packages that have received this award of excellence include: *Color Me,* a drawing program in which young children can add their own typed captions with results printed in color; *Mask Parade,* which children can use to create and print their own life-sized masks and badges; and *Muppets on Stage,* in which muppet characters invite children to engage in experiences with letters, colors, and numbers, providing an easy introduction to the computer (High/Scope, 1988).

While references can lead teachers to software that may be of interest to young children, they cannot replace the individual teacher's evaluation and ability to match the program with the interest and needs of the children in her or his classroom (Davidson, 1989).

Only the Best, Preschool–Grade 12 and *The Educational Software Review* are other references that may be used to find descriptions of currently available software (Dodge & Colker, 1992).

Computers can provide young children with another window into the world of literacy. Their use can encourage children to use language in meaningful context, interacting and creating in the process. The use of word processors encourages children to write more, be less concerned about mistakes, and experiment more with written language (Clements & Nastasi, 1992). The *Bank Street Writer* and *Primary Editor* are word-processing

programs that children can use in writing a story, developing a group composition, or creating an adaption of a favorite story. The teacher can also use the program as the children dictate a story, while they observe the recording and printing of their creations. The opportunity to see their ideas being produced on a large screen or by a printer can be an motivating experience for young children.

Other word-processing programs that promote both guided and unstructured learning are available for young children. *Stickybear Printer* includes pictures and graphic forms to go along with the writing of stories. Children can use *Color Me, Magic Crayon,* or *Mouse Paint* to draw illustrations, develop wordless books, and create pictures to serve as props for telling a story.

The *Explore-A-Story* series includes several different programs that are effective for young children. By using a mouse or arrow keys, young children can move animated objects or create their own stories. *The Bald-Headed Chicken,* a component in this series, has a book format, which includes a title page and four picture pages. Using this software, children can choose and move the characters or objects in the picture and add words to the illustrations. Their story can be saved for future editing or printed for immediate viewing. This design gives young children control over the content, which is then printed in book form.

Some available software directly relates to a specific story or character; for example *Clifford's Big Book Publisher* (Apple and MS-DOS). This program uses Clifford, the big red dog, as the main character, and the package includes clip art props that can be used in a variety of settings and story designs. This software can also be used to create different sizes of books and posters. *Write On!, Great Wild Imaginings* (Humanities Software), includes a series of writing activities created for use with *Where the Wild Things Are*. These encourage collaborative writing, with teacher and student working at the keyboard to complete ideas like, "What do you do when you feel wild?" or "What do your parents do when you get wild?" It includes ways to illustrate dreams, write chanting poetry, and participate in journal writing related to the book theme (Wepner, 1992).

Primary children can use programs such as *Print Shop* independently, to make signs for centers, directions for activities, or advertisements for plays and puppet shows. For primary children, who have had experience with computers, *The Newsroom* can be used. With this software, the children can create stories, develop news articles about happenings, and see them printed in the form of a newspaper. They can also develop a classroom newspaper that may be distributed to peers and parents, expanding their audience of readers. With *Story Weaver*, students can express ideas in words and pictures while creating colorful booklets with pages of text or in combination with graphics. The program provides a simple word processor, page decorations, background scenes, and cut-and-paste commands. These attractive booklets can be printed containing up to fifty pages. Having several selections of software in the classroom can help children begin to understand that computers can do many different things but that they are powerless until activated by the software and the child's operation.

For primary-aged children, literature-based software is being designed for emergent readers, which requires a CD-ROM drive. *Stories and More* is an example of the use of this new technology and includes thirty-six stories that come from original books. Each story has an activity to prepare the student for reading. Then, story time presents the voice-supported story, followed by thinking activities that help with story concept and going beyond to activities that encourage the child to express their ideas. *If You Give a Mouse a Cookie, Peter's Chair*, and *The Three Billy-Goats Gruff* are just a few examples of some of the stories included in the series. During the story time segment, children can read or listen and question at the end, stimulating original writing.

Software that can provide new capabilities, appropriate to use in classrooms that serve young children, is constantly being designed. For example, the *Big Book Maker: Favorite Fairy Tales and Nursery Rhymes* enables teachers

and students to combine graphics and simple word processing to create pages, books, and posters based on familiar poems and stories. After the stories have been created, they can be printed in four sizes including minibook and big, big book. *Puppetmaker* can be used to create shoe box, finger, and walking puppets, which can encourage children to write and perform plays. *Hyper Card*, software that permits multi media composition, is being used effectively with older students and shows potential for supporting young children's expression of ideas and stories (Char, 1990). Interactive stories are being used with upper elementary children. The software *Story Tree* allows the student to determine the directions of the story by selecting one of several options at various points in the plot. Instructions that are easy to understand and follow permit the technique incorporated in this software to be effectively utilized with young children (Henney, 1988).

The effective integration of the computer into early childhood programs requires careful attention to several factors. The computer should be integrated into the classroom environments so that children use it as another tool for learning. Computer use should be extended into all aspects of the program, including centers, special projects, and adult-child interactions. Children should be exposed to different uses of the computer so they can begin to understand that it is a tool that can be used in many different ways (Swick, 1989). Computers can be used to stimulate and support young children as literacy is emerging. They can be used during center time as a way of connecting pictures and words, as a way of writing and editing text, or cooperatively dictating ideas to the teacher, volunteer, or peers (Mayfield, 1992).

The arrangement of a special area can make a critical difference in the usefulness of the computer in the classroom. The computer should be located in a quiet part of the classroom close to the library area. The computer center should be out of high traffic areas but easily accessible to the children as an available activity choice. Good lighting in the area will make the screen more visible and actions easier to follow. A display area should be available for exhibiting the children's printed computer work. Two chairs should be placed near each computer so that children can work together, share techniques, and cut down on the long waits to use the computer. The area should also contain the software that the children can use to encourage their independent selection and use of the materials (Dodge & Colker, 1992).

Ross and Roe (1990) have developed helpful guidelines for using computers in the classroom. These steps can assist the teacher in planning for effective use of the computer with primary children:

1. Plan instructions related to the operations of the computer and software, and demonstrate a variety of uses.

2. Develop a schedule for each student to use the computer in class and for before and after school use.

3. Provide activities that encourage children to work together on the computer.

4. Use the computer and software to support the curriculum.

There are growing numbers of software programs available for use with young children in the classroom. The variety and interactive capability of this new software is only an indication of what will be developed for young children in the next few years. Some software is interesting, responsive, and appropriate, while some provides only drill and practice, which does not match the learning styles of young children. It is important that the early childhood educator continuously preview and study software as the options and possibilities increase. Inappropriate software should not be used simply because it allows the children use of the computer. The challenge to early childhood educators is to select software that, like other curriculum resources, reflects a sound developmental approach to young children as they learn through using computers (Haugland & Shade, 1988).

After a two and one half year study of young children using computers, Church and Wright (1986) concluded that the young child can effectively use the microcomputer as a multifaceted tool in graphic arts, language arts, and preprogramming. They recommend guided discovery combined with open-ended interactive programs that allow children to experience success as they invent and solve their own problems. After a review of research, Clements, Natasi, and Swaminathas (1993) concluded that open-ended programs can have many benefits in developing knowledge and problem-solving skills in ways that are developmentally appropriate for young children.

The computer provides one option in a classroom filled with many opportunities for learning. As teachers become sensitive to the trends that are influencing the child's world, they can guide these new forces in appropriate directions. Papert (1986), Campbell and Fein (1986), Davidson (1989), and Clements, Nastasi and Swaminathas (1993) emphasize that what children learn from the computer is greatly influenced by the teacher and the classroom environment. If the teacher encourages discovery, supports computer use, and provides opportunities for children to be successful, children will learn about the software and computer while enjoying the process.

Magazines Specifically for Young Children

Much has been written about the importance of the literacy environment and its subsequent influence on the emerging reader and writer. Durkin's study of early readers clearly identified the impact of the home that is language rich and includes printed materials such as books, newspapers, and magazines (Durkin, 1966). This and other studies have repeatedly recognized the importance of providing numerous opportunities for children to read a variety of materials containing interesting content. Magazines written specifically for children can provide an untapped resource for engaging children in pleasurable reading. Seminoff (1986 pp. 889-89) offered several benefits of using children's magazines in the classroom:

1. The material in magazines is current and relates to events that are occurring.

2. A range of content is offered in both areas of interest and difficulty of the material.

3. The format provides diverse experiences with language (crossword puzzles, finding hidden words, rebuses, poems, and short stories).

4. Articles present information in a concise form that the reader can complete in a short period of time.

5. The illustrations and photographs included are visually appealing and attract young readers to the content.

6. The low cost makes them very appropriate for the classroom.

Over the past few years, the number of children's magazines has increased significantly with many new publications designed for young children. Magazines can provide another medium for young children to explore as they develop an understanding of print and story. Since most of the magazines are educational as well as recreational, they provide a meaningful way for young children to enjoy using language. Many of the publications include attractive pictures and illustrations that captivate young children as they are developing their reading ability. Some of the magazines come with guides that can be used by the teacher before the material is shared with the children (Thomas, 1987).

Many young children have not had the opportunity to experience a magazine written for them, therefore they will need an introduction to this new medium. The teacher can discuss the content, show the pictures, read a story, or explain one of the interesting activities so that children can begin to understand how a magazine works. During orientation to this new material, young children observe their teacher reading and learn intriguing information.

Magazines make reading easily accessible to young children with a new supply of material arriving each month. The short story format with many illustrations often entices reluctant readers to the magazine when they might hesitate to pick up a lengthy book. Magazines provide a "quick read" that seems to be a reality in the modern world. Varied writing, entertaining activities, and current information make magazines a bridge to literacy. They are inexpensive, appealing, and support children's reading by engaging them in interesting articles (Cullinan, 1990).

The large and expanding number of children's magazines designed for use by young children necessitates that these publications be examined by the teacher or librarian before they are included in the classroom or library. A review can assist in the selection of magazines that will match the interest of specific children and be appropriate for their level of development. Donald Stoll, Executive Director of the Educational Press Association of America, estimates that in 1991 over 160 magazines were published for children. With this number of children's magazines available, it is difficult to know which ones are specifically useful for young children. *Magazines for Children* provides a listing of publications and includes a brief description, targeted age group, and subscription information. Even this publication, however, does not include some of the newer additions to the market.

Keep the following questions in mind when selecting magazines:

1. Is the content appropriate and clearly written for young children?

2. Do the illustrations, photographs, or cartoons support the written content presented?

3. Is the information included accurate and up-to-date?

4. Are the included activities developmentally appropriate for young children?

5. Are the articles and stories designed to encourage young children's reading?

6. Will the magazines be enjoyed by many of the children in the classroom?

7. Is the content varied, such as stories, poems, activities, and illustrations?

8. Will the magazine be useable next year?

The following magazines available for young children can add a dimension to the early childhood literacy environment. Single copies can be obtained from the publisher for teachers to evaluate and field test with young children.

SUGGESTED MAGAZINES FOR YOUNG CHILDREN

Children's Playmate Magazine—Children's Better Health Institute, for ages four to eight years, eight issues per year. This magazine focuses on health practices and includes stories, poems, jokes, word riddles, and recipes. Children are also encouraged to write questions to the doctor, and answers are published.

Happy times—Concordia Publishing House, for three-to five-year-olds with eleven issues per year. This magazines contains stories to read, cooking treats, crafts, and posters to supplement the content.

Lets's Find Out—Scholastic, Pre-K through Kindergarten, eight issues per year. Learning activities are focused around a monthly theme. The package includes coordinated materials, wall posters, and parents' letter.

My First Magazine—Scholastic, for ages three and four with six issues per year. Each issue focuses on a theme that is appropriate for young children. The magazine includes activities that involve children in storytelling, creative play, and social development. A big poster and teacher's guide accompanies four of the six children's magazines.

Your Big Back Yard—National Wildlife Federation, for ages three to five with twelve issues per year. This publication is designed to help children learn more about nature. Beautiful color photographs of animals add to the appeal of the content. A letter with suggestions to extend the pictures, games, and puzzles is sent with each issue.

Highlights for Children—For three- to twelve-year-olds, with eleven issues. Content focuses on thinking, reasoning, sensitivity and creativity. Includes cartoons, stories puzzles, and activities for a variety of developmental levels. Children are encouraged to send reactions and original artwork for publication. Guide for teachers provides suggestions for extensions.

Ladybug: The Magazine for Young Children—Carcus Publishing Company, 12 issues per year. Each issue contains stories by young children; many are written by well-known authors of children's literature. The colorful illustrations encourages young children to read the content. Songs, fingerplays, and other activities appropriate for young children are also included each month.

Lollipops, Ladybugs and Lucky Stars—Good Apple, for three- to five-year-olds with five issues per year. Includes games to teach basic concepts, poetry, songs, and bulletin board ideas.

Sesame Street—Children's Television Workshop, for ages three to eight with ten issues each year. The content is built around a theme and reinforces ideas shown on the television program. Includes a parent section with suggested activities. Available in Spanish and English.

Scholastic Let's Find Out—Scholastic Magazines, for five-year-olds, with ten issues per year. Includes four parts: sensory experiences, language arts, social studies, and math/science. A teacher's edition contains educational suggestions for use with young children.

Turtle Magazine for Preschool Kids—Children's Better Health, ages two to five with eight issues per year. Designed to challenge the intellectual needs of children while focusing on health issues. Includes stories, poems, rebuses, puzzles, and activities.

SUGGESTED MAGAZINES FOR PRIMARY CHILDREN

Cricket: The Magazine for Children—Open Court Publishing Co., for six- to twelve-year-olds, with twelve issues. Introduces children to some of the best literature and art from around the world. A variety of stories is included to stimulate children's imagination.

Chickadee Magazine—Young Naturalist Foundation, grades K through four with ten issues: A science and nature publication. Includes photos, easy-to-read animal stories, craft projects, and science experiments.

Disney Adventures—for seven- to fourteen-year-olds with twelve issues each year. This magazine includes feature stories, interviews, puzzles, games, short news items, letters from readers, and comic adventures.

Kid City (formerly The Electric Company)—Children's Television Workshop, for ages six through ten years, with ten issues annually. Uses themes to emphasize reading and writing. Includes photo essays, fiction, poetry, puzzles, and crafts.

Jack and Jill—Children's Better Health Institute. For ages six to eight, with eight issues per year. Includes short stories, artwork, stories, poems, and jokes.

Kids Discover—For six- to twelve-year-olds, published ten times a year. Each issue deals with a single subject, such as trees, the circus, or bubbles. Pictures and information are included along with puzzles, activities, and ideas to use in finding additional information on the topic.

Ranger Rick's Nature Magazine—The National Wildlife Federation, for ages five to eleven years, with 12 issues per year. Designed to increase understanding and appreciation of nature. Topics covered include personal adventures, animal life, natural history, photo stories, jokes, crafts, and poetry.

Shoe Tree—National Association for Young Writers, for ages six to fourteen, with three issues per year. This magazine contains stories, poems, and personal narratives by young writers and illustrators who are six to fourteen years of age. This magazine is designed to encourage young writers and artist by professionally publishing their work.

Stone Soup: The Magazine by Children—Children's Art Foundation, for ages six to twelve years, with six issues per year. A bimonthly publication that includes fiction, poetry, book reviews, and art by children. Each issue focuses on a topic related to children's lives and art from around the world, and includes photos of the children whose work is presented.

U*S*Kids—Richard J. LeBrasseur, ages five to ten, with eleven issues. The focus of this magazine is on understanding the world, encouraging reading and vocabulary development, and stimulating creativity. Issues include news, true to life stories and science and nature and activities (Stoll, 1991).

In a study of 110 library media centers, librarians were asked to list the magazines the children in their elementary school used most frequently. The magazines identified were: *Ranger Rick, National Geographic World, Boys' Life* and *Highlights*. It is interesting to note that they believed that the magazines were primarily used for recreational reading rather than information gathering (Swisher, Pye, Estes-Rickner, & Merriam, 1991). Although one of the positive outcomes of the inclusion of magazines in the classroom is that they are high interest materials that children enjoy reading, their usefulness as an informational source should not be overlooked. Teachers can demonstrate this feature as they search the content for a specific interesting fact or ask children to find an answer using a magazine as a reference.

In the early childhood classroom, magazines can be placed in many different areas. In the science center, *The Big Backyard, Ranger Rick's Nature Magazine,* or *Science Weekly* can relate to the display of nature items or problem-solving activities. In the writing center, children can be stimulated by reading works of other young writers in *Shoe Tree*. They can compare variations of the same tale presented by writers from various countries in *Children's World* or *Children's Digest*. In the library area, magazines can provide an additional reading choice for leisure browsing or information gathering. Magazines in this area can be enjoyed by one child, or several children can share a story or rhyme.

Magazines can also support the early childhood curriculum by providing additional materials for social studies as children learn about other parts of the world and expand their view of their country. Vocabulary can be developed through the use of magazines such as: *Highlights, 3-2-1 Contact,* and *U*S*Kids,* which include puzzles, word games, and challenging activities in which children use vocabulary in a functional way (Seminoff, 1986).

There are many children's magazines that publish children's writings and art work. The possibility of having a story or drawing published can be an exciting motivation for young children. Exposing children to periodicals that include original work can also nurture the idea that they too can make literary contributions. *Chickadee, Child Life, Children's Digest, Children's Playmate, Highlights for Children, Stone Soup,* and *Turtle: Magazine for Preschool Kids,* are just a few of the magazines that publish writings, artwork, and other materials by young children.

Newspapers published specifically for children can provide another way to experience stories and writings. For many years the most frequently used classroom newspaper was the *Weekly Reader*. This series of editions is designed for specific grade

levels and provides news stories, and articles on health, science, and safety. There are also summer editions designed to provide activities for children during their time away from school. *Scholastic News* is another weekly classroom newspaper, published in six separated editions for children in grades one through six that focuses on helping children understand major world and national news events.

In an exciting early childhood classroom, children participate in many different experiences presented in diverse ways. Magazines and newspapers add variety to the literacy environment of young children and provide an invitation to literature and reading.

Expanding the Literacy Environment for Today's Young Children

Early childhood educators must now move into the electronic age by using new tools to enrich the literacy experiences of young children. Both audio and visual media can support children's appreciation of literature and provide the cognitive framework for story comprehension (Rickelman & Henk, 1990; Wells, 1986). Experiences with varied media provides young children with opportunities to learn in different ways with diverse tools. The acceptance of the role of media, an understanding of the unique features of each medium, and its inclusion into the classroom help children make an important connection between literature and their world.

Creating a multimedia approach to literature can assist children in thinking about stories while developing new perspectives through the use of sound, images, and words (Char, 1990). Using a combination of books, audio cassettes, videotapes, computer programs, and magazines can be more effective than using a single medium in isolation. Rather than using one tool for learning, diverse media provide young children with opportunities to interact with technology in ways that enhance their learning. In early childhood programs the use of a variety of materials and approaches is stressed, since we understand that children learn in different ways and what captures one child's interest is ignored by another child. As with any material, diverse media work best when properly introduced, integrated in meaningful content, observed during use, extended through discussion, followed by hands-on activities, and related to books (Char, 1990). Media provide new challenges for young children in the classroom and opportunities to use visual images, auditory sounds, and interactive materials that will enrich their literacy environment today and in their future.

REFERENCES THAT INCLUDE REVIEWS OF MEDIA

There are a number of books that provide a quick reference to currently available media, including audio and videotapes, computer software, and magazines. These references can assist the busy educator in making selections for review, evaluation, and subsequent purchase.

The *Survey of Early Childhood Software*, published by High/Scope Educational Research Foundation, is a yearly guide to software that can be used with young children from three to six years of age. This review provides information on programs available and includes the latest information on new programs.

The American Library Association publishes the *Best of the Best for Children*, which includes librarian-recommended media that children can enjoy again and again. It includes videos, software, audio tapes, and magazines with short descriptions and the target audience for the media. This is a very effective reference for early childhood educators for it includes reviews for the divisions of: infant and toddler (birth to age two), preschoolers (ages three to five) and early grades (ages six to eight).

Success Story

Vanassa, the library media specialist, worked with the team of primary teachers to provide books and other media for their thematic units. In the previous years, all the teachers had needed the books at the same time, making it impossible for Vanassa to provide a variety of choices for the children in all the classrooms. The teacher's advanced planning and the decision to rotate the units of study allowed Vanassa to provide many more options for the children, expanding their opportunities for reading about the topic. She also suggested films, videos, audio tapes, and magazines that could be used in conjunction with the study allowing children different approaches and materials as they worked cooperatively on projects. In this expanded literacy environment, young children were able to chose the medium they preferred to use or combine several different approaches as they gathered information.

The primary teachers collected books, magazine articles, and reference materials that related to the videos and tapes to encourage the children to combine the audiovisual presentation with printed materials. This combination capitalized on the children's interest in media and encouraged them to include books and other printed materials in their learning experiences. As they participated in the unit activities, using a variety of media, they learned that literature can be presented and enjoyed in many different ways. Vanassa and the primary teachers developed units that included expanded literacy experiences that were appropriate for today's young children.

SUGGESTED LEARNING EXPERIENCES

1. Visit a library/media center in an elementary school. List the different types of materials that are available for the teacher to borrow for the early childhood classroom.
2. Watch a television program that uses a children's book as the content.
3. Visit a child care facility. Observe if there are televisions in the classrooms and how they are used with young children.
4. Identify an appropriate unit for the primary grades. Select audio and video materials that could be used to expand the study.
5. Observe young children using a computer. List the positive and negative aspects of the activity.
6. Review software that is available for use with young children. Select one that is appropriate for young children and use it with a young child.
7. Go to a children's bookstore and identify the magazines that are available for young children.
8. Check the titles of children's magazines available in a large supermarket. Notice how they are displayed.
9. Read a magazine to kindergarten children and ask them questions about the content presented.
10. Attend a planning meeting for a group of early childhood teachers. Keep a written record of their inclusion of media in their plan for their classroom.

REFERENCES

Anderson, D., & Collins, P. (1988). *The impact on children's education: Television's influence on cognitive development*. U.S. Department of Education. Office of Educational Research and Improvement. Washington, D.C.

Anderson, D., Field, D., Collins, P., Lorch, E. & Nathan, J. (1985). Estimates of young children's time with television: A methodological comparison of parent reports with time-lapse video home observations. *Child Development, 56*(5), 1345–1357.

Barcus, F. (1988, May). *Content and costs of children's video*. Paper prepared for the 38th Annual Conference of the International Communication Association, New Orleans Book Industry Study Group (1984).

Buckleitner, W. (1988). *Survey of early childhood software*. Yipsilanti, MI: High/Scope Educational Research Foundation.

Busch, J. (1978). Television's effects of reading: A case study. *Phi-Delta-Kappan, 59*(10), 668–671.

Campbell, P. & Fein, G. (Eds). (1986). *Young children and microcomputers*. Englewood Cliff, NJ: PrenticeHall.

Campbell, P., & Schwartz, S. (1986). Microcomputers in the preschool: Children, parents and teachers. In P. Campbell & G. Fein (Eds.), *Young children and microcomputers*. Englewood Cliff, NJ: PrenticeHall.

Char, C. A. (1990, April). Interactive technology and the young child: Insights from research and design. Paper presented at the American Educational Research Association, Boston, MA.

Chu, G., & Schramm, W. (1967). *Learning from television.* Washington: National Association of Educational Broadcasters.

Church, J., & Wright, J. (1986). Creative thinking with the microcomputer. In P. Campbell and G. Fein (Eds.), *Young children and microcomputers.* Englewood Cliff, NJ: Prentice-Hall.

Clements, D., & Gullo, D. (1984). Effects of computer programming in young children's cognition. *Journal of Educational Psychology, 76*(6), 1051–1058.

Clements, D., Nastasi, B., & Swaminathan, S. (1993). Young children and computers: Crossroads and directions from research. *Young Children, 48*(2), 56–63.

Clements, D., & Natasi, B. (1992) Computers and early childhood education. In S. Gettinger, N. Elliott, and T. Kratochwill (Eds.), *Advances in school psychology: Preschool and early childhood treatment directions* (pp. 187–246). Hillsdale, NJ: Lawrence Erlbaum.

Collins, W. (1982). Cognitive processing aspects of television viewing. In D. Pear, L. Bouthilet, & J. Lazar (Eds.), *Television and behavior: Ten years of scientific progress and implications of the 80's,* (Vol. 2 pp. 9–23). Technical Reports. Washington, DC: U.S. Government Printing office.

Collins, W. (1983). Interpretation and inference in children's television viewing. In J. Bryant & D. R. Anderson (Eds.), *Children's understanding of television: Research on attention and comprehension,* (pp. 125–150). New York: Academic Press.

Cooper, M. (1984). Televised books and the effects on children's reading. *Uses of English, 35*(2), 41–49.

Comstock, G. (1980). *Television in america.* Beverly Hills, CA: Sage.

Corder-Bolz, C. (1980). Mediation: The role of significant others. *Journal of Communication, 30*(3), 106–118.

Cullinan, B. (1990). Children's magazines: Fun and informative. In D. Stroll (Ed.), *Magazines for children.* Glassboro, NJ: Educational Press Association.

Davidson, J. (1989). *Children and computers together in the early childhood classroom.* Albany, NY: Delmar Publishers.

Deitch, G. (1978). Lecture delivered at Simmons College, Boston, MA: Weston Woods Archive, Weston, CT.

Dodge, D., & Colker, L. (1992). *The creative curriculum for early childhood* (3rd ed.). Washington, DC: Teaching Strategies.

Donavin, D. (Ed.). (1992). *Best of the best for children.* New York: Random House.

Dominick, J., Sherman, B., & Copeland, G. (1990). *Broadcasting/cable and beyond: An introduction to modern electronic media.* New York: McGraw-Hill.

Dorr, A., Graves S., & Phelps, E. (1980). Television literacy for young children. *Journal of Communication, 30*(3), 71–83.

Durkin, D. (1966). *Children who read early.* New York: Teachers College Press.

Educational Software Evaluation Consortium (1991). *Educational software preview guide.* Eugene, OR: International Society for Technology in Education.

Elkind, D. (1981). *The hurried child, growing up too fast too soon.* Reading, MA: Addison Wesley Publishing.

Gardner, H. (1983). *Frames of the mind: The theory of multiple intelligence.* New York: Basic Books.

Greenfield, P. (1984). *Mind and media: The effects of television, video games, and computers.* Cambridge, MA: Harvard University Press.

Henney, M. (1988). Reading and writing interactive stories. *The Computing Teacher. 15*(8), pp. 45–47.

High/Scope Early Childhood Computer Learning Report (1988, April). *Key notes, 4*(1).

Hollenbeck, A., & Slaby, R. (1979). Infant visual and vocal responses to television. *Child Development, 50*(1), 41–45.

Hougland, S., & Shade, D. (1988). Developmental appropriate software for young children. *Young Children, 43*(4), 37–43.

Huston, A. C., J. C., Rice, M. L., Kerkman, D. St. Pete's M. (1990). The development of television viewing patterns in early childhood: A longitudinal investigation. Washington, DC: US Department of Education, Office of Educational Research and Improvement.

Hyson, M., & Morris, S. (1985). "Computers? I love them!" Young children's concepts and attitudes about computers. *Early Child Development and Care. 23*(1), 17–29.

Lemish, D., & Rice, M. (1986). Television as a talking picture book: A prop for language acquisition. *Journal of Child Language, 13,*(2) 251–274.

Lull, J. (1980). The social uses of television. *Human Communication Research, 6,* 198–209.

Mayfield, M. (1992). *Organizing for teaching and learning in emerging literacy: Preschool, kindergarten, and primary grades.* (L. Ollida and M. Mayfield, Eds.). Needham Heights, MA: Allyn and Bacon.

McLulan, M. (1964). *Understanding media: The extensions of man.* New York: McGraw-Hill.

Meringoff, L. (1980). Influence of the medium on children's story apprehension. *Journal of Educational Psychology, 72*(2), 240–249.

Neil, S., & Neil, G. (1991). *Only the best: Preschool-grade 12 Annual guide to highest rated educational software.* Providence, NJ: Bowker.

Neuman, S. (1989). The impact of different story comprehension. *Reading Research and Instruction, 28*(14), 38–47.

Neuman, S. (1991). *Literacy in the television age: The myth of the TV effect.* Norwood, NJ: Ablex Publishing.

Noble, G. (1975). *Children in front of the small screen.* London: Constable.

Olson, D., & Bruner, J. (1974). In D. Olson (Ed.), *Media and symbols: The forms of expression, communication and education.* Chicago: National Society for the Study of Education.

Papert, S. (1980). *Mindstorms: Children and computers, and powerful ideas.* New York: Basic Books.

Pingree, S., & Hawkins, R. (1982). What children do with television: Implications for communication research. In B. Dervin & M. J. Voigt (Eds.), *Progress in communication sciences,* (Vol. 3, pp. 225–244). Norwood, NJ: Ablex Publishing.

Postman, N. (1985). *Amusing ourselves to death.* New York: Viking Penguin.

Potter, R. (1976). *New season: The positive use of commercial television with children*. Columbus, OH: Charles E. Merrill.

Quarfoth, J. (1979). Children's understanding of the nature of television characters. *Journal of Communication, 29*(3), 210–212.

Rickelman, R., & Henk, W. (1990). Children's literature and audio/visual technologies. *The Reading Teacher, 43*(9), 682–684.

Ross, E., & Roe, D. (1990). *An introduction to teaching the language arts*. Fort Worth, Tx: Holt, Rinehart and Winston.

Schindel, M. (1981). Children's literature on film: Through the audio-visual era to the age of telecommunications. *Annual of the modern language association division on children's literature and the children's literature association*. (Vol. 9). New Haven, CT: Yale University Press.

Scott, T., Cole, M., & Engel, M. (1992). Computers and education: A cultural constructionist perspective. In G. Grant (Ed.), *Review of research in education* (pp. 191–232) Washington, DC: American Educational Research Association.

Seminoff, N. (1986). Children's periodicals throughout the world: An overlooked educational resource. *The Reading Teacher, 39*(6), 889–894.

Sheingold, K. (1986). The microcomputer as a symbolic medium. In P. Campbell & G. Fein (Eds.), *Young children and microcomputers*. Englewood Cliffs, NJ: Prentice-Hall.

Signorielli, N. (1991). *A sourcebook on children and television*. New York: Greenwood Press.

Silvern, S. (1986). Video Games, affect, arousal and aggression. In P. Campbell & G. Fein (Eds.), *Young children and microcomputers*. Englewood Cliffs, NJ: Prentice-Hall.

Singer, J., & Singer, D. (1980). Implications of childhood television viewing for cognition, imagination and emotion. In J. Bryant & D. R. Anderson (Eds.), *Children's understanding of television: Research on attention and comprehension* (pp. 265–296). New York: Academic Press.

Singer, J., & Singer D. (1981). Television and reading in the development of imagination. *Annual of the modern language association division on children's literature and the children's literature association* (Vol. 9). New Haven, CT: Yale University Press.

Stoll, D. (Ed.). (1991). *Magazines for children*. Glassboro, NJ: Educational Press Association of America.

Swick, K. (1989). Appropriate uses of computers with young children. *Educational Technology, 29*(1), 7–13.

Swisher, R., Pye, L., Estes-Rickner, B., & Merriam, M. (1991). Magazine collections in elementary school library media centers. *School Library Journal, 37*(11), 40–43.

Thomas, J. (1987). Magazines to use with children in preschool and primary grades. *Young Children, 43*(1), 46–47.

Watson, J. A., Nita, R. & Shade, D. D., (1986). Educational issues concerning young children and microcomputers: Lego and Logo? *Early Child Development and Care, 23*, 229–316.

Wells, G. (1986). *The meaning makers: Children learning language and using language to learn*. London: Heinemann.

Wepner, S. (1992). Technology-based plans for primary students. *The Reading Teacher, 45*(6), 464–467.

Winn, M. (1977). *The plug-in drug*. New York: Viking Press.

Wright, J., & Anastasia, S. (1986). Play worlds and microworlds. In P. & G. Fein (Eds.), *Young children and microcomputers*. Englewood Cliffs, NJ: Prentice-Hall.

Wright, J., & Huston, A. (1983). A matter of form: Potentials of television for young viewers. *American Psychologist, 38*(7), 835–843.

Wood, I. (1992) Videos. In D. Donavin (Ed.), *American Library Association's best of the best for children*. New York: Random House.

CHILDREN'S LITERATURE REFERENCES

The authors and illustrators of children's books are listed, in all chapters, by their full names to help the reader become acquainted with them. If only one name is listed, the author also illustrated the book.

Andersen, Hans Christian. (1949). *The Emperor's New Clothes*. Illustrated by Nadine Bernond Westcott. Boston: Houghton Mifflin.

Andersen, Hans Christian. (1961). *Thumbelina*. Illustrated by Adrienne Adams. New York: Scribner.

Andersen, Hans Christian. (1965). *Ugly Duckling*. Illustrated by Tony Palazzo. New York: Scribner.

Bemelmans, Ludwig. (1977). *Madeline*. New York: Puffin Books.

Briggs, Raymond. (1978). *The Snowman*. New York: Random House.

Brown, Marc. (1990). *Arthur's Pet Business*. Boston: Joy Street Books.

Brown, Marcia. (1947). *Stone Soup*. New York: Scribner.

Burton, Virginia Lee. (1942). *Little House*. Boston: Houghton.

Dewey, Ariane. (1983). *Pecos Bill*. New York: Greenwillow.

Gág, Wanda. (1928). *Millions of Cats*. New York: Coward-McCann.

Geisel, Theodor (Dr. Seuss). (1957). *How the Grinch Stole Christmas*. New York: Random House.

Geisel, Theodor (Dr. Seuss). (1966). *If I Ran the Zoo*. New York: Random House.

Gramatkys, Hardie. (1939). *Little Toot*. New York: Putnam.

Grimm, Jacob. (1967). *Rumpelstiltskin*. Illustrated by Kinuko Craft. New York: Harcourt Brace Jovanovich.

Hoberman, Mary Ann. (1982). *A House Is a House for Me*. Illustrated by Betty Fraser. New York: Puffin Books.

Hutchins, Pat. (1986). *The Doorbell Rang*. New York: Greenwillow.

Irving, Washington. (1951). *The Legend of Sleepy Hollow*. New York: Macmillan.

Keats, Ezra Jack. (1962). *The Snowy Day*. New York: Viking Press.

Keats, Ezra Jack. (1967). *Peter's Chair*. New York: Harper & Row.

Keats, Ezra Jack. (1968). *A Letter to Amy*. New York: Harper & Row.

Keats, Ezra Jack. (1969). *Goggles*. New York: Macmillan.

Kipling, Rudyard. (1989). *The Elephant's Child*. Illustrated by Jan Mogensen. New York: Crocodile Books.

Lawson, Robert. (1962). *Ferdinand the Bull*. New York: Viking.

McCloskey, Robert. (1941). *Make Way for Ducklings*. New York: Viking.

McCloskey, Robert. (1943). *Homer Price*. New York: Viking Press.

Minarik, Else. (1957). *Little Bear*. Illustrated by Maurice Sendak. New York: Harper.

Parish, Peggy. (1971). *Come Back, Amelia Bedelia*. Illustrated by Wallace Tripp. New York: Harper & Row.

Rogers, Fred. (1985). *Going to Daycare*. Photographs by Jim Judkis. New York: G. P. Putnam.

Rogers, Fred. (1985). *Going to the Doctor*. New York: G. P. Putnam.

Rogers, Fred. (1988). *When a Pet Dies*. New York: G.P. Putnam.

Rylant, Cynthia. (1982). *When I Was Young in the Mountains*. New York: Dutton.

Rylant, Cynthia. (1985). *The Relatives Came*. New York: Bradbury Press.

Sendak, Maurice. (1963). *Where the Wild Things Are*. New York: Harper & Row.

Williams, Margery. (1922). *The Velveteen Rabbit or How Toys Become Real*. Illustrated by William Nicholson. New York: George H. Doran.

III

Literature Connections
to the Classroom,
the Curriculum
and the Home

*Designing an Inviting Classroom
for Children and Books*

*Five Early Childhood Teachers'
Stories—Children's Literature
in Classroom Practice*

Parents' Invitations to Literature

10

Designing an Inviting Classroom for Children and Books

Designing an Inviting Classroom for Children and Books

*P*art Three of *Stories: Children's Literature in Early Education* explains "Literature Connections to the Classroom, the Curriculum, and the Home." From this section, the reader will learn how to design an inviting physical environment, where books and stories in many forms are central to the classroom. Chapter 11 presents stories in which five early childhood teachers' face real-life classroom problems and dilemmas as they incorporate children's literature as the core of their programs. You will meet Anne, a lead teacher in a childcare center who develops methods to get parents interested in reading to their infants and toddlers. Emily is a preschool teacher who decides to include more literature in her classroom in some thought-provoking ways. Fran, an experienced kindergarten teacher, finds herself in a difficult position of dealing with a child who had been very successful in kindergarten, but who was having problems in first grade. April is moving to a new school to begin teaching in a multi-aged, continuous progress program in which the literacy program is literature-based. Lynnette, a third grade teacher, convinces the reading and language specialists in her school to stop delivering their services in a pull-out program and begin working with the children in the classroom.

Chapter 12 is devoted to ways teachers can work with parents to help them build literature-rich environments, inclusive of books, magazines, software, and videos, at home.

Mary Ann's Re-evaluation

Mary Ann was a kindergarten teacher for over twenty years. During those years she collected an array of valuable teaching tools, including bulletin board materials, manipulative items for display tables, children's books, and resource books for her own use. It seemed that each year her classroom grew smaller, the number of children increased and they were less interested in books. In the last few years, the school district incorporated more seat work for kindergartners and Mary Ann found herself storing away many of her "treasures" hoping to use them the next year.

While taking a course in literacy development and serving on a kindergarten curriculum revisions committee, Mary Ann decided to evaluate her classroom environment. Since one of her goals was to create an effective literacy environment, she began observing her children as they interacted with the materials she had included in her classroom. She questioned, "Are the children involved in hands-on literacy activities that are personally meaningful?," "Are the children choosing to go to the classroom library?," and "Does the environment encourage children's use of books throughout the day?"

The Classroom Environment

The environment communicates to young children what is important in the classroom. It conveys to young children what will be valued in this area and where certain activities will take place. The curriculum goals for children in the early childhood programs should directly influence the design, arrangement of the space, and the selection of materials that will be placed within the classroom. One of the long-term goals in an effective early childhood classroom is to nurture an interest in books and literature. For this goal to be accomplished, the space should be designed to clearly communicate to young children that this is a classroom where literature is a major component of the curriculum and that books are used frequently by both children and adults throughout the area.

Careful design of the space and appropriate selection of materials will encourage young children's literacy development and demonstrate that literature is the cement that holds their classroom together. The time and effort required to design a well-organized and attractive environment results in children who work more independently and with greater concentration. An integrated and evolving environment is designed to fit the characteristics of young children while still allowing the child to make changes to fit individual needs. These adjusting surroundings encourage children to move beyond the familiar situations to try new and challenging experiences (Rho & Drury, no date on publication).

THE FOCUS OF THE CLASSROOM: THE LIBRARY AREA

The classroom library is the central feature of an early childhood classroom, which is designed to encourage literacy. A library area that is carefully planned reflects the teacher's commitment to literacy and understanding of the unique needs of young children. An appropriate environment can draw young children to the library and help them find pleasure from interacting with books at their own pace. As young children become more involved with books for longer periods of time, they become more engaged with the literature. This deeper experience with books leads to more voluntary reading (Cullinan, 1989). How then, can young children be drawn into the library area and encouraged to become involved with books? An environment that is designed around the characteristics of young children can lead them to choose the library and enjoy their book experiences in this important area.

Characteristics of Young Children That Influence Library Design

Characteristics of young children as learners can be used to guide decision making:

1. Young children are active learners who construct knowledge as they interact physically and socially with their friends and the environment.

2. The physical development needs of young children require design considerations.

3. Socially, children need private and public space to be alone or to interact with peers and adults.

4. Young children are learners who rely heavily on visual information and hands-on exploration.

A classroom library that meets young children's needs must take into account their learning approaches.

Young Children Are Active Learners

Library corners are often considered the inactive and quiet area of the classroom. Perhaps this is one reason that Rosenthal (1973) and Morrow (1983) found the area to be the least frequently chosen center in the classroom. Rather than being an inactive area, the library center should convey the message that exciting things can happen here with books and active participation encouraged (Dodge, 1988).

To fully take advantage of young children's active natures, we must reexamine the size, arrangement, and contents of the library area. A larger library space shows young children that the area is valued by the teacher as an important component in the classroom. In addition, the larger space allows for the expanded activity level and more opportunities for a variety of interactions to take place in the library. The arrangement of the shelving and seating, as well as the placement of the contents of the center, can lead to active learning.

In addition to being concerned about the arrangement of the physical environment, teachers who want to design more effective environments need to plan for young children's more active participation with the books and materials in the area. Books and materials need to be placed so that they are easy to use. As Hickman states, "Books are not simply accessible but unavoidable [1983, p. 3]." Space needs to be available so children can respond naturally with movement to manipulative books. In the section on literacy materials that follows, there are numerous descriptions of books, displays, and props for story retelling that recognize the young child's need for active, physical manipulation of materials and responses to books.

Young Children's Physical Needs

Young children's small body proportions necessitate that the library area be designed in special ways to be comfortable for two- to eight-year-olds. It is important to include seating in this area to allow small children to be relaxed as they browse

through books. Morrow (1982) found that only half of the early childhood classrooms she studied had seating for the children in the library area.

Active young children change their positions frequently as they read books and therefore need a variety of seating choices. Pillows, low chairs, bean bags, low benches, stools, or floor cushions provide both low and flexible seating arrangements. Children can place small pillows covered with different fabric under their heads or pile them high for propping. Mats or air mattresses can be used to lounge on while enjoying an interesting story. These smaller moveable items allow the children to arrange different formations and spaces, giving them a variety of options for exploring books and props while choosing the positions they prefer.

YOUNG CHILDREN ARE SOCIAL

The classroom library should be a special space for sharing a book with a friend, a small group, or an adult. Talking about a book or "reading" to others makes this shared experience pleasurable and motivating (Raines & Isbell, 1991). A space large enough to accommodate five or six children allows room for movement and interaction. Braided or area rugs seem to draw children together to discuss a book or role-play a scene from a story. Small, partially enclosed spaces just right for two children, can also lead to cooperative reading.

In one library area, an old block storage unit was turned into an interesting and cozy space by covering the walls with reflective contact paper, adding a lawn chair pad and several small pillows covered in different textured fabrics. Inside, two children stretched out to share *Color Dance* by Ann Jonas. The book rested between the two children where first one child "read" the book and the other pointed out the pictures that explained the story. Then they switched roles with the other pointing to the appropriate pictures while the other child "read" the story. In this social interaction, the book became the focus of their attention and sustained their interest for at least two repeated readings.

Joint book experiences build positive attitudes toward reading as an enjoyable activity to share with a friend. When children do not initiate partner book experiences on their own, the teacher can suggest that they read a favorite book to a friend or tell a story to a small group. Preschool and kindergarten children increased their interactions with books when given these assignments by their teachers (Isbell, Fox, & Floyd, 1990; Martinez & Teale, 1988).

An adult in the library area encourages young children to share their ideas and have a person to read the books they select (Raines, 1990), and an adult reading model provides a powerful influence on the book interest behavior of young children. When children see the adult reading for pleasure, finding information from books, or reading to others, they imitate this behavior. They observe that reading is an activity that captures the interest of important adults. A volunteer or aide can be a special addition to the library area reading a book or sharing a favorite children's book. Adult readers are models for young children who are developing their interest in books and who are beginning to understand how reading can enrich their world.

While the library center can be a social area for children, they also need a place where books can be enjoyed privately. A private space needs clearly defined boundaries in order to function effectively. This separate place can be achieved by simply adding a large cardboard box with openings to let in light for reading. A more complex individual space can be created by the addition of a small rocket ship with detailed designs and twinkling lights or dome tent equipped with a battery operated lantern. These private spaces communicate that reading independently is a special thing to do. By providing the young child with a cozy place, she or he comes to understand that reading a book at one's own pace and looking at the pictures again and again can be an enjoyable experience. Inside this private space, the young child can retreat from "the traffic" while enjoying a book in a personal way.

YOUNG CHILDREN ARE VISUAL LEARNERS

Young children are visual learners who learn while examining and exploring appealing books, displays, equipment, and props. Recognizing that young children are visual learners means that the teacher should design an attractive classroom space with enticing displays, considering the visual impact of color, textures, and contents on the library area. Because of the young child's small size, short height, and movement patterns, their visual space differs greatly from adults. To plan appropriate displays and arrangement, adults need to view the area from the child's eye level and consider the space the child's body occupies, the materials and equipment they can reach easily, and what they see when they visually scan the space (Loughlin & Martin, 1987). A poster that may seem interesting to the teacher may provide young children with a boring view of the white border on the picture. Another concern is placing the literacy materials at a level so the children can visually explore their options without strain. These considerations will help the library area become a more pleasant place to spend time.

An old film strip projector in the book area can provide additional visual stimulation for the children in the center. The teacher, a volunteer, or a child can turn the filmstrip and see the story presented in yet another way. By adding the accompanying book to the area, the child can make the connection between the visual presentation and the printed content. A filmstrip such as Tafuri's *Have You Seen My Duckling?* combined with the book presents the story and illustrations in a larger form and provides opportunity for several children to see the content together. In a classroom where a projector and filmstrip were added, two four-year-olds were observed trying to figure out how to coordinate the pictures with those in the book. They talked about the visual details of the different pictures in the book and film until they successfully synchronized the two presentations. This problem solving by the children identified the importance of the illustrations to the story content. There are also 16 mm films available from public libraries that can be used in this area. A large showing of Lionni's *Swimmy* on a wall in the library area can provide another visual experience for the young children. During a showing of the *Swimmy* film, four young children were observed swimming through the colors and designs projected on a low wall in the library area. The children were moving inside the story and illustrations in a way never before possible. This experience captured their interest in the visual content while providing them with an opportunity to use their imaginations as they became small fish swimming in a colorful ocean.

A variety of colors and textures makes the book area visually appealing to young children. Bright colors stimulate intensive reactions, and used in small areas, accent interesting book displays. The bright accents draw children to these areas and help identify specific activities to be enjoyed. The use of neutral colors in larger spaces provides interesting contrast to the display areas, while patterns and designs add visual interest.

The use of a variety of textures can also add to the center's visual appeal. Covering walls and screens with carpet, contact paper, fabric, or tile helps children determine the activity level of the area. Soft textures added to the library help children feel secure, while soft rugs and cuddling toys add to the visual appeal and comfort level. When Jason was in the library area, he selected Freeman's *Corduroy* to read. Before he began to read, he went to the large laundry basket in the library filled with soft stuffed toys and carefully selected a well-loved teddy bear. He then took the book and the teddy bear to the private space where he turned the pages of the book while stroking the lovable teddy bear. Obviously the combination of book and fuzzy bear made this reading experience more enjoyable for him.

Design Considerations for the Library Center

When developing an effective library center, additional aspects should be considered. The placement of the center, displays, and materials available within the space will greatly influence young children's use of the library area.

PLACEMENT OF THE LIBRARY CENTER

The location of the library center in the classroom demonstrates the value the teacher places on the area and influences whether children choose to visit the center. The library area does not have to be in the corner of the classroom, but can be even more influential and tempting in the center of the room. A centrally located library functions as the hub of classroom activity (Stauffer, 1980). This placement emphasizes the importance of the library and the usefulness of books throughout the curriculum.

The boundaries of the classroom library can be defined by walls, storage units, or folding screens on at least three sides. It should be situated away from high noise-producing areas like blocks and the sand and water table, as well as away from large motor activities. To provide a sense of enclosure, the walls need be only 2.5 ft. to 3 ft. high. This height will not interfere with the teacher's view in the area but will help the children feel less distracted by other activities occurring in the classroom. The space can also be defined by draping fabric from the ceiling to make the area feel more intimate and special. Fabric pieces also add space for additional display of book covers and other story related items. Canopies, parachutes, and mobiles hung from the ceiling provide spatial variations and identification of the boundaries of the area (Greenman, 1988). Fabric-covered ceiling tiles can be suspended from the ceiling to identify the space while providing some insulation from sound produced in other parts of the classroom.

It is particularly important to consider available lighting for a library area where reading is encouraged. To avoid a dark, gloomy library area, it may be necessary to provide additional lighting. A floor lamp, clamp on lights, or spotlights can be used to highlight a specific portion of the space, to focus on an interesting display, or to direct light in a private cubby. A mixture of florescent light, natural light, and local lighting can create a variety of reading spaces, allowing the children to choose the source they find most effective and comfortable.

Arrangement of the Library Area

Regardless of the placement of the library center and whether the teacher is able to design a new space or use existing space in a different way, additional concerns about the arrangements of the contents of the center need to be considered. Early childhood educators want young children to feel a sense of control of their environment and to be able to use the materials independently with as little teacher assistance as possible. Any provisions for arranging, retrieving, and storing the contents of the library center should be guided by the goal of developing independence through child-directed activity. Books and literacy props should be arranged so that they invite interaction; but they should also be easily manipulated and stored so that the children feel comfortable in retrieving the materials and in returning them to their designated spaces. In other areas of the classroom, such as those designated for blocks and puzzles, there are special shelves, bins, and trays that children understand contain specific materials. The library center

was very evident that books with interesting covers were selected significantly more frequently than those without visual appeal. Book jackets can be laminated and attached to blank book covers to give the children visual clues about the contents and to capture their interest. If commercial book jackets are not available or have been lost, the children can become illustrators and draw covers for the books before they are placed in the collection. The teacher or a child can write the title of the book, which will help in the selection process and will encourage print awareness.

The library might also include a book check-out area. This addition provides opportunities for children to write their names, stamp the date, and play the roles of librarian and book user. The materials needed for this activity will include large blank cards placed in the backs of the books, a stamp pad, date stamp, pencils, magic markers, and a card file. Visits to a school library and public library help young children understand how the process works so they can role-play the activity in their classroom library.

also needs to function this efficiently and effectively for the children's use of the books, support equipment, and literacy props.

BOOK ARRANGEMENTS

Books should be easily accessible to young children in open shelving units and on low tables. Recommended shelf heights are 2 ft. 11 in. for toddlers, 3 ft. 1 in. for three- and four-year-olds and 3 ft. 3 in. for five-year-olds (Moore, Lane, Hill, Cohen, & McGinty, 1979). By adding additional height to shelves, 3 ft. 5 in. to 3 ft. 7 in., older children will be able to select books more easily. Visual and physical accessibility allow the children to find and select the books they want while encouraging independence and helping sustain interest in personally selected books.

Young children need to see the covers of the books and not the back spines neatly stacked together on the shelf. Interesting covers draw children in to handle the books and explore their content. Children do not select books with blank covers that lack identifying illustrations (Isbell, Fox, & Floyd, 1990). From observations of young children involved in book selection in the library area, it

LITERATURE RELATED DISPLAYS IN THE CLASSROOM LIBRARY

Displays in the library influence the area's attractiveness and children's interest in spending time there (Schickendanz, 1986). Literature related bulletin boards and posters can attract children to the library and spark their desire to read the featured books. Displays should be colorful, changed frequently, and relate to the specific books in the class collection.

Featured literature can be a "Book of the Week" or "Character of the Week," or works by important authors and illustrators. Selections can be highlighted by displaying drawings of main characters, story sequence, or special events. Presenting interesting portions from the book or unique illustrations will stimulate the children's curiosity about the book and encourage their involvement.

Working displays encourage children's physical interactions with books and their related materials. For example, a wall hanging with pockets can contain a place for the book and additional slots might hold items used to retell the story. One teacher created a wall hanging and used it to feature some of the children's favorite books. When she used Slobodkina's *Caps for Sale,* she filled the pockets with a variety of caps. When she featured Brett's *The Mitten,* she filled the pockets with mittens of different sizes and colors. This unique combination of books and props is especially effective with young children, for it links the text to concrete objects that are represented in the story. It encourages development of symbolic representation, since the pictures in the book are understood in relation to the real objects in the young children's world.

Unusual presentations of books also invite children to examine the content. A refrigerator box with several large holes to let in the light can be used as

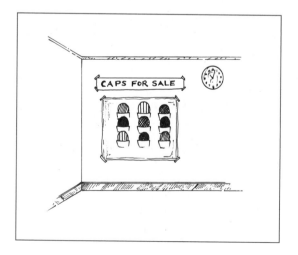

a special place for previewing a book. A sign on the outside of the box announces "New book just arrived." Placing a book inside this box with a flashlight may entice young children to explore the new addition to the library center. In a kindergarten classroom, the teacher created a book place by covering a table with a green sheet. Jessica crawled into the preview space after a new book, *Someday a Tree,* was placed under the table with a battery operated light. She spent several minutes examining the book on her own, turning the pages from beginning to end. She then called two other children, Ben and Allison, to join her to read the new book. This reading and rereading by three children was stimulated by the addition of a unique book preview space in their classroom.

PROPS FOR STORY RETELLING

Young children choose the library corner to have opportunities to read books, hear stories, and engage in story retelling. Morrow and Weinstein (1982) found that story cassette tapes were often responsible for children selecting the library area. Story tapes allow active children to manipulate a cassette player and control the starting and stopping of the story. Researchers also found that once the children were in the area, they interacted with other books in the collection.

When several children want to listen to a book, the listening station can be set up with headphones to encourage the sharing of story and book. The tape collection available can include both commercial materials and teacher-made tapes. Children will select their favorite stories and listen to them often. Tapes and accompanying books placed on a low table or shelf allow children to see their options and make personal choices. They can also be stored together in clear plastic bags and hung on pegs to vary the display and identify the literature available. Opportunities to make critical listening choices based on individual and small group preferences help build young children's confidence and encourage their attention to books.

In addition, a combination of tapes and books allows children to follow along with the text as it is being read and begin to establish the relationship of spoken words and print. Tapes of teachers reading are especially appealing to children of this age. After hearing his teacher read a book recorded on tape, a young child said, "Teacher, you are reading in the tape player." Other readers can also make tapes that will expose the children to different reading models, unique voices, and add variety to the collection. Parents, other adults, older siblings, and staff members in the school enjoy being asked to contribute their recorded readings of favorite books.

Flannel and magnetic boards are also inviting materials to use in the library center. The felt characters and magnetic items should relate to the books in the library and be adapted to books previously read aloud by the teacher. These items encourage the children to recall the characters and rehearse retelling the story while developing a sense of the underlying story structure.

The library corner should contain a large flannel board and materials for group story retelling, but it might also include small flannel boards for use by individuals. The child can dramatize the story privately and build confidence without concern for an audience response. When they are ready to share the story with a group, the larger flannel board is available for their presentation.

Flannel boards can be designed as freestanding or placed on an easel or chalkboard. A simple flannel board can be constructed by using a heavy piece of cardboard, display board, or plywood. The base is covered with flannel or felt fabric, which is then pulled smooth across the front and stapled on the back side. This attachment can be made more secure by adding cloth tape over the stapled area. It is important not to make the flannel board so large that it will make it too difficult for the teacher to move the board to different locations in the classroom. Fabric colors of light blue, light green, or a neutral beige should be used as these colors best serve as a background for most stories and will not distract from the story characters. Individual felt boards can be made using a smaller piece of cardboard or small cardboard boxes. Boxes used in gift wrapping can often be donated by local department or discount stores, or collected by parents. A benefit to using this type of flannel board is that the boxes can serve as both the story surface and storage of the story pieces. Felt glued on the box cover creates the story surface while the pieces can be stored inside the box when not in use. A printed story title on the side of the box will assist the child or teacher in making story selections and in organizing the storage of the materials. Flannel boards and story pieces are also available commercially from school suppliers. These options can provide additional materials for children to use in the retelling of stories.

Flannel-board story pieces can be made quickly and attractively by using interfacing fabric used in sewing. By placing the fabric over a page in a book and tracing the outline of the character, a pattern can be drawn and later colored with permanent markers. Characters and story props can also be made using construction paper covered with clear contact paper or laminating material. These items can be made to adhere to the flannel board if they have strips of felt or course sandpaper attached to the backs.

Figure 10.1 Suggested Flannel or Magnetic Stories

The Teeny Tiny Woman, Jill Bennett
The Turnip, Janine Domanska
Ask Mr. Bear, Marjorie Flack
Pocket for Corduroy, Don Freeman
Dandelion, Don Freeman
The Gingerbread Boy, Paul Galdone
The Little Red Hen, Paul Galdone
Fat Cat: A Danish Folktale, Jack Kent
Stone Soup, Ann McGovern
The House That Jack Built, Rodney Peppe
Caps For Sale, Esphyr Slobodkina
Over in the Meadow, Olive A. Wadsworth

Since these flannel board pieces are so simple to make, the teacher can provide many story selections and rotate them for the children to use.

Shaw's *It Looked Like Spilt Milk* can be effectively presented on a flannel board and the simple white clouds can be used for creative problem solving. By including additional felt clouds, not pictured in the book, young children develop their creative thoughts by imagining what else they see in the forms. Cumulative tales, such as *There Was an Old Lady Who Swallowed a Fly*, can be effectively adapted to flannel board presentations.

Magnetic stories provide an additional opportunity for children to retell a story while examining the properties of magnets. An inexpensive cookie sheet can be used to display magnet story items in the library corner and can be easily manipulated by the storyteller. Using a different tool, such as magnetic pieces, to assist in telling a story often captures the curiosity of the young children in the library area. Magnetic stories are easily made using poster board and a magnetic strip obtained from a craft store. Cookie sheet stories can be used by the teacher, groups of children, or an individual child to add variety to story presentations.

Whether using flannel board stories or magnetic boards, teachers need to consider ways to display and store the materials so that the children can view, retrieve, and replace them easily. Some teachers use pocket folders or clear plastic bags, and others use plastic boxes, which can be stacked in the area. Attention to the organization and storage of these materials and books can assist the children in making selections and encourage their use.

Puppets are an additional storytelling tool. They fascinate young children and are an exciting addition to the library area. The puppets can relate to characters from the books in the collection or be a simple sock puppet who narrates a variety of stories. Flexible puppets allow the children to creatively decide how they will be used in the story context. When Jason was in the library area, he used the generic sock puppet to be the storyteller, but Lucendia used the same puppet to be the old

man in the *Magic Fish* by Littledale. (See Chapter 8 for a more complete discussion of puppetry.)

Story boxes are also creative additions to the library area. Collections of interesting items that relate to a specific story can be placed in a shoe box, labeled, and displayed on a low shelf. Young children then explore the contents of the box and use their imaginations to retell the story. One teacher created a story box of Krauss' *The Carrot Seed* containing the book and props, such as a package of seeds, a small watering can, a toy spade, and a large plastic carrot. Using the props, three young children recreated the planting of the carrot seed. Tim and Maria assumed the roles of the mother and father and repeated the phrase "It Won't Come up!" At the conclusion of the play sequence, however, they were very anxious to help pull up the large plastic carrot that was included in the story box. Through dramatizations using books and real objects, children give concrete meaning to the story sequence and relate the props to items identified in text.

Another story box that the children enjoyed was based on the funny tale *It Could Always Be Worse* by Zemach. This box contained small plastic animals representing the ones the old man took to his house to make it quieter after getting advice from the wise man. David and Jeremy used the story box, a small covered cardboard box, as

the house where the man lived with his noisy family. They placed one animal at a time into the house, while making the appropriate sounds for each addition, and then together made the noises created by all the animals in the house. After all the animals had been included in the box, Jeremy, in the role of the wise man, said, "Now go home and take all the animals out." This story enactment helped the children understand the moral of the story, that "it could always be worse."

Children can listen to and retell stories in a variety of forms using tapes, flannel board characters, puppets, and story boxes that relate to the books in the classroom collection. This combination of materials and books increases the complexity of the children's play and promotes sustained involvement in the literacy activity. The variety of visual, auditory, and tactile stimulation attracts and helps maintain the interest of young children in an exciting story-filled environment.

A library area that is well designed and organized clearly indicates to young children that this a place were books and literature can be enjoyed: They know reading is a valuable activity in their classroom.

SPACE DESIGN FOR OTHER PARTS OF THE CLASSROOM

In a literacy classroom, books are used by both children and adults throughout the space. For this to be accomplished, the classroom must be organized so it is functional for both the children and adults in the environment. Is there a place for the teacher to store her or his collection of nursery rhymes that will be used in circle time? Is there a place to display reference books that can be used in finding answers to the thousands of questions posed by the young children? Are tapes available for the children to choose with a cassette recorder they can use easily?

ESSENTIAL CLASSROOM STORAGE

The varying needs of the adults and children in the classroom indicate the necessity for both open and closed storage. Closed storage is designed for adult use where materials, such as permanent magic markers, can be kept out of reach and sight. Open storage units place items low and make them easily accessible for young children while encouraging their independent use of the materials. Labels and/or symbols increase the children's understanding of the placement of book related materials so they can use and return them to the designated areas. It is also helpful if storage can be located near where the book, prop, or activity is used by the children. Clustering materials and work areas communicates to children which activities are available while they retain the control of their selection and participation. Transportable storage can also be used to change areas or redesign their use. Portable storage units can be as simple as mesh baskets or as complex as an old trunk where books and props are kept for story reading and dramatization.

In a classroom where young children must share space, it is important for each child to have a personal storage place. The young child will know here is a place that belongs to her or him that allows for responsibility for personal items. Here the child can keep coats, projects, books, and notes written to friends or parents (Vergeront, 1987).

ORDERED BUT CHANGING

Adequate storage allows the teacher to change materials in the classroom and centers rather than leaving everything out all of the time. The display of too many materials can overwhelm visually oriented young children and confuse them when making choices. By rotating materials and books out of storage, new interest is ignited each time they are reintroduced. A new book, an interesting puppet, or a slate board can encourage young children to participate in self-initiated activity. The effective early childhood classroom has order but does not become stagnant. In an interesting classroom, the environmental changes demonstrate the flexibility of space, materials, and uses. It is also acceptable for a young child to take an

interesting book from the library area to the block area or combine a creative drama with reading. If reading and literature are seen as a part of life rather than an activity contained in one spot, children have an opportunity to experience that understanding in many places within the classroom. When spaces and materials change regularly and in small ways, they spark new interest and capture the children's curiosity.

Bulletin Boards and Displays

Wall hangings, clustered objects, records of shared experiences, and bulletin boards also identify spaces. Signs help young children know that the space is theirs and useful for their activities. A creative bulletin board draws young children's attention to books, authors, and illustrators. Book jackets and illustrations are simple displays that can be easily changed by the teacher or by the children. For young children, the displays may relate to a theme, support a unit of study, or focus on an author or book character. The literature display can create visual interest by varying the background color and texture with materials such as foil, fabric, packing strips, egg cartons, and contact paper.

Working bulletin boards match the active learning style of young children. These boards are designed to involve children in interacting with the display. Here movable doors can be opened to see book characters or scenes from a story. The manipulation of these items can capture children's curiosity while actively involving them in the exploration of books.

Young children can also create wonderful displays that relate to the literature they are reading. They can illustrate their "cherished" book using tempera paint, magic markers, or a three-dimensional display using clay. Child-made displays are not only attractive, but they also demonstrate that the teacher values the children's work. Children's illustration can be framed or matted to complement their work and communicate to everyone, "Here is a special creation." Literature related pictures displayed at the door leading into the classroom signals that in this classroom illustrators and authors are held in high esteem. These changing displays will also draw curious young children to examine new books, reread books, and study illustrations.

A clothes line could be strung across the classroom for display with clothes pins available for use by the children to place story cards in sequence. Books authored by children in the classroom can be placed in plastic bags and hung for others to view. These books can also be borrowed to be read and provide inspiration for other children.

Expansion to Adjoining Areas: Dramatic Play Centers

Designing an environment that celebrates literature requires the enrichment of supportive areas such as dramatic play centers. Since young children assimilate their world through play and combine language with activity in these centers, it is an extremely effective place to add books and printed material. Selecting literature that follows the theme of their play, such as Hine's *Daddy Makes the Best Spaghetti*, provides young children in the housekeeping center with an opportunity to see pictures and words that represent families as they are involved in meaningful activity. This combination provides an avenue for young children to use in developing symbolic relationships through play and appropriate literature.

Including newspapers or phone books in this area exposes the children to functional print in a home setting and encourages them to assume the roles of mother and father using the items. Appropriate literature can extend the play of young children in the housekeeping center. By adding the book *The Man Who Didn't Wash His Dishes* by Krasilovsky and additional dishes as props, the play may change and new vocabulary used by the children. In the block center, Hutchins' *Changes Changes* can provide stimulation for play by visually presenting many different formations, including a house, fire truck, and boat. By combining the book and block building, young children begin to make the connection of real objects and pictorial symbolic representation. In a sand/water center, dePaolo's *The Quicksand Book* provides new possibilities for play.

The inclusion of literature and other printed materials in thematic centers demonstrates to young children that books are a part of all activities in their classroom and their world is filled with literacy opportunities. The veterinarian center and the book *Animal Doctors: What Do They Do?* by Greene can increase young children's understanding of the activities that occur in this setting while communicating that books provide information. In the veterinarian center, Kuklin's *Taking My Cat to the Vet* can add a book connection to the sociodramatic play. Cookbooks and recipe cards added to the bakery center demonstrates the usefulness of books in a concrete way. Lillegard describes the roles of the workers in a bakery in *I Can Be a Baker*. In a dance studio center, Gauche's *Dance, Tanya*, scarfs, and old dance costumes, as well as a recording of *Swan Lake* promotes creative movement. This book provides inspiration for creative expression while nurturing an interest in the arts.

These suggestions are supported by Morrow's (1990) research on literacy and dramatic play centers. In her experimental study, books and literacy materials were added to both thematic centers and dramatic play centers. She concluded that thematic centers stimulated the largest increase in the reading and literacy activities of the young children that she studied. Their literacy activities were focused on the themes, based on meaning, and increased their voluntary involvement with books.

THE ADJOINING WRITING CENTER

The writing center is another important part of every classroom designed to nurture the development of literacy through literature. In this center young children become the writers and creators of stories. Through effective design of the center's boundaries and displays, it is visually apparent to the young children that here writers can create individually, with a co-writer or in small groups. To encourage the beginning author, the space should be arranged to facilitate writing opportunities that match the abilities and interest of young children. Appropriate height and writing surfaces are needed so that children can stand while writing, walk away from their compositions, and return to writing after some physical activity. A table appropriate for standing activities should be approximately 17 in. for toddlers, 20 in. for pre-schoolers, and 24 in. for primary-aged children.

A variety of writing tools should be organized so they are easy to find and children can determine the writing instrument that works best for them or matches what they would like to create. Placing varied writing tools, such as magic markers, colored pencils, magnet letters, and chalk in clear plastic containers makes the children's choices more visible. Wall areas and peg boards can also be used to hang pockets or plastic baskets for easily accessible storage for writing tools. Using color-coded containers, such as tubs, crates, and boxes, keeps materials separated and easier for young children to use independently. These organized materials help the children keep track of materials and assume responsibility for their use and care.

A variety of sizes, colors, and textures of papers should be stacked in baskets or separated on shelves so the children will see what is available for selection. The varied options of materials provide additional stimulation for the beginning author. Stationery, greeting cards, and computer paper can be added to the traditional lined and unlined paper, colored construction paper, and news print, which is often included in the center. Chart paper, magic slates, and chalkboards also provide different surfaces for young children to use in their writing and will capture the children's attention because they are novel items. A "writing wall" can be constructed by covering one wall of the center with newsprint. The wall encourages children to construct stories together and provide large illustrations to accompany their writing. This technique is especially effective with young children who have less refined small-motor coordination and will feel frustrated when working on small pieces of paper with small writing tools.

Included in this area should be places where the children can store their work and return on another

day to complete their writing or editing. Cereal boxes can be covered with contact paper and decorated with the author's name for effective individual storage. Folders, files, and notebooks are other provisions that can be used to save and safely store the valuable writing. Low bulletin boards in the writing center can also provide a place for the display of the children's work when they feel it is ready for public viewing.

Adding a computer and/or typewriter to the center will provide another tool for children to use as they become writers. This equipment should work effectively and be simple to use to allow the children to be successful in using them. Toy typewriters, keyboards, or nonworking equipment are too frustrating for young children and discourages their interests in using the real equipment.

A small round table with several chairs in the writing area encourages partner or small-group writing and story sharing with a friend. This table can also be used by an adult, teacher, or volunteer who can become an important role model for writing. This adult writing model writes his or her own stories or assists the children with their beginning efforts. The writing adult demonstrates that writing is important and a valuable activity.

Other materials that will be helpful for older children are dictionaries, thesaurus, and rebus books, as well as books and magazines written by other children. This center helps make the connection that books are works written by real people and young children can be successful authors too.

THE ILLUSTRATORS' CENTER

Some of the most unusual ways teachers find to designate space can be seen in the effective illustrators' center. This creative area allows the teacher to experiment with different materials and techniques to communicate to young children that this is a space where they can set their creative thinking free and that unusual ideas are valued and encouraged. The possibilities for boundaries, displays, and activities are limitless and challenge both the teacher and children to explore the world of creative expression in new ways.

The illustrators' center should be designed to encourage creative productions. Here the space should be defined in unique ways that communicate to young children that creative illustrators work in this area. Unusual low walls can be made of plastic six-pack rings, egg cartons, fence wire woven with crepe paper, or lattice dividers, and demonstrate the creative problem-solving abilities of the teacher.

The illustrators' center should be located close to the library area and designed to provide creative inspiration for the children. Young children often draw their story or add pictures to stories dictated to teachers before they write independently. As they move from scribblers to writers, they begin to understand that their marks communicate meaning. Often young children are more interested in the pictures than the story (Lamme, 1989). By providing many forms of media in the art area, young children come to understand the pictures in their favorite books and the contribution of the illustrations to the story. By exploring firsthand techniques and materials used by illustrators, young children see that their stories can have many forms. While examining the crayon illustrations of Nancy Winslow and the collages of Carle and Lionni, children begin to appreciate their art work and understand the interrelationship with the story. In the illustrator area, young children can use techniques and tools that they select to communicate their story, while examining books with different illustrators. The children may compare the illustrations of Jan Brett and Yaroslava in Brett's and Tresselt's different versions of *The Mitten* and then create a third version uniquely their own.

The display spaces in this area should focus on color, texture, and design so that the children's illustration are complemented. Framing the children's illustrations is an especially effective tool in demonstrating the importance and beauty of their work. Frames can be made by the teacher from poster board and kept available so the children can select the design they would like to use with their illustration. Frames can be precut from poster board and constructed in sizes to match the paper available in the art area. Wood grain contact paper, foil, wrapping paper, wallpaper samples, and varied fabric are just a few of the options available to make the frames more attractive and realistic. The addition of these frames to the children's illustrations communicates to them that their work is special and being displayed in an important way.

This area can also be visually enhanced by displaying illustrations as mobiles hung from the ceilings at varying levels. This demonstrates yet another variation in the use of classroom space. The illustrator center could also contain an art gallery constructed from a large refrigerator box and smaller sized boxes grouped together to form a display area for illustrated treasures. Three-dimensional display units can be painted by the children with tempera paint or covered with paper, scrapes of fabric, and trim. Slightly crumbled, colored tissue paper applied with thinned white glue provides another background for their creations. This unique structure, three-dimensional and visually attractive, provides another avenue for encouraging creative writing and illustrating by young children.

Mary Ann's Success Story

Teacher success stories are measured by the children's effective uses of the space, books, and literacy props found in the learning environment. Mary Ann's success story was based on her use of some guiding principles to systematically examine her classroom and the changes she made for the children's literacy development. First, Mary Ann used the developmental characteristics of the young learner as the foundation for understanding the changes she chose to make. The basis for changes in her classroom came from recalling that young children are active, have unique physical needs, are social while also having a need for privacy and interaction with peers and adults, and that they are visual learners.

After consideration of these characteristics, Mary Ann decided she would create a new area in her classroom. During a visit to another school, she had seen a loft that was used as a play area. She, however, envisioned her use of this special area as a combination classroom library for groups of children upstairs and a private reading space below. She brainstormed the construction possibilities with her husband and a family friend who eventually helped construct the space from scrap lumber and lattice work at a cost of under $250. While not every teacher has a friend who is a carpenter or the resources to construct a loft, often a building project can be accomplished with parents, volunteers, or vocational students. A loft can provide more usable space in a crowded classroom and can identify the library area as special while remaining an essential part of the classroom.

Second, Mary Ann examined the design criteria for the library center, including placement, space, seating, and lighting. She added new elements to her collection of books, tapes, equipment, and props that she knew would engage the children's attention and sustain their interest in the literature. She arranged these materials so that they were easily accessible to the children because she understood their importance to the success of the library center. Mary Ann found that a library center that is well designed can attract children to the area where they will remain and enjoy books. The area can be the catalyst for literacy activities that are both active and meaningful to the young child. Here young children can participate in reading and language activities that develop their sense of story. Whether they are hearing a story read for the first time by the teacher, exploring a new book because of the appealing cover, or retelling a favorite folktale with flannel board pieces, the library can become an inviting place where child and story meet.

Mary Ann also studied her total classroom environment to determine where additional opportunities for interaction with books could be included. She wanted literature experiences to be happening throughout the classroom so more space and time could be used in these important activities. She understood the importance of play in the development of young children and identified dramatic play centers as a critical area where she would add books and printed materials. Her decision resulted in young children using books in meaningful ways as they read and played in traditional and thematic centers.

Finally, Mary Ann expanded her existing writing center to include many new tools and materials for children's selection in their writing process. She included books, magazines, and other children's writing as additional stimulus for their authorship. She also viewed the art center in a new way, transforming it to include an illustrator area where children could compose stories through pictures. This new addition helped young children understand the importance of illustrations while building their confidence as creators and illustrators.

After careful evaluation and appropriate changes, Mary Ann's kindergarten classroom was transformed into an active literacy environment where young children chose to go to the library center, select books to read in dramatic centers, and write and illustrate their own stories. Literature experiences in her classroom were not accidental or occasional, but rather major ingredients in a classroom environment that successfully nurtured the literacy development of her students.

SUGGESTED LEARNING EXPERIENCES

1. Visit an early childhood classroom and draw the layout of the space, including centers, circle area, and storage. Observe how children are using space and materials.

2. Interview three early childhood teachers. Ask them "Do you have a library area in your classroom? Do the children chose to go to that area? What books and materials are in the library area?"

3. Observe primary-aged children in a classroom library. List ways the classroom areas could be changed to stimulate interest in books and reading.

4. Volunteer to participate in a classroom library for several days. Take a textbook for reading but be available to read to the children if they so request. Write a paragraph describing the children's reactions to having an adult in the library area.

5. Create a bulletin board for a kindergarten teacher that features a book or author. After the board is displayed, ask the teacher to evaluate the effectiveness of the design.

6. Construct a flannel board that can be used in an early childhood classroom. Begin collecting stories that would be appropriate for use with the flannel board.

7. Create a design for a special space to introduce new books to young children. Include the materials that are needed for the construction and operation. Share the design in class and discuss the implementation of these ideas.

8. List free and inexpensive items that could be used for storage in an early childhood classroom. Combine this list with other class members to produce an extensive number of possible items.

9. Design an illustrator's or writer's area for a primary classroom. Draw a layout of the area and list the materials that can be included.

10. Visit an early childhood classroom and observe the design of the environment, the literacy opportunities for the children, and the library area. Determine the message the classroom communicates to young children.

REFERENCES

Cullinan, B. E. (1989). *Literature and the child.* New York: Harcourt Brace & Jovanovich.

Dodge, D. T. (1988). *The creative curriculum for early childhood.* Washington, DC: Teaching Strategies.

Greenman, J. (1988). *Caring spaces, learning places: Children's environments that work.* Redmond, WA: Exchange Press.

Hickman, J. (1983). Classrooms that help children like books. In N. Roser & M. Frith (Eds.), *Children's choices: Teaching with books children like* (pp. 1–11). Newark, DE: International Reading Association.

Isbell, R. T., Fox, J., & Floyd, S. (1990). Factors influencing young children's selection and use of books and related materials. Johnson City, TN: Center for Early Childhood Learning and Development. East Tennessee State University.

Lamme, L. L. (1989). Illustratorship: A key facet of whole language instruction. *Childhood Education, 66*(2), 83–86.

Loughlin, C. E., & Martin, M. D. (1987). *Supporting literacy: Developing effective learning environments.* New York: Teachers College Press.

Martinez, M., & Teale, W. H. (1988). Reading in a kindergarten classroom library. *The Reading Teacher, 41*(6), 568–572.

Moore, G. T., Lane, C. G., Hill, A. B., Cohen, U., & McGinty, T. (1979). *Recommendations for child care centers* (Report No. R 79–2). Milwaukee, WI: Center for Architecture and Urban Planning Research.

Morrow, L. M. (1982). Relationship between literature programs, library corner designs, and children's use of literature. *Journal of Educational Research, 75*(6), 339–344.

Morrow, L. M. (1990). Preparing the classroom environment to promote literacy during play. *Early Childhood Research Quarterly, 5,4,* 537–554.

Morrow, L. M., & Weinstein, C. S. (1982). Increasing children's use of literature through program and physical design changes. *The Elementary School Journal, 83*(2), 131–137.

Raines, S. C., & Isbell, R. T. (1991, April). Book interest and interaction behaviors of young children in the classroom library. Proposal for the Annual Conference of the Association for the Childhood Education International, San Diego, CA.

Raines, S. C. (1990). Book interest and interaction behaviors of young children in the classroom library. George Mason University Faculty Research Grant, Fairfax, VA.

Rho, L., & Drury, F. *Space and time in early learning.* Cheshire, CT: Board of Education. Publication funding under federal E.S.E.A. Title IV-C and P.L. 94–142. The Education of all Handicapped Children Act.

Rosenthal, B. A. L. (1973). *An ecological study of free play in the nursery school.* Unpublished doctoral dissertation, Wayne State University.

Schickedanz, J. A. (1986). *More than the ABC's: The early stages of reading and writing.* Washington, DC: National Association for the Education of Young Children.

Stauffer, R. G. (1980). *The language experience approach to the teaching of reading.* New York: Harper & Row.

Vergeront, J. (1987). *Places and spaces for preschool and primary (indoors).* Washington, DC: N.A.E.Y.C.

CHILDREN'S LITERATURE REFERENCES

The authors and illustrators of children's books are listed, in all chapters, by their full names to help the reader become acquainted with them. If only one name is listed, the author also illustrated the book.

Bennett, Jill. (1986). *The Teeny Tiny Woman*. Illustrated by Tomie dePaola. New York: Putnam.

Bunting, Eve. (1993). *Someday a Tree*. Illustrated by Ronald Himler. New York: Clarion.

Brett, Jan. (1989). *The Mitten*. New York: Scholastic.

dePaolo, Tomie. (1977). *The Quicksand Book*. New York: Holiday House.

Domanska, Janine. (1969). *The Turnip*. New York: Macmillan.

Flack, Marjorie. (1958). *Ask Mr. Bear*. New York: Macmillan.

Freeman, Don. (1968). *Corduroy*. New York: Viking Press.

Freeman, Don. (1964). *Dandelion*. New York: Viking Press.

Freeman, Don. (1978). *A Pocket for Corduroy*. New York: Viking Press.

Galdone, Paul. (1975). *The Gingerbread Boy*. Boston: Clarion Books.

Galdone, Paul. (1973). *The Little Red Hen*. New York: Scholastic.

Gauchi, Patricia Lee. (1989). *Dance, Tanya*. New York: Philomel Books.

Greene, Carla. (1967). *Animal Doctors: What Do They Do*. Illustrated by Leonard Kessler. New York: Harper & Row.

Hines, Anna Grossnickle. (1986). *Daddy Makes the Best Spaghetti*. New York: Clarion Books.

Hutchins, Pat. (1971). *Changes, Changes*. New York: Macmillan.

Jonas, Ann. (1989). *Color Dance*. New York: Greenwillow.

Kent, Jack. (1974). *Fat Cat: A Danish Folktale*. Harmondsworth, Middlesex, England: Puffin Books.

Krasilovsky, Phyllis. (1950). *The Man Who Didn't Wash His Dishes*. Illustrated by Barbara Cooney. New York: Doubleday.

Krauss, Ruth. (1945). *The Carrot Seed*. Illustrated by Crockett Johnson. New York: Harper & Row.

Kuklin, Susan. (1988). *Taking My Cat to the Vet*. New York: Bradbury Press.

Lionni, Leo. (1968). *Swimmy*. New York: Pantheon Books.

Lillegard, Dee. (1986). *I Can Be a Baker*. Chicago: Children's Press.

Littledale, Freya. (1986). *Magic Fish*. Illustrated by Ed Arno. New York: Scholastic.

McGovern, Ann. (1968). *Stone Soup*. Illustrated by Winslow Pinney Pels. New York: Scholastic.

Pelham, David. (1988). *Worms Wiggle*. Illustrated by Michael Foreman. New York: Simon & Schuster Books for Young Readers.

Peppé, Rodney. (1970). *The House That Jack Built*. New York: Delacorte.

Shaw, Charles Green. (1947). *It Looked Like Spilt Milk*. New York: Harper.

Slobodkina, Esphyr. (1940). *Caps for Sale*. New York: Harper & Row.

Tafuri, Nancy. (1985). *Have You Seen My Duckling?* (filmstrip). Westminster, MD: Random House/Miller-Brody for Newberry Award Records.

There Was an Old Lady Who Swallowed a Fly. (1973). Illustrated by Pam Adams. New York: Childs Play of England.

Tresselt, Alvin. (1964). *The Mitten*. Illustrated by Yaroslava. New York: Scholastic.

Wadsworth, Olive A. (1986). *Over in the Meadow*. Illustrated by Mary Maki Rae. New York: Penguin.

Zemach, Margot. (1990). *It Could Always Be Worse*. New York: Farrar, Straus and Giroux.

11

Five Early Childhood Teachers' Stories— Children's Literature in Classroom Practice

Five Early Childhood Teachers' Stories— Children's Literature in Classroom Practice

In this chapter, five teachers' stories are presented as examples of children's literature in actual classroom practice.[1] As you read the cases, decide what you would do if you were there as the main character in their stories, as the professional educator.

The early childhood teachers' stories are presented in three parts. The beginning of the case introduces the teacher and tells the context for the dilemma. Midstory, there is a pause for the reader to think about the problem the teacher faces and answer the key questions listed for reflection. Then, the ending of the teacher's story is told.

The first teacher you will meet is Anne, who is one of the lead teachers in a child-care center. Her main responsibility is supervising the infants and toddlers program and planning parent education. Anne wants to impress upon parents the importance of reading to their very young children.

The second teacher story is about Emily, a preschool teacher who learned more about emergent literacy and decided her role as a reading teacher was to increase three- and four-year-olds' interests in books and stories. The case presents some changes in Emily's classroom and her selection and use of good children's literature.

The third story is the case of Fran, a respected kindergarten teacher at a university lab school who hears reports that several of her former students are having difficulty in first-grade reading. The parents have turned to her for advice about their children who are graduates of her kindergarten.

The fourth story is April's case. Her challenge is to create a literature-rich classroom in a new school which is organized with a multiage grouping of six- and seven-year-olds.

The fifth and final case is Lynnette's, whose struggle is to find ways to work with the special services teachers in her literature-rich, third-grade class, rather than pulling out the children for remedial instruction. Lynnette's story is prompted by her concern for Byron, a child in her class.

This is a book about children's literature. Why should we be concerned about the teachers in these settings, with these dilemmas? The reality is that the teacher's use of children's literature does not occur in isolation. The teacher's eagerness to construct a literature-rich learning environment is dependent upon many factors, such as parents' concerns, the curriculum, expectations from teachers in higher grades, and ways to work with reading and language specialists. These five early childhood educators used children's literature as a major part of the solutions to their problems.

Anne, a Teacher of Infants and Toddlers

Anne was eager for the arrival of the guest speaker. As the lead teacher for the infants and toddlers in a large child-care center, she was responsible for the night parent meetings. Previous programs for parents' night had focused on a wide array of topics, but this was the first parent workshop on reading to infants and toddlers.

Impatient for the speaker's arrival, Anne walked into the multipurpose room and looked at the display of books: the photograph albums, board books, padded books, toy books, simple story and picture books, alphabet, song, and nursery rhyme books. The photograph albums the teachers had made were some of the children's favorite books. The poster on the easel announced the title of the session, "Reading Books to Infants and Toddlers." Anne checked the videotape and player to be certain that when she clicked it on, the scene of one of the infant caregivers reading to a six-month-old would appear. Her favorite part of the tape was when the child leaned forward and patted the picture in the book, gurgling and cooing as if to accompany the caregiver's reading.

QUESTIONS FOR REFLECTION

Often parents question the benefits of reading to children as young as their infants and toddlers.

- ☐ What would you tell them?

- ☐ What types of books would you recommend for infants and toddlers?

- ☐ As you read on, compare the effectiveness of Anne's two attempts at educating parents about the importance of reading to infants and toddlers.

AND NOW FOR THE REST OF ANNE'S STORY

Anne recognized that the young parents from the child-care center led very hectic family lives. Reading to their infants and toddlers was not high on the priority list nor did they feel confident about keeping the youngster's attention.

When Anne initiated the program of "reading to every child, every day," even her own staff had difficulty reading to the infants, the creepers, the crawlers, and the toddlers. This type of reading required the caregiver to interact with the book and still attend to the child. For the infants, helping them to focus on the book, pointing out pictures, turning the pages, then helping them look at the next pictures became a ritual. Often the caregiver sat in a rocking chair, holding the baby, and read and rocked. It did not appear to be important that the baby look at the book all the time, but hearing the language and rhythm of reading aloud seemed to be reassuring, soothing, and enjoyable. After only a few sessions, the infants become more excited when the caregiver approached them with a book in hand.

Five- to seven-month-olds who are manipulating everything, even putting their feet in their mouths, are eager to manipulate the pages of the books as well. The caregivers learned to allow for the children's patting the pictures, bouncing when they recognized a favorite scene, making noises while the adult read, and wiggling around. The caregivers learned to accept the movements and allowed the child to redirect his or her attention, then refocus on the book and listen more. The adults recognized that they must become attuned to the ebb and flow of the child's interest, not pushing for attention or thinking that when the child wasn't looking at the book that he or she had lost interest entirely. Often, given a moment's distraction, the five- to seven-month-olds returned again to the book for another period of interest.

Youngsters who were creeping and crawling often pulled up on the adult's slacks legs and tried standing up. One child in the videotape was seen holding onto a padded book with one hand and the slacks of the caregiver with another. The child came crawling to the adult as if to request a reading session. By this stage of development, the caregivers had abandoned the rocking chair as the favorite place to read. Instead they sat on the floor and began reading to a child, and were often joined by another child while the first one crawled away. As long as there was one child near, the caregiver interacted with the child and read the book. If both left, the caregiver waited for a moment or two, called attention to the book, and then the children usually crawled back again.

Many of the crawlers had reached the stage of staying from the beginning to the end of the book. They crawl into the caregiver's lap, snuggle close while the book is read, and help to turn pages. They often look up in the caregiver's face, pat the pages, and look down again, expectantly, as the page is turned. Some of the crawlers were book babblers. While the teacher was reading, they babbled and attempted to match their babbling to the adult's reading. When they found a favorite page, they giggled, looked up at the caregiver, and waited for recognition that the adult remembered the significance of the picture.

The caregivers found that toddlers, who walk around, were also a challenge for a reading session. They seemed to always be on the move. One caregiver described her reading sessions as a yo-yo. She was the wooden part and the child was holding onto the string. The child pulled far away, the full extent of the string, then rolled back up. As she read, she held the toddlers' attention for a while, then the child went away for a distance. As she read on, the child came back, went out again, back once more, and often plopped down onto her lap. When she first began reading to the toddlers, she thought they were not really interested and so would drop the book and go on to do other things in the room. Then, as she learned to stay in place and keep looking at the book, often continuing to read, they would return to her. The toddlers began spending longer and longer times on her lap or on the floor nearby. When a toddler saw a picture he or she liked, the child would point with an index finger, look up to the teacher, smile, talk, giggle, or even repeat a phrase from the book. One of the toddlers' favorite books was a photograph album which the teacher made by taking pictures of them

parents also found the modeling by the caregivers was very valuable. The videotape is still in constant circulation. As the children get older, the parents often check out the tape again to understand better how to read with their children who are a few months older. The list of books for holiday giving has become a tradition at the center. Anne was successful because she found ways to inform the parents about their youngsters' interests in books and modeled how they could interact with their children.

A Preschool Teacher— Emily's Story

Emily is a teacher of three- and four-year-olds in a church nursery school. Over the summer she attended staff development training on emergent literacy. When the director sent her the "invitation" to attend, Emily thought it was ridiculous; it was not her responsibility to teach children as young as three and four to read. But after the opening presentation, Emily realized that indeed she did teach reading. The books she read, how she read them, and the literature extensions she planned for the classroom influenced the children's interest in books and their beginning experiences with print (Fields, Spangler, & Lee, 1991). As Emily thought about the term *emergent literacy*, she liked the phrase. It sounded "developmental."

Circle time was story time in Emily's nursery school classroom. One of her favorite techniques was to hide an object in a paper bag and use it as the focus of the story she was telling or reading to the children. Emily read to the children everyday, sang songs, and did simple fingerplays with them. She planned many hands-on activities. Emily felt successful as a teacher, yet understood she needed more ways to invite the three- and four-year-olds to good books than by modeling good reading during circle time.

playing in different areas of their room and on the playground.

AFTER THE PARENT MEETING

Unfortunately, the attendance at the infant and toddler parents' session was smaller than for the usual parents' night programs. The librarian, accustomed to parents not recognizing the importance of the topic, knew to expect a small number and was not disappointed. But Anne was. She decided on another tact for getting the information to the parents. Since the videotape had been so successful with the few parents who attended, Anne decided to add some scenes to the tape. She hastily sketched out the significant milestones for different ages of infants and toddlers and the ways they interacted with the caregiver and the books.

In addition, since the winter holidays were nearing, she decided to make up a list of good books to purchase as gifts for reading with infants and toddlers. (See the suggested list in Chapter 2, Figures 2.6 and 2.7.) The videotape was tremendously successful. Anne wished it were not so amateurish in production quality, but the genuine "interactions" helped parents to see the importance of reading with infants and toddlers. The

Questions for Reflection

After the staff development sessions on emergent literacy, Emily decided there were two basic questions she needed to answer:

☐ How could she and the classroom aide encourage the preschoolers' interests in books?

☐ Which books would be good ones to place in play areas?

Emily's Successes With Encouraging Preschoolers' Interests in Books

Emily had quite a collection of children's literature books which she had accumulated over the years. Many of them were kept in her storage area. In the classroom, she had a simple shelf with books stacked on it. The book shelf was low and was near the front of the circle time rug. Any child who wanted to look at a book during free play could come to the stack and get one, sit on the carpet, and leaf through the pages. As Emily recalled, hardly anyone ever came to the bookshelf during free play. One of her former teacher aides had even used the book area as a punishment. If a child was having some behavior problem, she removed the child from the play group and sent him or her over to the carpet to sit and look at a book; hardly the message Emily wanted to convey to the three- and four-year-olds about enjoying good literature.

Instead of simply stacking books on a shelf, Emily created the library center with a display bookshelf, cushions, and a bulletin board. Because the rearrangement was new, the novelty of the redesigned space provoked a few more visits to the library center. However, helping three- and four-year-olds to want to go to the library area on a regular and sustained basis was not so simple. Emily found that if she read a good book in circle time and then announced she would read it again in the library corner several of the children would come over immediately to listen to the story again. Yet, Emily could not stay in the library corner during all of the center time, so she decided to enlist the help of the parent and grandparent volunteers.

She invited the regular volunteers to a special training session. While the volunteers were quite adept at reading to individual children, they expressed some reservations about selecting books to read aloud to groups of children. Emily asked them to take home any books they did not know and read them. They practiced reading with enthusiasm, noting how to engage the children and how to have the youngsters "read with" them when the book had a recurring phrase or the children knew the story so well they could join in by chanting some lines.

Emily pointed out that the volunteers' own enthusiasm for the book and the story was the best attraction for the children. She also provided a reading lamp for the library corner, an idea she heard at the training session (Raines & Canady, 1990). A lamp was placed in the library area and anytime there was an adult available to read, the lamp would be turned on. The children soon learned to look for the reading lamp and almost all of the children came at some time during the morning for a special reading session.

MORE BOOKS IN PLAY AREAS

Emily's second improvement in her classroom for three- and four-year-olds was to place more good books and print materials throughout the classroom. She placed related books in the play areas and special displays. For example, in the housekeeping area and dress-up corner, she added books about home decorating, cooking and recipe books, consumer magazines, and newspapers. Some were children's books and magazines, and others were adult versions which the children could pretend to read when they were role-playing being adults. In the pretend grocery store, she added cents-off coupons, grocery check lists, pencils, markers, poster board, and labels from cans and boxes, as well as books on foods and nutrition. In the block area, she displayed books on trucks, construction, and how things work.

The children noticed the books and materials and incorporated them into their play. They pretended to be mommy and daddy reading to their children, the dolls, and teddy bears. In the grocery store, they wrote pretend checks, matched pictures on food labels to the cents-off coupons, arranged the grocery shelves by cans and boxes, and bought children's and adults' magazines. In the block area, one child taped a picture with some scribbles on it onto the side of the long tractor-trailer rig he pushed through the maze of roads they built from blocks. He made his sign look similar to the one on the truck in Borden's *Neighborhood Trucker.* The science displays always included

children's nonfiction books on the topics, whether it was the aquarium or oceans. Simply adding the books to the area meant that the children began to associate books with the many activities of their preschool classroom (Schickedanz, 1986).[2]

The three- and four-year-old children's enjoyment of books and stories became a focal point of Emily's redesigned classroom. More children went to the library area and had books read to them, and leafed through them on their own. The parent volunteers and the teacher aide were also enthused with the changes and with their contributions to the children's interests in books. Books in the play areas became routine. At the beginning of each unit of study, Emily arranged a special display of books, introduced them to the children, and then scattered them throughout the classroom. (See the suggested list of books for three- and four-year-olds in Chapter 2.

A Kindergarten Teacher—Fran's Story

Fran teaches kindergarten in a lab school for a university. The five-year-olds in her classroom go on to a school system in which some of the teachers use worksheets and skills- based activities as their version of a reading program. The teachers present all the letter/sound symbol relationships and teach children to link each sound and read words. In some of the first grades, the children's reading is tested by presenting words in isolation from the text material and having the children attempt to read the list.

Fortunately, the kindergarten and lab school where Fran teaches has a developmentally appropriate practices philosophy (Bredekamp, 1987; Raines & Canady, 1990). The teachers described their program as active learning, with manipulatives and resource materials organized in learning centers. Fran spends much of her planning time selecting good books to read to children, organizing the classroom library with special displays that go along with the theme of the unit she is teaching, and pulling together activities that stretch the stories and make connections between the concepts in the books and the concepts she is teaching for the unit. Fran is a highly respected member of the faculty of the lab school and parents seek to have their children in her classroom by calling to register them over a year in advance.

Lately, Fran has been troubled by reports that one of her former kindergartners was not doing well in first grade. Concerned about Jason, Fran phoned the parents and asked about their son's progress. They confided that the parent conference after the first nine weeks of first grade had been a difficult one. While the first-grade teacher was pleased with Jason's behavior in school, she was quite displeased with his reading and blamed it on the fact that he did not have a good kindergarten preparation for first grade. While Jason was in kindergarten they thought Fran's classroom was wonderful, but they did not know what to do to help him in first grade. They remembered how he enjoyed books in kindergarten. They even recalled some of the titles of his favorites.

The parents implored Fran to visit Jason's first grade and advise them about ways to help him. Fran encouraged them to talk with Jason's teacher but they felt they had already tried and were not successful at getting specific suggestions. Fran hesitated but agreed to visit the school. She decided she would visit all of her former students' classes, not just Jason's.

QUESTIONS FOR REFLECTION

☐ What do you think Fran should say on the telephone as she asks the principal and the teachers if she can visit?

☐ What should she try to find out about the school, the teachers, and the success of her former kindergartners?

☐ Should she give advice to the parents of children who are now her former students?

FRAN'S SUCCESS STORY

As respected an educator as Fran was, she still felt a bit reluctant to call the principal and ask for a conference, but she mustered her courage and called anyway. She told the principal that she often checked up on her former kindergarten students and wondered if she might visit the first-grade classrooms and chat with the teachers. Ms. Bailey, the principal, was impressed at Fran's concern for her former kindergartners and called back in a few days to schedule the visits.

On the day of the visits, the receptionist gave Fran the classroom numbers and she proceeded down the hall. Upon seeing Fran at the door of their first-grade classrooms, the children in two of the first grades rushed over to her and gave her enthusiastic embraces. In the third classroom, the children sat in their seats and waved to her, one child rising from his chair and then looking over at the teacher before sitting down again. Instantly, Fran suspected this was Jason's classroom where her former students were reported to not be doing well. Fran felt quite at home in the first two classrooms, where the first graders were free to move around, select books and manipulatives from the shelves, and engage in a lot of artwork. When Fran asked to have her former students read to her,

the children enthusiastically approached her with books. The teachers and Fran enjoyed the shared pride of having taught the children.

In the third classroom of first graders, Fran found the children pouring over a stack of papers. After a few minutes of pleasantries, Fran asked if she could talk with Jason and if he might read to her. The teacher brought a stack of flashcards and a basal reader for Jason to read. He read in a halting manner, often stammering over words. Fran remembered that in kindergarten Jason had flown through *Jamberry*, *Green Eggs & Ham* by Dr. Seuss, *Whose Baby Are You?* and *Is Your Mama a Llama?* She wondered what had happened to his fluency. Jason did not do well with the flashcard exercise and seemed embarrassed, sitting kicking his feet back and forth, while he held on to the sides of his chair.

The teacher emphasized exactness, correcting every word which Jason said. If he paused the slightest, she insisted he sound it out and once chided him by saying, "Jason, you just saw that word on the last page," but did not allow him to turn back and look for it. After the reading session, the teacher had Jason stay in his chair and she and Fran stood up. The teacher began talking about Jason as if he were not there.

Fran immediately said, "I would be more comfortable if we could step outside in the hallway." Reluctantly, then with a snap of her fingers, the teacher pointed Jason back to his desk to finish his seatwork, the list of dittos printed on the chalkboard.

Taking a deep breath, Fran said, "Your children hardly moved while I was there." Unfortunately, the teacher took this as a compliment. She replied, "Well, first grade is where they start being real students. It's O.K. to play in kindergarten, I guess, but I have to teach them to read. You know how the parents are in this community. They have high expectations."

Fran acknowledged the parental pressures and then proceeded to refocus the conversation on Jason. She explained that Jason had read well on his own before he came to first grade. She told the first-grade teacher about the books she could recall Jason liking and reading. The first-grade teacher assured her that Jason was not reading those books in kindergarten, that he had memorized them. Now, he was reading, since he was learning to sound out the words.

Hesitantly, Fran tried to explain the reading strategies she used to teach kindergartners, always asking first what would make sense, using picture and context clues, and what the natural order of the language might be, and finally using beginning consonant sounds, if the child had not already figured out the word. The emphasis was on making sense of the text and Fran had not required exactness in every word. Sometimes children omitted words, substituted others, and guessed by saying what would make sense. The teacher did not agree with the strategies, except those which emphasized decoding with sounds.

The teacher had no interest in reading the articles Fran suggested on emergent literacy. Finally, Fran thanked the teacher for her visit and invited her to come to the lab school and see the kindergarten class. The teacher thanked her in return but said she taught first grade, not kindergarten, so she would not take time from her busy schedule to come over to the university lab school.

As Fran drove home from the elementary school, she thought about the three teachers. Two of them had accepted her invitation to come to the lab school for a visit. They had also asked for copies of the articles which Fran had collected for parents and the college students who

Figure 11.1 Whole Language Versus Skills-Based*

VIEWS OF		
Learner	CHILD CHOICE	TEACHER DIRECTED
Schedule	LARGE BLOCKS OF TIME	BRIEF SEGMENTS
Environment	ACTIVE LEARNING WITH ARRAY OF REAL MATERIALS	PASSIVE OR WORKSHEET DRIVEN
Language	TALK, PRINT, CHILD CREATED	QUIET, CONTROLLED
Reading Instruction	MEANING BASED TRADE BOOKS MAGAZINES, NEWSPAPERS ENVIRONMENTAL PRINT LIBRARY RESOURCES	SKILLS EMPHASIS BASAL READERS CONTROLLED TEXTS
Writing Instruction	MEANING BASED INVENTED SPELLING TOPIC SELECTED	SKILLS EMPHASIS SPELLING LISTS TOPIC DICTATED
Control	CHILD AS RISK TAKERS STRENGTHS EMPHASIS	CORRECTNESS EMPHASIS WEAKNESS EMPHASIS
Curriculum	UNIT TEACHING CONCEPT DEVELOPMENT	UNRELATED ACROSS SUBJECT AREAS
Sources	CHILD, FAMILY, COMMUNITY	TEACHER, TEXTBOOKS

*Teachers demonstrate varying degrees of each view.

had their practicum experiences in her classroom. Fran thought they might eventually establish a good working relationship.

When Fran called Jason's parents, she told them that Jason had lost his confidence as a reader. The children's literature books he enjoyed in her classroom were not a part of the reading instruction in his first grade. The parents discussed several options for helping Jason, everything from asking for a transfer to one of the other teachers' classrooms to placing Jason in a private school.

Figure 11.2 Sample of Predictable and Patterned Language Books for Confidence Builders*

RHYMING PATTERNS
Is Your Mama a Llama? (Guarino)
The Wheels on the Bus (Kovalsky)
We're Going on A Bear Hunt (Rosen)
Chicka Chicka Boom Boom (Martin)
Over in the Meadow (Wadsworth)

RECURRING PHRASES
Caps for Sale (Slobodkina)
Millions of Cats (Gág)
If You Give a Mouse a Cookie (Numeroff)
Teeny Tiny (Bennett)
What Do You Do With a Kangaroo? (Meyer)

REPEATED OR ADDED CHARACTERS
Jump, Frog, Jump! (Kalan)
The Mitten (Tresselt)
The Mouse and the Potato (Berger)
The Napping House (Wood)
Rooster's Off to See the World (Carle)

REPEATED PATTERNS OF INTERACTING
Are You My Mother? (Eastman)
Ask Mr. Bear (Flack)
Brown Bear, Brown Bear,
　　What Do You See? (Martin)
The Doorbell Rang (Hutchins)
The Three Billy-Goats Gruff (Appleby)

*Books are classified by their main feature.

A few hours after Fran's call to the parents, they called her back with an excellent suggestion. They decided to reestablish the pattern of reading with Jason which Fran had used in kindergarten. They collected a lot of Jason's favorite books from kindergarten, found others he liked at the library, and then began building his confidence by letting him read to them. When the teacher requested that the parents have Jason read from his reading book, the parents read to Jason instead, providing a read-aloud model, and then Jason echo read the sentences after them. Fran encouraged them to simply tell Jason what a word was or tell him to skip it, and keep reading. After Jason regained his confidence, the parent would read one page and Jason would read the next. They did not make him labor over each word sounding it out. The parents called this home reading. For Jason, there was home reading and school reading. He soon began to enjoy books again.

Meanwhile, even though the teacher had declined Fran's offer to read the articles, Fran enclosed an article in the thank you note for letting her visit in the classroom. Fran thought surely the teacher would be curious enough to read it. The article contained a list of predictable, patterned language books, similar to the ones listed in Figure 11.2. The article by Lynn Rhodes was from *The Reading Teacher*, "I Can Read! Predictable Books for Reading and Writing Instruction." The books are confidence builders for children as beginning readers. While we don't know if the article changed the first-grade teacher's approach, Fran does know Jason is reading well at home.

April's Story—Moving to a Multi-aged Classroom

April contemplated Ms. Dillon's invitation to move to the new school. It was one of the most difficult decisions she had been asked to make in her seven years of teaching. Ms. Dillon, who had been the assistant principal, announced that she had accepted the offer to become the principal of a new continuous progress school where children were in multiaged groups.[3] The curriculum was centered around thematic units and the reading program was literature based. She wanted April to move with her to the new school and teach a classroom of six- and seven-year-olds.

Although April did use some thematic teaching in her present first grade, she had always used basals as her method of reading instruction. Last year, however, she included more children's literature or trade books in her instruction, but she had not decided to leave the basals entirely. She feared that moving from a set scope and sequence of skills could mean the children might miss some important steps. However, when she visited one of the other first-grade teachers who was already

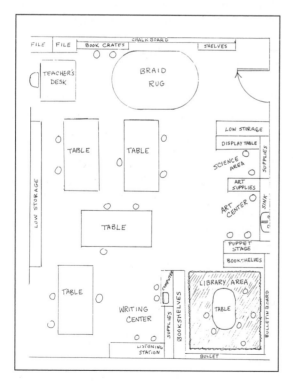

using trade books, she noticed the students were reading quite well. In fact, they were reading with more enthusiasm and not complaining about having to come to the reading circle.

It was the children's enthusiasm which had convinced April to consider using more children's literature books. April realized she needed to know a great deal about children's books to build a reading program around them and more about thematic units to plan the curriculum. The world of children's books was one she reserved mostly for the librarian. Over the summer, as April thought about her move to the new school, she found herself spending a lot of time at the neighborhood library and children's bookstores finding appropriate books for first and second graders, as well as books that would support an integrated unit approach. Eager to begin planning, April got the names of the other teachers who were moving to the new school and organized a meeting to see if they could combine some of the work and begin planning units together.

QUESTIONS FOR REFLECTION

☐ How will I manage my classroom in terms of space, time, resources, and supervision to teach using a literature-based reading approach?

☐ How will I plan the curriculum using thematic units?

APRIL'S SUCCESS STORY: USING LITERATURE TO TEACH READING

The transformation to a whole language classroom where literature was the source of reading instruction took many months for April to develop. She consulted with colleagues in the school, friends who were reading specialists, and scoured resource books and journals for

a listening station and puppet theater. The writing center with the computer was beside the library area and the art center was nearby.

Under the long chalkboard which covered one whole side of the classroom, April placed other half-sized plastic crates and let the children help sort books by genre or topic. They put all the imagination books in one crate. They had so many humorous books that they separated them into another bin. The children decided to group some like *Harry, the Dirty Dog* and all the *Clifford* books because they were all about dogs. As the year went on, the number of crates grew and the children often re-sorted them. Certainly, April had fulfilled the first requirement of any teacher who expects to engage children in reading books and that is to provide many books and to have them all around the classroom so that the children are constantly engaged with stories in print.

The writing center was another major area of the classroom, even though the children often wrote all around the classroom and not just at the small table in the center. In addition to the computer, the writing center was filled with interesting shapes of paper, a variety of writing and drawing pens, and a small chalkboard. It was an attractive place where children enjoyed brainstorming their writing ideas, often based on popular characters from books they were reading. Some of their favorites were the series books, such as Lobel's *Frog and Toad,* Parish's *Amelia Bedelia,* and Waber's *Lyle, Lyle Crocodile.*

TIME AND INSTRUCTION

One of April's major concerns was scheduling. She planned more time for children to read and write on their own, rather than more instruction time in reading and writing. April's day and the children's day looked quite different than when she taught mostly with teacher-directed materials. Literature groups replaced teacher-led basal reading groups.

relevant articles. But in the end, it was April herself who had to construct the changes she could handle and manage.

She thought in terms of four resources: space, books, time, and herself. She began by arranging the space into instructional areas. Space was the easiest to rearrange. She was pleased the new school had tables instead of desks. In the center of each table she placed half-sized plastic crates and filled them with some of the children's favorite books.

April arranged the classroom library by adding sets of book-shelves, a bulletin board, a reading lamp, chairs, a small table for displays, and some cushions. Adjacent to the area, there was

Listed below is a sample of April's day during the second semester in her multiaged class of six- and seven-year-olds.

LITERATURE GROUPS, READING AND WRITING TIME

The organization of the three literature groups was quite different from the former years when April organized reading groups by ability levels. She formed three literature groups which operated on a weekly basis. The first group was the free-reading group, composed of about a third of the children who read any book they wanted and wrote responses in their reading logs. The second group was reading from multiple copies of Lobel's *Frog and Toad are Friends*. The third group was reading from multiple copies of *We are Best Friends* by Aliki.

April lead the two literature groups' discussion of the stories they were reading. Their reading usually followed the sequence listed below.

Monday—Before reading the book, April asked the group to make predictions about the book, based on the cover, some key illustrations, and the title. She also found ways to use their background knowledge to connect to the content of the book. They discussed their predictions, knowledge of the characters and the setting, or made some associations with other books they knew by the author. April or one of the second graders would read the book aloud to the entire group.

Tuesday—At the beginning of the year, April read the book through again on Tuesdays, as a way to start the literature session. Later in the year as the children became better readers, they read the book silently on their own. The children talked about the

Multiage Class Schedule for Six- and Seven-Year-Olds	
8:30–8:45	Arrival, Greeting Time, Message Board
8:45–9:15	Meeting Time (Stories, reading strategies modeled, high-frequency words pointed out in context, and main ideas from units stressed)
9:15–10:00	Three Literature Groups
10:00–10:15	Snack Time
10:15–10:45	Writing, Choice of Centers
10:45–11:15	Outside Play or Gym
11:15–11:30	Read-aloud Selection, Washing up for Lunch
11:30–12:00	Lunch
12:00–12:30	Recap of Morning Activities, Author's Chair, Schedule Review for the Afternoon
12:30–1:15	Mathematics/Science Problem Solving and Project Emphasis
1:15–2:00	Science or Social Studies Units
2:00–2:30	Alternating Schedules for Specialists, Outside Play, and Centers
	This time period differed almost everyday. Three days a week, the children went out of the classroom to art, music, or the library. When they were not scheduled for a specialist, they went outside for play. Activity centers were used when there was bad weather.
2:30–2:40	Organization Time
	Children organized products and materials from specialists' classes and gathered books and personal belongings to go home.
2:40–3:00	End of the Day Summary, Rereading a Favorite Book or Poem, Dismissal

story, favorite parts, surprises, interesting phrasing, appealing illustrations, and so forth. To end the Tuesday session, each child read aloud a page or part of a page he or she chose. The child paraphrased the part of the story that preceded the one chosen for reading aloud.

Wednesday—The children brainstormed some creative responses to the story. Their ideas often included a mural for the bulletin board, a special display, a puppet show, and rewriting the story into a script. April required that each of the creative responses must include some writing. These activities became their assignments for the time which followed. They could work in small groups, with a partner, or alone. On Wednesdays, each child was also asked to take the book home and either read it to their parents or have their parents read to them.

Thursday—The children shared their work on their creative literature responses. April lead the discussion of what their projects illustrated—a picture of the main character with dialogue balloons, the mural with captions from the book, the script for the play, and even cue cards to help the puppets know what to say.

Friday—If needed, the children used this time to finish sharing their literature responses. Friday was also practice day. April asked the six-year-olds to read to their seven-year-old reading buddies and practice fluent reading. On Fridays, April also previewed the next focus books and the children made their selections of books they wanted to read the next week. The book they chose determined their literature group for the next week.

FREE-READING GROUP

While April was working with the two literature groups, the remaining children read any books they wanted, recorded what they had read in their reading logs, wrote a brief review of the book, or drew a picture of a favorite part of the book. They could read alone, with a reading buddy, or listen to a book on tape. They also selected at least one book a week to do a creative response. When they finished reading

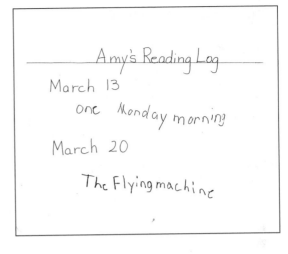

at least one book a day, they were free to go to the classroom learning centers.

LIMITED ENGLISH PROFICIENCY STUDENTS

The Limited English Proficiency (LEP) students were included in all of the activities with the two teacher-led literature groups and the free reading group. The LEP students also worked with a parent volunteer for additional modeling of good reading or to practice their own reading. The volunteers assisted the LEP students in recording what they had read in their reading logs, and drawing or writing in their journals.

APRIL'S SUCCESS STORY: USING CHILDREN'S LITERATURE TO PLAN CURRICULUM UNITS

When the new teachers meet to organize for their multi-aged classrooms, they were excited about sharing teaching ideas and concerned about planning the social studies, science, and literature study units. In the scene described below, April and a group of teachers are sitting around a large table in the media center.[4]

Taped on the wall are lists of the units from social studies and science that are usually taught to first and second graders. Along one wall of bookshelves, the librarian has collected and displayed books that could accompany the most common units. The teachers have chosen to visualize their planning by using webs. There are webs on posters and chart tablets around the room: curriculum webs, concept webs, activity webs, author webs, and literary element webs.

Characteristics of Webs

According to Karen D'Angelo Bromley in her book *Webbing with Literature* (1991), a web is a "graphic representation or visual display of categories of information and their relationships" (p. 2). The web as a planning device helps teachers build a curriculum plan that formulates categories of information and shows relationships. The use of webs as planning devices points out the connections between the major ideas and supporting information that build the concepts derived from the experiences.

As the illustrations of webs in this chapter reveal, there are some common parts of a web. In the center of the graphic display, the organizing concept or title of the social studies unit is printed. The lines radiating out from the center core indicate a relationship between the core and the parts. The connecting lines between the parts indicate the relationships between the categories.

CURRICULUM WEBS

The use of a web as a planning device points out the linkages between content, concepts, and activities. This dynamic of building connectors is an indicator of the teachers' views of curriculum development and how children learn. Jarolimek and Foster (1989), use the term unit teaching to mean, a "coordinated series of learning activities planned around a broad topic that will involve the whole class in a comprehensive study [p. 54]." The phrase *integrated thematic unit* is often found in curriculum planning materials. Integration refers to integration across the subject areas of the curriculum, such as music, art, science, social studies, mathematics, and language arts. Integration also refers to integrating new information with existing knowledge. Children will formulate broad general concepts, and specific, detailed information will also be integrated as a part of the unit. The broad generalizations and concepts that children develop are the byproducts of the activities, their past knowledge, and present experiences: Children, however, are eager consumers of interesting facts and concepts are expanded through supporting information. The key is the relationship of the factual knowledge to the overall concepts and to categorical understandings that children formulate as they think about the information and the inherent relationships between the whole and the supporting information.

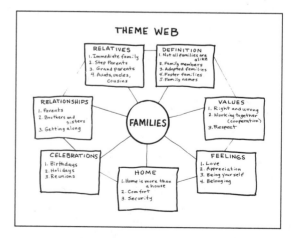

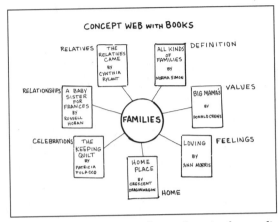

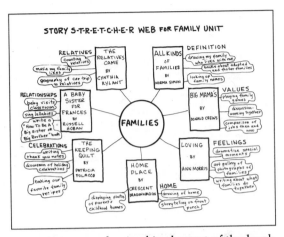

When the primary-grade teachers in the media center began discussing the unit they planned on families, they decided the key concepts were the definition of a family, the values one learns from family, the feelings families share, the significance of home, the ways families celebrate, the relationships between family members, and the extended family of other relatives. The web or graphic display of the main concepts, including the supporting ideas listed, helped the teachers plan what should be emphasized.

CONCEPT WEBS

With the help of the librarian, the teachers constructed a second web by adding titles of books that illustrate some of the main concepts they planned to teach through the unit on families. While many of the books had overlapping themes, each emphasized the main concepts well. The teachers planned to read aloud these focus books as selections for group discussion, and planned to use connecting activities to each book.

ACTIVITY OR STORY S-T-R-E-T-C-H-E-R WEBS

The third web illustrated the activities that are prompted by the theme of the unit and since the themes of the books are the same as the theme of the unit, the connections between the literature and the activities are displayed. The

concepts are emphasized in the text of the book and in the activities that the teachers select to s-t-r-e-t-c-h the stories into different areas of the curriculum. The children revisit the main ideas of the books and the unit themes through the activities the teachers and children select (Raines & Canady, 1992).

WEBS AND STORY MAPS TO SUPPORT LITERATURE STUDIES

Webs and story maps are also useful devices to help young children study stories and authors, make connections between literature selections, and understand literary elements. Older children can create literature webs on their own and younger children can work with their teachers.

Author Webs—One of the teachers from the planning group described an experience she had when a group of her former second graders identified some of their favorite authors. They liked Arnold Lobel, Pat Hutchins, Mercer Mayer, Marc Brown, Norman Bridwell, and Peggy Parish. The teacher created the author web by asking the children the titles of their favorite books. On index cards, they each wrote the names of their three favorite books and the authors' names. Then they made a tally showing which authors received repeated votes. Finally, they constructed a graph showing the top five vote-getters. Some of the authors were favorites because of one special book,

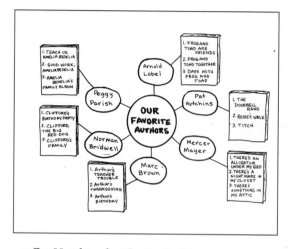

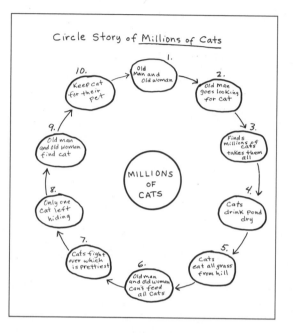

as Pat Hutchins for *The Doorbell Rang*. The children appeared to like knowing the format, the characters, and the predictableness of reading books in a series. Constructing the author web also encouraged children to read other books written by these authors.

Another way the teachers chose to use the author webs was to construct a second one later in the year and determine if the children's favorite authors had changed. In the first web of the year, many of the selections were books which the children liked to read on their own, such as the Clifford books and the Frog and Toad books. As the children's confidence grew in their reading skills, the teacher predicted that the variety of authors they will read will have more complex texts and themes.

Story Maps and Webs—Children become aware of the form of stories when they create story webs. Numerous types of webs can be used to illustrate story. Some of the simple ones are circle stories, which introduce the main characters, identify the problem and the steps needed in resolving the problem, and return again to the main characters. The story web of *Millions of Cats* by Wanda Gág is as an example of a circle story web.

Chained stories are another example of a type of story that young children can illustrate easily. For example, in the Ukranian folktale, *The Mitten* by Jan Brett, the predictable format of adding an animal to the mitten helps children sequence the chain of events. The creatures that crawl into the

mitten get progressively larger, until the tiny meadow mouse causes the mitten to explode. The animals arrive in this order: the mole, then the snowshoe rabbit, a hedgehog, an owl, a badger, a fox, a bear, and finally the meadow mouse. The teacher showed the size of the animals by printing the size of the letters progressively larger. Their story map for *The Mitten* was similar to the one below.

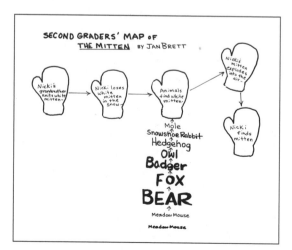

Literature Element Webs—Setting, characters, plot, including problem, events and the resolution of the problem, theme, style, and point of view can be shown graphically. While with young children we are less concerned that they can create webs that reflect the literary elements, teachers can use these devices as ways to represent story. In fact, many primary teachers refer to these webs as story maps. By far the most common story map is the sequence map that illustrates chronological occurrences in the story. See the story map of *The Little Red Hen.*

Characterization webs can be constructed to compare and clearly establish the good characters and the bad ones. Some plots use life-changing events to cause a change in the character. For example in the ever-popular Bill Peet book *Big Bad Bruce,* a bully of a bear terrorizes all the little creatures of the forest until he meets Roxy, the witch, who teaches him how it feels to be small and defenseless. After hearing *Big Bad Bruce* read aloud, the first graders helped their teacher construct the characterization web.

Circle stories, chain stories, comparison stories, and literature elements are excellent choices

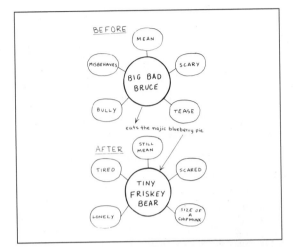

for literature webs because the graphic representations help children visualize the story. These devices are also excellent means for helping children to plan their own story writing. One teacher in the primary pod of the school had the children make a web of a book and then those who were interested wrote a sequel. A favorite one to sequel was *If You Give a Mouse a Cookie* by Laura Joffe Numeroff. In fact, the author's next book was a sequel, *If You Give a Moose a Muffin.*

After constructing a story map of *If You Give a Mouse a Cookie,* the teacher helped the children compose a group sequel. The children imagined what would happen if the mouse came to their classroom. She had the children visualize the little mouse knocking on the door of their classroom. She used one of the children in the writing group as a main character and said, "Scott hears a knock on the door, opens the door, looks down, and there is a little mouse asking for a chocolate chip cookie. What would happen next?"

The children went on to dictate the version. The teacher printed the story on large sheets of chart tablet paper, leaving room at the top of each sheet for illustrations. Later, the children constructed a cover of poster board and the teacher used the book as one of the class big books.

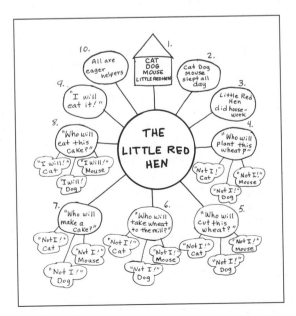

Figure 11.13 **Text of Dictated Sequel to *If You Give a Mouse a Cookie***

IF SCOTT GIVES A MOUSE
A CHOCOLATE CHIP COOKIE

"When Scott opens the door of the classroom, there is a Mouse.

Mouse asks for a chocolate chip cookie.

Scott gives him the biggest chocolate chip cookie.

When Scott gives the Mouse a chocolate chip cookie, he asks for a box of milk.

When Scott goes to the cafeteria to get a box of milk, the Mouse will ask to go too.

When Scott gets the box of milk, the Mouse will ask for a straw.

When Scott gives the Mouse the straw, he'll blow bubbles in his milk.

When he blows bubbles in his milk, he'll make a mess and ask for a napkin.

When he asks for a napkin, Scott will have to ask the cafeteria lady. (She can't hear mice talk.)

When Scott goes to ask for a napkin, the Mouse will take his chocolate chip cookie and run back to the classroom.

When Scott looks for him, the Mouse will be missing, but Scott will find him.

When Scott looks for him, he will follow the cookie crumbs down the hall from the cafeteria to the classroom.

When Scott gets to Mrs. Johnson's room, the custodian will tell him to sweep up the crumbs.

When Scott sweeps up the crumbs, he will see the crumbs stop at the classroom door.

When Scott comes back in our room, the Mouse will yell, 'Surprise!'

Then he'll ask for a chocolate chip cookie.

But don't give him one, because . . .

If you give a Mouse a chocolate chip cookie . . ."

Frog and toad played ball one day. It went in the the street. they were sad. frog said I have and idea. What is it said toad. When the wind blows. It will roll back. good idea siad toad. the blow and it rolled back and they were happy The End.

The Influence of Story on Young Children's Writing

In her group of six- and seven-year-olds, after finding out that the children's favorite books were Arnold Lobel's Frog and Toad books, April asked the students to write more Frog and Toad adventures. Each child wrote several drafts and the final version of a Frog and Toad story. The teacher bound the children's stories into books and placed them in the classroom library. Their class had the most extensive collection of Frog and Toad stories in the school. They were so popular that children from another primary pod came over and checked them out like library books.

The stories illustrated are examples from the classroom.

Text of "Frog and Toad Played Ball" by Carrie
"Frog and Toad played ball one day.
It went into the street.
They were sad.
Frog said, 'I have an idea.'
'What is it?' said Toad.
'When the wind blows, it will roll back.'
'Good idea,' said Toad.
The wind blew and it rolled back and they were happy. The end."

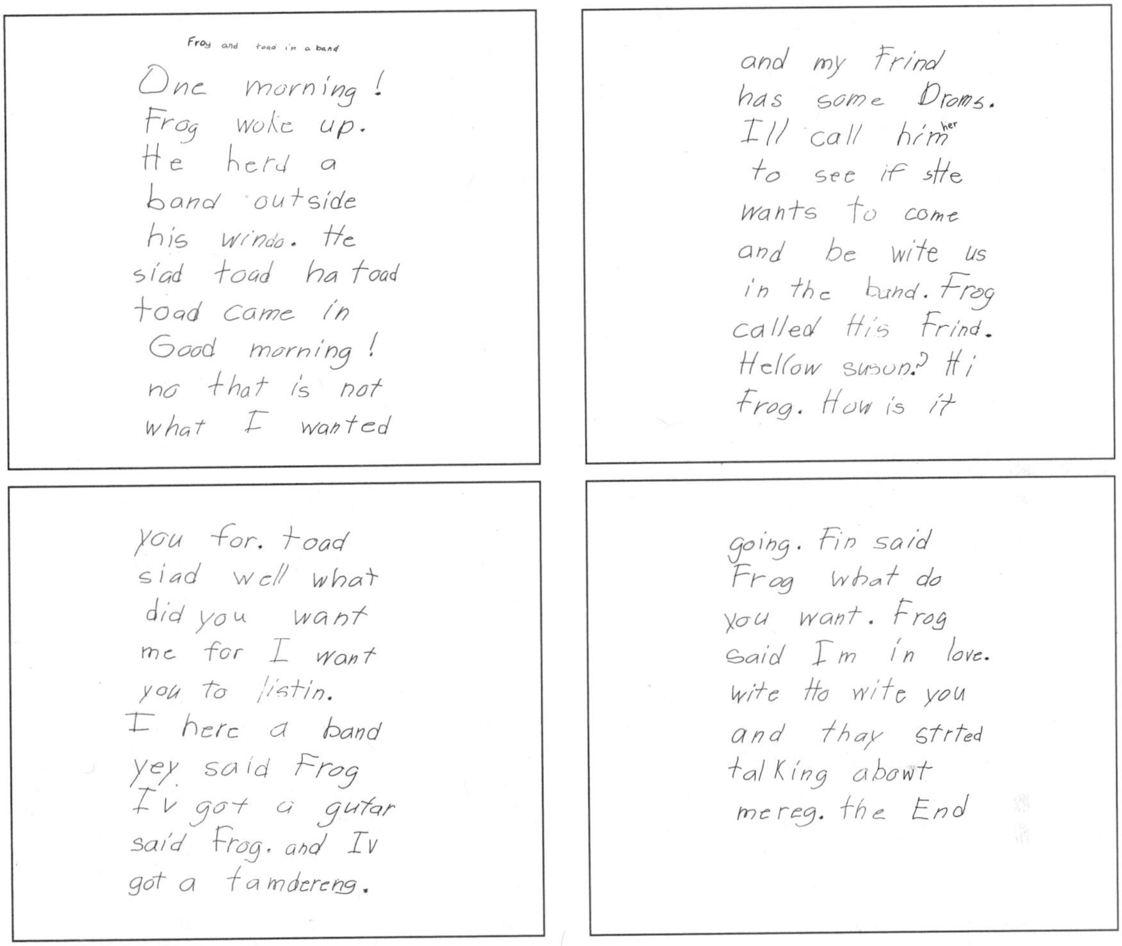

Frog and toad in a band

One morning !
Frog woke up.
He herd a
band outside
his windo. He
siad toad ha toad
toad came in
Good morning !
no that is not
what I wanted

and my Frind
has some Droms.
I'll call him[her]
to see if stle
wants to come
and be wite us
in the band. Frog
called His Frind.
Hellow suson? Hi
Frog. How is it

you for. toad
siad well what
did you want
me for I want
you to listin.
I here a band
yey, said Frog
Iv got a gutar
said Frog. and Iv
got a tamdereng.

going. Fin said
Frog what do
you want. Frog
said I'm in love.
wite Ho wite you
and thay strted
talking abowt
mereg. the End

Text of "Frog and Toad in a Band" by Janie.
"One morning, Frog woke up.
He heard a band outside his window.
He said, 'Toad, hey Toad, come in.'
'Good morning!' said Toad.
'No, that is not what I want you for.'
Toad said, "Well, what did you want me for?"
'I want you to listen. I hear a band. Yeah,' said Frog.
'I've got a guitar,' said Frog.
'And I've got a tambourine and my friend has some drums. I'll call her to see if she wants to come and be with us in the band.'

Frog called his friend, 'Hello, Susan!'
'Hi, Frog.'
'How is it going, friend?' said Frog.
'What do you want?'
Frog said, 'I'm in love with you, with you.'
And they started talking about marriage.
The end."

Throughout the year, April noticed the children's connections to stories in their everyday actions, their playful renditions of bits of stories, and their complimentary borrowing of story structure to write sequels or compose other similar stories. By writing using authors' stories as their models, the children internalized the structure of the stories and made them their own. Children should always be free to write their stories in any form they choose, but using the known story form is also beneficial. Imaginative teachers use the story formats as a means to get children started in writing and to plan their writing.

APRIL'S REFLECTIONS

An experienced, successful teacher, April found the decision to move with Ms. Dillon a challenging one. The reorganization of space, time, resources, and the curriculum had been troublesome at times, even for a seven-year veteran. In many ways, the move to literature-based reading instruction was easier than April had anticipated. The way she organized was different than the other teachers', but April felt her plan worked well for beginning readers.

While April had been quite comfortable with the social studies and science units, organizing literature units of study was a new experience for her. She began using the literature webs as a part of her instruction in reading and found herself emphasizing the structure of stories and making sense of the plots, as well as identifying the main problems of the story. She felt the literature units fit nicely with the structure of her literature reading groups as well.

April had tried a variety of ways of organizing social studies and science units. She always used the topic of the thematic unit for the main ideas of the "meeting time" instruction. She selected books which went along with the theme for the read aloud selections and found extra books for the class library, as well as books to display in the activity centers. April designed units around what interested the children. They were particularly drawn to units on animal life. Last year, the most successful unit was studying endangered species, which live in their area. The children were sensitive to the plight of the Florida manatee since they lived near the animal's habitat.

One day in March, the principal came by April's classroom to announce that some visitors were coming to see how their school operated. April anticipated some of the visitor's questions and remembered her frustrations, as well as her successes. She knew the teachers would ask: "How do you manage your time?," "How do you organize literature groups instead of reading groups?," "How do you integrate the theme across so many areas of the curriculum?" April looked back over her schedule and the collection of thematic units she and the other teachers had written together. She planned a handout of her daily schedule, made a list of units, and began thinking about how to describe her day, her year as a teacher in a multi-aged classroom.

A Third-Grade Teacher— Lynnette's Story

Lynnette liked third graders. They were so confident, loved their teacher, and were so eager to act and feel more grown-up. Lynnette was a community theater actor and thought that one of the best ways for the children to enjoy stories was to have them do readers' theater, write scripts of famous children's books, dramatize favorite scenes from stories, and write their versions of folktales from different cultures. Lynnette's classroom seemed to always be alive with activity.

Lynnette welcomed the school's decision to start teaching reading with trade books, incorporating writing workshop, and connecting the curriculum through children's literature. These changes fit perfectly with Lynnette's strengths in drama, music, and the arts which seemed to be the activities her students enjoyed.

The challenges were immense for Lynnette at Roosevelt Elementary, but the satisfaction of helping African-American, Mexican-American, and immigrant children from South and Central America gave Lynnette a great deal of satisfaction. While Lynnette, an African-American, grew up in a middle-class family, from her teaching she knew the struggles of the poor, whatever their race or ethnic backgrounds. Lynnette wanted all the children to succeed, to have a sense of pride, and to find in her classroom a compassionate teacher who would push them to achieve and find ways to make the classroom an enjoyable place where they wanted to return everyday.

She knew what she wanted to accomplish, but Lynnette had a major problem. There were so many special services at her school that her students were being pulled out of her classroom so often that she felt the day was disjointed for the children and the curriculum splintered. She wanted the children in the classroom with her, learning and being a part of the family she helped to create there.

Lynnette asked for a conference with Ms. Anson, the principal. She was surprised to learn that Lynnette felt her students were receiving too many special services. After Lynnette explained that over half of her third graders received some sort of special services and were out of the room for at least part of the day, Ms. Anson saw the magnitude of the problem. One child received Chapter One reading, Limited-English-Proficiency (LEP) services, speech therapy, saw the guidance counselor, and went to a special math lab for remediation. Lynnette felt Byron needed to be in her classroom. He hated leaving and often cried when he left, was sullen when he returned, and could not seem to get back into the swing of the activities that went on while he was out of the room. Lynnette could not keep up with what Byron had missed and she knew for certain that an eight-year-old could not. He felt left out of the wonderful drama, music, and art projects the other children were doing as a part of their multicultural literature responses.

QUESTIONS FOR REFLECTION

- ☐ To better identify with the children, follow a child who receives several special services for a day.
- ☐ What is the child's day like through her or his own eyes? Record what happens in a third-grade classroom for a day.
- ☐ What are the children missing in their regular classroom instruction while they are seeing the various remedial teachers?

LYNNETTE FACES THE DILEMMA

At first Ms. Anson, the principal, proposed that Lynnette work with all of the special teachers and try to coordinate Byron's work. Lynnette agreed to try, but returned in two weeks to say that it just was not feasible. She had not even been able to schedule a time when all of the different people who taught Byron could meet.

Ms. Anson called a meeting of the assistant principal, all the special teachers and Lynnette. Initially, the special teachers were defensive about their remedial roles and felt that if Lynnette would just work more closely with them that the problems could be resolved. It was at that point that Lynnette described all Byron was missing and his attitude when he returned from the special-services classes. The conversation focused on Byron's special needs and why he was so difficult to work with. Then Lynnette spoke up, rather forcefully and rather dramatically, saying, "The problem is not with Byron, the problem is with us!"

The Chapter One reading teacher proposed a solution. She told about a school where the reading specialist did not pull children out of the classroom for special services but instead went to the child in his or her own room. With some further discussion, Lynnette, the Chapter One teacher, and the LEP teacher met after school on Friday and talked about Byron, but they also discussed the other LEP children from Lynnette's third grade who received services. Lynnette was adamant that the children should not become like the "low-reading group."

The alternative was for the Chapter One teacher and the LEP teacher to meet with Lynnette's children during reading and writing time in the morning. The Chapter One reading teacher would focus on her four assigned students and assist them with their writing, do running records of their reading,[5] help them select classroom books to read on their own, and on occasion would read to the whole class from a book associated with a multicultural unit. The LEP teacher would work directly with the three LEP students, using the unit topic in Lynnette's classroom. In addition, the LEP teacher would spend some time instructing the parent

Figure 11.16 Multicultural Tales for Lynnette's Third Graders

African-American and African Tales Dramatized, With Music and Art Activities

McKissack, Patricia. (1988). *Mirandy and Brother Wind*. Illustrated by Jerry Pinkney. New York: Alfred A. Knopf.

Mirandy wins the cakewalk with Ezel, the friend she often teased, with some instruction in fancy stepping by Brother Wind.

San Souci, Robert D. (1989). *The Talking Eggs*. Illustrated by Jerry Pinkney. New York: Dial Books for Young Readers.

Adapted from a Creole tale, this is the story of Blanche who is like Cinderella, receiving wealth and moving away from her spiteful mother and sister.

Steptoe, John. (1987). *Mufaro's Beautiful Daughters*. New York: Lothrop, Lee & Shepard.

An African tale about how the kind sister is selected to become the new queen.

Caribbean Tales Dramatized, With Music and Art Activities

Bryan, Ashley. (1989). *Turtle Knows Your Name*. New York: Macmillan.

A young boy's long name is hard to learn until he and his granny dance a name dance by Turtle.

Buffett, Jimmy, & Buffett, Savannah Jane. (1988). *The Jolly Mon*. Illustrated by Lambert David. San Diego, CA: Harcourt Brace Jovanovich.

A golden-throated fisherman finds a bejeweled guitar and finds fame and fortune abroad but returns to save his people from evil pirates and becomes the new ruler.

Keens-Douglas. (1992). *The Nutmeg Princess*. Illustrated by Annouchka Galouchko. New York, Ontario: Annick.

The story of Petite Mama, a fruit seller, and the beautiful Nutmeg Princess who floated on a lake. She was only visible to Petite Mama until Petal saved Aglo from drowning. Nutmeg Princess blessed Petal for her kindness and bravery.

Mexican-American and Mexican Tales Dramatized, With Music and Art Activities

Garcia, M. (1978, 1987). *The Adventures of Connie and Diego/Las Adventuras de Connie y Diego*. San Francisco: Children's Book Press.

A fantasy tale of Connie and Diego, twins who have multicolored skin. They run away to a land where no one makes fun of them, eventually returning safely to their families.

Lattimore, Deborah Nourse. (1987). *The Flame of Peace: A Tale of the Aztecs*. New York: Harper Collins.

To prevent the outbreak of war, a young Aztec boy must outwit nine evil lords of the night to obtain the flame of peace from Lord Morning Star.

Rohmer, Harriet, & Gómez, Cruz. (1989). Mr. Sugar Comes to Town/La Visita del Sr. Azu'car. Illustrated by Enrique Chagoya. San Francisco: Children's Book Press.

Based on a puppet show, this is the story of evil Mr. Sugar and how he is conquered by good nutrition.

Teacher Resource Materials for Selecting Multicultural Books

Bararrera, R. B., Liguori, O., & Salas, L. (1992). Ideas a literature can grow on: Key insights for enriching and expanding children's literature about the Mexican-American experience. In V. Harris (Ed.), *Teaching multicultural literature in grades K–8*. (pp. 203–241).

Bello, Y. (1992). Caribbean children's literature. In V. Harris (Ed.), *Teaching multicultural literature in grades K–8*. (pp. 243–265).

Bishop, R. S. (1992). Multicultural literature for children: Making informed choices. In V. Harris (Ed.), *Teaching multicultural literature in grades K–8*. (pp. 37–53). Norwood, MA: Christopher-Gordon Publishers.

Fountain, J. (1993, April). Invitations to culturally diverse literature. Paper presented at the annual study conference of the Association for Childhood Education International, Phoenix, AZ.

Harris, V. (1992). Contemporary griots: African-American writers of children's literature. In V. Harris (Ed.), *Teaching multicultural literature in grades K–8*. (pp. 55–108). Norwood, MA: Christopher-Gordon Publishers.

Miller-Lachmann, L. (1992). *Our friends, our families, our world: An annotated guide to significant multicultural books for children and teenagers*. New Providence, NJ: R. R. Bowker.

reading volunteers about how to work more effectively in reading books with the three children. She also would read to the whole class in both Spanish and English. Ms. Rodriguez also agreed to teach the whole class some Spanish phrases.

At first, Lynnette was a bit self-conscious as she taught reading lessons in front of the reading specialist. It was a change for the reading specialist, as well, to plan reading lessons that were based on children's literature. She also found it challenging to help the students with writing. Eventually, she stayed in the classroom for the writing-workshop period to get a better grasp on what Lynnette was trying to do with the editing process when the children wrote their own stories, scripts, and retellings of folktales from many different cultures. She began by working with a small editing group, which included two of her special students.

The LEP teacher, however, liked the dual role immediately and found the process of working in the classroom exciting as she taught Spanish to the English speakers and helped the LEP Spanish students learn more English. The parent volunteers were happy to have the recommendations of a language specialist to guide them. Lynnette's enjoyment of art, music, and drama worked particularly well for the LEP students. They expressed their interest in the topic of some of the multicultural books by doing some creative activities in response.

Meanwhile, Lynnette began conversing with the art and music specialist about the possibility of doing some of their teaching in her classroom, when special equipment was not required for their lessons. Lynnette and the art and music teachers planned more emphasis on multicultural arts and crafts, as well as connections to music. Lynnette chose books, art, and music activities to focus on the heritage of the African-American and Mexican-American children, as well as that of two children who were recent immigrants from the West Indies. (See Figure 11.16 for titles of books and teacher resources the team of teachers used to select focus books for their units on different cultures.)

WHAT HAPPENED TO BYRON?

Lynnette's story, however, does not have a happy ending. Even though Byron was the motivation for Lynnette's collaboration with the many specialists and her emphasis on finding ways to integrate the curriculum, after only two weeks, he was not there to enjoy the classroom. Byron moved and Lynnette did not know where. No one called for his student records to be transferred. Lynnette should be used to this by now, but she wasn't. She was always concerned, deeply concerned when a family moved without leaving an address with the school. Usually it was to avoid the bill collectors. But schools do not give out information to bill collectors; they do inform teachers, teachers who care as deeply as Lynnette cares.

Concluding Remarks

These five early childhood teachers lived and worked in the ever-changing world of schools. That world included child care and preschool, as well as the changing arena of curricular needs, new methods of reading instruction, changing organizational patterns of primary schools, and the worries of a caring teacher who was prompted to action by a single child. Their teaching dilemmas went far beyond selecting the books they would read aloud to their classroom, but children's literature provided them a connection to solving the problems.

Anne knew that when parents read to their children, even from the youngest days of infancy, it lets the child know reading is important, but it also bonds the child and parent in a shared story. She learned that she must find new ways to help them understand how to read to their children.

When Emily, a preschool teacher, learned more about how children grow in their literacy, she incorporated more books and literacy materials in the classroom, without sacrificing the hands-on, playful learning environment of developmentally appropriate activities.

When a kindergarten teacher was courageous enough to talk with other teachers to find out how her former students were doing, she learned that she can not do anything about how other teachers teach. But, Fran did find a way to restore Jason's enthusiasm for good books.

When April was invited to move to a new continuous progress school that used a literature approach for reading instruction and integrated curriculum units, she began a massive reorganization project for her classroom of six- and seven-year-olds. She reorganized the space, the schedule, classroom resources, and her own use of time to manage the day and the curriculum.

When Lynnette, a third-grade teacher, focused on Byron's needs, she asked some difficult questions of the school. Her insistence caused the pull-out programs to be reevaluated and she learned that professionals can enjoy working and designing multicultural units together.

These teachers learned from the problems that were a part of their school. Each of the dilemmas required actions that the teachers took by thoughtfully reflecting on their teaching situations.

Authors' Note

To the beginning teacher, we heartily recommend finding a mentor, someone like Anne, Emily, Fran, April, or Lynnette, who can be a colleague.

Suggested Learning Experiences

1. Read the questions for reflection again. Do you agree with the decisions the teachers made? Would you feel comfortable facing these dilemmas? Which of the teacher's problems seemed most formidable to you?

2. Visit an infant and toddler program at a child-care facility. Look for books in the classrooms. Observe the caregivers and see if they read to the infants and toddlers.

3. Schedule a visit to a preschool classroom. Observe the teacher reading aloud to the three- and four-year-olds. Evaluate his or her reading effectiveness.

4. Examine at least five of the patterned language or predictable books listed in Figure 11.2.

5. Ask to read to kindergartners. Select a big book to read. Rehearse your presentation of the book.

6. Locate a continuous progress or multiaged group school in your community. Plan a visit and inquire about the daily schedule.

7. Observe a reading specialist who uses children's literature in remedial lessons.

8. Observe an LEP teacher and find out the titles of children's books he or she uses to instruct the limited-English-proficiency students.

9. Volunteer to read to an LEP child.

10. Discuss the pros and cons of remedial programs offered outside of the classroom and those coordinated with in-class instruction.

Endnotes

1. For the sake of anonymity, the names of the five teachers focused on in this chapter have been changed. We have selected five female teachers because our students were female. We did not change gender names.

2. For more suggestions, read: Morrow's *Literacy Development in the Early Years* (1993); Raines and Canady's *More Story S-t-r-e-t-c-h-e-r-s: Activities to Expand Children's Favorite Books* (1991); Schickedanz's *More than the ABCs: The Early Stages of Reading and Writing* (1986).

3. For additional information about continuous-progress schools, please read Barbour, N. H., & Seefeldt, C. (1993). *Developmental Continuity Across Preschool and Primary Grades*. Wheaton, MD: Association for Childhood Education

International; and Kasten, W., & Clarke, B. (1993). *Multi-age Elementary Classrooms.* Katonah, NY: Richard C. Owen.

4. The authors are indebted to the teachers at Centennial Elementary in Pasco County, Florida, and graduate students in Early Childhood and Elementary Education at the University of South Florida for sharing their curriculum planning and webbing processes.

5. For further discussion of this assessment procedure, see Johnston, Peter H. (1992). *Constructive Evaluation of Literate Activity.* New York: Longman.

REFERENCES

Bararrera, R. B., Liguori, O., & Salas, L. (1992). Ideas a literature can grow on: Key insights for enriching and expanding children's literature about the Mexican-American experience. In V. Harris (Ed.), *Teaching multicultural literature in grades K–8* (pp. 203–241). Norwood, MA: Christopher-Gordon.

Barbour, N. H., & Seefeldt, C. (1993). *Developmental continuity across preschool and primary grades.* Wheaton, MD: Association for Childhood Education International.

Bello, Y. (1992). Caribbean children's literature. In V. Harris (Ed.), *Teaching multicultural literature in grades K–8* (pp. 243–265). Norwood, MA: Christopher-Gordon.

Bishop, R. S. (1992). Multicultural literature for children: Making informed choices. In V. Harris (Ed.), *Teaching multicultural literature in grades K–8* (pp. 37–53). Norwood, MA: Christopher-Gordon Publishers.

Bredekamp, S. (Ed.). (1987). *NAEYC position statement on developmentally appropriate practice in programs for 4- and 5-year-olds.* Washington, DC: National Association for the Education of Young Children.

Bromley, K. D. (1991). *Webbing with literature: Creating story maps with children's books.* Boston: Allyn and Bacon.

Fields, M.V., Spangler, K. L., & Lee, D. M. (1991). *Let's begin reading right: Developmentally appropriate literacy.* New York: Merrill.

Fountain, J. (1993, April). Invitations to culturally diverse literature. Paper presented at the annual study conference of the Association for Childhood Education International, Phoenix, AZ.

Goodman, Y. M. (1978). Kidwatching: An alternative to testing. *Elementary School Principal, 57*(4), 41–45.

Harris, V. (1992). Contemporary griots: African-American writers of children's literature. In V. Harris (Ed.), *Teaching multicultural literature in grades K–8* (pp. 55–108). Norwood, MA: Christopher-Gordon Publishers.

Jarolimek, J., & Foster, C. D. (1989). *Teaching and learning in the elementary school.* New York: Macmillan.

Johnston, P. H. (1992). *Constructive evaluation of literate activity.* New York: Longman.

Kasten, W., & Clarke, B. (1993). *Multi-age elementary classrooms.* Katonah, NY: Richard C. Owen.

Miller-Lachmann, L. (1992). *Our friends, our families, our world: An annotated guide to significant multicultural books for children and teenagers.* New Providence, NJ: R. R. Bowker.

Morrow, L. M. (1993). *Literacy development in the early years.* Boston: Allyn and Bacon.

Raines, S. C. (1986). Teacher-educator learns from first and second grade readers and writers. *Childhood Education, 62*(4), 260–264.

Raines, S. C., & Canady, R. J. (1992). *Story s-t-r-e-t-c-h-e-r-s for the primary grades: Activities to expand children's favorite books.* Mt. Rainier, MD: Gryphon House.

Raines, S. C., & Canady, R. J. (1990). *The whole language kindergarten.* New York: Teachers College Press.

Rhodes, L. K. (1981). I can read! Predictable books for reading and writing instruction. *The Reading Teacher, 34*(5), 511–518.

Schickedanz, J. A. (1986). *More than the ABCs: The early stages of reading and writing.* Washington, DC: National Association for the Education of Young Children.

CHILDREN'S LITERATURE REFERENCES

The authors and illustrators of children's books are listed by their full names to help the reader become acquainted with them. If only one name is listed, the author also illustrated the book.

Appleby, Ellen. (1984). *Three Billy-Goats Gruff: A Norwegian Folktale.* New York: Scholastic.

Bennett, Jill. (1986). *Teeny Tiny.* Illustrated by Tomie dePaola. New York: G. P. Putnam's Sons.

Berger, Thomas. (1990). *The Mouse and the Potato.* Illustrated by Carla Grillis. Edinburgh, Scotland: Floris Books.

Brett, Jan. (1989). *The Mitten.* New York: G. P. Putnam's Sons.

Bridwell, Norman. (1988). *Clifford's Birthday Party.* New York: Scholastic.

Bridwell, Norman. (1988). *Clifford, the Big Red Dog.* New York: Scholastic.

Bridwell, Norman. (1984). *Clifford's Family.* New York: Scholastic.

Brown, Marc. (1989). *Arthur's Birthday.* Boston: Little, Brown.

Brown, Marc. (1986). *Arthur's Teacher Trouble.* Boston: Little, Brown.

Brown, Marc. (1983). *Arthur's Thanksgiving.* Boston: Little, Brown.

Bryan, Ashley. (1989). *Turtle Knows Your Name*. New York: Macmillan.

Buffett, Jimmy, & Buffett, Savannah Jane. (1988). *The Jolly Mon*. Illustrated by Lambert David. San Diego, CA: Harcourt Brace Jovanovich.

Carle, Eric. (1981). *The Very Hungry Caterpillar*. New York: Philomel.

Carle, Eric. (1972). *Rooster's Off to See the World*. Saxonville, MA: Picture Book Studio.

Carlstrom, Nancy White. (1986). *Jesse Bear, What Will You Wear?* Illustrated by Bruce Degen. New York: Macmillan.

Cohen, Miriam. (1971). *Best Friends*. Illustrated by Lillian Hoban. New York: Macmillan.

Cohen, Miriam. (1967). *Will I Have a Friend?* Illustrated by Lillian Hoban. New York: Macmillan.

Crews, Donald. (1992). *Big Mama's*. New York: Greenwillow.

Dragonwagon, Crescent. (1990). *Home Place*. Illustrated by Jerry Pinkney. New York: Macmillan.

Eastman, P. D. (1960). *Are You My Mother?* New York: Random House.

Flack, Marjorie. (1932). *Ask Mr. Bear*. New York: Macmillan.

Gág, Wanda. (1928). *Millions of Cats*. New York: Coward-McCann.

Galdone, Paul. (1973). *The Little Red Hen*. New York: Clarion.

Garcia, M. (1978, 1987). *The Adventures of Connie and Diego/Las Adventuras de Connie y Diego*. San Francisco: Children's Book Press.

Guarino, Deborah. (1989). *Is Your Mama a Llama?* Illustrated by Steven Kellogg. New York: Scholastic.

Heine, Helme. (1982). *Friends*. New York: Margaret K. McElderry Books.

Hoban, Russell. (1964). *A Baby Sister for Frances*. Illustrated by Lillian Hoban. New York: Harper & Row.

Hughes, Shirley. (1983). *Alfie Gives a Hand*. New York: Lothrop, Lee & Shepard.

Hutchins, Pat. (1968). *Rosie's Walk*. New York: Macmillan.

Hutchins, Pat. (1986). *The Doorbell Rang*. New York: Greenwillow.

Hutchins, Pat. (1971). *Titch*. New York: Macmillan.

Kalan, Robert. (1981). *Jump, Frog, Jump!* Illustrated by Byron Barton. New York: Scholastic.

Keens-Douglas. (1992). *The Nutmeg Princess*. Illustrated by Annouchka Galouchko. New York, Ontario: Annick.

Kennedy, Jimmy. (1983). *The Teddy Bears' Picnic*. Illustrated by Alexandra Day. San Diego, CA: Green Tiger Press.

Kovalski, Maryann. (1987). *The Wheels on the Bus: An Adaptation of the Traditional Song*. Boston: Little, Brown.

Lattimore, Deborah Nourse. (1987). *The Flame of Peace: A Tale of the Aztecs*. New York: Harper Collins.

Lobel, Arnold. (1979). *Days With Frog and Toad*. New York: Harper & Row.

Lobel, Arnold. (1970). *Frog and Toad Are Friends*. New York: Harper & Row.

Lobel, Arnold. (1971). *Frog and Toad Together*. New York: Harper Collins.

Malone, Nola Langer. (1988). *A Home*. New York: Bradbury Press.

Martin, Jr., Bill. (1983). *Brown Bear, Brown Bear, What Do You See?* Illustrated by Eric Carle. New York: Henry Holt.

Martin, Jr., Bill, & Archambault, John. (1989). *Chicka Chicka Boom! Boom!* Illustrated by Lois Ehlert. New York: Simon & Schuster.

Mayer, Mercer. (1974). *What Do You Do With a Kangaroo?* New York: Four Winds Press.

Mayer, Mercer. (1968). *There's a Nightmare in My Closet*. New York: Dial Books.

Mayer, Mercer. (1987). *There's an Alligator Under My Bed*. New York: Dial Books.

Mayer, Mercer. (1988). *There's Something in My Attic*. New York: Dial Books.

McKissack, Patricia. (1988). *Mirandy and Brother Wind*. Illustrated by Jerry Pinkney. New York: Alfred A. Knopf.

Morris, Ann. (1990). *Loving*. Photographs by Ken Heyman. New York: Lothrop, Lee & Shepard.

Numeroff, Laura Joffe. (1985). *If You Give a Mouse a Cookie*. Illustrated by Felicia Bond. New York: Harper & Row.

Parish, Peggy. (1988). *Amelia Bedelia's Family Album*. Illustrated by Lynn Sweat. New York: Greenwillow.

Parish, Peggy. (1976). *Good Work, Amelia Bedelia*. Illustrated by Lynn Sweat. New York: Greenwillow.

Parish, Peggy. (1977). *Teach Us, Amelia Bedelia*. Illustrated by Lynn Sweat. New York: Greenwillow.

Peet, Bill. (1977). *Big Bad Bruce*. Boston: Houghton Mifflin.

Polacco, Patricia. (1990). *Thunder Cake*. New York: Philomel.

Rey, H. A. (1941). *Curious George*. Boston: Houghton Mifflin.

Rockwell, Anne. (1975). *The Three Bears and 15 Other Stories*. New York: Crowell.

Rohmer, H., & Gomez, C. (1989). *Mr. Sugar Comes to Town/La Visita del Sr. Azu'car*. Illustrated by Enrique Chagoya. San Francisco: Children's Book Press.

Rosen, Michael. (1989). *We're Going on a Bear Hunt*. Illustrated by Helen Oxenbury. New York: Margaret K. McElderry Books.

Rylant, Cynthia. (1985). *The Relatives Came*. Illustrated by Stephen Gammell. New York: Bradbury Press.

San Souci, Robert D. (1989). *The Talking Eggs*. Illustrated by Jerry Pinkney. New York: Dial Books for Young Readers.

Scarry, Richard. (1974). *Richard Scarry's Cars & Trucks & Things That Go*. Racine, Wisconsin: Western Publishing.

Simon, Norma. (1976). *All Kinds of Families*. Illustrated by Joe Lasker. Niles, IL: Albert Whitman.

Slobodkina, Ephyr. (1940). *Caps for Sale*. New York: Harper & Row.

Steptoe, John. (1987). *Mufaro's Beautiful Daughters*. New York: Lothrop, Lee & Shepard.

Tresselt, Alvin. (1964). *The Mitten*. Illustrated by Yaroslava. New York: Scholastic.

Wadsworth, Olive A. (1986). *Over in the Meadow*. Illustrated by Mary Maki Rae. New York: Penguin Puffin.

Wood, Audrey. (1984). *The Napping House*. Illustrated by Don Wood. San Diego, CA: Harcourt Brace Jovanovich.

Wood, Don, & Wood, Audrey. (1989). *The Little Mouse, The Red Ripe Strawberry, and The Big Hungry Bear*. London: Child's Play.

12

Parents' Invitations
To Literature

Parents' Invitations To Literature

Raymond was hired to be the teacher in an overcrowded first-grade with thirty one children, in an inner city school, which he had attended as a child. As he prepared for his new job, he worked many hours to design a classroom environment that would nurture literacy in his young students. While writing lesson plans and constructing materials for his classroom, he thought about the information that he had obtained from classes in early childhood education. He tried to apply this learning to his new teaching situation. During this process, he remembered a comment that he had heard repeatedly during his training; "The best environment for young children is one where parents and teachers work cooperatively toward a shared goal." One of his goals was that his students develop an interest in books and reading. He struggled with the difficult questions, "How can I help my students' parents understand their important role in the literacy development of their children? How can they gain access to books and other printed materials when they don't have money for the necessities? and What can a teacher do to establish a cooperative relationship with diverse family units?"

The Importance of the Home Environment

Parents are their children's first teachers, influencing all areas of their development including intellectual, social, emotional, and physical growth (Ollila & Mayfield, 1992). Parents are also key contributors to their children's language and literacy development. Providing a nurturing environment that helps children reach their potential is a difficult task, and parents need support from family, friends, and professionals (Berger, 1991). Families grow in positive ways as they develop social networks, identify resources, and obtain assistance. A major responsibility for teachers of young children is to design and implement approaches that will provide support and continuity between the home and early childhood experiences (Swick, 1984).

Many research studies have shown that children are more successful in school if their parents have provided active support and encouragement for them to achieve success in school (Watson, Brown, & Swick, 1983). Rutter (1985) identified several parent behaviors that nurture children's intellectual development. These include providing a variety of experiences, allowing children to explore, encouraging their developing abilities, playing, and participating in their conversations. A study of federal programs found that parent participation fosters continuity between the home and the program while increasing parents' contributions to the education of their children (Lyons, Robbins, & Smith, 1983).

HOME INFLUENCE ON LITERACY

Many studies of young readers have clearly identified the importance of the home environment. Durkin's studies (1966) of children who read before they entered school identified factors that fostered their development. Durkin found that the early readers were in language rich homes where they were read to frequently. They were not taught to read but rather lived in environments that were filled with print, reading models, and adults who responded to their interest in books.

Clark (1976) interviewed parents on topics related to family background to determine the elements they perceived to contribute to their child's early reading. Parents responded that their children were exposed to and read a variety of print: nonfiction, fiction, comics, and even newspapers. The early readers had been read to frequently by their parents, and observed adults who read for pleasure and visited a library often.

In a detailed analysis of six children and their families, Taylor (1983) provided insight into how parents supported the development of literacy. She found that children, who grew up in a home where reading and writing were valued and shared by family members, had an advantage when they began to read and write. Children, who are careful observers, watch their parents as they read a book or share a story, thus impressions of the importance of literature are made upon them.

Feitelson and Goldstein (1986) studied children who succeeded in school and found they had been read to daily and had their own books in their home. Bailey (1990) identified three factors that were critical to reading success:

1. reading to children

2. talking and listening to them

3. helping to broaden their experiential background

Carol Chomsky's (1972) research with six- to ten-year-old children found that being read to continued to have positive effects on language development in later childhood. These and many other studies (Belcher, 1985; Rasinski & Fredericks, 1990; Wells, 1986) have recognized the importance of parents reading to their children and the powerful influence on language development. Holdaway (1979), Smithe (1978), and Clay (1979) all suggested that having stories read aloud is helpful to literacy development in children as they become readers and writers. Interactive behaviors that support the positive effects of parents reading include questioning, praising, discussion, and relating concepts to life experiences (Strickland & Morrow, 1990).

A partnership between parent and teacher has historically been recommended in early childhood program, but social and professional systems have often discouraged this orientation. Many educators have felt that they are only responsible for the education of children, not parents. Gordon (1977) and Ascher (1988), Dunst and Trivette (1988), Pence (1988), Berger (1991) and many others have challenged this view and emphasized that children learn within the ecology of the family and the larger systems of the community. This renewed interest in the family and their important role in the education of children has brought about changes in programs that serve young children. Programs that are based on the family-centered philosophy recognize parents as the key players in the education of their children as they carry out the parenting roles of nurturing, guiding, teaching, and modeling. Watson, Brown, and Swick (1983) found a significant positive relationship between the support the parent received from the environment and the support the family gave their children. As more and more educators are accepting the premise that children develop in a holistic way, there has been increased interest in strengthening the partnership between the teacher and parent. In a cooperative effort, teachers support learning while working with parents to build a partnership that will enrich their children's environment. Research has found that partnerships established in early childhood programs involving parents in meaningful learning experiences strengthens children's and parents' self-images. These partnerships also positively influence parent and teacher relationships (Powell, 1988; Swick, 1987). Parents who are involved in parent education programs in early childhood gain a sense of purpose and extend this concern into their involvement with teachers into the primary grades (Swick, 1991).

In the important publication *Becoming a Nation of Readers: What Parents Can Do* (Brinkley, 1988), the effect of parents on the reading process in emphasized. "Learning to read begins in the home and children learn a great deal about reading before they ever set foot inside a school building [Brinkley, 1988, p. 1]."

The U.S. Department of Education's book *What Works* (1986) describes approaches that have demonstrated their effectiveness in the increased learning of children. The publication emphasizes the "curriculum of the home" and the need to form a partnership with parents to insure that the home is a nurturing environment. This report stresses that one of the most promising aspects of the parent partnership is the development of children's literacy. "The best way for parents to help their children become better readers is to read to them—even when they are very young [U.S.

Department of Education, 1986, p. 9]." The importance of the parent and child talking together and having conversation while the reading is occurring is also mentioned.

Many young children, however, are raised in environments where parents are unable to read or do not know the importance of reading to their children. Some parents have not had the opportunity to learn from positive role models and are not aware of ways to encourage their children's literacy development. Children from these homes may be at a disadvantage since they have not had the opportunity to observe adults reading, to hear a story read, or to participate in the language interactions that often accompany the activity. Manning, Manning, and Cody (1988) concluded that if parents are made aware of the importance of reading to their young children they will increase the time given to this activity. Most parents want to help their children if they know what to do and the benefits of such efforts. During the early years, parents' interest is especially high and their involvement in the education of their young children can have greater benefits (Gordon, 1975).

CHANGING FAMILY UNITS

Today's families are varied and include many different people who participate in the care of young children. A family may include two parents, a single parent, or extended or blended families, but all are capable of giving the support and nurturance needed by children. The family that was once considered the traditional form, two parents and two children, is no longer the typical family in the United States. The roles of fathers have also significantly changed in recent decades with new emphasis being placed on their nurturing involvement in the lives of their children beginning in infancy (Lamb, 1986). By the year 2000, the United States is projected to have a population of more than 268 million people. This population will include Latin Americans, African Americans, Native Americans, Alaskan natives, Asians, Pacific Islanders, and Caucasians (Berger, 1991). The

United States is a nation of cultural diversity and includes many ethnic groups, a range of socio-economic levels, religious differences, and rural and urban variations. With the immigration of new minority groups into this country, there will be a continuing need to increase understandings of many cultures. Successful work with diverse parents must include accepting and appreciating differences and similarities of people while avoiding stereotyping. Early childhood educators must understand and accept children's families and work with them to positively influence the lives of their students (Berger, 1991). Swick (1991) identified four personal attributes of teachers that seem to enhance their interactions with parents of young children. Teachers are:

1. sensitive to the personal dynamics of the family and have the ability to respond to them in a concerned manner;

2. flexible in adapting to the individual child and parent needs;

3. reliable and consistent on issues related to the family and school; and

4. accessible to parents ideas related to their children's development and learning.

As teachers design ways to communicate with parents or guardians, they may plan meetings and distribute written materials. It is important for teachers to understand the families and special abilities of children with whom they work. Not surprising, Gordon (1975), Epstein (1986), and Swick (1991) found that parents felt that the children's most effective teachers were those who had encouraged high levels of parent involvement.

BEGINNING EARLY

Efforts to help parents recognize their role in supporting and teaching should begin during the first years of a child's life. Moving into partnership early promotes strong relationships between the parent and teacher and builds the foundation for many years of effective involvement.

Ira Gordon's landmark Florida Parent Education project (1977) provided a model for programs that work with parents of infants and toddlers. Home visitors demonstrated the construction and use of inexpensive toys while parents learned how to engage their children in play, language, and social activities. These home visitors were from the community and were parents themselves. Gordon found that the parents participating in the program gained confidence in their own abilities as well as those of their infants. This improved self-image helped them feel more competent as parents and capable of supporting their child's learning. This positive view of their capabilities affected their relationships with the child in the program and with subsequent interactions with other children. Parents continued to be interested in working with others, including teachers, in the education of their children in the years that followed the program.

The Parents as Teachers project, operated by the state of Missouri, is an example of using parent education to assist children's early development and learning. This project provides educational guidance and support for parents during the first three years of their child's life. The program includes: information to parents before the child is born; training in the home related to the child's social, language, and cognitive development; demonstrations of activities for the developmental level of the child; and a parent resource center at a school site. Each family receives a monthly home visit and can attend monthly group meetings with other parents. This program is an excellent example of a partnership that is established during the first three years of a chid's life and provides a foundation for future learning (White, 1988).

The Head Start program, in addition to providing a child development program, includes a strong commitment to family and parent education. From its inception in 1965, Head Start has assisted the family in many ways including providing information related to health and dental care, obtaining resources from the community, supplying nutritional food, and securing employment. In 1985, the National Head Start Parent Involvement Task

Force reaffirmed ways of strengthening this component including involving parents in decision making in local programs, increasing participation in the classrooms, and helping parents sustain and build on Head Start experiences as their children move into elementary school. The Task Force restated that parents must be involved to affect maximum impact on children's development (Commissioner's Task Force on Parent Involvement in Head Start, 1987).

A Home Environment That Nurtures Literacy

Oral language provides the base for literacy development. In the home, the child has the opportunity to interact in a small group and often in one-on-one situations with her or his parents or other adults. These very personal language exchanges are adjusted to the interest and level of development of the child and are individually paced for her or his continued involvement.

These conversations with parents are built around ongoing activities and provide opportunities for the child to ask questions to clarify what is occurring. Using words and sentences to accompany activity is an extremely effective way to enrich the language environment for a young child. The responsive adult listens to the young child and interjects more advanced vocabulary. The model constructs sentences that will extend the child's learning during interaction and builds on the child's language experience. These conversations may occur at different times during the day, at mealtime, while waiting at a doctor's office, or when taking a bath. These incidental learning experiences may provide many hours of language enrichment during the early years.

Often the child initiates the discussion with a question and sustains the interaction by asking additional questions. The parent may provide an answer or clarify the child's thinking by asking a question that will assist the child in constructing a response. These exchanges follow the contributions of the child, are responsive, and support the language attempts of the developing child.

If provided with these language-rich experiences, a young child will increase in her or his language competencies and broaden her or his understanding of the world. These experiences can also include information about the print in the environment—signs at the mall pet store, telephone books with a neighbor's number, menu items in a restaurant, and a birthday card from an aunt.

The parent and child's world is filled with print and this association helps the child understand that print carries meaning. The development of print awareness in the context of meaningful activities, combined with rich language interactions, provides an important foundation for literacy development. From these experiences a child builds concepts of the functions and use of language (Neuman & Roskos, 1993).

HELPING PARENTS READ WITH THEIR CHILDREN

One of the most important messages that can be communicated to parents during the early years is that reading to a child is essential. There are many ways the teacher can help parents recognize the need for reading. They include providing meetings that focus on reading to children, loaning books and videos on the topics and inviting parents into the classroom to observe and participate during reading times. Parents need to be informed of the importance of this activity and they need assistance in developing their ability to read effectively to their children. The reading of a story should be an enjoyable experience for the parent and the child so that both will want to continue the activity for many years.

An effectively shared reading experience may be demonstrated to parents so they are able to see and model the features of the interaction. During the modeling activity, the child should be in the parent's lap receiving individual attention from an adult whom she or he loves. The parent is giving the focused attention to the child that is so important to her or him. The reading will be interactive with the child and the parent, each contributing to the event.

The parent will read the story with expression and include the child in the activity by asking about the pictures, predicting what will happen next, or asking for phrases to accompany the reading. These book-related interactions will encourage the contributions of the child and will be paced to follow individual interest. If the child wants to hear the story again, the parent may reread the story, understanding that this will help the child's comprehension.

As this and other stories are shared, the child will develop preferences for certain books. These favorite stories will build the foundation for home reading as they are shared again and again. One of these frequently read favorites will often be the first book the child uses in pretend reading. First readings should be encouraged by the parent since they demonstrate the child's understanding of the story, a step on the road to independent reading. The child may make an effort to replicate the manner in which the parent reads the story, using the same inflections in the voice, repeating words, and concluding with, "Well that's all for tonight." Story time is a special event—enjoying books together, sharing the excitement about the content, and laughing at the antics of the characters. Story time may be the most pleasant time of the day for both the parent and child. In bedtime reading, for instance, there will be a routine known by both the adult and the child so the negotiations that may have characterized other activities during the day will not be present. Sharing a book, as the basis for interaction, may provide a pleasant atmosphere, making it easier to talk together, often concluding with a good-night kiss. This bedtime ritual will make these cherished moments between parent and child special while nurturing a positive attitude toward books (Schickendanz, 1986).

Children benefit from hearing a variety of people read to them: parents, grandparents, neighbors, teenagers, and older children. Each person has a special way of reading, of sharing stories, and

---

Figure 12.1 Helping Parents Choose Books for Their Children

1. Is the story appropriate for the child's age level?

2. Do the pictures add to the understanding of the story?

3. Are the characters in the story believable with some possessing good qualities?

4. Does the length of the book match the child's attention span?

5. Is a satisfactory conclusion reached at the end of the story?

6. Will your child enjoy hearing the story again and again?

of inspiring interest. Boys and girls will enjoy having a story read by mother, father, grandparents, and other significant adults. For example, as they snuggle with Daddy reading a story about *Feelings* (by Aliki), they will begin to understand that men can read and share feelings. When Johnson's *Tell Me a Story, Mama* (by Johnson) is read to a young girl, her mother can share other stories that were her childhood favorites. As grandmother reads *William's Doll* (by Zolotow), they will experience love and acceptance from an older person. When sister shares *The Purple Coat* (by Hest), they will see new capabilities in a family member.

Linda Lamme (1985 pp. 47-49) identified some general points that will be helpful for parents reading to their children:

1. Choose books to read with your child that you personally enjoy.

2. Stop reading when your child loses interest.

3. Read at specific times of the day establishing a pattern of routine reading.

4. Be supportive of your child's response to the story.

5. Make sure the book you have read is available to the child for several days.

6. Allow time after reading for talking about the book.

7. Extend the reading to other books on the topic.

Some adjustments will be needed when reading to children at different developmental levels. When reading to a baby, make sure she or he is comfortable and seems to be enjoying the experience. Watch the baby's responses to the language or pictures, and follow that interest by slowing the pace of presentation or repeating a section. When the baby's physical movements communicate that she or he has grown tired of the activity, bring the reading to a close, ending on a positive point.

Toddler reading sessions should be short, although those toddlers who were read to in infancy often are attentive for longer periods of time. Pointing out familiar objects in pictures, encouraging the toddler to participate, and including sound effects often help to sustain interest in the story. Because toddlers are busy people, it is helpful to read to them more frequently rather than for a long period of time in one setting.

Preschoolers like to hear favorite stories again and again. Reading some of the same stories frequently will help preschoolers learn the story and become familiar with the content so later they may be able to "read" the story for themselves. Preschoolers enjoy stories on tape and video, which can supplement—but never replace—parents' readings. Using tapes, children can repeat the story, stopping it and playing it again as they choose. Primary-aged children will enjoy reading for themselves and sharing this wonderful new ability with their parents. But it should be remembered that beginning readers have to work hard in the process and will still need parents, grandparents, and other people to read stories that they can relax with and enjoy. No matter how well children read, they will still benefit from hearing a story read aloud.

In a family where there are several children, a group story reading can be a special event. Older brothers and sisters will enjoy sharing a story with parents and younger siblings. Picture books and predictable books are especially effective in these sessions since they appeal to a wide range of abilities and can be understood by all listeners. This story time may also include reading by the parents of more complex literature, providing an opportunity to introduce quality literature and authors to the family.

Books may be used in many different family activities. The inclusion of literature in activities can demonstrate the usefulness of books to children. Information obtained from books and the enjoyment derived from the addition of books, may heighten the child's appreciation for literature. If a trip is planned, a book that describes some of the points of interest may be selected and family members may read and determine those places they want to visit. Stories about the area may be read before the trip or cassette tapes may be prepared by the parents so the children may listen to them in the car. Primary-aged children can take books with them for reading and finding information throughout the trip. If a children's production or puppet show is performed in the community, reading the book before attending the production may be interesting; and a rereading after attendance will highlight the differences in the book and the show. There are many ways books may be used by the family as a part of everyday activities. Understanding the importance of making this literature connection will help parents begin to identify the many opportunities for using books and increase meaningful book use in the home.

HELPING PARENTS MAKE APPROPRIATE BOOK CHOICES

With thousands of children's books published each year it is often difficult for parents to select appropriate books for their children or to decide which ones to purchase. The teacher can serve as a resource for parents by making suggestions for books that match the interest and developmental level of the children with whom they work. Several publications are available that assist the teacher and parent in selecting books or media to use with young children. One of the most helpful is *Parent's Choice* Newsletter, which includes reviews of outstanding children's books, audio/videotapes, computer programs, television, and toys. The description of the materials includes the age range appropriate for the material. Each year a panel composed of parents, children, grandparents, teachers, librarians, producers, critics, and other experts selects recently published storybooks that children have enjoyed and presents a Parent's Choice gold or silver award. These popular children's books are listed in the publication and are highly recommended for young children.

The American Library Association publishes *The Best of the Best for Children* (1992). This comprehensive volume includes books that librarians have found to be popular with children in different stages of development. Reviews are presented in sections appropriate for use with infant/toddlers, preschoolers, and primary-aged children. The teacher may use this reference to identify videos, computer software, and audiotapes that families may enjoy. A classroom library of appropriate tapes could also be available for parents to borrow and review at home.

GETTING BOOKS INTO THE HOME

A goal for every teacher should be that each child in her or his class have a book to take home and keep forever. This personal book will be a prized item for the child, but it will be especially meaningful to the one who has never owned a book. Reading Is Fundamental is a program designed to help the child have a book of her or his own. In participating schools and neighborhoods, children are able to select a book and take it home. In one instance at a school library, several children were trying to make their selection from the books furnished by the program. One little boy was having an especially difficult time making his selection. He carefully examined many books and returned them to the table before making his thoughtful final selection. He took it to the librarian and said, "I can keep this book, right? I don't have to bring it back tomorrow! Right?" This book was his. Book ownership is special since it provides a story that can be cherished, reread, and enjoyed whenever the proud owner chooses.

Children's bookstores are exciting places for young children and provide convenient access to many books that may be enjoyed at home. In these stores, books are displayed in an attractive manner and are easily accessible for examination by the curious young child. Children's bookstore managers are often very knowledgeable about new publications and may help the parent select books on a specific topic of interest or by a favorite author. These specialty stores often have visiting authors, storytellers, or workshops for parents, which can expand the family's literacy experiences.

Other methods for getting books into children's homes are book clubs and book fairs. Many schools participate in book clubs, sending forms home with children to make selections and placing book orders throughout the classroom. Although it is important to assist parents in the selection process, these clubs may provide an inexpensive way to increase the number of books in the child's home. An excellent time to have a parent workshop on "How to Share Your New Books" may be right before orders are received, capturing the excitement of the new books. This parent session may focus on practical suggestions for reading to young children.

Several distributors of children's books, such as Gryphon House and Scholastic, and children's bookstores work with teachers and schools to organize book fairs. They send books to the school to be sold at reasonable prices. The unsold books are mailed back to the company. Benefits of planning this type of presentation of books to children are that books are available at the school, they are easy for parents to view, the children may assist in the selection, and the book can be taken home immediately. The school or classroom will also expand the number of books it has for use by children since it will receive free books for displaying the materials and overseeing the purchases.

Some early childhood educators have found a new way to get books into the home. They have created book bags that children may take home and return, similar to the toy lending library approach (Nimnicht, 1972). The book bags contain a book, props that can be used with the story, and a card, signed by the child, to identify the borrower. One teacher described a book bag she found to be especially effective. It included a book, a story reading cassette, and an inexpensive tape player. The children in her classroom looked forward to getting this prized bag to take home and share with family members. At the end of the year, the book had never been lost and the tape recorder was still working. These book bags provide the best type of homework, encouraging literacy activities that can be enjoyed by both the parent and child.

Books may also be made by teachers, parents, and children. These easily constructed books may be made from poster board, wallpaper, construction paper, or contact paper. (See Appendix B for book binding directions). The stories may be dictated to the teacher or parent, and illustrations may be furnished by children; or the child may be both writer and illustrator. These books will be a treasure for parents, providing a story that can be shared at home—an example of the efforts of their developing young child. Since the child will have helped write the book, she or he can "read" it to her or his family, providing the family with an opportunity to show their admiration.

Of course the least expensive way to add books to the home environment is through the use of the school and community libraries. The school library provides immediate access to thousands of books that are appropriate for young children and can be enjoyed with families. The school librarian may assist the teacher, parent, and child in the selection of books that will match her or his interest and reading level. The community library can be an excellent center for family reading. Here the parent and child can select reading materials, view videos of stories, or enjoy a "story hour." Although many parents take their children to public libraries only before they enter school, the habit should be encouraged to continue after children go to elementary school. The public library provides diverse materials for selection by children and includes books and references for the adult reader. In this environment the child may observe adult readers making selections and may interact with her or his parents as they determine the books they want to borrow. In rural areas, the arrival of the bookmobile is an event anticipated by young children and their parents. These traveling libraries expand the world for the young reader and her or his family.

Reading Together is a unique program developed by Beginning with Books and the Carnegie Library of Pittsburgh. The goal of this program is to put quality children's literature into the hands of parents of infants and toddlers who have little money for books. Packets of quality books are given to parents at county health departments and well-baby clinics. Individual sessions, stressing the importance of reading to children and methods of book use, are also conducted. A six month follow-up study of the families has shown a significant increase in the amount of time parents spend reading to their very young children compared to time spent before the materials were made available to them. In 1990, over 6,000 parents participated in the book program in the Pittsburgh area. This program demonstrates one of the creative approaches being used to help low income families obtain books to read to their young children (Segel & Friedberg, 1991).

OTHER LITERACY-RELATED MATERIALS

Receiving children's magazines by mail can be a special monthly event for children and their parents. These colorful publications can include short stories, games, poems, children's writings, and many activities that will interest children in reading and writing. They provide another avenue for children to learn about the world and enjoy reading. Parents and children may discuss the content, participate in activities, and find new sources for books.

Many newspapers include in their publication on a weekly basis a Mini-Page (Universal Press Syndicate). This special section, distributed once a week, is designed for children and includes stories about famous people and interesting news events and games. Teachers can often obtain copies of these children's pages free from local newspaper offices. These can be given to the children to take home and share with family members. Some parents may read the section with their children and talk about the printed content.

There are many videos, related to children's literature, available for rental or purchase. These visual presentations of stories may be enjoyed by the child or shared with family members. Videos should be selected carefully and used sparingly so that they will serve as another avenue for enjoying stories rather than as replacements for books. Parents' Choice award winners in 1992 included wonderful selections such as *Mike Mulligan and His Steam Shovel* (Golden Book Video, 1958), *Shelley Duvall's Bedtime Stories* (MCA/Universal, 1992), *Stories From the Black Tradition* (CC Studios, 1992) and *Grandpa* (Sony Kids' Video, 1992). The use of these videos may lead to the understanding of story and the reading of related books.

ACCESSIBILITY OF BOOKS

Books should have a special place in the home. They should be placed in the child's room on low shelves so that they can be seen and easily accessed by the child. The space should include writing materials such as pencils, pens, and paper. A variety of books, children's magazine, a children's page from the local newspaper, and other materials should be available.

Young children can be responsible for the care of books and storage of the materials. They may also assist in returning borrowed books on the appropriate day to the community library. Responsibility for returning library books may be encouraged by providing a special storage place for library books and a calendar showing the day the books are to be returned. These procedures not only assist in the management of the returned books, but also add literacy activities to the child's world.

For the family with interest in computers, electronic encyclopedias may provide a new option for information storage and retrieval. Electronic encyclopedias often require CD-ROM equipment and include color pictures, animations, charts, and sounds such as bird calls, animal sounds, music, and famous speeches. Collections of children's stories, poems, and songs may also add to the variety of books used in the home and demonstrate the many forms of literature in the child's environment. Audio cassettes can be recorded by parents or professionally produced versions of stories can be purchased and added to the book area.

QUESTIONS FREQUENTLY ASKED BY PARENTS

There are a number of questions about reading and literature that parents frequently ask early childhood educators. It is helpful for the beginning teacher to consider these questions before they are asked. The following are suggested responses to some of those very difficult questions.

"When should I begin reading to my child?"—Even the day the child is born is not too soon to begin reading to a child. In the first edition of *A Parent's Guide to Children's Reading* (1958), Nancy Larrick recommends reading to infants and included books to be used with babies under one year of age. Lamme and Packer (1986) describe the behaviors of infants during book reading activities. Resnick, et al. (1987) studied maternal book sharing and the behaviors that maintained infants' interest in their readings. These and many other studies have strongly supported reading to infants during the first year of life. Examples of books that are appropriate to use with babies include: Oxenbury's series of baby board books, *Playing, Dressing, Family, Mother's Helper,* and *Shopping Trip;* Ormerod's series, *Reading* and *Messy Baby;* and Ahlberg's *The Baby's Catalogue.*

"My child is in Kindergarten and all the class does is read stories and play. Shouldn't they be teaching her to read?"—In a developmentally appropriate kindergarten, children are actively involved in learning experiences. They participate in centers, talk about their activities, and build with blocks. They work in groups on creative projects and listen to stories and dramatize the content. All of these activities may look like play but these are learning activities for children of this age. These active and appropriate experiences are providing the framework for reading and writing. Books and stories are integrated throughout the day and are accompanied by activities so that the child can understand how print relates to her or his world. In the block area are books about building. In the housekeeping center are recipe books they can examine. Young children also participate with their teachers in reading books that have repeated phrases, rhymes, and interesting repetitions. This experience allows them to "read" with the teacher and leads to "reading" the book for themselves as they repeat the phrases they have heard. These meaningful activities, combined with enjoyable literature experiences, provide the base for reading.

"My four year old makes up words to go with the pictures in the book. Should I correct her and tell her what the words really are?"—Your child is demonstrating a new ability. She can "pretend" she is reading and use many of the words she has heard you use in reading a story. This behavior should be encouraged since it is an important step in reading development. As she has more experience with books, she will be more concerned about the exact wording, but at present, enjoy this new emerging ability.

"My child has many fears. Are there books that I can share with him to help him resolve some of these concerns?"—It is not uncommon for young children to have fears. You should not be overly concerned about these feelings. However, there are many children's books that may be used to help your child begin to deal with these scary feelings, and may provide a way of beginning a discussion about his fears. Some of the books that may be used include:

Eugene the Brave, by Ellen Conford

Harry and the Terrible Whatzit, by Dick Gackenbach

The Little Old Lady Who Was Not Afraid of Anything, by Linda Williams

You're the Scaredy Cat, by Mercer Mayer

There's a Nightmare In My Closet, by Mercer Mayer.

Mama Says There Aren't Any Zombies, Ghosts, Vampires, Creatures, Demons, Monsters, Fiends, Goblins, or Things, by Judy Viorst

Although these books may be helpful and lead to a discussion between you and the child, they should not be the only means of addressing the problem. (When teachers suggest books to parents on difficult topics they should encourage the parents to read the book before they share it with the child to be sure that the content and explanations are in keeping with their views and the developmental level of their child.)

"My child is in the second grade and can read. Do I still need to read to him at home?"—It is important to continue to read to your child even after he has become a reader. Children can listen to the story and experience advanced vocabulary that they might not be able to read on their own for many years. A parent related an experience he had with his son, a talented reader who would often say, "I want to hear how it sounds when you read it." The parent continues to help the child learn how reading works and to provide the opportunity to creatively imagine the happenings. These special times shared with books are more than an intellectual activity, however, they are a time of focused attention, and that need is never outgrown.

"My child brings books home and wants to read to me, but he makes so many mistakes. Should I make him sound out the words?"—It is wonderful that your child wants to read to you and share his books with you. Although it sometimes takes patience to listen to beginning readers, it is important to remember that your child is learning to read by reading. Reading to you should be enjoyable for him. Appreciation of his effort should be acknowledged by you. If he reads a word that is not in the story, let him continue without interruption. When he comes to a word and obviously is waiting for you to pronounce it, simply tell him the word. Don't ask him to sound it out or criticize his inability to select the right word. It is more important that he understand the story and gain confidence in his growing reading ability than that he be "right." By making the sharing of a book with you a joyous event, rather than a pressure-packed time, you will encourage continued readings for years to come.

GETTING PARENTS INTERESTED IN LITERATURE ACTIVITIES

During the preschool years, real experiences help children develop oral language and assist them as they develop the ability to read and write (Ollila & Mayfield, 1992). Larrick (1982) explained that parents need to understand that reading is a two-way process. In the early years, children gather experiences that will help them gain meaning from the printed text. With this awareness, the early childhood educator can relate these important points to parents:

1. Read to your child every day.
2. Tell stories to your child.
3. Talk to your child about experiences as they are happening.
4. Encourage your child to write down ideas in their own way.
5. Read a variety of books to your child, including those that relate to the real-life experiences.
6. Keep interesting printed materials in the home.
7. Let your child see a parent model reading and writing.

Communicating With Parents

There are many different ways in which early childhood educators can communicate with parents. A variety of approaches may be used to meet the interest, needs, and diversity of parents. Harste (1989) suggested that effective programs view parents as partners in their children's learning and provide options for obtaining information so parents can chose the manner in which they participate. These varied approaches may help parents be more informed and interested in young children's emerging literacy in the home, while supporting the efforts of the teacher.

ONE-WAY COMMUNICATION

Newsletters—An effective way to communicate with parents is through a newsletter. This monthly newsletter may inform parents about the child's school program, about activities in which the child is involved, reading projects, field trips, and suggestions for literacy development at home. The newsletter may include explanations concerning the curriculum, units of study, new additions to the classroom, favorite songs or recipes of the children, and dramatic play center activities. Stories written by small groups or individual children may be included to help the parents appreciate the work of their children. Cartoons or jokes can add humor to the difficult responsibilities of teacher or parent. Television programs on films that children and parents can enjoy together may be another helpful addition. Ideas specifically related to literature may include: new books in the library; a recommended book that children have enjoyed during the month; a suggestion to the parent to reread the book at home; hours of story time at the local library; the time of a book fair; and a new video available. Suggestions for additional reading related to a unit being studied, magazines that young children would enjoy, and finger plays that are used in the classroom are additional elements of importance to be communicated in newsletters. A segment of an article about literacy may be included to help the parent better understand the appropriate developmental process and practices for the young child.

Newsletters should be written so parents will enjoy reading them and should not be filled with educational jargon. They should be proofed carefully so that they communicate the teacher's professional competency. It is a good idea to have another teacher read the newsletter before copies are made. The newsletter should be published at a specific time each month so that parents will anticipate its arrival.

A parent can read and discuss the newsletter with the child to further the benefits of the publication.

In some homes, parents are not able to read the newsletter because they are not English-speaking or cannot read. If there are non-English-speaking families represented in the classroom, the newsletter may be translated with the assistance of older children or neighbors.

Handbooks—Many early childhood programs distribute handbooks for parents, including important information relating to policies, curriculum, fees, breakfast and lunch programs, and a yearly calendar. This handbook is given to parents when the child enters the program or during a home visit before school begins. Handbooks help parents understand the program and eliminates many of the questions that teachers must address each year. Parent Handbooks should be updated as changes occur and should be written in a positive way to demonstrate teachers' interest in parents and their children. Included in the content of the handbook may be information concerning library use, parent materials, and professional comments supporting the importance of books and literature in the early childhood program. An invitation to visit the center or school should also be included so parents will know that they are welcomed by the staff.

Notes Home—In the past, notes went to the parent containing the "dreaded" request to schedule a conference to discuss a problem. Today, notes designed to spotlight an important accomplishment of a child, to share a story written, or to make a positive comment concerning the child, may open the door to communication. These brief messages can focus on positive learning experiences and let parents know what their child is learning at school. When the parents read the note they may share it with their child and communicate a positive attitude toward school and the child's efforts. A note may be attached to a book telling parents that this is a story their child enjoys reading. It may include the statement, "Let him read this book to you!" This will encourage them to listen to the child's reading and provide material for the child to read successfully. This book will have already been read and the child will be able to share it with the parent(s) without fear of being criticized. The book *What Do You Do With a Kangaroo?* is an example that provides a predictable text that is enjoyable to both parents and children. For other examples, see the list of predictable and patterned language books in Chapter 11.

Parent Bulletin Board and Library—In the classroom, a special area may be designed to provide information to parents. A bulletin board may focus on a topic or a specific question to be addressed. Included in this area may be articles about literacy that parents can take with them, booklets and pamphlets that are free, books that can be borrowed, and notices of events that may be of interest to families.

Figure 12.2 An Example of a Newsletter

Vol. 1, Issue 2　　**KINDERGARTEN NEWS**　　October 15,1994

BUSY DAYS FOR BUSY CHILDREN

Our Kindergarten class is always busy with new and exciting activities. Monthly plans are posted in the parent area so you can learn about the activities scheduled.

One of our units last month focused on the author, Leo Lionni. We read and enjoyed many of his excellent books. *Swimmy, The Biggest House in the World,* and *Frederick* were three of the children's favorites. In the art center, the children created illustrations using Lionni's techniques such as watercoloring, printing, and collage making. The children created their own books, inspired by his work.

Your child will enjoy hearing you read Lionni's books and talking about the stories again. The reading of books at school and at home provides wonderful learning opportunities and a special time to talk together.

SPECIAL ANNOUNCEMENT

Story time will be held at the community library each Saturday morning from 9:00 a.m. to 10:00 a.m., in January, February, and March.

Plan to talk to your child about attending some of these delightful sessions!

MAILBOXES

Our parent mailboxes have been moved. They are now located next to the main entrance. Check them frequently for recipes, birthday invitations, and special notices.

PARENT MEETING

Mark your calendars! March 21st, at 7:00 p.m., is the date of a special PARENT'S MEETING, "Developing Responsibility in Young Children," with Mary Letter, a school psychologist.

This is a topic many parents requested and will provide very practical information that you can use at home.

WINTERTIME FUN

We have learned many new winter songs, chants and fingerplays.

One we have enjoyed is sung to the tune of "I'm a Little Tea Pot." Here at our Kindergarten, we know it as "I'm a Little Snowman"....

> I'm a little snowman,
> Short and fat.
> Here is my broomstick.
> Here is my hat.
> When the sun comes out,
> I'll melt away.
> Down, down, down, down,
> **WHOOPS!** I'm a puddle!

CENTER TIME

We are setting up a new center for ice skating, skiing, and wintertime fun. In this winter center, your child will learn about winter sports, weather charts, new vocabulary, and have the opportunity to talk, read, and write about their experiences.

(Adapted from newsletter of East Tennessee State University's Child Study Center.)

Some pamphlets and brochures may be obtained from professional organizations. The following brochures are available for parents from International Reading Association at no cost and can be obtained by sending a stamped self-addressed envelope to:

International Reading Association
P.O. 8139
Newark, DE 19714–8139
Good Books Make Reading Fun for Your Child
You Can Encourage Your Child to Read
You Can Help Your Child Connect Reading to Writing
Summer Reading is Important
You Can Use Television to Stimulate Your Child's Reading Habits

Catalogs of resources are available, free of charge, on request from:

National Association for the
Education of Young Children
1509 16th Street, N.W.
Washington, DC 20036

and

Association for Childhood Educational International
11501 Georgia Avenue, Suite 315
Wheaton, MD 20902

Some professional publications include parent columns that are designed for teachers to copy for parents. These pages can be found in *Childhood Education*, "For Parents Particularly" and *Reading Today*, "Parents and Reading." The parent area can provide easy access to materials to read and discussion of topics that are of personal interest.

Groups of teachers working with similar age groups may write and produce their own brochure or one-page flyer that may be distributed to all involved parents. Short flyers such as "Using Books at Home," "Increasing Your Child's Interest in Books," or "Inexpensive Local Trips to Enjoy With Your Child" may focus on a specific topic.

This brochure should be attractive, easy to read, and should include practical suggestions for parents to use at home.

TWO-WAY COMMUNICATION

Parent Meetings—Parent meetings can provide an avenue for sharing information or educating groups of parents on a specific topic and may range from one session to a series of workshops. Burgess (1982) investigated the effectiveness of parent training in eight workshops that focused on children's language development. In this study, the first two-hour session was totally devoted to the importance of reading aloud and on how to read to children at home. At the conclusion of the session, two groups of children, the experimental and control groups, were compared. The kindergarten children whose parents participated in the workshops scored significantly higher on the language development test than those whose parents did not attend. The teacher will, however, need to determine the number and depth of training needed for the parents of the children in her or his classroom.

Parents will be more involved in the learning sessions if certain aspects are considered in the planning:

1. A positive climate is established.

2. Parents are recognized as contributing members.

3. The program addresses the concerns and needs of the parents.

4. Real examples are included to help understand the concepts presented.

5. Different approaches are used (demonstration, role-playing, discussion, or media).

6. Encouragement and positive feedback are provided.

7. Parents are able to conclude for themselves the need for change.
(Berger, 1991)

There are several different types of meetings that may be used by early childhood educators to increase parental awareness related to literacy. An orientation meeting may be held at the beginning of the year to help parents understand the

Figure 12.3 Example of Parent Handout

HOW TO INFLUENCE CHILDREN'S TELEVISION VIEWING

Young children watch a vast amount of T.V. Their average viewing time has been estimated to be four to five hours per day. We know that young children learn best when they are actively involved in their learning and T.V. viewing is a passive nonparticipatory activity. Parents have the greatest possible influence in bringing about changes in their young children's viewing habits. Together they can become selective T.V. viewers.

Some ways a parent can turn the T.V. experience into a more positive force are:

1. Keep a log of the hours and programs watched by your family.

2. Set limits on viewing time consistent with your children's needs. Be firm, but accompany your rules with an explanation.

3. Start regulating your child's T.V. viewing early, before age three, if possible.

4. Discuss and evaluate the content and quality of T.V. programs with your children.

5. Teach your child to select the program she or he wants to watch before turning on the set. Have him turn off the set when the program is over, so that additional viewing does not become automatic.

6. Watch T.V. with your child and talk about what she has seen and heard, about differences between make-believe and reality an about how T.V. characters could solve problems without violence.

7. Encourage children to communicate with others about what they watch on T.V. Television can be used as subject matter for meaningful conversation.

8. Screen the kinds of programs your children are allowed to watch. Sometimes children should be encouraged to watch a certain program, but many are unsuitable for children to watch.

9. Encourage involvement in active pursuits from an early age to help children develop their curiosity in the world around them, rather than becoming dependent on T.V. for entertainment.

10. Plan specific, exciting activities that can replace the T.V. viewing habit. This requires planning and participation by the parent.

11. Break up long periods of time that are usually spent watching T.V. with other activities.

12. Take an activity seen on T.V. and actually do it: make the recipe; build the kite. Turn the viewing experience into a firsthand experience for your child.

13. Have a fun night at home with the T.V. off. Plan and implement family projects on this special night.

14. Make props of costumes that children can use to dramatize T.V. programs. Discuss their roles as actors and actresses, and emphasize the "pretend" element.

15. The most inappropriate place to put a T.V. set is in a child's bedroom, where parents have the least control over what their children watch and learn from T.V.

Young children cannot break the T.V. habit alone. The parent must help children make the transition by spending time getting them started on active alternatives and taking a genuine interest in what they are doing.

ANALYZE YOUR USE OF T.V. WITH CHILDREN

_____ 1. Are your child's activities regulated by the T.V. schedule?

_____ 2. Do your children eat meals or snacks in front of the television?

_____ 3. Do you watch T.V. with the children?

_____ 4. Do you use T.V. as a babysitter for your children when you are busy?

_____ 5. Do you talk with your children about the programs you watch together?

_____ 6. Does the T. V. set occupy a prominent place in your home/center?

_____ 7. Do you suggest T.V. watching when your children seem bored or restless?

_____ 8. Do you turn off the T.V. when there is an uninteresting or violent program being aired?

Adapted from: Isbell, R. (1985). Feature Article: Taking Control of Children's Television Viewing. _Oklahoma Children_, 11(4).

program, the curriculum, and the book activities that the children will be involved in during the day. Slides and videotapes may show parents their children's involvement in the class activities while the teacher explains the learning occurring during the activities. Pictures that show the teacher reading to the children with an explanation of the importance of this activity and the influence of it on the child's literacy development may be included in the presentation. Books should be displayed in the room so parents can look at the materials their children are reading and hearing read to them in the classroom. It may also be helpful to provide a list of books that the children have enjoyed so parents may read them at home. Parent meetings may focus on a specific topic with information shared by a guest speaker or the teacher. A needs assessment or survey may be conducted at the beginning of the year to identify particular topics of interest to a group of parents. Some topics that might be included for parents of young children are:

1. How to Read to Your Child

2. Selecting Good Books for Young Children

3. Parent's Sharing: Books Your Children Love

4. Selecting Toys and Books for Gifts

5. A Positive Approach to Discipline

Since many parents put their children to bed at the conclusion of a television program instead of reading a story, an important topic for a group meeting might be, "How is television influencing your family?" This session may include information about the vast number of hours young children are watching television, activities conducive to development that young children might otherwise be involved in, and ways to make changes in television viewing patterns.

Children who watch television selectively, in moderation, in the company of their parents, and with opportunity to discuss what they are viewing can have their experiences broadened, rather than restricted, by television. Parents can help their children develop critical viewing skills that allow them to control their television viewing habits. As television is viewed more selectively, families can use the additional time in meaningful experiences that include more time for reading together.

There are a number of publications that have been developed by producers of television shows to help relate what children are watching to their reading. Some surveys, such as the one conducted by the Corporation for Public Broadcasting, have found that some programs, such as "Reading Rainbow," may increase library borrowing and book sales. In addition, the survey found that this series stimulates interest in summer reading. The publication that includes learning suggestions related to this series is *Reading Rainbow Gazette.*

Another possible topic for a parent meeting dealing with literature is "Family Storytelling." As our ancestors knew well, storytelling adds richness to life and families. The use of storytelling in the home provides an avenue for parents and children to share past experiences and discuss important issues. Parents can learn how to tell stories to their children by relating family memories of, "When I was a little girl, my mother use to take me . . . ," or retelling favorite stories of their childhood, such as, "My grandma used to tell me a story about a little boy who looked after sheep . . . " Sharing these special memories bonds family members and gives them a shared story history. Children enjoy listening to the humorous adventures of their parents or hearing a story that a parent has enjoyed in the past. As parents share family memories, children will begin to share their experiences in story form. They will include many of the features their parents use such as, "When I was in kindergarten, I . . . ," or, "My teacher told me a story about a . . . " This quality time spent in storytelling will provide a way for parents to communicate with their children. It will promote listening and understanding of story structure and introduce new vocabulary in an interesting context. Children will request the stories again and again since they are personally meaningful and provide a special understanding of their family. The most cherished stories may be written in a book so children can retell them and begin to see content in print. These stories may also be read by the child and shared with other family members during visits or holidays.

In some programs, a parent session may focus on computer literacy. Parents and teachers can work together selecting appropriate software to use in both the home and school settings. Parents and teachers may write stories, draw pictures, and create newspapers using available software. This hands-on session may help parents and teachers form partnerships as they discuss the child's use of the computer and the support of classroom learning.

Make-and-take workshops are a popular way to get parents involved in literacy activities. These parent sessions include materials, directions, and supervision for making activities that can be used at home with the child. Attendance at these sessions has built-in rewards, since the parent is able to take a new toy or book home at the conclusion of the meeting. The educational activities are constructed of inexpensive materials. As the parents are involved in the making of these materials, the teacher is able to discuss their educational benefits and suggest ways they may be used with their children. Through this approach, parents begin to understand their importance in the development of their child and the role they play in their child's emerging literacy. An example of an effective make-and-take workshop for parents occurred when out-of-date reading texts were going to be destroyed at one school. The primary teachers collected over fifty books that contained classic stories. They collected cardboard boxes, fabric pieces, wallpaper books, and several rolls of contact paper. During a Saturday morning session, they demonstrated to parents a method of constructing durable hardcover books from the collected materials. The parents then explored the outdated textbooks and laughed together at the old pictures of families included in the texts. Parents then selected stories that their children would enjoy today, including

classic fairy tales, folktales, and poetry. The parents combined the old stories with the new covers and included book pockets and cards in the back of each. As the parents were involved in making the books, teachers were able to discuss the benefits of reading to children and the importance of parental involvement in the reading process. They were also able to encourage parents to continue reading to their children even after they were reading independently. They discussed shared reading experiences and the positive relationship of attitude and reading abilities. These beautiful new books were constructed by parents and taken home to share with their children. This make-and-take workshop provided education to the parents as well as books that would enrich the home literacy environment.

Family Literacy Workshops—Family literacy has become a national concern and many programs are being developed to break the cycle of illiteracy. These programs vary in scope and depth but they all focus on the importance of the family in promoting literacy. Educators are becoming increasingly involved in family literacy as a part of parent education programs. An innovative example of programs of this nature is Partnership for Family Reading, in Newark, New Jersey. The goal for this family literacy program is "to help parents support the literacy development of their children and improve their own literacy in the process [Handel, 1992, p. 118]." The partnership includes parents, who are viewed as both learners and resources, and educators, who serve as guides in the process.

Parents and other family members attend interesting workshops and reading sessions using children's books. Six components are used throughout the workshop to organize the sessions. Introductory activities include asking the adult to recall and share a positive memory of his childhood that is related to storytelling or story reading. Next, the children's books are read to the adults. The books selected are multi-cultural, appealing to both adults and children, and from different genre. The reading of the books can be followed with a discussion of strategies that can be used to improve comprehension: predictions, formulating questions, and relating the story to personal experiences. After using these strategies, participants work in pairs to read and practice comprehension techniques. Group discussion follows these paired readings. The final section of the workshop is focused on preparing the parent for reading the book to her or his child at home. A variety of books is also available to be borrowed. Parents may choose those they feel most comfortable reading.

Family literacy projects such as Partnership for Family Reading have many positive outcomes. Parents who participated in the program were found to value family reading and felt the program fostered the reading relationship of the parent and child. There is also evidence that the amount of time spent reading in the home increased. Parents began serving as important reading models but they were also reading and learning in the process. Throughout the program parents were learning that school can be a pleasant place (Handel, 1992). Programs focusing on family literacy have rediscovered the knowledge that parents and teachers can effectively combine forces to provide a rich literature environment for adults and children.

Open Houses—Open houses are designed to encourage the parent to visit their child's classroom, talk to the teacher, and view the creation made by the child. At open house the teacher may discuss the importance that literature plays in the classroom. Book posters may be displayed around the room and in the library area, which includes tapes of books, puppets, and a variety of printed material. Books written and illustrated by the children may be examined and admired by the visiting parent.

When planning meetings it is important to determine the best time for parents to attend. With the growing number of parents working outside the home, it is often helpful to allow a parent to bring the child to the meeting since it is sometimes difficult to arrange care for her or him. If the child is included in the meeting, the child can participate along with the parents or participate in activities planned especially for her or him in another area. Separate activities allow the parent to focus on information discussed in a meeting, while meetings where the children participate can add to the understanding of orientations or classroom visitations. Two teachers may plan meetings on the same night, with one conducting a meeting for parents and the other providing interesting activities for children when separate sessions are needed. Teachers have found that attendance at parent meetings can be increased by including children, current interest topics, and events for the whole family.

INVOLVING PARENTS IN THE CLASSROOM TO NURTURE LITERACY

Parents are as diverse as their children. Their range of interest and capability varies significantly. Diversity should be respected by providing various opportunities for participation in the classroom. A short survey may be conducted at the beginning of the year to help identify ways parents may be involved in their child's program. Some parents may prefer to be involved by making items for the children's use in the classroom rather than actually working in the classroom. Possible ideas for this type of involvement include making book bags, cutting out flannel board stories, constructing cardboard books, collecting materials from local merchants (wallpaper books, carpet samples, display materials), building bookshelves, or typing children's stories. Parents may be invited to the classroom to observe the children using these creations, or photographs may be sent home for them to see how their work is contributing to the classroom success.

Some parents will enjoy assisting in the classroom as volunteers. It is important to remember that these parents are not teachers and they will need some instruction related to their involvement so the experience will be positive for them. They may participate as little as an hour, or as much as twenty hours a week. A workshop at the beginning of the year with a group of parents

interested in serving as aides may help this process. It is helpful for the teacher to demonstrate activities to the parents as well as to explain what learning is occurring and what approaches to use if the children are having difficulty. Parent involvement in the classroom may provide many additional opportunities for small group work, one to one interaction, and reading with an individual child. But the involvement also benefits the parents, since they learn about the program, gain a better understanding of the development of young children, and see techniques that may be used at home with their child.

There are many different ways in which parents may participate in the classroom related to the literature program. Some include reading to a child individually, reading in the library center, listening to a child read, assisting children making books, being a guest storyteller, working in the computer center, participating in a sociodramatic center that relates to the parent's particular interest, taping stories for the library area, creating stories with the children, or sharing a special talent or interest. Involving parents in the classroom requires planning, supervision, and patience, but the outcome is increased opportunity for children to interact with adults and enjoy

literature-related activities with them. These positive outcomes make the effort worthwhile.

LENDING LIBRARIES

Lending libraries contain a variety of materials that may be checked out by the parents and used in the home with their children. Resources may include books, cassette players and tapes, flannel board and story pieces, videos on children's literature, magazines, and computer software. The materials included may also relate to specific activities occurring in the classroom or activities to extend the classroom content. Parent education materials may also be included in the library so that reading may be done at home. Lending libraries provide inexpensive accessibility to materials that young children and their parents can enjoy and use in shared activities. It expands the materials available to many families that could not purchase the resources.

SUMMER ACTIVITIES

Although many programs are only open a portion of the year, children learn the year around. For many children summer is spent being shifted from teenage sitter to sitter and includes watching countless hours of television. Educators can provide parents with ideas related to literacy development and encourage the children's continued involvement with literature for the summer months. Some school systems provide a calendar of the summer months that contains simple ideas that can be implemented for children on each day of the vacation. Calendars of activities may serve as a guide for parents in planning interesting activities that encourage their child's continued involvement in meaningful activities during the summer months. Some teachers have developed a one-page handout that includes ideas for the summer months specifically related to the developmental level of the children that have completed the year with them. Some ideas related to language development that have been suggested include keeping a journal of events on a trip, developing a scrapbook with written descriptions of summer fun, collecting books and reading materials about a special activity, planning a summer party complete with invitations, exploring cookbooks for easy recipes, attending special summer activities at a local museum, enrolling in the library summer reading program, or events sponsored by parks and recreation departments.

Informed parents can have a positive influence on their young child's literacy development and be instrumental in the growing creation of an appreciation of literature. As the teacher works with parents, she or he may use a variety of approaches including demonstrating the reading of books, distributing informative newsletters, providing meetings on topics of parental interest, conducting workshops where materials are made, providing reading materials to borrow, and inviting parents into the classroom. Many different options allow parents to chose the involvement that matches their interests and capabilities. Parents' views are valued as the teacher shares activities and methods that will enrich the literacy environment for the child. The parent and teacher join together to insure that the child is connecting to books at home and at school. The love of books is one of the best gifts a parent and teacher can give a child.

Raymond's Success Story

Raymond worked diligently during his first year in his new school to provide an appropriate literacy environment for his first graders. An essential component of his plan was working with the parents, foster parents, grandparents, and guardians of his students. Parents were invited to Raymond's classroom and they were involved in a variety of activities. He conducted parent workshops on Saturday mornings enabling working parents to attend. Special activities were provided for the children during the meetings to support parent attendance. In the sessions, parents constructed books and other materials that could be used at school and at home. During the workshops he described ways the materials could be used and the adults discussed how they could adapt the ideas for their families. He started a collection of books, tapes, children's magazines, and newspapers that could be loaned to his families. Raymond was successful in stimulating his children's interest in books and reading. This was accomplished through

the carefully planned experiences he provided for the students. His success was also influenced by his effort to involve parents in his classroom and in their homes. His positive approach communicated to parents that they were valuable contributors to the education of their children. Raymond's efforts were rewarded by having more parent volunteers in his classroom than in any other classroom in the school.

SUGGESTED LEARNING EXPERIENCES

1. Remember a favorite book that you enjoyed at home or in another setting as a child. Write about the book and the shared experience. Include information about the reader, setting, and feelings related to the event.

2. Design a parent meeting for a specific first grade classroom that focuses on reading to children in the home. Develop an announcement of the meeting and an outline for the session. Include segments that involve parents.

3. Visit a local library and read *Parent's Choice*. Write a paragraph describing what information parents can obtain from this newspaper.

4. Design a book bag that could be used with primary-aged children. Include the book, props, and other materials that could be used to interest the children in reading the contents.

5. Visit a school or neighborhood that is participating in a program to get books into children's homes. Interview the person in charge of the local program and question her or him about the benefits of the book distributions.

6. Go to a community library and determine offerings they have for families and children.

7. Write a question often asked to early childhood teachers about literature or reading. Discuss the response in class and determine effective answers.

8. Determine a difficult issue that parents and young children are concerned about. Select a book that could be read to a young child and lead to a discussion of the topic.

9. Work with a preschool teacher to develop a newsletter that can be distributed to parents.

10. Read a column in a professional journal written for parents. Copy the article and bring it to class for a discussion of the appropriateness of the content for parents of young children.

REFERENCES

Administration for Children, Youth, and Families Head Start Bureau. (1987). *Commissioner's task force on parent involvement in head start: Final report*. Washington, DC: U.S. Department of Health & Human Services, Office of Human Services.

Ascher, C. (1988). Improving the school-home connection for poor and minority urban students. *Urban Review, 20*(2), 109–123.

Bailey, K. (1990, May). *Tune in and talk*. Paper presented at the meeting of Chapter 1, Region 6 Conference, Columbus, IN.

Becher, R. M. (1985). Parent involvement and reading achievement: A review of research and implications for practice. *Childhood Education, 62*(1), 44–50.

Berger, E. (1991) *Parents as partners in education*. New York: Macmillian.

Brinkley, M. (1988). *Becoming a nation of readers: What parents can do*. Lexington, MA: D.C. Heath.

Burgess, J. (1982). The effects of a training program for parents of preschoolers on the children's school readiness. *Reading Improvement, 19*(4), 313–318.

Chomsky, C. (1972). Stages in language development and reading exposure. *Harvard Educational Review, 42*(1), 1–33.

Clark, M. (1976). *Young fluent readers*. London: Heinemann Educational Books.

Clay, M. (1979). *Reading: The patterning of complex behavior*. Auckland, New Zealand: Heinemann Educational Books.

Compton's multimedia encyclopedia [computer file]. (1990). San Francisco: Encyclopedia Britannica.

Culligan, E. (1992). *Read to me: Raising kids who love to read*. New York: Scholastic.

Donavin, D. P. (Ed.). (1992). American Library Association Best of the Best for Children. New York: Random House.

Durkin, D. (1966). *Children who read early*. New York: Teachers College Press.

Dunst, C., & Trivette, C. (1988). A family systems model of early intervention and handicapped and developmentally at-risk children. In D. Powell (Ed.), *Parent Education as Early Childhood Intervention*. Norwood, NJ: Ablex.

Epstein, J. (1986). Parents' reactions to teacher practices of parent involvement. *The Elementary School Journal, 86*(3), 277–293.

Feitelson, D., & Goldstein Z. (1986). Patterns of book ownership and reading to young children in Israel. *Reading Teacher, 39*(9), 924–930.

Geta, J. (producer). (1986). *Drop everything and read!* [video]. Princeton, NJ: Films for the Humanities.

Gordon, I. (1977). *Parent oriented home-based early childhood education programs.* Gainesville, FL: University of Florida, Institute for Human Development.

Greater Vancouver Library Federation (producer). (1989). *Read to me too! Libraries, books, & young children.* Burnaby, British Columbia: The Federation.

Handel, R. (1992). The partnership for family reading: Benefits for families and schools. *The Reading Teacher, 46*(2) 116–126.

Harste, J. (1989). *New policy guidelines for reading: Connecting research and practice.* Urbana, IL: National Council of Teachers of English.

Holdaway, D. (1979). *The foundations of literacy.* Sydney, Australia: Ashton Scholastic.

Lamb, M. (Ed). (1986). *The father's role: Applied perspective.* New York: J. Wiley.

Lamme, L. (1985). *Growing up reading.* Washington, D.C.: Acropolis Books.

Lamme, L., & Packer, A. (1986). Bookreading behaviors of infants. *Reading Teacher, 39*(6), 504–509.

Larrick, N. (1982). *A parent's guide to children's reading* (5th ed.). Philadelphia: Westminster Press.

Lyons, P., Robins, A., & Smith, A. (1983). *Involving parents in schools: A handbook for participation.* Ypsilanti, MI: The High/Scope Press.

Manning, M., Manning, G., & Cody C. (1988). Reading aloud to young children: Perspectives of parents. *Reading Research and Instruction, 27*(2), 56–61.

Mini-Page (Universal Press Syndicate) 4900 Main Street, Kansas City, MO 64112.

Missouri Department of Elementary and Secondary Education. (1985). *New parents as teachers project: Executive evaluation summary.* Jefferson City, MO: Author.

Neuman, S., & Roskos, K. (1993). *Language and literacy learning in the early years: An integrated approach.* Fort Worth, TX: Harcourt Brace Jovanovich College Publishers.

Nimnicht, G., & Brown, E. (1972). The toy library: Parents and children learning with toys. *Young Children, 28*(2), 110–116.

Ollila, L., & Mayfield, M. (Eds.). (1992). *Emerging literacy: Preschool, kindergarten and primary grades.* Boston, MA: Allyn Bacon.

Pence, A. (1988). *Ecological research with children and families.* New York: Teachers College Press.

Powell, D. (1988). *Parent education as early childhood intervention.* Norwood, NJ: Ablex.

Rasinski, T., & Fredericks, A. (1990). Working with parents: The best reading advise for parents. *Reading Teacher, 43*(4), 344–345.

Resnick, M., Rothe, J., Aaron, P., Scott, J., Wolking, W., Larsen, J., & Barker, A. (1987). Mothers reading to infants: A new observational tool. *The Reading Teacher, 40*(9), 888–894.

Rutter, M. (1985). *Maternal deprivation reassessed.* Harmondsworth, England: Penguin Books.

Schickendanz, J. (1986). *More than ABCs: The early stages of reading and writing.* Washington, D.C.: National Association for the education of young children.

Segel, E. & Friedberg, J. (1991). "Is today library day?" Community support for family literacy. *Language Arts, 68*(8), 654–657.

Smith, F. (1978). *Understanding reading.* New York: Holt, Rinehart & Winston.

Strickland, D., & Morrow, L. (1990). Family literacy: Sharing good books. *The Reading Teacher, 43*(7), 518–519.

Swick, K. (1984). *Inviting parents into the young child's world.* Champaign, IL: Stipes.

Swick, K. (1987). *Perspectives on understanding and working with families.* Champaign, IL: Stipes.

Swick, K. (1991). *First: A rural teacher-parent partnership for school success.* Columbia, SC: U.S. Office of Education.

Taylor, D. (1983). *Family literacy: Young children learning to read and write.* Exeter, NH: Heinemann Educational Books.

Trelease, J. (1989). *The new read aloud handbook.* New York: Viking Penguin.

U.S. Department of Education. (1986). *What works: Research about teaching and learning.* (ERIC Document Reproduction Service No. ED 263 299). Washington, D.C.: U.S. Department of Education.

Watson, T., Brown, M., & Swick, K. (1983). The relationship of parents' support to children's school achievement. *Child Welfare, 72*(2), 175–180.

Wells, G. (1986). *The meaning makers: Children learning language and using language to learn.* Portsmouth, NH: Heinemann.

White, B. (1988). *Educating the infant and toddler.* Lexington, MA: D. C. Heath.

CHILDREN'S LITERATURE AND VIDEO REFERENCES

The authors and illustrators of children's books are listed, in all chapters, by their full names to help the reader become acquainted with them. If only one name is listed, the author also illustrated the book.

Ahlbert, A., & Ahlberg, J. (1983). *The Baby's Catalogue.* Boston: Little Brown.

Aliki, (1984). *Feelings.* New York: Greenwillow.

Conford, E. (1978). *Eugene the Brave.* Boston: Little, Brown.

Gackenbach, D. (1977). *Harry and the Terrible Whatzit*. New York: Houghton Mifflin.

Grandpa. (video). (1992). New York: Sony Kids Video.

Hest, A. (1986). *The Purple Coat*. Illustrated by Amy Schwartz. New York: Four Winds.

Johnson, A. (1989). *Tell Me a Story, Mama*. New York: Orchard Books.

Mayer, M. (1968). *There's a Nightmare in My Closet*. New York: Dial Press.

Mayer, M. (1973). *What Do You Do With a Kangaroo?* New York: Macmillian.

Mayer, M. (1974). *You're the Scaredy Cat*. New York: Parents Magazine Press.

Mike Mulligan and His Steam Shovel (video). (1958). Weston, CT: Children's Circle, Division of Weston Woods.

Ormerod, J. (1985). *Messy Baby*. New York: Lanthrop.

Ormerod, J. (1985). *Reading*. New York: Lanthrop.

Oxenbury, H. (1991). *Playing*. New York: Simon & Schuster.

Oxenbury, H. (1991). *Dressing*. New York: Simon & Schuster.

Oxenbury, H. (1991). *Family*. New York: Simon & Schuster.

Oxenbury, H. (1991) *Shopping Trip*. Dial Books for Young Readers.

Oxenbury, H. (1992). *Mother's Helper*. New York: Dial Books for Young Readers.

Shelley Duval's Bedtime Stories (video). (1992). Universal City, CA: MCA/Universal Home Video.

Stories From the Black Tradition (video). (1992). Weston, CT: CC Studios, Division of Weston Woods.

Viorst, J. (1973). *Mama Says There Aren't Any Zombies, Ghosts, Vampires, Creatures, Demons, Monsters, Fiends, Goblins or Things*. New York: Atheneum.

Williams, L. (1986). *The Little Old Lady Who Was Not Afraid of Anything*. New York: HarperCollins.

Zolotow, C. (1972). *William's Doll*. New York: Harper Trophy.

Appendices

Appendix A: Caldecott Medal and Honor Books

The Caldecott Medal and Honor Books are selected by the Association for Library Service to Children of the American Library Association. The annual award is given to the "artist of the most distinguished American picture book for children." The authors' and illustrators' names appear in the following list. If only one name is listed, the author also illustrated the book. The first book listed after a given year was the Caldecott Medal winner, and the books which follow were named as Caldecott Honor books. The authors' and illustrators' first names are also presented so that the reader can become familiar with the names.

1938

Fish, Helen Dean. (1937). *Animals of the Bible*. Illustrated by Dorothy O. Lathrop. New York: Frederick A. Stokes.

Artzybasheff, Boris. (1937). *Seven Simeons*. New York: Viking Press.

Fish, Helen Dean. (1937). *Four and Twenty Blackbirds*. Illustrated by Robert Lawson. New York: Frederick A. Stokes.

1939

Handforth, Thomas (1938). *Mei Li*. New York: Doubleday, Doran & Company.

Armer, Laura Adams. (1938). *The Forest Pool*. New York: Longmans, Green.

Leaf, Munro. (1938). *Wee Gillis*. Illustrated by Robert Lawson. New York: Viking Press.

Gág, Wanda. (Trans.). (1938). *Snow White and the Seven Dwarfs*. New York: Coward-McCann.

Newberry, Clare Turlay. (1938). *Barkis*. New York: Harper & Row.

Daugherty, James. (1938). *Andy and the Lion*. New York: Viking Press.

1940

d'Aulaire, Ingri, & d'Aulaire, Edgar Parin. (1939). *Abraham Lincoln*. Garden City, NY: Doubleday.

Hader, Berta, & Hader, Elmer. (1939). *Cock-a-doodle-doo*. New York: Macmillan.

Bemelmans, Ludwig. (1939). *Madeline*. New York: Simon & Schuster.

Ford, Lauren. (1939). *The Ageless Story*. New York: Dodd, Mead.

1941

Lawson, Robert. (1940). *They Were Strong and Good*. New York: Viking Press.

Newberry, Clare Turlay. (1940). *April's Kittens*. New York: Harper & Row.

1942

McCloskey, Robert. (1941). *Make Way for Ducklings*. New York: Viking Press.

Petersham, Maud, & Petersham, Miska. (1941). *An American ABC*. New York: Macmillan.

Clark, Ann Nolan. (1941). *In My Mother's House*. Illustrated by Velino Herrara. New York: Viking Press.

Holling, Clancy Holling. (1941). *Paddle-to-the-sea*. Boston: Houghton Mifflin.

Gág, Wanda. (1941). *Nothing at All*. New York: Coward McCann.

1943

Burton, Virginia Lee. (1942). *The Little House*. Boston: Houghton Mifflin.

Buff, Mary, & Buff, Conrad. (1942). *Dash and Dart*. New York: Viking Press.

Newberry, Clare Turlay. (1942). *Marshmallow*. New York: Harper & Row.

1944

Thurber, James. (1943). *Many Moons*. Illustrated by Louis Slobodkin. New York: Harcourt Brace & Company.

Jones, Jessie Orton. (Arrang. from *The Bible*). (1943). *Small Rain*. Illustrated by Elizabeth Orton Jones. New York: Viking Press.

Kingman, Lee. (1943). *Pierre Pidgeon*. Illustrated by Arnold Edwin Bare. Boston: Houghton Mifflin.

Chan, Chih-Yi. (1943). *Good-Luck Horse*. Illustrated by Plato Chan. New York: Whittlesey.

Hader, Berta, & Hader, Elmer. (1943). *Mighty Hunter*. New York: Macmillan.

Brown, Margaret Wise. (1943). *A Child's Good Night Book*. Illustrated by Jean Charlot. New York: W. R. Scott.

1945

Field, Rachel. (1944). *Prayer For A Child*. Pictures by Elizabeth Orton Jones. New York: Macmillan.

Tudor, Tasha. (1944). *Mother Goose*. New York: Oxford University Press.

Ets, Marie Hall. (1944). *In the Forest*. New York: Viking Press.

de Angeli, Marguerite. (1944). *Yonie Wondernose*. New York: Doubleday.

Sawyer, Ruth. (1944). *The Christmas Anna Angel*. Illustrated by Kate Seredy. New York: Viking.

1946

Petersham, Maud, & Petersham, Miska. (1945). *The Rooster Crows*. New York: Macmillan.

Brown, Margaret Wise. (1945). *Little Lost Lamb*. Illustrated by Leonard Weisgard. New York: Doubleday.

Wheeler, Opal. (1945). *Sing Mother Goose*. Illustrated by Marjorie Torrey. New York: Dutton.

Reyher, Becky. (1945). *My Mother is the Most Beautiful Woman in the World*. Illustrated by Ruth C. Gannett. New York: Lothrop.

Wiese, Kurt. (1945). *You Can Write Chinese*. New York: Viking Press.

1947

MacDonald, Golden. (1946). *The Little Island*. Illustrated by Leonard Weisgard. New York: Doubleday.

Tresselt, Alvin R. (1946). *Rain Drop Splash*. Illustrated by Leonard Weisgard. New York: Lothrop.

Flack, Marjorie. (1946). *Boats on the River*. Illustrated by Jay Hyde Barnum. New York: Viking.

Graham, Al. (1946). *Timothy Turtle*. Illustrated by Tony Palazzo. New York: Robert Welch.

Politi, Leo. (1946). *Pedro, Angel of Olvera Street*. New York: Scribner.

Wheeler, Opal. (1946). *Sing in Praise*. Illustrated by Marjorie Torrey. New York: Dutton.

1948

Tresselt, Alvin. (1947). *White Snow, Bright Snow*. Illustrated by Roger Duvoisin. New York: Lothrop.

Brown, Marcia. (1947). *Stone Soup*. New York: Scribner.

Geisel, Theodor S. (Dr. Seuss). (1947). *McElligot's Pool*. New York: Random House.

Schreiber, George. (1947). *Bambino the Clown*. New York: Viking Press.

Davis, Lavinia R. (1947). *Roger and the Fox*. Illustrated by Hildegard Woodward. New York: Doubleday.

Malcolmson, Anne (Ed.). (1947). *Song of Robin Hood*. Illustrated by Virginia Lee Burton. Boston: Houghton Mifflin.

1949

Hader, Berta, & Hader, Elmer. (1948). *The Big Snow*. New York: Macmillan.

McCloskey, Robert. (1948). *Blueberries for Sal*. New York: Viking Press.

McGinley, Phyllis. (1948). *All Around the Town*. Illustrated by Helen Stone. New York: Lippincott.

Politi, Leo. (1948). *Juanita*. New York: Scribner.

Wiese, Kurt. (1948). *Fish in the Air*. New York: Viking Press.

1950

Politi, Leo. (1949). *Song of the Swallows*. New York: Scribner.

Holbrook, Stewart. (1949). *America's Ethan Allen*. Illustrated by Lynd Ward. Boston: Houghton Mifflin.

Davis, Lavinia R. (1949). *The Wild Birthday Cake.* Illustrated by Hildegard Woodward. New York: Doubleday.

Krauss, Ruth. (1949). *Happy Day.* Illustrated by Marc Simont. New York: Harper & Row.

Brown, Marcia. (1949). *Henry-Fisherman.* New York: Scribner.

Geisel, Theodor S. (Dr. Seuss). (1949). *Bartholomew and the Oobleck.* New York: Random House.

1951

Milhous, Katherine. (1950). *The Egg Tree.* New York: Scribner.

Brown, Marcia. (1950). *Dick Whittington and His Cat.* New York: Scribner.

Will (William) Lipkind. (1950). *The Two Reds.* Illustrated by Nicolas (Mordvinoff). San Diego, CA: Harcourt Brace & World.

Geisel, Theodor S. (Dr. Seuss). (1950). *If I Ran the Zoo.* New York: Random House.

Newberry, Clare Turlay. (1950). *T-Bone the Baby-Sitter.* New York: Harper & Row.

McGinley, Phyllis. (1950). *The Most Wonderful Doll in the World.* Illustrated by Helen Stone. New York: Lippincott.

1952

Will (William Lipkind). (1951). *Finders Keepers.* Illustrated by Nicolas Mordvinoff. San Diego: Harcourt Brace Jovanovich.

Ets, Marie Hall. (1951). *Mr. T. W. Anthony Woo.* New York: Viking Press.

Brown, Marcia. (1951). *Skipper John's Cook.* New York: Scribner.

Zion, Gene. (1951). *All Falling Down.* Illustrated by Margaret Bloy Graham. New York: Harper & Row.

du Bois, William Pène. (1951). *Bear Party.* New York: Viking Press.

Olds, Elizabeth. (1951). *Feather Mountain.* Boston: Houghton Mifflin.

1953

Ward, Lynd. (1952). *The Biggest Bear.* Boston: Houghton Mifflin.

Brown, Marcia. (1952). *Puss in Boots.* New York: Scribner.

McCloskey, Robert. (1952). *One Morning in Maine.* New York: Viking Press.

Eichenberg, Fritz. (1952). *Ape in a Cape.* San Diego, CA: Harcourt Brace Jovanovich.

Zolotow, Charlotte. (1952). *The Storm Book.* Illustrated by Margaret Bloy Graham. New York: Harper & Row.

Kepes, Juliet. (1952). *Five Little Monkeys.* Boston: Houghton Mifflin.

1954

Bemelmans, Ludwig. (1953). *Madeline's Rescue.* New York: Viking Press.

Sawyer, Ruth. (1953). *Journey Cake, Ho!* Illustrated by Robert McCloskey. New York: Viking Press.

Schlein, Miriam. (1953). *When Will the World Be Mine?* Illustrated by Jean Charlot. New York: W.R. Scott.

James, M. R. (Trans.). (1953). *The Steadfast Tin Soldier.* Illustrated by Marcia Brown. (Adapted from Hans Christian Andersen). New York: Scribner.

Krauss, Ruth. (1953). *A Very Special House.* Illustrated by Maurice Sendak. New York: Harper & Row.

Birnbaum, Abe. (1953). *Green Eyes.* New York: Golden Press.

1955

Perrault, Charles. (1954). *Cinderella.* Illustrated by Marcia Brown. New York: Harper & Row.

de Angeli, Marguerite. (1954). *Book of Nursery and Mother Goose Rhymes.* New York: Doubleday.

Brown, Margaret Wise. (1954). *Wheel on the Chimney.* Illustrated by Tibor Gergely. New York: Lippincott.

1956

Langstaff, John. (1955). *Frog Went A-Courtin'*. Illustrated by Feodor Rojankovsky. New York: Harcourt Brace.

Ets, Marie Hall. (1955). *Play with Me*. New York: Viking Press.

Yashima, Taro. (1955). *Crow boy*. New York: Viking Press.

1957

Udry, Janice May. (1956). *A Tree is Nice*. Illustrated by Marc Simont. New York: Harper & Row.

Ets, Marie Hall. (1956). *Mr. Penny's Race Horse*. New York: Viking Press.

Tudor, Tasha. (1956). *1 is One*. New York: Oxford University Press.

Titus, Eve. (1956). *Anatole*. Illustrated by Paul Galdone. New York: McGraw-Hill.

Elkin, Benjamin. (1956). *Gillespie and the Guards*. Illustrated by James Daugherty. New York: Viking Press.

du Bois, William Pene. (1956). *Lion*. New York: Viking Press.

1958

McCloskey, Robert. (1957). *Time of Wonder*. New York: Viking Press.

Freeman, Don. (1957). *Fly High, Fly Low*. New York: Viking Press.

Titus, Eve. (1957). *Anatole and the Cat*. Illustrated by Paul Galdone. New York: McGraw-Hill.

1959

Cooney, Barbara (Ed.). (1958). *Chanticleer and the Fox*. New York: Thomas Y. Crowell.

Frasconi, Antonio. (1958). *The House that Jack Built*. New York: Thomas Y. Crowell.

Joslin, Sesyle. (1958). *What Do You Say, Dear?*. Illustrated by Maurice Sendak. New York: W. R. Scott.

Yashima, Taro. (1958). *Umbrella*. New York: Viking Press.

1960

Ets, Marie Hall, & Labastida, Aurora. (1959). *Nine Days to Christmas*. New York: Viking Press.

Goudey, Alice E. (1959). *Houses from the Sea*. Illustrated by Adrienne Adams. New York: Scribner.

Udry, Janice May. (1959). *The Moon Jumpers*. Illustrated by Maurice Sendak. New York: Harper & Row.

1961

Robbins, Ruth. (1960). *Baboushka and the Three Kings*. Illustrated by Nicolas Sidjakov. Berkeley, CA: Parnassus.

Lionni, Leo. (1960). *Inch by Inch*. New York: Obolensky.

1962

Brown, Marcia. (1961). *Once a Mouse*. New York: Scribner.

Spier, Peter. (1961). *The Fox Went Out on a Chilly Night*. New York: Doubleday.

Minarik, Else. (1961). *Little Bear's Visit*. Illustrated by Maurice Sendak. New York: Harper & Row.

Goudey, Alice. (1961). *The Day We Saw the Sun Come Up*. Illustrated by Adrienne Adams. New York: Scribner.

1963

Keats, Ezra Jack. (1962). *The Snowy Day*. New York: Viking Press.

Belting, Natalia. (1962). *The Sun is a Golden Earring*. Illustrated by Bernarda Bryson. New York: Holt, Rinehart and Winston.

Zolotow, Charlotte. (1962). *Mr. Rabbit and the Lovely Present*. Illustrated by Maurice Sendak. New York: Harper & Row.

1964

Sendak, Maurice. (1963). *Where the Wild Things Are*. New York: Harper & Row.

Lionni, Leo. (1963). *Swimming*. New York: Pantheon.

Leodhas, Sorche Nic. (1963). *All in the Morning Early*. Illustrated by Evaline Ness. New York: Holt, Rinehart and Winston.

Reed, Philip. (1963). *Mother Goose and Nursery Rhymes*. New York: Atheneum.

1965

de Regniers, Beatrice Schenk. (1964). *May I Bring A Friend?* Illustrated by Beni Montresor. New York: Atheneum.

Scheer, Julian. (1964). *Rain Makes Applesauce*. Illustrated by Marvin Bileck. New York: Holiday House.

Hodges, Margaret. (1964). *The Wave*. Illustrated by Blair Lent. Boston: Houghton Mifflin.

Caudill, Rebecca. (1964). *A Pocketful of Cricket*. Illustrated by Evaline Ness. New York: Holt, Rinehart and Winston.

1966

Leodhas, Sorche Nic. (1965). *Always Room for One More*. Illustrated by Nonny Hogrogian. New York: Holt, Rinehart and Winston.

Tresselt, Alvin. (1965). *Hide and Seek Fog*. Illustrated by Roger Duvoisin. New York: Lothrop.

Ets, Marie Hall. (1965). *Just Me*. New York: Viking Press.

Jacobs, Joseph. (1965). *Tom Tit Tot*. Illustrated by Evaline Ness. New York: Scribner.

1967

Ness, Evaline. (1966). *Sam, Bangs, and Moonshine*. New York: Holt, Rinehart and Winston.

Emberley, Barbara. (1966). *One Wide River to Cross*. Illustrated by Ed Emberley. Englewood Cliffs, NJ: Prentice-Hall.

1968

Emberley, Barbara. (1967). *Drummer Hoff*. Illustrated by Ed Emberley. Englewood Cliffs, NJ: Prentice-Hall.

Lionni, Leo. (1967). *Frederick*. New York: Pantheon.

Yashima, Taro. (1967). *Seashore Story*. New York: Viking Press.

Yolen, Jane. (1967). *The Emperor and the Kite*. Illustrated by Ed Young. Cleveland, OH: World.

1969

Ransome, Arthur. (1968). *The Fool of the World and the Flying Ship*. Illustrated by Uri Shulevitz. New York: Farrar, Straus and Giroux.

Dayrell, Elphinstone. (1968). *Why the Sun and the Moon Live In the Sky*. Illustrated by Blair Lent. Boston: Houghton Mifflin.

1970

Steig, William. (1969). *Sylvester and the Magic Pebble*. New York: Windmill/Simon and Schuster.

Keats, Ezra Jack. (1969). *Goggles*. New York: Macmillan.

Lionni, Leo. (1969). *Alexander and the Wind-up Mouse*. New York: Viking Press.

Preston, Edna Mitchell. (1969). *Pop Corn and Ma Goodness*. Illustrated by Robert Andrew Parker. New York: Viking Press.

Turkle, Brinton. (1969). *Thy Friend, Obadiah*. New York: Viking Press.

Zemach, Harve. (1969). *The Judge*. Illustrated by Margot Zemach. New York: Farrar, Straus and Giroux.

1971

Haley, Gail E. (1970). *A Story, A Story*. New York: Atheneum.

Sleator, William. (1970). *The Angry Moon*. Illustrated by Blair Lent. Boston: Little, Brown.

Lobel, Arnold. (1970). *Frog and Toad are Friends*. New York: Harper & Row.

Sendak, Maurice. (1970). *In the Night Kitchen*. New York: Harper & Row.

1972

Hogrogian, Nonny. (1971). *One Fine Day*. New York: Macmillan.

Domanska, Janina. (1971). *If All the Seas Were One Sea*. New York: Macmillan.

Feelings, Muriel. (1971). *Moja Means One: Swahili Counting Book*. Illustrated by Tom Feelings. New York: Dial.

Ryan, Cheli Duran. (1971). *Hildilid's Night*. Illustrated by Arnold Lobel. New York: Macmillan.

1973

Mosel, Arlene. (1972). *The Funny Little Woman*. Illustrated by Blair Lent. New York: Dutton.

Baskin, Hosea, Baskin, Tobias, & Baskin, Lisa. (1972). *Hosie's Alphabet*. Illustrated by Leonard Baskin. New York: Viking Press.

Baylor, Byrd. (1972). *When Clay Sings*. Illustrated by Tom Bahti. New York: Scribner.

Brothers Grimm. (1972). *Snow White and the Seven Dwarfs* (Randall Jarrell, Trans.). Illustrated by Nancy Ekholm Burkert. New York: Farrar, Straus and Giroux.

McDermott, Gerald. (1972). *Anansi the Spider*. : Holt, Rinehart and Winston.

1974

Zemach, Harve. (1973). *Duffy and the Devil*. Illustrated by Margot Zemach. New York: Farrar, Straus and Giroux.

Jeffers, Susan. (1973). *The Three Jovial Huntsmen*. New York: Bradbury.

Macaulay, David. (1973) *Cathedral*. Boston: Houghton Mifflin.

1975

McDermott, Gerald. (1974). (Adapted and Trans.). *Arrow to the Sun*. New York: Viking Press.

Feelings, Muriel. (1974). *Jambo Means Hello: Swahili Alphabet Book*. Illustrated by Tom Feelings. New York: Dial.

1976

Aardema, Verna. (1975). *Why Mosquitoes Buzz in People's Ears*. Illustrated by Leo and Diane Dillon. New York: Dial.

Baylor, Byrd. (1975). *The Desert is Theirs*. Illustrated by Peter Parnell. New York: Scribner.

dePaola, Tomie. (1975). *Strega Nona*. Englewood Cliffs, NJ: Prentice-Hall.

1977

Musgrove, Margaret. (1976). *Ashanti to Zulu: African Traditions*. Illustrated by Leo and Diane Dillon. New York: Dial.

Steig, William. (1976). *The Amazing Bone*. New York: Farrar, Straus and Giroux.

Hogrogian, Nonny. (1976). *The Contest*. New York: Greenwillow.

Goffstein, M. B. (1976). *Fish for Supper*. New York: Dial.

McDermott, Beverly Brodsky. (1976). *The Golem*. New York: Lippincott.

Baylor, Byrd. (1976). *Hawk, I'm Your Brother*. Illustrated by Peter Parnall. New York: Scribner.

1978

Spier, Peter. (1977). *Noah's Ark*. New York: Doubleday.

Macaulay, David. (1977). *Castle*. Boston: Houghton Mifflin.

Zemach, Margot. (1977). *It Could Always Be Worse*. New York: Farrar, Straus and Giroux.

1979

Goble, Paul. (1978). *The Girl Who Loved Wild Horses*. New York: Bradbury.

Crews, Donald. (1978). *Freight Train*. New York: Greenwillow.

Baylor, Byrd. (1978). *The Way to Start a Day*. Illustrated by Peter Parnall. New York: Scribner's.

1980

Hall, Donald. (1979). *Ox-cart Man*. Illustrated by Barbara Cooney. New York: Viking Press.

Isadora, Rachel. (1979). *Ben's Trumpet*. New York: Greenwillow.

Shulevitz, Uri. (1979). *The Treasure*. New York: Farrar, Straus and Giroux.

Van Allsburg, Chris. (1979). *The Garden of Abdul Gasazi*. Boston: Houghton Mifflin.

1981

Lobel, Arnold. (1980). *Fables*. New York: Harper & Row.

Plume, Ilse. (1980). *The Bremen-Town Musicians*. New York: Doubleday.

Bang, Molly. (1980). *The Grey Lady and the Strawberry Snatcher*. New York: Four Winds.

Low, Joseph. (1980). *Mice Twice*. New York: Atheneum.

Crews, Donald. (1980). *Truck*. New York: Greenwillow.

1982

Van Allsburg, Chris. (1981). *Jumanji*. Boston: Houghton Mifflin.

Willard, Nancy. (1981). *A Visit to William Blake's Inn: Poems for Innocent and Experienced Travelers*. Illustrated by Alice and Martin Provensen. San Diego, CA: Harcourt Brace Jovanovich.

Baker, Olaf. (1981). *Where the Buffaloes Began*. Illustrated by Stephen Gammell. New York: Warne.

Lobel, Arnold. (1981). *On Market Street*. Illustrated by Anita Lobel. New York: Greenwillow.

Sendak, Maurice. (1981). *Outside Over There*. New York: Harper & Row.

1983

Cendrars, Blaise. (1982). *Shadow*. Illustrated by Marcia Brown. New York: Scribner.

Rylant, Cynthia. (1982). *When I was Young in the Mountains*. Illustrated by Diane Goode. New York: Dutton.

Williams, Vera B. (1982). *A Chair for My Mother*. New York: Morrow.

1984

Provensen, Alice and Martin. (1983). *The Glorious Flight: Across the Channel with Louis Bleriot, July 25, 1909*. New York: Viking Press.

Bang, Molly. (1983). *Ten, Nine, Eight*. New York: Greenwillow.

Hyman, Trina Schart. (1983). *Little Red Riding Hood*. New York: Holiday House.

1985

Hodges, Margaret. (Adapted). (1984). *Saint George and the Dragon*. Illustrated by Trina Schart Hyman. Boston: Little, Brown.

Lesser, Rika. (1984). *Hansel and Gretel*. Illustrated by Paul O. Zelinsky. New York: Dodd.

Steptoe, John. (1984). *The Story of Jumping Mouse*. New York: Lothrop.

Tafuri, Nancy. (1984). *Have You Seen My Duckling?* New York: Greenwillow.

1986

Van Allsburg, Chris. (1985). *Polar Express*. Boston: Houghton Mifflin.

Rylant, Cynthia. (1985). *The Relatives Came*. Illustrated by Stephen Gammell. New York: Bradbury.

Wood, Audrey. (1985). *King Bidgood's in the Bathtub*. Illustrated by Don Wood. San Diego, CA: Harcourt Brace Jovanovich.

1987

Yorinks, Arthur. (1986). *Hey Al*. Illustrated by Richard Egielski. New York: Farrar, Straus and Giroux.

MacDonald, Suse. (1986). *Alphabatics*. New York: Bradbury.

Zelinsky, Paul O. (1986). *Rumpelstiltskin*. New York: Dutton.

Grifalconi, Ann. (1986). *The Village of Round and Square Houses*. Boston: Little, Brown.

1988

Yolen, Jane. (1987). *Owl Moon*. Illustrated by John Schoenherr. New York: Philomel.

Steptoe, John. (Adapt.). (1987). *Mufaro's Beautiful Daughters: An African Story*. New York: Lothrop, Lee & Shepard.

1989

Ackerman, Karen. (1988). *Song and Dance Man*. Illustrated by Stephen Gammell. New York: Knopf.

Stanley, Dianne. (1988). *The Boy of the Three-year Nap*. Illustrated by Allen Say. Boston: Houghton Mifflin.

Wiesner, David. (1988). *Free Fall*. New York: Lothrop, Lee & Shepard.

Marshall, James. (Adapt.). (1988). *Goldilocks and the Three Bears*. New York: Dial.

McKissack, Patricia. (1988). *Mirandy and Brother Wind*. Illustrated by Jerry Pinkney. New York: Knopf.

1990

Young, Ed. (Adapt.). (1989). *Lon Po Po: A Red Riding Hood story from China*. New York: Philomel.

Peet, Bill. (1989). *Bill Peet: An Autobiography*. Boston: Houghton Mifflin.

Ehlert, Lois. (1989). *Color Zoo*. New York: Lippincott.

Kimmel, Eric. (1989). *Herschel and the Hanukkah Goblins*. Illustrated by Trina Schart Hyman. New York: Holiday House.

San Souci, Robert D. (1989). *The Talking Eggs*. Illustrated by Jerry Pinkney. New York: Dial.

1991

Macaulay, David. (1990). *Black and White. Boston: Houghton Mifflin*.

Perrault, Charles. (1990). *Puss in Boots*. (Malcolm Arthur, Trans.). Illustrated by Fred Marcellino. New York: Farrar, Straus and Giroux.

Williams, Vera B. (1990). *"More More More," Said the Baby*. New York: Greenwillow.

1992

Wiesner, David. (1991). *Tuesday*. New York: Clarion.

Ringgold, Faith. (1991). *Tar Beach*. New York: Crown.

1993

McCully, Emily. (1992). *Mirette on the High Wire*. New York: Putnam.

Scieszka, Jon. (1992). *The Stinky Cheese Man & Other Fairly Stupid Tales*. Illustrated by Lane Smith. New York: Viking Kestrel.

Williams, Sherry Ann. (1992). *Working Cotton*. Illustrated by Carole Byard. San Diego, CA: Harcourt Brace Jovanovich.

Young, Ed. (1992). *Seven Blind Mice*. New York: Philomel.

Appendix B: Steps in Binding a Book

Steps in Binding a Book

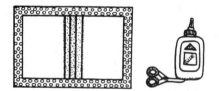

1. Cut two pieces of heavy cardboard slightly larger than the pages of the book.

2. With wide masking tape, tape the two pieces of cardboard together with ½-inch space between.

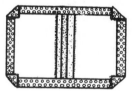

3. Cut outside cover 1½ inches larger than the cardboard and stick to cardboard (use thinned white glue if cover material is not self-adhesive.)

4. Fold corners over first, then the sides.

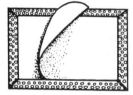

5. Measure and cut inside cover material and apply as shown.

6. Place stapled pages of the book in the center of the cover. Secure with two strips of inside cover material, one at the front of the book and the other at the back.

Appendix C: Wordless Picture Book Questionnaire

AVAILABILITY, SELECTION, AND USE OF WORDLESS PICTURE BOOKS.

Please answer the following questions as accurately as possible to reflect the use or non-use of wordless picture books in your teaching.

1. What age children do you teach? _____

2. What grade level do you teach? _____

3. How many years have you been teaching at this grade/age level? _____

4. Do you use wordless picture books in your classroom?

_____ Yes. If the answer is yes, please proceed to questions 5, 6, and 7.

_____ No. If the answer is no, please proceed to question 8.

5. How often do you use wordless picture books in your classroom?

_____ Daily, _____ Weekly, _____ Monthly, _____ 3–5 times a year.

6. Please check the way or ways you use wordless books in your teaching.

_____ Place them in the library corner for browsing.

_____ Use them myself in group time or whole-class presentation.

_____ Have children tell stories using wordless books.

_____ Use for concept teaching.

_____ Use to assess language/vocabulary development.

_____ Use to assess children's sense of story structure.

_____ Use with English as Second Language students.

_____ Have children write stories in response to wordless picture books.

Other ways you use wordless picture books in your classroom.

_____

_____

_____

7. Titles or authors of wordless picture books you recall using in your classroom. _____

_____

_____

Use the back of the form if additional space is needed to answer no. 7.

8. If you answered *no* to question 4, please complete this question.

Please check the reason or reasons you do not use wordless picture books in your classroom.

_____ Wordless picture books are for children who are not yet readers.

_____ There are few or no wordless picture books in our school or center library.

_____ I do not know how to select wordless picture books for the age children I teach.

_____ I do not know how to use wordless picture books.

_____ When I used wordless picture books in the past, my students did not respond well.

THANK YOU FOR YOUR TIME AND INFORMATION.

Appendix D: Resources Teachers May Use and Recommend to Parents

Parent's Choice: This publication provides reviews of books, television programs, movies, videos, computer software, music, toys, and games. Articles that relate to parenting are included. This comprehensive media evaluation provides information about the content, about what is educational, and about materials that children will enjoy.

Children's Choices: This publication reflects the choices of 10,000 children throughout the United States. And who knows better what is a good book for children, than children? The popular choices are briefly described to assist parents and teachers in selecting books that children will enjoy. Each year the selections are published in the November issue of *The Reading Teacher.* The selection process is jointly sponsored by the International Reading Association and the Children's Book Council.

BOOKS FOR PARENTS

Babies Need Books by Dorothy Butler (1988). London: Penguin Books. Focuses on reading to infants and includes books that are appropriate to use with this specific developmental level.

Read to Me: Raising Kids Who Love to Read by Bernice E. Cullinan, (1992). Scholastic. Includes practical ideas for parents as they help their children become readers. Includes a list of recommended children's magazines and effective read-aloud books. Available through International Reading Association.

The New Read Aloud Handbook by Jim Trelease, (1989). Viking Penguin Books. Discusses how parents can share the joys of reading with their children. Includes an annotated list of hundreds of titles that are proven successful in reading aloud to children.

Growing Up Reading by Linda Lamme, (1985). Acropolis Books. Describes how parents can create an environment that will nurture the natural development of reading. Includes practical suggestions that can be used with young children, beginning with infants. A helpful list of books and authors "too good to miss" is in the final section.

For Love of Reading by Masha Kabakow Rudman & Anna Markus Pearce, (1988). Consumers Union. Discusses all aspects of parenting young children and describes books appropriate to use at various stages of development. Annotated bibliography includes 800 books and recommended age level.

Family Storybook Reading by D. Taylor and D. Strickland, (1986). Heinemann. Describes how families have established ways to share books with their children. The connection between family book sharing and learning to read and write is also discussed.

VIDEOS FOR PARENTS

Drop Everything & Read (1986). Produced by Jan Greta, J.J. Films for the Humanities. This 30-minute video presents ways to help young children develop the habit of reading for fun. Encourages parents to read to their child each day.

Read to Me Too! (1989). The Federation. Tells the importance of continuing to read aloud to children five–eight years of age.

Foundations of Reading and Writing (1975). Campus Films. This film illustrates to parents that learning occurs while young children are involved in activities and play. Focuses on painting, building with blocks, clay modeling, and other activities that are included in early childhood programs. Can be used in parent meetings to explain curriculum.

CITED JOURNALS AND NEWSPAPERS

Childhood Education
Association for Childhood
Education International
11501 Georgia Avenue
Suite 315
Wheaton, MD 20902

Parent's Choice
Parent's Choice Foundation
Box 185
Waban, MA 02168

Reading Rainbow Gazette
648 Broadway
New York, NY 10003

Reading Today
International Reading
Association, Inc.
800 Barksdale Road
Box 8139
Newark, DE 19714–8139

The Reading Teacher
International Reading
Association, Inc.
800 Barksdale Road
Box 8139
Newark, DE 19714–8139

Appendix E: Children's Videos, Cassettes, and CDs Cited in Text

American School Publisher
P.O. Box 408
Hightstown, NJ 08520

Titles include:
Meet the Author Series
Meet Marc Brown
Meet the Newbery Author: Cynthia Rylant

Atlas Video
4915 Street & Elmo Avenue
Suite 305
Bethesda, MD 20814

Titles include:
The Storytellers Collection

Bank Street Read-Along Story Videos
Bank Street College of Education
900 Cuttermill Road
Great Neck, NY 11021

Titles Include:
Not Now Said the Cow

CBS/Fox Faerie Tale Theatre Programs
1211 Avenue of the Americas
New York, NY 10036

Titles include:
Faerie Tale Theatre
Aladdin and His Wonderful Lamp
The Dancing Princesses
The Nightingale

Children's Circle
Division of Weston Woods
C.C. Studios, Inc.
Weston, CT 06883

Titles include:
Corduroy and Other Bear Stories
The Maurice Sendak Library
The Snowman

Lightyear Video
Suite 5101
350 Fifth Avenue
New York, NY 10118

Titles include:
Stories to Remember

MGM/UA Home Video
10000 West Washington Boulevard
Culver City, CA 90232

Titles include:
*The Dr. Seuss Video Festival: Horton Hears
a Who and How the Grinch Stole Christmas*

Windham Hill Records
P.O. Box 93388
Stanford, CA 94309-9388

Titles include:
Rabbit Ears: Storybook Classics
We All Have Tales

Random House Home Video
400 Hahn Road
Westminster, MD 21157

Titles include:
Five Lionni Classics: The Animal Fables of Leo Lionni

Scholastic, Inc.
2931 East McCarty Street
P.O. Box 7502
Jefferson City, MO 65102

Titles include:
Moving Machines
Bugs Don't Bug Us

Warner Home Video
4000 Warner Boulevard
Burbank, CA 91522

Titles include:
The Ramona Stories

Weston Woods
389 Newton Turnpike
Weston, CT 06883

Titles include:
The Emperor's New Clothes
Homer Price
Make Way for Ducklings
Where the Wild Things Are
The Nutshell Library
The Snowy Day
Lentil
Books by Ezra Jack Keats

DISTRIBUTORS OF CITED AUDIO CASSETTES

Opportunities for Learning
20417 Nordhoff Street
Department KA2
Chatsworth, CA 91311

Titles Include:
Amelia Bedelia
Come Back, Amelia Bedelia
Little Bear
Stone Soup

Scholastic, Inc.
730 Broadway
New York, NY 10003

Titles include:
The Doorbell Rang
A House is a House for Me
The Snowy Day

Appendix F: Distributors of Cited Computer Software

Bank Street Writer
Broderbund Software
P.O. Box 1294
San Rafael, CA 94913–2947

Big Book Maker: Favorite Fairy Tales
and Nursery Rhymes
Pelican Software
768 Farmington Avenue
Farmington, CT 06032

Clifford's Big Book Publisher
Apple and MS-DOS
Scholastic Software, Inc.
2931 East McCarty Street
Box 7502
Jefferson City, MO 65102

Color Me
Mindscape, Inc.
3444 Dundee Road
Northbrook, IL 60062

Explore-A-Story Series
Collarmore Educational Publishing
D.C. Heath & Company
125 Spring Street
Lexington, MA 02173

High/Scope Educational Research
Foundation
600 North River Street
Ypsilanti, MI 48198–2898

IBM Educational Systems
P.O. Box 2150
4111 Northside Parkway, NW
Atlanta, GA 30055

Magic Crayon
C & C Software
5713 Kentford Circle
Wichita, KS 67220

Mask Parade
Springboard
7808 Creekridge Circle
Minneapolis, MN 55435

Mouse Paint
Apple Computer, Inc.
520 Madison Avenue, 34th Floor
New York, NY 10022

Muppets on Stage
Sunburst Communications, Inc.
39 Washington Avenue
Pleasantville, NY 10570

Primary Editor
IBM Educational Systems
P.O. Box 2150
4111 Northside Parkway, NW
Atlanta, GA 30055

The Print Shop
Broderbund Software
P.O. Box 1294
San Rafael, CA 94913-2947

Puppetmaker
Sunburst Communications
101 Castleton Street
Pleasantville, NY 10570

Stickybear Printer
Weekly Reader Software
245 Long Hill Road
Middletown, CT 06457

Story Tree
Scholastic, Inc.
P.O. Box 7502
Jefferson City, MO 65102

Story Weaver
Minnesota Educational Computing Corporation
6160 Summit
Brooklyn Center, MN 55430

Write On! Great Wild Imaginings
Humanities Software
P.O. Box 950
Hood River, OR 97031

Appendix G: Children's Magazine Information

Boys' Life Subscription Service
1325 Walnut Hill Lane
P.O. Box 152079
Irving, TX 75015–2079

Chickadee Magazine
P.O. Box 11314
Des Moines, IA 50340

Child Life
P.O. Box 10003
Des Moines, IA 50340

Children's Digest
P.O. Box 10003
Des Moines, IA 50340

Children's Playmate
P.O. Box 10003
Des Moines, IA 50340

Children's World
Vision Publishing House, Inc.
110 Ely Court
Elmont, NY 11003

Cricket: The Magazine for Children
P.O. Box 51144
Boulder, CO 80321–1144

Disney Adventures
Walt Disney Magazine Pubishing Group
500 South Burena Vista Street
Burbank Center Suite 100
Burbank, CA 91521–6018

Happy Times
Concordia Publishing House
3558 South Jefferson
St. Louis, MO 63118

Highlights for Children
P.O. Box 269
Columbus, OH 43272–0002

Jack and Jill
P.O. Box 10003
Des Moines, IA 50340

Kid City
200 Watt Street
P.O. Box 2924
Boulder, CO 80322

Kids Discover
P.O. Box 54205
Boulder, CO 80322

Ladybug: The Magazine for Young Children
Carus Publishing Company
315 Fifth Street
Peru, IL 61354

Let's Find Out
Scholastic
2931 East McCarty Street
P.O. Box 3710
Jefferson City, MO 65102–9957

Lollipops, Ladybugs and Lucky Stars
Good Apple, Inc.
1204 Buchanan
Carthage, IL 62321

My First Magazine
Scholastic, Inc.
2931 East McCarty Street
Box 3710
Jefferson City, MO 65102

Muppet Magazine
P.O. Box 10176
Des Moines, IA 50340

National Geographic World
P.O. Box 2330
Washington, DC 20077–9955

Ranger Rick
Membership Services
National Wildlife Federation
8925 Leesburg Pike
Vienna, VA 22180–0001

Scholastic Let's Find Out
Scholastic, Inc.
730 Broadway
New York, NY 10003

Scholastic News
2931 East McCarty Street
P.O. Box 3710
Jefferson City, MO 65102–9957

Sesame Street Magazine
P.O. Box 52000
Boulder, CO 80321–2000

Science Weekly
Subscription Department
2141 Industrial Parkway
Silver Spring, MD 20904

Shoe Tree
Membership Services
Department YW
P.O. Box 3000
Denville, NJ 07834

Stone Soup: The Magazine by Children
P.O. Box 83
Santa Cruz, CA 95063

3-2-1 Contact
P.O. Box 53051
Boulder, CO 80322-53051

Turtle Magazine for Preschool Kids
P.O. Box 10003
Des Moines, IA 50340

U.S. Kids
Field Publications
4343 Equity Drive
P.O. Box 16630
Columbus, OH 43216

Weekly Reader
Field Publications
P.O. Box 16630
Columbus, OH 43216

Your Big Back Yard
National Wildlife Federation
8925 Leesburg Pike
Vienna, VA 22180

Index

Note: Page numbers in **bold type** reference non-text material.